SIXTH EDITION

# Haimann's
# Supervisory
# Management
## for Healthcare
## Organizations

## ROSE T. DUNN, R.R.A., C.P.A., F.A.C.H.E.

Boston, Massachusetts   Burr Ridge, Illinois
Dubuque, Iowa   Madison, Wisconsin   New York, New York
San Francisco, California   St. Louis, Missouri

# WCB/McGraw-Hill

*A Division of The McGraw·Hill Companies*

Haimann's Supervisory Management for Healthcare Organizations

2  3  4  5  6  7  8  9  0  QPF/QPF  9  0  9  8

ISBN 0–697–25155–1

Publisher: *Michael D. Lange*
Sponsoring Editor: *Kristine Noel Tibbetts*
Developmental Editor *Kelly A. Drapeau*
Marketing Manager: *Keri L. Witman*
Project Manager: *Vicki Krug*
Production Supervisor: *Deborah Donner*
Compositor: *Shepherd, Inc.*
Typeface: *10/12 Times Roman*
Printer: *Quebecor/Fairfield*

**Library of Congress Cataloging-in Publication Data**

Dunn, Rose.
    Haimann's supervisory management for healthcare organizations/Rose Dunn.
    –6th ed.
        p. cm.
    Rev. ed. of: Supervisory management for healthcare organizations/
Theo Haimann, with contributions by Rose Dunn. 5th ed. c1994.
    Includes bibliographical references and index.
    ISBN 0–697–25155–1
    1. Health facilities—Administration.   I. Haimann, Theo
Supervisory management for healthcare organizations. II. Title.
    [DNLM: 1. Health Facilities—organization & administration.
    2. Personnel Management.   WX150 D923h 1988]
RA971. H22   1998
362.1'1'068–dc21
DNLM/DLC
for Library of Congress                                        97–10575
                                                               CIP

www.mhhe.com

# CONTENTS

# PREFACE

The challenge to today's healthcare providers in the United States is stronger than ever. Healthcare providers must keep pace with revolutionary and sophisticated breakthroughs in medical science and technology, an aging population, and a federal government trying to deliver affordable coverage. The highest quality of care might be replaced with "adequate" quality due to the strains of a financially driven system. Providers and patients are concerned that issues are being approached first on the basis of cost rather than need and quality.

Because of this challenge, survival has become an issue for many of today's healthcare organizations. Patients, providers, and payers all see the need for a more efficient healthcare system, and it is not surprising that major changes are taking place. Current market pressures are demanding new delivery methods, managed care contracting is a burning issue, and the movement toward a prospective payment system for outpatient care is continuing. Furthermore, physician practice arrangements are changing greatly, the traditional fee-for-service concept is all but eliminated, and standardized national fee schedules and managed care capitation arrangements are emerging.

At the center of all this activity is the manager, who has to bring and hold together the human resources, physical facilities, professional expertise, skills, technology, information systems, and other support systems necessary to deliver and/or monitor the care and services rendered. In addition, these tasks have to be accomplished within the fiscal constraints of a more efficient healthcare system. Therefore, it is necessary that healthcare managers understand the complexities of organization life, behavior, development, and climate. All managers—from the chief executive officer to the first-line supervisor—must be managers in the most professional sense.

In order to contribute to organizational effectiveness, administrators and managers must understand and know the practice of management. Most executive level positions are filled by individuals who have been exposed to formal health administration education. However, thousands of middle- and lower-level managerial positions, such as department heads and supervisors, are filled by health professionals and others who may not have had any formal education or training in administration, management, and supervision per sé.

This book is intended for these department heads and supervisors in all types of healthcare facilities: hospitals, ambulatory surgical centers, HMOs, physician's group practices, nursing homes, rehabilitation centers, long-term-care facilities, or other organizations of this type. These people became supervisors primarily because they did an outstanding job in their chosen healthcare professions. Yet they often find themselves in more and more demanding positions but have little or no familiarity with the administrative and managerial aspects of their newly attained rank. Suddenly they are confronted with the need to be an effective manager, to stay on top of a more sophisticated job, and to gain new perspectives and insights into human relationships. Such a supervisor may have changed from being a good nurse, for example, to becoming a head nurse, supervisor of nursing, or whatever the title may be. Thus, the job changes from being responsible for oneself to being responsible for former peers and motivating them to achieve departmental goals, institutional objectives, and their own personal goals.

This book is also written for students taking an introductory course in management and will acquaint them with their future roles in an organizational setting. It is intended to be used as a tool for nurses, medical technologists, dietitians, therapists, health information managers, and all other healthcare professionals. It can be used in any of the courses in which managerial, supervisory, and leadership concepts are studied.

Additionally, this text is intended to aid people in the healthcare field who are already faced with such supervisory tasks. Its purpose is to demonstrate that proficiency in supervision will better equip them to cope with the ever-increasing demands of getting the job done, will contribute more effectively to the overall goals of the institution, and at the same time will make them more valuable members of the organization's management team.

This book is introductory in that it assumes no previous knowledge of the concepts of supervision. Although the book does include sophisticated material, it is explained in terms that the inexperienced supervisor can easily understand. The book will also help newly appointed supervisors become acquainted with the many problems they will confront and offers practical advice for solving them. For experienced supervisors, this book is intended to refresh thinking, to introduce current ideas, and to widen horizons by taking a different and challenging look at both their own positions and of their employees.

Even though the text is written for supervisors, most of its content would be of great interest to chief executives and administrators as well. The common denominator in all levels of supervisors is the part they play as managers within the administrative hierarchy of the institution. Without going into the technical details of specific supervisory positions, the book discusses the managerial aspects common to every supervisory job, whether in nursing; the laboratory; radiology; physical, occupational or respiratory therapy; health information management; medical social work; housekeeping; dietary; pharmacy; security; laundry; practice management; engineering; or any of the other specialities found within the healthcare field.

The supervisory position in any field is the most critical point in the entire organizational structure. In all healthcare activities, the supervisor's position is exceptionally strategic since in most cases the recipient (patient) does not elect to receive the services provided, nor does the patient understand the technical aspects of these services. The supervisor must contend with emotional factors involved in the care of the patients and their loved ones under conditions that make effective supervision unusually difficult. Additionally, the supervisor is often torn between clinical, professional, administrative, legal, moral, and ethical considerations. Above all, however, the supervisor's activities must ultimately reflect the welfare of the patient. All these factors make it more imperative for the supervisor to be a capable manager of his or her work group.

External accrediting agencies and most internal levels of management have placed a new emphasis on quality of care. Many of the quality improvement concepts introduced in Japan after World War II are being adopted and implemented throughout the United States. Today's managers must comply with the performance improvement standards set by the Joint Commission on Accreditation of Healthcare Organizations and other regulatory agencies, plus respond to the demands of patients, peer department physicians, and insurers, to name a few. These managers must know how to delegate authority to their staff to insure customer service is accomplished.

To create a framework in which management knowledge can be organized in a practical way, the authors have chosen to use the *functions* of managers as the primary approach: planning, organizing, staffing, influencing, and controlling. Each function is thoroughly dealt with by breaking it down and explaining its relationship to the material already presented. This approach allows an new knowledge, whether from behavioral and social sciences, quantitative approaches, or any other field, to be incorporated at any point. All of the managerial functions are closely related; they represent an interlocking, interacting system. In practice, such a distinct classification of these managerial functions is not always discernible, but this type of academic separation allows a methodological, clear, and complete analysis of a supervisor's managerial functions.

The supervisor's job of getting things done with and through people has its foundation in the relationship between the supervisors and the people with whom they work. For this reason the supervisor must have considerable knowledge of the human aspects of supervision; that is, the behavioral factors that motivate the employees. This book attempts to present a balanced picture of such behavioral factors in the conceptual framework of managing.

In preparing this sixth edition we have retained the basic concepts and the emphasis on the five basic managerial functions. All the chapters of the previous editions have been revised and updated, and some of the subject matter has been rearranged to facilitate the reader's understanding of the concepts and their application. These concepts have been expanded and integrated with current practices, new knowledge and research, and recent developments to show the contemporary emphasis of this edition. The authors have given more attention to how the behavioral sciences affect the management of human resources. We have added new material on organizational design, performance appraisal, quality management processes, management by objectives, individual and small group behavior, motivation, sexual harassment, employee assistance programs, discipline without punishment, zero base budgeting, and many other aspects of managing.

The chapter focusing on the legal aspects of the supervisory job has been revised and updated by Brian L. Andrew, JD and the law firm of Polsinelli, White, Vardeman & Shalton. This chapter, however, is not intended to be a substitute for legal advice by lawyers.

Chapter 29, *Emerging Influences in Healthcare,* is new to this edition. The chapter discusses the impact managed care has had on healthcare providers, patient-focused care, teams, and the advantages of developing multiskilled practitioners.

Material for this text has come from the writings and research of scholars in the areas of management, and behavioral and social sciences, as well as from the practical experience of many supervisors, managers, and administrators in the field. In addition, this text also reflects the authors' experiences in teaching management, in consulting, in conducting many supervisory development programs, and in giving lectures to administrators and supervisors at different levels in the managerial hierarchy of hospitals and related healthcare facilities.

The reader of this will note that I continue to use "we" throughout the preface because I have attempted to retain as much of Theo Haimann's thoughts and words as possible. He was truly a great professor, but more so, a wonderful, talented teacher. I had the pleasure of taking two courses from Dr. Haimann and believe that it was his teachings that allowed me to be a successful manager. To his wife, Ruthe, and to his daughter, Carolyn, thank you for the opportunity to further his message. To my husband, Ray, thank you for your patience when I gave up so many weekends to work on this edition.

Finally, in writing such as this, we were indebted to so many persons that it is impossible to individually give due credit to all who have assisted over the two decades of the book's existence. Many hospitals and other healthcare organizations have willingly provided exhibits that are displayed throughout the text including BJC Health Systems, SSM Health Care System, HealthSouth Treasure Coast Rehabilitation Hospital, Lakeland Regional Medical Center, and Baptist Medical Center.

We acknowledge and thank the following for reviewing the manuscript and offering valuable suggestions: Jay I. Zuckerman, Adjunct Professor at St. Joseph's College in Patchogue, NY and Vice President of Southside Hospital in Bay Shore, NY and Cathy Cahill, St. Joseph's College. And . . . last, we also want to thank the following people at WCB/McGraw-Hill for their support: Kris Noel Tibbetts, Sponsoring Editor; Kelly Drapeau, Developmental Editor; Darlene Schueller, Senior Editorial Assistant; Vicki Krug, Project Manager; Karen Storlie, Permissions Coordinator.

# PART I
# STEPPING
# INTO
# MANAGEMENT

# *The Supervisor's Job*

*Chapter Objectives*

After you have studied this chapter, you should be able to:

1. Provide an overview of the rapidly changing healthcare environment and challenges it poses for managers and supervisors.
2. Define the terms *delivery of healthcare* and *management.*
3. Discuss the dimensions of the supervisor's job.
4. Review the aspects of the supervisor's position and the skills necessary to be successful.

**THE HEALTHCARE PERSPECTIVE**

The needs and demands for the highest-quality management in all healthcare delivery activities are intensifying to such a degree that survival has become an issue for some of today's healthcare organizations. No letup is in sight. The current market pressures are demanding new delivery methods. For example, in the past patients came to the healthcare center; now healthcare facilities are going to the patients with satellite outpatient services, outreach programs, mobile mammography units, health fairs, and so on.

Other changing trends affecting healthcare management include managed care contracting, an increasingly difficult issue for every healthcare institution. The further growth of managed care seems inevitable, and many healthcare centers are lacking the data they need for successful managed care contracting. The format of medical practice arrangements by physicians and surgeons also is changing greatly, and the traditional fee-for-service concept is undergoing radical rethinking. Fee schedules or limits on fees for certain services are defined by insurers and some managed care organizations have capitated the amount they will pay for the care rendered to a given insured during a period by paying the physician a fixed fee at the beginning of the month for the insured regardless of the amount of care rendered to the patient during the month by the physician.

In many instances new joint physician/hospital ventures are being set up. Additionally, new breakthroughs and technologies are likely to change key services, such as in the fields of cardiology, oncology, orthopedics, neurology, and women's health. Insurers are identifying a few hospitals to which the insured will be sent to receive high-tech care such as lung, heart, and pancreas transplants. Hospitals, in turn, are creating "centers of excellence" to focus limited resources on the growth and more profitable service areas and "niche" markets. Another challenge comes from healthcare facilities providing more and more services in the outpatient setting.

While in the past there was a danger of a shortage of nurses whose expertise and assistance was crucial to high quality healthcare, now the healthcare *providers* (hospitals, surgi-centers, physician groups or any entity or person who provides care to patients) have guarded against this possibility by training other staff to perform many of the nonregulated functions previously performed by nurses. These individuals, sometimes called "multiskilled professionals" or certified nurse assistants, record temperatures, pass medications, draw blood and other specimens, and perform some patient care services such as turning, exercising, and assisting patients when ambulating. Not only are these individuals readily employable, but their hourly rates are lower than nurses, thus reducing labor costs for the healthcare provider.

In addition to these factors, many other changes from all directions are affecting healthcare delivery. All of these challenges will continue to impose constraints on healthcare services and set higher expectations. These new developments, trends, and activities have something important in common: new "corporations" are being created for these new ventures and subsidiaries.

In order to pool resources and expertise, many facilities are merging with nearby hospitals, prior competitors, or other facilities strategically located to allow them to benefit from the larger, merged entity image. According to the American Hospital Association Section for Health Care Systems, 195 mergers took place from 1980 to 1991 involving 404 hospitals. While a sizeable number, the merger activity reported over this 11-year period was eclipsed in 1994 when *Modern Healthcare* reported that 674 hospitals and in 1995 when 735 hospitals were involved in mergers or acquisitions. Merging entities is not an activity limited to hospitals. Physician medical group mergers rose 58.5% in 1995 over 1994.[1] There were 103 such transactions between doctor groups, compared to 65 in 1994.[2] This type of activity requires extensive and sophisticated long-range planning and good control over internal affairs. In turn, all this radical reshaping of the healthcare field calls for more and better management. Managers, from chief executive officers down to first-line supervisors, are needed to help implement these changes and make them function effectively.

As stated, these changes are affecting organizational settings the most. The organization is the most important and critical element, providing the means for bringing the resources together. Managing is the process by which healthcare organizations fulfill this responsibility. Thus, it is the manager who is responsible for acquiring and combining the resources to accomplish the goals. As scientific, economic, competitive, social, and many other pressures change, it is not the nurse or the technologist that the organization depends on to cope with the change, it is the manager's responsibility. Management has emerged as a potent force in our society since the turn of the century and has become essential to the life of all healthcare endeavors.

Today's health services are almost exclusively delivered in organizational settings such as healthcare centers, nursing homes, clinics, surgical centers,

---

1. *Irving Levin Associates' Health Care Merger and Acquisition Report (New Canaan, Ct.) as reported in* AHA News, *March 4, 1996.*
2. Ibid.

health maintenance organizations, physicians' offices, home care programs, or any other type of healthcare institution. Only an organizational setting can bring together the physical facilities, professional expertise, skills, information systems, technology, and the myriad of other supports that today's health services delivery requires, whether these services are curative, rehabilitative, or preventive. Therefore, it is absolutely necessary that those involved in the delivery of healthcare services understand the complexities of organizational life, organizational behavior, development, and climate and the importance of expert administration in addition to their own professional areas of expertise.

Traditionally, healthcare professionals were primarily concerned with the scientific, technical, and clinical aspects of their work; being a good nurse meant mastering the field of nursing. This was true even of the director of nursing, who was a nurse first and a manager second. Now, because of the increased demands, the health professional must be equally concerned with both aspects of the job—the management and the profession.

*Delivery of healthcare* is a term that is becoming increasingly common in the press and in our daily conversations. What is generally meant by this term is the program or process of providing adequate healthcare services of all types, provided by a variety of healthcare providers (physicians, hospitals, nursing homes, etc.) intended to maintain and improve the health of all people regardless of age, race, locale, or ability to pay. *Healthcare delivery systems* are an organized association of different healthcare providers (hospitals, surgi-centers, clinics, physician groups, rehabilitation centers, home health agencies, etc.) that have affiliated or legally tied themselves together to provide comprehensive care and health maintenance options to people in their service area. The reason healthcare delivery systems are receiving such attention in the United States is that the cost of healthcare has risen more steeply than any other item in our national economy. Not only have the total expenditures in the health field services risen by leaps and bounds, but these expenditures have also become an ever-increasing percentage of the overall economy, as expressed in our gross national product. It is understandable that the delivery of healthcare has become a major national issue and that all institutions engaged in this service are receiving more scrutiny. The Clinton healthcare plan advocated the establishment of healthcare delivery systems not just on a metropolitan area basis, but rather on a regional basis. The association and consolidation of services encourages elimination of redundant services and channeling activity to a single, efficient provider rather than supporting multiple providers who cannot achieve economy of scale.

Moreover, since the delivery of healthcare largely means providing a service, which due to its nature is people intensive, it is understandable that about 60 percent of the total expenditures within the field are for wages and salaries, twice the amount of most industrial enterprises. Therefore, much criticism has naturally centered around employee productivity to justify such large wage and salary expenditures. What the U.S. needs is better and more effective administration of healthcare activities; that is, ultimately better supervision throughout the entire healthcare industry. It is the front-line management—the supervisor of the department regardless of the title and nature of work—who is responsible for

**Figure 1.1** The administrative pyramid.

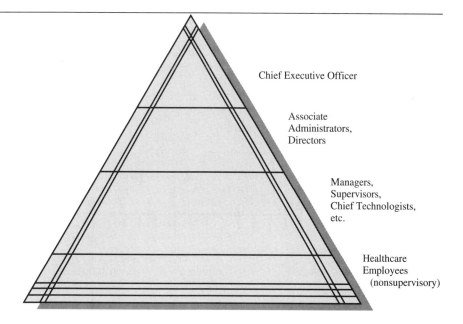

Chief Executive Officer

Associate
Administrators,
Directors

Managers,
Supervisors,
Chief Technologists,
etc.

Healthcare
Employees
  (nonsupervisory)

the department functioning smoothly and efficiently. It is essential, therefore, that due emphasis be placed on the need for the managerial development of effective supervisors within all phases of the healthcare field.

## THE DEMANDS OF THE SUPERVISORY POSITION

The supervisory position within the administrative structure of any healthcare facility, such as a medical center, nursing home, free-standing surgicenter, health maintenance organization, urgi-center, intermediate care facility, independent practice organization, or preferred provider organization, has long been acknowledged as a difficult and demanding one. You have probably learned this from your own experience or by observing supervisors in hospitals and related institutions as they go about their daily tasks. The supervisor, whether a head nurse or a chief technologist in the clinical laboratory, can be depicted as "the person in the middle," since he or she serves as the principal link between higher administration and the institution's employees. (See figure 1.1.)

If we look carefully at the job of almost any supervisor, regardless of who or what he or she supervises, we can see that it involves four major dimensions, that is, four areas of responsibility. First, the supervisor must be a good boss, a good manager, and a team leader of the employees who work in this unit. The supervisor must have the technical, professional, and clinical competence to run the department smoothly and see that the employees carry out their assignments successfully. The first responsibility—not in any order of importance—is toward the employees of the department. Second, the supervisor must also be a competent subordinate to the next higher manager. In most instances this person would be an

**Figure 1.2** Dimensions of the supervisor's job.

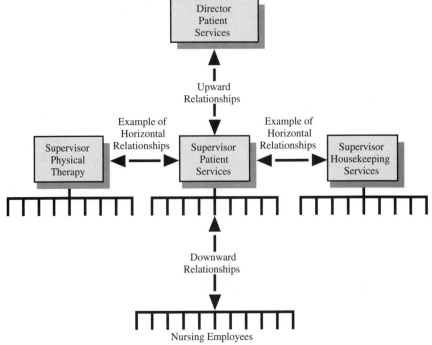

administrator, associate administrator, center executive, or director of a service. The second responsibility is toward administration and the "owners" of the organization.

Between these two dimensions of the supervisor's role is a third area of responsibility in which he or she acts as a connecting link between the employee and the administration. For example, employees such as laboratory technologists, technicians, and the clerical support see their supervisor, say the chief technologist, as the "administration." Their supervisor is their primary contact through whom the employees communicate their concerns to the true administration and from which comes the goals and policies established by senior administration for hospitalwide management. The supervisor is that member of the administration who must make certain that the work gets done.

The fourth and final part of the supervisor's role is to maintain satisfactory working relationships with the heads, leaders, and peer supervisors of all other departments and services. The relationship with these other department heads must be that of a good colleague who is willing and eager to coordinate the department's efforts with those of the other departments to reach the overall objectives and goals of the institution; that is, the best possible service and patient care regardless of which department or service gets "credit."

The four dimensions of the supervisor's job are shown more clearly in figure 1.2. The supervisor must be successful in vertical relationships downward with subordinates and upward with his or her superior. In addition, the supervisor must be skillful in handling horizontal relationships with other supervisors, since this will facilitate getting the job done for the benefit of the client.

Because of the complexity of these relationships, it is commonly acknowledged that the role of the first-line supervisor in any industrial or commercial undertaking is a most difficult one. It is even more difficult for supervisors within the healthcare field because their activities directly or indirectly affect people, the quality of patient care, and the smooth overall functioning of the institution. In addition to their many professional obligations, healthcare supervisors must always bear in mind the needs and desires of patients and their relatives who, at the time, are physically drained and emotionally upset. Thus, the supervisor should be informed of the problems of human relations among medical staff members, the other highly educated professionals and personnel of the institution or organization, and patients. All these considerations make the job of the healthcare supervisor a particularly demanding and challenging one.

For example, let us look at the long list of demands made on a head nurse in charge of a nursing unit. Whether the institution practices team nursing, primary care, or total patient care, the head nurse's duty still is to provide for and supervise the nursing care rendered to the patients in the unit. She does this partly by delegating a certain amount of her authority for the care of patients and the supervision of personnel to an assistant head nurse or to team leaders within her area. Still, the head nurse must plan, direct, and control all activities within the nursing unit. She must make the rounds of her unit with medical and nursing staff. She also is expected to make rounds to personally observe the condition and behavior of patients and to assess the need for and quality of continued nursing care. She may even have to assume general nursing functions in the care of those patients who have complex problems.

Furthermore, the head nurse must interpret and apply the policies, procedures, rules, and regulations of the facility in general and of nursing services in particular. She must provide coverage of the unit for twenty-four hours by scheduling to have the unit properly staffed at all times. She is to communicate and report to her nursing supervisor (assuming that the nursing supervisor is the immediate superior of a number of head nurses) all pertinent information regarding patients in her unit. She must orient new personnel to the unit and acquaint them with the general philosophies of the institution. She is also concerned with continued in-service education in her unit, in other words, with teaching personnel. Likewise, she participates in the evaluation of her subordinates.

In addition, it is part of the head nurse's job to coordinate the activities of her unit with unit managers if they are available. She also must coordinate her patient care with the care and therapeutic procedures of the various departments throughout the institution. Moreover, she is involved in the design and regular reevaluation of the budget. She serves on a number of committees, in addition to attending all head nurses' meetings. She might also be expected to help in the supervision and instruction of student nurses when necessary. Many additional duties are often assigned to a head nurse, depending on what the particular healthcare facility specifies in its description of this very demanding position.

Although it is difficult, if not impossible, to forecast when and how a new scientific or technological event will affect the supervisory position, every supervisor must continue to be better educated. It is important that supervisors prepare themselves and their employees professionally, scientifically, technologically, and psychologically for changes that will occur inevitably in the delivery of healthcare. In addition to the medical and scientific breakthroughs, increased automation and its concomitant benefits and challenges will continue to affect all supervisors. Adaptations and uses for desktop, personal, hand-held, and point-of-care computers will grow with the development of specialized software so that supervisors will have to be familiar with computer operations as part of their daily routines.

With a growing, complex society and increasing demands for more sophisticated and better healthcare, the job of any supervisor in the field is likely to become even more challenging. This is true whether the title is head nurse, health information manager, operating room supervisor, director of maintenance, foreman of the electricians, chief respiratory therapist, information systems leader, laboratory supervisor, chief technologist of radiology, food service supervisor, or supervisor of any one of the many other activities necessary for the smooth functioning of a healthcare center. The one aspect that will help the supervisor cope with all this is the continued advancement of his or her knowledge and skill in the managerial part of the job.

This supervisory position is usually the first step in a long career of administrative positions that will make increasing demands for demonstrated competent management skills as the individual moves up the administrative ladder. For instance, take the programmer analyst who is made programming manager. After having served in this capacity for some time, he is promoted to leader, information systems, then possibly to associate administrator, information services, and eventually to the organization's vice-president or chief information officer.

There is also the possibility of moving up the ladder in a less traditional way. For example, take the staff nurse who is selected to manage the admission reservations and scheduling activities. After having served in this capacity for some time and her good relations with a managed care company, she is recruited by that managed care organization to oversee the precertification unit with a title of precertification manager, then possibly to director of utilization management and eventually to assistant vice-president for customer service and medical management.

Most of the tens of thousands of managerial positions in healthcare today are filled by health professionals who have not had any formal administrative training or study in management or administration per se. It is therefore essential that the supervisor, department head, leader, or whatever the title may be, learn as much as possible about the meaning of being a competent first-line manager because this is his or her first step in the climb up the managerial and administration ladder.

## THE MANAGERIAL ASPECTS OF THE SUPERVISORY POSITION

The job of a supervisor can also be viewed in terms of three essential skills. First, the good supervisor must possess *technical skills*. These skills are primarily concerned with systematic procedures, so that he or she knows the clinical and technical aspects of the work to be done. In addition, two more skills are needed, namely human skills and conceptual skills. *Human skills* are those skills that concern working with people, motivating them, and understanding individual and group feelings. *Conceptual skills* enable the supervisor to visualize the big picture, and to understand how all parts of the organization contribute and coordinate their efforts. These human and conceptual skills are essential to the managerial aspects of a supervisor's job.

You may have observed various supervisors on different occasions and noticed that some of them are usually harassed, disorganized, and overly involved in doing the job at hand. They are muddling through and are knee-deep in work. Such supervisors put in long hours and are never afraid of doing anything themselves. They are working exceedingly hard but never seem to have enough time left to actually supervise. On the other hand, you may have observed supervisors who seem to be on top of the job and whose departments function smoothly and orderly. They have found time to sit at their desks at least part of the day and keep their desk work up-to-date. Why is there such a difference?

Of course, some supervisors are basically more capable than others, just as there are inept and proficient health information managers. However, if you compare two health information managers in two hospitals to discover why one is on top of the job and the other is constantly fixing things herself, you will probably find that one understands her job better than the other and has developed subordinate staff to whom she can delegate or entrust assignments. Let us assume that both are equally good professionals, both have graduated from health information management programs in the same community and have similar staffing ratios and technology available, and the conditions under which they perform are similar. Still, the results of one health information manager are significantly better than those of the other. Why is this? The answer is that the one is simply a better manager. She is able to supervise the functions of her department in a manner that allows her to get the job done through and with the people of her department. The difference between a good supervisor and a poor supervisor, assuming everything else being equal, is the difference in their managerial abilities.

Surprisingly enough, however, the managerial aspect of the supervisor's position has long been neglected. Rather, the emphasis has always been put on the clinical and technical competence for doing a particular job. Consider your own job, for example. It is very likely that you were appointed to this job from the ranks of one of the various professional services or crafts. As a result of your ingenuity, effort, and willingness to work hard, you were promoted to the supervisory level and were expected to assume the responsibilities of managing your unit. Little was done, however, to acquaint you with these responsibilities or to help you cope with the managerial aspects of your new job. More or less overnight you were made a part of administration without having been prepared to be a manager. Ever since, you have done the best you could by imitating and learning from your predecessors, and your department is probably functioning reasonably well. Still, there are likely to be some problems, which may be lessened by a better understanding of the supervisory aspects of your job, so that you will be the manager running the department instead of the department running you.

It is the aim of this text to show the supervisor how to become a better manager. This does not mean that one can neglect or underestimate the actual work involved in getting the job done. As you know, one of the requirements of a good supervisor is a thorough understanding of the clinical, professional, and technical parts of the operations. Often the supervisor is actually the most skilled individual of the department and can do a more efficient and quicker job than anyone else. He or she must not be tempted to step in and take over the job, however, except for purposes of instruction or in case of an emergency. Rather, the supervisor's responsibility is to see that the employees can do the job and do it properly. As a manager, the supervisor must plan, guide, and manage. Let us concentrate further on these managerial requirements of the supervisory position.

## THE MEANING OF MANAGEMENT

First, let us consider what is meant by management. The term *management* has been defined in many ways, generally as a process of coordinating and integrating human, technical, and other resources to accomplish specific results. The following is a more meaningful definition for our purposes: *management is the process of getting things done through and with people by directing and motivating the efforts of individuals toward common objectives.* You have undoubtedly learned from your own experience that in most endeavors one person can accomplish relatively little alone. For this reason people have found it expedient and even necessary to join with others to attain the goals of an enterprise. In every organized activity it is the manager's function to achieve the goals of the enterprise with the help of subordinates and fellow employees. Achieving goals through and with people is only one aspect of the manager's job. It is also necessary to create a working atmosphere, that is, a climate or a culture in which subordinates can find as much satisfaction of their needs as possible. In other words, a supervisor must provide a climate conducive for the employees to fulfill such needs as recognition, achievement, and companionship. If these needs can be met right on the job, employees are more likely to strive willingly and enthusiastically toward the achievement of departmental objectives, as well as the overall objectives of the institution. Thus, we must add to our earlier definition of management by saying that the manager's job is *getting things done through and with people by enabling them to find as much satisfaction of their needs as possible, while at the same time motivating them to achieve both their own objectives and the objectives of the institution.* The better the supervisor performs these duties, the better the departmental results will be. You may have noticed by this time that we have been using the terms supervisor, manager, and administrator interchangeably. Although the exact meaning of these titles varies with different institutions, the term *administrator,* or *executive, is generally used for top-level management positions,* whereas *manager* and *supervisor* usually connote positions within the middle or lower levels of the institutional hierarchy. There are some theoretical differences to consider, but for our purposes these terms will be used interchangeably.

Our reason for doing this will become clearer when you understand the somewhat surprising fact that the managerial aspects of all supervisory jobs are the same. This is true regardless of the supervisor's department or section or level within the administrative hierarchy. Thus, the managerial content of a supervisory position is the same whether the position is director of nursing services, head of the housekeeping division, chief engineer in the maintenance department, or lead clinical dietician. By the same token, the managerial functions are the same for the supervisor on the firing line (lowest-level or first-line supervisor), middle level of management, or top administrative group. In addition, it does not matter in which type of organization you are working. Managerial functions are the same for an industrial enterprise, commercial enterprise, not-for-profit organization, fraternal organization, government agency, or hospital or other healthcare facility. Regardless of the activities of the organization, department, or level, the managerial aspects and skills are the same.

## MANAGERIAL SKILLS AND TECHNICAL SKILLS

These managerial skills must be distinguished from the professional, clinical, and technical skills required of a supervisor. As stated before, all supervisors must also possess special technical skills and professional know-how in their field. Technical skills vary between departments, but any supervisory position requires both professional technical skills and standard managerial skills. Mere technical and professional knowledge would not be sufficient.

It is important to note that as a supervisor advances up the administrative ladder, he or she will rely less on professional and technical skills and more on managerial skills. If you will observe your own organization, you will find that the higher you go within the administrative hierarchy, the more administrative skills are required and the less technical know-how. Therefore, the top-level executive generally uses far fewer technical skills than those who are employed under him or her. In the rise to the top, however, the administrator has had to acquire all the administrative skills necessary for the management of the entire enterprise.

Let's consider a real-life example whose name has been disguised. Mr. Andrews, an English major in college, taught junior high for a few years prior to marrying. When the teaching position was inadequate to support his growing family, he joined an insurance company as a claims adjudicator (a base-level position). He noticed abnormalities in some claims from some providers and researched these for his superior. Eventually he was promoted to the fraud investigations unit and ultimately directed that operation until he was promoted to oversee all claims and investigations functions. He interacted well with physicians and insurance representatives alike. As he gained further experience he began negotiating arrangements with physician groups and hospitals for preferred provider organizations and health maintenance organizations. He was selected to be the chief executive officer of the health maintenance organization, which became national in scope and very successful. At each step of his advancement he built upon prior experience and knowledge, but did not need to personally perform all activities to ensure the success of his national health maintenance organization. He left the details to his proficient subordinates.

Similarly, the chief executive officer of a hospital is concerned primarily with the overall management of hospital activities; his or her functions are almost purely administrative. In this endeavor, the chief executive depends on the technical skills of the various subordinate administrators and managers, including all the first-line supervisors, to get the job done. The chief administrator in turn uses managerial skills in directing the efforts of all these subordinate managers toward the common objectives of the hospital. Therefore, throughout the organization the emphasis, content, and purpose of the managerial skills are the same.

## MANAGERIAL SKILLS CAN BE LEARNED

At this point you may be wondering how a supervisor acquires these very important managerial skills. First of all, let us emphatically state that the standard managerial skills can be *learned.* They are not something with which you are necessarily born. Although it is often suggested that good managers like good athletes are born, not made, this belief is patently false. We cannot deny that people are born with different physiological and biological potentials and that they are endowed with differing amounts of intelligence and many other characteristics. It is also true that a person who is not a natural athlete is not likely to run 100 yards in record time. Many individuals who are natural athletes, however, have not come close to that goal either.

A good athlete is made when a person with some natural endowment by practice, learning, effort, sacrifice, and experience develops this natural endowment into a mature skill. The same holds true for a good manager; by practice, learning, and experience he or she develops this natural endowment of intelligence and leadership into mature management skills. The skills involved in managing are as learnable and trainable as the skills involved in playing tennis.

If you currently hold a supervisory position, it is likely that you have the necessary prerequisites of intelligence and leadership and that you are now ready to acquire the skills of a manager. It takes time and effort to develop these skills; they are not acquired overnight. The supervisor has ample opportunity to apply the principles and guidelines discussed in this text to the daily work. By applying the content of this text, the supervisor will certainly prevent many difficulties from occurring, and before too long will reap the many benefits from practicing good supervision.

The most valuable resource of any organization is the people who work there, the human resources. It is the first-line supervisor to whom this most important resource is entrusted in the daily working situation. The best use of an organization's human assets depends greatly on the managerial ability and understanding of the supervisor, as manifested by his or her expertise in influencing and directing them. The supervisor's job is to create a climate of motivation, satisfaction, leadership, and continuous further self-development and self-improvement. This is a challenge to every supervisor because it ultimately means the need for his or her own further self-development as a manager.

## BENEFITS FROM BETTER MANAGEMENT

The benefits that you as a supervisor will derive from learning to be a better manager are obvious. First, you will have many opportunities to apply managerial principles and knowledge to your present job. Good management by a supervisor will make a great deal of difference in the performance of your department. It will function more smoothly, work will get done on time, you will probably find it easier to stay within your budget, and your team members or subordinates will more willingly and enthusiastically contribute toward the ultimate objectives.

The application of management principles will put you on top of your job, instead of being completely "swallowed up" by it. You will also have more time to be concerned with the overall aspects of your department, and in so doing, you will become more valuable to those to whom you are responsible. For example, you will be more likely to contribute significant suggestions and advice to your superiors, perhaps in areas about which you have never before been consulted but that ultimately affect your department. In these times of rapid change and facility mergers and acquisition, you will also find it easier to see the complex interrelationships of the various departments and organizations throughout the evolving healthcare system. This in turn will help you to work in closer harmony with your colleagues who are supervising other departments. Briefly, you will be able to do a more effective supervisory job with much less effort.

In addition to the direct benefits of doing a better supervisory job for the healthcare organization that employs you, there are other benefits for you personally. As a supervisor applying sound management principles, you will grow in stature. As time goes on, you will be capable of handling more important and more complicated assignments. You will be able to fill better and higher-paying jobs. You will move up within the managerial hierarchy and will naturally want to improve your managerial skills as you advance.

As stated earlier, an additional satisfying thought is that the functions of management are equally applicable in any organization and in any managerial or supervisory position. That is, the principles of management required to produce memory chips, manage a retail department, supervise office work, or run a repair shop are all the same. Moreover, these principles are applicable not only in the United States, but in other parts of the world as well. Aside from local peculiarities and questions of personality, it would not matter whether you are a supervisor in a textile mill in India, a supervisor in a chemical plant in Italy, a department foreman in a steel mill in Gary, Indiana, or a supervisor of the patient-focused care unit for trauma care in a hospital in Lakeland, Florida. By becoming a manager, you will become more mobile in every direction and in every respect.

Therefore, there are great inducements for you to learn the principles of good management. However, you cannot expect to learn them overnight. You can only become a good manager by actually managing, that is, by applying the principles of management to your own work situation. You will undoubtedly make mistakes here and there but will in turn learn from those mistakes. The principles and guidelines of management discussed in this book can be applied to most situations. They will help you avoid errors that often take a long time to correct. Your efforts to become an outstanding manager will pay substantial dividends. As your managerial competence increases, you will be able to prevent many of the difficulties that make a supervisory job a burden instead of a challenging and satisfying task.

**SUMMARY** The demands on good management in healthcare activities are increasing rapidly, making the role of the supervisor a most challenging one. To the employees in the department, the supervisor represents management. To a superior, he or she is a subordinate. To the supervisors in other departments, he or she must be a good colleague, coordinating efforts with theirs to achieve the organization's objectives. The supervisor must possess technical, human, and conceptual skills. The supervisor must have the clinical and technical competence for the functions to be performed in the department, and at the same time he or she must be the manager of that department.

Management is the function of getting things done through and with people. The way a supervisor handles the managerial aspects of the job will make the difference between running the department and being run by the department. The managerial aspects of any supervisory job are the same, regardless of the particular type of work involved or the position on the administrative ladder. As a supervisor climbs up this ladder, the managerial skills will increase in importance, and the technical and professional skills will gradually become less important. These managerial skills can be learned; a manager is not "born," he or she is made. A supervisor will benefit greatly both professionally and personally if he or she takes the time to study and acquire managerial expertise and excellence.

# *Managerial Functions and Authority*

## Chapter Objectives

After you have studied this chapter, you should be able to:

1. Identify the managerial role of the supervisor.
2. Discuss the two basic requirements of the managerial position: managerial functions and the concept of authority.
3. Enumerate and discuss the meaning of the five managerial functions, their interrelationships, and universal nature.
4. Discuss the concept of authority and its meaning as the foundation of the formal, organizational, and positional aspects of authority.

In chapter 1 we discussed the meaning of the manager's job, namely getting things done through and with people and motivating them to achieve the objectives of the organization and also the satisfaction of their own needs. We stressed the importance of the supervisor's role as the manager, the possibility and capability of learning the necessary skills, and the benefits of mastering them.

The supervisor's managerial role rests on two foundations: managerial functions and managerial authority. The first benchmark is the managerial functions a supervisor must perform to be considered a true manager. The second other major characteristic of the managerial position is the concept of authority inherent in the supervisory position. Authority is discussed later in this chapter in a brief and rudimentary manner and far more extensively throughout this book.

## THE MANAGERIAL FUNCTIONS

Managerial skills are the functions a manager *must* perform to be considered a manager. In this text, the five managerial functions are classified as: *planning, organizing, staffing, influencing,* and *controlling.* The labels used to describe these functions vary somewhat in management literature; some textbooks list one more or one less managerial function. Regardless of the terms or number used, the managerial functions collectively constitute one of the two major characteristics of a manager.

The managerial functions are the same, regardless of the technical functions in which the supervisor is involved; they are similar whether it involves the supervision of the dietary division, a laboratory, a claims unit, or a clinic registration department. Nor does it matter whether the supervisor is working in a not-for-profit organization, a government agency, a commercial enterprise, a school, or a nursing home. The primary managerial functions are the same regardless of the level within the managerial hierarchy; they are the same for the supervisor "on the firing line" or the person in top management.

A person who does not perform these functions is not a manager in the true sense of the word, regardless of title. The following explanation is only introductory, since most of the book is devoted to the discussion, meaning, and ramifications of each of these five functions.

## ■ Planning

Planning, the first managerial function, determines in advance what should be done in the future. This function consists of determining the goals, objectives, policies, procedures, methods, rules, budgets, and other plans needed to achieve the purpose of the organization. In planning, the manager must think of, contemplate, and select a course of action from a set of available alternatives.

Thus, planning is mental work that involves thinking before acting, looking ahead, and preparing for the future. Planning is laying out in advance the goals to be achieved, the road to be followed, and the best means to achieve these objectives. It is the collection of information and data from various sources to make decisions.

You may have observed supervisors who are constantly fighting one crisis after another. The probable reason is that they did not plan or look ahead. It is every manager's duty to plan; this function cannot be delegated to someone else. Certain specialists may be called on to assist in laying out various plans, but as the manager of the department, the supervisor must make departmental plans. These plans must coincide with the overall objectives of the institution as laid down by higher administration. Within the overall directives and general boundaries, however, the manager has considerable leeway in mapping the departmental course.

Planning must come before any of the other managerial functions. Even after the initial plans are laid out and the manager proceeds with the other managerial functions, the function of planning continues in revising the course of action and choosing different alternatives as the need arises. Therefore, although planning is the first function a manager must tackle, it does not end at the initiation of the other functions. The manager continues to plan while performing the organizing, staffing, influencing, and controlling functions.

## ■ Organizing

Once a plan has been developed, the manager's organizing function determines how the work is to be accomplished. The manager must define, group, and assign job duties. More specifically, through organizing the manager determines and enumerates the various activities to be accomplished and combines these activities into distinct groups—departments, divisions, sections, teams, or any other units. Then the manager further divides the group work into individual jobs, assigns these activities, and at the same time provides subordinates with the authority needed to carry out these activities.

In other words, to organize means to design a structural framework that sets up all the positions needed to perform the work of the department, and to then assign particular duties to these positions. The manager must align the authority relationships between the various subordinates. This means the manager must delegate a certain amount of authority to the subordinate managers, so that they can carry out the duties for which they are responsible. Organizing encompasses the following elements:

1. *Specialization*—the dividing of work activities into easily managed tasks and assigning the tasks to individuals based on their skills.
2. *Departmentalization*—the dividing of activities and people according to the needs of the organization or its customers.
3. *Span of management*—a concept that defines the optimum number of subordinates a supervisor can effectively manage.
4. *Authority relationships*—theories about individuals' rights to decide, make assignments, direct activities, etc., in managing human resources (people), materials, machinery, expenses, and revenues.
5. *Responsibility*—the obligation to perform certain duties.
6. *Unity of command*—the concept that each individual should have one person to report to for any single activity.
7. *Line and staff*—the theory of authority that defines whether one has the authority to direct (a line capacity) or advise (a staff capacity).

These and other factors will be discussed in the text. The result of the organizing function is creating an activity-authority network for the department, which is a subsystem within the total healthcare network, the overall organization.

## ■ Staffing

Staffing is the manager's responsibility to recruit and select employees to ensure that there are enough qualified employees to fill the various positions needed based on the organization of duties to achieve the plan, while at the same time remaining within the budgeted labor amount for the department.

Besides hiring them, staffing also involves training these employees, promoting them, appraising their performance, counseling them on how to improve their performance, and giving them opportunities for further development. In addition, staffing includes the task of compensating the employees appropriately. In most healthcare institutions, the department of human resources helps with the technical aspects of staffing. The basic authority and responsibility for staffing, however, remain with the supervisor.

## ■ Influencing

The managerial function of influencing means issuing directives and orders in such a way that staff will respond to these directives and accomplish the job.

Influencing also means identifying and implementing practices to help the members of the organization work together. This function is also known as *leading, directing,* or *motivating.*

The influencing function of a manager includes directing, guiding, teaching, coaching, and supervising subordinates. It is not sufficient for a manager to plan, organize, and staff. The supervisor must also stimulate action by giving directives and orders to the subordinates, then supervising and guiding them as they work. Moreover, it is the manager's job to develop the abilities of the subordinates by leading, teaching, and coaching them effectively. To influence is to motivate one's employees to achieve their maximum potential and satisfy their needs, and to encourage them to accomplish tasks they may not choose to do on their own.

Thus, influencing is the process around which all performance revolves; it is the essence of all operations. This process has many dimensions, such as employee needs, morale, job satisfaction, productivity, leadership, example setting, and communication. Through the influencing function the supervisor seeks to model performance expectations and create a climate conducive to employee satisfaction while achieving the objectives of the institution. As you may know from personal experience, much and perhaps most of your time is spent in influencing and motivating subordinates.

### ■ Controlling

Controlling is the function that ensures that plans are followed and objectives achieved. In other words, to control means to determine whether the plans are being carried out, if progress is being made toward objectives, and whether other actions must be taken to correct deviations and shortcomings. Again, this relates to the importance of planning as the primary function of the manager. A supervisor could not check on whether work was proceeding properly if there were no plans to check against. Controlling also includes taking corrective action if objectives are not being met, and revising the plans and objectives if circumstances require it.

**THE INTERRELATION-SHIPS OF MANAGERIAL FUNCTIONS**

It is helpful to think of the five managerial functions as the management cycle. A cycle is a system of interdependent processes and activities. Each activity affects the performance of the others. As shown in figure 2.1, the five functions flow into each other, and at times there is no clear line indicating where one function ends and the other begins. Because of this interrelationship, no manager can set aside a specific amount of time each day for one or another function. The effort spent on each function will vary as conditions and circumstances change. The planning function, however, undoubtedly must come first. Without plans the manager cannot organize, staff, influence, or control. Throughout this text, therefore, we shall follow this sequence of planning first, then organizing, staffing, influencing, and controlling.

**Figure 2.1**  Cycle of supervisory functions.

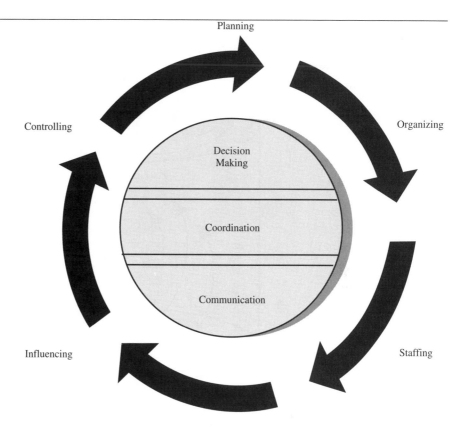

Although the five managerial functions can be separated theoretically, in the daily job of the manager these activities are inseparable. Again, each function blends into the other, and each affects the performance of the others. The output of one provides the input for another, all as elements of a system. (See figure 2.2.)

## UNIVERSALITY OF THE MANAGERIAL FUNCTIONS AND THEIR RELATION TO POSITION AND TIME

As stated earlier, these managerial functions are the responsibility of every manager, regardless of whether he or she is the chairman of the board, the president of the healthcare center, the vice-president for patient care, or the supervisor of the telephone operators. All of these managers perform all five functions. This idea is known as the principle of *universality of managerial functions.*

The time and effort that each manager devotes to a particular function will vary, however, depending on the individual's level within the administrative hierarchy. For example, a chief executive officer will usually exert more effort on planning, organizing, and controlling and less time on staffing and influencing. On the other hand, a supervisor of a department will probably spend less time on planning and organizing and more time on staffing, influencing, and controlling.

The CEO is likely to plan, for example, one year, five years, or even ten or twenty years ahead. A supervisor is concerned with plans of much shorter duration.

**Figure 2.2**  The inseparable elements of the supervisory management system.

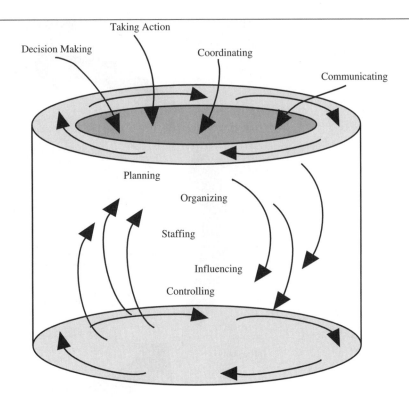

At times a supervisor will have to make plans for six or twelve months ahead but more frequently will just make plans for the next month, week, or even for the next day or shift. In other words, the span and magnitude of plans for the supervisor will be smaller.

The same is true of the influencing function. The CEO will normally assign tasks to subordinate managers, delegate authority, depend on their accomplishing the task, and spend a minimum of time in direct supervision. As a first time supervisor, however, you are concerned with getting the job done each day and throughout the day, and you will have to spend much time in this influencing or directing function. And similar observations can be made for organizing, staffing, and controlling. Therefore, we can conclude that all managers perform the same managerial functions, regardless of their level in the hierarchy, but the time and effort involved in each function will depend on their position on the administrative ladder. (See figure 2.3.)

## MANAGERIAL AUTHORITY

The second major characteristic of the managerial position is the concept of authority. Authority is the lifeblood of any managerial position. Without authority, a person in an organizational setting cannot be a manager. What is this authority that makes a supervisor a manager? Why is authority a characteristic that makes

**Figure 2.3**  Amount of time spent on each function.

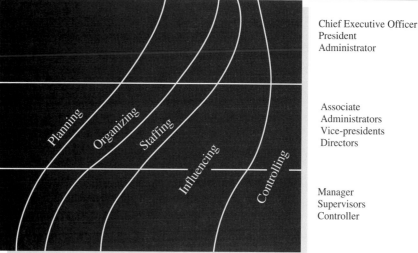

the managerial position? Briefly, at this point, authority will be defined as legal or rightful power—the right to act and to direct others. It is the power by which a manager can ask subordinates to do or not to do a certain task that the manager deems appropriate and necessary to realize the objectives of the department.

One must realize that this kind of organizational managerial authority is part of the formal position a manager holds and is not given to the manager as an individual. This formal, organizational authority gives the supervisor the power and right to make decisions, to give directives to the members of the department to achieve the objectives and tasks assigned to it. Our concept of authority must also include the possession of power to impose sanctions when necessary. Without such power to enforce an order, the enterprise could become disorganized, and chaos could result. If a subordinate refuses to carry out the manager's directive, this authority must include the right to take disciplinary action and possibly to discharge the employee.

This aspect of authority obviously has many restrictions. These may be in the form of legal restrictions, union contracts, or consideration of morals, ethics, and human behavior. For example, legal restrictions may make it necessary to take and fulfill many steps before an employee can be dismissed. Also, every successful manager knows that to influence and motivate subordinates to perform required duties it is best not to depend on this formal managerial authority but to use other persuasive ways and means to accomplish the job. In other words, it is far better not to depend on the negative aspects of dominance and authority.

In practice, most managers do not speak of authority at all. They prefer to speak of the responsibility, tasks, or duties they have. Such managers are right in saying that they have the responsibility for certain activities instead of saying that they have the authority to get the job done.

As a supervisor, however, you should know that having authority means having the power and right to issue directives. You should know that tasks and duties have been assigned to you and that you have accepted the responsibility for getting them done. Once you accept responsibility to achieve a certain project you can delegate authority to lower level staff to do certain activities to complete the project, but you cannot delegate the responsibility. The responsibility lies with you to achieve it as a supervisor through proper planning, organizing, staffing, influencing, and controlling. The concept of responsibility is always connected with authority. Regardless of how the supervisor applies authority, we emphasize again that the supervisory position must have this authority. If one is given the responsibility to provide maintenance services throughout an organization, but not given the authority to order plant engineering staff to perform them, the service will not be accomplished and chaos and frustration will follow.

Our discussion in chapter 9 on the meaning and various other bases of authority will shed additional light on this concept of authority. In chapter 11 we will look at how subordinates and workers react to authority and how authority is delegated. Delegation of authority means the process by which a supervisor receives authority from the superior manager, as well as the process by which some of the authority assigned to this position is delegated to subordinates. Just as authority is the foundation of any managerial position, delegating authority to the lower ranks within the managerial hierarchy makes it possible to build an organizational structure with effective managers on every level.

This point about authority will be discussed more fully throughout this text because it plays such an important role in supervisory management. This concept of formal positional authority will eventually become a part of an entire spectrum of influence, power, and authority. At this point, however, you need only to remember that authority is one of the basic characteristics of the managerial job. Without authority, managerial functions and the supervisor-subordinate relationship would be weakened and become meaningless.

## SUMMARY

The five managerial functions of planning, organizing, staffing, influencing, and controlling are one of the two benchmarks of the manager's job. Each blends into another, and each affects the performance of the others. The output of one provides the input for another. These five functions are universal for all managers, regardless of position in the managerial hierarchy and the nature of the enterprise. The time and effort involved in each function will vary, depending on where the manager is on the administrative ladder.

The second benchmark of the managerial job is authority; it makes the managerial position real. This organizational, formal authority is delegated to positions within the organization, permitting the incumbents to make decisions, issue directives, take action, and impose sanctions. To be successful, a manager must embrace the managerial functions and with the authority he or she has been given, use these functions to achieve the goals for which he or she is responsible.

# PART II
# CONNECTIVE PROCESSES

# Decision Making

## Chapter Objectives

After you have studied this chapter, you should be able to:

1. Discuss the importance of decision-making skills.
2. Discuss how problem solving and decision making are the essence of all managerial activities.
3. Explain the difference between programmed and nonprogrammed decisions.
4. Discuss five basic steps involved in the decision-making process that should be followed in their proper sequence.
5. Point out the possibilities of quantitative and scientific decision making.

If practicing managers were asked to define in one or two words the essence of their jobs, they probably would reply "making decisions." This process of decision making is the core of all managerial activities. Making decisions is a substantial part of everybody's daily activities. All of us have to solve problems at one time or another. Therefore, decision making should not be foreign to us. Decision making is a basic human activity that begins in early childhood and continues throughout a person's life.

Decision making can be defined as the process of selecting one alternative from a number of other alternatives. Decisions are an integral part of all five managerial functions, but they are most closely associated with the planning function. Although the manager acts within an organizational environment, in this text managerial decision making is considered an individual process.

At the heart of this process is the individual manager, whose decisions will be influenced by many other persons, various departments, the total organization, and a multitude of other factors such as the economy, technology, the state of the arts, governmental requirements, politics, and so forth.

## PROGRAMMED AND NON-PROGRAMMED DECISIONS

Many of the decision-making situations that confront us in our daily lives are not difficult to resolve because we have a standard solution. Solving these problems does not usually cause us much difficulty because we are quite familiar with them. These decisions are called *programmed decisions* because they refer to repetitive, structured, routine problems that have fixed answers, standardized operating procedures, methods, rules, and regulations.

For instance, a staff nurse finds that a patient has an elevated temperature. To verify this, the nurse measures it again with a different thermometer and finds out whether the patient just had a cup of hot coffee. The thermometer registers the same degree. Reinforced with these facts, the nurse has a solution for the problem, namely, to check again after a period of time. Again, the results are the same. The next decision is to see whether the attending physician left orders to cover this problem; if not, the nurse automatically decides to consult the physician for further action. The staff nurse had to make several decisions up to this point—programmed decisions based on standard procedure.

For other decision-making situations some of us can go to our computer where operations research has greatly aided in developing programmed decisions. For instance, in the purchasing agent's office, it is easy to determine the reorder point and the quantity to be ordered because a program has been designed for this particular problem. In some advanced organizations, the purchasing agent may not even be involved with this order, it may be electronically transmitted to the preferred vendor or to a vendor providing the lowest current bid price.

However, supervisors are frequently confronted with new or unusual problems—decision-making situations for which no standard solutions exist and no program has been designed. The supervisor is often confronted by a new problem where the dimensions and ramifications are not known or obvious. These situations call for the making of *nonprogrammed decisions.* Although programmed decision situations occur more frequently than nonprogrammed problems, the supervisor is constantly called upon to come up with a solution.

In these instances, the manager should use a logical, rational, and consistent decision-making process. When the problem being presented could impact other departments or areas, the supervisor should involve his colleagues from those areas, that is, if time permits for such team decision making. The following discussions are directed to these nonprogrammed decision-making situations.

## THE IMPORTANCE OF DECISION-MAKING SKILLS

As a supervisor, you are constantly called on to find practical solutions to problems that are caused by changing situations or unusual circumstances. Normally you are able to arrive at a satisfactory decision. One reason that you are in a supervisory position is that you have made many more correct decisions than wrong decisions as problems have presented themselves.

All managers at all levels make decisions. Decisions are not made in a vacuum, since each one affects the entire system. All managers go through, or should go through, the same process of decision making that you go through as a supervisor. The only difference is that the decisions made at the top of the administrative hierarchy are usually more far reaching and affect more people and areas than those decisions made by a supervisor. Thus, decision making, as with the five managerial functions, is an essential process that permeates the entire administrative hierarchy.

Once a decision has been made, effective action is necessary. Every decision made should be put into practice and carried out. A good decision is useless if nobody does anything about it. Obtaining effective action, however, is not our concern in this chapter.

Other chapters will deal mainly with ways the manager can achieve results. This discussion will explain the process that should come before the action, the process that you as a manager should go through to decide what action to take.

Let us be more specific about the timing of this decision-making process. When trying to imagine a person as a decision maker, we may think of an executive with horn-rimmed glasses bent over some papers, pen in hand, ready to sign on the dotted line. Or we may see a person in a board of directors meeting, raising an arm to vote a certain way. Such images have one point in common: they portray the decision makers at the very moment of choice, ready to select one alternative that leads from the crossroads down a particular path of action. This moment of decision making should not be emphasized here, since it does not describe the long, difficult process that must come before the final moment of selecting one alternative over the others.

Although long and difficult, it is worthwhile to learn and know the decision-making process. As with the managerial skills, the skills involved in decision making can be learned, and once learned they provide great benefits for the manager. Moreover, it is important to note that your managerial job involves not only making decisions yourself, but also seeing that those who work under you make decisions effectively.

Obviously a supervisor cannot make all the decisions necessary for running the department. Many of the daily decision-making activities you are responsible for as a supervisor will be delegated to your subordinates. It is therefore necessary that you also teach and train your subordinates in this process of making decisions.

## STEPS IN THE DECISION-MAKING PROCESS

The decision-making process involves several steps, and the decision maker must follow these steps in the sequence in which they are arranged:

1. Define the problem.
2. Analyze the problem.
3. Develop alternatives.
4. Evaluate the alternatives and select the best.
5. Take action and follow up.

### ■ Define the Problem

You may have heard more than one supervisor say, "I wish I had the answer," or "I wish I had the solution to this." All these "wishes" indicate that the supervisor is overly concerned with having an answer. Instead of seeking an *answer,* however, the supervisor should be looking for the real problem.

The first task is always to find out what the problem is in the particular situation; only then can one work toward the solution—the answer. As the saying goes, "There really is nothing as useless as having the right answer to the wrong question." In most cases, defining the problem is not an easy task. What often appears to be the problem might be merely a symptom. It is necessary to dig deeper to locate the real problem and define it. For example, a supervisor might be confronted with a problem of conflicting personalities within the department. Two employees often quarrel and cannot get along together. On checking into this situation, however, the supervisor may find that the problem is not one of personalities, but that the functions and duties of each employee have never really been delineated.

Thus, what appeared on the surface to be a problem of personal conflict was actually a problem of organization and structure. Only after the true nature of the problem has been realized can the supervisor do something about it. In the case of the quarreling coworkers, the chances are good that once the activities and duties of the two employees are delineated, the friction will stop.

Defining a problem such as this may be a time-consuming chore, but it is time well spent. The process of decision making cannot proceed further until the problem or problems are clearly defined. Clearly defining the problem cannot always be done from an office. Supervisors need to query staff and study processes to identify the problem completely.

## ■ Analyze the Problem

After the problem, not just the symptoms, has been defined, the manager can then set out to analyze it. The first step in this analysis is to assemble the facts. Only after finding a clear definition of the problem can the supervisor decide how relevant certain data are and what additional information may be needed. The supervisor will then gather as much information as possible.

Many supervisors complain, however, that they never have enough facts. Although it is normal for a supervisor to think that he or she does not have all the facts, this complaint is often just an excuse to delay a decision. A manager will never have *all* the facts available. Querying one's staff will provide additional facts but once again, *all* the facts may never be known. Therefore, it is necessary to make decisions on those facts that are available and also on those additional facts that the supervisor can gather without undue delay in time or excessive costs.

It is also wise to consider the behavioral impact on problem definition and to remember that what is believed to be a fact is somewhat colored by subjectivity. One cannot be completely freed of the subjective elements involved. As much as we may want to exclude prejudice and bias, we are only human, and subjectivity will creep in somehow, especially since employees are often involved. Of course, we should make an effort to be as objective and impersonal as possible.

This process of analysis, however, requires the supervisor to think not only of objective considerations, but also of intangible factors that may be involved. These factors are difficult to assess and analyze, but they do play a significant role, especially in healthcare institutions. Such intangibles may be factors of reputation, quality of patient care, morale, discipline, perception, ethics, etc. It is hard to be specific about such factors, but they should nevertheless be considered in analyzing the problem.

## ■ Develop Alternatives

After having defined and analyzed the problem, the manager's next step is to search for and develop various alternative courses of action and solutions. An absolute rule is to develop as many alternatives as possible. Always bear in mind that the final decision can only be as good as the best of the alternatives you have thought of.

It is almost unthinkable that a situation should not offer at least several alternatives. These choices, however, might not always be obvious, yet it is the duty of the decision maker to search for them. Also, some of the alternatives may not be desirable, but the manager should not decide this until all of them have been carefully considered. If this is not done, one is likely to fall into the "either-or" kind of thinking. The type of manager who thinks this way is too easily inclined to see only one of these two alternatives as the right one to follow.

Consider the following situation. Hospital regulations state that patients leaving their rooms after 10:00 A.M. will be charged a late-stay charge. This time limit is necessary to have the room vacated and cleaned in time for the new admission influx at 1:00 to 2:00 P.M. On July 1, at 2:00 P.M., a patient was admitted to the room and left at 11:00 A.M. on July 2. The bill arrived with an additional day's charge as the late-stay charge, but the patient stayed less than 24 hours and refuses to pay for 48 hours. Even in this unpleasant dilemma, several alternatives exist, although none of them is completely desirable.

The hospital could insist on having the patient pay the bill, although this would cause ill will. Second, one could ask the attending physician to justify why the patient could not be discharged earlier if the reason is medically related. This may be sufficient to have insurance coverage pay the charge if an insurer is involved. Third, the hospital could write off the charge.

Also, it is not enough for you as a supervisor to decide between the various alternatives that might have been presented by subordinates. The routine alternatives normally suggested by them may not include all the possible choices. It is your job as a manager to think of more, and possibly better, alternatives. Even in the most discouraging situations there are several choices, and although none of them may be desirable, the manager still has a choice to find the "least objectionable" solution.

*Brainstorming* is a tool often used to increase creativity in problem solving. If the decision situation is particularly vexing and if time permits, a brainstorming session with other supervisors or employees is a good tool to come up with as many alternatives as possible. This is likely to result in novel, unusual, and unorthodox alternative solutions.

Although a thorough discussion of brainstorming is beyond the scope of this text, the manager should know some of the main ideas. The participants must feel free to contribute as many alternatives as possible, no matter how extreme and wild these may be. The largest quantity of ideas should be sought, no matter how extreme. Even the wildest idea may have a grain of usefulness. The participants can build on ideas presented by others or "hitchhike" on them. In order to hear all ideas, criticism and ridicule, or even the appearance of them by nonverbal gestures for instance, during the brainstorming session cannot be allowed; such actions could kill a brainstorming session.

This creative problem-solving process is likely to increase the number of alternatives. The process also encourages dialogue amongst coworkers, which may build team spirit. Even a supervisor alone can "brainstorm" a problematic situation mentally and find additional alternatives.

An alternative to brainstorming in person, is utilizing the Internet. Many discussion groups exist on the Internet and enrollment in them is easy. Peers throughout the United States and around the world actively participate in the discussion groups and will share their experiences and outcomes to inquiries. The advantage to utilizing this resource is that alternative points of view are obtained from a variety of backgrounds.

## ■ Evaluate the Alternatives and Select the Best

The purpose of decision making is to select from the various alternatives the course of action that will provide the greatest number of wanted consequences and the smallest number of unwanted consequences. After developing the alternatives, the manager should test each of them by imagining that each has already been put into effect. Each alternative must be examined as to how feasible and satisfactory it is and what the consequences will be if it is chosen.

Once the supervisor has thought through the alternatives and appraised them along these lines, the decision maker will be in a position to select one. In this process, the supervisor should bear in mind the degree of *risk* involved in each course of action. No decision is without risk; one alternative will simply have more or less risk than another. It is also possible that the question of *time* will make one alternative preferable to another. There is usually a difference in the amount of time required to carry out each alternative, and this should be considered by the supervisor. Consider the time factor in a more personal instance. You are driving along the interstate at 65 mph and suddenly the car in front of you blows its rear tire and starts to swerve across the lanes. You rapidly brainstorm your alternatives and take decisive action, considering in a few swift seconds the risk of each.

Moreover, in this process of evaluating the different alternatives, the supervisor should also bear in mind the *resources, facilities, know-how, equipment,* and *records* that are available. Finally, the manager should not forget to judge the different alternatives along the lines of *economy of effort,* in other words, which action will give the greatest result for the least amount of effort and expenditure.

The decision must be of high quality, but it must also be *acceptable* to the group affected by it. If the highest-quality decision is not acceptable to the group, its effectiveness is probably diminished, since it will be carried out at best grudgingly, or it might even be quietly sabotaged. In such a situation it might be advisable for the supervisor to choose a more acceptable decision that is not of the highest quality. Acceptability is one more consideration in this process of choice.

Another consideration that plays a role in evaluating one alternative over another are aspects of *ethics.* Lately, most organizations have become extremely sensitive to business ethics. Business ethics refers to what is morally right and wrong as applied to executive behavior and decisions. In evaluating the alternatives, the manager must make certain that he or she complies with the corporate and professional ethical codes.

Using these criteria of feasibility, risk, timing, acceptability, ethics, resources, and economy, the manager often can see that one alternative clearly provides a greater number of desirable consequences and fewer unwanted consequences than any other one. In such cases, the decision is a relatively easy one. The best alternative, however, is not always so obvious. It is conceivable that at certain times two or more alternatives may seem equally desirable. Then the choice is simply a matter of the manager's personal preference. On the other hand, the manager also may believe that no single alternative far outweighs any of the others or is sufficiently stronger. In this case, it might be advisable to combine two of the better alternatives and come up with a compromise solution.

But what about a situation where the manager finds that none of the alternatives is satisfactory and that all of them have too many undesirable effects? As a supervisor, you might have been in a situation where the undesirable consequences of all the alternatives were so overwhelmingly bad that they paralyzed any action. You may have thought that there was only one available solution to the problem, namely, to take no action at all. Such a solution, however, is deceptive. A supervisor is wrong to believe that taking no action is as much a decision as deciding to take a specific action, although few people are aware of this. Most people think that taking no action relieves them of making an unpleasant decision. The only way for the manager to avoid this pitfall is to try to visualize the consequences of inaction. The manager needs only to think through what would happen if no action were taken and will probably see that in so doing, an undesirable alternative is chosen.

Having ruled out inaction in most cases, you may still be in a position where all alternatives seem undesirable. In such a case, you should search for new and different alternatives. Be a bit creative and try to develop at least a couple of new solutions. Also check to see that all the steps of the decision-making process have been followed. Has the problem been clearly defined? Have all the pertinent facts been gathered and analyzed? Have all possible alternatives been considered? Have you tried brainstorming? Chances are that some new alternatives will come up, and you can make a good decision. In making this decision, however, you might have to employ some additional factors, such as experience, intuition, and actual testing, or you may have to resort to scientific decision making.

## ◼ Experience

The manager's final selection from the various alternatives is frequently influenced and guided by past experience. Managers often decide wisely on the basis of their own experience or that of other managers. Managers can apply knowledge gained by past experience to new situations, and no manager should ever underestimate the importance of such knowledge. On the other hand, it is dangerous to follow past experience blindly. Experiential decision making is often seen in medicine.

A person appears at a urologist's office with lower back pain, and the urologist may consider it a bladder infection. If the person goes to an orthopedist with the problem, the physician may consider it a spur on a lumbar vertebra, while a neurologist may consider it a pinched nerve, and so on. Each physician is basing his or her *initial impression* on his or her experience, but before proceeding to treat the "initial impression," the physician gathers more facts because he knows that blindly accepting the first impression could result in the real untreated condition becoming more serious.

Therefore, whenever the manager calls on experience as a basis for choice among alternatives, the supervisor should examine the situation and conditions that prevailed at the time of the past decision. Current conditions may still be very similar to that of the previous occasion. More often than not, however, conditions have changed considerably, and the underlying circumstances and assumptions are no longer valid. In these cases, of course, the decision should not be the same.

Previous experience can also be helpful if the manager is called on to substantiate the reasons for making a particular decision. Experience is a good defense tactic, and many superiors use it as valid evidence. Past experience must always be viewed with the future in mind. The underlying circumstances of the past, present, and future must be considered. Only within this framework is experience a helpful approach to selecting an appropriate alternative.

## ■ Hunch and Intuition

Managers will admit at times that they have based their decisions on hunch and intuition. At first glance, certain managers may seem to have an unusual ability for solving problems satisfactorily by intuitive means. A deeper search, however, will disclose that the "intuition" on which the manager thought a decision was based was actually past experience or knowledge. In reality, the manager is recalling similar situations from the past that are now stored in his or her memory; this type of recall is labeled "having a hunch" or "gut feeling."

No superior would look favorably on a subordinate who continually justified decisions on the basis of intuition or hunch alone. These factors might come into play occasionally, but they must always be supplemented by more concrete considerations.

## ■ Experimentation

The avenue of experimentation, or testing, is a valid approach to decision making in the scientific world; conclusions reached through laboratory tests and experimentation are essential. In management, however, to experiment and see what happens is inappropriate and often too costly and time-consuming. Moreover, it is difficult to maintain controlled conditions and test various alternatives fairly in a normal work environment. There may be certain instances, however, when a limited amount of testing and experimenting is admissible, as long as the consequences are not too disruptive. For example, a supervisor might decide to test different work schedules or different locations for a new desktop computer. In this small, restricted sense, experimentation may at times be valid. In a supervisory situation, however, experimentation usually is at best an expensive way of reaching a decision.

## QUANTITATIVE DECISION MAKING

During the last five decades or so a new group of highly sophisticated tools has become available to aid the manager in decision making. These tools are quantitative, involving linear programming, operations research, probability, model building, and simulation. They are mathematical techniques applied by mathematicians, statisticians, programmers, systems analysts, or other scientists working with computers. A discussion of these tools is beyond the scope of this text, while a short description could not do justice to this important, large, and well-documented field of scientific decision making. The overall process is known as scientific decision making, or operations research.

Only certain types of management problems lend themselves to this type of quantitative analysis and solution. In a healthcare situation, for example, it could be applicable to problems involving scheduling, inventory, arranging for the best possible use of facilities and employees during various shifts, planning for the most effective use of existing resources, and so on. Such scientific problem solving is a complicated and costly way of reaching decisions, however, and it should be used only with the permission and knowledge of top administration when the magnitude of a problem warrants considerable effort and expenditure.

The problems confronting a single supervisor usually are not of this magnitude. If a major problem is affecting the entire organization, however, or if similar problems are found in several departments, it may be advisable for top management to employ the quantitative approach. Since most healthcare organizations today have access to computer systems, it should not be difficult to contact someone within information systems to see if they could lend some assistance in solving the problem. The programmers and systems analysts may produce not only an optimum solution, but their research may also lead to other findings that are welcome by-products. Management, however, should not forget that the process could be long and tedious, as well as expensive. If the problem is of sufficient magnitude, such effort and expense are certainly worthwhile.

### ■ Take Action and Follow Up

No matter what method has been used to arrive at the solution, effective action is necessary once the decision has been made. Going through the lengthy and tedious decision-making process is pointless unless the manager goes all the way and sees the decision carried out effectively. As stated before, nothing is so useless as a good decision that is not carried out. In other words, decision making is only one aspect of the manager's job; achieving effective execution of the decision is every bit as important.

Even after action has been taken, decision making is not complete without follow up to evaluate the effectiveness of the decision. This is the manager's control function. If all is well and the results are as expected and satisfactory, you have reached your goal. If the results are not as expected or if unanticipated consequences arose, however, or if something did not work out as decided, then the supervisor should look at the situation as a new problem and go through all the steps of the decision-making process again from a new point of view.

Action and follow up are impossible without two other essential processes, communication and coordination. Unless a decision is clearly communicated to the people who must carry it out and unless it is coordinated with other decisions and other departments, it will be meaningless. Thus, the two additional connective processes that are vital to management's overall task of "getting things done through and with people" must be examined.

---

## SUMMARY

Selecting the best alternative by facts, study, and analysis of various proposals is still the best way to make a managerial decision. If an objective, rational, systematic method is used in the selection, the manager is likely to make better decisions. The first step in such a method is to define the problem. After a problem is defined, you must analyze it. Then you must develop all the alternatives you possibly can, think them through as if you had already put them into action, and consider the consequences of each of them. By following this method, you will most likely be able to select the best alternative—the one with the greatest number of wanted consequences and the least number of unwanted consequences.

Not only can you learn this sound method of decision making, but as a supervisor you can teach the same systematic approach to your subordinates. In doing so, you are assured that whenever subordinates are confronted with a decision, they also will decide in a systematic and rational manner. Although this is not always a guarantee for arriving at the best decisions, it is likely to produce more good decisions than would otherwise be the case.

Scientific decision making, or operations research, is an approach to problem solving that involves quantitative analysis, models, and computers. If the problem is of sufficient magnitude to warrant such an expensive effort, sophisticated scientific decision-making techniques involving mathematicians, statisticians, systems analysts, and other specialists should be used.

# *Coordinating Organizational Activities*

*Chapter Objectives*

After you have studied this chapter, you should be able to:

1. Explain the increasing need for coordination due to increased work specialization and fragmentation of patient care.
2. Define the meaning of coordination as linking together a multitude of activities.
3. Differentiate between cooperation and coordination.
4. Discuss the obstacles inherent in achieving coordination.
5. Discuss how managers should not treat coordinating as a separate managerial function, but as a by-product of the five managerial functions.
6. Discuss the importance of good decision making and communication in achieving coordination.
7. Describe the three internal dimensions and one external dimension of coordination.

Division of work, or work specialization, means to break down a total job into smaller, more specialized tasks. Division of work and specialization, as discussed in chapter 10, involve separating employees into departments, divisions, units, sections, etc., based on their shared expertise. This method of work specialization is particularly common in the healthcare field. Having many specialized departments leads to large and complex organizational structures. This proliferation of specialties is necessary to assure the best possible care of patients as well as high standards of medical expertise. However, it creates additional problems for the management of healthcare facilities and even more difficulties within an integrated healthcare system, namely, the need for coordination—the process of linking together the activities of all the units in each of the affiliated organizations.

The reason for coordination is that all these healthcare entities depend on each other for services, resources, information, and communications. The interdependence is as great within a single organization as it is within a system. Patient care data is created and exchanged between patient service areas, e.g., from blood bank to surgery, from surgery to intensive care, and from intensive care to radiology. When many different specialized areas are interdependent on patient care data, more attention must be devoted to coordination.

Coordination of information in nonpatient care areas is as important as in patient care entities. If data is not accurately captured, reported, and assessed by management, then workflow will be negatively affected and goals will not be achieved.

## THE MEANING OF COORDINATION

We defined *supervisory management* earlier as the process of getting things done through and with people by directing their efforts toward common objectives. This means that management involves coordination of the efforts of all the members of an organization. Some writers have even defined management as the task of achieving coordination or, more specifically, of achieving the orderly synchronization of employees' efforts to provide the proper amount, timing, and quality of execution so that their unified efforts lead to the stated objectives. Other management experts have preferred to look at coordination as a separate managerial function. We look at coordination as the linking together of the activities in the organization to achieve the desired results. It is the process by which departments and tasks are interrelated to reach the objectives.

Thus, we prefer to view coordination not as a separate function of the manager and not as *the* defining characteristic of management, but as a *process* by which the manager achieves orderly group effort and unity of action in pursuit of the common purpose. The manager engages in this process *while* performing the five basic managerial functions of planning, organizing, staffing, influencing, and controlling. The resulting coordination, the resulting synchronization of efforts, should be one of the goals that the manager keeps in mind when performing each of the five managerial functions. Coordination, therefore, is a *by-product* the manager brings about while performing the five managerial functions appropriately. Coordination is a part of everything the manager does.

The task of achieving coordination is much more difficult on the top administrative level than on the supervisory level. The chief executive officer (CEO) has to achieve the synchronization of efforts throughout the entire organization. As a supervisor of only one department, you have to be concerned with coordination primarily within your own department and its relation to the other divisions. Achieving coordination is necessary, regardless of the scope of your division. As a supervisor, you should keep coordination at the forefront of your mind in everything you do. Synchronizing the efforts of subordinates should be a prominent consideration whenever you plan, organize, staff, influence, and control. Last, you should recognize that those activities that cut across and affect departments in addition to yours will result in a more complex maze of coordination efforts.

### ■ Coordination and Cooperation

The term *coordination,* however, must not be confused with *cooperation,* since there is a considerable difference between them. Cooperation merely indicates the willingness of individuals to help each other. Coordination is much more inclusive, requiring more than the mere desire and willingness of the participants.

For example, consider a group of people attempting to move a heavy object. They are sufficient in number, willing and eager to cooperate with each other, and trying to do their best to move the object. They are also fully aware of their common purpose. In all likelihood, however, their efforts will be of little avail until one of them, the manager, gives the proper orders to apply the right amount of force at the right place and time. Only then will their efforts be sufficiently coordinated to actually move the object.

Ensuring timely and accurate billing is a common activity in healthcare today that requires not only cooperation between several units but also coordination, primarily of data. Clearly, if correct insurance and patient identifying information is not collected at the time of admission or registration, the final billing function will be hindered. Regardless of the accuracy and completeness of the reports prepared by the physician and the coding applied by the health information coding staff, if this information links to an incorrect insurance number or patient whose name, for insurance purposes has a preceding initial before the first name, the bill may not clear. The coordination of information gathering is dependent upon each cooperating party performing his or her function with precision and then transmitting it to those other parties whose reliance upon it results in achieving the intended goal.

It is possible that by coincidence mere cooperation could bring about the desired result, but no manager can afford to rely on coincidence. Although cooperation is always helpful and its absence could prevent all possibility of coordination, its presence alone will not necessarily get results. Coordination is therefore superior to cooperation in order of importance. Coordination is a conscious effort to tie activities together.

## DIFFICULTIES IN ATTAINING COORDINATION

Coordination is not easily attained, and it is becoming increasingly difficult as the various duties in the healthcare field become more complex. As an organization grows, the task of synchronizing the daily activities becomes more and more complicated. As the number of positions in your department increases, the need for coordination and synchronization to secure the unified result increases. As stated before, specialization is another source that may cause problems of coordination. Also, human nature presents additional problems of coordination. Your employees are generally preoccupied with their own work because their evaluation is based on how they perform their jobs. Thus, they may have a narrow perspective and hesitate to become involved in other areas.

Coordination can be both hindered and helped by the use of automation. Some readers will acknowledge the difficulties they encountered when a new computer system was installed and then failed to interface adequately with other existing systems. Equally devastating is when an organization has become reliant upon a proprietary system that does not permit the integration of new technologies. The organization's investment is such that they cannot walk away from the asset they purchased, but they also cannot afford to do without the new technologies that may result in labor or other resource savings. This may be why "open architecture" systems are preferred since they allow different, yet compatible, systems from a variety of manufacturers to be used without a loss of coordination of data.

## COORDINATION AND THE MANAGERIAL FUNCTIONS

Coordination cuts through each of the managerial functions. We have already said that as a manager performs the managerial functions, coordination is one of the desired by-products. Let us look more carefully at how this important by-product is related to each of the five functions, as well as to the other connective processes.

When the manager *plans,* efforts for coordination must be made immediately. The planning stage is the ideal time to incorporate coordination. As a supervisor, you must see that the various plans within your department are properly interrelated. You should discuss these plans and alternatives with the employees who are to carry them out so that they have an opportunity to express any doubts or objections. By including employees in the process while plans are still flexible, you increase your chances for effective coordination.

The same concern for coordination should exist when the manager *organizes.* Indeed, the whole purpose of organizing is to ensure coordination. Thus, whenever a manager groups activities and assigns them to various subordinates, coordination should be in his or her mind. By placing related activities that need to be closely synchronized within the same administrative area, coordination will be facilitated.

Moreover, in the process of organizing, management should define authority relationships in such a way that coordination will result. Often poor coordination is caused by lack of understanding of who is to perform what, or by the failure of a manager to delegate authority and exact responsibility clearly. Such vagueness can easily lead to duplication of efforts instead of synchronization.

Coordination should also be an aspect of the *staffing* function. It is important that the right number of employees are in the various positions to ensure they properly perform their functions. The manager should see that they have the proper qualifications and training.

When a manager *directs* and *influences,* he or she is also concerned with coordination. The essence of giving instructions, coaching, teaching, and supervising subordinates is to coordinate their activities so that the overall objectives of the institution will be reached in the most efficient way. As some experts have stated, coordination is that phase of supervision devoted to obtaining the harmonious and reciprocal performance of two or more subordinates' responsibilities.

Finally, coordination is directly connected with the *controlling* function. By checking whether or not the activities of the department are proceeding as planned and directed, any discrepancy will be discovered and immediately corrected to ensure coordination after that point. Frequent evaluation and correction of departmental operations help to synchronize not only the efforts of employees, but also the activities of the entire organization. Thus, by its nature, controlling is the last process to bring about the overall coordination.

## COORDINATION AND DECISION MAKING

Since the process of decision making is at the heart of all managerial functions, achieving coordination must be foremost in every manager's mind whenever he or she is making decisions. When choosing from the various alternatives, the manager must never forget the importance of achieving synchronization of all efforts. Thus, that alternative most likely to bring about the best coordination will be selected. At times a certain alternative *taken by itself* may seem to constitute the best choice. A second choice, however, might result in better coordination. This is why chapter 3 stresses the importance of the solution's acceptability as one of the supervisor's considerations in choosing from alternatives. The supervisor would be better advised to follow the second solution, since achieving coordination is an important, if not overriding, objective.

## COORDINATION AND COMMUNICATION

In all coordination efforts, good communication is of immeasurable help. It is not enough for a manager to make decisions that are likely to bring about coordination; having decisions carried out effectively is at least as important. To achieve successful execution, the supervisor must first communicate the decisions to the subordinates so that they understand them correctly. Therefore, good communication is essential for achieving coordination. The importance of effective communication for achieving coordination will become even more clear when we discuss it in chapter 5.

Personal, face-to-face contact is probably the most effective means of communicating with others to obtain coordination. Other means, however, such as written communications, reports, procedures, rules, and bulletins, as well as electronic methods such as fax machines, also ensure the speedy dissemination of information to employees. Many organizations utilize E-mail, or Internet, technology today, which provides immediate response in written form and often facilitates communication between divisions that are geographically separated. National systems can use this technology to communicate new policies, findings, and reports to all locations within seconds. Individuals may access their E-mail wherever there is a modem and they have the designated software and computing capability. This access permits individuals to coordinate activities without delay.

## INTERNAL COORDINATION IN HEALTHCARE CENTERS

Because of the proliferation and specialization of medical sciences and technologies, healthcare centers have become large and complex organizational structures. More and more positions have had to be created, and this increasing specialization and division of work has generated a need for more and better coordination. As a result of such specialization, however, the synchronization of daily activities has become extremely complicated, and coordination has become increasingly difficult to attain. You know that as the number of positions in your department and in the hospital increases and as more specialized and sophisticated tasks are performed, the greater your need and effort becomes for coordination and synchronization to secure the unified result, namely, the highest-quality patient care.

Of course, the process of bringing about total coordination of *all* divisions and levels within a healthcare facility is ultimately the concern of the chief administrator. The CEO must deal with the fact that each department in the healthcare center is likely to stress its own opinion on how the best possible patient care should be accomplished. Each department, and each facility within a system, is likely to favor one route or another, depending on its particular functions and experience. This problem of different viewpoints also holds true among the numerous levels of the administrative hierarchy.

Considerable thoughtfulness and understanding is required of all managerial and supervisory personnel to coordinate the working relationships of the groups above, below, and alongside each department. Even with cooperative attitudes, self-coordination, and self-adjustment by most members of the healthcare organization, duplication of actions and conflicts of efforts may still result unless good administration carefully synchronizes all activities. Only through such coordination can management bring about a total accomplishment that exceeds the sum of the individual parts. Although each part is significant, the result can be of greater significance if management achieves coordination.

## TECHNIQUES AND METHODS OF COORDINATION

The techniques managers can use to achieve coordination are discussed in chapters 9 through 12, such as authority, span of management, delegation, and line and staff relationships. Policies, standard procedures, methods, rules, and performance standards are additional techniques used by managers to integrate activities. Good communications act as necessary lubricants in all these processes.

The techniques and methods to be used in an organizational setting will vary with the dynamics of the environment and the degree of specialization. If the manager cannot achieve coordination because of the dynamic nature of the environment, an individual in a liaison role might be called on to coordinate two or more independent units. That person, although without any formal authority, nevertheless is familiar with problems of both units and would facilitate coordinating needs. Some organizations engaged in high-performance and dynamic industries have even had to introduce an entire coordinating department into the organizational structure.

## DIMENSIONS OF COORDINATION

Working in any organization, one can see the need for coordination in three directions: vertically, horizontally, and diagonally.

### ■ Vertical Coordination

Coordination between the different levels of an organization can be considered as vertical coordination, such as between the CEO and the vice-president of facilities and between the vice-president of facilities and a director of housekeeping. Vertical coordination is achieved by delegating authority, assigning duties, and supervising and controlling. Although authority carries great power, effective vertical coordination is better achieved by performing the managerial functions wisely instead of relying on the weight of formal authority. (See figure 4.1.)

**Figure 4.1** Vertical coordination.

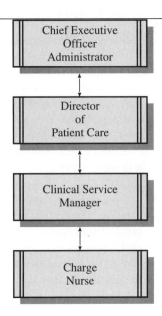

## ■ Horizontal Coordination

Horizontal coordination exists between persons and departments on the same organizational levels. For example, to achieve better hospital room utilization, the need for an earlier checkout hour has been targeted as the solution. To work out this problem, new arrangements have to be made between the various managers of the activities affected. Therefore, the director of admissions, together with the director of nursing, chief of the pharmacy, head of patient accounts, executive housekeeper, and director of ancillary escort services, who are all involved in the discharge process, will try to coordinate their activities to achieve this goal. (See figure 4.2.)

Each of the executives involved manages his or her own department and has no authority over the other executives. Horizontal coordination obviously cannot be ordered by any one of them. It is achieved by a policy and procedure stating that when necessary, the departments must interact, cooperate, and adjust their activities to achieve coordination. If horizontal coordination cannot be achieved, such a problem must be referred to a higher level in the managerial hierarchy with authority over all these departments. In all likelihood this is the CEO, who will simply issue the necessary directives to achieve better room utilization.

Some organizations that have experimented with a total quality management environment have succeeded in empowering their department leaders to solve problems that result from "glitches" in horizontal coordination. These quality improvement or performance improvement teams are permitted to assemble as needed and work through the issues. They use a variety of problem-solving techniques and participants have all been trained in the techniques and mores of this environment. Obviously, if those who must deal with the problems on a daily

**Figure 4.2**   Horizontal coordination.

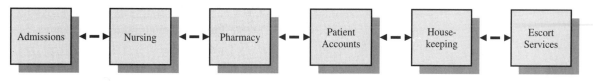

**Figure 4.3**   Diagonal coordination.

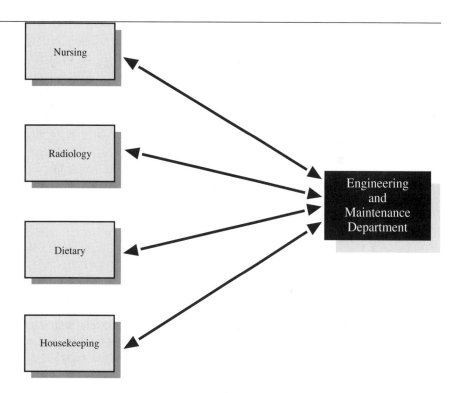

basis can gain consensus on the solution, implementation, future coordination, and cooperation will be enhanced.

## ■ Diagonal Coordination

Diagonal coordination cuts across the organizational arrangements, ignoring positions and levels. In a small day-surgery center, for example, close working relationships and short lines of communication make diagonal coordination easier than in a large organization. Even in this case, however, this process must be operative. For instance, in a hospital all departments need access to the engineering and maintenance department, a centralized service. This access has to be coordinated by negotiations between the users and the provider, who are responsible for working this out. (See figure 4.3.) Coordination cannot be accomplished simply by referring the problem up the line of command.

## THE COORDINATOR

Some healthcare entities do have positions labeled "coordinator"; these are often regular managerial and supervisory jobs and should be named as such. In these cases the title "coordinator" is a misnomer. For instance, instead of having a group of nurses, social workers, and health information professionals known as case managers, they might be called "case coordinators." Their positions, regardless of the title, as defined in their job descriptions are likely to be managerial to the extent that they manage a variety of healthcare resources. Some healthcare centers simply prefer the word *coordinator* to that of supervisor, for example, *shift coordinator.*

As stated before, however, the task of securing harmonious action and internal coordination within a healthcare center belongs primarily to those in managerial positions. This task should not be assigned to a specialist, often called a "coordinator." The managers are in a far better position than any specialist to view the various functions and determine how they should be coordinated to bring about the desired objective and get the job done. All managers must coordinate as they perform their five managerial functions. While some industries have found the coordinator or liaison position helpful, it is questionable whether the task of securing internal coordination within the healthcare center can be shifted or assigned to a special department or a number of individuals.

There are, however, several positions in many healthcare entities properly known and labeled as coordinators, such as in-service coordinator or education and training coordinator. These are usually staff positions providing service and assistance to whomever would need and benefit from their area of expertise.

## EXTERNAL COORDINATOR

In addition to the need for internal coordination, however, a need exists for coordination with factors *external* to the institution. These include changes in the method of reimbursement; governmental activities; medical, scientific, and technological advances; other providers; other provider or payor organizations; new user groups; joint ventures; and the social interests of the general public in healthcare.

In those situations where a hospital is trying to coordinate some activities with other healthcare institutions (such as long-term healthcare facility, surgi-center, joint venture, visiting nurses agency, etc.) or with any other external factor (social work agency, health maintenance organization, medicaid agency, etc.), a special coordinator or liaison person may be used. Such persons should be thoroughly familiar with the conditions and thinking of their institution, be able to explain these to the others, and communicate the findings and intentions back to their institution. Normally, however, an external coordinator does not have any authority to commit the institution to action. In most instances, it is necessary to check back with the administrator or executive director as to how far the institution will go to support whatever action has been chosen. In this situation, therefore, we are not dealing with a manager in the sense of the term used in this text.

Nevertheless, the importance of such external coordination should not be underestimated. The greater the degree of external coordination among healthcare centers and related institutions, the better our overall healthcare system will be. Thus, much is being said today about "interface relationships," i.e., analyzing behavior among healthcare providers and users at the point where they are tangent to one another.

Finally, management's ever-increasing problems of coordination, both internal and external, can only be offset by ever-increasing knowledge of how to perform the managerial job. Fortunately, management techniques are becoming more widely known because of: (1) the emergence of new tools and devices at reasonable costs, such as fully integrated management information and financial management systems, computer-based teaching software (CBT) on personal computers, bar code technology, optical imaging and storage, and E-mail; and (2) a more thorough understanding of the overall dependence and relationships among healthcare systems within the community, state, and country.

## SUMMARY

Coordination is a part of everything the manager does. Coordination is the orderly synchronization of all efforts of the members of the organization to achieve the stated objectives. It is not a separate managerial function but a by-product that results when the manager performs the five managerial functions. Coordination cuts across each of the managerial functions. A significant difference exists, however, between cooperation and coordination. Cooperation is always helpful in achieving coordination, but coordination is more encompassing.

As a supervisor plans, organizes, staffs, influences, and controls, he or she must remember that the ultimate goal is to achieve coordination or the synchronization of all efforts. The same thought should be foremost in the manager's mind whenever he or she makes decisions and communicates them to the employees. Achieving coordination is a valid consideration for all managers, regardless of their positions, level within the administrative hierarchy, or the type of enterprise in which they work. Because of the proliferation and specialization of the medical sciences and technologies, the task of obtaining coordination in a healthcare center has become increasingly difficult.

In addition to the need for internal coordination, a need exists for coordination with factors external to the institution, such as government agencies, local health councils, users, and other provider groups. To achieve this external coordination, facilities can use a liaison or special coordinator to provide the necessary contacts between the institution and outside entities.

# *Communicating*

## Chapter Objectives

After you have studied this chapter, you should be able to:

1. Describe the communication model and the roles of the senders and receivers.
2. Discuss how communication affects the organizational performance.
3. Identify and discuss the communication networks and channels.
4. Identify and explore communication problems caused by barriers.
5. Describe how managers can ensure more effective communication by overcoming the roadblocks.
6. Explain the operation of the grapevine and why it is important.

From the manager's point of view, communication is the process of exchanging information in such a way that mutual understanding is achieved between two or more people about work-related issues. It is a psychological process of sharing information to achieve a common understanding between ourselves and others.

Communicating is the process of transmitting information and understanding from one person to another. Almost all daily managerial activities involve communication, i.e., giving and receiving information. Communicating involves two or more persons. Therefore, behavioral processes such as motivation, attitudes, perception, leadership, experience, and feelings play an important role. When the supervisor sends a message, either by speaking, writing, or some form of electronic means, he or she encodes a message from a unique perspective. It is influenced by perceptions of the sender's world, making assumptions about the receiver's perspectives and how the message will be received. Backgrounds, perceptions, attitudes, values and so forth may differ widely among the individuals involved, all of which makes it difficult to achieve a mutual understanding of one another's ideas.

As with all organizations, valid information is needed by a healthcare facility. Communication provides the key to this important resource. A hospital devotes much activity to gathering and processing information from the moment the patient enters the facility until discharge. Serious consequences can arise when communications are minimal, become misunderstood, break down, or do not exist. The following incident is a spectacular example of the impact of no communication.

A few years ago a patient was "lost" for 25 hours in a Chicago area hospital. The patient, whose condition left him unable to speak or otherwise communicate and who needed support to sit up in a wheelchair, was secured to a wheelchair with a restraint belt, pillow, and lapboard. He had been receiving therapy in another level of the hospital and was wheeled by a volunteer escort supposedly back to his room. The escort wheeled him, along with another patient, to the passenger elevator. A second volunteer escort was to complete the assignment. About 45 minutes later, a nurse, assuming the patient was back in his room, could not locate him there. Intensive investigation began immediately, searching the hospital and adjoining buildings with the assistance of such people as the hospital security, unit staff, physicians, and nurses. The patient could not be located.

The search continued for 25 hours, when a hospital employee stepped onto an elevator to find the patient secured in a wheelchair but bent over. This person was unaware that the patient had been missing and leaned over to speak to him, offering assistance. The employee quickly observed that the patient was unable to respond, and after reading forms attached to the chair, returned the patient to his floor, where he was recognized by a medical student and returned to his proper room. During the "lost patient's" absence, several hospital employees who would have recognized the patient told investigators they rode the elevator on which he was later found and did not see him. An elevator repairman also said he and an inspector took the elevator out of service for some time during the patient's absence and that no one was on the elevator. Despite a thorough month-long investigation, the hospital was unable to account for the patient's whereabouts during the 25-hour period.

Communication is the third process that serves to link the managerial functions in an organization. Employees look for and expect communication, since it is a means of motivating and influencing people. Communication is vital to them not only for purposes of social satisfaction, but also to carry out their jobs effectively. Thus, the communication process fulfills both human needs and institutional needs. It is a process of pulling together the employees of the department.

You already know that as a supervisor your job is to plan, organize, staff, influence, and control the work of the employees and to coordinate their efforts for the purpose of achieving departmental objectives. To accomplish these goals, however, you must articulate plans and organize the arrangement of the work. You must give directives. You must describe to each subordinate what is expected of her or him. You probably will need to speak to each employee regarding his or her performance. All this is done by communicating.

As you continue supervising employees, you probably will come to realize that your skill in communication determines your success. Communication is the most effective tool for building and keeping a well-functioning team. Just consider your own job and you will quickly see why communication is essential to successful supervision. Communication is the only means a supervisor has to take charge of and train a group of employees, direct them, motivate them, and coordinate their activities. This ability to communicate is the essence of leadership. Is there any area of responsibility within your job as a supervisor that you could fulfill without communicating? Without effective communication, the organizational structure cannot survive.

---

## THE NATURE OF COMMUNICATION

Fundamental and vital to all managerial functions, *communication is a means of transmitting information and making oneself understood by another or others.* The exchange is successful only when mutual understanding results, i.e., when the meaning the sender wishes to convey has been transmitted. Agreement is not necessary as long as the sender and receiver have successfully exchanged ideas and understand each other, and the message received is close in meaning to the message intended.

As a supervisor, you spend most of your time in either sending or receiving information. One cannot assume, however, that real communication is occurring in all these exchanges. Also, being constantly engaged in encoding and decoding messages does not ensure that a supervisor is an expert in communicating.

Communication was defined as the process of passing on information and making oneself understood by another or others. The significant point here is that communication always involves two persons: a sender and a receiver. One person alone cannot communicate. For example, a person stranded on a deserted island who shouts for help does not communicate because there is no receiver. This example may seem obvious, but think of the managers who send out a large number of memoranda. Once a memorandum has been sent, many are inclined to believe that communication has occurred. However, communication does not occur until information and understanding have passed *between the senders and the intended receivers.*

Making oneself understood is another important part of our definition of communication. A receiver may hear a sender but still not understand what the sender means. Understanding is a personal matter between people. If the message received is close in meaning to the one intended, then communication has taken place. However, people may interpret messages differently. If the idea received is not the one intended, then communication has not taken place; the sender has merely spoken or written. "Simply telling" somebody something is not enough to guarantee successful communication. As long as there is no reception or imperfect reception of the idea intended, we cannot speak of having communicated.

Supervisors who use one form of communication will not be as effective in sending messages as those who communicate the same message in a variety of ways. Take the unit meeting, for example, this method allows attendees to hear your voice inflections and permits two-way communication because questions can be posed. However, if the messages communicated at the meeting are not written down and posted in minutes, they will be quickly forgotten. If any of the attendees were deaf and could not read lips, communication did not occur at all.

Some staff may lack the necessary prerequisites to read memoranda or minutes. These individuals will require the oral communication method. Others may find both the written and oral methods difficult to understand or retain. For these individuals, pictures, graphs, and charts may be a more meaningful method of communication. In summary, supervisors must try communication alternatives and utilize more than one method (such as written, oral, pictures) if they wish to ensure maximum communication. This chapter will discuss these methods and others in more detail later.

As stated before, communication does not require the receiver to agree with the statement of the sender. Communication occurs whenever the receiver at least understands what the sender means to convey. Two persons can fully understand each other and still not agree. Thus, your subordinates do not have to agree with everything you as a supervisor communicate to them, but they must understand it. No subordinate can be expected to comply with a directive unless he or she understands it. Similarly, supervisors must know how to receive knowledge and understanding in the messages sent to them by their subordinates, fellow supervisors, and superiors. Only through effective communication can policies, procedures, and rules be formulated and carried out. Only with such communication can misunderstandings be ironed out, long-term and short-term plans achieved, and activities within a department coordinated and controlled. The success of all managerial functions depends on effective communication.

## COMMUNICATION NETWORK

The organization structure will affect organizational communications. In chapters 10 through 14 we will discuss the formal organization structure and in chapter 15 we will learn that every organization also has an informal structure. Thus, in every organization the communication network has two distinct but equally important channels: the formal channels of communication and the informal channel, usually called the "grapevine." Each channel carries messages from one person or group to another in downward, upward, horizontal, and diagonal directions. (See figure 5.1.)

### ■ Formal Channels

The formal channels are established by the organizational hierarchy and formal reporting relationships. These channels follow the lines of authority from the chief administrator all the way down to employees. You are probably familiar with the expression that messages and information "must go through channels." This refers to the formal flow of communication through the organizational hierarchy.

#### *Downward Communication*

When it moves in a downward direction, this formal flow of communication flows from superiors to subordinates. The flow begins with someone at the top issuing a message, the next person in the hierarchy passing it along to those who report to him or her, and so on down the line. The downward direction is the one management relies on the most for its communication. Management devotes much time to communicate with subordinates through memos, meetings, and letters in order to explain objectives, policies, plans, and so forth. Supervisors send messages about these to their subordinates; they instruct employees through directives; inform them about work methods, procedures, and rules; and give feedback about performance, performance expectations, and so forth. Generally, downward communication starts action by subordinates; its content is mostly of a directive nature. The manager's position of higher authority requires effective downward communication. The manager should transmit the right amount of information, neither too little nor too much. Downward communication helps to tie the levels of the organizational structure together and to coordinate activities.

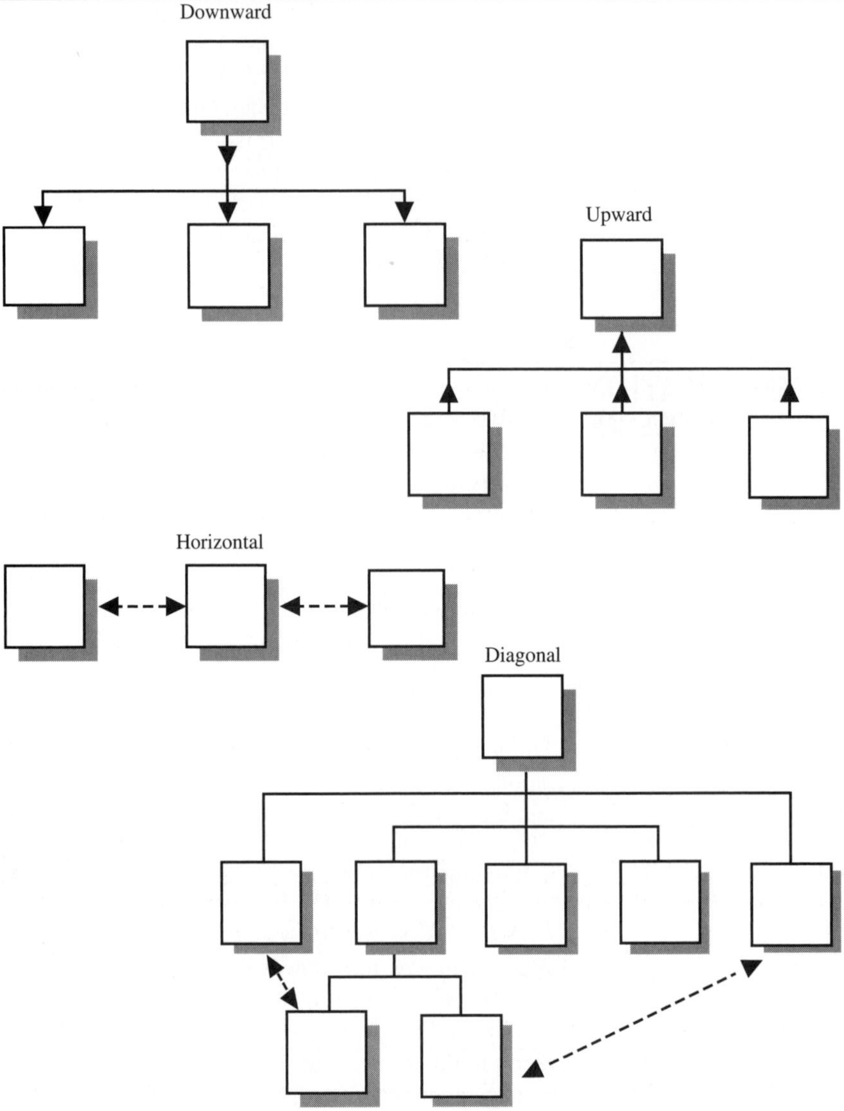

**Figure 5.1** The directions of information along formal communications channels.

*Upward Communication*

**Initiated by the Subordinate**

Upward communication is a second but equally important direction in which messages flow through the official network, but from subordinates to supervisors. Any person charged with supervisory authority also accepts an obligation to keep the superior informed. Subordinates must feel free to convey their opinions and attitudes to their superior and to report on activities and actions regarding their work. Usually, employees report on work progress, activities, and problems they have with their jobs; air complaints; and provide responses to inquiries. Much of this is predetermined and routine. Management should encourage a free flow of upward communication since this is the only means by which supervisors can determine whether their messages have been transmitted and received properly, and whether appropriate action is taking place. In addition to prescribed reporting procedures, an effective manager develops additional systems to encourage an upward flow of information.

As a supervisor, you should encourage and maintain upward communication channels and pay proper attention to the information transmitted through them. You must show that you want the facts and want them promptly. Unfortunately, the reaction of many managers to upward communication may be similar to that of ancient tyrants who executed the "bearer of bad news." In your supervisory capacity, you must make a deliberate effort to encourage upward communication by: (1) showing a genuine desire to obtain and use the ideas and reports of your subordinates, (2) being approachable, and (3) recognizing the importance of upward communication. Lack of an effective upward flow will throttle the will of your employees to communicate, lead to frustration, and ultimately cause them to seek different outlets, such as the grapevine.

### Initiated by the Supervisor

In addition to encouraging your employees to communicate upward to you, you must likewise communicate upward to your own superior. Persons who have been put into a supervisory position accept the obligation to keep their superiors informed. As stated at the outset, supervisors are the people in the middle. They are not only responsible for providing good communication downward to their employees, but they are also responsible for stimulating good communication upward *from* their workers and then passing this and other information to the next higher level in the administrative hierarchy. However, most supervisors will agree with the statement that it is much easier for them to "talk down" to their subordinates than to "speak up" to their superior. This is especially true if supervisors have ever had to tell their boss that they did not meet a deadline or that they forgot to carry out an order.

Nevertheless, it is the supervisor's job to keep his or her superior up-to-date on the department. The supervisor should inform the superior of any significant developments as soon as possible after they occur, even if the information reveals errors. If the boss were to learn such news elsewhere, this would indicate that proper upward communication was not allowed or that the supervisor was not providing it, or that he or she was not on top of the job. Superiors have a right to complete information, since they are still responsible if anything goes wrong.

Your superiors may have to act on what you report. Therefore, they must receive the information in time and in a form that will enable them to take the necessary action. As a supervisor, you must assemble all facts that are needed and check them carefully before passing them on to your boss. Bear in mind that upward messages are more subject to distortion than downward messages. Try to be as objective as possible. This may be difficult at times, since all subordinates want to appear favorably in the eyes of their boss. Thus, you may want to soften the information so that facts will not look as bad as they are. However, sooner or later the full extent of the malfunctioning probably will be discovered. When difficulties arise, it is best to tell your superior the complete score, even if this means admitting mistakes. Always keep in mind that your boss depends on you for upward communication, just as you depend on your employees to pass along their information to you.

### Horizontal Communication

In addition to downward and upward communication, a third direction of communication is essential for the efficient functioning of an enterprise. Horizontal, sideward, or lateral communication is concerned mainly with communication across departments or among peer managers, departments, and coworkers in charge of different activities. Horizontal communication is frequently used to coordinate activities, to inform others on the same level, and to persuade them. Horizontal communication occurs more among managers than among nonmanagerial personnel. For example, lateral communication will often occur between the recovery room supervisor and the head nurse on the surgical floor or the ER physician and the floor physician for an admission from the ER. This lateral channel is necessary to ensure coordination and to avoid misunderstandings. Horizontal communication also plays an important role in matrix and project organizations, as discussed in chapter 10.

### Diagonal Communication

Diagonal communication, on the other hand, is the flow of messages between positions that are on different lateral planes and activities of the organizational structure. Communication between line groups, such as nursing personnel, and between staff groups, such as the laundry department, are examples of diagonal communication, as are messages between the floor nurse and radiology, therapy, dietary, or laboratory departments. (See chapter 12.) To achieve coordination among the various functions in any organization, especially in a healthcare organization, a free flow of diagonal communication is essential. Without it, good patient care would be difficult to achieve.

## THE COMMUNICATION MEDIA

The media used most frequently for communication are verbal communication (oral and written words), visual media, and nonverbal (action and behavior) communication. Although spoken and written words are the most widely used media, one cannot ignore or underestimate the power of visuals and nonverbal communication.

### ■ Verbal Communication

Words are the most effective and most widely used forms of communication. They can be a real challenge to the supervisor, since words can be tricky and messages that mean something to one employee can have a completely different meaning to another. This leads to the problem of semantics. Semantics is concerned with the multiple meaning of words and phrases and how they are used in the context of messages. Therefore, supervisors must make an effort to improve their skills in speaking, writing, listening, and reading. (You may have heard the story about the maintenance foreman who asked the new worker to paint the canopy in the front of the hospital green. When the foreman checked on the job an hour later, he found that the waste container had been painted bright green. The new employee did not know what a canopy was. Perhaps he should have known, but no one had ever told him.)

## Oral Communication

The most prevalent form of communication in any organization is oral communication. Oral communication with your subordinates is superior to the written medium, since it normally saves time and achieves better understanding. This is true of both face-to-face and telephone communication. In daily performance, face-to-face discussions between the supervisor and subordinate are the principal means of two-way communication. Such daily contacts are at the heart of an effective communication system. Face-to-face discussions provide the most frequently used channels for the exchange of information, points of view, instructions, and motivation. No other form of communication can equal oral communication, especially the face-to-face type.

Oral communication is simple and can be done with little preparation and without pencil, paper, or PC. Therefore, effective supervisors will use this medium more than any other. They know that subordinates like to see and hear their boss in person. Also, oral communication is usually well received because most people can express themselves more easily and more completely by speaking than by writing.

Aside from these features, the greatest single advantage of oral communication is that it provides immediate *feedback,* even if the feedback is only an expression on the listener's face. By merely looking at the receiver, the sender can judge the reaction to what is being said. Oral communication thus enables the sender to find out immediately what the receiver is hearing or not hearing. Oral communication also enables the receiver to ask questions immediately if the meaning is not clear. Then the sender can explain the message more thoroughly and clarify unexpected problems. Moreover, the manner and tone of the human voice can endow the message with meaning and shading that even long pages of written words often cannot convey. The manner and tone create the atmosphere of communication, and the response is influenced accordingly.

There are some minor drawbacks to oral communications. No permanent record of what has been said exists. The sender may forget part of the message, or some noise (described later) or random disturbance may interfere. The many benefits, however, far outweigh these shortcomings.

## Written Communication

Regardless of the speed and effectiveness of oral communication, a well-balanced communication system will include both the written and the oral media. Although oral communication is used more frequently, written messages are indispensable and are especially important in healthcare activities. Often, detailed and specific instructions may be so lengthy and cumbersome that they must be put into writing so that they can be studied for a longer period. It is advisable to use the written medium for widespread dissemination of information that may concern a number of people. Furthermore, a degree of formality is connected with "putting it in writing," which spoken messages usually do not carry.

Written messages provide a permanent record that can be referred to as often as necessary. The spoken word, in contrast, generally exists only for an instant. Another advantage of written communications is that they are typically more accurate. The sender can take the necessary time to choose precise terminology, and to reread and redraft it before it is finalized. Written communication is preferable when important details are involved and a permanent record is necessary as "evidence." Many situations arise in the healthcare field where the written form is absolutely necessary.

## ■ Visual Media

Sometimes managers will also make use of visual aids as a way to communicate. Pictures are particularly effective in connection with well-chosen words to complete a message. Even without any words, however, visual media are a useful tool to convey a message. Many enterprises make extensive use of the pictorial language in such forms as blueprints, charts, graphs, models, posters, cartoons, and slides. Videos and comic strips offer clear proof of the power of the pictorial language to communicate and bring about understanding.

## ■ Nonverbal Communication

Although nonverbal communication normally does not use words at all, it can carry the same and even more meaning than words themselves. Sometimes it refers to situations where words are used in a manner that convey meaning beyond their narrow definition. *Actions* and *behavior* are the other media playing a part in nonverbal communication. As managers, supervisors must not forget that what they do is interpreted as a symbol or model by their subordinates and that often actions speak louder than words. Because of their managerial status, all observable acts communicate something to employees, whether supervisors intended them to or not.

The setting for the communication also can play a role as a nonverbal medium, expressing symbols of familiarity, power, etc. For example, consider the manager sitting in a manager's chair behind the desk and the receiver in the visitor's chair or standing up; this setting connotes the power and control of the supervisor. The manager's body position and facial expression also convey meaning. Managers who wish to convey "equality" will meet around a table or over lunch in the cafeteria, where the "turf" is neutral.

Purposeful silence, gestures, a handshake, a shrug of the shoulder, body movements, eye contact, a wink, interpersonal distance, a smile, and a frown can all have a lot of meaning. For instance, a frown on the supervisor's face at times gets the point across better than ten minutes of discussion. These are examples of nonverbal communication, sometimes also referred to as *body language.* Studies have shown that a large percentage of the impact of communication comes through facial expression, inflection, and tone of voice. By the same token, a manager's *inaction* is also a way of communication. An unexplained action can often communicate a meaning that was not intended. Suppose, for example, that a piece of equipment has been removed from the laboratory for overhaul and no explanation was given to the employees. To the technologists, who may be apprehensive of a reduction or change in procedures, such unexplained action could convey a message that the supervisor probably had no intention of sending.

The supervisor must always realize that nonverbal communication reinforces or contradicts what is expressed verbally. These "hidden" messages often are subtle and ambiguous and must be read with caution. They are, however, an important medium for the communicator.

## THE MANAGER'S ROLE IN COMMUNICATION

Since organizational effectiveness largely depends on its communication network working successfully, all managers must become familiar with what they can do to minimize communication problems and ensure its success. Most organizational structures today have many levels of supervision and long lines of communication. Breakdowns and distortions of communication can occur at any level of supervision.

All of you are familiar with the confusion, friction, and inconvenience that arise when communications break down. These breakdowns are not only costly in terms of money, but they also create misunderstandings that may hurt your teamwork, morale, and even patient care. Indeed, many managerial problems are caused by faulty communication. Moreover, most human relationship problems grow out of poor or nonexistent communication.

The way you as a supervisor communicate with your subordinates and your superior is the essence of your relationship. Always remember that no communication occurs until and unless the meaning received by the listener is similar to the meaning the sender intended to convey. The effective communicator must realize that the speaker and the listener are two individuals with separate backgrounds, experiences, values, attitudes, and perceptions. Both live in different worlds, and many factors can interfere and play havoc with the messages that pass between them.

## BARRIERS TO COMMUNICATION

The supervisor must realize that there are many barriers to effective communication that are sometimes referred to as "noise" in the system. First, we will discuss those factors that may create roadblocks to the intended meaning of a message, then we will examine the means of successfully overcoming these barriers.

Although many communication barriers exist, the more important ones can be grouped into three general categories: language barriers, status and position barriers, and general resistance to change.

## ■ Language Barrier

Normally, words serve us well and we generally understand each other. Sometimes, however, the same words suggest different meanings to different persons. The words themselves create a barrier to communication. An example of this word barrier is when a frustrating conversation ends with the people admitting "they are just not speaking the same language," yet both participants have been conversing in English. The term *language barrier* here does not refer to a difference in native tongue, but a breakdown in communication due to the communicator not speaking in terms, or in a style, the receiver understands. The sender should speak a language to which the receiver is accustomed. It is not a question of whether the receiver *should* understand it; the question is simply, does he or she understand the language? The supervisor must therefore use plain, simple words and direct, uncomplicated language.

In the healthcare field, concern about the language barrier is heightened. There are so many levels of unskilled and skilled positions in a healthcare facility, ranging from say the food service worker to the cardiothoracic surgeon. All of these people, however, must communicate in an understandable language in order to ensure patient care is delivered as planned.

This is difficult at times because one word in the English language may have several meanings. This problem is often referred to as one of *semantics.* For example, the word *round* has many meanings. We speak of round as a ball, a circle, a sphere, or a globe; he walks round and round, a round-trip, a round of beef, a round of boxing, round as a cylinder, round table, in round numbers, and so forth. When administration speaks of "increased productivity," these words may have a positive meaning for the manager and probably other, less positive connotations for the employees. When using words that have such different meanings, the communicator must clarify the exact meaning intended. The sender should not just assume that the receiver will interpret the word in the same way he or she does.

Many words in our language have reasonably similar meanings, but they convey different messages, as shown in the list following this paragraph. For most people, the words in list B convey a less favorable message than those in list A. When describing someone you care for, you are likely to use the words in list A. However, the listener tends to listen and interpret the language based on his or her own experience and frame of reference, not yours.

| **List A** | **List B** |
|---|---|
| Firm | Unyielding |
| Aggressive | Ruthless |
| Compassionate | Weak |
| Concerned with detail | Nit-picking |
| Confident | Cocky |
| Easygoing | Unconcerned |
| Selective | Arbitrary |
| Respects line of authority | Bureaucratic |
| An independent thinker | A nonconformist |
| Blunt and direct | Tactless |

## ■ Status and Position

An organizational structure and the resulting administrative hierarchy create a number of different status levels among the members of the organization. Status refers to how the members of an organization regard a particular position and its occupant. A difference in status certainly exists between the level of the president and that of the supervisors and also between the level of the supervisors and that of their employees. This difference in status and position often creates barriers that distort the sending and receiving of messages.

For example, when employees listen to a message from the supervisor, several factors come into play. First, the employees evaluate what they hear in relation to their own position, background, and experience, then they also take the sender into account. It is difficult for a receiver to separate what he or she hears from the feelings he or she has about the person who sends the message. Therefore, the receiver often adds nonexistent motives to the sender. Union members are frequently inclined to interpret a statement coming from administration in a negative manner because they are often convinced that management is trying to undermine the union. Often union members consider a hospital's newsletter the administration's propaganda mouthpiece, and its contents are viewed with suspicion. Such mental blocks and attitudes obviously do not make for good communication or understanding.

The supervisor who is trying to be an effective communicator must realize that these status and position differences influence feelings and prejudices of the employees and thus create barriers to communication. Moreover, not only might the employees evaluate the boss's words differently, but they might also place undue importance on a superior's gestures, silence, smile, or other nonverbal expressions. Simply speaking, the boss's words are not just words—they are words that come from a boss. This is how barriers caused by status impact the *downward* flow of communication.

Similar obstacles resulting from status and position also arise in the *upward* flow of communication, since all subordinates are eager to appear favorably in their boss's eyes. Therefore, employees may conveniently and protectively screen the information that is passed up the line. A subordinate, for example, is likely to tell the supervisor what the latter likes to hear and may omit or soften what is unpleasant. By the same token, supervisors are anxious to cover up their own weaknesses when speaking to a person in a higher position. Thus, supervisors often fail to pass on important information because they believe that such information would reflect unfavorably on their own supervisory abilities. After two or three selective filterings by different echelons of the administrative hierarchy, you can imagine that the final message may be considerably distorted.

## ■ Resistance to Change

Resistance to change can constitute another serious barrier to communication because often a message is meant to convey a new idea to the employees, something that will change either their work assignment, position, daily routine, working environment, or social networks. Most people prefer things as they are and do not welcome changes in their working situation. There are many reasons for resistance to change, but the most common one is that many employees feel that it is *safer* to leave the existing environment in its present state. (See chapter 19 for further discussion of the reasons for resistance to and facilitation of change.)

Ultimately, all of us find our niche in an organization where we feel comfortable. Our work area in a large department, our locker, our desk, our chair—all become part of this small workplace world. Consequently, many employees may be suspicious of a message that threatens to change their niche in the organization or their routine. Their listeners' receiving apparatus works as a filter, rejecting new ideas if they conflict with what listeners already believe. They are likely to receive only the portion that confirms their present beliefs and ignore anything that conflicts. Sometimes these filters work so efficiently that the receivers do not listen at all. Even if they hear the entire message, they will either reject that part of the message as false, or they will find some convenient way of twisting its meaning to fit their preconceived ideas. In the end, the receivers hear only what they wish to hear. If they are insecure, worried, or fearful in their position, this barrier to receiving communication becomes even more impermeable.

This filtering process can become a barrier to progress. Joel Barker, a well-known speaker and author on this subject, uses the example of the Swiss watchmakers who, in 1970, rejected a digital watch proposal from one of their own because they thought no one would want a nontraditional watch—one without a face, hands, and gears. Texas Instruments and Seiko then recognized the idea as a breakthrough in technology, and we all know what has happened since. Unfortunately, the Swiss were locked in gear and unable to progress past their own watch paradigm.

As a supervisor, you may have been confronted with situations in which it appeared that your subordinates only half listened to what you had to say. Your employees were so busy and preoccupied with their own thoughts that they only paid attention to the ideas they had hoped to hear. They simply selected those parts of the total communication that they could readily use. The information your employees did not care for, did not apply to their situation at this time, or considered irreconcilable was conveniently brushed aside, not heard at all, or easily explained away. The selective perception of information constitutes a serious barrier to a supervisor's communications, particularly when the message was intended to convey a change, a new directive, or anything that could conceivably interfere with the employees' routine or working environment.

### ■ Additional Barriers

In addition to the barriers already mentioned, many other roadblocks to communication arise in specific situations. For example, obstacles are caused by emotional reactions, such as deep-rooted feelings, biases, and prejudice. The subordinate's perception of the sender as not being trustworthy is likely to cause distortion. Other obstacles result from physical conditions, such as inadequate telephone lines, voice mail, overload of messages, lack of a private place to talk, temperature conditions, or noise. Indifference, complacency, or the "they-don't-care" attitude also may prevent communication. A supervisor who will not or does not take the time to listen is his or her own worst barrier to communication. In such a case, the message may get through, but it is acted on only halfheartedly or not at all.

Unless managers are familiar with barriers to communication, they are in no position to overcome them. Supervisors should not just assume that the messages they send will be received as intended; in fact, it may be more realistic, although discouraging, to assume the opposite. Since the effectiveness of the supervisory job depends largely on the accurate transmission of messages and instructions, managers must do everything possible to overcome these barriers and improve their chances for enhancing their communication effectiveness.

## OVERCOMING BARRIERS TO IMPROVE COMMUNICATION EFFECTIVENESS

Supervisors can prevent and overcome major communication barriers through adequate preparation, credibility, feedback, direct language, effective listening and sensitivity, appropriate actions, and some repetition. Becoming familiar with and using these techniques will increase your likelihood for successful communication.

### ■ Adequate Preparation and Credibility

Do not initiate communication before you know what you are going to say and what you intend to achieve. You must think the idea through until it becomes solid in your mind; do not just proceed with imprecise thoughts and desires that you have not bothered to put into final form. Only if you understand your ideas can you be sure that another person will understand your instructions. Therefore, know what you want to communicate and plan the sequence of steps necessary to attain it.

For example, if you want to make a job assignment, be sure that you have analyzed the job thoroughly so that you can explain it properly. If you are searching for facts, decide in advance what information you will need so that you can ask intelligent, pertinent, and precise questions. If your discussion will entail disciplinary action, be certain that you have sufficiently investigated the case and have enough information before you reprimand or penalize.

If supervisors are not a reliable source of information, problems of credibility may arise. If communication senders are well prepared and honest, however, credibility will not be a problem. Supervisors must overcome the barriers caused by their managerial position and by the employees' likely interpretation of the message's meaning. Some reactions should be anticipated, and the message should include clarifications of some questions it may cause.

## ■ Feedback

Probably the most effective tool for improving communication is feedback. It is the link between receiver and sender that makes certain that effective communication has taken place. Managers must always be on the alert for some signal or clue indicating that they are being understood. Merely asking the receiver and getting a simple "yes" is not usually enough. Usually more is required to make sure that the message is received as intended and that understanding is actually taking place. The medium used in the communication affects the type of feedback you may receive.

The simplest way to obtain such reassurance is to observe the receiver and judge the responses by nonverbal clues, such as a facial expression of understanding or bewilderment, the raising of an eyebrow, or a frown. This form of feedback is only possible in face-to-face communication, of course, which is one of the outstanding advantages of speaking to someone in person.

Another way of obtaining feedback in any oral communication is for the senders to ask the receivers to repeat in their own words what the sender has just said. This is much more satisfactory than merely asking the receivers whether or not they understand or if the instruction is clear, both of which require only a "yes." If the receiver can restate the content of the message, then the sender will know what the receiver has heard and understood. At the same time, the receiver may ask additional questions that the sender can answer immediately. This direct feedback is probably the most useful way to make certain that a message has gotten across.

Additional feedback can be obtained by observing whether or not the receivers behave in accordance with the communication. If direct observation is not possible, such as occurs with a written message, the senders must watch for responses, for reports, and as a last resort, for results. If these are as expected, the sender can assume that the message was received correctly.

## ■ Direct Language

Another helpful way to overcome blocks in communication is for the manager to use words that are as understandable and simple as possible. The communication should be on an adult basis, and the supervisor should not "speak down" to the employees. Long, technical, complicated words and jargon should be avoided, unless both the sender and the receiver are comfortable with them. The sender should also be aware of the possible different meanings that words can have for different receivers, as discussed earlier. Again, the single most important question is not whether the receiver should have understood it, but did he or she understand it at all?

## ■ Effective Listening and Sensitivity

An additional means for overcoming barriers to communication is to spend more time listening to the receiver effectively. Because of our different backgrounds, the working world or environment of the subordinate is often significantly different from that of the supervisor. Some common ground still is necessary for understanding. Therefore, you must give the other party a chance to explain what is on his or her mind. The only way you can convince the other party of your interest in and respect for his or her opinions is to listen carefully and completely; this means putting the other party at ease and not interrupting. Good listening means more than a mere expression of attention. It means putting aside biases, listening without a fault-finding or correcting attitude, and paying attention to the meaning of the idea rather than to only the words. (See figure 5.2.)

The supervisor who pays attention and listens to what the subordinate is saying learns more about the employee's values and relationships to the working environment. Understanding, not agreement, is essential. It may even be advisable for the supervisor to state occasionally what has been expressed by asking the common question, "Is this what you mean?" The listener must patiently listen to what the other person has to say, even though it may seem unimportant. Such listening will greatly improve communication, since it will reduce misunderstandings. Being sensitive to the receiver is necessary in order to communicate effectively. This means being sensitive to the receiver's perspective and position, and possibly even expressing empathy. Careful listening and sensitivity allow a speaker to adjust the message to fit the responses and world of the receiver. This adjustment opportunity is another advantage of oral communication over written messages.

## ■ Actions Speak Louder Than Words

Supervisors communicate by actions as much as by words. In fact, actions usually communicate more than words; that is, what a supervisor does speaks louder than what he says. Consider the accounting supervisor who preaches that all staff must be at their desks and working by 8:00, but he arrives routinely

**Figure 5.2**    Effective listening guide.

1  **Stop talking!**
   You cannot listen if you are talking.
   Polonius *(Hamlet):* "Give every man thine ear, but few thy voice."

2  **Put the talker at ease.**
   Help a person feel free to talk.
   This is often called a permissive environment.

3  **Show a talker that you want to listen.**
   Look and act interested. Do not read your mail while someone talks.
   Listen to understand, rather than to oppose.

4  **Remove distractions.**
   Don't doodle, tap, or shuffle papers.
   Will it be quieter if you shut the door?

5  **Empathize with talkers.**
   Try to help yourself see the other person's point of view.

6  **Be patient.**
   Allow plenty of time. Do not interrupt a talker.
   Don't start for the door or walk away.

7  **Hold your temper.**
   An angry person takes the wrong meaning from words.

8  **Go easy on argument and criticism.**
   These put people on the defensive, and they may "clam up" or become angry.
   Do not argue; even if you win, you lose.

9  **Ask questions.**
   This encourages a talker and shows that you are listening.
   It helps to develop points further.

10  **Stop talking!**
   This is first and last, because all other guides depend on it.
   You cannot do an effective listening job while you are talking.

• Nature gave people two ears but only one tongue,
  which is a gentle hint that they should listen more than they talk.

• Listening requires two ears,
  one for meaning and one for feeling.

• Decision makers who do not listen
  have less information for making decisions.

From Keith Davis and John W. Newstrom, *Human Behavior at Work: Organizational Behavior*, 7th ed., New York: McGraw-Hill Book Company, 1985, p. 413. Reproduced with permission of The McGraw-Hill Companies.

somewhere between 8:20 and 8:40. Therefore, one of the best ways to give meaning to a message is to behave accordingly. Managers who fail to bolster their talk with action fail in their job as a communicator, no matter how capable they are with words. Whether supervisors like it or not, their superior position makes them the center of attention for the employees. The boss communicates through all observable actions, regardless of whether or not they were intended.

Verbal announcements backed up by appropriate action will help the supervisor overcome barriers to communication. If the supervisor says one thing but does another, however, sooner or later the employees will "listen" primarily to what the boss "does." For example, the director of central supply services who says she is always available to see a subordinate will undermine the verbal message if the door to the office is kept closed or if she becomes irritated whenever someone comes in.

### ■ Repetition

At times it is advisable for a supervisor to repeat the message several times, preferably using different words and means of explanation. A certain amount of redundancy is especially advisable when the message is important or when the directives are complicated. The degree of redundancy will depend both on the content of the message and on the experience and background of the employee. The sender must be cautioned, however, not to be so repetitious that the message may be ignored because it sounds overly familiar or that the listeners feel patronized by the constant reminding. If in doubt, a degree of repetition is safer than none.

## THE GRAPEVINE: THE INFORMAL COMMUNICATIONS NETWORK

Although it is essential to develop sound formal channels, the dynamics of organizational life tend to create additional channels of communication. This informal communication network among people in the organization is commonly referred to as the *grapevine*. Every organization has its grapevine, a network of spontaneous channels of communication. Informal communication is a logical and normal outgrowth of the informal and casual groupings of people, their social interaction, and their natural desire to communicate with each other. People exchanging news through the grapevine must be looked on as a perfectly natural activity. It fulfills the subordinate's desire to be kept posted on the latest information. The grapevine also gives the members of the organization an outlet for their imagination and an opportunity to relieve their apprehensions in the form of rumors.

Attempts to eliminate the grapevine will be in vain. An efficient manager will acknowledge the grapevine's presence and possibly put it to good use. For example, by learning who the key members are, the manager can sound out employee reactions to contemplated changes before making a decision. An informal communication network also enables the manager to surreptitiously feed some information into this channel and obtain some valuable information from it. Being attuned to the grapevine will give the supervisor excellent insight into what the subordinates think and feel.

### ■ Operation of the Grapevine

Sometimes the grapevine carries factual information and news, but most often it passes on inaccurate information, half-truths, rumors, private interpretations, wishful thinking, suspicions, and other various bits of distorted information. The grapevine is active twenty-four hours a day and spreads information with amazing speed, often faster than most official channels could. The telephone and such electronic technologies as fax machines, voice mail, and E-mail via computers, help news to travel even faster via the grapevine and reach more people at the same time. The grapevine has no definite pattern or stable membership. It carries information in all directions—up, down, horizontally, diagonally, etc. The news is carried in a flexible, meandering pattern, ignoring organization charts. Its path and behavior cannot be predicted, and the path it followed yesterday will not necessarily be the same as today or tomorrow.

Most of the time only a small number of employees will be active contributors to the grapevine. Most employees hear information through the grapevine but do not pass it along. Any person within an organization is likely to become active in the grapevine on one occasion or another. However, some individuals tend to be active more regularly than others. They believe that their prestige is enhanced by providing the latest news, and thus they do not hesitate to spread the news or even change it, so as to augment its "completeness" and "accuracy." These active participants in the grapevine know that they cannot be held accountable, so it is understandable that they exercise a considerable degree of imagination whenever they pass information along. The resulting "rumors" give them, as well as other members of the organization, an outlet for getting rid of their apprehensions.

During periods of insecurity, upheaval, and great anxiety, the grapevine works overtime. In general, it serves as a safety valve for the emotions of all subordinates, providing them with the means to say freely what they please without the danger of being held accountable. Since everyone knows that tracing the origins of a rumor is nearly impossible, employees can feel quite safe in their anonymity as they participate in the grapevine.

## ■ Uses of the Grapevine

Because the grapevine often carries a considerable amount of useful information, in addition to distortions, rumors, and half-truths, it can help to clarify and disseminate formal communication. Informal communication often spreads information that could not be disseminated through the official channels of communication. For instance, the nursing director "resigns" suddenly. Although top administration does not want to say publicly what happened, it does not want to leave the impression that she was treated unfairly or discriminated against. In such a situation, someone in administration may tell someone in the hospital, who "promises" not to spread it further, what really happened.

Managers should accept that they can no more eliminate the grapevine than they can abolish the informal organization that develops among employees. It is unrealistic to expect that rumors can be stamped out; the grapevine is bound to flourish in every organization. To deal with it, the supervisors must be attuned to the grapevine and learn what it is saying. Normal grapevine listening is not unethical behavior by supervisors; they must look for the meaning of the grapevine's communication, not merely for its words. They must learn who the key members are and who is likely to spread the information. They must also learn that by feeding the grapevine facts, they can counter rumors and half-truths. This is one way to use the grapevine's energy in the interest of management.

Rumors can be caused by several different factors, such as wishful thinking and anticipation, uncertainty and fear, or even malice and dislike. For example, it is common for employees who want something badly enough to start suddenly passing the word. If they want a raise, they may start a rumor that management will give everybody an across-the-board pay increase. No one knows for certain where or how it started, but this story spreads like wildfire. Everyone wants to believe it. Of course, it is bad for the morale of a group to build up their hopes in anticipation of something that will not happen. If a story is spread that the supervisor realizes will lead to disappointment, the manager should move vigorously to debunk it by presenting the facts. A straight answer is almost always the best answer. If the supervisor has been able to build a climate of trust, the employees will believe the manager.

The same prescription applies to rumors caused by fear or uncertainty. If, for example, the activities of the institution decline, and management is forced to lay off some employees, stories and rumors will quickly multiply. In such periods of insecurity and anxiety, the grapevine will become more active than at other times. Usually the rumors are far worse than what actually happens. Here again, it is better to give the facts than to conceal them. If the supervisor does not disclose the facts, the employees will make up their own "facts," which are usually a distortion of reality. In many instances, much of the fear and anxiety can be eliminated by maintaining open communication channels. Continuing rumors and uncertainty are likely to be more demoralizing than even the most unpleasant facts. Thus, it is usually best to explain immediately why employees are being laid off. When emergencies occur, when new procedures are introduced, or when policies are changed, explain the reasons why. Otherwise, your subordinates will make up their own explanations, often which are incorrect.

Other situations may arise, however, in which you as a supervisor do not have the facts either or the facts are so confidential that they cannot be revealed. In such instances, let your superior know what is bothering your employees. Ask your superior for specific instructions as to what information you may give, how much you may tell, and when to give it. Next, meet with your assistants and lead employees. Give them the story and guide their thinking. Then they can spread the facts before anyone else can spread the rumors.

Although this procedure may work with rumors caused by fear or uncertainty, it might not be appropriate for rumors that arise out of dislike, anger, or malice. Once again, the best prescription is to try to be objective and impersonal, and to come out with the facts, if possible. Sometimes, however, a supervisor will find that the only way to stop a malicious rumor peddler is to expose him or her personally and then reveal the untruthfulness of the statement.

A superior should always bear in mind that the receptiveness of any group to rumors is directly related to the strength of the supervisor's leadership and the trust the subordinates have in the manager. If employees believe in your fairness and good supervision, they will quickly debunk any malicious rumor once you have exposed the person who started it or have given your answer to it. Thus, although there is no way to eliminate the grapevine, even its most threatening rumors can be counteracted to the management's advantage. Every supervisor, therefore, will do well to listen to the informal channels of communication and develop the skill of dealing with them.

### ■ When Communication Breaks Down Among Employees

Occasionally, disagreements will arise between staff and sometimes between supervisors as well. Your role as a manager is to ensure these disagreements are settled quickly and fairly, and that all points of view are considered. The Alexander Hamilton Institute of New Jersey offers the following advice.[1]

How to Deal with Conflict

To handle conflict among team members:

- **Ask those** who disagree to paraphrase one another's comments. This may help them learn if they really understand one another.
- **Work out** a compromise. Agree on the underlying source of conflict, then engage in give-and-take, and finally agree on a solution.
- **Ask each** member to list what the other side should do. Exchange lists, select a compromise all are willing to accept, and test the compromise to see if it meshes with team goals.
- **Have the** sides each write 10 questions for their opponents. This will allow them to signal their major concerns about the other side's position. And the answers may lead to a compromise.
- **Convince team** members they sometimes may have to admit they're wrong. Help them save face by convincing them that changing a position may well show strength.
- **Respect the** experts on the team. Give their opinions more weight when the conflict involves their expertise, but don't rule out conflicting opinions.

---

**THE IMPACT OF NEW TECHNOLOGY**    New information technologies are influencing and changing organizational communications. Price Pritchett explicitly demonstrates the impact of such technologies in his handbook *New Work Habits for a Radically Changing World* with such facts as: "Since 1987, homes and offices have added 10,000,000 fax machines, while E-mail addresses have increased by over 26,000,000."; "Close to 19,000,000 people now carry pagers, and almost 12,000,000,000 messages were left in voice mailboxes in 1993 alone."; and "Communication technology is radically changing the speed, direction, and amount of information flow, even as it alters work roles all across organizations. As a case in point, the number of secretaries is down 521,000 just since 1987." Teleconferencing—two-way communication between

---

1.   Reprinted with permission from "Making Teams Succeed at Work," by Alexander Hamilton Institute, Inc., 70 Hilltop Road, Ramsey, NJ 07446. To order, please call (800) 879–2441.

persons at different locations by video and audio equipment—telephone-answering devices, closed circuit television, videophones, electronic mail, Internet, faxing, and so forth undoubtedly have had major consequences on communications. Although the new technology has permitted a whole new way of communicating, all of the fundamentals outlined in this chapter will continue to remain essential for successful communications.

## SUMMARY

Communication is the process of transmitting information and making oneself understood by another or others. As long as two persons understand each other, they have communicated, although they may not agree. Agreement is not necessary for communication to be successful. To perform the managerial functions, a supervisor must realize the crucial importance of good communication.

Throughout every organization there are formal and informal channels of communication. These channels carry messages downward, upward, horizontally, and diagonally. The formal channels are established mainly by the organizational structure and authority relationships. The position of the supervisor plays a strategic role in the communication process in all these directions.

Although spoken word is the most significant medium of communication, one must not overlook the importance of nonverbal language as another meaningful medium. In addition, action is a communication medium that often speaks louder than words. In the healthcare field, the written word is a major medium of communication. Of all media, however, oral face-to-face communication between supervisors and employees is still the most widely used and the most effective, since it provides immediate feedback.

There are many reasons that messages frequently become distorted or are not accurately received. The manager must be aware of the major barriers to effective communication; some can be attributed to the sender, the receiver, the interaction of the two, or the environment. Efforts must be made to be aware of these obstacles and how to overcome them.

In addition to the formal channels, an informal network exists, usually referred to as the "grapevine." This is the personal network of information among employees fostered by social relationships; it is a natural outgrowth of the informal organization and the social interactions of people. The grapevine serves a useful purpose in every organization. Instead of trying to eliminate it, the supervisor should accept the grapevine as a natural outlet and safety valve of the employees. The supervisor should tune in to it and at times even feed, cultivate, and put it to good use.

New communication technologies such as electronic mail, faxing, and so forth have had an impact on how business is being done without changing the fundamentals for communicating successfully.

# Legal Aspects of the Healthcare Setting

Revised by Brian L. Andrew, JD and the law
firm of Polsinelli, White, Vardeman & Shalton
Carolyn A. Haimann, JD, Lynne Morgenstern, JD,
and the law firm of Lewis, Rice, and Fingersch

*Chapter Objectives*

After you have studied this chapter, you should be able to:

1. Understand basic information on legal issues affecting the healthcare environment.
2. Outline the basis of institutional responsibility for healthcare rendered to patients.
3. Recognize key causes for liability.
4. Identify employee litigation issues.
5. Understand the key concepts of both the Americans with Disabilities Act and sexual harassment.

Enormous pressures on the healthcare industry continue to create a legal environment of change and uncertainty. Courts have demonstrated an increasing willingness to adopt new theories of liability for healthcare institutions as providers of medical services and as employers. Government agencies continue to issue regulations that constrain hospital activities in an attempt to meet two distinct and possibly conflicting goals: holding down healthcare costs and improving the quality of care.

Healthcare institutions have lost their traditional role as charitable providers of medical care. Instead, hospitals, integrated delivery systems, home health agencies, managed care organizations, and a host of ancillary providers and payers are now recognized as business entities that, tax-exempt or not, must maintain a bottom line profitability to survive. These providers can no longer escape the legal liability that general business has had to cope with for decades. Advertising and marketing projects developed to address the present competitive climate in the industry require reflection on their legal implications.

Further, the development of Integrated Delivery Systems (IDSs) increases the potential for spreading liability over an entire network of healthcare entities and thus compels the need to recognize high-risk activities. These IDSs will need to be concerned with liability based on the various traditional agency doctrines.

There is no question that in order to function effectively in this atmosphere, today's healthcare managers must be aware of the legal considerations that may arise from their activities and decisions. All persons involved with the operation of a healthcare institution should recognize the importance and effect of law in healthcare delivery. All of these people apply laws and legal principles at times in their daily routines. This is true of the problems faced not only by the members of the board, administrators, and physicians, but also by all supervisors, department heads, and possibly everyone involved in healthcare delivery in a private healthcare setting.[1]

This chapter is intended to provide general and basic information in nonlegal language and should not be used in place of the advice of or consultation with legal counsel. The purpose is to give department heads and supervisors a general perspective on some of the legal aspects of their positions. The reader should be aware that problems of healthcare liability evolve from state and federal statutes and also from court decisions based on principles of common law and that they can vary from jurisdiction to jurisdiction. As with all aspects of law, health law and court decisions applying these principles evolve and change on a continuous basis.

For example, for a long time the courts protected hospitals and other charitable institutions from lawsuits that might infringe on the assets of a charitable institution. This was generally known as the doctrine of charitable immunity. As discussed later in this chapter, nearly every state has now established the doctrine that charitable organizations are obliged to compensate for injuries caused by them.

## LIABILITY

Liability is a word and a problem that has become more and more familiar to administrators, supervisors, and employees in any healthcare organization. This type of liability primarily relates to torts and related actions, as distinguished from liabilities associated with the organizational aspects of a healthcare entity (*e.g.,* antitrust, tax, fraud and abuse, insurance, or regulatory issues). Managers and employees at all levels are constantly being reminded of the potential for liability and its resulting costs to the institution. The need for in-house legal counsel, risk managers, consent forms, incident reports, and numerous requirements for documentation are reminders of the litigious environment within which the healthcare team works. Liability is on everyone's mind, and the burgeoning number of multimillion-dollar judgments against institutions and their staffs has become an albatross around the necks of management and physicians.

Just as charitable institutions were able to avoid liability that was traditionally applied to general business corporations, so too have managed care entities been able to avoid the liability concerns that were pervasive throughout the healthcare industry. However, a growing number of courts have expanded the utilization of traditional vicarious liability doctrines to managed care entities, particularly to

---

1. *This chapter does not cover situations in facilities operated by the Veterans Administration, Army, Navy, Air Force, Public Health Service, or other federal agencies.*

health maintenance organizations (HMOs). HMOs, a hybrid between health insurers and healthcare providers, are now subject to the same liabilities as a traditional healthcare provider, including negligence and ostensible agency actions. This includes an HMO being liable for the medical malpractice of a physician if it creates the appearance that the physician is its employee, regardless of his or her actual status. Thus, all of the discussion in this chapter of potential legal concerns to healthcare providers and institutions will naturally apply to managed care organizations as well. The following section addresses some of the various aspects of liability for the healthcare institution, the supervisor, and the employee.

## ■ The Institution's Direct Responsibility

Although liability is frequently imposed on institutions for negligence resulting in injuries to visitors and employees, most lawsuits filed against healthcare facilities involve patient injuries and allegations of negligent care. Therefore, this discussion focuses on the institution's liability for injuries to its patients and its responsibility for the medical care rendered by its physicians.

The law requires that any organization, such as a hospital, that the public relies on for its safety, has a duty to exercise ordinary care to prevent injury. The duty owed by the hospital to its patients varies to some degree from jurisdiction to jurisdiction and also varies depending on the particular circumstances involved. Generally speaking, however, in most jurisdictions a hospital owes a duty of due care to its patients to provide that degree of skill, care, and diligence that would be provided by a similar hospital under the same or similar circumstances. More specifically, a hospital has a legal duty to provide its patients with, among other things, premises kept in a reasonably safe condition, appropriately trained and skilled staff, reasonably adequate equipment, and proper medications. Whether the hospital has breached any of its duties to the patient in a particular situation usually will be decided by a jury. If a jury finds that a hospital has failed to meet the various standards of care owed to its patients thereby breaching its duty, then the hospital can be found negligent.

## ■ Respondeat Superior

Not only is the institution directly responsible for its actions in relation to the patient, but it is also indirectly liable for patient injuries. It is legally responsible for the actions of those persons, employees, and staff over whom it exercises control and supervision. This vicarious liability arises from the doctrine of *respondeat superior*. Under this doctrine, the institution-employer is legally responsible for the negligent or wrongful acts or omissions of the employee even though the facility itself committed no wrong; the negligence of the employee is imputed to the employer. If an employee commits a negligent act that is the direct cause of injury to a patient, then the employer may be liable for the damages awarded to the injured party. The doctrine of *respondeat superior* applies only to civil actions, thus an employer is not responsible for the criminal actions of its employees.

In order for the institution to be liable under *respondeat superior,* it is necessary that the employer have the right to control the actions of employees in the performance of their duties (*i.e.,* the method, time, and manner of work performance). If the jury determines that this is the case and that the employee (or agent) was acting within the scope and course of employment, then the institution will be liable. An act will generally be considered within the scope of employment when the employee is acting on behalf of or perceives himself or herself to be acting for the benefit of the institution.

The doctrine of *respondeat superior,* however, does not absolve the employee of liability for his or her wrongful act. The employee as well as the employer may be found liable in damages to an injured third party. Under the law, the employer may pursue indemnification from the employee for damages paid on his or her behalf under *respondeat superior.* In other words, the institution can seek recovery for the financial loss from the employee when his or her actions caused the facility to be responsible for the loss. This occurs infrequently since the adverse effect on employee morale outweighs the benefit of attempting to collect monies from the employee.

A hypothetical example will illustrate the application of liability under *respondeat superior.* Let us assume Joe Smith has been employed by hospital X for the past five years as a full-time registered nurse on its medical floor. He has a good job record with no incidents of poor performance or poor exercise of nursing judgment. While Joe Smith is on duty during his assigned shift on his assigned floor, he is responsible for passing evening medications to the patients. One day Joe fails to carefully check the order for patients Ms. Jones and Ms. Brown, and administers the medication ordered for Ms. Jones to Ms. Brown instead. As a direct result of the wrong medication being administered to her, Ms. Brown suffered a severe, sudden drop in blood pressure resulting in shock. Ms. Brown recovered, but not until after an extended hospital stay in the intensive care unit. She then sued the nurse and the hospital for negligence. The jury found the nurse liable for negligence and found the hospital vicariously liable because it was the employer. The jury awarded a single sum of money, $50,000, against both the hospital and the nurse jointly, even though the nurse was negligent and the hospital's responsibility was based solely on the theory of *respondeat superior.* The hospital paid the $50,000 to Ms. Brown and, in accordance with its policy, did not exercise its right of indemnification. It did not ask Joe Smith to pay the hospital $50,000.

In this example, the employer-employee relationships existed; Joe Smith was a salaried employee, whose hours of work, type of duties, and procedures for carrying them out were all controlled by his employer, the hospital. Furthermore, the wrongful act, giving the wrong medication to the wrong patient, occurred while Joe was on his assigned shift performing his assigned duties, and thus the act was "within the scope and course of his employment."

Just as the hospital in this example was responsible for the acts of its nurses, it is also responsible for the acts of all other employees, professional and nonprofessional, over whom it exercises the requisite degree of control. Thus, an institution will be liable for the negligent acts of technicians, orderlies, transporters, housekeepers, dietary personnel, etc.

The "borrowed servant" theory and the related "captain of the ship" doctrine are often mentioned in connection with the principle of *respondeat superior.* The "borrowed servant" doctrine applies in certain situations when a private physician has "borrowed" the employee from the hospital to aid him and thus the physician has assumed the right to control and direct the employee in the performance of a duty or task. Thus, the physician and not the facility-employer will be liable for that employee's negligent acts.

The "captain of the ship" doctrine, a narrower concept than the "borrowed servant" theory, applies in the operating room setting. Under this doctrine, the surgeon is considered the "captain of the ship"; that is, he or she has complete and total control and supervision over the personnel assisting him or her. Thus, the surgeon is responsible for the employee's negligent acts that occur during the procedure. The "captain of the ship" doctrine does not apply outside the operating room setting. It is important to note that this doctrine has been increasingly rejected by the courts in various jurisdictions. The current trend is to hold the institution, rather than the surgeon, responsible under *respondeat superior* for the actions of its operating room personnel.

In both the "borrowed servant" and "captain of the ship" situations, the key element is the extent and right of control the physician has over the employee whose acts caused the alleged injury. Courts carefully examine and juries decide whether or not an employee truly has become the "borrowed servant" of the physician before vicarious liability can be imposed on the physician for the employee's negligent acts. Generally speaking, in nonoperating room settings, a physician will not be held liable for negligence of an institution-employed nurse in carrying out the physician's order in the regular course of the nurse's duties. If a physician issues a medically inappropriate order, a court may apportion a measure of the liability to the nurse, and therefore to the institution, if another nurse possessing the same skill and training would have questioned the order rather than carried it out.

The concept of *respondeat superior* also plays an important role in the question of the institution's responsibility for actions of certain members of its medical staff. The facility is liable under *respondeat superior* for the actions of those physicians who are employed by the facility or are under its direct control and supervision. Interns and residents in a training program, for example, are considered hospital employees. They are salaried by the hospital to render care to its patients, they do not have private patients, and they are under the control and supervision of the hospital usually through a chief physician who is a hospital employee. Because interns and residents fall within the "employee category," because they do not contract privately for services with their patients, and because the hospital has a right of control over them, hospitals are almost always held vicariously liable for their actions.

Usually, however, hospitals (and other healthcare institutions) are not held liable for the actions of their private physicians practicing in the hospital or for other physicians who act as "independent contractors" and over whom the hospital exercises no direct control. The private physician is considered an independent contractor because he or she has an independent relationship with the patient apart from the hospital. The private physician makes independent judgments regarding care of the patient and is not compensated by the hospital for patient care services. He or she is merely making use of the institution's facilities and support staff for the benefit of the patient, the facility exerts no control over the patient's choice of physician and has no right of control over the physicians' actions regarding their patients.

## ■ Ostensible Agency

A clear trend has emerged in which the hospital has been held vicariously liable for the actions of an independent contractor private practice physician when no employer-employee relationship exists. In these situations, several courts have held that if the hospital caused the patient to believe that the physician rendering care to him or her was a hospital employee or agent, and if the patient did not choose the physician himself or herself, then the hospital was held responsible for the physician's acts under the theory of "ostensible agency."

This principle is most often applied in circumstances where a group of private physicians has contracted with the hospital to render special services, such as anesthesiology, pathology, radiology, or emergency room coverage. These physicians are considered independent contractors, not hospital employees. Some courts have held, however, that patients who come for treatment to the emergency room of a hospital that uses these contracted services do not know, and are not expected to know, that the physicians are not hospital employees and do not choose which physician they want to attend them. In fact, the courts hold that it appears to the patient that the physician is the hospital's employee. The same applies when a hospitalized patient is taken for tests to the radiology department staffed by private physicians who have contracted with the hospital to provide services. In most cases, the patient does not select an individual radiologist to conduct the test; the patient accepts treatment from the radiologist assigned. Although the radiologist is a private physician and an independent contractor, he or she appears to the patient to be a hospital employee who was provided to the patient by the hospital to render care. The courts that have adopted this doctrine have made it clear that the patient cannot be expected to know or understand the specific contractual relationship between the hospital and the treating physician.

Since hospitals routinely contract with outside entities to provide services formerly rendered entirely by hospital departments, the risk of this type of exposure is great in those states that have adopted this doctrine. A carefully drawn contract can afford a modicum of protection for the institution, although a contract's provisions cannot constitute an absolute bar to a court finding the institution liable for the acts of an independent contractor.

The courts have found a variety of factors that determine whether vicarious liability or ostensible agency exists. While it is not necessary that all of the following factors be present before such liability may be imposed, any combination may result in a court determining such. The following factors in some combination may suggest vicarious liability or ostensible agency:

1. The healthcare entity invites patients to utilize its services.
2. A patient receives treatment at the hospital by a physician provided by the hospital without specific selection by the patient.
3. The hospital fails to advise the patient that the Emergency Room (E.R.) physician or other hospital-based physician was not an agent or employee of the hospital.
4. The hospital arranges for a specific group of physicians to provide exclusively certain types of medical service.
5. The hospital directly bills patients for services of the E.R. or hospital-based physician.
6. The hospital undertakes to collect the accounts receivable of the E.R. or the hospital-based physician.
7. The hospital shares the E.R., radiology, anesthesiology, or pathology collections with physicians or guarantees them a minimum compensation level.
8. The E.R. or other hospital-based physician is prevented by a contract with the hospital from conducting a private medical practice or from practicing at any other hospital.
9. The hospital owns the equipment and operates the department utilized by E.R. or hospital-based physicians.
10. The hospital through its employees indicates that the physician is an agent of the hospital (*e.g.,* referring to the physician as "our" doctor).
11. The hospital's management controls the appointments of physicians.

Healthcare institutions should take steps to address these factors if their entities are located in a jurisdiction favoring the ostensible agency doctrine.

## ■ Institutional Responsibility for Medical Care and Treatment Rendered to Patients

Traditionally, nonprofit, tax-exempt healthcare institutions (most often hospitals) were not considered legally responsible for the negligence of private physicians chosen by the patients themselves and therefore were protected by the doctrine of charitable immunity. The hospital was considered to be merely the provider of the physical premises where the physician carried out his or her work. The hospital did not "practice medicine," only the physician did. The hospital's legal responsibility for the quality of care rendered by private physicians in its facility, however, has expanded greatly in recent years. This legal responsibility on the part of the hospital is known as corporate negligence.

The corporate negligence doctrine is primarily the result of case law beginning in 1965 with the Illinois Supreme Court case of *Darling v. Charleston*

*Community Memorial Hospital.*[2] In this case, the plaintiff sustained a fracture in his leg during a football game and was taken to Charleston Community Hospital for treatment. There the leg was casted, but severe complications arose, resulting in the eventual necessity for amputation of the plaintiff's leg. The plaintiff brought suit against the physician and the hospital. The Illinois Supreme Court held the hospital liable for the patient's injuries and held that the hospital owed a direct duty of care to the patient. This was a landmark decision because it imposed on the hospital the duty to monitor the quality of patient care.

The *Darling* case has been cited, followed, and expanded on by courts in most other states. The implications of the *Darling* decision for hospitals has been widely debated. The general trend since the *Darling* decision, however, has been toward holding the institution directly responsible for the medical care rendered to its patients. The court in the *Darling* case said:

> *The conception that the hospital does not undertake to treat the patient, does not undertake to act through its doctors and nurses, but undertakes instead simply to procure them to act upon their own responsibility, no longer reflects the fact. Present-day hospitals, as their manner of operation plainly demonstrates, do far more than furnish facilities for treatment. They regularly employ on a salary basis a large staff of physicians, nurses, and interns, as well as administrative and manual workers, and they charge patients for medical care and treatment, collecting for such services, if necessary, by legal action. Certainly, the person who avails himself of "hospital facilities" expects that the hospital will attempt to cure him, not that its nurses or other employees [ ] will act on their own responsibility.*

Clearly at this point, although the hospital is not legally responsible for the negligent acts of its private physicians acting as independent contractors, a hospital has a legal duty to monitor the quality of patient care and the care given by its private physicians. A hospital usually will be held directly liable under the corporate negligence doctrine for failing to select and retain only competent physicians on its medical staff; regularly and routinely review the activities of its physicians; formulate, adopt, and enforce adequate rules and policies to ensure quality care; and take necessary action against those physicians when the hospital has knowledge or reason to know that they are not performing according to set standards, are incompetent, or are endangering patient welfare.

In fact, state and federal legislation (*e.g.,* the Health Care Quality Improvement Act of 1986) imposes peer review responsibilities on hospitals that include reporting disciplinary actions and lawsuits against physicians on the hospital's staff to government agencies (*e.g.,* through the National Practitioner Data Bank). Some states have extended the reporting requirements to include nurses.

Liability exposure has also resulted from changes in reimbursement for healthcare services, primarily due to increased managed care products. As the principal method used to manage healthcare under a health benefit plan is utilization review, a medical insurance company, for example, will designate a

---

2. *Darling v. Charleston Community Memorial Hospital, 33 Ill.2d 326, 211 N.E.2d 253, 14 A.L.R.3rd 860 (1965), cert. denied, 383 U.S. 946 (1966).*

specified number of days for hospitalization of a plan enrollee. If complications develop and the patient requires a longer stay, the physician must seek third-party payer approval for the additional time. If that request is denied, the hospital will not be paid for the extended stay. These developments have given rise to the perception, whether or not it is true in practice, that patients are being prematurely discharged. Suits for injuries caused by premature discharge may not only be brought against hospitals, but against physicians and third-party payers as well.

Thus, in those situations where hospitals act as the managed care entity, there is increasing concern about potential liability for medical treatment decisions that may arise out of adverse payment determinations. The notable California Appellate Court case known as *Wickline vs. State of California*[3] held that third-party payers could be held liable to a patient if their prior authorization programs were administered in such an arbitrary or negligent manner so as to injure the plaintiff. However, in this case, the court absolved the payer from liability, ruling that the responsibility for deciding the course of the medically necessary treatment, including when to discharge a patient from the hospital, belonged to the treating physician rather than to the third-party payer. In those situations where hospitals have significant oversight of physician practices, it is incumbent upon the hospital to ensure that the physicians utilize to the extent possible all appeals and other grievance mechanisms set forth by the payer.

The growth of sophisticated information systems and the increased demand for data mean that more outsiders have access to hospital information. As it becomes increasingly difficult for healthcare entities, providers and payers alike, to maintain the confidentiality of patient records, patients are becoming more concerned with release of what they consider to be personal information. As health information management moves toward the fully automated patient record, information becomes increasingly accessible to providers, payers, employers, and other organizations. Recent federal and state moves for complete healthcare information automation and broad interchange of such information requires greater concern about the confidentiality and security of patient records. Healthcare entities must consider all these factors in developing procedures to provide the maximum protection of patient information. Although it is the institution's responsibility to develop these procedures, it is a supervisor's responsibility to make employees aware of these procedures and to monitor compliance.

## NEGLIGENCE AND MALPRACTICE

*Malpractice* is a term often used synonymously with *negligence* in reference to the actions or wrongful acts of physicians, nurses, and other health professionals. In fact, these terms are not identical but are similar. *Negligence* is defined in *Black's Law Dictionary* as:

3. *239 Cal. Rptr. 810 (Ct. App. 1986) review granted, 231 Cal. Rptr. 560 (1986), review dismissed, remanded, ordered published 239 Cal. Rptr. 805 (1987).*

*The omission to do something which a reasonable man, guided by those ordinary considerations which ordinarily regulate human affairs, would do, or the doing of something which a reasonable and prudent man would not do.[4]*

*Malpractice* is the term for negligence of professional persons. *Malpractice* is defined in *Black's Law Dictionary* as:

*Professional misconduct or unreasonable lack of skill. This term is usually applied to such conduct by doctors, lawyers, and accountants. Failure of one rendering professional services to exercise that degree of skill and learning commonly applied under all the circumstances in the community by the average prudent reputable member of the profession with the result of injury, loss, or damage to the recipient of those services or to those entitled to rely upon them. It is any professional misconduct, unreasonable lack of skill or fidelity in professional or fiduciary duties, evil practice, or illegal or immoral conduct.[5]*

Any individual can be negligent, such as when one drives carelessly and strikes another vehicle or when a home owner fails to rope off a hole in his front walk that is not easily visible. Only a professional person such as a physician, however, can commit malpractice.

To determine what does or does not constitute negligence, the law has developed a measuring scale called the "standard of care." Generally speaking, this standard of care is determined by what a reasonably prudent person would do under similar circumstances. This "reasonably prudent person" is, more specifically, a hypothetical person with average skills, training, and judgment. This is the yardstick for measuring what others should do in similar circumstances. The performance of the person being accused of being negligent is then measured against what the reasonably prudent person would have done in similar circumstances. If someone's performance fails to meet the standard, then there is negligence. Also, if it was foreseeable that failure to meet that standard would cause injury and if the negligence was the direct and proximate cause of injury, then liability will be imposed.

There are a number of elements necessary in order to maintain an action for negligence. There must be an injury to someone, a duty that must be owed to the injured person, a breach of that duty, and the breach of this duty must have been the proximate cause of the injury. If any one of these elements is missing, a negligence claim theoretically cannot be maintained successfully. The standards of care that medical professionals must meet are higher than those imposed on laypersons. An example of how these elements of negligence apply in the hospital setting in reference to a professional person follows.

Let us assume Jane Doe is a registered nurse in a jurisdiction that permits recovery against nurses for malpractice. Ms. Doe is assigned to give medicine to Mr. James, a patient under her care. She misreads the order, which is for 40 mg of the antibiotic gentamicin, and instead gives him 400 mg of gentamicin. This drug is extremely potent, and Ms. Doe knows that an excessive dose can cause

4. Black's Law Dictionary, *6th ed., St. Paul; MN: West Publishing, 1990, p. 1032.*
5. Black's Law Dictionary, *p. 959.*

renal problems. Mr. James suffers renal shutdown and has to be hospitalized for several more weeks. Applying the elements as previously outlined, Nurse Doe has a duty to the patient to possess that degree of skill and learning ordinarily possessed by nurses. She also has the duty to meet the standard of care for nurses in this same situation, that is, to act as a reasonably prudent nurse would have acted. In this case, this means that in meeting that requisite standard of care, she should have given the ordered medication to the right patient, in the ordered dose, at the ordered time, and by the ordered mode of administration. This is what a reasonably prudent nurse would have done in this same situation. Ms. Doe deviated from the standard of care (breaching her duty) by failing to give the correct dosage and was thus negligent. If her negligence was the proximate cause of harm to the patient, then she will be liable for damages. The burden is on the plaintiff to prove the standard and deviation from it. The jury must then decide whether the negligent act was in fact the proximate cause of the injury.

Despite the perceptions of most plaintiffs, it is important to recognize that not all bad results or unexpected outcomes are the result of negligence or mean liability for the person committing the act. Let us assume Jane Doe gave the correct dosage of medication to the patient. Let us assume further that Mr. James had never taken the medication before and on inquiry had said he had no known allergies to any drugs. Five minutes after he received the medication, he suffered a severe, unanticipated allergic reaction resulting in a cardiac arrest. In this case, although the medication caused injury to Mr. James, Ms. Doe will not be liable. She met her duty of care. She gave the correct dose to the right patient, at the right time, and in the correct manner of administration. She had no reason to anticipate that Mr. James would have an allergic reaction. Since she did not breach her duty she was not negligent. Therefore, without committing negligence, Ms. Doe cannot be found liable.

Oftentimes the most difficult element to provide in a negligence action is causation. One may be negligent but not held liable if the negligent act is not the proximate cause of harm to the other party. If Jane Doe gave the wrong dose of medication to Mr. James but he suffered no ill effects, she is still negligent. Because her negligent act caused no harm, however, she probably will not be held liable for damages. Further, as the time between the negligent act and the injury lengthens, the more difficult it becomes to prove causation.

We have taken a brief look at some of the various types of liability for the healthcare institution, corporate negligence, and *respondeat superior*. General reference has also been made to the employee's own liability for his or her acts. Let us now turn our attention to the liability of the supervisor.

## SUPERVISOR'S LIABILITY

We have seen how the healthcare professional can be held personally liable for his or her actions. Many members of this group are supervisors by title and supervise others as a regular part of their job duties. What about this aspect of their job? Can the supervisor be held personally liable for his or her negligent actions as a *supervisor* as well?

The supervisor is not liable for the acts of those supervised on the basis of *respondeat superior* because the supervisor is not the employer of those he or she supervises. The institution is the employer, and the supervisor has only administrative responsibility for those he or she directs. A supervisor is also not liable just because someone under his or her supervision acts negligently and causes injury to a third party.

Using the prior elements for establishing liability, a supervisor's performance may be measured against the standard of care for a reasonably prudent person in the same or similar supervisory position. If a supervisor fails to meet the standard, he or she might be held liable as a supervisor for the harm caused. If a supervisor permits or directs someone to perform a duty that he or she knows (or reasonably should know) the person is not trained to perform, then the supervisor may be held liable for negligent supervision if that person causes harm.

Let us assume Betty Green is a head nurse in hospital X. The hospital has a provision stating that no nurse employed less than three months shall be allowed to do endotracheal suctioning without assistance unless the head nurse is familiar with and has reviewed and approved the new employee's performance of that task. Ms. Burnside, a new employee, has been working under Ms. Green's supervision for one month. Ms. Green has observed Ms. Burnside help another nurse suction a patient and concluded that Ms. Burnside does not perform the task adequately and needs some additional in-service training. Mr. Kane, a patient, has an order to be suctioned if needed, and Ms. Green tells Ms. Burnside to suction him. Ms. Burnside does so, but incorrectly, causing injury to the patient's tracheal wall. Ms. Green will probably be held liable for negligent supervision. She had reason to know that Ms. Burnside by herself could not yet adequately and skillfully perform suctioning on a patient.

Liability for the nursing supervisors frequently arises as a result of the actions of nursing students under their direct control and supervision. Supervisors need to exercise particular care in not permitting nursing students and others in training to perform tasks and duties for which they are not yet trained or do not have adequate skill, information, or experience.

Remember the example given earlier in which Joe Smith gave the medication intended for Ms. Jones to Ms. Brown? In this case, Joe had worked on his floor for five years with a good record and no incidents of poor performance or faulty nursing judgment. His head nurse, as supervisor, would not be liable for Joe's negligent act. Since the head nurse is not Joe's employer, she is not liable under *respondeat superior*. Also, she is not liable as a supervisor because she had no reason to think Joe was not able to perform properly the task of passing out medications. If, on the other hand, Joe had made ten similar mistakes in the past several months and the supervisor was aware of this and took no action to counsel Joe or make sure he was performing properly, then the supervisor might be held liable for negligent supervision.

As a practical matter, legal actions against healthcare supervisors are not as common as those against healthcare professionals, primarily because the potential for injury to plaintiffs is relatively remote.

## ADDITIONAL POTENTIAL CAUSES FOR LIABILITY

Many other areas of healthcare activities have potential for liability of the institution, its supervisors, and its employees. These include obtaining informed consent from patients; following proper admission and discharge procedures to avoid charges of false imprisonment, negligent failure to render treatment, or abandonment of care; negligent selection or credentialing of providers; and ensuring a safe work environment for employees. Institutions and personnel must also deal with controversial issues fraught with philosophical, moral, legal, and ethical complexities, such as abortion, sterilization, and the right to die with dignity. A discussion of these and other issues, however, is beyond the scope of this chapter.

## EMPLOYEE LITIGATION

Employees are becoming increasingly aware of their legal rights, resulting in an explosion in the number of legal actions brought by employees against their current or former employers. Oftentimes these claims involve a former employee alleging unlawful discharge by the employer. This is a recent phenomenon, since historically the law viewed the employment relationship as one "at will." That is, if there was no contract for a specific term, the employee or employer could terminate the employment relationship at any time and for any reason.

The first exceptions to this legal principle originated with statutory and constitutional prohibitions against discrimination based on race. More recently sex, national origin, age, handicap, and pregnancy discrimination have been prohibited by statute and regulation. Following on the heels of these legislated exceptions, the courts in many states have begun to acknowledge other situations where an employer cannot rely on the "employment at will" doctrine. Courts have recognized claims where an employee was discharged for refusing to perform an illegal act, for "whistle-blowing" against the employer, or for breaching what the employee alleged to be an express or implied contract. In many states, employees have successfully claimed that employee handbooks are essentially valid written contracts or that statements made during job interviews constitute implied contracts.

Employee litigation, however legitimate, places additional burdens on supervisors, since it is their responsibility to treat an employee fairly, to follow institutional policy regarding discipline, and to monitor and document the employee's performance accurately. If a supervisor fails to follow proper procedures and to document incidents and the manner in which employees discharge their duties, the institution is left open to claims that an employee was disciplined for discriminatory or wrongful reasons and not for poor performance.

### ■ Americans with Disabilities Act

The Americans with Disabilities Act ("ADA") is a comprehensive federal statute that was enacted to protect those with physical or emotional disabilities. It makes it illegal for most entities to discriminate against individuals with disabilities in such areas as employment and public accommodations. The ADA has spawned a variety of novel claims that could not have been predicted even a short time ago. Therefore, expert healthcare employment relations' legal counsel should be consulted for additional information.

The act identifies a disability as a past, current, or perceived physical or mental impairment of a major life activity. Employers are prohibited under the ADA from doing any of the following:

1. Limiting, segregating, or classifying a disabled job applicant or employee in a way that adversely affects job opportunities or status.
2. Participating in an arrangement that has the effect of discriminating against a disabled individual.
3. Utilizing standards, criteria, or methods that have the effect of discriminating on the basis of disability.
4. Denying equal jobs or benefits to individuals based upon their relationship or association with an individual known to be disabled.
5. Using standards or tests that screen out disabled individuals unless the standard or test is job related and consistent with business necessity.

The ADA imposes upon employers a duty to "reasonably accommodate" a disabled individual's ability to perform essential job functions. Such reasonable accommodation includes the following:

1. Making facilities accessible to and usable by disabled persons.
2. Job restructuring.
3. Modifying work schedules.
4. Reassigning a disabled person to a vacant position.
5. Acquiring equipment or devices.
6. Adjusting or altering tests.
7. Providing training materials.
8. Furnishing readers or interpreters.
9. Making other similar adjustments to a job.

A reasonable accommodation need not be the best accommodation available, as long as it is effective for the purpose.

An employer may not use qualification standards or selection criteria that screen out or tend to screen out an individual with a disability on the basis of his or her disability, <u>unless</u> the standard or criterion is <u>job related and consistent with business necessity</u> (the standard or criterion must be a legitimate measure or qualification for the specific job for which it is being used and must relate to the essential functions of the job). In screening applicants for positions, though, an employer is not required to lower existing production standards applicable to the quality or quantity of work for a given job in considering the qualifications of an individual with a disability, if these standards are applied uniformly to all applicants and employees in that job.

Under the ADA, an employer may not inquire into an applicant's medical condition or disabilities prior to making a conditional offer of employment. An employer, though, may ask a job applicant about his or her ability to perform specific job functions, tasks, or duties, as long as those questions are not phrased in terms of a disability. An employer also may ask an applicant to describe or demonstrate how he or she will perform specific job functions, if this is required of everyone applying for a job in this job category, regardless of disability.

An employer may not require a job applicant to take a medical examination, to respond to medical inquiries, or to provide information about workers' compensation claims before making an offer of employment. An employer, however, may condition a job offer on an applicant's ability to pass a medical examination if it requires all applicants within the same job classification to satisfy that condition.

While an employer may not discriminate against a drug addict because of a history of drug addition, if the individual is not currently using drugs and has been rehabilitated, an employer may do the following:

1. Prohibit the illegal use of drugs and the use of alcohol at the work place.
2. Test for the illegal use of drugs.
3. Discharge or deny employment to persons who currently engage in the illegal use of drugs.
4. Discipline, discharge, or deny employment to an alcoholic whose use of alcohol impairs job performance or conduct to the extent that he or she is not a "qualified individual with a disability."
5. Require employees who use drugs or alcohol to meet the same standards of performance and conduct that are set for other employees.

## ■ Sexual Harassment

Workplace harassment has become a heavily litigated area in the field of employment law. The recent media attention to sexual harassment will likely increase such claims.

Claims of sexual harassment can be brought under either federal or state law. The applicable federal statute is Title VII of the Civil Rights Act of 1964 and the amendments thereto, enacted under the Civil Rights Act of 1991. Title VII prohibits discrimination generally on the basis of sex. Most states now have antidiscrimination statutes that likewise prohibit sexual harassment. Relief in a Title VII case, as amended by the 1991 Civil Rights Act, includes "make whole" damages, meaning back pay and lost benefits, plus attorney's fees, front pay (*i.e.,* wages into the future) when reinstatement is impossible or impractical, and now includes compensatory damages (*i.e.,* monetary loss, emotional pain, mental anguish, etc.) and punitive damages. In addition, the 1991 Act provides for jury trials. The amount of damages are, however, limited, depending on the size of the employer. In general, under state law, the broader range of remedies is available, including emotional distress and punitive damages.

Guidance on acts that constitute sexual harassment at your healthcare organization can be obtained from the Human Resources Department.

**SUMMARY**    The healthcare institution's legal responsibility for what occurs on its premises or by its employees and agents is cause for concern by administrators, supervisors, and employees alike. The professional members of the healthcare team also are being held to stricter and higher standards of care and continue to be held liable for their negligent acts. Those practicing in the healthcare field are well advised to familiarize themselves with the various aspects of their job that could result in liability to themselves or their institution. They must be able to recognize potential legal issues, understand the practical ramifications, and exercise caution and care in the performance of their duties.

# PART III
# PLANNING

# *Managerial Planning*

## *Chapter Objectives*

After you have studied this chapter, you should be able to:

1. Describe the planning function and its importance as a primary function.
2. Discuss the various planning periods and how they are integrated.
3. Relate goals and objectives to organizational planning.
4. Describe how management by objectives (MBO) can be used to implement plans.
5. Distinguish between standing plans and single-use plans.
6. Discuss the various types of standing plans and their effects on the managerial decision making.
7. Describe the types of single-use plans and their purposes.

Planning is the primary managerial function. It is the process of deciding in advance what is to be done in the future. Logically, planning must come before any of the other functions because it determines the framework in which the other functions—organizing, staffing, influencing, and controlling—are carried out. Planning begins with decision making, the process of selecting from alternatives. Modern healthcare activities operate in an environment that is always changing in ways institutions can neither control nor predict precisely. This increases the need for planning. The only way healthcare organizations can survive is to plan rationally and prepare for change. Although many plans are not carried out exactly as planned due to changing circumstances, experience has shown that those institutions that did plan tend to be more successful than those that did not plan at all.

Every organization must plan ahead because it dare not face the future unprepared. In planning, management is concerned with formulating a strategy, establishing the objectives (or critical success factors) to be achieved, and determining how to achieve them. Planning information is assembled, the external and internal environments are studied, planning premises are set out, and decisions are made to reach organizational goals. The decisions made in planning provide the operational units of the organization with their objectives and with the standards against which performance is measured.

Thus, when the manager plans a course of action for the future, he or she attempts to insure a consistent and coordinated operation aimed at achieving the desired results. Plans alone do not bring about these results; to achieve them, effective operation of the healthcare center by managers knowledgeable of the plan is necessary. Without plans, however, random activities by all managers would prevail, resulting in confusion and possibly even chaos. The plan serves as the road map for managers to follow as they chart their path in contributing to successfully reaching the goal.

# THE NATURE OF PLANNING

## Planning as a Continuous Mental Process and Primary Function

No substitute exists for the hard thinking that planning demands. One should think before acting and base action on facts rather than guesses. For this reason, planning is the primary function that must come before the manager can intelligently perform any of the other managerial functions. Only after having made the plans can the manager organize, staff, influence, and control. How could he or she properly and effectively organize the workings of the department without having a plan in mind? How could the department head effectively staff and supervise the employees without knowing which avenues, policies, procedures, and methods to follow and without knowing what the objectives are? And how could the activities of the employees possibly be controlled? None of these functions could be performed without having been planned first.

However, planning does not end abruptly when the manager begins to perform the other functions. It should not be a process used only at occasional intervals or when the manager is not too engrossed in the daily chores. Rather, planning is a continuous process that must be done every day. With day-to-day planning, the supervisor realistically anticipates future problems, analyzes them, determines their probable effect on the activities, and decides on the plan of action that will lead to the desired results.

## ■ Planning as a Task of Every Manager

It is the job of every manager to do the planning, whether chairman of the board, chief administrator of a clinic, executive director of a nursing home, or supervisor of a small department. By definition, all of these people are managers and therefore all of them must do the planning. The importance and magnitude of the plans will depend on the level at which plans are determined. Planning at the top level of administration is more fundamental and more far-reaching than at the supervisory levels of management, where the scope and extent of planning become narrower and more detailed.

Thus, the chief administrator is concerned with the overall aspects of planning for the entire healthcare organization, such as constructing new facilities, adding new services, aligning with other organizations, and enlarging outpatient services. Planning for new buildings encompassed most of healthcare's long-range planning during the 1960s. In the 1980s, management developed plans that would reduce inpatient costs to respond to prospective payment systems using diagnosis related groups (DRGs). In the 1990s, managed care began its ratcheting efforts on healthcare provider reimbursement. Today's long-range planning must make certain that the healthcare center's services are appropriate, timely, and competitive; it probably will also include plans for shared services and affiliations with other healthcare providers; and above all, it must improve the quality of care. As managed care penetrates more communities, today's managers must attempt to plan programs that will be cost-effective and *managed health.*

An example of a Chief Information Officer's long-range planning may include setting objectives for achieving a paperless environment for the organization. The information systems supervisor who is knowledgeable about this plan will define priorities (which areas should be involved, what equipment is needed, etc.), write new procedures, and determine activities to fulfill these objectives. A supervisor is more concerned with plans for getting the job in the department done promptly and effectively each day or, as some say, "operationalizing" the plan.

Although planning is the manager's function, this does not mean that others should not be called on for advice. Some healthcare institutions have full-time employees known as "planners," usually in a staff position. They are normally employed to help the chief executive officer (CEO) in his or her long-term strategy and planning decisions. It is unlikely that supervisors would need such planners' help. However, at times a supervisor may think that certain areas of planning require special knowledge, such as with human resources, (scheduling due to transcriptionist shortages), information systems (implement an optical imaging system), and accounting procedures (how to budget a lease), or with professional and technical aspects. In such instances, the supervisor must feel free to call on specialists within the organization to help with the planning. In other words, a manager should avail himself or herself of all possible help to plan effectively. However, it is still the manager's (and no one else's) personal responsibility to plan.

## ■ Benefits of Planning

Planning is a rigorous process of establishing objectives; deciding on strategies, tactics, and activities to achieve them; and formally documenting expectations. It makes for purposeful organization and activities, which in turn minimize costs and reduce waste. Deciding in advance what is to be done—how, by whom, where, and when—promotes efficient and orderly operations and reduces errors. All efforts are directed toward a desired result, so that haphazard approaches are minimized, activities are coordinated, and duplications are avoided. Minimum time is needed to complete each planned activity because only the necessary amount of work is done. Facilities are used to their best advantage and guesswork is eliminated. Thus, planning has many benefits that no manager can afford to neglect.

Effective management demands optimum use of the organization's resources. As a supervisor, you are entrusted with the management of both the employees and physical resources of the department. You have to work with people and also with such factors as space, equipment, tools, and materials. How all these resources are used is your primary responsibility and the basis on which your managerial performance is judged.

Only by planning will you be able to make the best possible use of these resources and bring out the best in your employees, the most valuable resource you have. Plans for the proper use of physical resources are also essential because of the capital investment that the healthcare center has made in them.

| THE STRATEGIC PLANNING PROCESS | As a supervisor, you may be asked to contribute information for consideration during the strategic planning sessions typically attended by the board of trustees or directors and senior management or administration of the healthcare organization. In addition, the strategic planning facilitator may invite external experts to guide the thinking. Such experts may include the organization's external auditors, professional association leaders, and community leaders. |
|---|---|

## ■ Steps of the Process

One of the first steps during any strategic planning process is to validate the organization's *mission,* a statement describing concisely what the organization does today. A mission statement may be: "We provide long-term, skilled nursing and rehabilitative services for individuals residing in our facility in a cost-effective and high-quality manner."

With the merger of organizations, the mission of one entity may have changed when it merged with another or the mission may have changed naturally over time as new services were added by the organization. Consider the changes to the above cited mission if this organization now offers home health services.

As mentioned above, much information is needed to plan effectively. The information review is known as the *environmental assessment* and is not limited to internal information. To be able to predict the impact of changing or adding services, linking with another organization, etc., one must know what is happening outside the walls of the organization and in the healthcare industry in general. Therefore, the *environmental assessment* includes a comprehensive analysis of information about: the organization's current, past, and potential future customers; competitors in the region and those who may "invade" the region served by the organization; societal changes such as demographic shifts in the aged population, movement of the population, or expectations from society in general of healthcare providers; industry indicators and comparative data; and, of course, how your own organization is performing (financially; in terms of patient outcomes and volume; staff and patient satisfaction; licensure issues, etc.).

The last component, the internal organization review, often includes what is known as a *SWOT analysis.* The SWOT (**S**trengths, **W**eaknesses, **O**pportunities, and **T**hreats) analysis evaluates the internal organization based on its strengths compared to competitors and regional/societal demands, weakness compared to competitors or just the internal functions, opportunities for advancing ahead of competitors or serving a patient population not served or well served currently, and threats from external or internal agents that could stymie the organization's success.

## ■ Identifying Critical Success Factors or Objectives for the Organization

Once the environmental assessment and analysis has been completed, the leadership of the organization (those participating in the strategic planning activities) will formulate a *vision.*

The *vision* of an organization is a statement about where the leadership sees the organization going in the next, 5 years perhaps or what it will look like in say 5 years. The next step is to prioritize those actions indicated for the organization to continue to succeed and deliver its mission. To expand upon our earlier example, the vision may look like: "Shady Oaks Nursing Home will by 2004 have three nursing homes to provide high-quality residential care for those needing skilled nursing and rehabilitative care, as well as one location providing residential housing for those who can care for themselves in a continuing care community located in the suburbs of our community."

## ■ Determining the Critical Success Factors or Objectives

Once the vision is determined and the analysis of the environmental data completed, leadership will establish broad strategic thrusts to achieve the vision. The thrusts for our example may include: (1) a fund-raising program to raise the money needed to build or acquire two additional nursing homes and the property and buildings for the residential housing; (2) identifying any legislative or regulatory hurdles that would prevent the organization from achieving its vision; (3) identifying consulting firms to assist management; etc. In effect, the strategic planning group could be perceived as sitting on the seat of a bicycle and pedaling it down a path toward the vision.

In addition to the strategic thrusts, the information from the environmental assessment will identify critical success factors. One may be obtaining state approval prior to a competitor for a given community location or establishing an effective marketing campaign to support the fund-raising program.

With the vision, strategic thrusts, and critical success factors defined, senior management and administration take over identifying the objectives that will support critical success factors and bring the vision to reality. The burden of the effort to make the organization successful lies with management and staff. The full strength of this group must be mustered to achieve the vision. As a supervisor, you will meet with your administrative superior and define the objectives for your department, their impact on your daily work processes, and the interdepartmental relationships that must be established or strengthened for total organizational success. To continue the analogy, you and your staff are now pedaling the bicycle. (See figure 7.1)

---

**OTHER PLANNING CONSIDERATIONS**

### The Planning Period

The length of time for which the manager should plan is called the planning horizon. Usually you should make a distinction between long-term, intermediate, and short-term planning. The exact definitions of long-term and short-term planning depend on the manager's level in the hierarchy, the type of institution, and the kind of activity in which it is engaged.

Generally, *short-term* planning covers a period up to one year, while planning of activities to be carried out over a period of one to five years is known as *in-*

**Figure 7.1** Strategic planning model.

*"Courtesy of Kevin McArdle of McArdle Enterprises, Inc., St. Louis Park, MN."*

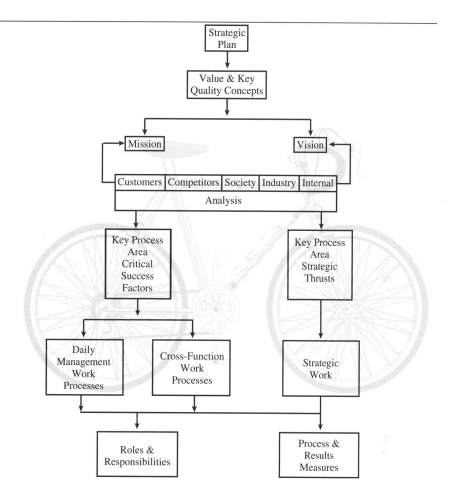

*termediate* planning. This planning horizon contains fewer uncertainties than the long-range planning, which has to contend with highly uncertain conditions of several decades hence. Thus, *long-term* planning usually involves a considerably longer horizon—generally, any plan that extends beyond five years. Recently, administrators, such as board members and CEOs, have begun to plan for as long as several decades ahead. This is difficult to do with political change that can occur potentially every four years.

The supervisor's planning period probably will be short range, that is, for one year at the most or perhaps for six months, one month, one week, or even one day. There are some activities in certain departments for which a supervisor can definitely plan three, six, nine, or twelve months in advance, such as the planning of preventive maintenance. On the other hand, with other activities in a healthcare facility, supervisory planning will be for a shorter time—a week, a day, or only a shift. Such short-range planning is frequently needed in nursing services. It is more desirable if the supervisor is able to make longer-range plans, but for practical purposes, proper attention must be given to seeing that the work of each day is accomplished. This short-range planning requires the supervisor to take the time to think through the nature and amount of work that is to be done each day by the department, who is to do it, and when. Furthermore, this daily planning must be done ahead of time; many supervisors prefer to do it at the end of the day or shift, when they can size up what has been accomplished to formulate plans for the following day or shift.

Occasionally, a supervisor will also be involved in intermediate and long-term plans. For example, the boss may want to discuss planning for new activities for the institution. A supervisor may be informed of a contemplated expansion or the addition of new facilities, for instance a nursing home, and will be asked to propose what the department can contribute or what will be needed. If a hospital plans for an enlarged outpatient surgical center, the director of nursing, as well as the operating room supervisors, will be deeply involved in such a plan.

From time to time the administrator might request the supervisor to look into the future and project the long-term trend of a particular activity, especially if it is apparent that such activity will be affected by major breakthroughs in medical science and technology. It is important for the supervisor to participate in such long-range planning because the plans may require some employees to be reassigned or others to acquire additional skills.

The long-range plans also may indicate that subordinates with completely new skills and education are needed and that a search for them must start now. Learning new procedures and techniques might be necessary as a result of new and different ways of diagnosing and treating medical conditions. For instance, consider the transition from the old X-ray department's functions to the variety of sophisticated imaging and noninvasive diagnostic procedures. Even though these technologies were readily available, due to their high cost and the time it took to acquire the capital, their implementation date was often placed in the long-range plan. In these situations, the supervisors must participate in long-range planning to insure adequate space, staff training, etc.

## ■ The Integration and Communication of Plans

Integrating, coordinating, and balancing the long-range, intermediate, and short-range plans is essential. Therefore, the supervisor's short-range plans must support intermediate plans, which in turn should support long-range plans. Long-range planning should not be viewed as an activity separate from or contrary to short-range planning. Top-level administrations must keep all managers well informed on the intermediate and long-range plans of the institution. The better informed the middle-level and lower-level managers are, the better they will be able to integrate their plans.

All too often, however, there is a gap between the knowledge of top management and lower-level management concerning planning. This gap is often justified by the claim that many of the plans are confidential and cannot be divulged for security reasons. Most employees know that very little can be kept secret in any organization; therefore, internal security cannot always be used as an excuse. On the other hand, supervisors should realize that some limitations exist and that top-level administration does not have to disclose all their plans as long as lower-level managers are informed of those plans that will affect their particular activities.

To the extent necessary, plans should be communicated and fully explained to subordinate managers so that they are in a better position to formulate derivative plans for their departments. Along the same line, supervisors should always bear in mind that their own employees will be affected by the plans that they make. Since employees are needed to execute whatever has been planned, the supervisor is well advised to take them into his or her confidence and explain in advance the plans for the department. The manager may even want to consult the employees and ask for suggestions, since some may be in a position to make helpful contributions. The supervisor should also remember that well-informed employees always are better employees. Such employees appreciate that they have not been kept in the dark.

## THE USE OF OBJECTIVES IN PLANNING

### Organizational Goals and Objectives

All planning has the purpose of achieving success, that is, achieving the organization's goals and objectives. Therefore, the first step in planning is to develop a statement of the goals and objectives for the institution that becomes the target, the end results that the institution seeks to attain through organized efforts and toward which all activities are directed. These goals and objectives must be expressed clearly and communicated fully so that all managers have a common understanding around which to coordinate their activities. The objectives will largely determine how the managers go about their organizing, staffing, and influencing functions. Also, controlling would be meaningless without objectives as guidelines.

Effective management is always management by objectives. This holds true for the CEO of a hospital, for the supervisor on the "firing-line," and for all managers on the levels in between. Formulating objectives should therefore be foremost in every manager's mind. Once the goals have been established, additional plans, such as policies, standard procedures, methods, rules, programs, projects, and budgets, are then designed to achieve the objectives.

### ■ Primary Objectives

The first step in planning is a statement of the overall, or primary, objectives to be achieved by the enterprise. Every member of the organization should be familiar with this statement of objectives, since it outlines the multiple goals and end results toward which all plans and activities are directed. These objectives constitute the purpose of the healthcare center, and without them no intelligent planning can take place. Setting these overall objectives is a function of top-level administration, the board, and the CEO.

In general, many healthcare centers have such primary objectives as: providing primary, secondary, or tertiary care to the sick and injured; providing healthcare at a reasonable cost; doing research; working toward advancement of medical knowledge; helping in the maintenance of health and in the prevention of sickness; recruiting outstanding graduates from medical schools; providing education; and training employees in all the professional and nonprofessional activities customarily associated with a healthcare institution. In addition to these goals, a healthcare facility can have many other objectives, such as achieving total quality management, maintaining a fine reputation among hospitals, practicing the best possible medicine, establishing a good and caring image in the community, discharging numerous social and charitable responsibilities, achieving cost effectiveness and cost containment. Moreover, another essential objective, even for not-for-profit healthcare facilities, is to ensure fiscal integrity, operate within available financial resources, and balance a present budget. For those healthcare activities organized as a for-profit undertaking, profit certainly is also one of the major objectives.

A healthcare institution also will strive toward many other less tangible objectives. In relation to its employees, for instance, the goal is being a good and fair employer. The objective in this case is to establish the reputation of being a good place for people to work.

Any organization has many objectives, and the real difficulty lies in ranking and balancing them. This is especially true for healthcare facilities. Although it would be beyond the scope of this book to discuss all the objectives of the different types of healthcare facilities, the previous lists of objectives show sufficiently well the multiplicity and complexity of objectives and the reasons top-level administration is constantly challenged in balancing and achieving them. If the CEO chose a single objective and excluded all the others, the effectiveness of the institution's overall performance could be jeopardized. Because healthcare activities must function in a constantly changing and increasingly challenging environment, it is necessary to continually reevaluate past objectives and add new ones.

## ■ Secondary or Departmental Objectives

The goals established for an institution as a whole are called the primary objectives, and those set up for each of the institution's various departments can be called secondary, operative, supportive, or derivative objectives. Since each department or division has a specific task to perform, each must have its own clearly defined goals associated with the functions as a guide. These secondary goals and objectives of the departments must stay within the overall framework set by the primary objectives and must contribute to the achievement of the overall institutional objectives.

Because they are concerned with only one department, however, the secondary objectives are necessarily narrower in scope. Whereas the overall objectives are general, the objectives of a department have to be much more specific to serve as guidelines for subordinate units. They enable departmental managers to operate at their own discretion, although always within the limits of the overall institutional goals. For instance, the objective that "the welfare of the patients is the foremost concern in our institution" will affect all secondary goals.

This may become clearer if we use as an example the stated objectives of the facility's medical records department, now known also as medical information services or health information services. The objective is to systematically collect and maintain all patient demographic and medical data and to facilitate analysis of it so that the resulting information benefits the user. The medical record is compiled during the treatment of each patient and preserves all information about a person's illness or injury as noted by, and in the treatment rendered by, the medical team. It is used as a permanent record of conditions treated and may serve as an aid in treating future illnesses. Furthermore, the patient's record is the primary data source for: (1) reimbursement, (2) clinical and statistical research, (3) administrative planning and program evaluation, and (4) litigation for the patient, institution, and physician. Additional objectives of the medical information services department are: (1) to generate the diagnostic codes for billing; (2) to collect, analyze, and publish various hospital and diagnostic statistics; and (3) to review concurrently and retrospectively the quality of care and utilization of services.

In another example, the nursing department's objectives may state that its mission is to provide superior patient care within selected specialties in which it has demonstrated ability. This might include primary care, secondary care, and possibly tertiary care. The objectives may state further that this care is to be provided in the context of a medical education program and possibly in an academic medical center setting. Figure 7.2 gives an example of the mission and philosophy of the nursing service in a large teaching hospital.

Obviously, these departmental objectives are specific, but their fulfillment contributes significantly to the achievement of overall institutional goals. In fact, the primary objectives could not be achieved if these and all other departmental objectives were not fulfilled.

## ■ Integration of Objectives

All supervisors and their employees must clearly understand not only the objectives of their own department but also those of the entire institution. The two sets of objectives must be carefully defined and stated so that they can be integrated, coordinated, and explained on the departmental level. The supervisor must bear in mind that the successful completion of a task depends on the full understanding of its purpose by those who have to carry it out. It is therefore good management to make certain that all employees at all levels are thoroughly informed about the objectives to be achieved.

## ■ Review of Objectives

Planning is a dynamic process. Since all healthcare activities operate in an increasingly complex and dynamic environment, new situations and new information will

---

Document Number _____
Reviewed _____

I.   <u>POLICY STATEMENT</u>

The primary mission of Barnes Hospital Nursing Service is to provide high quality patient care. This is achieved through empowering nursing personnel to assume responsibility, accountability, and authority for the continuous improvement of their clinical practice. Primary nursing is the delivery of care model that ensures each patient receives nursing care coordinated by one professional nurse. The leadership of nursing service has the responsibility to give nursing staff the support systems needed to work most efficiently and effectively.

Nursing is the process of assisting patients and their families as they progress through changing levels of health to achieve outcomes reflecting an improved level of function and self-care or a peaceful death. Our Nursing Service values maintaining the quality of life for individual patients. The standards of care provide a framework in which individual professional nurses utilize the nursing process. Through application of the nursing process the professional nurse assesses a patient's needs, indentifies nursing diagnoses or relevant health problems, selects appropriate nursing therapies, and evaluates the patient's progress toward recovery. The professional nurse coordinates a patient's care all the way through discharge by making ongoing clinical decisions, instructing patients and families, keeping patients and families informed of clinical progress, initiating and revising nursing therapies, and collaborating with the patient, family, and other healthcare professionals.

The nurse is the patient's advocate and thus must respect the patient's values when decisions regarding healthcare are made. At the same time, the professional nurse relies on knowledge and the experience of clinical practice to make ethical decisions influencing the patient's care. The patient has the right to respectful care and is to be treated with dignity and compassion.

A climate for professionalism requires ongoing research activities to evaluate and improve clinical practice. Competency in nursing practice is enhanced through the ongoing education of nurses. The level of satisfaction patients express about their care is an impetus to make changes and innovations. Finally, all professionals must act responsibly in the appropriate utilization of resources.

---

**Figure 7.2**   Nursing service philosophy. Courtesy of Barnes-Jewish Hospital, St. Louis, MO.

necessitate revising and updating the long-range and intermediate plans. This in turn will create the need for a change in the objectives. Objectives must be flexible and adaptable to changes in the internal and external environments. Therefore, revising, updating, and reviewing the objectives on an increasingly frequent basis is a managerial duty on all levels.

# MANAGEMENT BY OBJECTIVES

To achieve specific results from setting these departmental objectives, organizations use a process called *management by objectives* (MBO). The term and concepts were first introduced by management expert Peter Drucker in the early 1950s and have become very popular since then. Managers in healthcare organizations should be familiar with the MBO concept, since its use in their activity is increasing.

Management by objectives is an integrative management concept, containing elements of the planning function, together with participative management, motivation, and controlling. It is the process of collaborative goal setting by the manager and subordinate. In evaluating and rewarding the subordinate's performance, the degree to which goals are accomplished will play a major role. Management by objectives demonstrates the interrelationships of the managerial functions and the systems approach to management. Therefore, management by objectives will also be discussed in other appropriate sections of this text. At this time, however, we are primarily concerned with the meaning of MBO in connection with setting and achieving objectives.

When a facility begins an MBO program, top administration must communicate that this method will start at the top of the organization. Top management must also state the reason why MBO has been adopted and what results it will produce. All managers and employees need to be educated and informed about what their role in it will be.

Management by objectives is concerned with goal setting for individual managers. In this process, a manager at any level and his or her immediate subordinate jointly develop goals in accordance with the organizational goals. Once institutional goals are clarified, the manager and the subordinate, on a one-to-one basis, should develop and agree on the subordinate's goals during a stated period. To be operational, these performance objectives must be *specific, measurable (quantifiable),* and *challenging,* but realistically *attainable* by the subordinate within the *time frame* established. This means that each objective must provide a plan showing what work is to be done, the time frame, and the individual who will do it. It is also necessary to specify the resources the subordinate will need to get the job done. There also must be quantitative indicators to measure what work is achieved.

To be realistic, it should be possible to carry out the activity within the time frame set—a period long enough to meet the objective, but short enough to provide timely feedback and still permit intervention if necessary. In general, the goals should meet the three criteria of *specificity, conciseness,* and *time frame.* The degree to which these goals are achieved will be a major factor in evaluating and rewarding the subordinate's performance.

It is an important point that these goals be jointly established and agreed upon ahead of time. At the end of the period, both supervisor and employee participate in the review of the subordinate's performance to see how results for the period compare with the objectives he or she set out to accomplish. If the goals were achieved, new goals will be set for the next period. If a discrepancy exists, efforts are made to find steps to overcome these problems, and the manager and subordinate agree on new goals for the next period. Management by objectives clearly is a powerful tool in achieving involvement and commitment of subordinates.

## ADDITIONAL TYPES OF PLANS

Once the objectives have been determined, managers must design numerous plans necessary to achieve fulfillment of the goals. Several different types of plans are devised to implement objectives: policies, procedures, methods, rules, programs, projects, and budgets. All these plans must be designed to reinforce one another; that is, they must be internally consistent, integrated, and coordinated. Since every manager will probably have to devise or at least use each type of plan at some time, he or she should be familiar with the meaning of all of them. The major plans are formulated by top administration, but department supervisors will have to formulate their own departmental plans accordingly. The purpose of all these plans is to ensure that the thinking and actions taken on different levels and in different departments of the institution are consistent with and contribute to the overall objectives.

These different types of plans can be divided into two major groups: *repeat-use* plans and *single-use* plans. Objectives, policies, procedures, methods, and rules are commonly known as repeat-use, or standing, plans. They are used for problems that occur regularly. Repeat-use plans are applicable whenever a problem situation presents itself that is similar to the one for which the standing plan was originally devised.

The opposite of repeat-use plans are single-use, or single-purpose, plans. They are used for nonrecurring situations. These plans are no longer needed once their objective is accomplished. Within this single-use plan category are programs, projects, and budgets.

## POLICIES

Policies are probably the most important and frequently invoked repeat-use plans among the various plans a manager must depend on. Generally, they are issued and set by the top management of the organization. *Policies are broad guides to thinking* providing managers with a general guideline for decision making. They are general statements that channel the thinking of all personnel charged with decision making. Because they are broad, policies do not have definite limitations and boundaries. Policies reflect constraints, and as long as a supervisor stays within these limitations, he or she will make an appropriate decision, one that conforms to the policy.

Thus, policies serve to keep decision makers on the right track, and in this way they facilitate the job of both managers and subordinates. They ensure uniformity of decision making throughout the organization. Policies are standing plans that express the organization's general response to a problem or situation. Thus, top management directs decisions toward the achievement of the organizational goals, expressing values and ideas it deems important. They help to coordinate activities and as the organization grows larger and more complex, the need for policies increases.

### ■ Policies as an Aid in Delegation

Policies cover the various areas of the organization's activities: some relate to the managerial functions (*e.g.,* a promotion-from-within policy); others relate to operational functions (*e.g.,* patient care policies, public relations, and marketing); and still others cover the safety and health of the employees. By issuing all these policies, top-level administration sanctions in advance the decisions made by subordinate managers, as long as they stay within the broad policy guidelines. After having set policies, a higher-level manager should feel reasonably confident that whatever decisions the subordinates make will fall within policy limits. In fact, the subordinates will probably come up with decisions comparable to those the manager would have made. Thus, policies make it easier for the higher-level manager to delegate authority to the subordinates.

Policies are a great help to the subordinate managers as well. They provide guidelines that help subordinates make decisions and at the same time ensure uniformity of decisions throughout the enterprise. Therefore, the clearer and more comprehensive the policy guidelines are, the easier and more effective they will be for the higher level managers to delegate authority and for the subordinate managers to exercise authority.

## ■ The Origin of Policies

Policies are determined by management, particularly by the higher administrative levels. Formulating policies is one of the most important functions of top-level management. These managers are in the best position to establish the various types of policies that will help achieve the enterprise's objectives. Once the corporate policies have been set by the top-level administrator, they in turn will become the guidelines for various policies covering divisions and departments, such as patient care policies. Such divisional and departmental policies are *originated* by the various managers lower in the managerial hierarchy. This type of policy formulation, originated by the top administrative level and pursued by the lower managerial levels, is the most important source of policies.

Occasionally, however, a supervisor may have a problem situation not covered by existing policy. Here the supervisor has only one choice: go to the boss and simply ask whether or not any of the existing policies are applicable. If none applies, then the supervisor should appeal to the boss to issue a policy to cover such situations.

For instance, suppose that one of your employees asks for a leave of absence. To make the appropriate decision, you would prefer to be guided by policy so that your decision would be in accord with all other decisions regarding leaves of absence. You may find, however, that the administrator never issued any policies on granting or denying a leave of absence. Instead of making an ad hoc decision (a decision that pertains to this case only), you ask your boss to issue a policy, which you will be able to refer to whenever leaves of absence are requested in the future. You probably will not have to make such a request very often because a good administrator usually foresees most of the areas in which policies are needed. On occasion, however, you may have to appeal to your own boss, stimulating the formulation of what is known as an *appealed policy.*

In addition to originated and appealed policies, some policies are *externally imposed* on an organization by external factors, such as the government, accrediting agencies, trade unions, and trade associations. The word *imposed* indicates having to comply with compulsory rules. For instance, to be accredited, hospitals and other healthcare facilities must comply with certain regulations issued by the accrediting agency, the Joint Commission on Accreditation of Healthcare

Organizations. These regulations must be translated into institutional policy, and all employees must abide by them.

The Joint Commission requires hospitals to have formal written policies on patient care matters. Another example of externally imposed policies are those mandated by the Equal Employment Opportunity Commission. Unless the healthcare center was an equal opportunity employer before federal and state fair employment codes were legislated, such a policy statement can be regarded as one that was externally imposed on the institution.

## ■ Clarity of Policies

Because policies are such a vital guide for thinking and thus for decision making, it is essential that they be stated simply and clearly. Policies must be communicated so that those in the organization who are to apply them understand their meaning. This is no easy task. It is difficult to find words that will be understood by all people in the same way, since different meanings can be attached to the same word. Although there is no guarantee that even the written word will be properly understood, it still seems more desirable to put all policies in writing. This at least will avoid the added ambiguity of trying to remember someone's spoken words.

In addition to better comprehension, other benefits are derived from written policies:

1. The process of writing policies requires the top-level administrator to think them out clearly and consistently.
2. Written policies are easily accessible; the subordinate managers can read them as often as they wish.
3. The wording of a written policy cannot be changed by word of mouth because it can always be consulted.
4. Written policies are especially helpful for new managers who need immediate help in solving a problem.

Although these advantages are significant, one disadvantage is connected with written policies. Once policies are in writing, management may become reluctant to change them. Thus, some enterprises prefer to have their policies communicated by word of mouth because they believe that this is more flexible, allowing the verbal policies to be adjusted to different circumstances with greater ease than with written policies. The exact meaning of a verbal policy might become scrambled, however, making it difficult to apply the policy properly. For this reason, written policy statements are generally considered far more desirable and necessary.

## ■ The Flexibility of Policies

Although policies must be consistent to successfully coordinate the activities of each day, they must also be flexible. Some policies even explicitly state this flexibility using such words as "whenever possible," "whenever feasible," or "under usual circumstances." For instance, one of the most widely practiced policies today is: "Our enterprise believes and practices promotion from within whenever possible." If these clauses are built in, then the manner in which the supervisor applies the policy will determine its degree of flexibility. The supervisor must intelligently adapt the policy to the existing set of circumstances. Such flexibility, however, must not lead to inconsistency; policies must be administered by supervisors in a consistent manner.

## ■ The Supervisor and Policies

Although supervisors seldom have to issue policies, they must constantly use them. Supervisors primarily apply existing policies in making their daily decisions, but must also interpret and explain the meaning of policies to the employees of their departments. Therefore, it is essential that they clearly understand the policies and that they learn how to apply them appropriately.

A manager who heads a major department, such as the director of nursing services, a department that normally comprises half of the institution's employees and has many subdivisions within it, may find it necessary to issue and write policies for the department. In fact, the Joint Commission on Accreditation of Healthcare Organizations will examine these "nursing policies." All of them must reinforce and be in accordance with the overall policies of the healthcare center. Among these policies will probably be a nursing policy stating that the welfare of the patient is the foremost concern of the nursing service and that it takes precedence over all other considerations. In all likelihood, the institution's overall policy of fairness and nondiscrimination will also show up in a nursing policy. The policy may state that patients shall be accorded impartial access to treatments or accommodations to the extent that these are available and medically indicated regardless of race, color, creed, or national origin. The policy also may state that the patient's right to privacy shall be respected, consistent with medical needs, etc.

The director of nursing services certainly will see that a policy exists for cardiopulmonary resuscitation, also referred to as "no code" or "DNR" (do not resuscitate) orders. No code policies set forth the circumstances under which a no code order will be considered appropriate and may be written. (See figure 7.3.)

## ■ Periodic Review of Policies

Changes in the healthcare environment, accompanied by changes in an institution's own goals, are reasons older policies must be periodically reviewed, revised, or removed, regardless of how well thought out the policies were when originated. Such a review may uncover policies that contradict other policies, or it may uncover policies that have become so outdated that no one follows them. In such cases, top-level administration must either rewrite or abandon the questionable

Document Number _____
Reviewed _____

I.  POLICY STATEMENT

    A.  Cardiopulmonary Resuscitation (CPR)

        1.  Cardiopulmonary resuscitation will be initiated on all patients unless there is an order written not to resuscitate.

        2.  In order to clarify as precisely as possible for the professional staff the intent and scope of the planned therapy, orders must clearly state what measures are to be excluded. These include: no CPR, no intubation, no defibrillation, and no pressors.

        3.  Guidelines for "Do Not Resuscitate" orders are as follows:

            a.  On covered services: the intern or resident may write "Do Not Resuscitate" orders following discussion with the attending physician. The house officer must indicate, in the medical record, that the attending physician has been contacted and that the plan of care has been discussed with the patient and/or family. The attending physician must sign the order within 24 hours.

            b.  On uncovered service: The attending physician may give a telephone "Do Not Resuscitate" order only to another member of the medical staff on the hospital premises. He/she will record it in the orders. This order must be signed by the attending physician within 24 hours and a note placed in the medical record indicating that the plan of care has been discussed with the patient and/or family.

        4.  Any CPR-trained employee may initiate CPR.

        5.  RNs, LPNs and PCTs are to be CPR retrained annually.

            NOTE: If CPR is initiated, the procedure approved by the American Heart Association is used. Nursing personnel have been trained in this procedure.

    B.  Defibrillation/Cardioversion

        1.  The physician is responsible for electrical defibrillation/cardioversion.

        2.  Nursing staff may not defibrillate except on designated nursing divisions.

        3.  Elective cardioversion is done in CCU (8200) or another ICU.

        4.  If patient goes to 8200ICU for cardioversion, an RN from the sending floor needs to accompany patient.

            NOTE: Procedure for cardioversion may be found in the ICU Policy & Procedure Unit Manual.

        5.  Safety precautions are to be followed at all times and include:

            a.  Do not touch patient, bed or other cabinet surfaces when trigger is fired, including anything in contact with patient, IV line, etc.

            b.  Physician/nurse should alert other personnel by calling out "all clear" and allow other members of team to step away.

            c.  Defibrillator mode selector is always turned to "off" position when not in use.

    C.  Code 7

        1.  The patient's managing resident will assume charge of the medical aspects of the resuscitation. In his absence, the medical resident on the arrest team will assume control.

**Figure 7.3**  Nursing service: cardiopulmonary resuscitation (CPR) policy statement. Courtesy of Barnes-Jewish Hospital, St. Louis, MO.

2. The charge nurse will assume charge of the nonmedical aspects. In a nonpatient area, this responsibility passes to the Nursing Director/Nursing Supervisor. (Arrangements have been made with CSR and Dispatch to bring an infusion pump, AC suction, and saline to Code 7 occurring in nonpatient care area, i.e., QT Lobby.)

   a. Assignment of staff during code — ideally 3 RNs needed:

      1. One RN at bedside to push drugs/suction/start or secure IVs.

      2. One RN at crash cart to distribute medications and equipment needed.

      3. One RN to record on cardiac arrest work sheet.

      If three are not available, other (qualified) personnel can be substituted.

   b. Removal of excess furniture and equipment and nonessential personnel from the area.

   c. Disposition of any roommates, visitors, and other nonstaff people.

   d. Determination that all members of the arrest team (Medical Resident, Surgical Resident, Anesthetist, Nursing Supervisor, Respiratory Therapist, EKG Technician, and Dispatch) have arrived. (Central paging, ext. 2–1242, will call the nursing division to check if all the arrest team has arrived.) Central paging will reach those who have not arrived.

   e. Initiation of call to house staff, if not present, and the attending physician of any private patient.

   f. Assurance of physician's notification of family, if not present.

## II. PROCEDURE

Purpose:   To efficiently manage the acute patient.

| NURSING ACTIONS | KEY POINTS |
|---|---|
| **A. Assessment**<br><br>Patient is found pulseless, breathless, and/or unresponsive. | |
| **B. Plan**<br><br>1. Call code 7 — dial 2–2700. Start CPR. | |
| 2. After code team arrives other nursing responsibilites are: | No code nurse will show up with code team. Staff nurses on the floor are responsible for working the crash cart. |
|   a. Set up IV fluids.<br>  b. Preparation and administration of IV medications.<br>  c. Maintenance of the cardiac arrest.<br>  d. Disposition of specimens.<br>  e. Supportive care for family members present.<br>  f. After code procedure, cart needs to be checked and restocked. | |
| **C. Evaluation/Charting**<br><br>Nursing Flowsheet<br><br>CPR W/S | Document change in patient's condition/see cardiac arrest work sheet. The document needs to be signed by the physician. |

policies, since an institution certainly cannot afford to let its various subordinate managers decide which policies are still current or whether or not they should still be observed. Thus, it is essential for policies to be periodically reviewed by top-level management and kept up-to-date.

## ■ Procedures

Procedures are repeat-use plans for achieving the institution's objectives. They are derived from policies, but are much more specific. *Procedures are guides to action,* not guides to thinking. Procedures specify a set of actions to be followed step-by-step. They outline a chronological order for the acts that are to be performed. (See figure 7.3.) In brief, procedures prescribe a path toward the objectives; they describe in detail how a recurring activity is to be performed and are commonly used in the daily operations. For example, let us recall the policy that stated: "Our institution promotes from within whenever possible." The purpose and objectives of this policy are clear. The procedure designs the steps to be taken in a chronological sequence to fulfill the meaning of the policy. These steps might be stated as follows:

1. Every opening in the institution must be posted on the employees' bulletin board in the employees' cafeteria for two weeks.
2. The potential candidates should be able to obtain a job description from the manager in whose department the job is open.
3. Potential candidates must inform their present boss before arranging for an interview.
4. An interview between the applicant and the head of the department where the opening is will be arranged with the assistance of the personnel department.

There are literally hundreds if not thousands of procedures in a healthcare center. Just think of the number in nursing services alone, such as the procedures for administering medications, intravenous medications, radiologic techniques, examination of critically ill patients, epidermal injections, and discharge of patients. Consider, for instance, the need for cardiopulmonary resuscitation in connection with the nursing policy that resuscitative measures must be initiated on all patients who have experienced cardiac arrest unless a "no code order" has been written by the responsible physician. (See figure 7.3.) Or consider the detailed surgical procedures a doctor follows to help ensure good results or those an anesthesiologist uses during surgery.

Although supervisors will not have much opportunity to issue policies, there will be many occasions for them to devise and issue procedures. Since supervisors are the managers of the department, they determine how the work is to be done. The level of detail in written procedures may differ, depending on the skill and/or educational level of the staff. As educational levels increase, more freedom to act based on tested and demonstrated experience is permitted. Effective work procedures designed by the supervisors for the institution will result in definite advantages.

One of these advantages is that the process of preparing a procedure requires analyzing the work to be done. Moreover, once a supervisor establishes a procedure, it ensures consistent and uniform action. Procedures try to establish a predictable outcome. In addition to these benefits, procedures provide the supervisor with a standard for appraising the work of the employees. Since a procedure specifies the sequence of actions, it also decreases the need for further decision making. This makes the supervisor's job, as well as that of the employees, easier. The supervisor is also more likely to assign work fairly and to distribute it evenly among the employees.

A good supervisor will spend considerable time and effort in devising efficient procedures for the department. From time to time, of course, it will be necessary for the supervisor to review and revise departmental procedures, since some are likely to become outdated. Because of the advances in medical science, new activities are frequently introduced into the department. Then the supervisor's first duty is to write appropriate procedures for them.

## METHODS

A method is also a standing plan for action, but it is even more detailed than a procedure. Whereas a procedure shows a series of steps to be taken, a method is concerned only with a single operation, with one particular step. The method tells exactly how this particular step is to be performed. (See figure 7.4.) For instance, one typical nursing procedure guides nurses step-by-step in how to account for controlled substances at the beginning of each shift by both the nurse going on duty and the nurse going off duty. For each step in this procedure, there exists a method. For example, one method explains exactly what is to be done in case of unavoidable spilling or accidental destruction of narcotics—the nurse involved must record what happened. The remnants, if possible, are to be returned to the pharmacy or wasted altogether. Another professional nurse must verify the spill and witness the report form.

For most work done by the employees of a department, there exists a "best method," that is, a best way for doing the job, and it is up to the supervisor to specify for the employees exactly what is considered the best method in their healthcare center. Indeed, a large amount of the supervisor's time is spent in devising methods. Once a method has been devised, it carries with it all the advantages of a procedure already stated such as uniformity of action, predictability of outcome, and standard for appraisal. In determining the best method, a supervisor may occasionally need to enlist the help of another professional, such as a physician, surgeon, pathologist, biochemist, or a management engineer (a specialist in motion and time study,) if such a person is available in the organization. Most often, however, the supervisor's own experience is probably broad enough to allow him or her to design the "best" work methods.

**Figure 7.4**   The relationship of policies, procedures, and methods.

*Adapted from Theo Haimann and William G. Scott,* Management in the Modern Organization, *Boston: Houghton Mifflin Co., 1970, p. 105. Reprinted with permission of the publisher.*

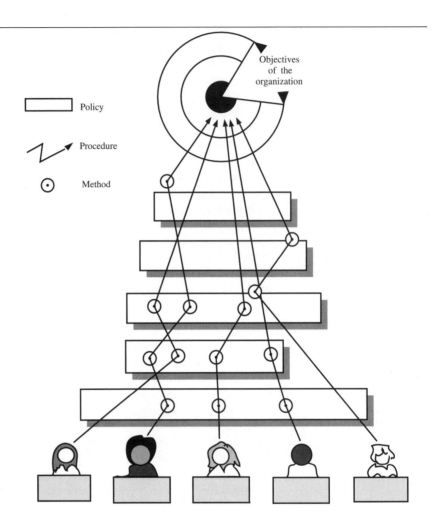

## STANDARD PROCEDURE AND PRACTICES

In some healthcare activities, there will be less need for the supervisor to be overly concerned with devising procedures and methods because the employees will already have been thoroughly trained in standard practices and procedures. For example, nurses, therapists, technologists, technicians, and medical specialists receive many years of schooling and training, during which great emphasis is placed on the proper procedures and methods for performing certain tasks. In managing a department in which such highly skilled employees are at work, the supervisors job is simplified. One of the main concerns is to ensure that good, generally approved procedures and methods are performed in a professionally accepted way.

However, even then, most healthcare centers "do things differently from everyone else." Even after many years of good schooling and experience in other healthcare settings, new employees have to become familiar with the procedures, methods, and idiosyncrasies of the new facilities. The same holds true for recent baccalaureate graduates of nursing programs. Regardless of how much experience a nurse had in another hospital, and regardless of how much a technologist has been taught in school, each healthcare center has its own way of doing things: documentation and charting, collecting specimens, administering medication, handling emergency measures, etc. Therefore, new employees probably will go through an orientation program of many weeks to familiarize them with the procedures and methods of the institution. This is often done by placing them under a preceptor (instructor) on the workplace to which they are assigned.

## RULES

A rule, probably the most explicit kind of a standing plan, is a statement that either forbids or requires a certain action or inaction without variation, e.g., no smoking, speed limit, or a stop sign. A rule is different from a policy, procedure, or method, although it is also a standing plan that has been devised to attain the enterprise's objectives. A rule is not similar to a policy because it does not provide a guide to thinking; it does not leave any discretion to the party involved. A rule is related to a procedure, insofar as it is a guide to action and states what must or must not be done. But a rule is not the same as a procedure because it does not specify a time sequence for the particular action. Rules pertain whenever and wherever they are in effect. A no smoking rule for instance is one issued by management and is probably just one of a long list of safety rules. This rule is a guide to action, or more precisely a guide to inaction. No order of steps is involved, however; it is simply "no smoking" wherever and whenever it is in effect.

Rules develop from policy; they are not part of it. For example, the institution's safety policy is to make the facility a safe place for the patients, employees, and visitors. Safety considerations play an important role in all procedures and methods, and the no smoking rule is just an outgrowth of the original safety policy. The same applies to the rule issued by the supervisor of the clinical laboratories that all employees are to wear gloves and impervious gowns at all times.

It is the supervisor's duty to apply and enforce the rules and regulations of the healthcare center uniformly, whether they are defined by higher management or set by the supervisor. There will be many occasions when supervisors have to set their own departmental rules. For example, the dress code may state that employees must come to work "appropriately attired" for their job. This general rule gives the director of nursing services the right and obligation to devise a more detailed dress code for the nursing personnel. The operating room supervisor in turn would decide on a special dress code for those working in the surgical areas. Since supervisors have the obligation to see that rules are observed, they should be involved in the formation of these rules. Again, these rules are developed from overall hospital policies and must reinforce and support them.

## SINGLE-USE PLANS

In the preceding sections, we have discussed various repeat-use plans, such as objectives, policies, procedures, methods, and rules, which are followed each time a given situation is encountered. The opposite of repeat-use plans are single-use plans or plans that once their objective is accomplished or the time is over, will not be repeated or needed in the future. Programs, projects, and budgets are the three types of single-use plans.

## PROGRAMS AND PROJECTS

A *program* is a single-use plan with a complex set of activities to reach a specific major objective. The program may have its own guidelines, such as policies, procedures, and budgets, and may extend over several years. For instance, building a new extended care facility within a healthcare system is a major one-time undertaking. Or, for instance, the merger of two independent healthcare institutions can be the objective of a program. Such a program involves many derivative plans, each of which can be considered a project. Such plans would include selecting the architects and contractors for the new construction, arranging public information for the local community, providing information for the local medical society, and recruiting the needed personnel. Arranging the financing itself would be a project.

A *project* therefore is similar to a program but is smaller in scope. It is an undertaking that can be planned and executed as a distinct entity within the overall program; all projects must be coordinated and synchronized so that the major program will become reality. Programs and projects are single-use plans; once they are achieved, they are filed away. Occasionally someone may look at them again but probably only to show patrons (donors) the project's history. Once accomplished, these single-use plans have served their purpose and are finished. Planning such a program is usually top-level administration's concern, whereas department heads and supervisors will often be involved in one of its many projects. It is also possible for a project to come up without a connection to a major program—for instance, recruiting nurses in Ireland due to the shortage in the United States, or a wage and salary survey.

## BUDGETS

Budgets are usually thought of only in connection with the controlling function, but this is too narrow a view. In this context, we look at budgets as plans that express the anticipated activities and results in numerical terms. Such terms may be dollars and cents. However, most items start out in other measurable terms such as nursing hours, hours per patient day, or kilowatt hours; tests to be run; output; materials; computer time; inventory levels; or any other unit used to perform work or measure specific results. Since the overall budgets for the entire institution are ultimately expressed in the one common denominator of dollars and cents, and since most values are convertible to monetary terms, all budgets are eventually translated and expressed in monetary terms. Although budgets are an important tool for controlling, preparing and making a budget certainly are part of the planning function. As we know, planning is the duty of every manager. Using the budget and living with it is part of the manager's controlling function, which will be discussed in chapter 26.

Since a budget is a plan expressed in numerical units, it has the distinct advantage that it is stated in exact and specific terms instead of in generalities. The figures put into a budget represent actual plans that will be seen as goals and standards to be achieved. These plans are not mere projections or general forecasts; they will be considered as a basis for daily operations, cost effectiveness, and the bottom line. They are ambiguous guidelines about the institution's expectations.

Budgets usually cover a time period of one year, although further breakdowns by quarters or months are common. They are established for the whole organization and the various divisions and functional departments. A healthcare center designs a number of budgets, such as income or revenue budgets, capital expenditure budgets, and expense budgets. Of all these, the *expense budget* is the supervisor's major concern because it defines the limits of the various departmental expenditures for a stated period, usually one year. All the following comments refer to budgets of this type because the departmental expenses for salaries and wages, materials, supplies, utilities, equipment rentals, travel, etc., are of great concern to the department head.

Because budgets are so important for the daily operations of every department, supervisors who have to use them should participate in their preparation. It is only natural that people resent arbitrary orders, and this applies to having to abide by budgets they see as arbitrary. Thus, it is necessary that all budget objectives and allowances be determined with the full input of those who are responsible for executing them. All supervisors should actively participate in the budget-making process for their units, and this should not be mere "pseudo-participation." They should participate in what is commonly known as "grass roots budgeting." The subordinate managers also should be allowed to submit their own budgets. (This participation becomes even more involved in zero based budgeting practices, as discussed in chapter 26.)

Each supervisor will have to substantiate the budget proposals in a discussion with the boss and possibly with top-level administration, where the budgets are finalized. This is what is meant by active participation in budget making, and it ensures the effectiveness of the process. Such participation, however, should not be construed to mean that the suggestion of the supervisor will always or completely prevail. The supervisor's budget should not be accepted if the higher-level manager believes it is based on plans that are inadequate, overstated, or incorrect.

Differences between budget estimates should be carefully discussed by the supervisor and higher-level manager, but the final decision rests with higher management. Nevertheless, if a budget is arrived at with the participation of the supervisors, then the likelihood that they will live up to it is higher than if it had been handed down to the supervisors by their boss.

In conclusion, it is important to remember that the budget is a single-use plan. When the period is over, the budget is no longer valid. A new budget will have to be drawn up, and a new planning period will be established. In traditional budgeting, the previous year's budget serves as a guideline for next year's budget, unless the healthcare center practices zero base budgeting. Zero base budgeting (see chapter 26) is a fairly new concept. Instead of accepting current expenditures as a base for the new budget, zero base budgeting requires that all expenditures new and existing must be justified, reassessed, and approved from the very beginning.

---

**SUMMARY**   Planning is the managerial function that determines in advance what is to be done in the future. It is the function of every manager, from the top-level administrator to the supervisor of each department. Planning is important because it ensures the best utilization of resources and economy of performance. The planning period at the supervisory level is usually much shorter than the period at the top administrator's level. Nevertheless, the short-range plans of the supervisor must coincide with the long-range plans of the enterprise.

Setting objectives is the first step in planning. Although the overall objectives are determined by the top-level administration, many secondary objectives must be clarified by the supervisor and must be in accordance with the primary objectives of the overall undertaking. One useful technique for implementing plans is management by objectives (MBO), which is a process of collaborative goal setting leading to evaluation. To reach all the objectives, different types of plans must be devised. The broad range of plans can be grouped into repeat-use and single-use plans. The first group is designed for a course of action that is likely to be repeated several times, whereas the latter is designed for a course of action that is not likely to be repeated in the future.

Policies, the major type of repeat-use plans, are guides to thinking and most originate with the chief administrator. In most cases, the supervisor's concern with policies is primarily in interpreting them, applying them, and staying within them whenever decisions are made for the department. Although supervisors do not usually originate policies, they will often be called on to design procedures, methods, and rules, which are other repeat-use plans. These plans are guides for action, not guides for thinking. Supervisors also participate in the establishment of budgets, which are single-use plans expressed in numerical terms. Occasionally supervisors are involved with programs and projects, two more examples of single-use plans.

# *Supervisory Planning*

## Chapter Objectives

After you have studied this chapter, you should be able to:

1. Discuss the need for and extent of forecasting, which provides the background for managerial planning.
2. Suggest a number of tactical considerations the supervisor can use.
3. See why the supervisor has to plan for the many resources entrusted to him or her.
4. Understand the importance of time management for the employees and for the supervisor.

Planning, as we said, is deciding in advance what is to be done in the future. Although the future is fraught with uncertainties, managers must make certain assumptions about it in order to plan. These assumptions are based on forecasts of what the future will hold. Forecasting will provide information on which the enterprise bases its planning premises; this is done by scanning the external and internal environments. This information gained from the environmental assessment will provide the background and assumptions on which the institution's plans for the future are based. Since the appraisal of future prospects is inherent in all planning, the success of an enterprise greatly depends on the skill of management first in forecasting and then in preparing for the future conditions.

## FORECASTS AS THE BASIS OF PLANNING

### Administrative Forecasts

To plan intelligently, all managers must make some assumptions about the future. The chief executive officer (CEO), in cooperation with his or her board of directors or trustees, however, must forecast the future in a much more far-reaching manner and scope than a supervisor. Since both the CEO and a supervisor are managers, however, both must make forecasts. Such forecasts are possible in widely diverse areas.

Management typically confines its forecasting effort to factors that experience suggests are important to its own planning. Thus, the chief administrator of the healthcare facility selects those forecasts that have a direct material bearing on the healthcare field in the broadest sense.

In trying to make predictions, the administrator will consider the general economic, political, labor, and social climates in which the healthcare institution must operate during the next few years. This information comes from looking at forecasts on government policies, legislation and regulation, government spending, merger and consolidation activities, and insurer penetration, and then determines how these might ultimately affect the activities of healthcare providers.

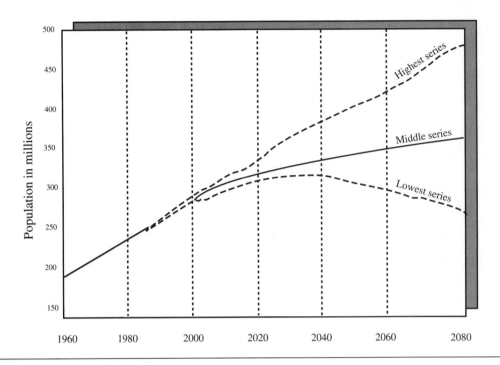

**Figure 8.1** Estimates and projections of total population: 1960 to 2080.

*Source: Data from 115th Edition,* Statistical Abstract of the United States, 1995 The National Data Book, *U.S. Department Commerce, Economics, and Statistics Administration, Bureau of the Census.*

Thus, top-level administration does not actually perform the research and statistical analysis for all their forecasts. They frequently use data published in government and trade publications or made available by hospital or healthcare organizations, hospital system corporate research staffs, and other experts in various fields. The administrator will then try to predict the general trends for the delivery of healthcare as it affects the various providers and users, in relation to cost effectiveness, and so forth.

With the turn of the century approaching, top-level management will be vitally interested in forecasts of changes in our population. In the year 2000, for example, using the highest series, the U.S. population is expected to reach 285 million people, about 381 million in 2040, and approximately 475 million people in the year 2080. Projections showing this increase from 257 million in 1989 are based on first-series assumptions for future fertility, mortality, and net immigration levels. (See figure 8.1.) We will see the impact of these factors on every organized activity because population trends are critical planning premises that affect long-range strategies of most organizations, especially those in the healthcare field.

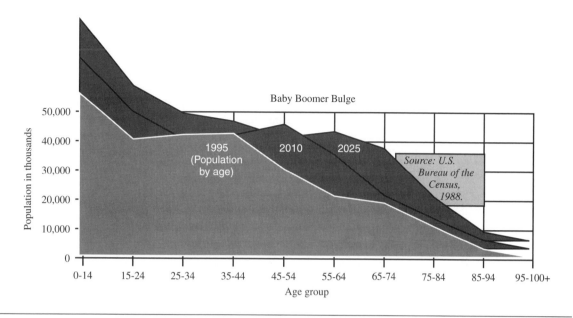

**Figure 8.2**    Baby Boomer Bulge.

*Source: Data from 115th Edition,* Statistical Abstract of the United States 1995, The National Data Book, *U.S. Department Commerce, Economics, and Statistics Administration, Bureau of the Census.*

The breakdown of population figures by age and sex will be even more meaningful, depending on whether administrators are planning for a general short-term hospital, long-term healthcare facility, nursing home, etc. (See figure 8.2.) This graph shows us that the babies born during the baby boom that occurred after World War II will be reaching Medicare age shortly after the turn of the century. The boom creates a surge of 60 year olds starting in 2010 that will continue to ride the timeline horizon through 2030+/– and will place demands on the healthcare system for treatment and care. These demands are similar to the ones that occurred in the early 1950s for schools and teachers to accommodate the school age children created by the baby boom.

All these environmental, economic, and political conditions will affect the future operations of a healthcare facility. Since the administrator's and board's job is to take the long-term outlook, making forecasts in these far-reaching fields is necessary. Although not directly concerned with making such overall assumptions, all middle- and lower-level managers will ultimately be affected by them because they will need to implement the plans that will achieve the goals to accommodate the forecasts.

■ Supervisory Forecasts

### Scientific and Technological Developments

When supervisors make departmental forecasts, their assumptions about the future will cover a much narrower field than will those of administrators. A supervisor should forecast mostly those factors that may have some bearing on the future of his or her department. For example, supervisors should determine whether there is a growing trend for more sophistication or simplification of the function they oversee or whether this function seems to be of increasing or decreasing significance to the healthcare institution. It is important to keep abreast of the rapid and often revolutionary developments in the medical field, in technology, and automation. Of course, there are some broader assumptions with which supervisors also will have to contend, e.g., cost containment, government involvement, staff recruitment, skill requirements, and others that concern the healthcare field.

Based on past events, the supervisor should make some assumptions on what the future will hold. In making such assumptions, he or she can look to the sources of supplies, available technology, and equipment used for assistance. The supervisor can also learn by attending lectures, national meetings, and exhibitions; by joining professional organizations; and by reading journals. Advances in the medical sciences and technology are progressing so rapidly that in several years a department's functions and staff's responsibilities may be significantly different from what they had been or are today. Consider, for instance, the impact of further computerization and automation in laboratories, where current automated analyzers are likely to be obsolete in three to five years. Such projections are essential for the planning done by supervisors in clinical laboratories: Will more, less, or about the same number of employees be needed with the same or different education or additional training? Should the equipment be bought or leased? The supervisor must consider these and similar questions.

### Employees and Skills

Supervisors will also have to make forecasts about the types of employees who will be working in the department in the future. The Industrial Age has given way to the Information Age. The Department of Labor estimates that by the year 2000 at least 44% of all workers will be in data services—for example, gathering, processing, retrieving, or analyzing information.[1] Most healthcare activities probably will create a need for some employees who have been educated and trained in completely new and advanced scientific fields capable of coping with new state of the arts. These employees may possess knowledge and skills unknown and unneeded at present. For example, more knowledge in chemistry, physics, genetics, electronics, mechanical engineering, use of artificial intelligence, neural networks, computers, etc., will be helpful to healthcare personnel.

1.   *Price Pritchett,* New Work Habits for a Radically Changing World *(Pritchett & Associates, 1994).*

Employees also will need skills in handling data. The explosion in computing power geometrically increases the amount of data available for decision making. However, the key to quality decision making is the conversion of data to *information*. Some experts indicate that data supplies double every five years. Pritchett states that there has been more information produced in the last 30 years than during the previous 5,000.[2] Given this explosion, data management, manipulation, massaging, and display skills will be a premium asset for employees to possess.

The forecast may include the need for employees who are educated in new fields of knowledge, are more skilled, and whose increasing demands the department must be ready to meet. This refers both to monetary demands and to demands that the position offer enough of a challenge. For example, supervisors may find that the current pattern of hours, wages, and fringe benefits will not be satisfactory in the future, and they would be well advised to plan accordingly at an early time.

In addition, supervisors may find that department reorganization could result in the need for less employees, but those who have skills in a variety of areas. In 1993, the Report of the Pew Health Professions Commission was published. This report represented the thinking of representatives from all health professions. One theme that permeated the report is that "Schools must develop strategies that will create an environment conducive to the education of a generalist practitioner." The report goes on to say that "It will require the alteration of some organizational structures and the development of new and different relationships with affiliated institutions and community-based practitioners. In part, these needs will be met by working across professional lines in clinical settings and by courses aimed at instilling the value of primary care, providing the skills necessary to maintain primary care, and promoting the team work skills vital to participation in primary care." In effect, the Pew Report encourages staff who are multiskilled or able to perform multiple tasks rather than staff who are specialized and unable to "jump in" where needed because of skill limitations.[3] As healthcare transitions from a "sick care" approach to one of promoting "health care," individuals with diverse skills will be needed.

Now consider a healthcare entity that has decided to pursue a patient-focused approach in its facility. Under this approach, all services are directed to the patient and if necessary "come" to the patient. This should be contrasted with what occurs in many healthcare facilities, where the patient "comes" to the service. For example, the patient comes to registration to be admitted; goes to the laboratory or EKG area for tests on the way to his/her room; once in his/her assigned bed, if radiological tests need to be taken, he/she goes to the radiology department; if therapy is required. . . . to the physical therapy department, and so on.

Further, in a patient-focused environment, the laboratory technician, cardiology technician, and radiology technician will do most of the testing in the patient's room. In fact, the patient knows which floor to go to when he/she enters

2. *Ibid., pp. 20–21.*
3. Pew Health Professions Commission Report, *February 1993, pp. 13–22.*

the facility so the patient does not stop in registration. Registration, as a centralized service, really does not exist.

In this example, a multiskilled patient care practitioner might be an individual who could register the patient upon his/her arrival to the patient care division, take the patient to his/her room, draw blood or take other specimens and run simple laboratory tests, perform the EKG and chart the preliminary report, and take routine radiology films. Clearly, multiskilling requires training in a variety of disciplines and individuals with an aptitude to learn and retain a multiplicity of skills.

Similarly, supervisors should be aware of the noneconomic demands that young people coming out of school—whether a university, junior college, vocational training program, or high school—expect to fulfill on their jobs. Meeting all types of demands, such as material, psychological, and professional, will be particularly important if supervisors have to find people who possess skills that up to now have never been known or required in the department or perhaps anywhere in the institution.

Consider figure 8.2. The time is now that the administrator and his/her medical director and director of nursing should be evaluating adding more skilled nursing facility (SNF) beds and recruiting geriatric trained staff or providing in-house training for existing staff to serve the surge of older patients that will come to the facility seeking care. If a general shortage of certified nurse aides is in the forecast, plans should be made now on how to cope with such an event.

## BENEFITS OF FORECASTING

One should always remember that at the base of all forecasts lie certain assumptions, approximations, opinions, and judgments. Forecasting is an art, not a science. As of yet, no infallible way of predicting the future exists; however, forecasting accuracy increases with experience. As time goes on, making assumptions about the future should become a normal activity for all managers, from the administrator down to the supervisor. Managers should exchange ideas, help each other, and supply information whenever available. They most likely will act as a check on each other, and their analysis of what the future holds will probably be quite reliable.

Even if some of the events that have been anticipated do not materialize or do not occur exactly as forecasted, it is better to have foreseen them than to be suddenly confronted with them. Having foreseen these events, supervisors have prepared themselves and the state of affairs to be able to incorporate changes whenever they are needed. Although this task may sound formidable for supervisors, their job is to be alert to all possible changes and trends. This is the only way supervisors can prevent their own and their employees' obsolescence.

## TACTICAL CONSIDERATIONS IN PLANNING

While planning, supervisors must keep in mind how these plans will affect others. Success or failure of planning will depend largely on the reaction of those involved in the plans, whether they are employees, supervisors of other departments, the boss, top-level administration, the medical staff, or many others. Several tactical or political strategies are at the supervisor's disposal to help minimize negative reactions and facilitate the success of the plans. One or a combination of these political or tactical considerations may be used, depending on the situation at hand.

Since timing is a critical factor in all planning, the manager may choose the strategy that tells him or her to *strike while the iron is hot.* This strategy advocates prompt action when the situation and time for action are propitious. On the other hand, the supervisor may prefer to use the *wait and see* strategy, which takes the approach that *time is a great healer.* This is not an endorsement of procrastination, but of moving more slowly and seeing if factors take care of themselves after a short while.

When significant changes are involved in planning, the supervisor may use the strategy known as *concentrated mass offensive.* This strategy advocates a quick pulling together of all resources and taking radical action all at once to get immediate results. Another approach may be *team involvement.* This strategy involves using employees, who utilize various techniques such as brainstorming, to solve "what if" questions. Team involvement takes time but also provides for buy-in on plans by the employees while at the same time tapping into an information resource. On the other hand, the supervisor may prefer to just *get a foot in the door.* This tactic implies that it may be better to propose merely a portion of the plan in the beginning, especially if the program is of such magnitude that its total acceptance would be doubtful.

Sometimes one supervisor's plan may involve changes that could come about more easily if supervisors of other departments would join in the action. It may therefore be advisable to seek allies to promote the change, that is, to adopt the strategy that states there is *strength in unity.* For example, if a supervisor plans to propose to increase the salaries of the employees, it may be expedient to try to get the other supervisors to join the effort in presenting a general request for higher remuneration to the management. This may involve the *you-scratch-my-back-and-I'll-scratch-yours* strategy. This tactic of reciprocity is practiced not only in political circles and by businessmen, but also among colleagues who wish to present joint action on a particular issue.

The choice and application of these political tactics will depend on the people involved, magnitude and urgency of the objective, timing, means available, and various other factors. Mentioning these tactical considerations, however, should not be construed to mean that they are always recommended. Properly applied, however, they can minimize difficulties and increase the effectiveness of the supervisor's planning.

## PLANNING THE UTILIZATION OF RESOURCES

Every supervisor is entrusted with a large number of valuable resources to accomplish the job. The supervisor has a duty to plan specifically how to use the resources available so that the work of the unit can be managed efficiently and cost effectiveness can be achieved. This means that detailed plans must be made for the proper utilization of the equipment, instruments, space, materials and supplies, and supervisor's and employees' time.

## ■ Utilization of Patient Care Equipment and Other Machinery

The supervisor must plan the proper utilization of the equipment, analyzers, and instruments provided for the department. The institution has made a substantial investment in the equipment. Therefore, plans for its efficient use must be made to ensure the proper utilization and return on the investment. In many departments, much of the equipment's usage will depend on the orders of the physicians and surgeons. However, it is the supervisor's job to see that employees respect the equipment and instruments and treat them carefully.

Furthermore, the supervisor must ensure that the equipment of the unit is properly maintained. Equipment that is poorly maintained and does not function properly could possibly lead to an incident resulting in a patient's lawsuit for damages. When the supervisor finds out that there seems to be a malfunctioning piece of equipment, he or she should immediately determine whether the employee is operating the equipment properly or if a maintenance problem exists. The proper steps to remedy the malfunction should be taken at once. Supervisors should work closely with the maintenance department or biomedical services and plan for periodic maintenance checkups.

Most facilities have an established program to check equipment at regular intervals in accordance with the manufacturers' guidelines. Records of these checks should be maintained. If a single piece of equipment becomes troublesome due to many repairs or downtime, these records will provide the supervisor with evidence to support replacement. In addition, such records of maintenance, repair, and corrective action are often reviewed by regulatory and accrediting agencies at the time of facility inspections.

It is the supervisor's job to ascertain if the equipment serves its purpose and if better facilities are available for doing the work. This does not mean that a supervisor must always have the very latest model available; however, the supervisor should plan to replace inefficient equipment. The medical staff working in this area should be actively involved in deciding to update the equipment and recommending the replacement models and/or manufacturers as well. If the enterprise uses an outside biomedical service, supervisors would be wise to obtain its advice on replacement brands since the service may have encountered a more reliable model or brand elsewhere.

Once supervisors decide to replace old equipment or introduce new equipment, they must plan such replacements very carefully. In addition to consulting with the medical staff, they must read professional journals and literature circulated by hospitals and related associations, listen to sales presentations of equipment and instruments, and keep themselves abreast of current developments within their fields. Only with this type of background can the supervisor submit intelligent plans and alternatives for the replacement of equipment to the immediate superior or the administrator. The recommended changes should be well substantiated and supported. The proposal should include such items as projections of better patient care, utilization, cost effectiveness, community need, collaboration required, payback or return expected, customer sensitivity, and the important considerations of leasing versus buying.

## ■ Financial Considerations when Proposing the Purchase of New Equipment

Every year department managers submit requests for new equipment. The requests are often evaluated by an administrative or board committee generally known as the capital expenditures committee. Funds for the equipment, or *capital* as it is often called, are derived from an accounting process that sets aside a portion of monies each month or year in a fund called "accrued depreciation."

Competition for the accrued depreciation is usually high. All managers want to update their equipment and furnishings. Furthermore, new technologies for patient care purposes may be requested by members of the medical staff. When preparing a capital expenditure request, a manager should consider the following points recommended by Sweeny and Rachlin: 1) Is the request supportive of, and consistent with, the organization's strategic plan? 2) Is the request responsive to the needs of the customers served as described by the marketing department? 3) Is the request responsive to the needs of the operating department? Will is solve an operational problem? 4) Has the request been fully justified by analysis of the benefits it will offer the organization/department? 5) Is the proposal supported by firm price quotations by vendors and contractors? and 6) Is the request financially fundable?

*Source: H. W. Allen Sweeny and Robert Rachlin,* Handbook of Budgeting, *2d edition, page 103, 1987, John Wiley & Sons, Inc., New York, NY.*

The final decision, however, remains with higher management. Even if the request is turned down, the supervisor has demonstrated that he or she is on top of the job, planning for the future. Eventually the plans for replacing equipment probably will be accepted, and the administrator will realize that the supervisor planned for the department's equipment with foresight.

## ■ Work Methods and Procedures

In discussing the planning process, we pointed out that the supervisor is deeply involved in designing, developing, and writing procedures and methods. The supervisor should continually review and, if necessary, revise procedures and make plans concerning improved work methods and processes in the department. The difficulty is that many supervisors work under considerable pressure and find little time for this type of planning. Moreover, the supervisor is often so close to the jobs performed in the department that he or she believes the prevailing work methods are satisfactory and that not much can be done about them.

Nevertheless, to maintain a high level of efficiency and the best possible patient care, occasionally the supervisor must study the operations performed in order to plan improvements. If the department begins doing something that has not been done before, then the supervisor has to write a complete set of new procedures and methods for this new activity. For example, if the hospital gets involved in some new laser techniques, the manager of that unit has to develop new procedures for this operation. The manager will do so with the help, information, and support from medical specialists, technologists, and possibly the maker of the equipment.

The supervisor should try to look at all of the department's operations from the point of view of a newcomer visiting the department for the first time. In other words, he or she should look at the current operations objectively. The supervisor should ask: Is each operation really necessary? What is the reason for it? Could the procedure be combined with another operation? Are the various steps necessary? Are they performed in the best possible sequence? Are there any avoidable delays?

In this effort to devise more efficient work methods, the supervisor may be able to enlist the help of a staff specialist, such as a nurse clinician, systems analyst, or methods engineer. The supervisor should also seek ideas from employees who are doing the job, since they often can make valuable suggestions for improved methods and procedures. The use of *teams* of employees can be very useful in developing new procedures and identifying external barriers to performing their jobs effectively. These barriers may require the supervisor to work with peer supervisors outside of her department to improve the flow of work inside.

Supervisors also may be asked to establish productivity standards for their staff. To do so will take time as production history, methods to improve production, equipment used, and industry or local use of standards must be assessed. Supervisors must be able to define not only the quantity expected but also the quality of the activities expected. The definitions form the framework within which management establishes the standards of performance. Once the standards are established, a simple and timely reporting mechanism must be developed as a control system. (Control will be discussed later in this text). It is outside the realm of this text to discuss in depth various techniques to gauge production and establish productivity standards. Supervisors are encouraged to obtain more information on these techniques prior to embarking on a program of establishing standards.

## ■ Safety

Traditionally, healthcare providers have been very much aware of the need for safety for their patients, employees, and visitors; after all, many accident victims end up in hospitals. This makes every healthcare employee doubly aware of the importance of safety. Also, a safe environment for patients, employees, and visitors of a healthcare center is an ever-present consideration in the training and education of most healthcare professionals.

Although almost all healthcare facilities have a safety committee, or even a safety department, this alone cannot fulfill the institution's obligation to create and maintain a safe environment for clients, visitors, and employees. As part of their responsibilities, managers and supervisors must diligently watch their areas and attempt to eliminate safety hazards. The recent flood of liability suits against hospitals has put additional emphasis on the need for safety.

A hospital patient is entitled to expect the hospital to keep its premises reasonably safe. The same is true of any healthcare facility, be it ambulatory or residential in nature, of its obligation to its patients. The same care must be taken regarding equipment, instruments, and appliances so that they are adequate for use in the diagnosis or treatment of patients. If defective equipment causes injury to a patient, the hospital may be liable. Patients have brought suits against hospitals because of defective beds, broken thermometers, inoperative patient call systems, improperly calibrated X-ray equipment, and improperly prepared food, to name a few. These are all examples of why JCAHO stresses the Life Safety Code.

Another impetus for safety came with the Occupational Safety and Health Act (OSHA) of 1970, which places greater responsibility on employers to provide employees with a safe and healthy work environment. Since OSHA's scope is so vast, the supervisor cannot possibly be familiar with all of it or with its most important aspects. Therefore, supervisors should be in close touch with the person in the healthcare center who is the expert, such as the safety director.

However, it is the supervisor's duty to keep his or her staff informed of chemical agents with which staff may come in contact. When chemical agents of any type, such as detergents, "white out," printer toner, or laboratory chemicals and reagents are used in the work setting, a Material Safety and Data Sheet (MSDS) should be prominently posted in the work area. These MSDS sheets provide staff with "need to know" information such as what to do to treat the employee if the chemical is ingested, gets in the eyes, etc. This OSHA requirement helps to ensure staff safety and knowledge of the chemicals to which they may be exposed. In any event, OSHA has added to the supervisor's responsibility for planning and maintaining a healthier and safer work environment.

Although many healthcare centers have a safety director, safety committee, or committee for claim prevention and loss control, the true responsibility for safety lies with every manager, from the CEO down to the supervisors. The supervisor, being the person on the spot, must stress safety more than anyone else and enforce safety procedures. Safety must be foremost in the supervisors' and employees' thoughts, and must be a constant consideration in all supervisory planning. It must be integrated in all policies, procedures, methods, practices, and directives, so that accidents and incidents do not occur or at least are significantly reduced.

## ■ Use of Space

Supervisors must also plan for the best utilization of space. First, they should determine whether or not the space assigned to the department is being used effectively. Some industrial engineering help, if available, may be requested to make this determination. If such help is not available, the supervisor should make a layout chart, showing the square footage of the department, the location of equipment and supplies, and the work paths of the employees. Such a chart can then be studied to determine whether the allocated space has been laid out appropriately or whether areas need to be rearranged so that the department's work can be done more efficiently.

For example, say the chief technologist of the clinical laboratories shows that their annual workload has been increasing by approximately 10 percent annually, which would result in nearly doubling the workload in approximately nine years, from 40,000 to 70,000 tests. She also points out that the increased volume requires additional instrumentation that will require more square feet of room. She may also show how long the laboratories have occupied the same space. The chief technologist then draws up a typical laboratory space plan, showing a layout for separate work units or technical sections—hematology, urinalysis, biochemistry, histology, serology, bacteriology, immunology, blood bank, and the support areas. At the same time, the supervisor points out that laboratory facilities should preferably be on the first floor near the emergency room and patient registration areas, and should be easily accessible to surgery, rather than on the present upper floor location. The supervisor also discusses the "feasibility of moving the labs to an off-site location." She then presents these materials and her discussion to the administrator and the medical director of the laboratory.

This type of layout planning might show the need for additional space and/or a different location. If such a request is placed before the administrator based on thorough planning of the space currently allotted, then the likelihood that it will be granted is greater. In this case, the chief technologist most likely will be competing with many other managers who probably also requested more space and another location. Even if the request is denied, these plans will not have been drawn up in vain. They most likely will alert the supervisor, in this case the chief technologist, to some of the conditions under which the employees are working, and perhaps that information can be used to plan more efficient work methods according to the existing conditions.

## ■ Use of Materials and Supplies

The supervisor must plan for the appropriate use, security, and conservation of the materials and supplies entrusted and charged to the department. At the nursing station, these would include such supplies as gloves, masks, bandages, adhesive tape, cotton balls, tongue blades, alcohol wipes, syringes, needles, IV insertion materials, single-use disposable clinical thermometers, medicine cups, and paper goods, or the tray of supplies in the patient's room hall closet. In most departments, the quantity of materials and supplies used is substantial. Even if each single item represents only a small value, the aggregate of these items adds up to sizeable amounts in the budget of a healthcare facility. Proper planning will ensure that materials and supplies are used as conservatively as possible, without compromising sterility, asepsis, and sanitary requirement. Supervisors must teach their employees proper use of supplies because many workers are careless and do not realize the amount of money involved.

Another problem is the loss and theft of materials, often done by the employees themselves. Supervisors must take adequate precautions to minimize this source of loss. They must consider "pocket loss," that is, those supplies that leave the facility (innocently in most cases) in the pockets of lab coats or uniforms. When this author managed a hospital department, she noted increased supply usage—specifically, pencils, pens, and tablets—in September, coinciding with the start of school. Although proper planning for the utilization of materials and supplies will help significantly in performance, it will not prevent all waste.

## ■ Management of Time

Supervisors also must plan the use of time. Managers must not only plan their employees' time, but they must also consider at least as carefully the management of their own time.

## ■ Managing the Employees'Time

When planning for the effective use of the subordinates' time, much will depend on the supervisors' basic managerial strategy and their assumptions about human nature. According to Douglas McGregor, a well-known author and professor of management, most managers base their thinking on one of two sets of assumptions about human nature, which he calls Theory X and Theory Y. The Theory X manager believes that the average employee dislikes work, will avoid work, and tries to get by with as little as possible. The employee has little ambition and has to be forced and closely controlled in each and every job.

The Theory Y manager operates with a drastically different set of assumptions regarding human nature. He or she believes that most employees consider work natural and that most are eager to do the right thing, will seek responsibility under the proper conditions, will exercise self-control, and do not need to be constantly reminded to do their work. Theory Y further states that external controls and threats are not a good means of producing results. Rather, since work is as natural to people as play or rest, they will not avoid it.

Although there may be some situations in which a manager has no choice but to follow Theory X, practice and belief in Theory Y is preferred. Much more will be said about McGregor's theories in chapters 19 and 21, but it is appropriate to bring them up now because they are important when planning for the effective utilization of employees' time.

For example, if a supervisor is a Theory Y manager, he or she will expect employees to do the right thing and to turn in a fair day's work. Since one cannot expect employees to work indefinitely at top speed, however, the plans for their time will be based on a fair output instead of a maximum output. Allowances will be made for fatigue, personal needs, unavoidable delays, and a certain amount of unproductive time during the workday.

In planning employees' time, as in other aspects of planning, the supervisor may be able to get assistance from a specialist employed by the healthcare provider, preferably a motion and time specialist. However, most supervisors usually can figure out what can be expected of their employees. Managers are generally capable of planning reasonable performance requirements that their employees accept as fair. Such requirements are based on average conditions and not on emergencies. These reasonable estimates of employees' time are necessary because the supervisor must depend on the completion of certain tasks at certain times. The supervisors themselves may have been given deadlines, and to meet them, they must have a reasonable estimate or idea of how fast the job can be done.

In some situations, the subordinate's time is paced and is set by someone other than the supervisor because of the nature of the activity performed. For instance, the time an operating room nurse or technician spends on a case is determined by the type of surgery and the speed and skill of the surgeon. In the clinical laboratories and even in the food service dish room, the time required is set by the speed of the automated equipment. Furthermore, unexpected complications may add to the time normally necessary to complete the job. In these cases, average time estimates can still be made, but the time allotted must allow for the various contingencies that can arise.

In addition to planning for the normal employee time, it may be necessary to plan for overtime. Overtime should be considered only as an emergency measure. If the supervisor finds that overtime or working a double shift is regularly required, then plans need changing by altering work methods, obtaining better or more equipment, or hiring more part-time and full-time employees. The supervisor must also plan for employee absences. One cannot plan for those instances in which employees are absent without notice, but one can plan for holidays, vacations, leaves of absence, or layoffs for overhaul. Plans for these absences should be worked out in advance so that the functioning of the department will suffer as little as possible.

## ■ Flexible Work Schedules

Work schedules for many employees in different organizations have become more flexible. The idea behind this is that employees should have some autonomy to adjust their work schedule to fit their lifestyles and to choose the hours they would prefer to work. The plans are designed to give employees greater opportunities to enjoy their life *off,* as opposed to *on,* the job. "Flex time" enables employees to choose a schedule that fits into their off-the-job activities. It enables working parents or others with responsibilities at home the opportunity to combine work with family life. The concept of flex time has been successfully introduced into various private and public organized activities and in healthcare centers. Flexible work schedules probably will become even more popular in the future, especially for professional and clerical work.

It is well known that some healthcare professionals, especially nurses, have left their field of expertise because they were dissatisfied with several factors, among which grueling hours and schedules loomed large. Many nurses cannot or do not want to work the old and traditional five-day, forty-hour week of rotating shifts, 7:00 to 3:00, 3:00 to 11:00, and 11:00 to 7:00. Therefore, it was necessary to do away with the traditional pattern of nursing staff scheduling. To alleviate these dissatisfactions, flexible work hours have been introduced. Varied plans are available, including the "4-40," which is four days at ten hours; seven days on and seven days off, using the ten-hour workday; 24-hour weekend shifts; two 16-hour shifts on a weekend; or the three-day weekend plan. In this situation, the introduction of flexible work schedules certainly has been a good idea and probably will be expanded.

Flexible working schedules undoubtedly create some additional scheduling and planning problems for supervisors. Furthermore, such schedules cause problems for proper supervision of the employees during different shift arrangements and in supervisors' coordination of activities with other departments. There also is the real concern that schedules with long hours can potentially cause fatigue and an increase in errors. These concerns and others are additional challenges for supervisors. However, as long as flexible working schedules produce good results (*e.g.,* easier staff recruitment, better staff retention, higher morale, fewer absences, less tardiness, less dissatisfaction, and better patient care), supervisors will make every effort to overcome these problems by better planning and supervision.

## ■ Managing the Supervisor's Time

Time is life. It is irreversible and irreplaceable. To waste your time is to waste your life, but to master your time is to master your life and make the most of it.

Time is one of the most valuable resources that cannot be renewed or stored. If supervisors want more time, they have to "make" it themselves. The supervisor's own time is one of the resources for which he or she is responsible. Every supervisor has probably experienced days that were so full of pressures and demands that he or she began to feel as though all the matters that needed attention could never be resolved. The days and weeks were just too short. The only way to keep such days at a minimum is for the supervisor to plan the time for the most effective use.

Unfortunately, the supervisor's problems come up constantly but without any order of importance or priority. Thus, the first thing the supervisor must do is to "triage," that is, to sort and grade the problems by deciding which ones he or she must attend to personally and those that can be assigned to someone else. The supervisor cannot delegate some matters, but most can be assigned to one of the employees. Every time the supervisor dispenses with one of the duties by assigning it to an employee, time is gained for more important matters. This delegation of tasks is worthwhile even if some valuable time must be spent training one of the employees in a particular task. In case of doubt, therefore, the supervisor should be inclined to delegate. Then the available time must be planned so that it is divided among those matters to which the supervisor alone can attend. These matters again have to be classified according to their urgency.

Stephen R. Covey, in his popular book, *The Seven Habits of Highly Effective People,* describes a time management matrix wherein he defines the four ways we spend time.

If managers follow Covey's advice, they will attempt to concentrate their time in proactively preparing for the future rather than being driven by it when the future arrives, thus causing a crisis. In addition, Covey provides guidance in setting priorities. Two factors that define an activity according to Covey are *urgent* and *important. Urgent,* he says, means it requires immediate attention. It's "Now!" Urgent things act on us, for example a ringing phone is urgent Covey says. *Important,* however, has to do with results and those *important* actions contribute to the manager's mission, values, or goals, states this author.

Unless supervisors distinguish between those matters that *must* be done and those that *ought* to be done, they are inclined to pay equal attention to all matters before them. Then planning and the more important items may not receive the attention they truly deserve. By distinguishing between the two, supervisors will be giving priority to those matters that need immediate attention. A supervisor should therefore plan the time so that the most important things to attend to will appear at the top of the schedule. The supervisor must make certain, however, that some free time is left in the time schedule because not every contingency can be anticipated. There will be some emergencies that a supervisor must deal with when they arise. The flexibility will make it possible to take care of these situations without significantly disrupting the other activities planned on the time schedule.

Many techniques have been devised to help supervisors control their time schedules. One of the simplest methods is to use a desk calendar to schedule or a "to do list of" those items that need attention, such as appointments, meetings, reports, and discussions. The supervisor should schedule these events far in advance, then they will automatically come up for attention when they are due.

Another effective way of planning each week's work, as well as knowing what is being accomplished as the week progresses, is to keep a planning sheet. Such a planning sheet is prepared at the end of one week for the week to follow. It shows the days of the week divided into morning and afternoon columns and a list of all items to be accomplished. Then a time for accomplishment is assigned to each task by placing it in the morning or the afternoon blocks of the assigned day. As a task is accomplished, its box is circled.

Those tasks that have been delayed during the day must be rescheduled for another time by placing them in an appropriate block on a subsequent day. Those tasks that are planned but have not been accomplished during the week (the ones that remain uncircled) must be rescheduled for the following week. Such a record will show how much of the original plan has been carried out at the end of the week and will provide a good answer to the question of where the supervisor's time went. Based on this record, the supervisor will then be able to plan the next week and so on. Regardless of whether this particular system or another is used, the supervisor must schedule the time periods each week and have some method of reporting the tasks that are planned and those that have been accomplished. (See figure 8.3.)

## ■ Time-Use Chart

A manager can best figure out how his or her time is spent by keeping a time-use chart or a time log. At least twice a day—at noon and before leaving in the evening—the supervisor should list all his or her activities on a half-hour basis; or in order not to forget anything, the supervisor should write down all of his or

**Figure 8.3** Sample planning sheet.

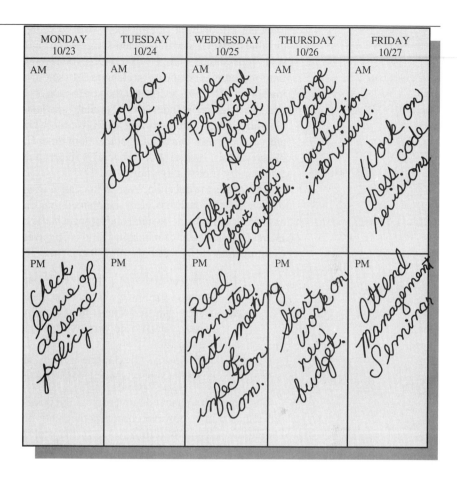

| MONDAY 10/23 | TUESDAY 10/24 | WEDNESDAY 10/25 | THURSDAY 10/26 | FRIDAY 10/27 |
|---|---|---|---|---|
| AM | AM *Work on job descriptions* | AM *See Personnel Director about Helen* / *Talk to maintenance about new fl outlets.* | AM *Arrange dates for evaluation interviews:* | AM *Work on dress code revisions* |
| PM *Check leave of absence policy* | PM | PM *Read minutes, last meeting of infection con.* | PM *Start on work on new budget.* | PM *Attend management seminar* |

her activities every half hour. This log should be kept during a fairly typical workload for at least one or two weeks. At the end of the week, a review of this log will tell the supervisor how much time he or she spent in counseling and instructing employees, on the phone, answering letters, in meetings, on personal chores, socializing, or having lunch. Then the supervisor should create some broad classifications for daily activities, such as routine duties, regular supervisory duties, special duties, emergencies, and innovative thinking.

The supervisor may find that 20 percent of the time was spent on *routine work,* which could and should be assigned to some of the subordinates. A large percentage of time was devoted to *regular supervisory duties,* such as checking performance, giving directives and instructions, evaluating and counseling employees, and promoting and maintaining discipline. These are supervisory duties that the manager alone should do. Then the supervisor should find out how much time he or she spent on *special duties* such as: serving on committees, attending professional meetings, planning next year's budget, changing the dress code, and reviewing procedures. Again, all this time is probably spent wisely.

A certain amount of time also will be spent on *emergencies,* i.e., unpredictable events that will demand some of the supervisor's attention. In addition, some time should be open for *creative and innovative thinking,* which is essential for planning advances or changes for the department and the progress of the institution. The boss evaluates the supervisor on how well the department's job gets done, which includes his or her innovative changes and suggestions.

Studying the time-use chart will illustrate where the time went and in which areas a supervisor can "make" some more time. Unless the supervisor has a clear picture of this, routine tasks probably will creep in and reduce the time available for the truly supervisory duties.

This raises the question, Who is in control of the supervisor's time? Throughout our discussion it has been maintained that only he or she can control time, and that it is his or her responsibility for what is done with it. However, another interesting approach to managing time is suggested by Oncken and Wass. They examine three different kinds of management time:

1. *Boss-imposed time* is time used by an individual to accomplish those activities that the boss requires and the supervisor cannot disregard.
2. *System-imposed time* is time used by an individual to give support to peers and to cooperate with and coordinate activities of the organization.
3. *Self-imposed time* is time used by an individual to accomplish the items the supervisor originates and agrees to do himself or herself.

The supervisor cannot do much about the boss- and system-imposed time. The self-imposed time, however, becomes the major time frame of his or her concern. During the self-imposed time, some of the supervisor's time is taken up by the subordinates, which can be called *subordinate-imposed time.* Subordinate-imposed time can be consumed by such things as counseling, idle chitchat, seeking direction, and settling disputes. The latter has become a significant time consumer (see figure 8.4). The remaining time is called *discretionary time.* To increase discretionary time, the supervisor must reduce the subordinate-imposed time.

In summary, effective time management increases the manager's discretionary time for managerial tasks and innovative thinking. Another important benefit of time management is that stress can be controlled and reduced if the individual does a good job of managing time.

## ■ Utilization of the Workforce

The employees in a department are the most valuable resource. Therefore, planning for their full utilization must be foremost in every manager's mind. Although a supervisor must plan for the use of equipment, tools, and space; improved work methods and processes; conservation of materials and supplies; and proper use of time, the most important planning of all is utilizing the workforce.

**Figure 8.4**  Playing peacemaker.

*Reprinted with permission from The Journal of Accountancy, copyright 1996 by American Institute of CPAs, Opinions of the authors are their own and do not necessarily reflect policies of the AICPA.*

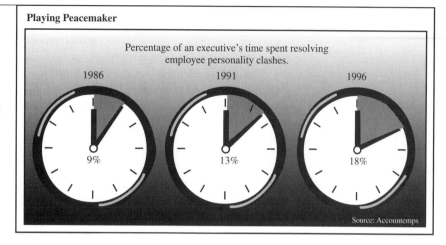

This, of course, does not mean planning to squeeze an excessive amount of work out of each employee. Rather, proper utilization means giving employees as much satisfaction as possible in their jobs. To plan for the best utilization of the workforce also entails developing methods for recruiting good employees, searching for all available sources of employees, and working for their retention. Furthermore, proper utilization means conducting an ongoing search for the best ways to group employees' activities and includes training, supervising, and motivating the employees.

Finally, effective use of workers means the continual appraisal of their performance, appropriate promotions, adequate plans for compensation and rewards, and at the same time, fair disciplinary measures.

All these considerations play an important role when the supervisor plans for the best utilization of the department's employees. Only through such human resource planning can a situation be created in which workers willingly contribute their utmost to achieve both personal satisfaction on the job and the department's objectives. Employees will amply reward a supervisor who considers their personal satisfaction important. Planning for the best utilization of employees is at the heart of expert supervision.

## SUMMARY

All planning must be done with forecasts of the future in mind. Since the future is uncertain, one must make various assumptions as to what it will hold. Overall forecasts or assumptions are made by the top-level administrator, and the supervisor narrows these down to forecasts for the departmental activity. Based on such forecasts, the supervisor will then make plans for the department.

Plans must be made for the full utilization of all the resources at the supervisor's disposal. More specifically, he or she must plan for proper use of equipment and instruments, work methods, and processes. The supervisor should plan to effectively use the space available and the materials and supplies under his or her supervision. The efficient use of time also must be planned. Even more important, the supervisor must plan for the best overall utilization of the employees in the unit. This means, among other things, seeing that employees are able to find satisfaction in their work.

Throughout all planning, the supervisor should be concerned with the effects of these plans on other members of the organization. At times, the manager may need to resort to various tactical considerations that will be helpful in getting the department's plans accepted and effectively performed.

# PART IV
# ORGANIZING

# *9* *Fundamental Concepts of Organizing*

*Chapter Objectives*

After you have studied this chapter, you should be able to:

1. Discuss why organizing is an important managerial function.
2. Identify the organizing function as the process of designing the structural framework and establishing authority relationships based on major principles.
3. Enumerate and discuss two fundamental organization underpinnings, namely authority and span of management.
4. Describe the meaning and major sources of formal, positional authority.
5. Explain the importance of the span of management and the relationships of span to levels leading to a flat or tall organization.
6. Discuss the major factors that will influence the width of the span.

Planning defines the goals and objectives of the institution. Organizing is closely related to it. It defines and arranges the activities needed to accomplish these objectives and establishes the relationships among various functions. Organizing is the process of deciding how best to group and relate organizational activities and resources. These activities and functions form subsystems that are synchronized and coordinated into a larger system, called the *formal organization.* Organizing means setting up this formal structure of activities and authority relationships.

How this structure looks and works depends on the organization's objectives and size, state of the arts and science, technology, culture, and many other factors. The managerial function of organizing is an impersonal function, which means that the organization is designed with the activities in mind and not around individual personalities to perform them. Of course, the organization must be a structure that can be inhabited by people, the most valuable asset of any organization. It must be a structure in which people can function and thrive. The human element obviously is important, and we will discuss all these considerations in the staffing and influencing functions. When the manager designs the structure, however, it is done without thinking of specific persons. Organizing means setting up a formal structure of activities and authority relationships based on major principles.

Formal organizational theory rests on several major principles:

1. *Authority* is the lifeblood of the managerial position, and the *delegation of authority* makes the organization come alive.
2. The *span of management* sets outside limits on the number of subordinates a manager can effectively supervise.
3. The *division of work* is essential for efficiency.
4. The *formal structure* is the main network for organizing and managing the various activities of the enterprise.
5. *Unity of command* must prevail.
6. *Coordination* is a primary responsibility of management and is fulfilled by performing the managerial functions properly.

These major principles of organization are a primary concern of the chief operating officer (COO). He or she must translate them into a formal organizational structure so that the institution operates smoothly and accomplishes its objectives.

Since the application of these formal organizational principles involves all levels of management, it is also necessary for you as a supervisor to understand them and know how they are used. This knowledge will help you organize your own department and coordinate its activities with those of the rest of the institution. As a supervisor, you will certainly be asked to carry out (and may even be asked to help make) such decisions involving reorganization, departmentalization or the division of work, the span of supervision, and the delegation of authority.

As you move up the managerial hierarchy, you will probably be called on to participate in more and more organizational decisions. Thus, although the COO initially applies the formal principles to establish the organization's overall structure and activities, the department heads, supervisors, and other middle- and lower-level managers must make these principles and the resulting structure work. This is why it is essential for us to discuss the organizing process on an overall, or institutional, basis before we can discuss it on the departmental, or supervisory, level.

The many contingencies facing management are a constant challenge, and the dynamic nature of organizing enables the manager to bring about change and to absorb and accommodate change as the need arises. This will enable the enterprise to pursue and achieve its objectives continuously.

## AUTHORITY AND SPAN OF MANAGEMENT

Although organizing is a dynamic process, it rests on two fundamental concepts: *authority* and *span of management,* which this chapter examines. Authority, the right to direct others and to act and give orders, is one of the bases through which the manager gets the job done. It is the underpinning of the organization. The span of management deals with another dimension—the scope of supervision—the number of people who report to a particular manager.

**AUTHORITY**   In chapter 2, we referred briefly to how important authority is to the managerial position. Our discussion of authority at that point merely stated that it is the lifeblood of the supervisory position and one of the characteristics of a manager. Also we mentioned that delegating authority breathes life into an organization; without it, an organization cannot and does not exist. Therefore, we must first examine and understand the concept of authority.

### ▪ The Meaning of Authority

Authority is a difficult concept; it has many interpretations and meanings, including the one we have used before: the key to the managerial job. In this sense, authority refers to the formal or official power of a manager to obtain the compliance of the subordinate by using directives, communications, policies, and objectives. Such authority is associated with the manager's function in the organization; it is vested in organizational roles or positions. As long as an individual holds the position, he or she has the privilege of exercising the authority that is inherent in it.

Since positions are meaningless unless they are occupied by someone, we generally speak of the authority of the manager, the authority that is delegated to the manager, and so forth. Although it would be more precise to speak of the authority of the managerial *position* itself or the authority delegated to that position rather than to the person who occupies it, the difference is generally regarded as semantic. As long as we understand that authority in this sense resides in the position, we may speak rather loosely of the authority of the manager, supervisor, etc.

### ▪ Source of Nature of Authority

As stated, authority is a difficult concept, with many interpretations and meanings. The definition of authority as "legitimate power" to give orders was first clearly expressed by Max Weber. The subordinates' compliance rests on the belief that it is legitimate for managers to give orders and illegitimate for subordinates not to obey them. This kind of authority is vested in organizational roles and positions, not in the individuals who occupy these positions. As long as an individual holds the position, he or she has the privilege of exercising the authority that is inherent in it. Once a manager leaves an organizational position, he or she loses the authority inherent in it, and the authority will go to the successor.

While examining the foundation for this organizational authority, Weber identified three bases of authority: *tradition, rules and regulations,* and *charisma.* Traditional authority "rests on the belief in the sacredness of the social order." For instance, in a patriarchal society, the father receives legitimacy as an authority through custom. Rules and regulations form a second base.

Subordinates will comply with order because, in a bureaucratic organization, superior-subordinate authority relationships are defined by rules and regulations. In charismatic authority, the compelling personal characteristics and charisma of the leader make the subordinates and followers carry out the orders. The concept of leadership is further discussed in chapter 21.

In addition to these explanations of the meaning and sources of authority, other views have been developed and expressed. In reference to the *source of authority,* there are two contradictory views: *the formal authority theory* and the *acceptance theory.* In *formal authority theory,* authority originates at the top of the organizational hierarchy and is delegated downward *from superiors to subordinates.* On the other hand, in *acceptance theory,* a leader's authority originates at the bottom of the organizational pyramid and is determined by his or her subordinates' willingness to comply with it. Let us look at each of these theories more carefully to gain further insight into the authority concept.

## ■ Formal Authority Theory

The formal authority theory is the top-down theory. It traces the flow of authority downward from top-level management to subordinate managers. You can trace your authority directly from your boss, who has delegated it to you. He or she in turn receives authority, for example, from an associate administrator, who receives authority from the chief administrator, who traces authority directly back to the board of directors, who receive their authority from the owners or the stockholders. In private corporations, therefore, one may say that the actual source of authority lies in the stockholders, who are, loosely speaking, the owners of the corporation. These owners delegate their power to administer the affairs of the corporation to those whom they have put into managerial positions. From the top administrator that power flows down through the chain of command until it reaches the supervisor.

## ■ Limitations of Authority

There are limitations to the authority that a manager has by virtue of his or her position in an organization. These limitations can be either explicit or implicit. Moreover, some of them stem from internal sources and others from external sources. *External limitations* on authority include such factors as our codes, folkways, and lifestyle, along with the many legal, political, ethical, moral, social, and economic considerations that make up our society. For example, laws referring to collective bargaining and resulting contractual obligations, fair employment practices, etc., are specific examples of external limitations on authority.

In contrast, *internal limitations* on authority are set mainly by the organization's articles of incorporation and bylaws. In addition to these overall internal restrictions, each manager is subject to the specific limitations spelled out by the administrator when duties are assigned and authority delegated. Generally, there are more internal limitations on the scope of authority the further down one goes in the managerial hierarchy. In other words, the lower the rung on the administrative ladder, the narrower is the area in which authority can be exercised. This is known as the *tapering concept of authority,* as shown in figure 9.1.

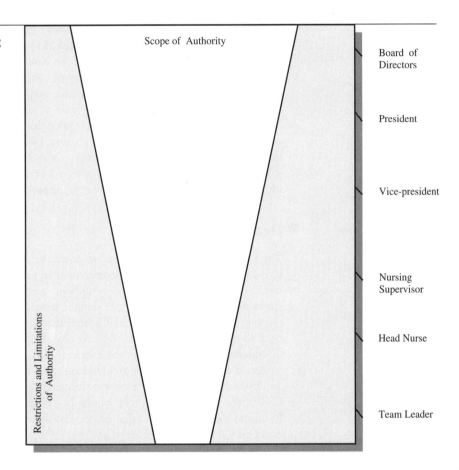

**Figure 9.1**  The tapering concept of authority.

All these limitations are explicit, fairly obvious restrictions on authority. In addition to these, a number of more implicit limitations, such as biological restraints, exist simply because human beings do not have the capacity to do certain things. No subordinate should be expected to do the impossible. Thus, physical and psychological restrictions on authority must be recognized and accepted. In today's society, such considerations significantly limit the scope of authority of every manager.

Thus far, our discussion has centered on the formal way of looking at the origin of authority as a power that results from our recognition of private property. According to this theory, then, the ultimate sources of all managerial authority in the United States would be the constitutional guarantee of the institution of private property. Since the Constitution was created by the people and is subject to amendment and modification by the will of the people, it follows that society is the source from which authority flows.

This theory is in agreement with Weber's definition of formal authority, since management's right to give orders is legitimate and the employees are obliged to carry out these orders because the orders are legitimate. There could be a problem, however, when such an order seems unethical to the employee or outside the limits of the job. This raises the question of whether the subordinate has some say in this matter.

## ■ Acceptance Theory of Authority

The acceptance theory of authority addresses the role of subordinates and managerial authority. It is a bottom-up approach in which employees give managers their authority. In addition to Barnard, other experts do not agree with the formal theory and maintain that management has no meaningful authority unless and until subordinates confer it. These writers claim that formal organizational authority is effective only to the extent that subordinates accept it. They state that unless your subordinates accept your authority, you, as a manager, actually do not possess that authority. In reality, subordinates often do not have a real choice between accepting or not accepting authority. The only choice they have is to leave the job. Nevertheless, this is a worrisome thought, indicating that there is considerable merit in looking at authority as something that must be accepted by your employees.

Advocates of the acceptance theory state that in most cases a manager does not have a real problem; an employee, on accepting a job, knows that the boss of the department has the authority to give orders, take disciplinary action, and do whatever else goes with the managerial position. Whenever an employee decides to work for a healthcare institution, he or she agrees, within the limits of the job, to accept orders given by the organization. The decision whether an order has authority, however, lies with the person to whom it is addressed and does not reside in "persons of authority" or those who issue these orders.

## ■ Formal Authority Theory versus Acceptance Authority Theory

To repeat, the origin of authority can be considered from two viewpoints. The formal way views authority as something that originates with private property, formally handed down from the owners at the top to the lowest line supervisor. In contrast, the acceptance idea views authority as something that is conferred on the supervisor by the subordinates' acceptance of this authority. It is not the author's intention to go further into this academic argument here. This difference of opinions is discussed because it significantly influences the practice of supervision, that is, the manner and the attitudes with which supervision is approached.

This will become more obvious when we realize that adhering to the acceptance theory does not necessarily rule out the downward delegation of authority from upper to lower levels of management. The acceptance theory can be thought of as merely adding another dimension to the formal concept of organizational authority. That is, in addition to having formal authority delegated from above, managers must also have such authority accepted from below. All managers must be aware that they possess formal authority and, if need be, can resort to it as a final recourse.

Today no one wants to rely exclusively on the weight of this formal authority to motivate workers to perform their jobs. At times, however, every manager will have to make full use of this authority and power; it is hoped that these occasions will be the exceptions and not the rule. Even when the manager must invoke this authority, the manner in which it is done will make a difference in whether it is resented or accepted without resentment. If such actions are accepted graciously most of the time, the manager will know that the subordinates have chosen to recognize and respect the authority that superiors have formally delegated to him or her.

## ■ Types of Authority

In the past, it might have been sufficient for a manager to rely on authority based on the legitimacy of the social institution—the concept of property rights—to get the job done. This approach alone, however, is no longer appropriate for a manager in any organized activity, especially in a healthcare institution. Therefore, it is necessary to examine the various types of organizational authority: positional, functional, and personal.

*Positional authority* is based on organizational position and, as stated, rests on the legitimacy of the manager's position as the agent of a socially valid organization. This authority is vested in the position and in the organization and is impersonal. Positional authority exists in all types of organizations: healthcare, educational, business, military, religious, fraternal, etc. We may not like or care for a particular individual, but we recognize and accept the legitimacy of that person's position and authority.

*Functional authority* is based on expertise and knowledge. We accept expert advice and recognize that this person is an "authority" in a particular specialty. Functional authority exists in all branches of learning and crafts and comes from specialization. Healthcare institutions are a prime example of the role and importance of functional authority. The "specialist's" statements and directives are accepted because he or she is the "authority in this field" and carries the weight and power of functional authority.

Whereas positional authority is impersonal, functional authority in this sense is highly personal. It adheres to the individual whose knowledge and expertise make him or her the "authority." Whereas positional authority can and must be delegated, functional authority cannot be delegated; it remains with the individual wherever he or she may be and work. Although it is highly personalized, functional authority has some aspects of positional authority because some organizations, especially healthcare centers, demand that certain positions can only be filled by individuals with special skills and expertise. A hospital abounds in examples and applications of functional authority, probably more than any other organized activity. Functional authority rests on acceptance, but it stems from an individual's knowledge and not from society.

*Personal authority* is based on an individual's characteristics, magnetism, and charisma. Subordinates and followers accept personal authority because their needs are consistent with the leader's goals. Personal authority motivates the subordinates to work willingly and enthusiastically toward the achievement of the objectives. This concept of personal authority can be equated with leadership, which is discussed in chapter 21.

## ■ Integrated Approach to Authority

To be an effective manager in a healthcare institution, it is not enough to depend on the weight of positional authority based on legitimacy, although occasionally this may be the last resort. It is much more desirable if the manager relies on a combination of all three types of authority—positional, functional, and personal—to manage effectively. This is even more important in the healthcare field because of the occupational and professional character of the people involved.

New fields of scientific advances and new technologies make greater expertise a necessity, leading to more and more functional authority. For instance, the lead coding professional should not rely on only positional authority as the "lead" of the coding team; he or she should also use personal expertise and knowledge in this field as well as leadership ability and charisma. Reliance on all three types of authority will create a highly desirable and motivating organizational climate.

## THE SPAN OF MANAGEMENT

Another important underpinning of the organization is the number of people who report to a particular manager. This defines the span of management, also known as *span of authority, span of supervision,* or *span of control.* This concept deals with the scope of supervision, the number of people any one person can supervise effectively. Should it be relatively narrow, with few subordinates per manager, or reasonably wide, with many subordinates per manager? In order to make these reporting relationships become effective, organizations must create departments in different areas of activities and place someone in charge of each.

The establishment of departments in an organization is not an end in itself. It is not desirable per se because departments are expensive; they must be headed by various supervisors and staffed by additional employees, all of which runs into large sums of money. Furthermore, creating departments is not intrinsically desirable because the more there are, the more difficulties will be encountered in communication and coordination. However, as discussed earlier, departments do make the division of work possible. Equally important, they allow an organization to incorporate the *principle of the span of management,* or the span of supervision. This principle states that *there is an upper limit to the number of subordinates a manager can effectively supervise.* This is a very crucial factor in structuring organizations.

## ■ The Relationships of Span to Levels

Almost every manager knows that a limit exists to the number of employees he or she can effectively supervise. The problem is caused by the many superior-subordinate interactions that are possible: (1) *direct relationships* between the superior and the immediate subordinates, (2) *direct group interactions* between the superior and different groupings of the subordinates, and (3) *cross-relationships* among the subordinates themselves. The number of superior-subordinate interactions that can be handled is limited.

Since no one can manage an infinite number of subordinates, the administrator must create departments, or distinct areas of activities, over which a manager is placed in charge. The administrator delegates authority to this manager. The manager in turn will re-delegate authority to some subordinates, who in turn will supervise only a limited number of employees. In this manner, not only are departments and subdepartments created, but also the *span of supervision,* or the number of employees under each manager, is established. The number of managerial *levels* in the organization is determined as well.

To examine this relationship between the span of supervision and the levels of an organization, imagine a hypothetical organization in which eighty-one subordinates report to one chief executive, thus representing an organizational level (See figure 9.2.) Then let us assume that eighty-one subordinates are too many and that only three should report to the top administrator. Under each of these three associate administrators there would now be twenty-seven employees. By creating associate administrators, however, we have established two levels of organization and have a total of four executives. Now, assuming that twenty-seven subordinates are still too many, and that this number is reduced to nine, the organization will require a third managerial level, increasing the total number of managers to thirteen. Each of the four executives on the upper two levels will have three subordinates, and each of the nine supervisors on the lowest level will have nine subordinates. The span of supervision has thus been reduced drastically from the original eighty-one to a maximum of nine.

This obviously extreme example shows what occurs when one begins to narrow the span of supervision. The narrower the span becomes, the more levels of management have to be introduced into the organizational setup. As with departments, this is not desirable per se because it is expensive. Every manager costs money, not only in salaries, but also in supporting salaries. Many levels complicate communication, since the dangers of distortion, omission, and misinterpretation are increased. Finally, adding levels to an organization creates problems with morale because it increases the distance between employees and upper administration. Therefore, a constant conflict exists between the width of the span and the number of levels: the narrower the span, the more managerial levels. The problem is whether to have a broader span of supervision or more levels, or vice versa. This problem is one that all managers face throughout their entire career and one to which we have still not found a clear solution. Thus, there is no definitive answer to the question: How many subordinates should report to a given manager? One can only say that there is an upper limit to this figure.

Although we do not know exactly what the upper limit should be, it is interesting that in many enterprises the top-level administrator has only from five to eight subordinate managers reporting directly to him or her. Descending down the managerial hierarchy, we find that the span of supervision generally in-

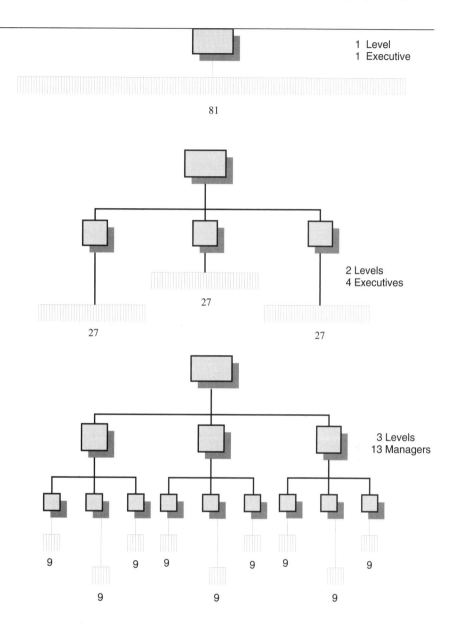

**Figure 9.2** Relationship between the span of supervision and the levels of an organization.

1 Level
1 Executive

81

2 Levels
4 Executives

27

27

27

3 Levels
13 Managers

9          9     9          9     9          9

9               9               9

creases. It is not unusual to have anywhere from fifteen to twenty people report-ing to the supervisor. On closer inspection, we find that the number of subordi-nates who can be effectively supervised by one manager actually depends on nu-merous different contingency factors. These factors determine not only the actual number of relationships, but also their frequency and intensity. Therefore, before deciding the proper span of supervision in a particular organization, it is necessary to examine the more important contingencies that influence the magnitude of the span.

## ◼ Factors Determining the Span of Supervision

One of the factors that influences the magnitude of the span is the *competence of supervisors*—their quality of management, experience, and know-how. Some supervisors are capable of handling more subordinates than others. Some are better acquainted with good management practices; others have had more experience and are simply better all-around managers. A person who is a "good manager" probably can supervise more employees. Limitations still exist, however, on the human capacity and the amount of time available during the working day.

What the manager does with this time is of utmost importance in determining the span. For example, a supervisor needs more time to make an individual decision for every problem that arises than to make initial policy decisions that anticipate problems that might arise later. Clear and complete policy statements reduce the volume of, or at least simplify, the personal decision making required of a manager and thus can increase the span of supervision. The same applies to other managerial processes that determine in advance definitions of responsibility and authority, procedures, methods, and performance standards. Predeterminations such as these reduce the number of decisions the manager has to make and likewise increase the potential span of management.

Another factor that will determine how broad a span a manager can handle is the *competence and makeup of the subordinates*. The greater the capacities and self-direction of the employees, the broader the manager's span can be. The schooling and training possessed by the subordinates is also important. The better their background, the less they will need their supervisor, thus freeing the manager to increase the span.

Another contingency on the manager's span is the amount and availability of *help from staff specialists* within the organization. If a hospital has a range of experts who provide various kinds of advice, support, and service, then the manager's span can be wider.

The number of subordinates who can be supervised will also depend on the *nature and importance of the activities* performed by them. If these activities are complicated, are highly important, carry critical consequences, or change frequently, the span of supervision will have to be small. The simpler, less complicated, or more uniform the work, the greater can be the number of persons supervised by one supervisor.

Closely related factors that have a bearing on the span of supervision are the *dynamics and complexity of a particular activity*. Some aspects of a hospital routine are most certainly dynamic, whereas others are more stable. In those departments engaged in dynamic, critical, and unpredictable activities, the span will have to be very narrow. In those departments concerned with more or less stable activities, such as food production in the dietary department, the span of supervision can be broader.

Another factor that will determine the span of supervision is the degree to which a fairly comprehensive set of *standard procedures* and *objective standards* can be applied. If enough of them exist and are available for subordinates to gauge their own progress, they will not need to report to and contact their boss constantly. Objective standards and standard procedures will result in less frequent relationships, freeing the manager for a broader span. Although we have now discussed most of the major factors that influence the span of supervision, we still cannot state a definite number of subordinates that a supervisor can effectively manage in each case. The optimum span will always depend on the particular circumstances.

Finally, a fairly new approach to expanding the span of control is the use of *self-directed teams.* These teams further "compartmentalize" a department. Each team has a *leader* who is formally appointed or selected by the team. The team assumes some of the traditional supervisory duties, thus relieving the supervisor of some duties. Duties and authority assumed by the team may include assigning workload to team members, scheduling vacations or weekend duty, checking each other's work, and even preparing performance reviews. Team management allows authority to be shared, broadens the span of control, and encourages staff to work together rather than compete with one another. With broader spans of control, the organization also functions with fewer supervisors.

## SUMMARY

Authority and the span of management are two basic underpinnings of the organizing function. Authority is the right to give orders and directives and to expect that they are carried out. Much has been said and written about the source of authority. The formal top-down opinion views authority as coming from our Constitution, the recognition of private property, social institutions, owners, stockholders, board of directors, higher management, and so on down the line to the supervisor.

The opposite view, the acceptance theory, views authority as coming from the bottom up. This theory states that managers have no authority unless and until the subordinates accept their authority, and they will normally accept only those directives they perceive to be legitimate.

Several bases of authority exist: traditional, rules, and charisma. These bases lead to three major types of organizational authority. Positional authority is based on the position in the organization; functional authority is based on knowledge and expertise; and personal, or charismatic, authority comes from the subordinates' needs being consistent with the leader's goals.

A second basic concept in the organizing process is to determine the span of supervision at each level and the number of managerial levels. The span of supervision states that there is an upper limit to the number of managerial levels. The actual width of this span is determined by such factors as the competence of the supervisor, and the competence and experience of the subordinates to be supervised by one manager. The manager knows, however, that when the span of supervision is decreased, meaning that the number of employees to be supervised is reduced, an additional supervisor has to be introduced for the excess employees.

In other words, the smaller the span of supervision, the more levels of supervisory personnel are needed. This will shape the organization into either a tall, narrow pyramid or, in the case of a broad span of supervision, a shallow, wide pyramid. Team management enhances the shallow pyramid structure and allows employees to manage their own activities without consuming a manager's time to do so.

# *10* Division of Work and Departmentalization

*Chapter Objectives*

After you have studied this chapter, you should be able to:

1. Describe the importance and benefits of division of work, that is, job specialization.
2. Describe the rationale for departmentalization.
3. Describe departmentalization methods.
4. Discuss new forms of organization and their implications for management.

As stated in the previous chapter, organizing means deciding how best to group the activities and resources of the organization. Formal organization theory, also as stated earlier, rests on several major principles or premises. Two of them are division of work and departmentalization. *Division of work,* or *job specialization,* means the degree to which the task of the organization is broken down into component parts. This is essential for efficiency, for the overall performance of healthcare activities, and for the achievement of objectives.

*Departmentalization* is the process of grouping the many activities into distinct units according to logical arrangements. Departmentalization is the building block for the formal structure, the main network for managing the various activities of the enterprise. In this chapter, we discuss the division of work and the design of the formal structure.

These two major premises of organization are a primary concern of the chief executive officer (CEO) in a smaller organization or chief operating officer (COO) in a larger organization. He or she is the one who must translate them into a formal organizational structure for the institution. Since the application of these formal organizational principles involves all levels of management, it is also necessary for you as a supervisor to understand them and to know how they are used. This knowledge will help in organizing your own department and in coordinating its activities with those of the rest of the institution. In your supervisory capacity, you will certainly be asked to carry out, and maybe even help make, decisions involving departmentalization and division of work. As you move up in the managerial hierarchy, you will probably be called on to participate in many more such organizational decisions.

## DIVISION OF WORK: JOB SPECIALIZATION

Division of work is as an age-old practice. Consider the division of work in many tribal societies: women plant and maintain the gardens and wash clothes while the men hunt for food and protect the tribe. Job specialization is the degree to which the overall task is broken down and divided into smaller parts. For example, the building of a car has many tasks, one set of workers place bumpers on the vehicles, others install the windshield, and still others paint the car. Thousands of years ago human beings divided work in this manner because they realized a group of people, each performing a small specialized part of the overall job, could accomplish more than the same-size group in which each individual was trying to do the whole job alone. Furthermore, each individual learns how to do his or her task exceptionally well. In other words, the division of work results in greater efficiency and higher production. This explains the mass production capabilities due to specialization achieved in industrial settings in the United States and the rest of the world in the twentieth century.

This acceptance of specialization and division of work theory is particularly true in healthcare organizations. Continuous advances in medical sciences and technology resulted in greater specialization of professionals, facilities, and equipment and in increased fragmentation of the delivery of care. Physicians and surgeons attain a high degree of specialization in extremely challenging occupations. Because of the proliferation and specialization of medical sciences and technologies, healthcare centers have become very large and complex organizational structures.

This proliferation of specialties has clear advantages for patients in terms of their receiving state-of-the-art care. However, this specialization creates problems in administrating healthcare institutions, due to the need for the varied organizational structures to coordinate these specialties. It also causes problems for the patients who can no longer go to one physician for everything that ails them.

Hospitals are not alone in the specialization arena. Managed care organizations (MCO) have found it necessary to specialize as well. Some specialization is along product lines such as services that support the Health Maintenance Organization (HMO) that may not be the same as those that support the Preferred Provider Organization (PPO). Therefore, staff have been employed and trained to work in the HMO but this need is not necessary in the PPO since the providers have greater independence. The MCO may have employed staff specifically to perform provider relation functions for the PPO, but these individuals do not serve the HMO.

In essence, as healthcare as an industry becomes more sophisticated, higher degrees of expertise are required, thus forcing specialization of the professionals and staff who work within its confines. We will discuss later in this book the impact specialization may have on motivating your workforce.

## DEPARTMENTALIZATION

Because the division of work into such specialized tasks produces a much more efficient operation, almost every organization must departmentalize. As stated, departmentalization is the process of grouping various activities into natural units by logical arrangements. A department is such a unit; it is a distinct area of activities over which a manager or supervisor has been given authority and has accepted responsibility. The terminology may vary and a department may be called a division, service, section, unit, office, bureau, or similar term, but it still represents a closely related set of activities. Departmentalization relies on specialization, which is the core determinate. By departmentalizing the organization, a horizontal grouping of specialized activities is attained.

The major departments in an organization are established by the CEO or COO. The top-level executive is the one who groups the various activities as departments. Some departments established this way will be small and will require no further subdivision. In a healthcare institution, however, many departments will be so large that their managers will have to further subdivide, that is, set up subdepartments, smaller units, or teams. For this reason, every manager must become acquainted with the various alternatives available for grouping activities.

The process of departmentalization can be done on the basis of: (1) functions, (2) process and equipment, (3) territory (location), (4) customer (patient), (5) time, or (6) product. We now explore each of the six alternatives more fully.

## ■ Functions

The most widely accepted practice of departmentalizing is to group activities according to functions or according to the common tasks to be done. All activities that are alike or similar and involve a particular function are placed together into one department under a single chain of command (figure 10.2). For instance, a director of nursing services would be put in charge of all nursing activities throughout the center, and a director of dietary services is put in charge of all food- and nutrition-related activities. (See figures 10.1 and 10.3.) A rather new but fairly common functional grouping is that of information management, where all information generating departments (health information management, health information systems, registration/admitting, utilization review, risk management, and patient accounts) are organized under the Chief Information Officer (CIO) (figure 10.1).

As the institution grows and undertakes additional work, these new duties are added to the already existing departments. For instance, when a hospital adds an outpatient surgical center performing surgery with reasonably low risk on patients who do not stay overnight, this new activity would logically be assigned to the operating rooms department and its director. Such increased activities, however, will require adding more employees and levels of supervision within the functional departments, a topic that was discussed in chapter 9.

To departmentalize by function is a natural, logical way of arranging the various activities in any enterprise and certainly in such facilities as hospitals and nursing homes. This kind of departmentalization takes advantage of specialization by combining the functions that belong together and that are performed by experts in that functional field with the same type of education, background, equipment, and facilities. The experts for each function are brought together under a supervisor for the area. Each functional supervisor is concerned with only one type of work and concentrates all of his or her energy on it. This leads to an efficient use of resources.

Functional departmentalization also facilitates and enhances coordination, since one manager is in charge of one type of activity. Coordination is easier to

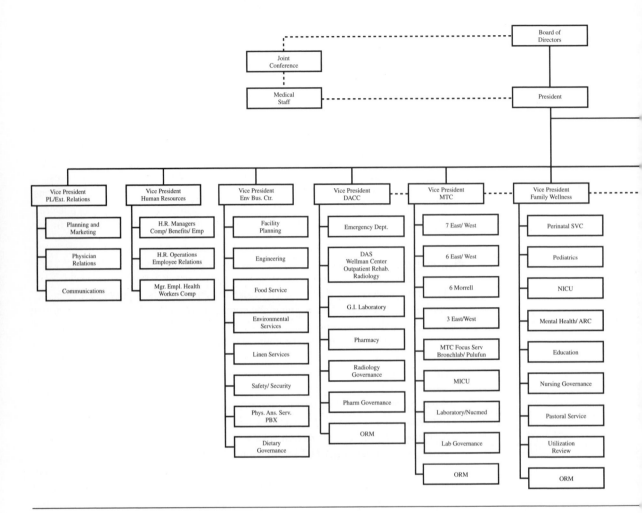

**Figure 10.1**   Organization chart of Lakeland Regional Medical Center, Lakeland, FL.

*"Courtesy of Lakeland Regional Medical Center, Inc., Lakeland, FL"*

achieve in this way than it would be in an organization where the same function is performed in several different divisions. Another advantage of functional departmentalization is that it makes the outstanding abilities of one or a few individuals available to the enterprise as a whole.

Functional design also facilitates in-depth skill development and allows for clear career paths. For example, an employee may start out at the technician I level, then after a year, move to the technician II level. If the technician has three or more years of experience, he or she may qualify for the team leader position, after five years, the day supervisor position, and so forth. Because func-

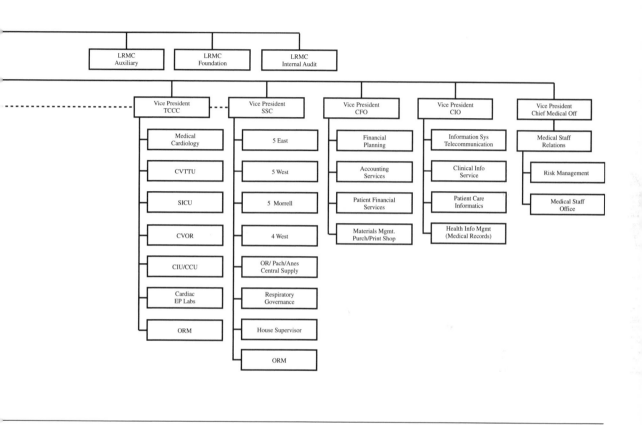

tional departmentalization is a simple and logical method, and has all these advantages, it is the most widely used way of setting up departments.

There are some disadvantages to functional departmentalization that have arisen in large industrial organizations, especially when the undertaking grows in size. One problem arises when robotics are introduced—what then should the organization do with the displaced employees? Lay them off? Retrain them? In a healthcare setting, however, such weaknesses are less likely to occur, and should not prevent management from opting for functional departmentalizations.

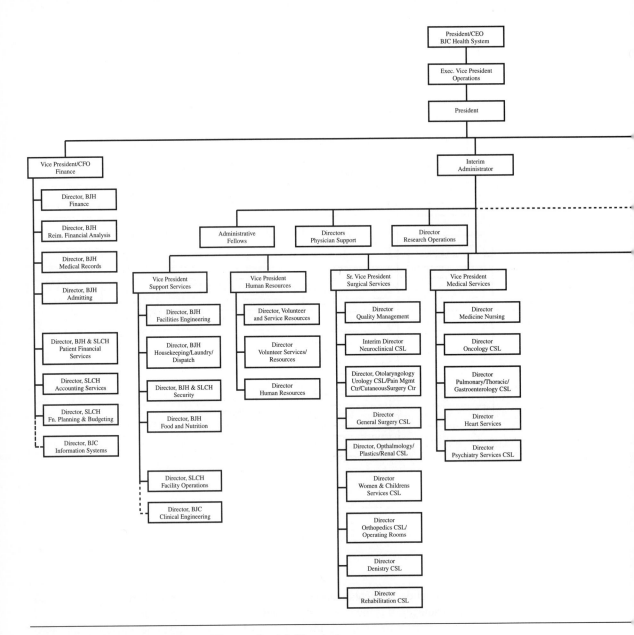

**Figure 10.2** Organization chart of Barnes-Jewish Hospital.

*Courtesy of BJC Health System, St. Louis, MO.*

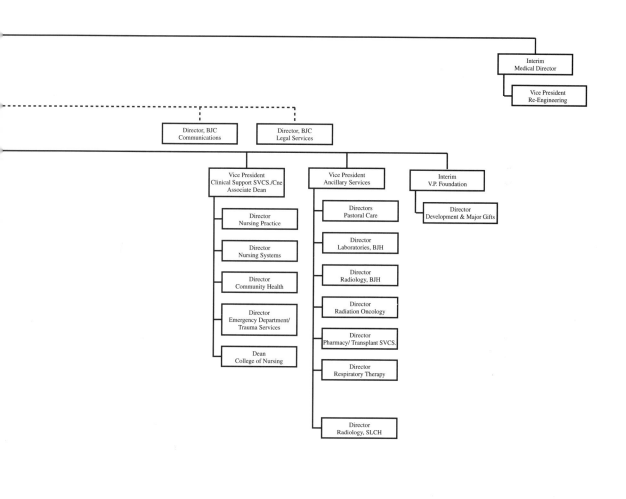

# Baptist Medical Center of Columbia

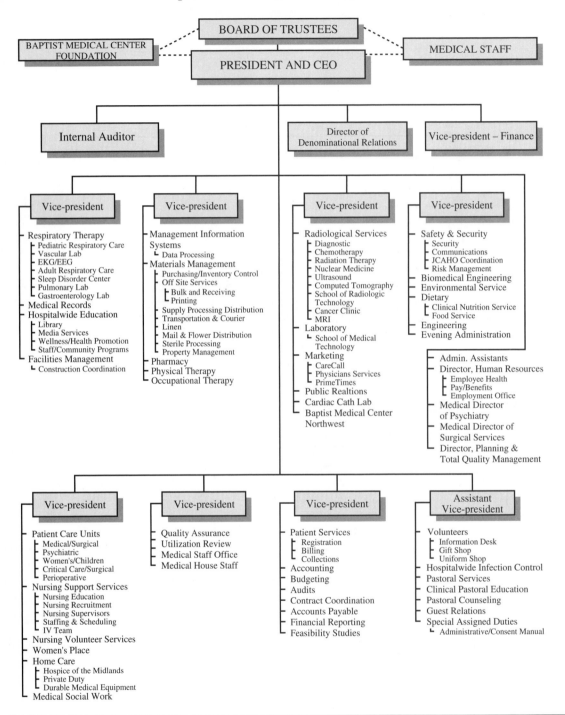

**Figure 10.3**   Organization chart of Baptist Medical Center of Columbia, SC.

*Used by permission of Baptist Medical Center, Columbia, SC.*

## ■ Process and Equipment

Activities can also be grouped around the equipment, process, and technology involved. This way of departmentalizing is often found in hospitals because they usually operate sophisticated equipment and handle certain processes that require special installations, training, and expertise. Every task involving the use of certain equipment and technology is then referred to its special department. This type of organizational structure is similar to functional departmentalization, the major difference being the emphasis on person-machine relationships. For instance, in an imaging department, specific equipment is used but only certain functions are performed. Another area where organizing occurs around equipment is in large laboratories. Here staff may be assigned to work with the microbiology equipment or the chemistry equipment and remain in this area for their career. Organizing by equipment, process, and technology will result in the staff becoming very specialized in the defined area. In the laboratory and in radiology specifically, the aligning of similar areas under the same umbrella is likely. That is, the alignment of groups of staff who are equipment, process, and technology specific with laboratory equipment will be linked together and functionally organized under one director or manager. Therefore, departmentalization by function and by equipment frequently becomes closely allied.

## ■ Territory (Location)

An alternative way to departmentalize is according to location. This means setting up departments on the basis of defined geographic areas or sites. The extent of the area may range from the entire hemisphere to a number of cities, a few blocks of a large city, or different floors in the same building. Again, this type of departmentalization is more important in industrial enterprises and government entities, such as the U.S. Post Office, the Federal Reserve Bank, and police departments. But healthcare institutions can also be set up this way. For example, a hospital or nursing home in a large city may have several physically dispersed units, such as St. Mary's East on one side of town and St. Mary's West on the other. If the same functions are performed in different locations and different buildings, then geographic departmentalization is necessary. The same considerations are applicable even if all activities are performed in one building, but on different floors and wings, such as a medical-surgical nursing unit, third floor, west wing, and another on the fourth floor, south.

One of the advantages of territorial departmentalization is placing decision making close to where the work is done. This departmentalization has the disadvantage of possible duplications of efforts; on the other hand, it provides opportunities for the development of more managerial talent.

## ■ Customer (Patient)

At times, management may find it advisable to group activities based on customer (patient) needs and characteristics, hence the term *customer departmentalization.*

Two examples of nonindustrial organizations that have departmentalized along customer lines are universities and hospitals. In some universities, night programs and day programs comply with the requests and special needs of the "customers," namely, part-time and full-time students. With hospitals, certain services and activities are grouped for outpatients and inpatients, such as outpatient surgery. In so doing, the healthcare center delivers its services to more people, especially in such supporting services as the laboratory, X-ray, or therapy departments. Healthcare services delivered on an outpatient basis are on the rise, are a significant factor in a hospital's revenue picture, and ultimately result in fewer overnight patients. This is "customer" departmentalization, which emphasizes the characteristics and needs of the patient and demonstrates the reasons that a hospital would consider this method of departmentalization.

## ■ Time

Some organizations find it helpful and necessary to group activities according to the period during which they are performed. An enterprise such as a hospital or public utility, which operates around the clock, must departmentalize activities on the basis of time, at least to a certain extent. In other words, the institution must set up different time shifts, usually day, afternoon, and night, or only day and night. The many working hour arrangements currently practiced by healthcare personnel may necessitate different time shift demarcations. Activities typically are grouped first on some other basis, such as by function, and then are organized into shifts. The activities to be performed on the other shifts are largely the same as those performed during the regular day shift. Thus, such groupings often create serious organizational questions of how self contained each shift should be and what relationships should exist between the regular day shift supervisors and the off shift supervisors.

## ■ Product

This departmentalization approach is similar to customer departmentalization. Industry frequently uses the concept of product departmentalization and this approach has gained acceptance in healthcare institutions. To departmentalize on a product basis in industry means that a product division is responsible for a single product or groups of closely related products. In product departmentalization, the emphasis is shifted from the function to the output, or product. For example, a hospital supply company may have a separate department for furniture, another for surgical supplies, and a third for uniforms.

Product departmentalization in a healthcare facility would involve dividing it into departments based on the "product" turned out, for example, maternity, surgery, oncology, cardiology, and psychiatry. Each such department would have its own supervisor of nursing, its own dietary supervisor, its own maintenance staff, etc., and each such "product" department would have its own boss—the director of surgery, the director of maternity, etc. These directors would be in charge of all functions within their product departments, including nursing activities, therapy, food services, laundry, and maintenance.

As you can see, such product departmentalization would result in duplication of effort. Instead of a single director of nursing, there would be as many as the number of existing departments. Moreover, coordinating all nursing services and ensuring that the same level of care is rendered would be difficult, since each supervisor reports to a different boss. The same difficulties would be found in every department. However, as hospitals have had to compete for market share, they have had to enhance and to some extent exploit those areas that are in demand by the population served. Some hospitals have created geographically separate facilities dedicated to one product, such as women's services or mental health services. Further, the increased technology and advances in medicine in some product areas have forced healthcare enterprises to organize by product to permit the manager or product leader to focus on the product, the technology serving it, and the impact of medical advances on its future. Thus, product departmentalization, as practiced in healthcare institutions, also has encouraged specialization.

## ■ Mixed Departmentalization (Composite, Hybrid Structure)

Departmentalization is not an end in itself. In grouping activities, management should not attempt to merely draw a balanced organizational chart. Its prime concern should be to set up departments that will help bring about the institution's objectives and coordinate its functions. There are advantages and disadvantages to each method of departmentalization. Choosing a method is a question of balance and deciding which works most effectively. In so doing, management will probably have to use multiple bases of departmentalization and end up with a hybrid structure, that is, a mixed departmentalization; for example, a nursing supervisor (functional) on the surgical unit (subfunction), west wing, third floor (location), during the night (time). In practice, almost all hospitals have this composite type of departmental structure, combining function, location, time, and many other considerations. Any mixture is acceptable, as long as it works and is consistent with the overall objectives of the institution.

## ■ Organizational Design

So far our discussion of organizational structure has centered around what is often called *traditional structure*. There are many reasons to discuss and understand this approach first and foremost. Traditional structure is the most often used structure in all types of organized activities. It is the most studied and researched form of organization and has a long history of successful performance. Traditional structure is a contemporary design and is not inflexible or rigid. This structure functions successfully under most prevailing conditions and is capable of producing and accommodating change and adapting to contingencies as they arise.

Of course, even the best-designed organization cannot be left without change forever. Changes in the state of the arts, the environment, human and social processes, organizational size, the workforce, economic trends, regulatory activities, and so forth have to be accommodated. The institution must design a structure that works best under these contingencies. The organization is an open system, which means that every change in one part of it affects the activity in another part. The organizational concepts discussed thus far are applicable even under those new contingencies. An example of this flexibility is the recent matrix design of organization, basically a combination of functional and product departmentalization.

## ■ Matrix Organization (Matrix Design)

One of the newer organizational structures building on traditional concepts is the matrix organization. Matrix organization, also known as *project,* or *grid, organization,* does not do away with the traditional organization—it simply builds on it and, under certain contingencies, improves on it. It is superimposed on functional organization, creating a grid, or a matrix. It thus provides horizontal dimensions to the traditional vertical orientation of the functional organization. It is an organizational design that combines technical expertise and product coordination simultaneously.

During recent years, high-technology industries found a need to create project organizations to focus resources and special talents for a given time on a specific project. For example, if we were emphasizing oncology (cancer) care we would bring into the oncology division the dietitian, radiation therapy techs, pharmacists, nurses, lab techs, and physicians who specialize in cancer care. These members would define the services we would offer to cancer patients. They would then develop the plans, recruit the staff needed, organize the functions needed to serve the patients, and deliver the care. Management and the customer would become increasingly interested in the end result—the product, cancer care. The essence of matrix management is a compromise between functional and product departmentalization in the same organizational structure. Figures 10.1 and 10.4 shows possible matrix arrangements in a healthcare institution in which the functional managers are in charge of their professional function, with an overlay of project managers who are responsible for the end product—a specific project.

The concept of matrix organization gives an enterprise the potential of conducting several projects simultaneously. For example, the president of the hospital sees the need for three projects to be phased into the institution within the next two years, such as a unit-dose pharmaceutical system, a hospitalwide computer-based patient record system, and preparation for the hospital's accreditation. These three projects could be assigned to three different project managers, and matrix organizations could be established for obtaining these objectives.

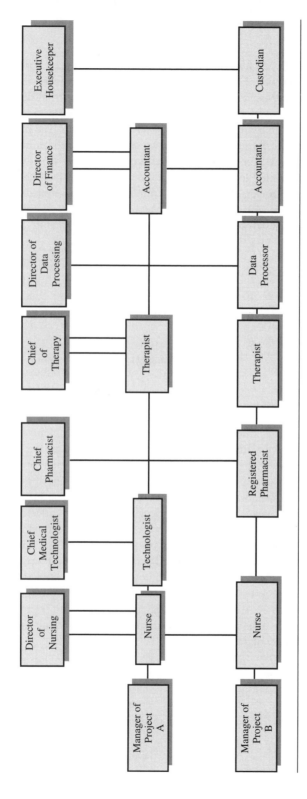

**Figure 10.4** Matrix Organization.

By establishing a project organization, better coordination can be achieved than would be possible in a traditional organizational structure. As the project proceeds, it is assigned to a project manager from the beginning to its completion, and people from the functional areas needed for this project are assigned either on a full- or part-time basis to this project. The matrix is an overlay on conventional structure; it draws on traditional structure for the various skills required for this project. The project manager sees the project through from the beginning to the end. When the project is finished, the specialized personnel return to their functional departments or are reassigned to a new project; the same occurs with the project manager.

The advantages of matrix organization are that it:

1. Offers an effective way to phase new projects in and out of operation;
2. Improves coordination and establishes lateral relationships;
3. Offers greater flexibility to innovative ideas;
4. Creates teams quickly to cope with a sudden change or need;
5. Dissolves teams without too much repercussion on the overall structure;
6. Exposes members of a project to interaction with experts from other areas, thus offering an opportunity for personal development; and
7. Affords top-level management an additional way to delegate and decentralize.

Matrix design also creates a number of problems. Most result from the team members finding that during the project, their roles have not been clearly defined. Matrix organization is a system in which employees are supervised by two bosses, namely their functional director and the project manager. The professional, when assigned to a project, may then be faced with duality of command because conflicting directives may come from the two bosses. Additionally, the employees on the project may not be certain to whom they are supposed to report and whose assignments take priority. This is even more confusing when one person is assigned part-time to two or more projects.

Further sources of frustration for the professional are that while assigned to the project, he or she may also feel isolated from the mainstream of his or her expertise. Also, since the assignment is only temporary, evaluations and possible promotions are usually vested in the functional department head and not in the project manager.

Most of these problems are caused by poor project preparation and a lack of concise and clear statements of authority relationships. At the start of the project, the enterprise executive should try to clarify these relationships. He or she should clarify the authority and responsibility of the functional directors, for example, those of the chief medical technologist in figure 10.3 and those of the manager of project A. The project manager should have full authority and responsibility over the integrity of the design and over the budget; he or she must act as decision maker and coordinator for the duration of the project. There must be clear statements about the project manager's frequency of reporting and the scope of the project. The project manager must decide on schedules and work out priorities with the functional managers. The functional managers should be responsible for the integrity of the service or products their departments supply to the project. Statements concerning these decisions and responsibilities are necessary for the guidance of the project manager and of the functional managers whose departments are involved in the project.

Despite the best preparations and clarifications, misunderstandings may still arise. For example, the priorities between the project managers of two projects who are both vying for a functional manager's services may become an issue. Provisions to resolve such a dilemma should probably be made by referring such a dispute to higher management. Thorough preparation and clarifying authority and responsibility when the project is established will minimize many of these problems. Some borderline cases involving problems of dual command may still arise. Remember that all organizational structures can create some problems occasionally. Matrix organization provides a system with a contemporary proven method of implementing a complex new task of relatively short duration.

Figure 10.5 is an example of a matrix organization in which the project involves the computerization of the laboratories. This is a one-time undertaking, a project that is to be completed within a certain time. To phase this project into the organization and have it completed within the allocated period, the administrator decides that a matrix, or project, organization would be the best vehicle to get the job done. After appointing the project manager, several functional specialists needed to accomplish this task are assigned to it. A project manager is put in charge of this project with a clear objective as to what should be accomplished and when it should be finished.

To implement this laboratory computerization project, it is necessary to have input and coordination from the laboratories, data processing, pathology department, accounting, and administration. These specialized employees work under the supervision and guidance of the project manager assigned to the project on either a full- or a part-time basis. The administrator is able to draft these specialists for the duration of the project; he or she clearly states whether and to what extent the project manager is in charge and is their line superior on this project. The project manager sees the project through from the beginning to the end. On completion, the specialized personnel return to their functional departments, as does the project manager, or some may go on to another project where their special skills are needed.

Project: Introduction of a computer system into the clinical laboratories.

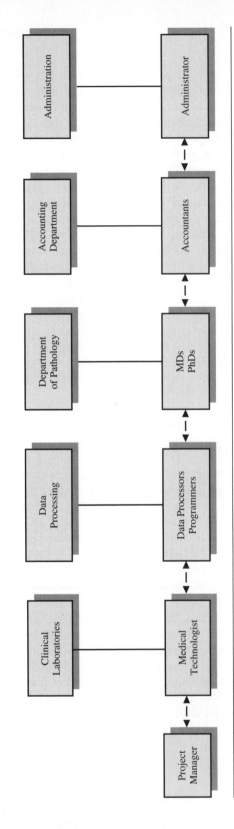

**Figure 10.5**  Project organization.

**SUMMARY**  Management's overall organizing function is to design a formal structural framework that will enable the institution to achieve its objectives. The CEO or COO establishes this framework initially, using the basic principles of formal organizational theory as guidelines. He or she begins with the principle that specialization, the division of work, is necessary for efficiency. This means grouping the various activities into distinct departments or divisions and assigning specific duties to each. The administrator can approach this departmentalizing task in several ways. The most widely used concept of departmentalization is grouping activities according to functions, that is, placing all those who perform the same functions into the same department. Besides departmentalization by functions, it is possible to departmentalize by process and equipment, geographical (territorial) lines, customers (patients), time (shift), or product. However, a composite structure made up of several of these alternatives is most often used.

These guidelines lead to the design of an organizational structure that is sometimes referred to as "traditional." This traditional structure is as contemporary as the manager wants it to be. Besides having a long history of successful performance, this conventional form of organizational structure can accommodate contingencies and changes as they occur.

One of the newer developments in organizational design is the matrix organization. This stresses horizontal relationships and combines functional and product departmentalization. Matrix design is employed for achieving a special project with a definite result by superimposing a matrix over the traditional organizational structure. At the project's inception, the CEO or COO must state the authority relationships to the project manager in charge, the functional personnel assigned to the project for the duration, and their functional department heads. This is necessary to minimize possible problems of dual command, dual allegiance, and other conflicts.

# Delegation of Organizational Authority

*Chapter Objectives*

After you have studied this chapter, you should be able to:

1. Discuss authority as the lifeblood of the managerial position, and describe how the flow of authority throughout the organizational structure makes it operative.
2. Explain how delegating authority is key to creating an organization.
3. Identify delegation of authority as the process of partially distributing authority to subordinate managers for making decisions and performing tasks.
4. Describe the concepts of the scalar chain and unity of command.
5. Explain the three major parts of the process of delegation: duties and tasks, clarity and sufficiency of authority, and responsibility.
6. Describe decentralization as the degree of delegation.
7. Describe the spectrum of delegation with centralization on one end and decentralization at the other end.
8. Identify the advantages and disadvantages of extensive delegation.

The formal organization structure, as stated in the previous chapter, is based on the division of labor and departmentalization. Once this has been accomplished, the second essential step for creating an organization is delegation of authority. Authority is the lifeblood of the managerial position; without authority the manager's job is meaningless. The process of delegating authority breathes life into the organizational structure. The same process of delegation that brings authority to the manager is used to delegate it farther down the line of command. As one divides managerial responsibilities, one creates additional levels in the chain of command. The degree to which authority is delegated throughout the institution will indicate the extent of decentralization. Some institutions' organizational structures are more centralized, whereas others are more decentralized.

## THE MEANING OF DELEGATION

Delegation of authority makes the organization operative. Although the formal structure of an organization may have been meticulously designed by the chief administrator and carefully explained in manuals and charts, the organization still will not have life until and unless authority is delegated throughout its entire structure. Through this process of delegation, *the subordinate manager receives authority from the superior.* In other words, if authority was not delegated, there would be no subordinate managers and thus no one to occupy the various levels, departments, and positions that make up the organizational structure. Only in delegating authority to subordinate managers is the organization actually created. Only with such delegation can the administration vest a subordinate with a portion of its own authority, thereby setting in motion the entire managerial process and life of the organization.

Delegation of authority, however, does not mean that the boss surrenders all of his or her authority. The delegating manager always retains the overall authority to perform his or her functions. If necessary, all or part of the authority granted to a subordinate manager can be revoked and reallocated. A good comparison can be made between delegating authority and imparting knowledge in school. A schoolteacher shares knowledge with the students, who then possess this knowledge, but the teacher still retains the knowledge as well.

## ■ The Scalar Chain

The line of vertical authority relationships from superior to subordinate is the *scalar chain,* or the *chain of command.* Through the process of delegation, as we have said, formal authority is distributed throughout the organization. It flows downward from the authority at the top, through the various levels of management, to the supervisor, and from there possibly to lower line supervisors. The broad authority necessary to run a private healthcare center is usually delegated by the board of directors or trustees to the president (also known as the administrator or CEO), who in turn must delegate authority to subordinate managers (vice-presidents, etc.), who then delegate authority farther down the line, and so forth.

This line of direct authority relationships throughout the organization is commonly known as the scalar chain. It is a clear line from the top authority to the lowest managerial ranks. The chain of command must be clearly understood by every subordinate and must be closely adhered to, or the risk exists of undermining authority. By the time this "flow of authority" reaches the supervisory level, it probably has narrowed down quite a bit, thus focusing the supervisor's range of authority on the function for which he or she is responsible. Nevertheless, it can be traced directly upward to the top authority.

Let's look at an example. In most organizations, there is a finance division headed by the Chief Financial Officer (CFO). This individual may have authority to sign contracts and authorize expenditures up to $500,000. The division may have several departments: accounting, patient billing, accounts payable, cashiers, and auditing. Each department leader (manager or director) also may have contract signing privileges and expenditure authorization limits, generally at a substantially lower level, perhaps to $50,000. Amounts above $50,000 to $500,000 must be approved by the CFO, and amounts above $500,000 must be approved by his superior.

As we travel down the chain of command we will reach the accounts payable clerk who will have no contract signing privileges nor expenditure authorization rights. Everything he or she allows to be paid has been authorized by another more superior in rank individual. These scalar relationships are based on positional authority, as discussed in chapter 9. They are also based on another important managerial principle: unity of command.

### ■ Unity of Command

Delegation of authority flows from a single superior to a single subordinate. Each subordinate reports and is accountable to only one superior, namely, that person from whom he or she receives authority. This is known as *unity of command.* A superior manager can have a number of subordinates reporting to him or her, but for each of these subordinates, the one-to-one relationships (unity of command) still prevail.

The scalar chain provides the major route along which the process of delegation moves. Unity of command is a critical organizational concept; it enables the administration to coordinate activities, pinpoint responsibility and accountability, and define and clarify superior-subordinate relationships. An analogy may be in order. The scalar chain serves as a road map for staff to follow when seeking direction and/or guidance. If the road splits or the map becomes blurry, consternation about the best route to take to get to a destination and hesitation may arise. Whenever this principle of unity of command is violated or compromised, management must anticipate complications. Some will appear as employee frustration; others in staff turnover; and poor employee morale may surface as well.

## THE PROCESS OF DELEGATION

Every manager must be thoroughly familiar with the process of delegation. It consists of three components, all of which must be present. These three components are inseparably related, so that a change in one of them will require an adjustment of the other two.

The three essential parts of the delegating process are as follows:

1. The assignment of duties by a manager to the immediate subordinates.
2. The granting of permission (authority) to the subordinates to make decisions and commitments, use resources, and take all the actions normally necessary to perform their assigned duties.
3. The creation of an obligation (responsibility) on the part of each subordinate to the delegating superior to perform the assigned duties satisfactorily.

Unless all three of these steps are taken, the success of the delegating process cannot be ensured. This is true no matter which level of management is doing the delegating. All managers, from the chief administrator down to the line supervisors, must do their part in delegating authority throughout the entire organization.

The chief administrator does the initial delegation when he or she groups activities, sets up line and staff departments, and assigns them their duties. Then the managers of each department or division must subdivide and reassign these duties within their own section and at the same time delegate the appropriate amount of authority and exact responsibility to carry them out. Whether it is the chief administrator who delegates authority to the associate administrators and directors, or the line supervisor who delegates authority to the nonmanagerial subordinates, the steps in the process of delegation are the same. In the following discussion of these essential steps, we will approach the delegation process mainly on the departmental level rather than on the administrative level, since this book is primarily written for departmental supervisors.

## ■ Assigning Duties

In assigning duties, the supervisor determines how the work in the department is to be divided among the subordinates and the supervisor. All the tasks that must be accomplished in the department will be considered; the supervisor decides which ones he or she can assign to a subordinate and which he or she must do.

First, the supervisor should assign routine duties to the regular subordinates. Second, she should assign duties that require special knowledge to those subordinates who are particularly qualified to do them. Third, the supervisor must decide which functions he or she only should perform.

In all likelihood, many duties can be delegated to the two subordinate groups. In such cases, much will depend on the supervisor's general attitude and on the availability of subordinates, but some logical guidelines can aid the manager when assigning duties. It is better that the assignments be justified and explained on the basis of such logical guidelines, rather than on personal likes and dislikes, or hunch and intuition. Assigning duties logically is important because the supervisor will be subject to pressures coming from different directions. Some subordinates will want to do more work, whereas others will believe that they should not be burdened with certain duties. Thus, despite the guidelines, the supervisor will often have difficulty deciding who should do a certain task.

One way of doing this is to assign the activity to those employees who will be involved with it most of the time. One also may be inclined to assign an activity to employees who already have the skills and interest to perform the work, for they are the ones who will best carry out the activity.

By considering such factors, the supervisor should be able to assign work so that everybody gets a fair share and can do his or her part satisfactorily. To achieve this distribution of work, the supervisor must clearly understand the nature and the content of the work to be accomplished. Furthermore, one must be thoroughly acquainted with the capabilities of the employees. All this is not as simple as it might appear at first. The supervisor is often inclined to assign heavier tasks to those employees who are more capable because it is the easiest way out. In the long run, however, it would be far more advantageous to train the less capable employees so that they also can perform the more difficult jobs. If the manager relies heavily on one person or a few persons, the department will be in a bad situation in their absence. Thus, it is always a good idea to have a sufficient number of available employees who have been trained in the department's more difficult tasks. Also, the supervisor's problems of assigning various duties will become simpler by building up the strength and experience of all the employees.

The manner and extent to which the supervisor assigns duties to the employees will significantly affect the degree to which they respect and accept the supervisor's authority. Much of the manager's success will depend on the skill in making assignments. This function will be discussed further throughout the text. We should emphasize again that the first step in delegating authority is to assign certain tasks or duties to each subordinate.

## ■ Granting Authority

The second essential part in the process of delegation is granting authority, that is, granting permission to make decisions and commitments, use resources, and take all those actions necessary to get the job done. As pointed out earlier, duties are assigned and authority is delegated to *positions* within the institution rather than to people. Since these positions are staffed by people, however, one typically refers to delegating authority to subordinates instead of to subordinate positions.

To be more specific, granting authority means that a supervisor confers on the subordinates the right and power to act and make decisions within a predetermined and limited area. The manager always must determine in advance the scope of authority that is to be delegated. The range of delegated authority is usually specific when a task is routine and more general when the task is less formalized.

How much authority can be delegated will depend on the amount of authority that the delegating manager possesses and on the type of job to be done. Generally, enough authority must be granted to the subordinate to perform what is expected adequately and successfully. There is no need for the degree of authority to be greater than necessary, but it must be sufficient to get the job done. If employees are expected to fulfill the tasks assigned to them and make reasonable decisions for themselves within this area, they must have enough authority to perform.

The degree of authority delegated is intrinsically related not only to the duties assigned but also to the results expected. Whenever management delegates authority, it is necessary to inform the subordinate of the expected results. For example, the employee should know how fast you expect him or her to accomplish the job or how "perfect" you expect the work to be. For this purpose, standards of performance are established to provide a basis for judging work done and to facilitate management's control. These standards are discussed more fully in the section on control in chapter 25.

At this point, it is sufficient to say that you as a supervisor must be specific in telling each employee just what authority he or she has and what results are expected while exercising that authority. If this is not stated clearly, the subordinate will have to guess how far the authority extends, probably by trial and error. As a supervisor, you may have experienced this confusion when your own boss was not explicit about how much authority you really had. To avoid this happening to your subordinates, you should explain the scope of authority and results you expect. As time goes on, less explanation will be necessary. Remember, however, that if you change an employee's job assignment, you must check to see that the degree of authority you have given is still appropriate. Perhaps it is more than needed, then you may have to revoke some of the delegated authority. Whenever conditions and circumstances of an employee's job change, he or she will need additional clarification of the scope of authority.

## ■ Limitations to Authority

As discussed in chapter 9, a manager's authority is limited due to his or her position in an organization. These limitations can be either explicit or implicit; some stem from internal sources and others from external sources. Generally, more internal limitations on the scope of authority are present the farther down one goes in the managerial hierarchy. In other words, the lower the rung on the administrative ladder, the narrower is the area in which authority can be delegated and exercised. This is known as the tapering concept of authority. (see figure 9.1 in chapter 9).

## ■ The Exception Principle

Although the scope of authority clearly delineates the area of decision making, the supervisor may be confronted by a problem beyond and outside of this area. Then the *exception principle* comes into play. These problems are exceptions and must be referred to the supervisor's delegating manager for decision making. The latter must make certain that this is truly an exception, since a danger exists that some subordinate managers may refer too many decisions upward when their own authority would be sufficient. In those situations, the superior should refrain from deciding and refer the problem back to the subordinate manager. If it is truly an exception, however, and is beyond the scope of the subordinate's authority, then the superior manager must decide.

## ■ Only One Boss

In granting authority, the principle of unity of command must be followed. Employees must be reassured that all orders and all positional authority can come only from the immediate supervisor, the only boss they have. This principle should be stressed, since situations do occur in which two superiors issue directives and delegate authority to one subordinate. Dual command is bound to lead to unsatisfactory performance by the employee, and it definitely results in confusion about lines of formal authority. The subordinate does not know which of the two "bosses" has the authority that will contribute most to his or her success and progress within the organization. Eventually, such a situation will result in conflicts and organizational difficulties.

## ■ Revoking Delegated Authority

As stated before, delegating authority does not mean that management has divested itself of its authority. The delegating manager still retains authority and the right to revoke whatever part of the authority he or she delegated to a subordinate. Occasionally, as activities change, there is a definite need to take a fresh look at the organization and to realign authority relationships. Managers frequently speak of reorganizing, realigning, reshuffling, and so forth. What is meant by these terms is the revoking of authority and reassignment of it elsewhere. Naturally, such realignments of authority should not take place too often, since frequent changes create uncertainty, which affects morale. However, periodic reviews of authority delegations are not merely advisable, they are necessary in any organization. This applies to top-level administration as well as to the lowest-level manager.

## ■ Creating Responsibility

The third major aspect of delegating authority is creating an obligation on the part of the subordinate toward the boss to perform the assigned duties satisfactorily. The acceptance of this obligation creates responsibility. Without responsibility, the process of delegation would not be complete.

The terms *responsibility* and *authority* are closely related. Both terms are often misused and misunderstood. Although you may hear phrases such as "keeping subordinates responsible," and "delegating responsibility," these phrases do not describe the actual situation because they imply that responsibility is handed down from above, whereas it really is accepted from below.

Responsibility is the *obligation of a subordinate* to perform the duty as required by the superior. By accepting a job, by accepting the obligation to perform the assigned tasks, an employee implies acceptance of responsibility. This responsibility cannot be arbitrarily imposed on a person; rather, it results from a mutual agreement in which the employee agrees to accomplish the duties in return for rewards. Thus, although the authority to perform duties flows from management to subordinate, the responsibility to accomplish these duties clearly flows in the opposite direction, from the subordinate to management.

It is essential to bear in mind, however, that responsibility, unlike authority, cannot be delegated. Responsibility cannot be shifted. Your subordinate accepts responsibility, but you still have it. The supervisor can assign a task and delegate the authority to perform a specific job to a subordinate. However, the supervisor does not delegate responsibility in the sense that once the duties are assigned, the supervisor is relieved of the responsibility for these tasks. A supervisor can delegate authority to a subordinate, but not responsibility.

The healthcare administrator must delegate a great deal of authority to the associate administrators in order for them to oversee the performance of various tasks and services. These associate administrators, in turn and of necessity, have to delegate a large portion of their authority to the managers below them, but none of them delegates any responsibility. Each still accepts all the responsibility for the tasks originally assigned. Similarly, when you as a supervisor are called on by your boss to explain the performance within your department, you cannot plead as a defense that you have "delegated the responsibility" for such activity to some employee. You may have delegated the authority, but you have remained responsible and must answer to your boss.

Every supervisor should clearly understand this vital difference between authority and responsibility. When managers delegate the authority to do a specific job, they reduce the number of duties that they have to perform. They also conditionally divest themselves of a certain amount of authority, which can be taken back at any time if conditions are not fulfilled. In this process, however, managers do not reduce the overall amount of responsibility originally accepted. Although subordinates also accept a certain amount of responsibility for duties assigned to them, this does not in any way diminish the manager's responsibility. It does add another layer or level to the overall responsibility, thereby creating *overlapping obligations.* Such overlapping obligations provide double or triple insurance that a job gets done correctly and responsibly.

Thus, even though responsibility is something you accept, you cannot rid yourself of it. This thought should not make you overly anxious. After all, delegations and re-delegations are necessary to get the job done. Although as a supervisor you will try to follow the best managerial practices, you cannot be certain that each of your subordinates will use his or her best judgment all the time. Therefore, allowances must be made for mistakes. In evaluating your performance as a supervisor, your boss should notice how much you depend on your subordinates to get the work of your department accomplished. Although the responsibility has remained with you, your boss will understand that you cannot do everything yourself.

In appraising your skill as a manager, your boss will consider how much care you have shown in the following areas: selecting your employees, training them, providing constant supervision, and checking their activities. All these matters will be taken into consideration in evaluating your ability in the event that something goes wrong in your department.

## ■ Equality of the Three Essential Parts

Always bear in mind that these three components—duties, authority, and responsibility—must blend together to make delegation of authority a success. There must be enough authority (but not more than necessary) granted to your subordinates to do the job, and the responsibility you expect them to accept cannot be greater than the area of authority you have delineated. Subordinates cannot be expected to accept responsibility for activities if they have not been handed any authority. In other words, do not try to "keep your subordinates responsible" for something that you have not actually delegated to them.

Inconsistencies between delegated authority, responsibility, and assigned tasks will generally result in difficult and undesirable outcomes. You may have worked in organizations where some of the managers had much authority delegated to them but had no particular jobs to perform. This created misuses of authority and conflicts. You also may have been in positions where responsibility was exacted from you when you did not have the authority to fulfill an obligation. When responsibility exceeds authority, it is nearly impossible to do the job. This, too, is a most embarrassing and frustrating situation. Therefore, you must make certain that the three essential elements for successful delegation are of equal magnitude and that whenever one is changed, the other two are changed simultaneously.

Some rare occasions occur when responsibility and authority are not equal. For example, in emergencies managers are often inclined and even forced to exceed their authority. One hopes this is the exception and not the normal state of affairs.

## DECENTRALIZATION: THE DEGREE OF DELEGATION OF AUTHORITY

As discussed earlier, delegation of authority is the key to the creation of an organization. If no authority has been delegated, one can hardly say an organization exists. Thus, from an organizational point of view, the problem is not whether to delegate or not delegate authority, but rather *how much* authority will be delegated to middle- and lower-level managers. The question involves the *degree* of authority to be delegated. Centralization and decentralization represent opposite ends of this delegation continuum.

This question about the degree of delegation is extremely important because it will determine the answer to another highly significant organizational question: To what extent is the organization decentralized? How much of what authority should be given to whom and for what purpose? Variations in the extent of decentralization are innumerable, ranging from a highly centralized structure, in which the concept of an organization barely exists, to a completely decentralized organization, in which authority has been delegated to the lowest possible levels of management. In the first instance, the chief executive is in close touch with all operations, makes all decisions, and gives almost all instructions. Hardly any authority has been delegated and, strictly speaking, it cannot be said that an organization has been created. Many small enterprises regularly operate along these lines. Often such one-man shows will collapse if their chief executive becomes incapacitated, dies, or for some other reason leaves the enterprise.

A much less extreme situation is found in organizations where authority has been delegated to a limited degree. In such organizations, the major policies and programs are decided by the top-level manager of the enterprise, and the task of applying these policies and programs to daily operations and daily planning is delegated to the first level of supervision. Few or no other levels exist between the top-level manager and the supervisors. This type of arrangement is often found in medium-sized enterprises. It is advantageous because it limits the number of managers that the general manager must hire, thus keeping expenses down. Furthermore, the particular knowledge and good judgment the general manager possesses can be applied directly. A considerable number of enterprises in the United States have this type of organization with a limited degree of delegation of authority.

At the other end of the centralization-decentralization continuum, we find those organizations in which authority has been delegated as far down the chain of command as possible. To find out if an organization is this decentralized, one must determine the type of authority that has been delegated, how far down in the organization it has been delegated, and how consistent the delegations are. In other words, one must ask how significant a decision can be made by a manager and how far down this occurs within the managerial hierarchy. The more important the decisions made farther down in the hierarchy are, the more decentralization is prevalent. The number of such decisions and the functions affected by them also serve as indicators of decentralization. Also, the less checking that is done by upper-level management, the greater the degree of decentralization.

The answers to all these questions will indicate whether or not you are dealing with an organization that has delegated authority to the greatest extent possible. Most healthcare institutions probably find broad delegation of authority and decentralization advisable and necessary because of the nature of the activities involved and the background and expectations of the personnel. Today's better educated and more sophisticated healthcare workforce wants and expects more authority and responsibility to use individual judgment.

Timing also plays a role in solving the degree of delegation problem. Although centralization of authority or limited decentralization may be the most logical organizational form to use in the early stages of an enterprise, later stages will usually require the CEO to face the problem of delegating more authority and decentralizing the organization to a greater extent. Such decentralization of authority becomes necessary when centralized management finds itself so burdened with decision making that the top executives do not have enough time to perform their planning function adequately or maintain a long-range point of view. This type of situation usually occurs when an organization expands. This lack of time to plan should indicate to top-level management that they should delegate authority to lower echelons. In other words, there should be a gradual development toward decentralization of authority commensurate with the growth of the enterprise.

## ■ Advantages and Disadvantages of Delegation

There are numerous advantages to delegating and decentralizing authority; these advantages become even more important as the enterprise grows in size. Remember our time management matrix in chapter 8; by delegating authority, the senior manager is relieved of much time-consuming detail work. Subordinates can make decisions without waiting for approval. This increases flexibility and permits more prompt action. In addition, such delegation of decision-making authority may actually produce better decisions, since the manager on the job usually knows more pertinent factors than the manager higher up, and speedy decisions are often essential. Delegation to the lower levels also increases morale and interest and enthusiasm for the work. It also provides a good training ground. All these advantages serve to make the organization more democratic and more responsive to the needs and ideas of its employees, which ultimately will result in delivery of better patient care.

Some disadvantages to considerable delegation also may exist. For example, the supervisor of a department may believe that he or she no longer needs the help of upper-level managers and can develop his or her own supporting services. This could easily lead to duplication of effort. Another disadvantage could be a possible loss of control, although the delegating manager can take steps to see that this does not happen. In most situations, however, the advantages of broad delegation far outweigh the disadvantages.

As stated before, the environment and contingencies of healthcare institutions are such that to deliver the best possible patient care, authority must be delegated broadly. It is a question of balance, of finding the degree of decentralization that works. No two healthcare centers are alike. Each has its own tradition, history, problems, challenges, workforce, and environment to integrate into an organizational structure that works. This is an ongoing process. One must constantly monitor and adjust the degrees of delegation and decentralization as the environment and the institution change.

## SUMMARY

In earlier chapters we defined authority as the power that makes the managerial job a reality. Authority is the lifeblood of the managerial position, and the process of delegation of authority breathes life into the organizational structure. Good managers must know how to use formal authority and how to delegate it to their subordinates. Through the process of delegating authority, management actually creates the organization. This process of delegation is made up of three essential parts: assigning a job or duty, granting authority, and creating responsibility. All three are inseparably related, and a change in one will necessitate a change in the other two.

This process of delegation is the only way to create an operative organization. Thus, the question is not whether top-level management will delegate authority, but rather how much or how little authority it will delegate. A centralization-decentralization continuum exists in all organizations. If authority is delegated freely all the way down to the lowest levels of supervision, then the organization is highly decentralized. If most authority is in the hands of higher level managers, the organization is highly centralized. Although centralization might be appropriate when an enterprise is just getting started, far greater advantages arise from decentralization, or broad delegation of authority.

# Line and Staff Authority Relationships

## Chapter Objectives

After you have studied this chapter, you should be able to:

1. Discuss the need to add staff specialists to the organization as an additional consequence of specialization.
2. Describe the typical line and staff organization.
3. Describe the primary chain of line command to achieve unity of command.
4. Discuss and contrast line and staff departments and explain their positions in the organizational hierarchy.
5. Discuss the staff's function to provide support, advice, and counsel in specialized areas such as discrimination, affirmative action, legal affairs, and economic consulting.
6. Discuss the typical relationships between line and staff.
7. Define functional authority and explain how it is an exception to the typical relationship between line and staff.
8. State the benefits and shortcomings of functional authority.

All of the chapters in part IV of this text are concerned with building an effective organization. Therefore, we first discussed horizontal organization, meaning how to divide the work into departments. Then we looked at dividing the managerial work vertically by delegating authority. Now, as another consequence of specialization, we have to add staff to the organization. We are creating lateral and diagonal relationships by adding line and staff relationships, another essential building block of the organization.

In healthcare facilities, one usually speaks of different staffs such as the nursing staff, medical staff, plant engineering staff, and administrative staff. In this context, the word *staff* applies to a group of people who perform similar jobs, such as nurses, physicians, and maintenance engineers. In the general field of management and administration, however, the meaning of the term *staff* is very different. "Staff" is spoken of in connection with "line," and both these terms refer to authority relationships, which are discussed in this chapter. In the following discussion, any reference to *staff* will mean *line/staff,* not the meaning that most people working in healthcare centers usually associate with staff, such as medical staff.

Since no one, not even the chief executive officer (CEO), could possibly have all the knowledge, expertise, skills, and information necessary to manage a modern organization, staff becomes an essential and critical part of the institution. *Line* managers retain the administrative and authoritative parts of the activities, whereas *staff* representatives supply expert advice and support, the scientific, technological, technical, and informational aspects. Without these aspects, the institution could not function properly.

## ORIGIN OF STAFF

We've been discussing the informal meaning of staff, that is, the grouping of individuals together who perform a similar task. In management theory, however, the term *staff* has another meaning, one that developed over time since the days of ancient Athens and Rome. The technical definition refers to an individual or individuals who serve in an advisory capacity to the manager(s) of an organization. Consider the President of the United States. He has many issues he must keep abreast of and does so through the use of a team of staff advisors. These staff positions may also serve in an "extender" role, that is, they may perform portions of a task or prepare pieces of a project or study for the manager when the manager cannot do everything himself or herself. In the previous section we referred to this "extender" role for the manager who could no longer supervise any more supervisors.

As organizations grow in size and complexity, and as the environment changes and impinges more and more on them, the duties of the managers increase. Then managers add subordinate managers by creating more departments and delegating authority. Sooner or later, however, the manager's span of management is so large that no more additional supervisors can be added because the manager cannot pay proper attention to them. At this point, they add personal staff, which means one or more assistants to do the work that cannot be delegated. (See figure 12.1.)

Again, sooner or later the assistant's knowledge becomes too general and not sufficiently qualified. Furthermore, other members of the organization also require the help of experts in many difficult areas, such as fair employment practices and healthcare law. This is where organizational staffs are added to advise and support any member of the institution who needs this kind of help and support. Today staff activities are increasing, as is the number of people working in them.

## LINE AND STAFF ORGANIZATION

At this point, it is important to distinguish between line and staff. Staff personnel are advisory in their duties, whereas, line personnel have direct responsibility to insure goals are achieved through their subordinates. While a line manager or supervisor may seek advice from a staff advisor, the line supervisor will determine what action must be taken next and then direct the subordinates to carry it out.

A common staff department is human resources. The director of human resources serves the management of the organization in a staff capacity. If the

# Stages of Staff Development

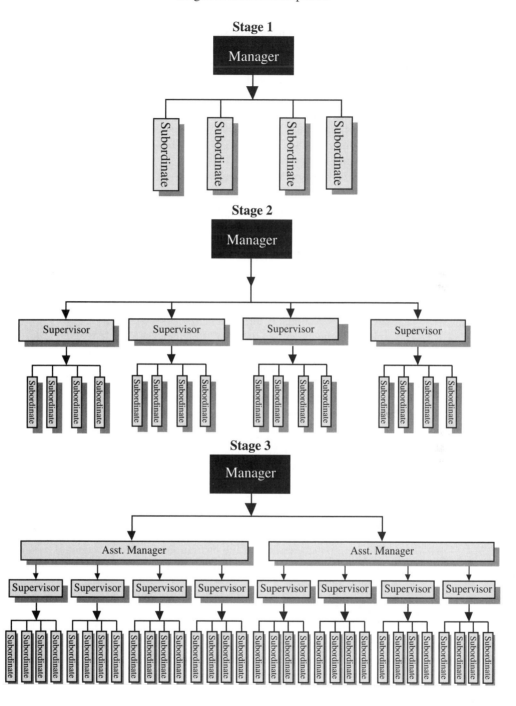

**Figure 12.1**  Stages of staff development.

director has subordinates (*i.e.,* supervisors of recruitment, benefits, employee relations, etc.), then he or she also has line duties for the ongoing activities of the department. Much has been written and said about the concepts of line and staff, and probably no other area in the field of management has evoked as much discussion as these concepts. Many of the difficulties and frictions encountered in the daily life of an organization probably result from line and staff problems. Misconceptions and lack of understanding as to what line and staff really are can cause bitter feelings and conflicts of personalities, disunity, duplication of effort, waste, and lost momentum.

As a supervisor of a department, you should know whether you are attached to your organization in a line capacity or a staff capacity. You might be able to find this out by reading the job description, and, if that does not clarify it, by asking your superior manager. Line and staff are not characteristics of certain functions; rather, they are characteristics of authority relationships. Therefore, the ultimate way to determine whether a department is related to the organizational structure as line or staff is to examine the intentions of the CEO. The CEO confers line authority on certain departments and places others into the organizational structure as staff. Staff are not inferior to line authority, or vice versa; they are just of a completely different nature. As we discuss these differences, keep in mind that the objectives of the staff elements are ultimately the same as those of the line organization, namely, achievement of the institution's overall goals of delivering the best possible care.

## ■ Line Organization

The simplest of all organizational structures is the line organization, which depicts the primary chain of command and is inseparable from the concept of authority. Thus, when we refer to line authority, we mean a superior and a subordinate with a direct line of command running between them. In every organization, this straight direct line of superior-subordinate relationships runs from the top of the organization down to the lowest level of supervision. Figure 12.2 depicts an example of one direct line of authority running from the board of directors to the president of the institution, the vice president of patient care services, a nursing director, a head nurse, a team leader, and finally to the other nursing employees.

### *Unity of Command*

The uninterrupted line of authority from the president to the team leader in figure 12.2 ensures that each superior exercises direct command over the subordinate and that each subordinate has only one superior to whom he or she is accountable. This is known as the principle of unity of command, as discussed in chapter 11. Unity of command means that one person in each organizational unit has the authority to make the decisions appropriate to his or her position. Each employee has a single immediate supervisor, who in turn is responsible to his or her immediate superior, and so on up and down the chain of command. Thus,

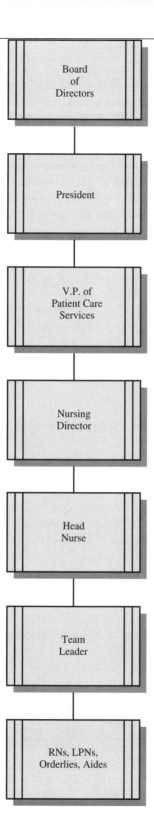

**Figure 12.2** A direct line of authority.

Board of Directors

President

V.P. of Patient Care Services

Nursing Director

Head Nurse

Team Leader

RNs, LPNs, Orderlies, Aides

everyone in the line organization knows precisely who the boss is and who the subordinates are. The individual knows exactly where he or she stands, to whom orders can be given, and whose orders have to be fulfilled.

From what we have said thus far, it is easy to see that line authority can be defined as the authority to give orders, that is, to command. It is the authority to direct others and require them to conform to decisions, plans, policies, and objectives. The primary purpose of this line authority is to make the organization work by evoking appropriate action from subordinates. Directness and unity of command have the great advantage of ensuring that results can be achieved precisely and quickly.

This type of direct line structure, however, does not answer all the needs of the modern organization. This structure was adequate when organizations and their environments were not as complex as they are today. In most enterprises now, activities have become so specialized and sophisticated that an executive needs assistance to direct all his or her subordinates properly and expertly in all phases of their activities. Line management today definitely needs the help of others to make the right decisions. That is, to perform the managerial functions properly, almost every line executive needs someone to lean on, someone who has the information and expertise, and who can give advice and service. In short, a staff is needed.

## ■ Staff Organization

Staff is auxiliary in nature; it helps the line executive in many ways. Staff provides information, counsel, advice, and guidance in any number of specialized areas to all members of the organization whenever and wherever a need may exist. However, staff cannot issue orders or command line executives to take their advice. Staff can only make recommendations to the line. That advice can be accepted, ignored, rejected, or altered by the line. Because staff is an expert in its specialty, the advice is usually heeded, but it does not have to be. When the line accepts the staff's suggestion, this suggestion becomes a line order. Line authority is based on superior-subordinate relationships; it is positional and managerial. Staff's authority is based on expertise; it is advisory and not managerial. Obviously, staff is not inferior to line and line is not inferior to staff. They are just different, and both are needed to complement each other to achieve the objectives.

Although the right to command is not part of staff authority, there are two exceptions to this. First, within each staff department there exists a line of command with superior-subordinate relationships just as in any other department. Staff's own chain of command, however, does not extend over to the line organization. Rather, it exists alongside the line organization as shown in figure 12.3. The second exception arises when staff has been given functional authority by the CEO. This very important concept is discussed fully later in the chapter.

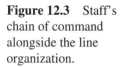

**Figure 12.3** Staff's chain of command alongside the line organization.

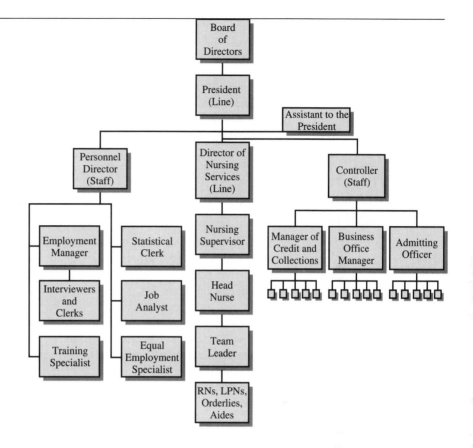

You can probably now see more clearly why all supervisors must know whether their position is attached to the organization in a line or a staff capacity. They must know this so that they will understand their function and relation to the other members of the organization. If it is staff, then the function is to provide information, guidance, counsel, advice, and service in their specialized area to whomever may ask for it. As far as the supervisor's own department is concerned, however, it will not matter whether the position is line or staff. Within every department the supervisor is the line manager. He or she is the only boss, regardless of whether the department is attached to the organization in a staff or a line capacity.

At this point, we must distinguish between *personal staff,* briefly mentioned already, and *specialized staff.* When executives find themselves in a position where they need a personal aide (sometimes referred to as an "administrative assistant" or "assistant to", such as "assistant to the President") who will help them in the performance of duties that they cannot delegate, a personal staff position may be created. The person in this position is a staff aide to the particular executive rather than to the organization at large; for example, the assistant to the president shown in figure 12.3.

Eventually, however, a personal staff member may become inadequate because this person may not be sufficiently qualified and specialized in the many areas challenging the executive; furthermore, many other members in the organization also need expert advice and guidance. At this juncture specialized staffs and possibly staff departments are introduced into the institution to provide counsel and advice in various special fields to any member of the organization who needs it. Our discussion in this chapter refers to these specialized staff positions.

## RELATIONSHIPS BETWEEN STAFF AND LINE

Conflict over organizational and operational problems may occasionally arise between line and staff, regardless of how well the relationships were defined. This is because of the two types of authorities at work: positional and formal on one side, with the weight of expertise and knowledge on the other. In most organizations, line and staff work together harmoniously. Harmonious cooperation between line and staff is especially important in a healthcare institution, since the input of so many specialists is necessary for the delivery of good healthcare. Much will depend on the sensitivity and tact of the staff people and the clarity of organizational arrangements.

It is common practice for certain activities in each organization to be undertaken as staff activities. This does not mean, however, that one can assume these are always staff activities. Line and staff, as stated before, are characteristics of authority relationships and not of functions. Thus, even a title will not offer any clue in recognizing line or staff. In industrial enterprises, one typically finds a vice-president of engineering, a vice-president of human resources, and a vice-president of production. None of these titles, however, indicates whether the position is line or staff. The little square box on the organizational chart also does not offer any help in this dilemma.

The same situation applies in hospitals and related healthcare facilities. For example, most hospital personnel managers are often known as vice-president of human resources, and their departments operate in a staff capacity, although this is not obvious from their titles. The function of a staff human resources department is to provide advice and service on personnel matters to all the other departments of the institution. The human resources department is there to recruit, screen, and test applicants; keep personnel records; help provide reasonable wage and salary administration; and advise line managers when difficult problems of fair employment practices or discipline arise. Whenever a line manager has a personnel problem, therefore, the specialized services of this staff department should be requested. Someone in the department of human resources certainly is best qualified to supply the current advice and information.

All the human resources manager can do, however, is submit suggestions to the line manager, who in turn can accept, alter, ignore, or reject them. If the line manager believes that the suggestions of the human resources department are not feasible, he or she is at liberty to make a different decision. Since the reason for establishing a staff in most instances is to obtain the best current advice, however, it is usually in the interest of the line manager to follow staff suggestions. After all, staff members are the ones who really ought to know best. For all practical purposes, the "authority" of the staff lies in their expertise in dealing with problems in their field. They will sell their ideas based on their *authority of knowledge,* not on their power to command. A person who acts in a staff relationship must know that his or her task is to advise, counsel, and guide, and not to give orders, except within his or her own department. If any of the suggestions of the staff are to be carried out, they are carried out under the name and authority of the line officer, not that of the staff person.

## ■ Functional Authority

As stated before, in most instances it is correct to say that staff provides advice and counsel to line managers but that staff lacks the right to command them. As mentioned briefly before in this chapter, an important exception to this concept of staff exists: a staff office may have been given functional authority. *Functional authority* is authority restricted to a narrow area; it is a special right given to someone who normally would not have authority and therefore could not command. Although functional authority is limited to this area, it is full authority and gives this staff member the right and power to give orders outside of normal authority lines in this limited area. This right is based on expertise in the specialized field.

For example, an administrator decides that the human resources director's office should have the final word in cases of employee dismissal. In recent years, the laws, regulations, court decisions, and interpretations referring to fair employment practices have become an important area of managerial concern and a specialty that requires daily attention by someone in the organization. The department of human resources probably is best suited to keep up-to-date in this area. To avoid and minimize problems of this nature for the healthcare center, the administrator decides to confer final operations decisions on the human resources department. In this instance, the administrator has conferred functional authority on staff (assuming that the human resources department in this institution is a staff activity) in the special area of dismissals. Now the human resources director, rather than the line supervisors, has the authority to discharge employees. This is an example of functional staff authority.

Functional authority undoubtedly violates the principle of unity of command. This principle, as you will recall, states that the subordinate is subject to orders from only one superior regarding all the functions. Functional authority, however, introduces a second superior for one particular function, such as the discharging of employees in our example. Functional staff orders have to be carried out by the line supervisor to whom they are directed. If the line supervisor should disagree strongly, he or she can appeal to the superior manager up the line. However, unless these orders are changed, which is unlikely, the supervisor has to comply with them.

Functional authority is advantageous because it allows for the maximum effective use of a staff specialist, leading to improved operations. It enables staff to intervene in line operations in situations designated by top-level management. Assigning functional authority is an effective way to use staff because, while still maintaining the over-all chain of command, we make use of the specialized staff expertise. There is a price for this intervention—violating unity of command—and this may cause friction in some organizations. It is up to the administrator to weigh the advantages versus the disadvantages before functional authority is assigned.

### ■ Assistants-to

The assistant-to is a personal staff position attached to a single executive, such as the assistant to the president in figure 12.3. This person does a variety of jobs for the executive such as gather information, do research, and relieve the executive of detail work. This position is also often used to train and develop junior managers to acquaint them with how higher-level executives function. The assistant-to position has no line authority. This individual, however, often plays a role in the channels of informal communications and in the workings of the informal organization.

## THE AUTHORITY OF ATTENDING PHYSICIANS AND SURGEONS

At this point, we must discuss another line of internal authority found only in a healthcare setting such as a hospital, HMO, clinic, or the like, the authority exercised by physicians and surgeons. Here we are referring to those physicians who are members of the medical staff group. They are full-time chiefs of a medical specialty, physicians under contract by the hospital or HMO to serve in various "director" roles, and other "private" or "part-time" physicians and surgeons who are members of the medical staff.

With the many changes that have been happening during the last decade, some or all of these physicians may be compensated by the hospital. In the past, the chiefs usually received some compensation from the hospital while the others did not. The part-time or private physicians were compensated through their own efforts on a fee-for-service or some other clinic compensation arrangement. The growth of managed care organizations (MCOs) and the acquisition of physician practices by healthcare systems have resulted in a variety of compensation arrangements as well as changed the roles physicians hold in these new healthcare enterprises.

The potential exists for tensions and misunderstandings between administration and members of the medical staff. This is understandable. The administration must consider the entire healthcare entity or system as an organized activity, its relationships with all its employees, financial viability, and its role in the community. The physician's interests, however, are likely to be geared to the patient and at times to the physician's own economic well-being. Members of the medical staff often wonder whether the administrative staff really understands their problems, and vice versa. Normally in most hospitals, clinics, and HMOs, these frictions are minimal, since both groups strive toward the best results for the healthcare center.

In most situations, a natural partnership exists between administration and the medical staff, the first providing the necessary facilities and personnel, and the latter providing the practice of medicine. There may also be conflicts between the full-time and part-time members of the medical staff. These may relate to policies established by the full-time members that adversely affect the part-time members; control over the care plan of the patient, especially if a full-time physician is directing the care, say in the ICU and a part-time physician admits his or her patient to the ICU; or teaching obligations that may be imposed on part-time physicians whose compensation is directly related to the amount of time they have to serve patients in their offices.

There is little doubt that the physicians direct the care of the patients they admit into the hospital or serve in their offices. In this connection they have clinical-therapeutic-professional authority and exercise substantial influence throughout the healthcare entity at many organizational levels and in many functions. These physicians allowed to practice at the hospital or clinic, usually referred to as the medical staff, are not shown on the hospital organizational chart in any direct line or staff relationship under the CEO unless they are employees of the hospital or clinic. They are usually placed in a vague relationship to the board of directors on the chart. They practice medicine at the hospital, but they are outside of the administrative line of authority. They are "guests" who are granted practice privileges to perform certain services, but they have much authority over various people in the hospital. Their authority is exercised over the patient and especially over the nursing staff when it comes to the medical issues. They also give orders to and expect compliance from many other employees of the hospital, for example, personnel in the respiratory therapy department, laboratories, and cardiac diagnostic services.

As a second line of "authority," such orders from the physician or surgeon clearly violate the principle of unity of command. While in the operating room, the surgeon is known as the "commander of the ship." This may lead to a situation in which operating room personnel in particular are accountable to two "bosses"; that is, they must take orders from and are responsible to their supervisor and to the physician on the case. This can cause difficulties when orders from the administrative source of authority and the medical professional source of authority are not consistent. Nevertheless, in a hospital the physician can give orders to an employee without being the line supervisor. In other words, the physician constitutes an outside source of authority who can marshal the resources of the hospital without being in the chain of command. The physician also is not responsible to the administrator, except for his or her professional medical responsibility to the medical world and to the hospital policies, rules, and regulations governing the medical staff.

This dual command obviously creates administrative and operational problems, as well as difficulties in communication, discipline, and organizational coordination. Moreover, dual command can cause considerable confusion in cases when it is not clear where authority and responsibility truly reside. This may lead to the attending physicians trying to circumvent administrative channels. Additionally, the administration may think that the physicians, through their power and authority, are interfering with administrative responsibilities. There probably will need to be some clarifications concerning this situation as hospitals' overall legal responsibilities are defined more clearly in the future. Regardless of all the complications inherent in this duality of command, it is an integral part of every hospital and exists in most other healthcare facilities as well.

## SUMMARY

Management's organizing function is to design a structural framework that will enable the institution to achieve its objectives. First, we divided the work to be done horizontally into departments, then divided the managerial work vertically by delegating authority. Another result of specialization is adding of staff to the organization. No manager could possibly possess all the knowledge, expertise, and information necessary to manage a modern healthcare institution, or any other organized activity, without the expertise and knowledge of specialists.

The CEO must decide whether a department is attached to the organization in a line or in a staff capacity. Since line and staff are quite different, it is essential for every supervisor to know in which capacity he or she serves. The supervisor in a straight direct chain of command that can be traced all the way to the top-level administrator is part of the line organization. The line organization generally follows the principle of unity of command, which means that each member of the organization has a single immediate superior.

The person who is not within this line of command is attached to the organization as a staff person to provide expert counsel and service in a specialized field to whomever in the organization needs it. Staff people are not inferior to line staff, or vice versa; rather, they represent different types of authority relationships. The line manager has the authority to give orders, whereas the staff manager usually only has the authority to make recommendations. The advice can be accepted, ignored, rejected, or altered by the line manager who requested it. Because staff represents expertise in a specialty, however, the advice is usually accepted. Staff's authority is based on expertise; it is advisory, not managerial authority.

This situation changes in the case of functional authority. Sometimes the CEO may decide to confer functional authority on a staff office, that is, the right to give orders in a narrow area based on the staff person's expertise in a specific area. Although functional authority is limited to this area, it is full authority and the right and power to command outside of normal lines. Such functional authority violates the principle of unity of command. A similar difficult situation of duality of command is created by the attending physician's clinical-therapeutic authority. These additional channels of command result from the nature of healthcare delivery. Many areas of functional authority exist in most healthcare centers.

# *13* *Organizing on the Supervisory Level*

## Chapter Objectives

After you have studied this chapter, you should be able to:

1. Describe how the guidelines and principles for the organizing function depended upon by top administration are the same for supervisors in designing and building their departments.
2. Discuss the supervisor's goal to design the "ideal" departmental structure.
3. Explain the need to design the departmental structure based on principles, not on people in the various jobs.
4. Review the various approaches available for organizing and reorganizing such as reengineering, job design, and patient-focused arrangements.
5. Discuss the importance of delegation of authority to the broadest extent.
6. Explain the need for the supervisory understudies and backstops.
7. Discuss the process of developing suitable understudies.
8. Explain how broad delegation of authority ultimately amounts to general supervision on the lowest employee level.

Thus far, we have discussed the organizing process from an overall institutional point of view. We have explored how the chief executive establishes the formal organization structure and makes it come alive by selecting the right supervisors to whom organizational authority is delegated.

Most department heads and supervisors are not likely to be involved in the major decisions concerning the overall organizational structure of their healthcare institution. However, they will be greatly concerned with the structure of their own department. Logically, we could not discuss the organizing process on the departmental level until we have understood the basic principles of organizing and how they are applied in the design of the overall structure.

With this broad understanding, we are now ready to approach the organizing function more specifically from the supervisor's point of view of the departmental goals and objectives, daily operations and activities, and existing personnel and resources. In other words, we will now look at organizing on a narrow scale, zeroing in on the microcosm known as the department. We will focus attention on how a supervisor actually goes about organizing and delegating within his or her own department.

It should not be surprising to find that the organizing process is basically the same, whether it is performed by the CEO, COO, or the lowest line supervisor.

Organizing involves grouping activities for purposes of departmentalization or subdepartmentalization on the supervisory level, assigning specific tasks and duties, and most importantly, delegating authority. In essence, this means that the basic organizational principles must be understood and applied by supervisors when they are setting up their own department, just as they were by the chief administrator when the overall institution was structured. Let us see how a supervisor might go about applying these principles, using them on a day-to-day basis so that they are not just abstractions, but parts of a healthy departmental body.

<table>
<tr>
<td>

**IDEAL ORGANIZATION OF THE DEPARTMENT**

</td>
<td>

Most supervisors are placed in charge of an existing department; only a few will ever have the opportunity to design a structure for a completely new department. When designing or rearranging the organizational structure of the department, the supervisor should conceptualize and plan for the ideal organization. The word *ideal* in this instance is not intended to mean *perfect;* rather, it is used to mean the *most desirable* organization for the achievement of stated objectives. It is the supervisor's job to design an organizational setup that will be best for this particular department. In so doing, the principles and guides of organizing must be observed. Following these is no guarantee that the department will not have any problems. A significant number of problems will be avoided, however, because the organizational network has been designed based on sound and proven principles and is likely to function smoothly in most cases.

</td>
</tr>
</table>

The manager must bear in mind, however, that certain organizational concepts and arrangements that work well in a very large organization may not be applicable to a smaller organization. It is conceivable that in a fifty-bed hospital a supervisor may be supervising two different activities, such as purchasing and health information management. In other words, supervisors must not blindly follow the idea that what is good for one enterprise is also good for another. Moreover, it is not essential that the manager's organizational plans for the department look pretty on paper or that the organizational chart appear symmetrical and well balanced. Rather, this ideal design should represent the most appropriate arrangement for reaching the departmental objectives. It should be uniquely tailored to suit the conditions under which the manager works, instead of some abstract image of what an "ideal" department should look like.

In planning this ideal, but realistic, organization, the supervisor must consider it as something of a standard with which the present organizational setup can be compared. The ideal structure should be looked on as a guide to the short- and long-range plans of the department. Although the supervisor should carefully plan for the ideal structure on becoming the department's manager, this does not mean that the existing organization should be forced to conform to the ideal immediately. Each change in the prevailing organization, however, should bring the existing structure closer to the ideal. In other words, the ideal organization of the department represents the direction in which the supervisor will move as time passes.

## INTERNAL DEPARTMENTAL STRUCTURE

At this point, you might be a bit unclear as to exactly how supervisors would go about designing the ideal departmental structure. What does this involve, how is it done, and are supervisors really equipped to do it? In most cases they are equipped to do so because essentially they are being asked to subdepartmentalize, to establish subdivisions or subunits within their department, just as the chief administrator established the overall divisions or units for the whole organization. Three examples of how a director of nursing services might subdepartmentalize or set up the internal departmental structure are shown in the organizational charts in figures 13.1, 13.2, and 13.3. Additional information on this can be found in the appendix of this book.

More specifically, what supervisors are being asked to do is to consider the groupings of activities in the department, the various existing positions, and the assignment of tasks and duties to these positions. Is what he or she finds the best possible arrangement for achieving departmental and institutional objectives? Are all the present positions necessary, or could some be eliminated or combined with others? Does each position have a fair assignment of tasks and duties, commensurate with its status and salary? Are the positions related so that there is no duplication of effort and that coordination and cooperation are facilitated? In other words, is the department well organized? Does it function in the most efficient manner? Are there any changes at all that the supervisor would like to see in the internal organizational structure of the department?

If there are any such changes, then these will become the basis for what we have been calling "the ideal organization of the department." They will become the organizational goals toward which the department head will strive when structuring the department.

If a supervisor is setting up a new department or working in a newly established institution, much of this ideal structure can probably be implemented in the beginning. This would be the most desirable situation but is not usually the case. Generally, the supervisor is forced to implement organizational goals gradually while working within the existing departmental structure and with existing personnel.

### ■ Organization and Personnel

The supervisor should design this ideal organization based on sound organizational principles, regardless of the people with whom he or she has to work. This does not mean that departments could exist without people to staff their various positions. Without people, of course, there can be no organization. The problems of organization should be handled in the right order, however; the sound structure comes first, then the people are asked to fulfill this structure.

If the organization setup is planned first around existing personnel, then existing shortcomings will be perpetuated. Because of incumbent personalities, too much emphasis may be given to certain activities and not enough to others. Moreover, if a department is structured around personalities, it is easy to imagine what would happen if a particular employee is promoted or resigns. If, on the

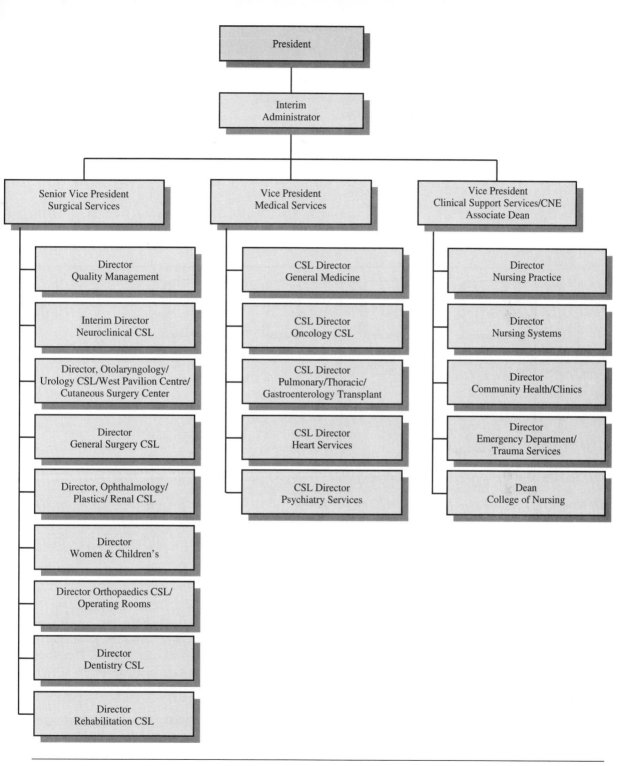

**Figure 13.1** Internal departmental structure of a nursing service.

*Courtesy Barnes-Jewish Hospital, St. Louis, MO.*

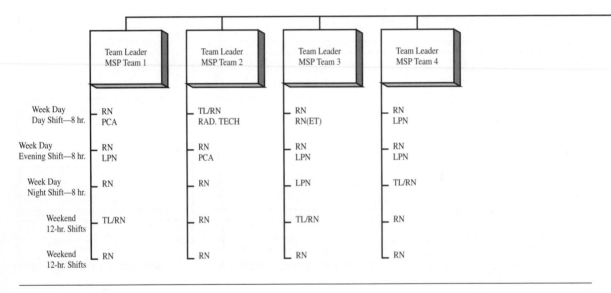

**Figure 13.2**   Internal departmental structure of a nursing service.

*"Courtesy of Lakeland Regional Medical Center, Inc. Lakeland, FL."*

other hand, the departmental organization is structured impersonally on the general need for personnel rather than on the incumbent personalities, it should not be difficult to find an appropriate successor for a particular position. Therefore, an organization should be designed first to serve the objectives of the department, then the various employees should be selected and fitted into departmental positions. This, however, is easier said than done.

In most instances, the supervisor has been put into a managerial position in an existing and fully staffed department without having had the chance to decide on the present structure or personnel of the department. Frequently, some of the available employees do not fit well into the ideal structure, but they cannot all be overlooked or dismissed. In such cases, the best the supervisor can do for the

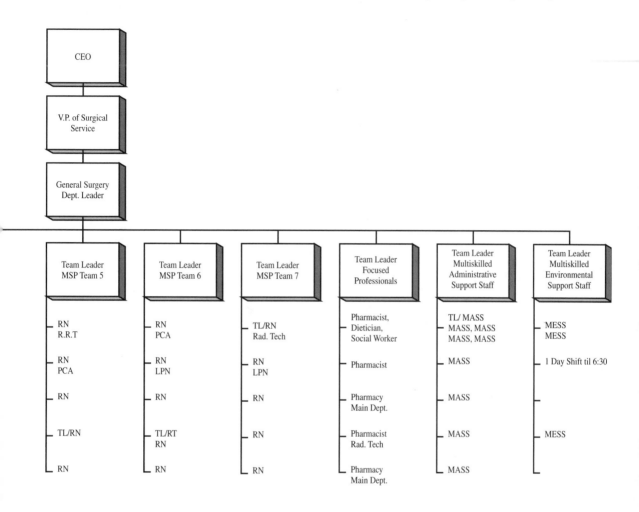

time being is to adjust the organization to use the capacities of the employees he or she has. It should be realized that this is an accommodation of the ideal plan to fit present personalities and should be regarded as temporary. Such personnel adjustments are sometimes necessary, but fewer of them will be required if the supervisor has already made a plan of the organization he or she would like to have if the ideal human resources were available. Then, as time goes on, the supervisor will strive to come closer and closer to the ideal departmental setup.

## ■ Reorganization

One must keep in mind that organizational structure is not static. The organization is a living institution and therefore needs a certain amount of adjustment as time goes on. For this reason, the manager's organizing function is constant;

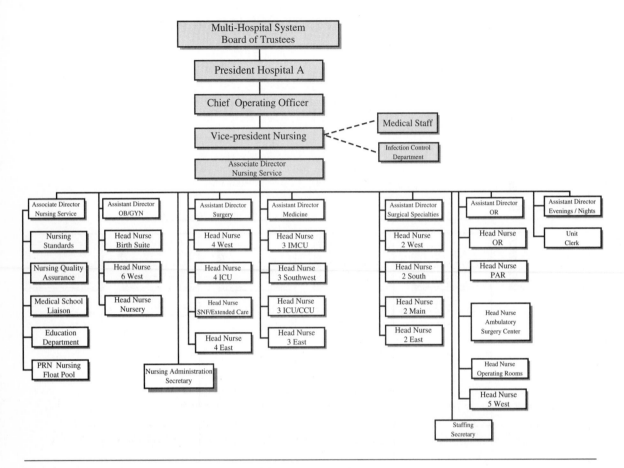

**Figure 13.3**    Internal departmental structure of a nursing service.

checking, questioning, and appraising the soundness and feasibility of the departmental structure are an ongoing process. Organization is not an end in itself, but rather a means to an end—the accomplishment of the objectives of the department. A manager must be on the lookout for new developments, practices, and thinking in the field of organization. The supervisor must be willing to *reorganize* the department if developments warrant it or if it is indicated that the existing structure does not permit effective functioning.

The term *reorganization* has all types of different connotations. In our discussion, this term will refer to changes in the organizational structure, departmentalization, the assignment of activities, or authority relationships. From time to time, a manager makes such changes because of scientific and technological advances, the dynamic and changing nature of the department's activities, or a change in supervisors. As noted previously, reorganization also may be necessary to overcome existing deficiencies.

Let us look at a recent example of reorganization to overcome existing deficiencies. In the past, many nurses found themselves burdened with too much secretarial and clerical work that kept them away from actual patient care and bedside nursing. This was an undesirable situation, since the thrust of their education and purpose was the care of patients. Finally, it became apparent that many of these functions could be performed by someone else without a nursing education just as effectively. This led to the creation of positions now commonly known as nursing assistants. The care of "things" was assigned to them, whereas the actual care of "people" reverted back to where it should be, the nurses.

The job of the nursing assistant is to perform a variety of clerical duties, such as preparing, maintaining, and compiling records in the nursing unit. This person copies information from nurses' records, writes requisitions for laboratory tests, dispatches messages to other departments, transcribes physicians' orders, and so forth. The nursing assistant also makes appointments for patient services in other departments as requested by the nursing and medical staff, maintains an established inventory of stock supplies for the unit by verifying supplies and making requisitions, and performs many other duties that the nursing personnel previously had to do. This is an example of reorganization where duties were reassigned and new authority relationships had to be established between nursing assistants, nurses, and head nurses.

The success of this reorganization was pursued and studied. As nursing shortages continued to threaten healthcare facility viability, patient care assistants evolved. These individuals, after extensive training, perform some of the patient care duties previously performed by nurses. By employing patient care assistants, the number of nurses needed decreased, the cost of patient care staff declined, and the talents of nurses were used for those patient care activities requiring their education.

Once this or any other type of reorganization has been decided on, it can be carried out either as a long-term, gradual, or continued change or as a one-time change covering only a short period. The latter approach has typically been called the "earthquake" or "shake-up" technique, indicating that the full shock of the reorganization is felt all at once. The long-range, or long-term, plan, on the other hand, provides for a period of more gradual adjustment to the organizational changes. No doubt this approach is less disturbing and creates fewer upsets than the earthquake approach.

## REENGINEERING

An approach introduced in the 1990s is known as *reengineering*. According to Michael Hammer, "the simplest way to define reengineering is to say it means taking a 'clean sheets' approach to forget how you've done things in the past and to ask what's the very best way to get your work done. It's about rethinking how you do your work, working backwards from what customers need and then determining what's required to deliver it." Hammer contends that the concept has nothing to do with profit and loss, and it is not about buying and selling, merging or divesting. "It's about serving customers' needs."[1]

Deloitte & Touche LLP's April 1996 issue of *Health Care Review* identified potential reengineering questions for healthcare organizations as:

> *What is the best way to care for patients?*
> *To organize the work involved in acquiring members?*
> *To manage care across the continuum?*
> *To acquire and distribute materials in the hospital?*

In an effort to prepare for the future, healthcare organizations concluded that the trend toward more sophisticated specialization and computer literacy would continue and that employees with higher levels of technical skills would replace lower-skilled employees because higher levels of technical skill will be needed to treat future acute care patients. A higher level of computer literacy would also lend itself to *telecommuting,* or working from home and transmitting work accomplished via modem. A common activity performed at home is medical transcription. Some anticipate that the advent of a fully computer-based patient record will permit the functions of patient account bill editing, medical record coding, analysis, quality assurance, and cancer registry to all be performed at home. *Money Magazine's* February 1996 issue projected that by the year 2000 more than 10% of the workforce will be telecommuting. Given these technological advances and changes in the "workplace," reengineering may be approached to respond to questions like those posed by Deloitte & Touche.

O. J. Kralovec of First Consulting Group (CA) contends that the underlying premise of reengineering is that business processes should be designed around related and interdependent tasks that together produce an outcome that fulfills a defined customer need.[2] Given this, reengineering has the potential to re-create organizations to improve quality and customer responsiveness, reduce costs, and streamline operations. One key difference from other approaches is that this approach relies heavily on employee teams coordinated by management to accomplish the change.

In a healthcare organization, often there may be more than one customer. Reengineering must begin with identifying the different customers served, followed by a clear delineation of their needs and how well the organization is meeting them. The Deloitte & Touche interview with Hammer identifies the second characteristic of reengineering as a process that is focused, which means that it is a process of end-to-end sets of activities that provide value to the customer. This may include crossing all kinds of organization boundaries. Terrence Noetzel, Deloitte & Touche's partner, points out, "A patient care process frequently crosses different entities in the care continuum. Redesigning the work across entities as a single, integrated process is a giant leap in a traditionally fragmented industry."

1. *Deloitte & Touche LLP,* Health Care Review. *(Washington, DC: April 1996).*
2. *Rhonda Bergmann, "Reengineering Health Care,"* Hospitals and Health Networks. *February 5, 1994, p. 28.*

"By improving the quality of the work performed for customers while seeking to lower the cost of providing results, reengineering aims for what sounds like an unachievable goal," Hammer says in the Deloitte interview, "But the goal—to simultaneously do a better job and spend less—is eminently achievable. The key is, you get rid of work that doesn't add value—the approvals and hand-offs and supervisions that consume a lot of money and yet manage to degrade quality."

The April 1996 issue of Deloitte and Touche's *Health Care Review* elaborated on the results of successful reengineering by giving examples and indicating that they are evident in a broad spectrum of entities, including hospitals, academic medical centers, HMOs, and other healthcare plans. One hospital gained significantly improved patient satisfaction and public recognition, while at the same time cutting the cost of care by more than 20 percent.

At a comprehensive cancer center treatment, volume in radiation services has been increased by 18 percent, referral to treatment time has been reduced from 47 to 7 days, and unit costs have been cut by 38 percent. Reengineering meant a total redesign of the radiation process to improve access while maintaining quality. A new caregiver role was defined, and a multidisciplinary team approach was structured to assure greater treatment value to patients.

Another example is reengineered physician group practices in which cost savings have exceeded 30 percent, while patient "stops" during an average visit have decreased from 5 to 2, adding to the satisfaction of patients. In addition, patients are able to schedule follow-up appointments more quickly and easily as the result of an improved scheduling process.

Reengineering has made it possible for a large healthcare insurer to restructure its customer service process, reducing the time it takes the plan to respond to member inquiries by 85 percent. Another insurer, deeply involved in care management, has saved $75 million annually through improvements in how the delivery process is managed from beginning to end.

First Consulting Group compared reengineering to reorganization (see table 13.1).[3] Even with this comparison, reengineering is difficult to distinguish from other traditional approaches to organizing, so at this point it may be helpful to describe some additional terms that may help differentiate it from other organizational processes we have discussed or will discuss later in the text.

*Job design* is the process managers complete to define the specific tasks, methods, and relationship of a given job or position to others in the organization. *Job redesign* is the process in which the manager reviews the various tasks assigned to a job or position and alters the assignments to improve productivity, enhance quality, or enrich the employee's work experience. *Job enlargement* is a method used in redesigning the job by adding variety to it via more tasks of a similar nature. *Job enrichment* is similar to job enlargement in that it is a method used to redesign jobs but in the process of doing so, the employee is allowed more participation in decision making by increasing the depth of the employee's

3.   Ibid., *p. 32.*

**TABLE 13.1**

|  | Reengineering | Reorganizing |
| --- | --- | --- |
| *Goals* | Dramatic improvements | Moderate cost reduction |
| *Approach* | Top down | Top down |
| *Focus* | Strategic | Cut costs |
| *Action* | Replace processes | Collapse layers |
|  | Leverage automation |  |
| *Type of Change* | Radical | Layoffs |
| *Employee Role* | Reengineering teams | Victim |
| *Timing of Results* | 2–4 years | Quick |
| *Role of Automation* | Key enabler | None |

authority and adding a variety of tasks to the job. It is anticipated that employees in the future will expect to participate more in the decisions that affect their daily work routines, thus requiring managers to consider redesign activities that will result in job enrichment.

*Patient-focused redesign* has been referred to in this text previously and requires that the healthcare environment (resources and personnel) be designed around the patient. However, some organizations have chosen to pursue *product line redesign.* This approach to redesign requires the environment to be designed around the services or products delivered. All of the approaches mentioned in this section are methods of organizing (and reorganizing).

The difference between the above approaches and reengineering is best described by Michael Hammer and James Champy, authors of the article "Don't Automate. Obliterate" that appeared in the *Harvard Business Review,* who some refer to as the "fathers" of reengineering. In their book *Reengineering the Corporation,* they assert that reengineering is the fundamental rethinking and *radical* redesign of critical systems and business processes to achieve dramatic improvements in contemporary measures of performance, such as cost, quality, service, and speed.[4]

In a reengineered airline company, not everyone would fly first-class, but everyone would receive first class service. The reason being that if you don't provide the service, your competitors will, according to Hammer and Champy.[5] Consider the impact of this philosophy on healthcare services by reorienting staff's thinking from single products to whole procedures, or episodes of care. Once this mindset is established, staff begin to think across the artificial boundaries that have developed in healthcare organizations, often along professional specialty lines.

4.  Gayle Hanson, *"New Currents Recharging the Workaday World,"* Insight. *July 26, 1993, p. 17.*
5.  Ibid., *p. 19.*

John Hargrove of Ohmeda, Inc. describes reengineering as "an ongoing process that requires:

- collaboration
- commitment
- compromise
- compensation
- comprehension
- compliance
- consensus, and
- constant communication."

Further, he says, "the bottom line is that the key to reengineering success is not managing by some academic process where people are the last ingredient. The key is managing people to validate the real process of change."[6]

One must remember that changes are always disturbing to those who are affected by them, regardless of how well intended they are. A manager who frequently changes the department's organizational structure runs the risk of damaging the morale of the subordinates. To the supervisor suggesting the reorganization, it might seem trivial, but to the subordinates it will probably appear frightening because it implies changes in their working environment, status, and security. The wise supervisor will have to learn how to strike a happy medium in the desirable amount of organizational change. In most instances, the supervisor will probably find that most subordinates quickly adjust to changes if they are properly explained and if the need for them is demonstrated. A more detailed discussion of the introduction of change will be given in chapter 19.

As stated briefly in our discussion on delegation of authority, from time to time it is necessary also to review the degree of authority that has been delegated. The supervisor may believe that he or she has lost control over certain activities and that it has become necessary to "tighten up" or to *recentralize.* Another reason to "tighten" or recentralize is resulting from the merger of healthcare facilities. Many services are no longer needed at multiple locations when healthcare facilities merge. For example, human resource, purchasing, accounting, patient accounting, and even telecommunication departments are being centralized at one location. This centralization effort streamlines the services, reduces staff, and requires the realignment of authority held by the remaining incumbents.

If recentralization of authority is called for, authority must be revoked or realigned. This is another form of reorganization that presents a difficult task for the supervisor, since feelings of suspicion, hurt, discouragement, and insecurity on the part of the subordinate are likely to surface. To mitigate these tensions,

6. *"Managing Change: People, Partnerships, Process, and Persistence,"* Journal of Healthcare Resource Management, *July/August 1996, vol. 14, no. 6.*

the supervisor must explain the reasons for this action. Such an unpleasant situation can be lessened by taking great care in the choice of a subordinate when delegating authority in the first place.

Since organizing is a dynamic process, it should be emphasized that regardless of the difficulties and unpleasant aspects involved, it is necessary for a supervisor to make organizational adjustments occasionally to keep the department as viable as possible.

| DELEGATION OF AUTHORITY ON THE SUPERVISORY LEVEL | Once a supervisor has organized or reorganized the department's structure, or at least planned the changes that are needed and recorded them in an ideal organizational design or position description, he or she is ready to delegate or redelegate authority in accordance with the organizational structure. We assume that the supervisor has been given sufficient authority and that he or she is in charge of all the activities within this section. Just as any other manager, supervisors are faced with the necessity of delegating some of the authority that has been handed down to them. As mentioned previously, unless this is done, an organization has not been created. This is certainly the case when there are many employees. In other words, the supervisor must assign tasks, grant authority, and create responsibility within each of the subunits and for each of the positions in the department. |
| --- | --- |

If a supervisor is taking over an existing department consisting of a large and substantial number of employees, broad delegation of authority probably is in effect. It still is necessary, however, to check carefully whether all of it is consistent with the ideal organizational plans. The supervisor should check the amount and type of authority delegated to each position and whether the three essential steps in the process of delegation were followed. In other words, he or she should refer back to the specific procedure outlined in chapter 11 to see that authority is delegated properly in the department.

Let us now turn to the situation in which the number of employees in the supervisor's department is rather small. Such a department would consist merely of a supervisor and a few employees (three to six). The supervisor may wonder if in these circumstances it is necessary to delegate authority. The answer is yes. Even in a small department, the supervisor will need someone who can be depended on to take over if the supervisor should have to leave either temporarily or for any length of time. Even in the smallest department, there should be someone who can work as the supervisor's *backstop.*

It is a sign of poor supervision when no one in a department can take over when the supervisor is sick or has to be away from the job. The supervisor also may miss a promotion because there is nobody to take charge of the unit. Thus, sooner or later every supervisor needs a backstop, understudy, assistant, or whatever this person may be called. It would be appropriate for the supervisor to discuss this intention with his or her immediate boss as well.

## ■ Availability of Trained Subordinates

The process of delegation assumes that there is someone available who is willing to accept authority. As a supervisor, you may have wanted to delegate more and more authority to some of your subordinates and to make one of them your assistant, but you had no one within your department who was willing to accept this arrangement and to take charge of an area of activities. You may not have anyone working for you who is capable of handling more authority. In such a case authority, for the moment at least, cannot be delegated and must be withheld.

On the other hand, you may find yourself in a vicious circle, complaining that without better trained subordinates you cannot delegate. Without delegating additional authority, however, your subordinates still have no opportunity to ever obtain the necessary exposure. With additional experience and training, their judgment could be improved and they could become more capable subordinates. Although this lack of trained subordinates is often used by supervisors as an excuse for not delegating authority, they must always bear in mind that unless they begin to delegate authority, no subordinate capable of being a backstop and of taking over the department (if necessary) will ever be available.

It is the supervisor's duty to develop and train such a person, and in the process more authority most likely can be delegated not only to the individual selected as a backstop but to other employees as well. Moreover, this process of training for increased delegation will give the supervisor a much clearer view of his or her own duties, the workings of the department, and the various jobs to be performed. Bringing subordinates to the point where they can finally be given considerable authority is a slow and tedious process, but it is worth the effort. In the early stages the degree of authority granted will be small, but as subordinates grow in their capacities, more and more authority can be delegated to them.

### *The Supervisor's Hesitancy to Delegate*

Often supervisors do not like the idea of creating a backstop; they may be reluctant to delegate authority because they know that they cannot delegate responsibility. Since the responsibility remains with the supervisors, they may think it is best to make all decisions themselves. Thus, out of fear of their subordinates' mistakes, many supervisors are not willing to delegate authority and, as a result, continue to overburden themselves. Their indecision and delay may often be costlier than the mistakes they hoped to avoid by retaining their authority. Always remember the likelihood exists that the supervisor may make mistakes as well. Moreover, if employees are permitted to learn from some of their own mistakes, they will be more willing to accept greater authority.

The supervisors' reluctance in delegating such authority is understandable in view of their continued accountability for the results. The traditional picture of a good supervisor was one who rolled up his or her sleeves and worked right alongside the employees, thus setting an example by his or her efforts. Such a description is particularly true of a supervisor who has come up through the ranks and for whom the supervisory position is a reward for hard work and professional or technical competence. This person has been placed in a managerial position without having been equipped to be a manager and is faced with new problems that are difficult to cope with. This person therefore retreats to a pattern in which he or she feels secure and works right alongside the employees. Occasionally such participation is needed, for example, when the job to be performed is particularly difficult or when an emergency has arisen. Under these conditions the good supervisor will always be right on the job to help. Aside from such emergencies and unusual situations, however, most of the supervisor's time should be spent carrying out the supervisory job, and the employees should be doing their assigned tasks. It is the supervisor's job not to do, but to see that others get tasks done.

Frequently, however, supervisors will still think that if they want something done right, they have to do it themselves. Often they believe that it is easier to do the job than to correct the subordinate's mistake. Even if the supervisor lets the subordinate do it, the supervisor may feel a strong temptation to correct any mistakes rather than explain to the subordinate what should have been done. It is frequently more difficult to teach than to do a job oneself. Moreover, supervisors often believe that they can do the job better than any of their subordinates, and they are probably right. Sooner or later, however, they will have to get used to the idea that someone else can do the job almost as well as they can, and at that point they should delegate the necessary authority. In this manner they will be able to save their own time for more important managerial jobs, for thinking and planning. If supervisors are willing to see to it that employees become more competent with each job, then their own belief and confidence in their employees' work will also grow. This mutually advantageous relationship will permit the supervisor to carry out the basic underlying policy of delegating more and more authority as the employees demonstrate their capability in handling it.

Despite the fact that a certain amount of authority must be delegated to create an organization, some supervisory duties cannot be delegated. The supervisor should always apply and interpret policies, give general directions for the department, take necessary disciplinary action, promote employees, and appraise them. Aside from these duties, however, their subordinates should perform most tasks by themselves.

### Selecting a Backstop

As we have said, this process of delegation of authority should include making one particular subordinate into an assistant for the supervisor. The first step is to select the right person for the job. The supervisor undoubtedly knows which employees are more outstanding. These would be the ones to whom the other employees turn in case of questions and who are looked on as leaders.

Outstanding employees, moreover, know how to do the job very well, seem to be able to handle problems as they arise, and do not get into arguments. They should also have shown good judgment in the way they organize and go about their own job, should be open-minded, and should be interested in further development and moving into better positions. Without such ambitions, even the best training would not achieve any results. Outstanding employees must have shown a willingness to accept responsibility and must have proven dependability.

Sometimes a worker may not have had the opportunity to show all these qualities. Whatever qualities have remained latent, however, will show up rather quickly during the actual training process.

If the supervisor has two or three equally good employees in the department, training all of them for greater delegations of authority on an equal basis should begin. Sooner or later it will be obvious which one has the superior ability, and this individual will then become the major trainee for the backstop position. Once the selection of a single person is made (or in a large department there could be several backstops), it is not necessary to come out with general formal announcements in this respect. Of course, the supervisor should discuss and explain the intentions fully to the employee chosen. More importantly, the supervisor must follow through by laying a thorough groundwork for good training so that the one who has been chosen will work out as an understudy.

### The Reluctant Subordinate

The delegation of authority and especially the development of an understudy are two-sided relationships. Although the supervisor may be ready and willing to turn over authority, the subordinates may sometimes be reluctant to accept it. Frequently subordinates may feel unsure of themselves, unsure that they will be able to handle the job assigned to them. They may be reluctant to leave the security of their job and their coworkers. Merely telling them to have more self-confidence will have little effect. The supervisor, as we have said, must create this self-confidence by carefully coaching and training the subordinate to undertake more and more difficult assignments. Then, and only then, will the subordinate be able to accept the increased responsibility that goes along with harder tasks and greater authority.

### Training a Backstop

Although the phrase *training a subordinate* is frequently used, the term *training* is really not appropriate. It would be more fitting to speak of the development, mentoring, or even self-development on the subordinate's part. Understudies must be eager to improve themselves and show the initiative to be self-starters.

The supervisor should gradually let understudies in on the workings of the department, explain some of the reports to them, and show them how needed information is obtained. The supervisor should tell them what is done with these reports and why it is done. The supervisor should also introduce an understudy to other supervisors and other people in the organization with whom they must associate and contact; sooner or later the understudy should contact them himself or herself. It is advisable to take the understudy along to some of the institution's meetings after this person has had a chance to learn the major aspects of the supervisor's job. On such occasions the supervisor should show how the work of the department is related to that of the other departments in the healthcare facility.

As daily problems arise, the supervisor should let understudies participate in them and even try to solve some of them for themselves. By letting understudies come up with some solutions to problems, the supervisor will have a chance to see how well they analyze and how much they know about making decisions. In time the supervisor should give the understudy some areas of activities for which he or she will be entirely responsible. In other words, gradually more duties and authority should be assigned.

This whole process requires an atmosphere of confidence and trust. The boss must be looked on by the understudy as a coach and friend, not as a domineering superior. Supervisors should caution themselves that in their eagerness to develop the understudy as rapidly as possible, they do not overload them or pass on problems that are beyond the backstop's capabilities. The supervisor must never lose sight of the fact that it takes time to be able to handle problems of any magnitude.

All of this will require much effort and patience on the supervisor's part. With increased responsibilities there should also be commensurate positive incentives for the backstop. These may be in the form of pay increases, bonuses, a fancier title, recognized status within the organization, or other rewards of a tangible and intangible nature. Such rewards will include the self-satisfaction that the subordinate feels when he or she is able to handle increased responsibility and is moving up in the organizational ranks. Conceivably, just about the time the understudy comes to the point of being truly helpful, he or she may be transferred to another job outside of the supervisor's department. This may be discouraging for the moment, but the supervisor may rest assured that the administrators will give credit for a training job well done.

## ACHIEVING DELEGATION OF AUTHORITY

Broader delegations of authority are not always easily put into practice. To be effective, a sincere desire and willingness to delegate must permeate the entire organization. Top-level management must set the mood by not only preaching but also by practicing broad delegation of authority. Although top management's intentions may be the best, at times the desired degree of decentralization of authority may not be achieved. For instance, top management may find that authority has not been delegated as far down as it intended because somewhere along the line there is an "authority hoarder," a person who simply will not delegate authority any further. This person grasps all the authority delegated to him or her without redelegating any of it.

There are several reasons why managers might resist further decentralization of authority in this manner. To some, the delegation of authority may mean a loss of status or a loss of power and control. Others may think that by having centralized power they are in closer contact with top-level administration. Still other managers are truly concerned with the expenses involved in delegating authority. Moreover, it is difficult for many managers to part with some of their own authority and still be left with full responsibility for the decisions made by their subordinates.

There are several ways to cope with this problem and to achieve the degree of decentralization that is desired by the top-level administration. As stated before, the entire managerial group must be indoctrinated with the philosophy of decentralization of authority. They must understand that by carefully delegating authority they do not lose status, nor do they absolve themselves of their responsibilities. One way of putting this understanding into practice is to request that each manager have a fairly large number of subordinate managers reporting to him or her. By stretching the span of management, the subordinate manager has no choice but to delegate authority. Another way to achieve broader delegations of authority is for the enterprise to adopt the policy of not promoting a manager until a subordinate manager has been developed who can take over the vacated position. By doing this, as noted in the discussion of backstops, the manager is encouraged to delegate as much authority as possible at an early stage. Moreover, this process creates an ideal organizational climate in which the subordinates can find maximum satisfaction for many of their most important needs.

## DELEGATION AND GENERAL SUPERVISION

There is an end to delegation, in the strict sense of the word, when we reach the point of execution of daily duties; in other words, when we reach the level of employees who are actually doing the work. When we have reached the level where no more authority can be delegated, the question now arises as to how a supervisor can effectively reap the benefits of delegation, that is, how he or she can take advantage of the motivating factors of delegation in the daily working situation. The answer to this question can be found at the point where the philosophy of delegation takes on the form of what is commonly referred to as *loose,* or *general, supervision.*

General supervision means merely giving orders in broad, general terms. It means that the supervisor, instead of watching every detail of the employee's activities, is primarily interested in the results achieved. The supervisor permits the subordinates to decide how to achieve these results within accepted professional standards and organizational requirements. He or she sets the goals and tells the subordinates what is to be accomplished, setting the limits within which the work has to be done, but the employees are to decide how to accomplish these goals. This gives each employee maximum freedom within the constraints of the organizational and professional standards.

### ■ The Employee's Reaction to General Supervision

Most employees accept work as a part of normal, healthy life. Accordingly, most managers display the underlying managerial attitude of McGregor's Theory Y (see chapters 19 and 21) toward their employees. Such managers understand that in their daily jobs employees seek a satisfaction that wages alone cannot provide. Most employees also enjoy being their own bosses. They like a degree of freedom that allows them to make their own decisions pertaining to their work. The question arises as to whether this is possible if one works for someone else, whether such a degree of freedom can be granted to employees if they are to contribute their share toward the achievement of the enterprise's objectives. This is where the ideas of delegation of authority and general supervision can help.

The desire for freedom, for being one's own boss, can be enhanced and fulfilled by delegation of authority, which in a working situation means general supervision. In the daily work environment, this broad, general type of supervision on the employee level has the same motivating results as the delegation of formal authority throughout the managerial hierarchy.

## ■ Advantages of General Supervision

Significant advantages result from this approach to supervision and are similar to those cited in our discussion of the process of delegation. The supervisor who learns the art of general supervision will benefit in many ways. First, he or she will have more time to be a manager. If the supervisor tried to practice close, detailed supervision and tried to make every decision personally, he or she would probably be exhausted physically and mentally. With delegation, however, the supervisor will be freed from many of the details of the work and will thus have time to think, plan, organize, and control. In so doing, the supervisor will be freed to receive and handle more authority and responsibility.

Moreover, the decisions that general supervision allows employees to make will probably be superior to those made by a harried supervisor trying to practice detailed supervision. We have already pointed out that the employee on the job is closest to the problem and therefore is in the best position to solve it. Furthermore, opportunities to make decisions will give the employees a chance to develop their own talents and abilities and become more competent. It is always difficult for a supervisor to instruct employees on how to make decisions without letting them make them. They can really only learn by practice.

This leads us to the third advantage of general supervision: it enables employees to take great pride in the results of their decisions. As stated before, employees enjoy being independent. Surveys reveal that the one quality employees most admire in a supervisor is the ability to allow them to be independent by delegating authority. Employees want a boss who shows them how to do a job and then trusts them enough to let them do it on their own. In this way the supervisor provides on-the-job training for them and a chance for better positions. Thus, we can see that general supervision allows for the progress not only of supervisors themselves, but also of the employees, the department, and the enterprise as a whole.

Much more will be said about general supervision when we discuss the managerial function of influencing. Let us briefly state that practicing the general approach to supervision, instead of an autocratic, dictatorial, detailed approach, provides much of the satisfaction employees seek on the job, which money alone does not cover. Because this approach fulfills many of their needs, employees are motivated to put forth their best efforts in achieving the enterprise's objectives.

## ■ Attitudes toward General Supervision

It seems appropriate at this stage to point out that the general approach to supervision and the idea that one must help motivate employees were not always as widely accepted as they are today. In the past, some managers believed that emphasis on negative authority was the best method of motivating employees. Those who depended on the force of authority as their major means of motivation—and a few may still erroneously believe in this today—believed that managing consisted of forcing people to work by threatening to fire them if they did not. Their assumptions were that the only reason people work is to earn money and that they will work only if they fear losing their jobs. This approach ignores the fact that employees want many other intrinsic satisfactions from their work besides the salary. It also assumes that people do not like work and that they try to get away with doing as little as possible. On this basis the need for close supervision is justified. The supervisor must tell the workers precisely what is to be done every minute of the day and not permit them any chance to use their own judgment. The older school of managerial thought was based on Theory X (see chapters 19 and 21) as its underlying assumption.

Such reliance on the sheer weight of authority has lost most of its followers. This approach was possible in the early days of the Industrial Revolution when workers were close to starvation and would do anything to obtain food, clothing, and shelter. In recent years, however, employees have begun to expect much more from their jobs. This is particularly true when most of the employees are professionals and when times are good and employment is high. We also find that the educational process of our youth has had a significant influence on recent attitudes. Many years ago children were accustomed to strict obedience toward their elders. Now schools and homes emphasize freedom and self-expression, and it is therefore becoming more and more difficult for the young employee to accept any kind of autocratic management on the job. In addition to this, legislation, regulations, and the impact of unions have made it more difficult for a supervisor to fire an employee.

Perhaps the most important change in current attitudes is the increased awareness that the "be strong" form of "motivation" provides no incentive to work harder than the minimum required to avoid punishment and discharge. Under these conditions employees will probably dislike work, which, if workers are not unionized, can lead to slowdowns, sabotage, and spoilage. Management will probably react by watching workers even more closely. This in turn will encourage the employees to try to outsmart the administration. Thus, a vicious circle is started with new restraints and new methods of evading them. Sooner or later such a circle will produce aggression, arguments, fights, and a general devastating effect on the entire organization.

## SUMMARY

In this chapter we considered the organizing process from the supervisor's point of view. Basically, organizing on the departmental level involves the same general steps as organizing the overall institution, that is, grouping activities or sub-departmentalizing, assigning specific tasks and duties, and delegating authority. The supervisor should supplement these steps, however, by designing an ideal organizational structure specifically for his or her particular department. Such a structure represents the way the supervisor would organize the unit if starting from scratch with ideal resources and personnel. In most cases, however, the supervisor comes into an existing department and cannot immediately implement an ideal organizational design. One reason may be that the available personnel do not fit into this model. What must be done instead is to plan changes or completely reorganize the department to make it come closer to the ideal. Such reorganization is a normal and important part of managerial life; however, it should not be done so frequently that it undermines the security and morale of employees. Organizational changes can be implemented either all at once or gradually, depending on the imminence of the need for them.

After reorganization has been accomplished or at least planned, the supervisor can proceed to delegate or re-delegate authority in accordance with the departmental structure. In a large or medium department the process of delegation will be like the one outlined in chapter 11—assigning duties, granting the authority to carry them out, and encouraging employees to accept responsibility for them. In a small department, the delegation of authority will take the form of developing a backstop, an understudy who can take over when the supervisor is not there. This is a long and tedious process because it involves careful development and progressively increasing delegations of authority. It is well worth the effort, since it will contribute to high motivation and morale among employees. Moreover, unless the supervisor does train someone to be the backstop and does grant authority to that person, the supervisor will not have created any organization. Then the department is bound to collapse if the supervisor is absent for any length of time or leaves the scene.

This decentralization of authority is not as easily achieved as it might seem. Management frequently runs into obstacles that must be overcome to achieve broad delegation. These obstacles may be caused by an authority hoarder somewhere down the line, a subordinate's reluctance to shoulder authority and responsibility, or the unavailability of suitable subordinates to whom authority can be delegated.

At some point in the organization further delegation of authority is not possible. This is at the interface between the supervisor and nonmanagerial employees as they go about performing their daily tasks. At this level, delegation of authority expresses itself in the practice of a general, or loose, type of supervision that involves giving employees a great amount of freedom in making decisions and determining how to do their jobs. In other words, general supervision is an application of Theory Y and not Theory X (see chapters 19 and 21). It enables the employees to use their own judgment, and, in so doing, they will receive greater satisfaction from their jobs. Such general supervision is probably also the best way to motivate employees, whereas dependence on the sheer weight of authority would normally bring about the least desirable results. Occasionally the manager must fall back on formal authority, but with the newer attitudes and expectations of our society, the general trend is toward more freedom and self-determination in management, as well as in other aspects of life.

# Committees as an Organizational Tool

## Chapter Objectives

After you have studied this chapter, you should be able to:

1. Explain the need for committees in today's organizational setting.
2. Describe the committee as a formal group with defined purposes and reporting relationships, created with authority and responsibility for work-related results.
3. Discuss the various types of committees and their functions.
4. Describe the benefits and limitations of committees.
5. Discuss the major considerations to bring about effective committee operation.
6. Discuss the importance of the conference leadership role played by the chairperson.

A committee is a formal group with defined purposes and relationships within an organization. For example, the healthcare center's board of directors has a permanent position, a defined structure, and purpose at the top of the management hierarchy. Although individual members may change, the nature of the group is stable.

We find committees, boards, task forces, commissions, and teams everywhere—in business, government, schools, churches, and certainly in healthcare organizations. An institution's growth in size and specialization makes its administration and coordination by the chief executive officer (CEO) and associates more and more difficult and, at the same time, more necessary. One method to cope with this difficulty is to establish committees and turn specific problems over to them.

Committees are an organizational tool that, if utilized properly, can be of great help in the smooth functioning of an enterprise. A *committee is a group of people who function collectively by working together,* whether their purpose is to make a decision, submit a recommendation, solve a problem, conduct an investigation, manage a government agency, or so forth. It differs from other units of management insofar as committee members normally have regular full-time duties in the organization and devote only part of their time to committee activities.

The amount of time management spends in committee activities is increasing. According to the *Successful Manager's Handbook,* managers spend between 25% and 75% of their working hours in group meetings.[1] There is definitely a

---

1.   Brian L. Davis, Lowell W. Hellervik, Carol J. Skube, Susan H. Gebelein, and James L. Sheard, Successful Manager's Handbook-Development Suggestions for Today's Managers *(Personnel Decisions, Inc. 1992) p. 101.*

growing emphasis on committee meetings within today's organizations. This is true for several reasons. First, since most enterprise activities have become more complex and specialized, there is a more urgent need for coordination and cooperation. Conferences and meetings have proved to be a good means of answering this need. Another reason for the emphasis on meetings is that administrators now understand the fact that people are more enthusiastic about carrying out directives and plans they have helped to devise rather than those handed down from above. Thus, committees are an additional means for effectively combining the formal and the acceptance theories of authority, giving employees more freedom, greater delegation of authority, and more motivation.

Although we often hear people complain that there are too many meetings and that they take up too much time, committees are still a widely used device in all organizations, especially in healthcare centers. They seem to have no substitutes. Without committee meetings, it would be almost impossible for an organization of any size to operate efficiently and effectively. Of the many ways of obtaining ideas and opinions on how to handle certain problems, there is really no better way than by holding a meeting. The real criticism of meetings is probably not that there are too many, but that the results produced often do not warrant the time and effort invested.

No doubt you have sometimes been annoyed at being tied up in a meeting in which the chairperson rambled along in all directions, without any purpose whatsoever. In the meantime, more important work accumulated on your desk. It is very likely that the chairperson had not properly prepared for the meeting, and that the performance did not increase your respect for his or her managerial ability. After an experience of this type, you can quickly see how important it is for supervisors to acquaint themselves with committee meetings and with committee or conference leadership techniques. In other words, supervisors should learn how to run committees well and how to obtain effective participation. Meetings will then become increasingly interesting and stimulating because the participants will have the satisfaction of knowing that the meeting is accomplishing something.

Therefore, all supervisors must familiarize themselves with the workings of a committee. There may be occasions when the supervisor will find it necessary to establish an intradepartmental or interdepartmental committee or to chair a committee. At other times, the supervisor may only be an ordinary member of the committee. Also, there will be many instances when the supervisor will have to act as a conference leader or chairperson of a committee made up only of department employees.

## THE NATURE OF COMMITTEES

### Definitions and Characteristics

A committee is a formal group of people with defined purposes and reporting relationships within the organization to whom certain matters have been committed. They meet for the purpose of discussing those matters that have been assigned to them.

Committees function collectively, and their members normally have other duties, making their committee work merely a part-time assignment. Because committees function only as a group, they differ considerably from other managerial devices.

Committees can be found at all organizational *levels,* and chances are that at some time a committee exists or existed for every organizational activity.

Committees can be in *line* or *staff capacities.* The committee works on the problem to which it is assigned. When a solution is reached, a committee that has line authority will make a decision. If the committee is acting in a staff capacity, however, it will merely make a recommendation after having analyzed and debated the problem.

Committees can be classified as *standing* or *temporary.* A standing committee has a formal, permanent place in the organization. Typically it deals with the same set of recurring issues on an ongoing basis. In a hospital, for instance, the quality assurance, surgical review, infection control, pharmacy and therapeutics, safety and new products, and many other committees would be considered standing committees. The nature and purpose of a permanent committee remain the same although the individual members may change. A temporary committee, on the other hand, is one that has been appointed for a particular short-term purpose, and will be dissolved as soon as it has accomplished its task. This type is also known as an *ad hoc* committee. At times, it is called a *task force* or a *team.*

## ■ Functions of Committees

### *The Committee as a Place to Inform or to Discuss*

Most committee meetings may be described as either informational or discussional. In an *informational meeting,* the leader or chairperson does most of the talking to present certain information and facts. Assume, for example, that a supervisor wants to make an announcement and a meeting is called as a substitute for posting a notice or speaking to each employee separately. It may be expensive to take the entire workforce away from the job, but, on the other hand, it guarantees that everyone in the department is notified of the subject at the same time. Such a meeting also gives subordinates a chance to ask questions and discuss the implications of the announcement. Care should be taken, however, that questions from participants are largely confined to further clarifications of the supervisor's remarks so that the meeting will not stray from its purpose.

In the *discussional meeting,* the chairperson encourages more participation of the members to secure their ideas and opinions. The supervisor could ask the individuals singly for suggestions, but it is probably better to call a meeting to allow them to make recommendations. Although it is up to the supervisor to make the final decision and to determine whether or not to incorporate some of the employees' suggestions, the employees will nevertheless derive great satisfaction from knowing that their ideas have been considered and may even be used. The employees will probably offer good suggestions and they will most likely implement them more enthusiastically if they participate in finalizing them. In this case the committee acted in a staff capacity.

The supervisor can also go beyond merely asking for suggestions. A meeting may be called for the sole purpose of having the employees of the department fully discuss and handle a problem themselves, that is, come up with their own decision. As discussed next, this involves using the committee as a sort of collective managerial decision maker.

### Decision-Making Committees

In addition to committees whose purpose is to spread information or merely discuss a matter and make recommendations, other committees are delegated formal authority to make decisions. Just as a supervisor can delegate decision-making authority to an individual subordinate, so can a committee be formed and authority delegated to the group to decide on a solution to a problem. In these instances the committee has decision-making power, in other words, line authority.

Many questions in a healthcare center are of such magnitude and affect so many departments that it is far better to have the decision made by committee members representing several functions than by the administrator or one of the associate administrators alone. The same situation can exist within a department. For example, employees are frequently dissatisfied with the allocation of overtime and weekend work, regardless of the supervisor's efforts to be fair. Naturally the supervisor can make a decision for the employees on these matters, but it would be better if they could find a solution themselves. In such a case, management is not really concerned with precisely what decision is made so long as it falls within the limits set; for example, that the time allotted for overtime is not exceeded. By letting the group make this type of decision, it will come up with an acceptable solution. Even if such a solution is only adequate and not necessarily the best, it is still better if it is implemented by the group with greater enthusiasm than a "perfect" decision that meets with their resistance. There are many problems and areas in which management is not concerned with the details of the decision as long as it remains within certain predetermined boundaries.

## ■ Benefits of Committees

There is little doubt that a group of individuals exchanging opinions and experiences often comes up with a better answer than any one person thinking through the same problem alone. This is perhaps the major benefit of group discussion. Various people will bring to a meeting a wide range of experience, background, information, perspective, and ability far beyond that of an individual; and as new members join the group, they bring new ideas and perceptions. All of this would not be available if the subject had been committed to an individual decision maker. Indeed, many problems are so complicated that a single person could not possibly have all the necessary knowledge to come up with a wise solution. The forum for evaluating alternatives and ideas among several people will stimulate and clarify thinking.

Group deliberation can also be a real help in promoting coordination and co-operation. Members of the committee often become more considerate of the problems of other employees, supervisors, and of the administration. They become more aware of the advantages of and the need for working together to seek solutions. By being involved in the analysis, logic, rationale, and solution of a problem, individual members are more likely to accept and implement what has been decided. In reality, it matters little how much a person actually contributed to the plan, as long as this individual was a member of the committee and sat in on the meeting. Probably the most significant benefit of committees in health services organizations is promoting coordination and cooperation between the various units of the institution.

Committees have a number of additional benefits. They produce continuity in the organization; few committees replace all their members at the same time. Furthermore, they are a good environment for junior managers and executives to learn how decisions are made, absorb the philosophy and thinking of the hospital, and see how it functions. It provides a forum for potential leaders to be identified. Also it gives representatives from the various departments a chance to be heard and involved in the affairs of the organization.

## ■ Disadvantages of Committees

Despite all these beneficial features, the committee has often been abused. Sometimes committees are created to delay action, and many people have come to think of the committee as a debating society. Jokes about committees are numerous. They have been defined as a group "that keeps minutes but wastes hours," "where the unwilling appoint the unfit to do the unnecessary," "where the camel is a horse designed by a committee," and so forth. Remarks are often made that there are meetings all day long without leaving any time to get the work done. Indeed, one of the most often voiced complaints about committees is that they are exceedingly *time consuming*. This is true, since each member is entitled to have his or her say, and often certain individuals carry on too long about how valid their points are.

In addition to their cost in terms of time, committees also cost *money*. It is clear that time spent in committee meetings is not spent otherwise. Thus, every hour taken up by a meeting costs the institution. Furthermore, there might be expenses involved for travel and for the preparation of meetings.

Another shortcoming of committees is that there are limitations to the *sense of responsibility* that they evoke. When a problem is submitted to a committee, it is submitted to a group and not to individuals. Responsibility does not weigh as heavily on the group's shoulders as it would on an individual's shoulders. The committee's problems become everybody's responsibility, which in reality means they are nobody's responsibility. It is difficult to criticize the committee as a whole, or any single member, if the solution proves to be wrong, since each person may be quick to say that the "committee" made the decision. Members are willing to settle for less than the best solutions and blame the committee if the solution does not work out. The thinning out of responsibility is natural, and there is no way to avoid it.

The dangers of a *weak compromise decision* and *tyranny of the minority* are other shortcomings of committees. It has often become a tradition to reach decisions of unanimity based on politeness, cooperative spirit, mutual respect, and other considerations; however, this often leads to committee action that is a weak, watered-down, undesirable compromise, frequently using the lowest common denominator instead of the optimum solution. Also, in their efforts for unanimous or nearly unanimous conclusions, committees may be tyrannized by a minority or a dominant individual who holds out as long as possible. Finally, the majority might allow itself to be dominated by such a minority or a dominant personality because of lack of time, interest, or sense of responsibility. This may even lead to a strain in working relationships outside of the committee.

Another danger is that committee members may become victims of the *groupthink* phenomenon. Groupthink is a way of thinking in which one's true deliberations are dominated by a desire to concur with the group at any expense. Under this influence, the group is likely to make decisions that are not in the best interest of the organization in order to avoid conflict and dissent.

## THE EFFECTIVE OPERATION OF A COMMITTEE

Most healthcare facility administrations have established a number of committees, since ultimately, they will contribute to the smooth functioning of today's sophisticated organizational climate. A number of these committees exist to fulfill the requirements of the Joint Commission on Accreditation of Healthcare Organizations or other accrediting agencies, such as the National Committee on Quality Assurance.

Therefore, supervisors must familiarize themselves with the means for ensuring effective committee operation and conference leadership. It is not easy to make committee meetings and conferences a success because the goals are numerous and difficult to achieve. As we have already indicated, the goals of committee meetings are: (1) to come up with the best suggestions or solutions for the problem under consideration; (2) to arrive at suggestions or solutions with a majority or, ideally, unanimity or consensus; and (3) to accomplish objectives in the shortest time. It is a challenge for any committee to fulfill these goals, but the task will be made easier if the following discussion is used as a guide for effective committee operation and conference leadership.

### ■ Scope, Functions, and Authority of the Committee

The first thing a committee must have is a mandate; it must know its scope and functions to operate effectively. The executive establishing the committee must define the subjects to be covered and the functions that the committee is expected to fulfill; there must be a description of its job. It must also be stated how the committee relates to other units within the organization. This will prevent the committee from floundering and will enable the manager to check on whether it is meeting the expectations.

In addition to its functions and scope, the degree of authority conferred on the committee must be specified. (See example below.) As briefly mentioned before, it must be clearly stated whether the committee is to serve in an advisory (staff) capacity or decision-making (line) capacity. For example, in many hospitals the human research committee (sometimes referred to as the investigational review board) has line authority to make decisions as to whether a proposed research project should be approved or not. In reaching the decision, this committee, guided by federal rules and regulations governing human experimentation issued by the U.S. Department of Health and Human Services and the Federal Drug Administration, clearly has line authority. On the other hand, in most hospitals the medical executive committee acts in an advisory (staff) capacity when it deals with a physician's or surgeon's application for hospital privileges. This committee simply makes a recommendation to the board of directors, and they will decide. In such an instance, the medical executive committee clearly acts as a staff committee.

For a formal, standing committee, all such information should be set down in writing in the organizational manual.

Documents stating all this information for the various committees are also usually required by the Joint Commission on Accreditation of Healthcare Organizations. For a temporary committee, scope, functions, and authority must also be explicitly stated but perhaps not so formally. It is extremely important that an

---

*PQN Medical Policy & Peer Review Committee*

**Criteria for Physician Committee Members and Committee Composition**

Each physician appointed to this committee must have an initial Health Advantage (HA) medical efficiency estimate of at least 80%.

Committee members and the physician Committee Chairman are appointed by the Chairman of the HMO Partners (HMOP) Board of Directors.

This physician committee is composed of nine (9) Partners in Quality physicians representing a cross section of physician specialties and Central Region geographic areas.

At least six (6) committee physicians must be present in order for the committee to make recommendations.

**Health Advantage Medical Policy**

The PQN Medical Policy & Peer Review Committee will recommend to the Health Advantage Executive Committee (HMOP Board of Directors) medical policy intended to promote high-quality, efficient medical care.

HA Medical Policy is used *both* in determining medical benefits payable to HA members and as criteria in retrospectively estimating an individual physician's medical efficiency displayed in medical practice patterns observed through data-based physician profile reports, focused medical chart audits, and all other relevant information from other sources.

In formulating Health Advantage medical policy, there will often be preliminary review and full development of medical policy issues by ad hoc Specialty Physician committees composed of PQN Specialty physicians. These ad hoc committees will recommend medical policy to the PQN Medical Policy & Peer Review Committee.

(box continues on page 212)

---

**PQN Medical Efficiency Estimates & QIS Score Based (FFS) Physician Reimbursement**

This committee will become familiar with all aspects of PQN retrospective medical efficiency estimates and recommend various improvements likely to improve the accuracy of medical efficiency estimates.

The Chairman of the PQN Medical Policy & Peer Review Committee will recommend to the HA Executive Committee "best estimates" of medical efficiency ratings (QIS Scores) for all HA physicians.

These QIS Scores, when approved by the HA Executive Committee, will then be the basis for HA physician reimbursement. The committee is also asked to address other issues touching on the terms of an individual physician's participation in the various HA physician networks serving various HA product lines and membership groups.

Any changes in an individual HA physician's QIS Score will also be recommended to the HA Executive Committee by the PQN Medical Policy & Peer Review Committee.

**Committee Meetings: Time, Place, and Minutes**

The PQN Medical Policy & Peer Review Committee will meet as often as needed to accomplish the work of the committee but no less frequently than monthly.

Committee members will be reimbursed for each meeting plus any travel expense.

The place of meetings will be the HMOP Board Room unless otherwise determined by the committee.

The Minutes of the committee meetings will be prepared by HMOP staff and approved/signed by the Committee Chairman.

The Chairman of the PQN Medical Policy & Peer Review Committee will typically present the recommendations of the committee to the Health Advantage Executive Committee (or full Board of Directors).

*Courtesy of Health Advantage/Arkansas Blue Cross Blue Shield, Little Rock, Arkansas*

---

ad hoc committee only be established for a subject worthy of group consideration. If a topic can be handled by one person or over the phone, there is no need to establish a committee.

## ■ Composition of the Committee

Since the quality of committee work is only as good as its members, care should be exercised in choosing people to serve on committees. Members should be capable of expressing and defending their views, but they should also be willing to see the other party's point of view and be able to integrate their thinking with that of the other members. If possible, members should be from approximately the same organizational rank so that they can contribute freely without the complications of a direct superior-subordinate relationship. If committee members are chosen from different departments, the problems of rank are more easily overcome. Sometimes the composition of a committee is dictated by outside regulations.

The committee device is a good opportunity for bringing together the representatives of several different interest groups. Specialists of different departments and activities can be brought together in such a way that all concerned parties are properly represented. This will result in balanced group integration and deliberation. The various representatives will then be assured that their interests have been heard and considered. Administration should see that this concern with proper representation is not carried too far. It is more essential to appoint capable members to a committee than merely representative members. The ideal solution is to have a capable member from each pertinent activity on the committee.

## ■ Size of the Committee

No definite figure can be given as to the ideal size of a committee for effective operation. The best that can be said is that the committee should be large enough to provide for thorough group deliberation and broad resources of information. It should not be so large, however, that it will be unwieldy and unusually time consuming. Usually smaller committees with about four to ten members seem to work best. If the nature of the subject under consideration requires a very large committee, it might be wise to form subcommittees that will consider the various aspects of the problem. Then the entire committee can meet to hear subcommittee reports and decide on a final answer.

## ■ Effective Conference Leadership

Since the success of any meeting will depend largely on the chairperson's ability to handle it, he or she must be familiar with effective *conference* or *committee leadership* techniques to guide the meeting to a satisfactory conclusion. The individual members of a committee undoubtedly bring to the meeting their individual patterns of behavior and points of view. The chairperson must know how to fuse the individual viewpoints and attitudes so that teamwork will develop for the benefit of the group. It will take considerable skill, time, and patience on the chairperson's part to create a closely knit group out of a diverse membership, but this is generally the best way to achieve integrated group solutions. Let us look more carefully at the chairperson's role.

### *Adequate Preparation*

Successful committee work requires good preparation. First, the chairperson must carefully outline the strategy and establish an agenda before the meeting. He or she should list the discussion topics in the proper sequence, and decide how long the meeting will last. The chairperson may even want to establish, for his or her own guidance, an approximate time limit for each discussion item to ensure better control of the situation. If possible, the agenda should be distributed to the members before the meeting so that they can better prepare themselves for the coming discussion.

Furthermore, additional background information should be gathered either by the chairperson, the committee's own staff, or by the organization's staff services. This information should be distributed to the members before the meeting for their perusal and study. Meetings should be planned far enough in advance to give the members adequate notice and time to review any materials that will be discussed. Written minutes of the previous meeting should be sent along for review and approval. All this preparation allows the committee members to minimize conflicting responsibilities since they often serve on several committees.

## The Role of the Chairperson

The chairperson is the most important member of the committee. This person is expected to play and succeed in two roles: (1) to bring about the fulfillment of the task, and (2) build and maintain successful group interaction. Since the committee is made up of individuals, great skill is required to help these individuals interact productively.

The first step, once the committee has convened, is to ask someone to volunteer to be the recorder. Next, the chairperson needs to help the members agree on the nature of the problem under discussion so that everybody understands the issues. Too often people think first of how a new proposition will affect themselves and their own working environment, which can lead to unnecessary friction in a committee setting. Also, people tend to see the same "facts" differently. Words can mean different things to different people. Thus, the chairperson has to find out what the participants *think* the issues are in order to learn whether or not they understand the issues as they *actually* are. Remember, don't compete with members. Give their ideas precedence over yours.

Finding out everyone's interpretation of the issues however, is easier said than done. A frequent comment about committees is that the issues on the conference table are really not as difficult to deal with as the people around the table. Individuals at a meeting will often react toward each other rather than toward their ideas. For instance, just because person A talks too much, everything he or she suggests may be rejected; B might automatically reject whatever someone else suggests; and C may be that member of the committee who never speaks. If you are running the meeting, listen to everyone. Paraphrase what participants have said when appropriate, but do not judge the merits of their comments. Avoid putting anyone on the defensive. As the meeting leader you must assume that everyone's ideas have value.

It is the chairperson's job to minimize these personality differences by using the legitimate tools of parliamentary procedure. Attempt to control the dominant people without alienating them. The speaking time of each participant can be limited so that one person will not monopolize the entire meeting. Also, one should be especially careful to call on people who seldom speak. Sooner or later, with the help of such leadership techniques, the committee will start reacting toward the meeting content and not the individuals around the table. For a meeting to be successful, the various members need to forget about their personalities and outside allegiances, and work together as a team toward a meaningful solution of the problem at hand. In all this, the chairperson plays a critical mediating role.

The quality of the solution will also depend to some extent on the amount of time spent in reaching it. Too much haste will probably not produce the most desirable solution. On the other hand, most meetings have a time limit. If they do not, the members become bored and frustrated. Remember, as the chairperson that your interest and alertness are contagious. It is the chairperson's job to give every member a chance to participate and voice his or her suggestions and opinions. This is especially important when the committee members are also expected to execute the decisions they make. Then the chairperson may need to persuade the minority to go along with the decision of the majority. On other occasions, the majority might have to be persuaded to make concessions to the minority. All this takes time and may result in a compromise that does not necessarily represent the best possible solution. If the solution has been arrived at democratically, however, the chairperson's leadership abilities will have been demonstrated, and the major purpose of the meeting, finding a solution, will have been accomplished.

It is important to keep all participants informed about the committee's actions. Keep notes during the meeting on a flip chart or board that everyone can see. This helps members to keep track of what they have discussed and what has been decided. At the end of each meeting, distribute copies of the minutes and decisions made at the meeting with a reminder of the next meeting and any assignments made during the meeting.

## *The Chairperson's Opinions*

It has often been stated that the function of a good chairperson is to help the members of the group reach their own decisions, to work as a catalyst to bring out the ideas present among the committee members. If the chairperson *expresses his or her own views,* the members of the committee may hesitate to argue further to express their opinions, especially if they disagree. This is even more likely to occur if the chairperson also happens to be their boss or holds a position higher up in the hierarchy. On the other hand, in many situations it would be unwise and completely unrealistic for the chairperson not to express his or her views. This individual may have some factual knowledge or sound opinion, and the value of the deliberations would be lessened if these were left unknown to the members of the committee.

On the whole, it is best for the chairperson to express his or her opinions and, at the same time, let it be known that they are subject to constructive criticism and suggestions. After all, silence on the leader's part may be interpreted to mean that he or she cannot make a decision or does not want to do so for fear of assuming responsibility. On certain occasions, however, the chairperson must use sensitive judgment as to whether or not or to what extent his or her opinions should be expressed.

### The Leadership Style

There also is the question of how much of a *formal leadership role* the chairperson should display. The variations of this role can run from the one extreme of an autocratic dictator to the other extreme of simply a moderator. At times it may be necessary for even a very permissive chairperson to use tight control over the meeting, although on most occasions the loosest sort of control will be employed. Indeed, it has often been found that if the group of participants consists of mature people, little or no control and formal chairpersonship are really necessary.

Although this may be true for some higher-level committee meetings, on the lower levels the need frequently exists for a stable structure and strong leadership from a chairperson. If the group has a formally elected or appointed chairperson, the members will naturally look to that person to keep the meeting moving along so that it will come to an efficient conclusion. Under most conditions, the formal leadership of the chairperson is necessary to ensure that group decision making is effective. If the chairperson lacks leadership ability, some other member of the committee will rise to be the *de facto* chairperson. This is a natural event in group dynamics.

### Setting Up the Meeting

At least initially, attempt to set a time when all the members are available. Once the committee has met several times at a consistent time and its schedule is established, members should take it upon themselves to book the time in their schedules to attend future meetings. Always allow sufficient time between meetings to prepare for the next meeting and gather any information required.

Select a location that is convenient to all attendees. It should be comfortable and have the facilities required to conduct the meeting effectively, such as a white board, flip chart, etc. Set up the room to maximize participation. Either set up the room around a table or in a semi-circle so all participants can see each other and hear the comments shared.

## ■ The Agenda and Task Control

Working with a *well-prepared agenda* is the best way to achieve task control, that is, keeping meeting members from too much digression. Although the agenda designs the overall strategy and sequence, it must not be so rigid that there is no means for adjusting it. The chairperson should apply the agenda with a degree of flexibility so that if a particular subject requires more attention than originally anticipated, the time allotted to some other topic can be reduced. In other words, staying close to the agenda should not force the chairperson to be too quick to rule people out of order. What seems irrelevant to him or her may be important to some of the other committee members. Some irrelevancies at times actually help create a relaxed atmosphere and relieve tension that has built up. Since it is the chairperson's job to keep the meeting moving along toward its goal, it is a good idea to pause at various points during the meeting to consult the agenda and remind the group of what has been accomplished and what still remains to be discussed. A good chairperson will learn when the opportune time has arrived to summarize one point and to move on to the next item in the agenda.

The agenda should state the purpose of the meeting and any specific goals that need to be achieved. It should also state the start and stop time with a stop time that is natural, such as lunch or end of shift. Occasionally, a meeting may not progress as planned. If the meeting does not appear that it will end as scheduled, ask the group if they wish to extend this meeting or table discussion of the remaining topics. If the latter is chosen, you as the chairperson must make sure these topics appear on the next agenda. To assist the members and the chair to remain on schedule, some chairpersons establish time limits for the topics. Using the agenda as a guide and referencing it often will keep the group aware of the time and their progress.

## THE COMMITTEE MEETING

Now that we are familiar with some of the guidelines for effective committee operation, we are ready to examine how these guidelines can be applied in a typical committee meeting. In other words, we want to see how a diverse group of people can, with the help of an effective conference leader, hold a meaningful discussion and arrive at satisfactory answers to the problems under consideration.

### General Participation in the Discussion

Always start the meeting on time. After a few introductory remarks and social pleasantries, the chairperson should make an initial statement of the problem to be discussed. This will open up an opportunity for all members of the meeting to participate freely. Any member should be able to bring out those aspects of the problem that seem important to him or her, regardless of whether or not they seem important to everyone else. The chairperson should facilitate the discussion to eventually get to the relevant points.

There are always some members at the meeting who talk too much and others who do not talk enough. One of the chairperson's most difficult jobs is to encourage the latter to speak up and to keep the former from holding the floor for too long. There are various ways and means to do this. For example, after a long-winded speaker has had enough opportunity to express his or her opinions, it may be wise not to recognize that member again, giving someone else the chance to speak. It might also help to ask him or her to please keep the remarks brief or to arrange the seating at the conference table so that it is easy not to recognize his or her request to have the floor. Most of the time, however, the other members of the committee will find subtle ways of getting past those members who have too much to say.

This does not mean that all members of the meeting must participate equally. Some people know more about a given subject than others, and some have stronger feelings about an issue than others. The chairperson must take such factors into consideration but should still stimulate overall participation. The chairperson should accept everyone's contribution without judgment and create the impression that everyone should participate. Controversial questions may have to be asked merely to get the discussion going. Once participation has started, the chairperson should continue to throw out provocative, open-ended questions that ask why, who, what, where, and when. Questions that can be answered with a simple yes or no should be avoided.

Another technique that the chairperson can use is to start at one side of the conference table and ask each member in turn to express thoughts on the problem. The major disadvantage of this technique is that instead of participating in the discussion spontaneously, members will sit back and wait until called on. The skilled chairperson, however, will watch the facial expressions of the people in the group. This may very well provide a clue as to whether someone has an idea but is afraid to speak up. Then a special effort should be made to call on that person.

If a meeting involves many participants, it may be advisable for the chairperson to break it up into small groups, typically known as *buzz sessions.* Each of the subgroups will hold its own discussion and report back to the meeting after a specified period. In this way those people who hesitate to say anything in a larger group will be more or less forced to participate and express their opinions. Buzz sessions are usually advisable whenever there are more than twenty or so participants.

In using all these techniques to encourage general participation in the discussion, the chairperson should try to stick to the agenda and see that the discussion is basically relevant. Sometimes a chairperson who is inexperienced at holding meetings is so anxious to have someone say something that much discussion for discussion's sake will occur. This usually is not desirable because it confuses the issues and delays the even more important decision-making phase of the meeting.

## ■ Group Decision Making

Once a problem has been considerably narrowed down and understood in generally the same sense by all members of the group, try to get to the facts as objectively as possible. Only by looking at all the relevant facts will the group be able to suggest alternative solutions. The chairperson knows that the best solution can only be as good as the best alternative considered. Therefore, the members at the meeting should be urged to contribute as many alternatives as they can possibly think of so that no solution is overlooked. The chairperson may have the members brainstorm, a highly interactive approach. Brainstorming encourages the participants to be spontaneous, creative, and have complete freedom of expression, regardless of how far out the suggestion is.

The next step is to evaluate the alternative solutions and discuss the advantages and disadvantages of each. In so doing, the field can eventually be narrowed down to two or three alternatives on which general agreement can be reached. The committee members, by unanimous consent, can probably eliminate the other alternatives. The remaining options must be discussed thoroughly to bring about a solution. The chairperson should try to play the role of a middle person, or mediator, by working out a solution that is acceptable to all members of the group.

Often the best procedure is to find a solution that is a synthesis of all the important points raised by the members. Throughout this process the chairperson has the difficult job of helping the minority to save face. It is easier to placate the minority if the final decision of the group incorporates something of each person's idea so that everyone has a partial victory. This can be a long and tedious process, and as we have said, such a compromise may not always be the strongest solution.

Sometimes, however, the group may not be able to reach a compromise or to come to any decision on which the majority agrees. This happens more often when the group is hostile. In such a situation the chairperson has to find out what is bothering the group and discuss it. Committee participants may think first of what is objectionable about a new idea rather than think of its desirable features. Discussing such objections may dispel unwarranted fears and may allow participants to see the positive aspects of a certain alternative. Also, the objections may be strong enough to void the proposition. In any case, the group must have a chance to voice negative feelings before a positive consensus can be reached.

## ◼ Taking a Vote

The chairperson is often confronted with the problem of whether a vote should be taken, or whether the committee should keep on working until the group reaches a final unanimous agreement, regardless of how long it would take. Offhand, many people would say that voting is a democratic way to make decisions. Voting does accentuate the differences among the members, however, and once a person has made a public commitment to a position by voting, it is often difficult to change his or her mind and still save face. Also, if this individual is a member of the losing minority, he or she cannot be expected to carry out the majority decision with great enthusiasm. Therefore, whenever possible, it is better not to take a formal vote but to work toward a roughly unanimous agreement.

As pointed out previously, one of the disadvantages of reaching a unanimous conclusion is that it can cause a serious delay in the meeting. Also, the price of unanimity is often a solution that is reduced to a lower common denominator and may not be as ingenious and bold as it would have been otherwise. The situation and the magnitude of the problem involved will determine whether or not unanimity is worth this price. In most instances it is not as difficult as one might think to come up with a unanimous decision.

The skilled chairperson can usually sense what the members are feeling, and all he or she needs to say is that such and such a solution seems to be the consensus of the group. At this point, especially in a small meeting, the group can probably dispense with parliamentary procedure and a formal vote. In a large meeting, of course, unanimity may be an impossible goal, and decisions should be based on majority rule.

### ■ Follow-Up of Committee Action

Regardless of whether a committee was acting merely to come up with a recommendation or whether it has final decision-making authority, its results need a follow-up. After the chairperson has reported the committee's findings to the superior who originally channeled the subject to the committee, it is the superior's duty to keep the chairperson or the committee posted about what action has been taken. It is common courtesy to give the committee some explanation. Inadequate statements or no statements at all will cause the committee to lose interest in its work. When the committee has had authority to make a final decision, then the problem of carrying out the decision usually belongs to the committee itself. The chairperson will generally oversee this, or the particular executive who normally deals with the subject matter may execute the decision. In any event, the committee members must be kept informed as to what has happened.

---

**SUMMARY**   Every supervisor has probably been involved in committees either as a member or as an organizer. Committees have become an extremely important device for augmenting the organizational structure and the functioning of an enterprise. They allow the enterprise to adapt to increasing complexity without a complete reorganization. They permit a group of people to function collectively in areas a single individual could not handle. The advantages of committees are offset to a certain extent by their limitations and shortcomings. Despite the disadvantages and other criticisms leveled against committees, they can be of great value if properly organized and led.

Because today's organizations are larger and more complex, committees are more necessary. Thus it is essential for the supervisor to familiarize himself or herself with the workings of a committee. Committee meetings are called either to disseminate information or to discuss a topic. If discussion is involved, a distinction should be made between whether the committee is to arrive at a final decision on the question under discussion and take action based on this decision, or whether it is to merely make recommendations to the line manager who appointed the committee. A committee can be in a line or staff capacity.

Regardless of the committee's purpose, it is likely that group deliberation will produce more satisfactory and acceptable conclusions than one formally handed down from above. Decisions will be carried out with more enthusiasm if members of the organization have had a role in making them or in making recommendations. For group decisions and recommendations to be of high quality, however, it is necessary that the committee members be carefully selected. In the composing of a committee, one must represent as many interested parties as possible. The people chosen as representatives should be capable of presenting their views and integrating their opinions with those of others. As to the size of a committee, there should be enough members to permit thorough deliberations, but not so many as to make the meetings cumbersome.

In addition to these factors, the success of committee deliberations depends largely on effective committee or conference leadership. This means that the chairperson's familiarity with effective group work will make the difference between productive and wasteful committee meetings. The chairperson's job is to produce the best possible solution in the shortest amount of time and, it is hoped, with unanimity. In trying to achieve these goals, the chairperson is constantly confronted with the problem of running the meeting either too tightly or too loosely. Control that is too tight may frustrate the natural development of ideas, may create conclusions before the committee has considered all alternatives, and in general, may create resentment. On the other hand, if the control is too loose, members of the meeting may feel aimless and confused.

The chairperson will have to depend on his or her perception of the "mood and climate of the meeting" to know exactly how to lead it and bring it to a successful conclusion. Thus, the chairperson will have to sense when there has been enough general participation in the discussion, when alternative solutions have been properly evaluated, and when and if a vote is necessary to arrive at a group decision. In all these matters, the conference leadership abilities of the chairperson will be of utmost importance.

The question of superiority of either group or individual decision making is a difficult issue. When questions involve time and technical constraints, individual decision making is probably superior to group decision making. But when problem solving calls for a diversity of view points, skills, and insights, group decisions are usually superior. The same is true when broad-based acceptance is needed.

# 15 Informal Organizational Structures

## Chapter Objectives

After you have studied this chapter, you should be able to:

1. Discuss the origins of the informal organization that exists apart from the formal organization.
2. Describe how informal small groups evolve from personal interaction, sentiments, and social activities of employees.
3. Describe the benefits and costs of the informal organization for its members and the power it can exert on the functioning of the formal organization.
4. Discuss how small informal groups have the potential to develop into an informal organization with status positions, standards, norms, and sanctions.
5. Discuss the impact that informal organization and its informal leaders can have on the supervisory position.
6. Suggest ways the supervisor can react to informal groups and their leaders in order to improve relationships to achieve increased organizational effectiveness.

In almost all enterprises, informal structures arise evolving from personal interactions, social activities, sentiments, friendship, common interests, and needs. This invisible, shadow organization produces intricate patterns of influence beyond the lines of the formal organization. These informal structures are not written down, and do not have manuals, charts, or titles. But they are very influential on the functioning of the formal organization and can be supportive of or disruptive to management authority.

Whenever people work together, informal relationships exist and become a powerful source of influence on the formal organization. The formal task structure, goals, and functioning of the organization are affected by a social subsystem known as the *informal organization*. Early scholars maintained that an inherent conflict exists between the goals of the formal organization and informal relationships. Today we know that both formal and informal relationships are essential subsystems of a complex system and that the informal relationships help the functioning of the formal organization by providing individual satisfaction and group morale, which otherwise would be lacking.

The informal organization found in almost all enterprises is closely related to the workings of groups, committees, and group participation, but it is quite different in origin. The informal organization is a powerful source of influence that interacts with and modifies the formal organization. Although many managers would like to conveniently overlook its existence, they will readily admit that to understand the nature of organizational life fully, it is necessary to "learn the ropes" of the informal organization. In almost every institution such an informal structure will develop. It reflects the spontaneous efforts of individuals and groups to influence their working conditions. For example, two or three people who do not work in the same area may meet daily for lunch because they enjoy each other's company, or people may join together because they have similar ideas about how a task could be improved upon and they want to approach their supervisor to discuss changing it. Whenever people associate with each other, social relationships and groupings are bound to come about. The informal organization can make a positive contribution to the smooth functioning of the enterprise or can be disruptive. Therefore, the manager must understand its workings, respect it, and even nurture it.

To be more specific, informal structures arise from the social interactions of people as they associate with each other. Such interactions may be accidental or incidental to organized activities, or they may arise from personal desire or gregariousness. At the heart of informal organization are people and their relationships, whereas at the heart of formal organization are the organizational structure and the delegation of authority. Management can create or rescind a formal organizational structure that it has designed, but it cannot rescind the informal organization because management did not establish it. As long as people work together in a department, there will be an informal organization consisting of the informal groupings of employees.

## THE INFORMAL GROUP

At the base of all informal organization is the small group, consisting of a few people (five for example) or a few more who share physical proximity and contact; this brings about an interplay of sentiments and interaction sharing ideas, feelings, and opinions. The group interacts regularly to accomplish a common goal or purpose. The first question that comes to mind is why people join such groups. We may wonder what advantages they gain from groups, since they are already members of a department where their duties are specifically assigned, channels of communication exist, a line of authority has been established, and they are a significant part of a formal organizational structure. The answer to this question is that employees have certain needs that they would like to have satisfied, but apparently the formal organization leaves unsatisfied. One of the needs is for *achievement,* and the other is for *emotional satisfaction.* People have a basic need to associate with others in groups small enough to permit intimate, direct, and personal contact among individuals. The satisfactions derived from these types of relationships generally cannot be obtained from working within a large organization. Thus, the small group provides the individual with satisfactions that are uniquely different from those that can be obtained from any other source.

## ■ Benefits Derived from Groups

People join groups for various reasons, including interpersonal attraction, group goals, group activities, and social needs. First, group participation provides a sense of *satisfaction.* An individual in a group is usually surrounded by others who share similar values. This reinforces his or her own value system and interests, and gives him or her confidence, since it is always more comfortable to be among people who think along the same lines. There is also the need for *friendship and companionship* that the group fulfills. The employee needs and enjoys the social contact with fellow workers, sharing experiences, joking, and finding a sympathetic listener. The group thus will fulfill the need for *belonging,* the need to associate with others who have similar attitudes, personalities, economic standing, and the same purposes and goals.

Another need satisfied by belonging to a small group in many instances is the need for *balance and protection.* Social interaction may balance routine and tedious work, but a small group offers protection from what the members may think of as an imposition or an encroachment by management, such as protection against increased output standards, changes in working conditions, or reduced benefits. We are all familiar with the old saying, "there is strength in unity." In this respect the small group is a source of *security, support,* and *collective power.* Often when people enter an organization for the first time they are anxious. The surroundings are unfamiliar and much uncertainty exists. When several people are in the same circumstance, a small group may form on this basis alone, providing temporary support in an unfamiliar environment. Whenever people sense the need for protection, they form small groups.

An additional need that a small group fulfills is *achieved status,* because the group enables an employee to belong to a distinct little organization that is more or less exclusive. It also gives the individual an opportunity for self-expression, and a kind of audience of sympathetic listeners. Another reason why people join groups is to have access to the informal communications network and to secure *information* to reduce their uncertainties. The grapevine works very effectively in small groups, providing speedy, although at times inaccurate, information. Groups tend to form around an individual who seems to be the focal point in a communications network. An individual who has information is able to satisfy the communication needs of others, even though the information transmitted may be false or distorted.

In addition to these emotional needs, there exists the need for achievement, for getting things done. Groups are a means of getting a *task* accomplished by interacting, communicating, and collaborating. Informal groups help employees to accomplish tasks that may be impossible to accomplish alone. They also serve to bring the goals of these tasks more into the realm of the employee. The objectives and goals of the formal organization may appear remote and meaningless to the average employee. It is much simpler to identify with the objectives and goals of one's immediate work group. Often employees will readily forego some of their own goals and replace them with the goals of the group.

It is important for the supervisor of a department to be aware of all these needs employees want satisfied. If the supervisor understands the many reasons why employees tend to join informal groups, an attempt can be made in daily supervision to use these groups constructively rather than to be suspicious of them or try to destroy them.

## INFORMAL GROUPS AND THE INFORMAL ORGANIZATION

Small informal groups, as we said, are at the basis of informal organization, and all small informal groups have the potential to become informal organizations existing in and interacting with the formal structure of the institution. In every organization, unless it consists of only a few individuals, there is an informal, also known as an invisible, organization; as stated before, it does not have a printed chart, written manuals, written policies, procedures, and so forth. Also, the informal organization probably differs from the lines of the formal organization, but it is a functioning entity. (See figure 15.1.)

The informal organization develops when small groups acquire a more or less distinct structure and a set of norms and standards, as well as ways to exert pressure for conformity and procedure, to invoke sanctions to ensure conformity to the norms. The informal organizational structure is determined largely by the different status positions that people within the small group hold.

### ■ Status Positions

Generally, there are four status positions: the group's *informal leader,* the members of the *primary group,* the members who have only *fringe status,* and those who have *out status.* (See figure 15.2.) The informal leader of the small group is the person around whom the primary members of the group cluster; their association is close, and their interaction is intense. This is normally considered the small nucleus group of which newcomers would like to become members.

These newcomers are usually new employees of the department. They remain on the fringe of the group while they are being evaluated by the small nucleus for acceptance or rejection. Eventually these individuals will either move into the nucleus, are gradually integrated and become bona fide members of the small group, or they will move into the outer shell because they have been rejected.

The people in the outer shell are still a part of the department, even though they have not been accepted as members of the core group. Such rejection, however, can have serious behavioral effects, especially if a person strongly wishes to belong to the nucleus group. This is true because in essence the group is a system of interaction that causes members to modify their own behavior and to significantly affect the behavior of persons in the fringe shell or the outer shell. If the rejection is mutual, the person in the outer shell can survive very well on his or her own.

Although leadership will be discussed fully in chapter 21, a few words should be said at this time about *informal leadership.* The person who plays the role of the informal leader is usually the dynamic force of the group. As with the

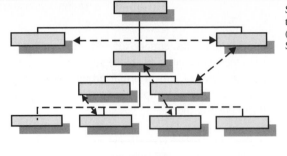

Social relationship:
the special friendships in the organization.
("I'll talk to my friend Jane in purchasing.
She"ll know what to do.")

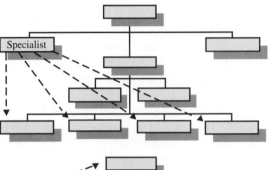

Specialist

Functional relationships:
the direct relationship between specialists
and operating departments. ("You have to
see someone in Personnel for approval to
take that course.")

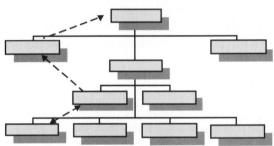

Decision relationships:
the flow of significant decisions in the
organization. ("Don't worry about Joe. He
doesn't get into this. Our next step is to
go topside.")

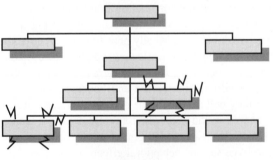

Power relationships:
the centers of power in the organization.
("Before you go any further, you'd better
clear that with Maria in production
planning.")

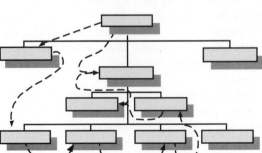

Communication relationships:
the route of telephone calls on a particular
matter. ("If we had to go through channels,
we'd never get anything done around here!")

**Figure 15.2** A model of informal relationships.

*Haimann, Theo. William G. Scott, and Patrick E. Connor,* Management, *Fifth Edition. Copyright © 1985 by by Houghton Mifflin Company. Adapted with permission.*

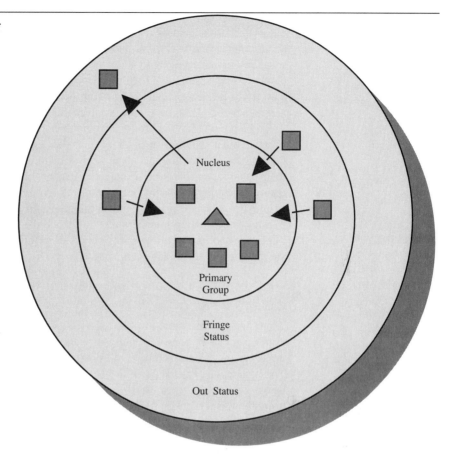

committee chairperson, this individual engages in leadership activities, crystallizes opinions, and sets objectives. This group leader is generally democratically chosen by the group. The leadership role is created by consensus. This person usually possesses communicative skills, sensitivity, and intelligence, and helps the members achieve their tasks and emotive needs. The informal leader gains status, although without rank, and satisfies the group members' need for a leader to whom they can turn for support. Occasionally one might find small groups in which the leadership is shared and in which different leaders perform different functions, sometimes only for a brief time. For example, one leader may deal with administration, whereas another may deal with the union, and another may try to maintain internal cohesiveness and morale. Most of the time, however, there is only one informal leader with whom the supervisor will have to deal.

## ■ Norms and Standards

Besides status positions, there are norms and standards that regulate group behavior. Norms are expectations about how members of the group ought to behave.

They define the boundaries between acceptable and unacceptable behavior. In addition to these standards for behavior between group members, norms relate to quality and quantity of work and to many other areas, such as honesty, loyalty, squealing to management about a coworker, or anything else the group deems important. Norms promoting high performance, creativity, and an honest day's work are clearly desirable, whereas, cheating, leaving work early, and limiting output are not beneficial. Norms of one group cannot be generalized to another group.

To be admitted to the group, the employee must be willing and eager to comply with such standards instead of his or her own. Since groups are capable of granting or withholding the advantages of membership, individuals must modify their behavior so that it corresponds to that of the group. This is why the informal organization has such a significant influence over the behavior and work of employees who are primary group members. In addition, the interactions between primary group members also influence the behavior of those who are in the fringe shell and even possibly someone in the outer shell, since all of them are members of the total system.

## ■ Sanctions

Along with norms, there must be an effective procedure for invoking sanctions if a group member does not conform to the standards set. If individuals violate group norms, group members will exert pressure for conformity to these norms. These sanctions can range from being elusive and evasive on the one hand, to being overt on the other. At first sanctions can be very mild; the group may try to bring the nonconformist back in line by friendly communication. If this does not produce the desired results, friendly comments may stop, and threats, ridicule, or possibly physical abuse may follow. The most powerful sanction is ostracism—rejection. Employees who consistently do not comply with the group's norms will soon be on the outside. Their life can then be made miserable, their work can be sabotaged, and eventually they may want to leave the institution completely. All these sanctions of the informal organization, whether subtle or strong, serve to see that group members adhere to the group's ideas of correct on-the-job behavior.

## ■ Additional Characteristics

One of the reasons people form small groups is the need for information to reduce their uncertainties. These groups provide their own unofficial channel of communication, the *grapevine,* and access to it. This manifestation of the informal organization has already been fully discussed in chapter 5. Briefly, again, the grapevine is the major connecting link of the informal organization, just as communication through regular channels serves to link the formal organizational structure. The informal organization influences the behavior of employees regardless of the status they occupy within the informal group. This is important for a supervisor to remember because one cannot hope to understand individual behavior without understanding the behavior of the organizational forces that shape it.

Another characteristic of the informal organization is inflexibility, especially *resistance to change.* It resists especially those changes that could be interpreted as a threat to the informal group. Over time, the small group has developed very satisfying social relationships, and any change that may challenge its equilibrium and stability will be greeted with resistance. This resistance can take the form of complaints, work slowdown, excessive absenteeism, and reduction in the quality of the job performed. It is essential for a supervisor to understand the dynamics of these types of group behavior in order to introduce change successfully. This is discussed further in chapter 19.

## INTERACTION BETWEEN INFORMAL AND FORMAL ORGANIZATIONS

Often it might appear that the informal organization makes the job of the supervisor more difficult. Because of the interdependence between informal and formal organizations, the attitudes, goals, norms, and customs of one affect the other. Informal organizations do frequently give life and vitality to the formal organization, but this is not always the case. Informal organizations can have either a constructive or hindering influence on the formal organization and on the realization of departmental objectives. The way the supervisor manages the informal structure will have much to do with whether that influence is positive or negative.

The supervisor must respect the informal organization for the power it has; it cannot be ignored, and attempts to suppress it should not be made. It is important for the supervisor to be aware that these informal groups are very strong, and they may often govern the behavior of employees to an extent that interferes with formal supervision. Sometimes it can even go so far that the pressure of the informal group frustrates the supervisor in carrying out objectives that the superior manager expects the supervisor to achieve. The wise supervisor, therefore, should make all possible efforts to gain the cooperation and goodwill of the informal organization and the informal leader, and to use them wherever possible to further the departmental objectives.

Both formal and informal relationships are parts of the system and they interact, each modifying the other. They may be mutually reinforcing or conflicting. The supervisor should remember that informal groups provide the satisfaction of some needs that the formal organization leaves unsatisfied. Informal relationships make a contribution to the organizational climate; they keep the organization flexible and can be a strong ally.

### ■ The Supervisor and the Informal Organization

One way the supervisor can put the informal organization to the best possible use is to let the employees know that its existence is accepted and understood. Such an understanding will enable the supervisor to group employees so that those most likely to comprise a good team will be working with each other on the same assignments. The supervisor's understanding of how the informal organization works will also help him or her avoid activities that would unnecessarily threaten or disrupt the informal group. The manager should do his or her utmost to integrate the interests of the informal organization with those of the formal organization.

The supervisor should exhibit this positive approach because he or she knows that there are positive attributes in a cohesive informal group. Morale is likely to be high, turnover and excessive absences tend to be low, and the members work smoothly as a team. This can make supervision much easier because the supervisor avoids hearing a lot of bickering; it can also ease the burden of communication, since the group provides its own effective, although informal, channels.

Supervisors who encourage informal group leaders and informal relationships are likely to make their own job easier by gaining allies. However, supervisors who suppress informal relationships risk creating enemies and retaliation. By integrating formal and informal organizations effectiveness is increased.

## Group Decision Making

A supervisor can do even more to bring out the positive aspects of informal groups if he or she shares the decision-making authority with them, that is, by practicing group decision making. When problem solving demands a diversity of viewpoints and skills, and when broad-based acceptance is needed, group decisions usually are superior. They enable the group to exercise control over their own activities and to make certain that all their interests are taken into account, with the result that no one comes out a loser. The group has a broader information base and a greater number of different approaches to the problem because of their different educational backgrounds, experiences, and perceptions. The group decision-making process also produces a broader understanding of the solution, which in turn brings increased acceptance and commitment. Thus, groups generally produce better decisions.

A popular group discussion and decision-making technique is brainstorming. According to GOAL/QPC[1] "this tool allows the group to expand their thinking to include all of the dimensions of a problem or solution. Brainstorming is used to help a group create as many ideas as possible in as short a time as possible.

Brainstorming can be used in two ways:

1. Structured: In this method, every person in a group must give an idea as their turn arises in the rotation or pass until the next round. It often forces even shy people to participate but can also create a certain amount of pressure to contribute.

2. Unstructured: In this method, group members simply give ideas as they come to mind. It tends to create a more relaxed atmosphere but also risks domination by the most vocal members.

In both methods the general "rules of the road" are the same:

- Never criticize ideas.
- Write on a flip chart or blackboard every idea. Having the words visible to everyone at the same time avoids misunderstandings and reminds others of new ideas.

---

1. GOAL/QPC, The Memory Jogger, A Pocket Guide of Tools for Continuous Improvement. *(13 Branch Street, Methuen, MA 01844), p. 69.*

- Everyone agrees on the question or issue being brainstormed. Write it down, too.
- Record on the flip chart in the words of the speaker; don't interpret.
- Do it quickly; 5–15 minutes works well."[1]

The next step in this approach is to determine which idea to work on. GOAL/QPC describes a commonly used technique known as the Nominal Group Technique (NGT).[2] (See page 232.)

Group problem solving has some shortcomings as well. Usually group decisions take longer. Often there is group pressure for conformity and consensus, possibly caused by one dominant individual; this at times may lower the quality of the decision, leading to undesirable compromised results. Furthermore, the danger exists that the group may become a victim of groupthink. This phenomenon, as discussed in chapter 15, is when the individuals lose track of the facts at hand and put the importance of the group's endeavor first. Although these are serious shortcomings, generally the advantages far outweigh them. (See figure 15.3.)

The supervisor should establish certain ground rules for a group decision-making process, otherwise, it could bring about opposite results. First, the supervisor must sincerely believe in group decision making and want it. Second, the topic must be clearly set. For instance, if the group is to arrange its own vacation schedule, it should be stated how many employees with a special skill must always be present, what the time limits are, and so forth. Third, it must be clear whether the group is merely asked for suggestions or whether

---

**Figure 15.3** Assets and liabilities of group decision making.

*"From INTRODUCTION TO ORGANIZATIONAL BEHAVIOR, 3rd Edition by Richard M. Steers. Copyright © 1988, 1984, 1981 Scott, Foresman and Company. Reprinted by permission of Addison-Wesley Educational Publishers, Inc."*

| Assets | Liabilities |
|---|---|
| ■ Groups can accumulate more knowledge and facts. | ■ Groups often work more slowly than individuals. |
| ■ Groups have a broader perspective and consider more alternative solutions. | ■ Group decisions involve considerable compromise that may lead to less than optimal decisions. |
| ■ Individuals who participate in decisions are more satisfied with the decision and are more likely to support it. | ■ Groups are often dominated by one individual or a small clique, thereby negating many of the virtues of group processes. |
| ■ Group decision processes serve an important communication function, as well as a useful political function. | ■ Overreliance on group decision making can inhibit management's ability to act quickly and decisively when necessary. |

---

2. *Ibid. pp. 70–71.*

### Nominal Group Technique (NGT)

When selecting which problems to work on and in what order, it often happens that the problem selected is that of the person who speaks the loudest or who has the most authority. This often creates a feeling in the team that *"their"* problem will never be worked on. This can lead to a lack of commitment to work on the problem selected, and the selection of the *"wrong"* problem in the first place. The **Nominal Group Technique** tries to provide a way to give everyone in the group an equal voice in problem selection. The steps in the process are as follows:

1. Have everyone on the team write (or say) the problem that he/she feels is most important. If members of the team do not write the problem out, you need to get them written on a flip chart or blackboard (or somewhere visible), as they are being communicated. If people do produce written problems, collect them when they are finished. Everyone may not feel comfortable writing, but it may make them feel safer talking about sensitive problems at the beginning.

2. Write the problem statements where the team can see them.

3. Check with the team to make sure that the same problem hasn't been written twice (but may be in slightly different words). If a problem is repeated combine them into one item.

4. Ask the team members to write on a piece of paper the letters corresponding to the number of problem statements the team produced. For example: if you ended up with five (5) problem statements, everyone would write the letters "A" through "E" on the paper.

5. Make sure that each problem statement has a letter in front of it. Then ask the team members to vote on which problem is most important by putting a five (5) next to that problem's letter. For example, the problem list would look like this:
   A. Space
   B. Safety
   C. Housekeeping
   D. Quality going down
   E. No Preventive Maintenance

the authority to find a solution and make a decision has been delegated. Finally, the supervisor should choose a problem in which the enthusiastic acceptance and execution are at least as important as, if not more important than, the specifics of the decision itself. Under these conditions, group decision making can be an additional means of bringing out the positive aspects of informal organization.

Each member's paper would look like this:

A. _____
B. _____
C. _____
D. _____
E. _____

So, if someone thought *"quality is going down"* was the #1 problem it would look like this:

A. _____
B. _____
C. _____
D. __5____
E. _____

Everyone then has to complete the list by voting what's second most important, third most important, etc.

A. 2, 5, 2, 4, 1
B. 1, 4, 5, 5, 5
C. 4, 1, 3, 3, 4
D. 5, 2, 1, 1, 2
E. 3, 3, 4, 2, 3

An alternate ranking approach involves the "one half plus one" rule. Especially when dealing with a large number of items, it may be necessary to limit the items to be considered. This rule suggests ranking only one-half of the items plus one. For example, if 20 items were generated, team members would only rate 11 ideas.

6. Add up each line of numbers across. The item with the highest number is the most important one to the total team. In this case "B" (Safety) would be the most important item with a total of "20." You would add up the numbers for each item and put them in order.

7. You would then work on item B first, and then move through the list.

## ■ The Supervisor and the Informal Group Leader

Informal leaders are powerful because of their status and power of authority; they can be a great help when they work in the best interest of the institution. When informal leaders work against the goals of the organization, however, they can cause great difficulties. Therefore, supervisors should maintain a positive attitude toward the informal group leader. Instead of viewing this person as a "ringleader," supervisors will do better to consider this individual as someone "in the know" and respect and work with him or her. In an effort to build good relations with the informal leader, supervisors can pass information on to that person before giving it to anyone else. They can ask for advice on certain problems, and, particularly if a rearrangement of duties is under consideration, they may want to discuss it with the informal leader first to get some feedback. Or supervisors may ask the informal leader to "break in" a new employee in the department, knowing full well that he or she would have done it anyway.

In taking this approach, however, the supervisor must be careful not to cause the informal leader to lose status within the group because working with the supervisor means working with management. In other words, the supervisor should not extend too many favors to the informal leader, since this would ruin the latter's leadership position within the group at once. This discussion assumes that an informal group leader is easily visible in the department. Often it is difficult, however, for a supervisor, especially a new supervisor, to identify the informal leader of a group. Observation is probably the best means to find out. The supervisor should look for the person to whom the other employees turn when they need help, the person who sets the pace and who seems to have influence over them. The supervisor must continually and closely observe this because the informal group will occasionally shift from one leader to another, depending on the purposes to be pursued. Regardless of who the leader is, the supervisor should do all he or she possibly can to work *with* the informal leader instead of against that person.

---

**SUMMARY**   In addition to the formal organization, there exists in every enterprise an informal organization based on informal groups. These groups satisfy certain needs and desires of their members, which apparently are left unsatisfied by the formal organization. For example, an informal group can satisfy the members' social needs. It gives them recognition, status, and a sense of belonging. Informal information transmitted through the grapevine provides a channel of communication and fulfills the members' need and desire to know what is going on. The informal organization also influences the behavior of individuals within the group and requests them to conform with certain norms the group has set up. Informal organization can be found on all levels of the enterprise, from the top to the bottom. It exists in every department, regardless of the quality of supervision.

Informal organization can have either a constructive or hindering influence on the formal organization. To make the best possible use of informal organization, the supervisor must understand its workings and be able to identify its informal leaders. Then the supervisor can work with them in a way that will help accomplish the objectives of the department. Instead of dwelling on the informal organization as a source of conflict, the supervisor should remember that both the formal and the informal organizations are part of a complex system interacting with each other. Instead of viewing it as something antagonistic, the supervisor should approach this group positively and emphasize its potential for the good of the enterprise. One way to emphasize the positive is to practice group decision making by the informal groups. The supervisor must not suppress the informal relationships. Formal and informal relationships should be integrated to increase organizational effectiveness.

# PART V
# STAFFING: HUMAN RESOURCES MANAGEMENT

# *16* *The Staffing Process*

## *Chapter Objectives*

After you have studied this chapter, you should be able to:

1. Explain why human resources management has always been important and is becoming more so.
2. Define the staffing function as the sum of activities required to attract, develop, and retain people with the knowledge and skills needed to achieve the objectives.
3. Describe how equal opportunity laws and fair employment regulations affect the staffing function.
4. Describe the relationships between the human resources department and line management.
5. Discuss the growing influence of the human resources people in managerial decision making.
6. Explain the steps in human resources planning, such as determining the need, kind, and number of employees necessary.
7. Describe the importance of job description and job qualifications based on job analysis.

People are the most important and valuable asset of an organization, not sophisticated equipment, facilities, or buildings. Staffing is the managerial function concerned with the procurement and maintenance of the human resources to fulfill the institution's goals. It is the sum of activities needed to attract, develop, and retain people with the necessary skills and knowledge to achieve the objectives. Once goals have been determined, departments set up, and duties and task relationships established, people must be found to give life to what would otherwise be an empty structure. It is the manager's responsibility to vitalize the department by staffing it properly.

Human resources management begins with planning for the present and future human resources needs. Staffing begins with *recruitment* and *selection; recruitment* is the process of locating qualified candidates and *selection* is the process of choosing from the pool of applicants. Staffing also involves making sure the department's subordinates are properly oriented, placed, trained and developed, and compensated and given benefits. The manager's staffing duties also include judging the employees' work and evaluating their performance, promoting them according to effort and ability, rewarding them, transferring them, and, if necessary, disciplining or even discharging them. Only if a manager performs all these duties can one say that the managerial staffing function has been truly fulfilled. Additionally, the manager will get help and support from the human resources or personnel department.

Staffing is a difficult task, and the importance of human resources management has expanded greatly in recent years. Good resource planning and maintenance have a major impact on the performance of the organization. Poor resource planning can result in severe shortages, and improper recruiting practices can lead to embarrassing situations. Much of these shortages or improper practices are caused by today's complex legal environment affecting human resources management. Thus, the supervisor depends heavily on the expertise of the human resources (or personnel) department. Most organizations with more than just a few employees usually have a department of human resources to assist the line managers in their task.

Many supervisors may believe that some of the previously mentioned duties are the responsibility of the human resources department. In many healthcare facilities some of these activities are performed by the personnel department. In such institutions this department has very broad jurisdiction. Nevertheless, good management still considers human resources management the responsibility of all operating managers. Although the supervisor may be assisted by the human resources staff in performing these functions, they are still the supervisor's responsibility. For example, the human resources department will do the recruiting and the initial screening, but the final hiring should be made by the supervisor of the department. Also, the evaluation of the employees' performance should be made by the line supervisor, although the system, procedures, forms, and so forth are designed by the human resources people. All this will be discussed in detail in the following pages.

## THE STAFFING FUNCTION AND THE HUMAN RESOURCES DEPARTMENT

Throughout this text, the terms *human resources department* and *personnel department* will be used interchangeably. This department is a staff department as defined in our discussion of line and staff capacity. Its usefulness and effectiveness will depend largely on its ability to develop a good working and sharing relationship with line supervisors. This will be governed in part by how clearly and specifically the CEO has outlined the activities and authority of the human resources department. In determining its scope and relationship to the staffing function of line supervisors, it is necessary for line managers to understand the historical place of the personnel department in organizations. Only then will one be able to establish a structure that is meaningful in terms of current needs and environment.

### ■ Historical Patterns

The personnel department started primarily as a record-keeping department. It kept all employment records for the employees and managers, all correspondence pertaining to their hiring, application blanks, background information, various positions held within the enterprise, dates of promotions, salary changes, leaves of absence granted, disciplinary penalties imposed, and other information on the employee's relationship to the enterprise.

Proper maintenance of these clerical records is still of great importance today, especially with the growing emphasis on equal opportunity employment, pension and benefits, insurance programs, unemployment claims, seniority provisions, and promotional and developmental programs. By assigning such clerical service activities to the personnel staff, the administrator knows that they will be handled competently and efficiently due to the department's members' specialization. If such a service were not provided by the personnel department, each supervisor would have to keep these records for his or her own department, which would be a time-consuming task. Therefore, line supervisors are pleased to have the personnel clerical staff perform these services for them.

In the 1920s, many managers in industry believed unionization might be thwarted if the industries gave employees such benefits as cafeterias, better recreational facilities, bowling teams, and company stores. Management thought that these additions would make the employees happier and less resentful. Since none of these activities fit into the regular line departments of the enterprise, however, the personnel department took responsibility for many of them.

During the 1930s, another shift in the emphasis of the personnel department took place. With the increase of union activities, the personnel department was expected to take direct charge of all employee and union relations. It often assumed full responsibility for hiring, firing, handling union grievances, and dealing with general labor problems. In other words, management believed that by having a personnel department, all personnel questions could be handled by it, leaving the line supervisors with practically no staffing function.

This led to serious difficulties, however, because while the duties and power of the personnel department increased significantly, the standing of the supervisor as a manager decreased. The more power the personnel director acquired, the weaker the supervisor's relationship became with his or her own employees. The demoralized supervisor justifiably complained that it was impossible to manage the department effectively without having the power to select, hire, discipline, and reward the employees. The employees no longer regarded the supervisor as their boss. Because someone in the personnel department hired the employees, established their wages, and promoted, disciplined, and fired them, employees looked to someone in the personnel department as their supervisor. Since this led to a bad state of affairs in many organizations, good management had to clearly differentiate between the functions of the personnel department in a staff capacity and the supervisor's role as the department's operating manager.

## ■ Current Patterns

During the last decades, most organizations have recognized the need for constant interaction and proper balance of influence and authority between the line managers and the human resources staff. Good management dictates that supervisors and personnel people must work together and share the burden because their work is intertwined; however, their areas of authority and their roles must be clearly stated. Sound management principles advocate that the primary job of the human resources department is to provide the line supervisors with advice, suggestions, and counsel concerning personnel problems and to help them in every possible respect. Going beyond this could lead to a fragmentation of the supervisor's job and make it difficult for the supervisor to be an effective manager. Of course, the supervisor must manage within the framework of the organization's personnel policies, procedures, and regulations. Line supervisors should take full advantage of the expertise and assistance that is available within the human resources department, but they must retain the basic responsibility for managing their department.

An example that emphasizes the distinction between management and human resources is found in a passage from the text *The Management of Human Resources.*

---

### *"We Don't Have an HR Department"*

An article in the *Personnel Administrator* described Nucor Corporation as the most productive steel mill in the world. When students in a human resource management class heard that a Nucor mill was located nearby, they thought it would provide an excellent field trip. One of the student leaders, Rebecca, called to arrange the visit. When she phoned she asked to speak with their human resource manager.

"I'm sorry, we don't have a human resource manager."

"Then could I speak with your personnel director?"

"We don't have a personnel director either."

"Then what do you call that position?"

"I'm sorry ma'am, but we simply don't have that position."

Assuming they had a special title for the position, Rebecca asked, "Who handles your compensation and benefits?"

"Our benefits are managed by our controller but our compensation is directed by a payroll clerk. Would you like to talk with her?"

"Is she also the one who manages the recruiting, hiring, and performance evaluation?"

"No, those activities are performed by our supervisors. Is there something I could help you with?"

Finally, Rebecca realized that they did not have a human resource manager or a personnel department. Eventually her call was directed to the general manager, who explained how the personnel functions were performed at that steel mill. Although Nucor Steel did not have a human resource manager at each mill, they had a manager of personnel services at the corporate headquarters who was responsible for creating personnel policies and programs for the mills.

The general manager explained that 335 employees worked at that location and all but 55 of them were directly involved in producing steel. These 55 included the supervisors, the clerical support staff, and six vice presidents. Although none of these people had the title human resource manager, they all performed various human resource functions. Wages, salaries, and benefits were distributed by the payroll clerk; health and accident insurance was supervised by an insurance clerk. The supervisors were responsible for most of the remaining personnel functions, including interviewing, hiring, discipline, safety, and training. Recruiting was not assigned to anyone since they had a long waiting list of job applicants and turnover was negligible.

(box continues on page 240)

> The supervisors received a salary for 52 weeks per year, plus an annual bonus, whole production workers received hourly pay plus generous productivity bonuses that were calculated daily and weekly. Everyone also participated in an annual profit-sharing plan. The productivity bonuses generally accounted for over two-thirds of the production workers' pay. Employees who came to work late forfeited their daily production bonus, and if they were absent they lost their weekly production bonus. Consequently, tardiness and absenteeism were not problems at this mill.
>
> Rebecca asked if it would be possible to bring the student group on a field trip to visit the plant.
>
> "I'm sorry, but we cannot accommodate you. It's not that we dislike visitors or want to be secretive, we simply don't have anyone to show you around. We are in the business of producing steel, not guided tours."
>
> Nucor Steel is good at making steel. The top five steel mills in the United States average 347 tons of steel per employee per year, while the top five integrated steel mills in Japan average 480 tons of steel per employee per year. Nucor produces approximately 950 tons of steel per employee per year.
>
> *"Nucor's Ken Iverson on Productivity and Pay,"* Personnel Administrator *October 31, 1986: 46, 106.*

Since it is the supervisor's job to accomplish the work within the department, he or she must make managerial decisions that concern the department's employees. Generally, this means that the supervisor defines the specific qualifications expected from an employee who is to fill a specific position. It is the human resources department's function to develop sources of qualified applicants within the local labor market. This department must let the community know what jobs are available and in general create an image of the organization as an employer. This can be accomplished by fostering good community relations and recruiting from high schools, training schools, colleges, and other sources of employees.

The human resources department should conduct screening interviews with applicants to determine whether or not their qualifications match the requirements as defined by the supervisor. They will also perform tests if the position requires them. This department should make necessary reference checks about previous employment dates and past records and should not further consider those applicants who do not meet job requirements. Those candidates who meet the stated requirements should be referred to the supervisor.

It is up to the supervisor to interview, select, and hire from among the qualified available candidates. The supervisor normally should make the final decision, sometimes in collaboration with the direct line superior. The supervisor assigns the new employee to a specific job, and has the responsibility to judge how this new employee's skills can best be used and developed. It is the human resources department's job to inform the new employee about the healthcare center's benefits, general rules, shifts, and hours. The supervisor, however, should introduce the employee to the specific details about the job—wages, departmental rules, hours, and rest periods. The supervisor instructs and trains the new employee on the job and assesses performance to determine whether he or she should be retained. The supervisor also monitors compensation within the pattern of remuneration and later decides whether or not this person should eventually receive a pay adjustment or be promoted into a better job. If the need to take disciplinary measures should arise, it is clearly the supervisor's duty to do so. During the time an employee is with the organization, the complete employment record is maintained by the human resources department.

Throughout the entire staffing procedure the supervisor will be greatly aided by the personnel department. The latter maintains all the clerical services and keeps the records. As previously mentioned, this is particularly essential because of the importance of nondiscriminatory employment, insurance, pension, promotion, and other practices. The human resources department is also there to provide expertise, advice, counsel, and guidance whenever personnel problems arise. In making decisions, the supervisor can follow, ignore, reject, or alter the personnel department's advice and counsel. In today's societal and legal environment affecting the staffing function, however, the input of the human resources employees has become very vital and has a strong impact on the practice of management.

Sometimes supervisors will welcome the human resources department's willingness to help them out of a difficult situation. Frequently supervisors ask the personnel department to make a decision for them so that they will not become burdened with so-called personnel problems. They gladly accept the staff person's decision, believing that if the decision is wrong, they can always excuse it by saying it was the personnel department's decision. In other words, the line supervisor is only too ready to capitulate to the personnel person in many instances. In so doing, one can "pass the buck" to the human resources department.

Although it is understandable that the supervisor may be reluctant to question and disregard the advice of the staff expert, he or she must bear in mind that the staff person sees only a small part of the entire picture, and is not responsible for how the department performs. There are usually many other factors involved in the overall picture that will affect the department, factors that the human resources staff is not as familiar with as is the line supervisor. The supervisor cannot always separate his or her functions between personnel problems and performance problems. Every situation has certain personnel implications, and it is impossible to separate the various components of each problem within the department. Only the supervisor is likely to see the broad picture.

In the daily operations, the human resources people constantly interact with other managers. Unless the managers have a clear understanding of the line-staff relationships and expectations, these interactions can easily produce conflicts and misunderstandings. This is increasingly important because of equal employment opportunity laws and similar requirements.

## STAFFING AND LEGAL IMPLICATIONS

During recent years the staffing function has become more complex due to numerous federal, state, and local laws; executive orders and guidelines; and court decisions. Employment practices and policies must comply with these regulations, which in general prohibit discrimination against applicants and employees on the basis of race, sex, color, religion, or national origin. Also, employers cannot use age as a criterion of selection among applicants between forty and seventy years old. Other laws might request that an organization hire handicapped persons and veterans. Affirmative-action programs might dictate that the institution give hiring preferences to minority members who are qualified or have the potential to fill available jobs.

A detailed discussion of equal employment opportunity (EEO) is beyond the confines of this text; however, supervisors must be aware of this concern because it affects their staffing function. Figure 16.1 is a partial listing of the major laws on equal employment opportunity requirements and the enforcement agencies. Equal employment is discussed in more detail in chapter 17. It would be impossible for a line supervisor to keep abreast of all the equal employment opportunity and antidiscrimination laws. This is where the expertise of the human resources department comes into play. The human resources department must make sure the organization complies with the multitude of laws and regulations.

## FUNCTIONAL AUTHORITY AND THE HUMAN RESOURCES DEPARTMENT

At the beginning of this chapter, we stated that the human resources department is attached to the organization in a staff position, which means that staff's job is to advise and assist line managers. During the last few years, however, many CEOs of healthcare institutions, industry, and businesses have decided to limit the supervisor's authority to terminate an employee. Thus all dismissals have to be approved by the human resources director. Such a change is necessary in order to protect the organization from expensive wrongful discharge suits. The top-level administrator has the authority to make such a provision, and in this instance *functional* staff authority, as discussed in chapter 12, has been conferred on the human resources department. In other words, top-level administration wants human resources to make the final decision as to whether or not an employee, who has been working in the institution longer than the customary probationary period, should be dismissed. The administrator is removing this portion from the supervisor's authority and conferring it on the human resources department.

There must be solid reasoning behind such a decision since it clearly runs counter to the principle of unity of command and weakens the authority of the line manager's position. A CEO would probably make such a decision based on the need and desire to comply with all possible fair and nondiscriminatory employment practices and regulations. Also, there could be other reasons why a CEO would delegate this final authority to fire an employee to the director of human resources.

In addition, the human resources department often has sole responsibility for many other activities, such as personnel record keeping, EEO/affirmative action,

| Legislation | Concern or content | Administrative agency |
| --- | --- | --- |
| Title VII of the Civil Rights Act of 1964† | Sex | EEOC‡ |
| Equal Pay Act of 1963 | Sex | EEOC |
| Title VII of the Civil Rights Act of 1964† | Color | EEOC |
| Title VII of the Civil Rights Act of 1964† | Race | EEOC |
| Title VII of the Civil Rights Act of 1964† | Religion | EEOC |
| Title VII of the Civil Rights Act of 1964† | National origin | EEOC |
| Age Discrimination in Employment Act of 1967, as amended in 1978 | Age (protection for those 40 to 70 years old) | EEOC |
| Rehabilitation Act of 1973 | Handicapped persons | U.S. Department of Labor |
| The Vietnam–Era Veteran Readjustment Assistance Act of 1974 | Vietnam-era veterans | U.S. Department of Labor |
| Various executive orders, principally no. 11246 and revised order no. 4 | *All* the above as part of affirmative action programs | Office of Federal Contract Compliance, U.S. Department of Labor |
| The Americans with Disabilities Act of 1990** | Handicapped persons | EEOC |

*Effective at the time of publication of this text. This is a partial list of the framework of laws, regulations, and administrative agencies that govern employment policies and decisions.

† As amended by the Equal Employment Opportunity Act of 1972 and the Pregnancy Discrimination Act of 1978.

‡Equal Employment Opportunity Commission.

**Effective 7/26/92.

**Figure 16.1** Examples of current laws and regulations affecting employment policies.

insurance benefits administration, exit interviews, outplacement services, unemployment compensation, employee assistance programs, attitude surveys, and others.

Of course, it is always desirable for the personnel director to disseminate current information regarding fair employment practices to all first-line supervisors. For example, the department of human resources should familiarize the supervisors with recent issues and government provisions. Also, the various possibilities of conscious and unconscious discriminatory practices and sexual harassment should be brought to the attention of the supervisors. Supervisors should also understand the meaning of affirmative action.

Furthermore, administration should explain the importance of documentation, and line supervisors should be urged to keep meaningful personnel and recruitment records that they and the institution can refer to if necessary. If supervisors are kept up to date on these issues, it is unlikely that, for example, they will contemplate discharging an employee unless all possible ramifications have already been considered. Under these circumstances the director of human resources probably will go along with a proposed dismissal, since the supervisor has a well-documented and substantiated case that can become a valid defense. It is desirable, therefore, that the personnel director who has been given the final authority on discharge and other issues will use it with discretion.

---

## THE SUPERVISOR'S STAFFING FUNCTION

The staffing function is an ongoing activity for the supervisor, not something that is required only when the department is first established. More typically, the supervisor will have to handle the staffing of an existing department with a certain number of employees already in it. Although there is a nucleus of employees to start with, the composition of the department rarely stays the same for long. Since every supervisor depends on employees for the department's results, it is his or her responsibility to make certain that there is a supply of well-trained employees to fill the various positions.

### ■ Determining the Need for Employees

To make certain that the department can perform the jobs required of it, the supervisor must determine both the number and type of employees who will be needed for the department. By type, we mean, what competencies staff must possess that will be most significant to the department's success. Some competencies may be *achievement orientation, customer service orientation, flexibility, teamwork, conceptual thinking, self-confidence, assertiveness, persuasive ability, professional aspirations,* and *developing others.* Once the competencies are known, the supervisor can design a behavior-based interview approach and query applicants in these competency areas.

If the supervisor has set up the structure of the department, he or she has designed an organizational structure in which the functions, competencies, and jobs are shown in their proper relationships. If the supervisor takes over an existing department, it is necessary to become familiar with the organizational structure by drawing a chart of the existing jobs and functions, and assessing the competencies of the current incumbents. For example, the supervisor of the maintenance department may find that there are groups of painters, electricians, carpenters, and other skilled *persons* within the department. After taking this inventory of personnel, the supervisor should determine how many skilled *positions* there are or should be within this department and if the current incumbents are able to support the department's needs, consider budgetary constraints. The working relationships between these positions should also be examined and defined by the supervisor.

After determining the needs of the department, the supervisor may have to adjust the ideal setup to existing necessities. Several positions may have to be combined into one if there is not enough work for one employee. Then the competencies of the employee must be assessed to determine if he or she needs additional training to be able to perform successfully in the restructured position. Only by studying the organizational setup of the department can the supervisor determine what and how many employees are needed to perform the various jobs.

To fill the various positions with appropriate employees, the supervisor needs to match the available jobs in the department with the qualifications of prospective employees. The supervisor makes such a match with the help of job descriptions and job specifications. The *job description* tells exactly what duties and responsibilities are contained within a particular job. It describes what the employees do, how they do it, and the working conditions. A *job specification,* also at times referred to as job qualification, identifies and describes the minimum acceptable qualifications required of a person holding a job; it typically contains general qualification requirements, such as experience and training, education, and knowledge and skills. Frequently, these requirements are incorporated into the job description.

Job descriptions and job specifications are based on the *job analysis;* this is a study of the jobs within the organization. It consists of analyzing the activities the employee performs; the equipment, tools and work aids the employee uses; and the working conditions. The supervisor who is taking over an already established department will often find a set of job descriptions available. If none is available, however, the human resources director will help establish a set. However, no one is better equipped to describe the content of a job than the supervisor. He or she is responsible for the accomplishment of the department's tasks, and knows (or should know) the content of each position. Although the final form of the job description may be prepared in the personnel office, the supervisor should determine its specific content.

Only by closely analyzing the job requirements is it possible to ascertain the skills necessary to perform the job satisfactorily. Even if the position is already in operation, it is still advisable to determine the major duties and responsibilities. Then the supervisor should compare this list of duties with the current job description and with the employee's actual duties. If the older job description no longer fits the current content of the job, the supervisor should update it. Even if the job in question is a new position, the supervisor should proceed along similar lines. The supervisor should determine the job's duties and responsibilities, and, with the help of the personnel department, draw up a job description. Once the content of the job has been listed, the supervisor should then specify the knowledge, education, degrees, experience, and skills required of the prospective employee.

In every job, an employee must know certain facts before he or she can perform the job effectively. For example, a certain position may require the ability to read simple blueprints or have skills in mathematics. If a knowledge of mathematics is needed for a certain job, the specific type of mathematics required should be clearly defined. The word *mathematics* could imply knowledge far beyond a working knowledge of simple arithmetic, or a knowledge of simple arithmetic might be all that is required in the job. The more precisely you define the required job knowledge, the easier it will be for you to select from among available applicants.

When stipulating the skills needed for a particular job, the supervisor should not ask for a higher degree of skill than is absolutely necessary. One way to avoid this is to check the requirements drawn up with the qualifications of employees who are doing the same or similar work. Such an investigation may quickly reveal whether a high school education is necessary for a certain job. The supervisor may discover that an experienced person without a high school diploma can perform this work.

Equal employment opportunity laws and rulings require that job descriptions must not discriminate against certain classes and that they must be job related. Here the supervisor should consult the human resources department. To comply with these laws and regulations, many personnel departments have assumed responsibility for the final draft of the job descriptions. The supervisor should realize that by setting employment standards unrealistically high, the task of finding the person to meet these specifications will become unnecessarily difficult. There is no need to specify a certain number of years of formal education and experience if all that is required is simply job know-how. This does not mean that the job specifications should ask for less than what is needed, but should specify the requirements realistically. If the requirements are set too high, you may end up employing an overqualified person. This particular employee may prove to be unhappy and bored with the position. It is just as disastrous, however, to ask for less than the necessary requirements. Once placed on the job, the employee may turn out to be unsatisfactory. Many of these difficulties can be avoided if the supervisor thoroughly analyzes the job content and specifies the necessary job knowledge and skills.

The human resources department will be a great help in drawing up these job descriptions. The supervisor should be cautioned, however, not to totally turn over this job to personnel. The content must be specified by the supervisor. Once these job descriptions have been drafted, the supervisor should consult with some of the people who are holding these jobs to compare the job descriptions with the actual positions in question. Once all difficulties have been ironed out, these job descriptions are maintained in the human resources department and also in the supervisor's file. Whenever the supervisor needs to fill a certain job, the personnel staff is informed of the opening. Personnel will recruit applicants and quickly screen out those who are obviously unsuitable because they do not have the knowledge, necessary skills, or other requirements. All who seem to fulfill the requirements will then be referred to the supervisor for his or her acceptance or rejection.

Since job descriptions should be kept up-to-date, the supervisor occasionally must review the contents of the job. Without regular reviews, descriptions may become inadequate. Many activities in the healthcare field change considerably through new technology, scientific advances, and sometimes because of the creative efforts of the person occupying a position. Ambitious employees may enlarge the scope of their own activities, whereas other employees lose or forego portions of theirs. The extent and character of change must be determined so that accurate information is contained in the job description. This is necessary because the job description is constantly referred to when the human resources department recruits candidates, when the supervisor hires new employees, when the employees' performance is appraised, and when establishing equitable wage patterns within the department.

If staffing decisions are to possess any validity, they must be based on comprehensive job descriptions that are systematically revised to reflect the current job situation as accurately as possible. Furthermore, they must reflect the current requirements of equal employment opportunity and nondiscrimination.

## ■ How Many to Hire

Normally, the supervisor is not confronted with the situation in which many employees have to be hired at the same time. Such a situation could exist when a new department is created and the supervisor has to staff it completely from scratch. More typically, the question of hiring an employee will occur from time to time. Generally, a department's composition of employees does not stay the same for a long time.

A supervisor will usually need to hire a new worker when one of the employees leaves the department voluntarily, is dismissed, or leaves for some other reason. In such instances, there is little doubt that the job must be filled. Occasionally changes in the technical nature of the work take place, and manual labor may be replaced by machinery or sophisticated instruments. In this case a replacement may not be needed or a new employee with the necessary technical skills will be hired unless a present member can be trained.

Other situations arise when additional employees have to be added. For example, when departmental activities have been enlarged or when new duties are to be undertaken and no one within the department possesses the required job knowledge and skill, the supervisor has to go out to the open market and recruit employees. Sometimes a supervisor is inclined to ask for additional help if the workload is increased or if the supervisor feels added pressure. Before requesting additional employees under those conditions, the supervisor should make certain that the persons currently within the department are working up to capacity and that additional people are absolutely necessary. Due to these shifting situations the manager is involved in the staffing function much of the time.

If vacancies exist within the department, the supervisor should inform the human resources staff in order for them to start recruiting. Recruiting is the process of attracting and seeking a pool of applicants from which to choose a qualified candidate. The personnel department accomplishes this task by consulting the various job descriptions in order to know which type of people to recruit. Then the personnel staff interviews those applicants whose resumes or applications seem to show they have proper requirements for the job. Those candidates who seem to be generally acceptable and have the required knowledge and skills will then meet with the supervisor.

In sum, the actual hiring decision is not to be made in the personnel office, but rather by the supervisor in whose department the employee is to work. Although the supervisor may believe that he or she need not be involved in filling an unskilled job, the supervisor should not relinquish his or her prerogative and duty to do the hiring. Whether the job is nonskilled, semiskilled, or skilled, it is up to the supervisor to hire the employee. Since all applicants are screened by the human resources department, the supervisor knows that all those sent to him or her possess the minimum qualifications prescribed for the job. It is the supervisor's job to pick out the one who will probably best fill the job. This is not an easy task, but as time goes on the supervisor will gain more and more experience in selecting the "right" applicant. The selection process is discussed in chapter 17.

## SUMMARY

People, the organization's human resources, are the most important asset. Staffing is the managerial function of procuring and maintaining the department's human resources, a function every supervisor has to perform. Staffing means to attract, select, place, train, retain, evaluate, promote, discipline, and appropriately compensate the employees of the department. All this is the supervisor's line function. The human resources department aids the supervisor in fulfilling this duty. In most enterprises, this department is attached to the organization in a staff capacity, and its purpose is to counsel, inform, and service all other departments of the enterprise. Sometimes, to be of service to the line manager, the human resources department may be inclined to take over line functions such as hiring and disciplining. Supervisors must caution themselves not to turn over any of their line functions to the personnel department, although at times it might seem expedient to let them handle the problems.

Before the manager can undertake the staffing function, the number and types of employees and competencies needed in the department must be clarified. The organizational chart combined with job descriptions will help the supervisor decide what workers are needed to fill the various jobs. In addition, the supervisor must consider the amount of work to be performed and the positions allocated in the budget. In all these supervisory duties the human resources department is available for assistance and service. It is the supervisor's function, however, to select, place, develop, evaluate, promote, reward, and discipline all the employees within the department.

During the last decades, numerous federal, state, and local laws and regulations as well as executive orders have been enacted regarding equal employment opportunities, fair employment practices, and nondiscriminatory practices. All staffing practices and policies must comply with these requirements. Making sure the organization is complying with these regulations is best handled by specialists in the human resources department. Because of the vast impact this has made on the activities of all managers and because of the importance of compliance, the influence of the human resources department within an organization has increased substantially. The CEO recognizes and deals with the need for a proper balance of influence and authority between the line managers and the human resources people.

In a number of organizations, functional authority has been conferred on the human resources department, especially when the problem involves dismissals and fair employment practices. The average line supervisor could not possibly be or remain aware of new laws, court decisions, and so forth. Therefore, it makes good sense that the authority of the human resources department has been greatly increased, even if this means narrowing the supervisor's line authority.

# *The Selection Process and the Employment Interview*

*Chapter Objectives*

After you have studied this chapter, you should be able to:

1. Discuss the selection process as the choosing and hiring of employees from among those candidates recruited for the organization.
2. Describe the interview as a universally used and reliable means of selection.
3. Discuss the difference between directive (structured) and nondirective (unstructured, counseling) interviews.
4. Describe the functions of nondirective interviews.
5. Discuss the employment interview as an example of a directive interview.
6. Discuss the importance of concluding the employment interview and making a decision.

The purpose of the selection process is to hire the best employees available for the organization. This process involves choosing the candidate who best meets the job demands, is likely to perform well, and also will stay with the organization. Since selecting the right employee contributes significantly to the effectiveness of the department, the final decision should rest with the candidate's prospective superior. In so doing, the selector can be kept completely responsible for how the selected candidate performs. Opinions of others, such as the selector's superior, those who will have working relationships with the candidates, and specialists from the human resources department, can help the supervisor make his or her decision. The final decision on selection, however, rests with the department supervisor.

After all the preliminary work has been performed by the human resources department, such as recruitment, preliminary screening interviews, obtaining biographical data, and relevant testing, it will have reduced the pool of applicants to three or five possible candidates. Line managers then interview these applicants, see them, talk to them, and select the one who will best fill the vacant job. This is a decisive step for the candidate and the supervisor. This is the moment when the supervisor must match the applicant's capability with the demands of the job, the authority and responsibility inherent in the position, the working conditions, and the rewards and satisfactions it offers. The personal interview between the supervisor and applicant is an essential part of the selection process.

Although some people question the interview as a reliable means of selection and as a predictor of performance, it is an almost universally used selection device. It involves two-way communication, enabling the interviewer to learn more about the applicant's background, interests, and values, and enabling the applicant to ask questions about the institution and the job. The interview is not a precise technique, and it is difficult to interview skillfully. Since no fixed criteria exist for success or failure, prejudiced interviewers too easily evaluate an applicant's performance according to their own stereotypes. Also, job applicants react differently to different interviewers. As a major means for deciding, however, interviews are probably more valid for predicting employee behavior than decisions made on tests alone. It is not easy to appropriately appraise someone's potential during a brief interview. Interviewing is much more than technique; it is an art that can and must be developed by every supervisor.

## INTERVIEWS

The supervisor will come to learn that there are several types of interviews. These include preemployment, or selection, interviews between the supervisor and prospective employees; discussions when employees are fired; and counseling sessions during which the abilities and deficiencies of an employee are discussed. Other interviews occur when an employee voluntarily leaves the job, as well as when an employee wants to discuss complaints, grievances, and any other problems. In general, all these can be grouped into two kinds of interviews: *directive* (structured) and *nondirective* (unstructured or counseling). Throughout our discussion we will separate these two approaches, but some interviews have aspects of both categories. For example, the appraisal interview (see chapter 18) is primarily a directive interview, but the discussion may take on some aspects of a nondirective counseling interview.

### ■ Directive Interviews

Normally, a directive interview, also known as a structured interview, is a discussion in which the interviewer knows beforehand what facts will be discussed and what the goals, objectives, and areas of discussion are. The employment interview in which the supervisor selects one applicant over another is an example of a directive interview. In a structured interview, a predesigned format is followed. The interviewer will try to obtain the necessary information by encouraging the interviewee to volunteer as much as possible, and then, by asking the interviewee additional direct questions. In a structured interview, the interviewer frequently follows a standardized list of questions, making for consistent, job-related, nondiscriminatory questions. The benefit of structured interviews is that all pertinent aspects are covered and that their contents can be compared.

## ■ Nondirective Interviews

Although we will be primarily concerned with the directive interview in this chapter, the supervisor should be aware of what it means to conduct a nondirective, or counseling, interview. It is unstructured, no checklist is used, and the format develops as the interview unfolds. In a nondirective interview, the interviewer encourages the interviewee to express his or her thoughts freely.

This type of interview is usually used in problematic situations in which the supervisor is eager to learn what the interviewee thinks and feels. The supervisor may conduct a nondirective interview when an employee has a grievance or an off-the-job problem. Or the supervisor may use this approach in an exit interview when the employee voluntarily leaves the job. Another reason a nondirective interview may be held is to obtain opinions about the overall operation of your department or satisfaction with recent changes. While the interview may be held with the supervisor of the subordinates, occasionally a level of supervision is skipped and the department manager may meet one-on-one with subordinates of a supervisor. Affording your subordinates the opportunity of counseling interviews is a vital aspect of good supervision.

Supervisors must encourage subordinates to come to them with their problems. They must show them that they are willing to hear employees out. Otherwise minor irritations may turn out to become major problems. The supervisor must realize that inherent in the managerial position is an invisible barrier between the supervisor and the subordinates. Some employees will have little difficulty speaking to their supervisors, but many may be more timid. Therefore, the supervisor must make an effort to encourage those who are reluctant to reveal their thoughts. The supervisor should see that time is always available to listen to the subordinates. If time is not available at the moment, then the interview, if possible should be postponed for a few hours; the supervisor must allow enough time and not rush through the discussion.

The principal function of the nondirective interview is to give the supervisor a clue as to what the interviewee really thinks and feels and what lies at the root of a particular problem such as excessive turnover, absenteeism, or complaints about work or the department. In addition, it gives the interviewee a feeling of relief and helps the subordinate develop greater insight into his or her own problems, often finding solutions while "thinking out loud." Many sources of frustration exist within and outside the working environment, and unless frustration is relieved, it may lead to all forms of undesirable responses.

The ground rule for conducting a nondirective interview is to let the interviewee say whatever he or she wants to say. Conducting such an interview is more difficult than conducting a directive interview. It demands the concentrated listening and continuous attention of the supervisor. The supervisor must exert self-control and hide his or her own ideas and emotions during the interview. He or she should not interrupt, argue, or change the subject. The supervisor should not express approval or disapproval even though the employee may request it. This may prove exasperating, but it is essential.

In such a counseling interview, the employee must feel like he or she can speak openly. In all likelihood, as soon as all the negative feelings have been expressed, the employee may start to find some favorable aspects of the very same things that he or she had criticized earlier. When the employee is encouraged to verbalize problems, he or she may gain a greater insight into them or possibly may arrive at an answer or course of action that will help solve the difficulties. The employee must be permitted to work through difficulties alone, without being interrupted and advised by the counselor regarding the best course of action. If the problem concerns the job, work, and organization, however, the supervisor may have to be directive so that the solution is consistent with the needs of the institution.

The supervisor should normally exercise great care not to give advice or become burdened with the task of running the subordinate's personal life. Most of the time the interviewee wants a sympathetic and empathic listener and not an advisor. The average supervisor is not equipped to do counseling, and this is not part of the job. If necessary, the subordinate should be referred to trained specialists, for example one of the institution's social workers or psychologists, or the organization's employee assistance program. This may be necessary when sensitive areas and deep-seated personality problems are involved. The patient-psychiatrist relationship is not applicable to that of subordinate and boss.

At first, the nondirective interview is difficult to conduct, but as time goes on a good supervisor will learn to exercise self-control and, by concentrated listening, grasp the feelings of the employee. The counseling interviews can often be very time consuming. Although the supervisor is under many pressures and may not have much time for listening, time for such interviews must be made. The supervisor will find out that by listening, relationships with subordinates will be better and probably fewer personnel problems will arise.

Skillful listening is an art that can be learned with training and experience. It can be learned better by practice than by reading books on the subject. The supervisor can gain this practice almost every day on the job. Eventually the supervisor will develop a system of listening that is comfortable and fits his or her personality and at the same time puts the employee at ease. A common purpose of both directive and nondirective interviews is to promote mutual understanding and confidence. The nondirective approach is not a cure for all human relations problems.

Occasionally, as stated before, the supervisor has to be directive in the solution stage of the discussion. After fully listening to the subordinate, the supervisor may still have to overrule the employee so that the solution is in accordance with the needs and within the limits of the organization.

## THE EMPLOYMENT INTERVIEW

The employment interview, also known as the preemployment, or selection interview, will be discussed as an example of the directive, or structured, interview. The interviewer knows ahead of time what facts will be discussed, what the objectives are, and what areas the discussion will cover. The structured interview is conducted using a set of standardized questions asked of all applicants; this produces data that can be compared and provides a basis for evaluating the applicants. The interviewer should prepare the questions in advance. This does not mean that the structured interview must be rigid. Although the questions preferably should be asked in a logical sequence, the applicant should have ample opportunity to explain the answers. At times, the interviewer has to probe until a full understanding has been reached. The supervisor wants to learn as much as possible first by letting the interviewee volunteer information and then by asking direct questions.

## ■ Preparing for the Employment Interview

Since the purpose of the directive employment interview is to collect facts and reach a decision, the supervisor should prepare for it as thoroughly as possible. First, it is essential that the supervisor become acquainted with the available background information. By studying all the information assembled by the personnel director, the supervisor can sketch a general impression of the interviewee in advance.

The supervisor should identify the competencies the "ideal" candidate will have in advance of the interview. (Some competencies were discussed in chapter 16.) However, if the supervisor is interviewing for a lead microfilm clerk for the micrographics section, some competencies may include: ability to develop/train others, technical expertise with the camera or other equipment used, good customer relations, positive perspective, history of high productivity, desire to do things right the first time, etc. Given these competencies, the supervisor should structure his or her questions to encourage the applicants to discuss issues and experiences related to these competencies.

The *application* is a form that seeks information about the applicant's background and present status. (See figure 17.1.) It supplies a number of facts, such as the applicant's schooling and degrees; training; previous work experience, including nature of duties, length of stay, and salary; and other relevant data. The application is handed to the candidate on his or her first visit to the personnel department, and these data are evaluated there to decide whether the applicant merits further consideration.

The information contained in a completed application is somewhat limited because of laws, regulations, and court decisions regarding equal employment opportunities and discrimination. Generally, except under certain bona fide, job-related circumstances, federal regulations and guidelines prevent requiring applicants to state religion, sex, ancestry, marital status, age, birthplace of the applicant or parents, and other data. More details will be discussed later concerning what questions an interviewer is allowed to ask of the interviewee. An application may sample the candidate's abilities to write, organize thinking, and present facts clearly. The application indicates whether the applicant's education has been logically patterned and whether there has been a route of progression to better jobs. Also, it gives the interviewer points of departure for the formal interview.

NAME _____
last        first        middle

CURRENT ADDRESS _____
# street     city     state     zip code

PERMANENT ADDRESS _____
# street     city     state     zip code

(     ) _____
telephone number                   ---- ---- ---- ---- ---- ---- ---- ---- ---- ---- ---- ----
social security number

Are you younger than 18 years of age?   If yes, birth date      | Date you can begin work:      | Salary requirements:
❑ Yes   ❑ No

Employment status desired:
❑ Full-time ❑ Part-time ❑ Temp ❑ Per-diem

Shift preference:
❑ Day ❑ Evening ❑ Night ❑ Rotation

Can you work weekends/holidays?
❑ Yes ❑ No

POSITION DESIRED    1) _____    2) _____

Indicate the days and times of your availability:

Have you ever been employed by any facility in the BJC Health System?   ❑ Yes   ❑ No

If yes, facility ------------------------------    Date(s) ----------------   Position(s) ------------------------
Supervisor(s) ------------------------------    Under what name(s) ------------------------------------------

| SCHOOL | NAME AND LOCATION | COURSE OF STUDY | DID YOU GRADUATE? | DIPLOMA/DEGREE RECEIVED |
|---|---|---|---|---|
| High School | | | DID YOU GRADUATE OR RECEIVE A G.E.D.? ❑ Yes ❑ No | |
| | # street   city   state   zip | | | |
| Vocational/Technical | | | ❑ Yes ❑ No  Dates Attended: --------- to --------- mo./yr   mo./yr | |
| | # street   city   state   zip | | | |
| College/University | | | ❑ Yes ❑ No  Dates Attended: --------- to --------- mo./yr   mo./yr | |
| | # street   city   state   zip | | | |
| Graduate/Other | | | ❑ Yes ❑ No  Dates Attended: --------- to --------- mo./yr   mo./yr | |
| | # street   city   state   zip | | | |

Special courses, training, or experience acquired (to include special training in the military).

| Office Skills | Knowledge of software: | |
|---|---|---|
| ❑ Typing   wpm    ❑ Dictaphone  ❑ Shorthand   wpm    ❑ PBX  ❑ Ten key by touch    ❑ Word processor  ❑ Medical terminology    ❑ Personal computer | I am proficient at: | I have a working knowledge of: |

We appreciate your interest in the BJC Health System. We are an equal opportunity employer and do not discriminate on the basis of race, color, religion, sex, national origin, age, disability, or veteran status as provided by law.

SMOKE-FREE AND DRUG-FREE WORKPLACE

**Figure 17.1**   Typical employment application form used by healthcare institutions.

*Continued*

*Courtesy of BJC Health System, St. Louis, MO.*

**Licenses/Certifications**

| Are you currently: ☐ Registered ☐ Licensed ☐ Certified | Are you eligible for: ☐ Registration ☐ Licensure ☐ Certification | | | |
|---|---|---|---|---|
| Professional Licenses, Certifications, Registrations | | State | ID Number | Expiration Data |
| | | | | |
| | | | | |
| | | | | |
| | | | | |

**Employment History**

Starting with your most recent employer, list all positions for the past 10 years and account for periods of unemployment. Please list significant experience more than 10 years ago. **Resumes are welcome;** however, **completion of the application is required. Incomplete applications cannot be considered.** Additional sheets are available if needed. List most recent employer first.

**❶ Employer** | Address | | Telephone number ( )
City | State | Zip

☐ Full-time ☐ Part-time | Your position title | Dates employed From: To: | Starting salary | Ending salary | Shift diff. | Supervisor's name and title

Describe your responsibilities: | Reason for leaving

**❷ Employer** | Address | | Telephone number ( )
City | State | Zip

☐ Full-time ☐ Part-time | Your position title | Dates employed From: To: | Starting salary | Ending salary | Shift diff. | Supervisor's name and title

Describe your responsibilities: | Reason for leaving

**❸ Employer** | Address | | Telephone number ( )
City | State | Zip

☐ Full-time ☐ Part-time | Your position title | Dates employed From: To: | Starting salary | Ending salary | Shift diff. | Supervisor's name and title

Describe your responsibilities: | Reason for leaving

**❹ Employer** | Address | | Telephone number ( )
City | State | Zip

☐ Full-time ☐ Part-time | Your position title | Dates employed From: To: | Starting salary | Ending salary | Shift diff. | Supervisor's name and title

Describe your responsibilities: | Reason for leaving

**PLEASE COMPLETE**

| **Please explain any gaps in your employment history** | Have you ever been employed or attended school under another name? If yes, what name(s)? | May we contact your present employer(s)? ☐ Yes ☐ No    If no, please explain. |
|---|---|---|
| From: To: Reason: | | |
| From: To: Reason: | How many days were you absent in the last year?_ _ _ _ _ Last five years?_ _ _ _ _ | May we contact your previous employer(s)? ☐ Yes ☐ No    If no, please explain. |

We appreciate your interest in the BJC Health System. We are an equal opportunity employer and do not discriminate on the basis of race, color, religion, sex, national origin, age, disability, or veteran status as provided by law.

SMOKE-FREE AND DRUG-FREE WORKPLACE

**Figure 17.1**—*Continued*

U.S. Military - complete this section if you served in the U.S. Armed Forces.

Branch of Service _____ Dates of Service (Mo./Yr.) _____ to _____

Describe duties and any special training _____

_____

Rank at Discharge _____

---

**Other**

Have you ever been convicted of a misdemeanor or felony (other than a parking violation)? ☐ Yes ☐ No

If yes, explain _____

The type and seriousness of the crime, along with your entire work history, education history, and the position for which you are applying will be considered. A "Yes" response to the above question will not automatically disqualify you from consideration for employment with the BJC Health System.

---

**References**

Please give two references (not relatives or persons previously listed) who are acquainted with your training or activities during the past five years. If recent college graduate, professors and faculty advisors in your field of concentration are particularly helpful.

| Name | Address | Telephone number | Occupation | Years known |
|------|---------|------------------|------------|-------------|
|      |         |                  |            |             |
|      |         |                  |            |             |

---

**Remarks**

Make any comments thaqt you feel are important to your application.

---

The reponses given above are true and correct. I have not withheld any fact which might adversely affect my application, and understand that any omissions of fact or any false or misleading statements will be considered just cause for immediate dismissal, no matter when discovered. I further understand there may be no positions currently available. I agree that all former employers, or any other persons, may furnish any member of the BJC Health System with all information regarding my character and qualifications, and I release all such employers and persons from any liability regarding the provision or use of such information. I understand that if I am offered employment, I am not required to furnish any information which is prohibited by federal, state or local law, and that I may request reasonable accommodations, if needed due to disability, in order to participate in the overall application process. I will be required to successfully complete a job-related health screening provided and paid for by member of the BJC Health System, along with pre-employment testing for drug use. I also relinquish any claims and ownership of any specimen provided to any member of the BJC Health System. I will also provide such documents as required by " The Immigration Reform and Control Act of 1986." I understand that my employment application, including past references, a reference from my present supervisor, including disciplinary actions, if any, and attendance records may be made available to any member of the BJC Health System to which I have applied for transfer. I also agree that if transferred to another member of the BJC Health System, all personnel records and employee health records will be transferred to that member.

_____                    _____
Applicants signature                                Date

## HOW DID YOU HEAR ABOUT THIS JOB? CHECK ONE BOX NEXT TO THE APPROPRIATE RESPONSE:

| | |
|---|---|
| Advertisement In: | Harris Stowe College ____ hsc |
|   Post Dispatch ____ advpd | International Institute ____ ii |
|   Suburban Journal ____ advsj | New Southside Employment Coalition ____ nsec |
|   Other Magazine ____ advot | Project JESS ____ jess |
| I Know Employee Working Here Referred Me ____ eref | St. Louis Community Colleges ____ slcc |
| Called Hot Line for Jobs List ____ cal | St. Vincent DePaul ____ svd |
| Job Fair ____ jf | Technical Schools ____ tech |
| Job Service-Missouri/Illinios ____ jsvc | Temporary Agencies ____ ts |
| Mailed in ____ mal | Urban League ____ ul |
| I Worked Here Before ____ reh | Universities: |
| My Relative Working Here Referred Me ____ rref |   Southern Illinois Univ ____ usiu |
| Walk In On Own ____ wlk |   Univ of Missouri-St. Louis ____ umsl |
| Assoc. of Retired People ____ aarp |   Other ____ uot |
| Cardinal Ritter Institute ____ cri | Worker ReEntry ____ wre |
| Catholic Community Service ____ ccs | Others ____ |

We appreciate your interest in the BJC Health System. We are an equal opportunity employer and do not discriminate on the basis of race, color, religion, sex, national origin, age, disability, or veteran status as provided by law.

SMOKE-FREE AND DRUG-FREE WORKPLACE

---

**Figure 17.1**—*Continued*

While studying the application before the interview, the supervisor should keep in mind the job for which the applicant will be interviewed. If some questions arise while studying the application blank, the supervisor should write them down so that they will not be forgotten and will be asked. For example, all previous jobs are stated in chronological sequence; however, these data might reveal a gap of six months during which the applicant did not work or go to school. Careful questions about this may reveal that the candidate spent the time as unemployed, receiving rehabilitation for a substance abuse problem, traveling abroad or that a car accident required a lengthy hospital stay. Some questions may concern results of skill and aptitude tests given by the department of human resources, and any questions in this area should be clarified by the supervisor before the interview takes place.

Be careful not to ask questions that could be considered discriminatory or illegal. Your Human Resources Department will be able to assist you in designing your questions to avoid certain pitfalls. Examples of appropriate and inappropriate questions follow:

| Appropriate Questions | Inappropriate Questions |
|---|---|
| 1. What did you like best about your present (most recent) job? Why? What did you like least? | 1. Were you born in Cuba or the United States? |
| 2. What special assignments have you taken on in the past (or your current job) that will make you successful here? | 2. Will your husband (wife) have any problems with your working hours? |
| 3. Have you ever been convicted of any crime or misdemeanor other than parking violations? | 3. Have you ever been arrested for any crime? |
| 4. Is there anything that would preclude you from traveling out of town overnight or working overtime? | 4. Do you have babysitters arranged for your children? |
|  | 5. Did you dislike your current job because you were reporting to a woman? |

Some additional information can also be gained from a *reference check.* (See figure 17.2.) Such reference checks with previous employers are best handled by the human resources department; special care is advisable because of emerging personal privacy regulations and potential exposure to damage claims. The points to be checked should be job related. All reference checks should be done with the knowledge and permission of the applicant.

Since the purpose of the employment interview is to gather information to make a hiring decision, the supervisor should prepare a schedule or plan for the interview. The interviewer should jot down all those areas that need further clarification. Once all these key points have been written down, one is not likely to

** I HEREBY AUTHORIZE THE HOSPITAL TO CONTACT MY FORMER EMPLOYERS CONCERNING MY
   PRIOR RECORD OF EMPLOYMENT.

_____

Signature of Applicant

Name _____     Date _____
        Last                    First               MI

Organization _____     Employed from _____ to _____

Position _____     Social Security Number _____

The above applicant has given your name as a previous employer and reference that we may contact. Would you please verify the information concerning employment and complete the evaluation below:

I.      Please check the appropriate box:

| | EXCEPTIONAL* | SATISFACTORY | SOME DEFICIENCIES | UNSATISFACTORY |
|---|---|---|---|---|
| ATTENDANCE | | | | |
| ADAPTABILITY | | | | |
| ABILITY TO FUNCTION INDEPENDENTLY | | | | |
| INITIATIVE | | | | |
| PERFORMANCE RE: PATIENT CARE | | | | |
| PERFORMANCE RE: STAFF RELATIONS | | | | |
| ABILITY TO ASSUME LEADERSHIP | | | | |
| ABILITY TO COMMUNICATE (Verbal and written) | | | | |

* Exceptional:   Exceeds expectation of average candidate

II.     Do you feel the applicant can work in a situation where he will be judged on his/her abilities to participate as a member
        of an integrated team?   _____ Yes   _____ No

III.    Would you rehire?  Yes_____   No_____

IV.     Additional comments: _____
        _____
        _____
        _____
        _____
        _____
        _____

_____     _____     _____
Signature                   Title                       Date

**Figure 17.2**  Typical form for reference check.

forget to ask the interviewee about them. Conceivably, the supervisor may be interrupted during the interview, and the applicant might be dismissed before the supervisor has had a chance to ask about certain points that still lack information. Writing them down beforehand will prevent such an occurrence. Having thought out the various questions in advance, the supervisor can devote much of the attention to listening and observing the applicant. A well-prepared plan for the employment interview is well worth the time spent on it.

In addition to obtaining background information and making out a plan for the interview, the supervisor should be concerned with the proper setting for conducting the interview. Privacy and some degree of comfort are normal requirements for a good conversation. If a private room is not available, the supervisor should create an aura of semiprivacy by speaking to the applicant in a corner or in a place where other employees are not within hearing distance. That much privacy is a necessity. If it can be arranged, precautions should be taken to avoid any interruptions during the interview by phone calls or other matters that could distract your attention from the applicant. This gives the interviewee additional assurance of how much importance the supervisor places on this interview.

## ◼ Conducting the Interview

In conducting the employment interview, the supervisor should make certain that a leisurely atmosphere is created and that the applicant is put at ease. The good supervisor will think back about when he or she applied for a job and recall the stress and tension connected with it. After all, the applicant is meeting strange people who ask probing questions and is likely to be under considerable strain. It is the supervisor's duty to relieve this tension, which is certain to be present in the applicant, and possibly in the supervisor as well. The applicant might be put at ease by opening the interview with brief general conversation, possibly about the weather, traffic, or some other topic of broad interest. The interviewer may offer a cup of coffee or may employ any other social gesture that will put the applicant at ease and build rapport such as taking the applicant for a walk through the work area. A good starting question would be to ask how the applicant learned about this job opening.

This informal "warming-up" approach should be brief, and the interviewer should move the discussion quickly to job-related matters. Excessive nonjob-related informal conversation should be avoided. Studies have shown that sometimes the interviewer makes a selection decision in the first minutes of the interview, and it would be wrong to do this without having discussed job-related matters.

In addition to obtaining information from the applicant, the interviewer should see to it that the job seeker learns enough about the job to help the applicant decide whether he or she is the right person for the position. The supervisor, therefore, should discuss the details of the job, such as working conditions, wages, hours, vacations, who the immediate supervisor would be, and how the job in question relates to other jobs in the department. The supervisor must describe the situation completely and honestly. In his or her eagerness to make the job look as attractive as possible, especially to professionals who are in short supply, the supervisor conceivably may state everything in terms better than they actually are. The supervisor must be careful not to oversell the job by telling the applicant what is available for exceptional employees. If the applicant turns out to be an average worker, this will lead to disappointments.

After outlining the job's details, the supervisor should ask the applicant what else he or she would like to know about the job. If the interviewee has no further questions at this time, the supervisor should proceed with questioning to find out how well qualified the applicant is. The supervisor will have some knowledge about his or her background from the application; there is no need to ask the applicant to restate information already given. However, the interviewer will need to know exactly how qualified the interviewee is in relation to the job in question. By this time the applicant has probably gotten over much of the tension and nervousness and will be ready to answer questions freely. Most of this information will be obtained by the supervisor's direct questions. The interviewer should be careful to phrase these questions clearly for the applicant. In other words, only terms that conform with the applicant's language, background, and experience should be used. Questions should be asked in a slow and deliberate form, one at a time, so as not to confuse the applicant.

The interviewer should take care not to ask "leading" questions that would suggest a specific answer. For example, the supervisor should refrain from questions such as, "Do you have difficulty adjusting to authority?" or "Do you daydream frequently?" This form of questioning can only lead to antagonism.

Frequently, supervisors take notes during or, preferably, immediately after the interview. This can be helpful, especially if several candidates are being interviewed. It is difficult to remember in such a situation what each of the applicants said and not to get their statements confused. There is no need to take notes on everything; only the key factors should be jotted down.

All questions the supervisor asks should be pertinent and job related. This brings up the area of those questions that, although not directly related to the job itself, can become relevant to the work situation. Problems of a personal nature, although only indirectly connected with the job, may be relevant to the work situation. A supervisor will have to use good judgment and tact in this respect, since the applicant may be sensitive about some of the points to be discussed. By no means should the supervisor pry into personal affairs that are irrelevant and removed from the work situation merely to satisfy his or her own curiosity.

## ■ Equal Employment Opportunity Laws

Before the 1960s, the interviewer could ask almost any question that was job related in some way. Today, interviewing has become far more complicated and sophisticated because of the many laws, executive orders, and court decisions affecting equal employment opportunities, discrimination, and affirmative action. A number of questions are still perfectly lawful; for example, the interviewer can ask for the applicant's first and last names, current address, previous employment, educational background, etc. Questions that are for the most part unlawful include those about race or color, sex, religion, birthplace, and arrest record. Some questions are potentially unlawful to ask. For instance, it is certainly lawful to ask the applicant what other languages he or she speaks—it is desirable, even sometimes necessary, to speak Spanish for some jobs. However, this question should not lead to asking the applicant's native language and the one used at home. It would be presumptuous to provide a comprehensive list of what to ask and not ask in this text since each situation could involve legal restraints and has to be judged in the local context, relatedness to the job, and the particular circumstances.

It is far better for supervisors to consult with the human resources department periodically to learn what can be asked and in which way and what should not be asked. The laws and regulations are numerous and ever changing, and in some case may be state specific. New decisions are made by the courts and administrative agencies almost daily, so it is a full-time job to stay abreast of them. The staff in the personnel division are usually familiar with the most recent developments and proper current practices. The interviewer should consult with them to learn which questions are appropriate, lawful if properly worded, and unlawful. The interviewer may also receive some suggestions as to how to obtain information that is necessary but cannot be asked directly. For example, rather than asking "How would your spouse feel about you traveling a lot or working long hours" the supervisor may have to resort to questions such as, "Can you be away from home overnight if the job requires it?" or "Will your home responsibilities permit you to work around the clock?"

## ■ Evaluating the Applicant

The chief problem in employment interviews is how to interpret the candidate's employment and personal history and other pertinent information. It is impossible for supervisors to eliminate completely all their personal preferences and prejudices. Interviewers should face up to personal biases and make efforts to control them. A supervisor cannot claim that he or she has no biases, and should be able to clearly write down the reasons why one applicant has been selected over another. It is essential that the interviewers take great care to avoid some of the more common pitfalls while sizing up a job applicant.

The first of these pitfalls is making *snap judgments*. It is difficult not to form an early impression and look for evidence during the rest of the interview to substantiate this first impression. The interviewer should collect all the information on the applicant before making a judgment. This will also help the interviewer not to become a victim of the halo effect, which occurs when an interviewer lets one prominent characteristic overshadow other evidence. It means basing an applicant's entire potential for job performance on only one characteristic and using this impression as a guide in rating all the other factors. This may work either favorably or unfavorably for the job seeker. In any event, it would be wrong for the supervisor to form an overall opinion of the applicant on a single factor, such as the ability to express himself or herself fluently. If an applicant is articulate, there is no reason to automatically assume the rest of his or her qualifications are top notch. A glance at the employees in the department will remind the supervisor that there are some very successful employees whose verbal communications are rather poor.

Another common pitfall is that of *overgeneralization*. The interviewer must not assume that because an applicant behaves in a certain manner in one situation that he or she will automatically behave the same way in all other situations. There may be a special reason why the applicant may answer a question in a rather evasive manner. It would be wrong to conclude from this evasiveness in answering one question that the applicant is underhanded and probably not trustworthy. The halo effect would be there if the interviewer lets, for example, an applicant's alma mater overshadow other aspects. People are prone to generalize quickly.

Judging the applicant by *comparisons* with current employees in the department is another common mistake. The interviewer may wonder how this applicant will get along with the other employees and with the supervisor, and how the candidate will fit into the corporate culture. The interviewer may believe that any applicant who is considerably different from current employees is undesirable. This thinking may do great harm to the organization because it will only lead to uniformity, conformity, and thus mediocrity. This should not be interpreted to mean that the interviewer should make it a point to look for "oddballs" who obviously would not fit in the department. Just because a job applicant does not exactly resemble the other employees is no reason to conclude that the person will not make a suitable employee.

The interviewer should realize that the applicant may often give responses that are socially acceptable but not very revealing. The job seeker knows that the answer should be what the interviewer wants to hear. For example, if the interviewer asks a nurse what his or her aspirations are, the reply probably will be to be a head nurse one day. He or she settles for aspiring to be a head nurse rather than the director of nursing to avoid appearing conceited or presumptuous, because the applicant knows that a certain amount of ambition is socially acceptable.

Another hazard for the interviewer to avoid is *excessive qualifications*. Eager to get the best person for the job, the supervisor may look for qualifications that exceed the requirements of the job. Although the applicant should be qualified, there is no need to look for qualifications in excess of those actually required. An overqualified applicant would probably make a poor and frustrated employee, who will quickly become bored with the job. These are some of the more common pitfalls in interpreting the facts brought out during an interview. Supervisors should make an all-out effort not to fall into these traps when evaluating applicants.

## CONCLUDING THE INTERVIEW AND MAKING THE DECISION

The final step in the selection process is choosing an individual for the job. It is difficult to make a judgment based on all the information gathered. However, if our previous suggestions have been followed, the chances of making a successful decision are improved. We assume that it is within the supervisor's sole authority to decide and that the organization's policies and procedures do not require checking first with the line superior or someone in the human resources department. At the conclusion of the employment interview, the supervisor is likely to have the choice of three possible actions: hire the applicant, defer the decision, or reject the applicant. The applicant is eager to know which of these actions the supervisor is going to take and is entitled to an answer. No particular problem exists if the supervisor decides to hire this applicant; the person will be told when to report for work, and additional instructions may be given. The supervisor also may decide to defer a decision until several other applicants for the same job have been interviewed. In this case, it is necessary and appropriate for the supervisor to tell the interviewee and inform this person that he or she will be notified later. Preferably the supervisor will set a time limit within which the decision will be made.

Such a situation occurs frequently, but it is not fair to use this tactic to avoid the unpleasant task of telling the applicant that he or she is not acceptable. Under such circumstances, telling the applicant that the interviewing supervisor is deferring action raises false hopes. While waiting for an answer, the applicant may not look for another job and consequently may let some other opportunities slip by. It is unpleasant to tell an applicant that he or she is not suitable, but if the supervisor has decided that an applicant will not be hired, he or she should be told in a clear but tactful way. Although it is much simpler to let the rejected applicant wait for a letter that never arrives, the applicant is entitled to an honest answer. If the job seeker does not fulfill the requirements of the job, it is preferable to say so.

It is better not to state the specific reasons beyond a general turndown phrase. Supervisors may have experienced that stating reasons for not hiring someone encourages arguments and comparisons, and can lead to many other problems, especially since the chances for being misquoted and misunderstood are great. It is best to turn the applicant down by stating, in a general way, that there is not sufficient match between the applicant's qualifications and the needs of the job. It is also not fair to tell the applicant that he or she will be called if something suitable opens up if the interviewer knows that no hope exists.

The supervisor should always bear in mind that the employment interview is an excellent opportunity to build a good reputation for the institution. The applicant knows that he or she is one of several candidates and that only one person can be selected. A large percentage of applicants are not hired. The way they are turned down, however, can have an effect on their impression of the institution. The only contact the applicant has with the organization is through the supervisor during the employment interview. Therefore, the supervisor should remember that the interview will make either a good or a bad impression of the institution on the applicant. It is necessary, therefore, that an applicant leave the interview, regardless of its outcome, at least with the feeling that he or she has been courteously and fairly treated. Every supervisor should bear in mind that it is a managerial duty to build as much goodwill for the organization as possible and that the employment interview presents one of the rare opportunities to do so.

## ■ Documentation

In recent years, the need for documentation has become increasingly necessary, since the supervisor's decision about a job candidate might be challenged. Therefore, the interviewer must write down the reasons for not hiring a certain applicant and/or why the one was hired in preference to the others. It is essential to have this documentation because the supervisor could not possibly remember all the various reasons, and he or she may be asked to justify the decision later.

Generally speaking, the department of human resources will inform the line managers of what to do in this respect. Such documentation is even more important now because the decision to hire or reject an applicant should be based on job-related factors and should not be discriminatory. In some cases, supervisors might be pressured by the personnel department or higher management to give preferential hiring considerations to minorities or women. Supervisors should realize that the organization may have to meet certain affirmative action goals. Again, only by careful documentation will supervisors be able to justify their decisions. Notes on a separate piece of paper attached to the application will serve the purpose.

## ■ Temporary Placement

Sometimes, although the applicant is not the right person for a particular job, he or she may be suitable for another position for which no current opening exists. The supervisor might be tempted to hold this desirable employee by offering temporary placement in any job that is available. The applicant should be informed about this prospect by the supervisor. At times, however, temporary placement in an unsuitable job causes misunderstanding and disturbance within the department. It is usually strenuous for an employee to mark time on a job that he or she does not care to perform while hoping for the proper job to open up. Normally such strain causes dissatisfaction after some time, which is usually communicated to other employees within the work group. Also, the expected suitable job may not open up. Therefore, generally speaking, interim placements should be approached with great care.

## SUMMARY

There are two ways of filling available job openings: to hire someone from the outside or promote someone from within the organization. In hiring from outside, the supervisor is aided by the human resources department, since it performs the services of recruiting and preselecting the most likely applicants. It is the supervisor's function and duty, however, to interview the various candidates appropriately and to hire those who promise to be the best ones for the jobs available. To accomplish this, the supervisor must acquire the skills needed to conduct an effective interview. The employment interview is primarily a directive, or structured, interview, in contrast to the nondirective interview often encountered in the supervisor's daily work.

During the employment interview, the supervisor tries to find out whether the applicant's capability matches the demands of the job. The objective is to hire the person most suitable for the position available. To carry out a successful interview, the supervisor should become familiar with background information, list points to be covered and questions to be asked, be prepared in advance, and have the proper setting. In addition to securing information from the applicant, the interviewer should discuss with the interviewee as many aspects of the job as possible. There will be a number of additional questions and answers before the interviewer is ready to conclude the employment interview, evaluate the situation, and make a decision. All this must be accomplished while giving proper attention to the many aspects of equal and fair employment practices and other legal considerations.

In addition to conducting directive interviews, the supervisor is often called on to carry out nondirective interviews. This form of interview usually covers problematic situations and gives the employees the opportunity to freely express their feelings and sentiments. Many sources of frustration exist within and outside the working environment that can easily lead to a variety of undesirable responses. Giving subordinates the opportunity for a counseling interview is another vital duty of the supervisory position.

# Performance Appraisals, Promotions, and Transfers

*Chapter Objectives*

After you have studied this chapter, you should be able to:

1. Describe the purpose of periodic performance appraisals.
2. Discuss the role of the supervisor in performing the appraisal.
3. Outline problems in performance ratings.
4. Review the relationship between wage and salary structure and employee retention and recruitment.
5. Describe the purpose and methods of promotion.

The performance appraisal system is the ongoing process of gathering, analyzing, evaluating, and disseminating information about the performance of its employees. These appraisals not only guide management in selecting certain individuals for promotion and salary increases, but also are useful for coaching employees to improve their performance. Appraisals are an important part of long-range personnel planning and the supervisor's staffing function. In addition, well-identified and described appraisal methods and procedures will contribute to a healthy organizational environment of mutual trust and understanding. This type of atmosphere is necessary if the healthcare center wants to bring about increased productivity and better patient care. A performance appraisal system helps to identify work requirements, performance standards, analysis and appraisal of job-related behaviors, and recognition of such behaviors.

Performance appraisals are central to organizational and management development. Their purpose is to provide a measure of the employee's job performance that leads to counseling (motivation) and his or her further development (training). Since a performance appraisal is a formal system of measuring, evaluating, and influencing an employee's job-related activities it identifies the types of training experiences that may enhance the employee's performance. (See figure 18.1) Performance appraisal is a control system that serves as an audit of the effectiveness of each employee. Decisions regarding an employee's continued employment, promotion, demotion, transfer, salary increase, or possible termination are made on the basis of the performance appraisal. Performance

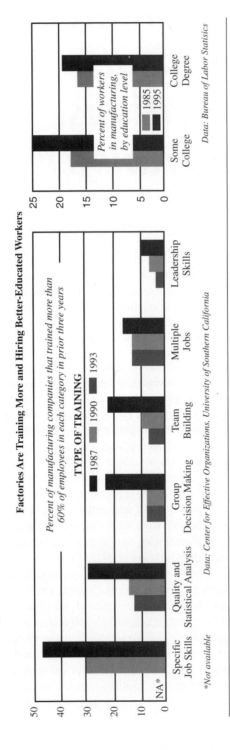

**Figure 18.1** Factories are training more and hiring better-educated workers.

*Reprinted from September 30, 1996 issue of Business Week by special permission, copyright © 1996 by the McGraw-Hill Companies, Inc.*

appraisals are important to maximize employee motivation and productivity, and to minimize the chances of litigation suits. In the typical organization, every employee is subject to a periodic performance appraisal. Every organization needs valid information that enhances management's effectiveness in the directing of human resources.

## THE PERFORMANCE APPRAISAL SYSTEM

The appraisal of an employee's performance is central to the supervisor's staffing function. It points to the need for further development, shows how effectively various subordinates contribute to departmental goals, and helps management identify those employees who have the potential to be promoted into better positions. It is important for a supervisor to be in a position to assess objectively the quality of the employees' performance in the department. Therefore, most organizations request that their supervisors carry out the provisions of the institution's formal appraisal system and periodically appraise and rate their employees. (See figure 18.2.) This formal appraisal system is also known as *employee evaluation, employee rating,* or *merit rating.* For our purposes it is assumed that the system has been designed so that it is legally defensible and not discriminatory in any way.

### ■ Purposes of the Performance Appraisal System

The performance appraisal system serves many purposes, such as to provide a guide for possible promotion, further development, and a basis for merit increases. Another purpose is to translate the performance, experience, and qualities of an employee into objective terms and then to compare them with the requirements of the job. The formal appraisal system is designed to consider such criteria as job knowledge, ability to carry through on assignments, judgment, attitude, cooperation, dependability, output, housekeeping, and safety. Such a system of evaluations helps the supervisor to take all factors into account when considering merit increases or a promotion. It also provides a rational basis for decision making, since it reduces the chances for personal bias.

Such a formal appraisal system forces the supervisor to observe and scrutinize a subordinate's work not only from the viewpoint of how well the employee is performing the job, but also from the standpoint of what can be done to improve the employee's performance. It is difficult to make such judgments because in most healthcare settings one is not dealing with concrete performance measures such as units produced, but with concepts of leadership, teamwork, and cooperation. Since an employee's poor performance and failure to improve may result from inadequate supervision, a formal appraisal system is also likely to improve supervisory qualities.

A formal evaluation system also serves another purpose. Employees have always expected security from their work. In addition to it, they seek satisfying and interesting work that enables them to grow. A well-designed appraisal system reduces ambiguity concerning job requirements and uncertainty by providing employees with information about what is expected from them and feedback on how they have performed.

**BJC HEALTH SYSTEM NON-MANAGEMENT PERFORMANCE APPRAISAL / FORM A**

| | | | | | |
|---|---|---|---|---|---|
| Employee's Name | | | | | Employee Number: |
| Title: Dept.: | | | | | Entity: |
| Appraisal Period From: 7/1/19__ through 6/30/19__ | | | | | Purpose of Review: Annual ______ Other ____________ |
| E = Exceeds Expectations M = Meets Expectations I = Inconsistently Meets Expectations | | | | | |
| Principal Accountabilities | Weight | E | M | I | COMMENTS |
| #1 | | | | | |
| #2 | | | | | |
| #3 | | | | | |
| #4 | | | | | |
| #5 | | | | | |
| #6 | | | | | |
| #7 | | | | | |
| Total Weight Must Equal: | 8 | E | M | I | CIRCLE THE OVERALL RATING<br>Superior — Min. 6 E's; No I's<br>Exceeds Expectations — Min. 4 E's; No I's<br>Meets Expectations — Max. 1 I<br>Inconsistently Meets Expectations — Max. 3 I's<br>Unacceptable — 4 or more I's |
| TOTAL: | | | | | |

8610-100 NEW 1/94

**Figure 18.2** Example of a performance appraisal form: weighting format.

*Courtesy of BJC Health System, St. Louis, MO.*

Attendance - Comments on the Employee's Attendance and Punctuality

**EMPLOYEE GROWTH AND DEVELOPMENT PLAN**

Directions: Describe the agreed upon action plan for improving performance in the employee's current job and/or developing the employee for possible future responsibilities within the organization. Include both the role of the supervisor and the role of the employee in implementing the plan.

| Areas for Growth, Development and/or Improvement | Action Plan: Plans should be realistic, yet require effort and be stated in measurable terms. | | |
|---|---|---|---|
| | | | |

Current Rate: _____    Total Increase: _____ %   (Base: _____ %    Lump Sum: _____ %)    New Rate: _____    Effective Date of Increase: _____

**Signatures:**

Employee Signature: _____    Date: _____
(Your signature indicates neither agreement nor disagreement, but it does indicate that this evaluation has been discussed with you.)

Immediate Supervisor's Signature: _____    Date: _____

Second Level Supervisor's Signature: (optional) _____    Date: _____

Employee Comments:

Distribution: Original: Entity Human Resources          Copies: Department File and Employee

**Figure 18.2**—*Continued*

271

| CRITERIA-BASED JOB DESCRIP- TION AND PERFORMANCE STANDARDS | **Position Title** Multiskilled Administrative Support Staff (MASS) | **Hospital** Lakeland Regional Medical Center |
|---|---|---|
| | **Responsible To** Within-the-Team Leader and/or Department Leader(s) | **Date** November 16, 1995 |
| | **Department** | **Page** 1 |
| | **Typist** | **Approved By** |

All the criteria-based duties and standards within this document will be performed according to established policies, procedures, and guidelines within the department and the Hospital.

## ■ Job Summary

The Multiskilled Administrative Support Staff (MASS) is responsible to Within-the-Team Leader and/or Department Leader(s). Works as an empowered member of a self-directed work team committed to a common purpose and goals, and holds self mutually accountable for team outcomes, under the general supervision of a Within-the-Team Leader. Shares 24-hour, 7 day/week responsibility for all aspects of department administrative support. Performs miscellaneous duties as assigned.

## ■ Primary Job Duties

1. Makes decisions consistent with the principles and tenets of patient-focused care.
2. Demonstrates continuous learning and improvement of competence in own job role and actively participates in departmental performance improvement program so that patient outcomes are improved and costs are reduced.
3. Takes personal responsibility for self and accountability for actions in a self-directed work team environment, as well as sharing the work of the team.
4. Promotes patient, physician, and staff satisfaction.
5. Responsible for performing all data collection and computer entry to service, discharge, and transfer functions.
6. Contacts appropriate payor source to verify and interpret benefit availability for each patient.
7. Contacts patients scheduled for service to communicate billing instructions and set up payment schedules as required.
8. Insures appropriate financial counseling is provided to each patient to include collection of required deposits, and identification and management of problem accounts.

9. Contacts physicians to have admissions classified as required.
10. Insures the appropriate payor order is established in the patient record and notifies utilization review as appropriate.
11. Schedules patients for preadmission, admission, and bed placement.
12. Collects, archives, and reports all pertinent department and/or center statistical information related to census or regulatory requirements.
13. Performs a variety of department-specific clerical duties as required. Examples include basic word processing and other computer skills, time keeping, payroll, maintenance of the medical record, filing, mail distribution, ordering and stocking of supplies, and charging and posting of supplies utilized.
14. Performs receptionist duties as required including beeper, intercom, and telephone communications; as well as providing information to patients, visitors, employees, and physicians.

---

| | | |
|---|---|---|
| **TEAM/UNIT QUALITY OF WORK-OUTCOME** | **1.0** | The following standards relate to the team's performance in the categories of quality, productivity and interpersonal relations. All performance demonstrates an understanding of the care of patients utilizing the principles of Patient-Focused care. |

- Resources must be patient-focused and fully utilized.
- All operations must be responsive to patient and physician needs.
- Individuals at all levels must be accountable and satisfied.
- Patients must readily perceive value in their care.

1.1 10% Continuously improves the cost-effectiveness, efficiency, and quality of care to patients so that the OPIP unit or team relative value score is between 3.2 and 2.8. Distinguishes the OPIP trending data that is applicable to the MASS role and formulates improvement action plans.

**Source of Information:** Organizational Performance Improvement Plan Scores.

**Measurement Criteria:** Exceeds if relative value score is < 2.8

1.2 10% Consistently performs 100% of the Stage 2 behaviors in team development matrix, so that the team functions effectively to perform the total work of the team as evidenced by the use of Patient-Focused Tenets*.

| | |
|---|---|
| * Seek the Source | * Work it out |
| * Team with the docs | * Focus on care |
| * Serve the patient | * Lend a hand |
| * Keep it simple | * Keep it current |
| * Be the best | * Keep the continuity |

**Source of Information:** Supervisory Observation—10%
Documented Team Examples—50%
Input from patient/physician satisfaction surveys—30%
Peer Review—10%
**Measurement Criteria:**
Meets: Can demonstrate 100% of the behaviors at Stage 2 using 5 tenets consistently within/across team(s).

Exceeds: Consistently performs 100% of the behaviors at Stage 4 of Team Development.

1.3   10%   The team consistently demonstrates a willingness and flexibility to assume a workload level resulting in efficient/productive team utilization. All team members are flexible to provide coverage across all shifts and to adjust staffing related to the work of the unit as needed so that paid hours for the team are within budget.

**Source of Information:**
FTE management reports (monthly)
**Measurement Criteria:**
Meets: Team FTE/OT are 98–100% of budget.
Exceeds: Team < 98% of budget.

1.4   20%   Records are reviewed for complete and accurate documentation, including demographic, guarantor/insurance, and financial (i.e., charge posting) follow-up resulting in positive reimbursement outcomes.

**Source of Information:**
Team-based file review (2/member/yr) to be completed within the team—25%
MASS II review (2/member/yr)—50%
Number of reimbursement denials/errors. (Provided by finance)—25%
Total number of errors divided by the number of admissions.
**Measurement Criteria:**
Meets: Overall accuracy rate of 95–97%.
Exceeds: Overall accuracy rate is greater than 97%.

---

**INDIVIDUAL QUALITY OF WORK OUTCOMES**   2.0   Each individual must take personal responsibility for self through demonstrated competence, continuous learning, active participation in the departmental performance improvement program as well as sharing the work of the self-directed team. The process of continued team development is based on the success of this individual's development, which is measured in the performance standards below:

2.1   15%   Demonstrates technical competence of all primary job duties for MASS, as specified at the advanced beginner or competent level so that desired outcomes are met or continually improved.

**Source of Information:** Department—identified tools of assessment (written and oral tests, observed skills, demonstration, etc.). Team-based file review (2/member/yr) to be completed within the team—25%.
MASS II review (2/member/yr)—50%.
**Measurement Criteria:**
Meets: Advanced beginner/competent skills and file reviews indicate 95–97% accuracy.
Exceeds: Demonstrates expert performance with > 97% accuracy.

2.2    5%    Demonstrates positive interpersonal skills/relationships with both customers and peers as demonstrated by positive guest relations, good phone etiquette, offering assistance/direction to guest/peers, and initiating direct and honest communication.

**Source of Information:**
Supervisory Observation—20%
Peer Review—40%
Documented examples—40%
**Measurement Criteria:** See Subjective Criteria

2.3    10%    Optimize outcomes through appropriate follow-up, seeking appropriate resources as needed and initiating independent actions based on judgment. (i.e, Initiation of referrals to outside agencies for unfunded patient admission.)

**Source of Information:**
Documented examples—40%
Chart/folder review—40%
Supervisory observation—20%
**Measurement Criteria:** See Subjective Criteria

2.4    5%    Actively supports the LRMC Culture through consistent demonstration of the six fundamental components. Meets with Department Manager/Leader to: (1) ensure understanding of the Culture's fundamental components, (2) seek assistance in identifying opportunities for improvement, and (3) establish a personalized set of goals and objectives for continuous improvement.

**Source of Information:**
Direct observation by manager/leader, team feedback, patient/customer feedback.
**Measurement Criteria:**
Meets if consistently demonstrates five of the six fundamental components.

Exceeds if consistently demonstrates continuous improvement in at least three of the six components.

2.5    5%    Consistently meets job expectations and does not exceed budgeted authorized hours during performance appraisal period unless specifically approved by department manager.

**Source of Information:**
Department FTE and payroll reports.
**Measurement Criteria:**
Meets if hours paid are 98–100% of budgeted authorized hours. Exceeds if hours paid are less than 98% of budgeted authorized hours. Does Not Meet if hours paid are more than 100% of budgeted authorized hours.

2.6    10%    Performs a variety of department-specific clerical duties as required. Examples include basic word processing and other computer skills, time keeping, payroll, maintenance of the medical record, filing, mail distribution, ordering and stocking of supplies, and charging and posting of supplies utilized.

**Source of Information:**
Direct observation by manager/leader, within-the-team leader.
**Measurement Criteria:**
Subjective criteria demonstrates positive outcomes.

*Courtesy of Lakeland Regional Medical Center, Inc. Lakeland, Florida.*

Every employee has the right to know how well he or she is doing and what can be done to improve their work performance.

One can assume that most employees are eager to know what their supervisors think of their work. In some instances, the employee's desire to know how he or she stands with the boss can be interpreted as asking for reassurance about his or her future in the organization. In other instances this expressed desire has different interpretations. For example, a supervisee may realize that he or she is doing a relatively poor job but hopes to find that the boss is not aware of it. On the other hand, another subordinate who knows that he or she is doing an outstanding job may wish to make certain that the boss is aware of it. This supervisee will want to receive more recognition.

Regular appraisals are important incentives to the employees of an organization. In a large, complex organization employees can easily feel that they and their contributions are forgotten and lost. Regular appraisals assure employees that the potential exists for improving oneself in the position and that one is not lost within the enterprise. It assures employees that supervisors and the entire organization care about them.

Some organizations are experimenting with an approach known as *empowerment*. It permits individuals within a work team to make certain decisions about their work assignments, schedules, and other related items. When we discussed *teams* earlier in the text, this decision-making freedom was in the context of delegation and authority. If you and your subordinates are working in an environment that supports *empowerment* and *team* structures, then it may be appropriate to allow team members to prepare or contribute to the performance appraisal of a member of the team. Team members often know the strengths and weaknesses of a fellow team member better than the supervisor. Caution must be exercised not to overly criticize or praise an individual without adequate substantiation of the facts.

The appraisal program is a critical tool at the disposal of the supervisor, since it influences all personnel functions. It is a determinant in the planning, developing, and recognition of the organization's human resources. Performance appraisals motivate employees, which benefits the organization. The supervisor will have ample opportunity to include the topics of motivation, such as Theories X and Y and hierarchy of needs (see chapter 20), in the appraisal procedure, particularly during the appraisal interview. These motivational theories can be incorporated into the performance appraisal, thus leading to an environment of trust.

In addition to creating a healthy organizational climate of trust, performance appraisals help management make decisions about compensation and employees' developmental and training needs. Appraisals provide an inventory of human resources suitable for promotions. They aid the supervisor because they show whether an employee is in the right job. They identify for the boss those employees who are moving ahead and those who are not progressing satisfactorily. Appraisals show whether the supervisor is succeeding in the job as a coach and teacher.

Another *inventory* that may result from performance appraisals is known as a *skills inventory.* It is often the output from the development section of a performance appraisal. In the development section, both the employee and his supervisor discuss the individual's skill strengths and weaknesses. Skills used both on the job and off the job should be noted. The strengths of all staff are captured in the inventory. Strengths may include such things as "Internet skills," "calligraphy," "public speaking experience at the Chamber of Commerce," "pilot in-training," etc. The benefit of a skills inventory for the organization is obvious. The inventory allows the organization to search "within" the organization for new or unusual skills before filling a position with an external applicant.

As mentioned, an appraisal program also has many advantages for employees. It reflects the quality of their work and gives them a sense of being treated fairly and not being overlooked. The employee knows what he or she can do to be promoted to a better job. Appraisals give the subordinate an opportunity to complain and criticize and to express personal goals and ambitions. In this respect, appraisals are motivational because they create a learning experience for subordinates that inspires them to improve.

## TIMING OF APPRAISALS

Appraisals must be conducted regularly to be significant to the employee and the organization. A one-time performance measure is of little importance. Therefore, the supervisor should formally appraise all the employees within the department at regular intervals at least once a year. This formal appraisal means completing special forms and a follow-up evaluation interview. One year is normally considered a sufficient period. Ideally, employees should be evaluated several times throughout the year to ensure that they receive timely feedback on their performance and to separate the performance review from the timing of a wage adjustment.

If an employee has just started in a new or more responsible position, however, it is advisable to make an appraisal within three to six months. These periodic appraisals will assure the employee that whatever improvement was made will be noticed and that he or she will be recognized for this progress. As time goes on, periodic ratings and reviews will become an important determinant of an employee's morale. It reaffirms the supervisor's interest in the employees and in their continued development and improvement.

Annual formal appraisals and their review do not take the place of the feedback on performance that is part of the day-to-day coaching responsibilities of the supervisor. Employees should receive feedback daily; it is well known that performance feedback is most effective when it occurs immediately after the event to which it relates. This applies equally to feedback on below-par performance and to recognition of above-par performance. Without this ongoing daily feedback, formal, once-a-year appraisals would not suffice.

## WHO IS THE APPRAISER?

A major difficulty in effective performance appraisal is that we as human beings can only make subjective appraisals. This creates *intellectual* and *perceptional problems,* leading to the rater's own interpretation of reality and not necessarily absolute reality. To minimize these shortcomings, some organizations devise an appraisal system in which the employee is evaluated by various appraisers. This may include self-appraisals and peer appraisals; in some systems, the appraisals are subject to reviews by those higher up in the administrative hierarchy. A few organizations have assessment centers for evaluating employees for their future potential as managers. (This concept is discussed more fully toward the end of this chapter.)

With the exception of *team-cultured* organizations, almost all organizations, however, have come to the conclusion that at lower- and middle-management levels, the appraisal is best performed by the individual's immediate supervisor. Formal authority inherent in the managerial hierarchy means, among many other aspects, the supervisor's right to make decisions in reference to the subordinate's performance. Among all other appraisers, the immediate supervisor is the person who should know the duties of the jobs within the department best. The immediate supervisor has the best opportunity to observe the appraisee on the job and provide feedback. Furthermore, most subordinates want to receive performance-related feedback from their immediate superior and feel more comfortable in discussing the appraisal with him or her.

Therefore, it is best for the immediate line supervisor to make the evaluation. Sometimes it may be necessary for the first-line boss to call on the help of the next higher supervisor. In some institutions the appraisal is made by a committee made up of the first-line supervisor, his or her boss, and possibly one or two other supervisors, as long as the appraisers have adequate knowledge of the performance of the person being rated. This also has the advantage of reducing some of the immediate supervisor's personal prejudices. Alternative sources to supervisory appraisals are particularly necessary in situations in which the superior has little opportunity to observe the employee on the job; this is a problem concerning all enterprises that work around the clock.

*Self-appraisal,* or *self-rating,* is an alternative source of supervisory appraisals. There are several advantages to self-ratings: they (1) often contain less halo error; (2) show the supervisor how the employee perceives the responsibilities and problems of the position; (3) help to identify differences of opinions; and (4) are particularly useful when employees work in isolation. However, self-appraisal can often lead to a conflicting situation when the supervisor's appraisal differs significantly from an inflated self-rating by the employee. Often the appraisal system combines self-appraisals and supervisory appraisals.

At times, *peers* are used as appraisers. They can provide valuable information about their colleagues because of their daily interactions if they have close contact with one another. They can observe how an employee interacts with them, the subordinates, and the boss. Peer appraisals offer independent judgment and have often proved to be good predictors of performance when used as a basis for promotion.

However, some powerful influences in organizational life may distort or cloud a peer's perception. Most employees have a strong need for security and work for present and future rewards from the employer. If someone else receives additional rewards, the chances for additional rewards become smaller for everyone else, since the resources are limited. This competition for current or future employer rewards, whether readily apparent or not, could possibly distort a peer's perception of a colleague's performance and potential. In addition, friendships and stereotyping may bias the rating. Friendship does not relate only to individuals, but also to groups. For instance, the appraiser may evaluate some peer in a group of which he or she was once a member. The appraiser may be tempted to rate members of that particular group higher than individuals in another group. Also, at times peers are not willing to evaluate each other, considering it to be an inducement to snitching on one another.

For all practical purposes, appraisal done by the immediate supervisor should suffice, and in most organizations the immediate supervisor is the primary, if not the only, appraiser of employee performance. However, the use of multiple sources of appraisals is likely to obtain a more comprehensive evaluation.

Performance appraisal consists of two distinct steps: the preparation of the performance rating and the appraisal interview that follows.

---

## PERFORMANCE RATING

To minimize and overcome the difficulties in appraising an employee, most enterprises find it advisable to use some type of appraisal form. These appraisal forms are prepared by the personnel department, often in conjunction with outside consultants and with the supervisors' suggestions. As mentioned, great care must be exercised to make certain that the system used is legally defensible.

Although innumerable types of appraisal forms are available, most of them specify job-related and important criteria for measuring job performance, intelligence, and personality traits. In addition to determining criteria, standards must be clarified to determine how well employees are performing. The instrument most used in the appraisal process will be based on both behavior and traits. The following are qualities and characteristics that most frequently are rated. For nonsupervisory personnel, typical qualities rated are quantity and quality of work produced, job knowledge, dependability, cooperative attitude, supervision required, housekeeping, unauthorized absenteeism, tardiness, safety, and personal appearance. For managerial and professional employees, typical factors are analytical ability, judgment, initiative, leadership, quality and quantity of work produced, knowledge of work, attitude, dependability, and emotional stability. For each of these factors the supervisor is supposed to select the degree of achievement attained by the employee. In some instances, a point system is provided to arrive at a numerical scoring. The form is usually a "check-the-box" type and reasonably simple to fill out. (See figure 18.3.)

Despite the outward simplicity of some rating blanks, the supervisor will probably run into a number of difficulties. First, not all supervisors agree on what is meant by a simple adjective rating scale, such as unsatisfactory, marginal, satisfactory, above average, and superior. It is advisable, therefore, that the form contain a descriptive sentence in addition to each of these adjectives: for *unsatisfactory,* "performance clearly fails to meet minimum requirements"; for *marginal,* "performance occasionally fails to meet minimum requirements"; for *satisfactory,* "performance meets or exceeds minimum requirements"; for *above average,* "performance consistently exceeds minimum requirements"; and for *superior,* "performance clearly exceeds all job requirements." Instead of the adjective, the supervisor might choose from descriptive sentences the one that most adequately describes the employee.

For example, in rating a nurse's degree of emotional stability, the appraiser may have the following choices:

1. "Unreliable in crises; goes to pieces easily; cannot take criticism"
2. "Unrealistic; emotions and moodiness periodically handicap his or her dealings; he or she personalizes issues"
3. "Usually on an even keel; has mature approach to most situations"
4. "Is realistic; generally maintains good behavior balance in handling situations"
5. "Self-possessed in high degree; has outstanding ability to adjust to circumstances, no matter how difficult"

## Problems in Performance Rating

Doing a performance rating of an employee is frequently subject to a number of errors and weaknesses because it is a subjective process. Some of these errors are more common than others. The supervisor should be aware of these pitfalls in order to minimize the errors in processing, storing, and recalling observed behavior. Some supervisors have a tendency to be overly *lenient* in their ratings, rating appraisees higher than normal. They are afraid that they might antagonize those being evaluated if they rate them low, thus making them less cooperative.

---

### PERFORMANCE REVIEW FORMAT

EMPLOYEE: _____

JOB TITLE: Registered Nurse and Graduate Nurse

DEPARTMENT: Nursing

SUPERVISOR: Clinical Coordinator

DATE OF HIRE: _____

TYPE OF REVIEW: ___ PROBATIONARY ___ ANNUAL ___ TRANSFER/PROMOTION ___ OTHER

---

<u>JOB SUMMARY</u>:

The Registered Nurse maintains the delivery of quality patient care by assuring that the Nursing Care Plan is carried out. She/he may serve as charge nurse in the absence of the supervisor. The position combines the activities of direct and indirect patient care.

The Graduate Nurse carries out these activities under direct supervision of a Registered Nurse. She has no charge nurse responsibilities.

**★★**

The performance review addresses the overall requirements of the above stated employee in a criteria-based format. There is an area to delineate accomplishments and goals not specifically described in the basic criteria. The reviewer is to check the appropriate category and summarize the employee's performance over the past year.

<u>DIRECTIONS</u>:

1. Check each performance standard competency

   I   =   Does not meet standard

   II   =   Meets standard

   III   =   Exceeds standard

2. Enter comments deemed necessary in space provided after each competency.

| A. Written Communication | I | II | III |
|---|---|---|---|

– –consistently utilizes the appropriate charting format.
  a. Documents appropriately on chart forms in a timely manner.
  b. Documents legibly.
  c. Utilizes only approved abbreviations.
  d. Demonstrates an understanding of the legal implications of charting.
  e. Nursing Assessment – within 24 hours of admission.
  f. Weekly Summary – within 48 hours of the 7-day period.
  g. Discharge Summary – within 48 hours.
  h. Nursing Care Plan – within 48 hours of admission.
  i. Treatment Plan – Initial, Updates, Discharge preparations for presentation at Team Conference.
  j. Monthly Summaries – within 48 hours of the 30-day period.
  k. FIM Admitting – within 72 hours of admission.
  l. FIM Discharge – within 24 hours of discharge.

---

**Figure 18.3**  Example of a performance appraisal form: check-the-box format.

*"Courtesy of HealthSouth Treasure Coast Rehabilitation Hospital, Vero Beach, FL"*

*Continued*

|  | I | II | III |
|---|---|---|---|

– –completes admission documentation within 24 hours
of admission.
– –uses communication forms appropriately, e.g., Transfer Sheets, Incident
Reports, etc.
– –documentation on patient's chart correlated with Nursing Care Plan.

Written Communication Comments:

B.  Verbal Communication
– –demonstrates effective interviewing skills to elicit information from patient
and/or family that is necessary to plan, implement, and evaluate nursing
care.
– –applies verbal and nonverbal communication skills to identify and reduce
anxiety in patient and/or family.
– –verbalizes patient care expectations to co-workers in goal-directed report
throughout the shift.
– –gives and seeks feedback to and from rehabilitation team members regarding
patient's progress towards goals.
– –suggests appropriate contacts with other disciplines and resources in order
to achieve patient care/nursing goals.
– –assists with Nursing's role in Team Conference.

Verbal Communication Comments:

C.  Teaching Methods
– –explains procedures, tests, and treatments in understandable terms to
patient, family/others and documents the same.
– –assists in implementing teaching programs for patients and families.
– –maintains a positive environment to create an atmosphere conducive
to learning.
– –exhibits knowledge of teaching principles/information.
– –utilizes aids relative to area being taught.
– –participates in orientation and staff development — a preceptor.

Teaching Methods Comments:

D.  Decision Making
– –incorporates nursing process in clinical practice based on continuing
education.
– –sets and revises priorities in response to situation and on-going change/
evaluation.
– –recognizes crisis situations and takes appropriate and immediate action to
resolve the situation.
– –takes responsibility to complete interventions.
– –makes decisions that reflect consistency with hospital philosophy,
policies, and procedures and is supportive of them and administration

**Figure 18.3**—*Continued*

| | I | II | III |
|---|---|---|---|

and staff.
– –evaluates effectiveness and implications of own decisions and assumes responsibility for the same.
– –identifies patient rights and serves as patient advocate.

Decision Making Comments:

E. Discharge Planning
– –documents discharge information and/or home situation on Nursing Care Plan within 24 hours of admission.
– –demonstrates basic understanding of the discharge process by recognizing need to involve resource persons with appropriate documentation.
– –completes details of discharge consistent with hospital guidelines.

Discharge Planning Comments:

F. Safe Physical and Psychological Care
– –identifies needs on head-to-toe physical assessment and delivers safe care following prescribed therapies.
– –has ability to assign meanings to symptoms and initiate appropriate action to relieve or reduce symptoms.
– –maintains safe patient environment.
– –initiates and documents actions taken to prevent and/or correct risk situations to patient, families, co-workers, and self.
– –performs technical functions and directs patient care consistent with scientific principles and hospital policies and procedures.
– –has to identify and communicate significant abnormalities in patient's data to appropriate rehabilitation team member.
– –recognizes emergency situations and takes corrective action.
– –consults resources when confronted with new or unfamiliar task or situation and follows through with nursing intervention.
– –has to recognize a correlation between emotional stresses and physical manifestations.
– –demonstrates preservation of human dignity and confidentiality to patients and families.
– –uses proper technique to transfer and move patients. Uses a gait belt.

Safe Physical and Psychological Care Comments:

**Figure 18.3**—*Continued*

*Continued*

COMMENTS:

EMPLOYEE COMMENTS:

I have received, read, and understand my job evaluation.

Days Absent     _____

Days Tardy     _____

CPR Exp. Date     _____

License Exp. Date     _____

_____
Employee Signature

_____
Supervisor Signature

_____
Date

GOALS TO BE ACHIEVED OVER THE COMING REVIEW PERIOD:

**Figure 18.3**—*Continued*

Other supervisors are overly harsh in rating their employees and appraise them lower than the average appraiser. To give consistently low ratings is equally damaging as being too lenient. A low rating for an individual being evaluated may also reflect on the supervisor's own inability to motivate his or her subordinates.

For example, the nursing personnel on one station may be consistently appraised higher than those on the next station. Thus, it is difficult to determine whether this is because of one head nurse's strictness or the other's leniency, or whether this reflects real differences in the employees' abilities and performance.

Another common error is *central tendency,* in which the appraiser rates the employees as average or around the midpoint, although the employees' performance warrants a higher or lower rating. Such a supervisor is often reluctant to rate employees high or low. This tendency shows that the supervisor may be unprepared for the formal appraisal and avoids being decisive. Another subjective error of the appraiser is to be influenced by the *halo effect* (discussed in chapter 17), which is the tendency of many appraisers to let the rating they assign to one characteristic influence their rating on all subsequent characteristics. This works in two directions. Rating the appraisee excellent on one factor influences the rater to give the employee another high rating or higher rating on other qualities than he or she actually deserves. On the other hand, rating the employee unsatisfactory on one factor influences the appraiser to give the appraisee another low rating or lower-than-deserved rating on other factors. One way to minimize the halo effect is to rate all employees on a single factor or trait before going on to the next factor. In other words, the supervisor only rates one factor of each employee at a time and then goes on to the next employee for the same factor, and so on. This enables the supervisor to standardize the ratings. Additionally, it is not necessary that the distribution of ratings resemble a normal, or bell-shaped, curve.

A further distortion can be caused by interpersonal relations and bias. The ratings may be influenced by the supervisor's likes and dislikes about each individual working in the department. This is especially apparent when objective standards of performance are difficult to determine or not available.

Another error in making appraisals is the *similar-to-me* tendency. Some raters are tempted to judge more favorably those employees whose attitudes resemble their own.

Another source of difficulty arises from *organizational influences* the way administration uses the ratings. Often raters are lenient when they know that pay raises and promotions depend on the appraisals. If the organizational emphasis is on further employee development, appraisers are inclined to be harsh and emphasize weaknesses.

The supervisor's judgment must be based on the total performance of the employee. It would be unfair to appraise a subordinate based on only one assignment on which he or she had done particularly well or poorly. Also, instead of recognizing the employee's performance during the entire appraisal period, the supervisor may just rate the appraisee's most recent behavior. If periodic appraisals are performed at intervals throughout the evaluation period, a supervisor is less likely to judge an individual on the most recent experience.

Supervisors must caution themselves not to let random or first impressions of an employee influence their judgment, which should be based on the employee's total record of performance, reliability, initiative, skills, resourcefulness, and capability. Obtaining input from peers and customers served by the employee, and combining these observations with the supervisor's impressions, will result in fairer assessment of the individual's performance.

Supervisors also should not allow past performance appraisal ratings to influence current ratings unjustly either way. An aid to minimize these errors and biases is to document employee behavior as soon as possible after the occurrence. When the formal appraisal takes place, supervisors can refer back to the documentation, thus minimizing biases and other pitfalls in rating.

Observing all these problems in rating will help supervisors overcome subjectivity in processing, storing, and recalling observed behavior when evaluations are made. Although the results are not perfect, many human errors can be significantly reduced and counteracted by the top-level administration emphasizing training for those who do the appraising. Such training is necessary because appraisals that are biased, inaccurate, or distorted will not increase an employee's motivation. These errors may lead to poor promotion and retention decisions, and even possibly to charges of discrimination. Training supervisors in how to observe behavior is an ongoing process. The success of the performance appraisal largely depends on the supervisor's ability to obtain accurate information and then to discuss it with the appraisee in a non-threatening and constructive manner. The evaluation interview that follows the appraisal fulfills this function.

## THE APPRAISAL INTERVIEW

The second step in the appraisal procedure, the appraisal interview, takes place when the immediate superior who has prepared the formal evaluation sits down with the individual being evaluated to discuss the appraisee's performance. Some supervisors would prefer to shy away from having to tell their subordinates how they stand in the department and what they should do to improve. They are reluctant because, unless it is done with great sensitivity, this type of interview can lead to hostility and even greater misunderstanding. Many employees distrust anything that relates to their review, starting with the validity of the measuring instrument used, the appraiser's ability to observe, and so forth. Employees may be reluctant to discuss their workplace behavior. However, this discussion is absolutely essential to ensure effective appraisals.

The institution should provide supervisors with learning opportunities to carry on appraisals in such a way that they are effective. Therefore, many facilities provide training in conducting appraisals in such forms as practice sessions, behavior modeling training programs, role-playing experiences, in-basket exercises, and assessment centers, and so forth. All this is done to increase the supervisors' effectiveness in dealing with those being evaluated, to improve their observer accuracy, and to aid them in carrying out appraisal interviews effectively. According to some experts the four major formats for this interview are (1) the tell-and-sell approach, (2) the tell-and-listen format, (3) the problem-solving approach, and (4) a mixed interview combining all these formats.

Although experienced supervisors probably do not need to follow a formalized system, administration does often suggest that supervisors follow a standardized outline. According to this approach, the supervisor should first state the purpose of the evaluation procedure and the interview. The supervisor should proceed to a discussion of the evaluation itself, first stating the subordinate's strong points and then the weak points. Next, there should be a general discussion, giving the employee an opportunity to state his or her opinions and feelings.

Another possible procedure is to let subordinates appraise themselves first. This gives the appraisees the opportunity to state their side of the story first. It is easier for many subordinates to criticize themselves than to take criticism from the supervisor. The interview should end with a discussion of what the subordinate can and wants to do about any deficiencies and what the supervisor will do for the employee in this regard. Although such suggested schemes will help some supervisors, it is better not to formalize this process. As supervisors gain experience, they will devise their own plans, and each supervisee probably will be approached in an individual manner.

Everything regarding general techniques of interviewing (see chapter 17) is applicable to the appraisal interview. Additional skills are necessary, however, since the direction of evaluation interviews cannot be predicted. At times it may be very difficult for the supervisor to carry on this interview, especially if the subordinate shows hostility when the supervisor discusses some negative evaluations. Of course, employees need to know if and where their performance is inadequate. Positive judgment can be communicated effectively, but it is difficult to communicate criticisms without generating resentment and defensiveness. It will take much practice and insight to acquire skills for handling the evaluation interview.

Some supervisors do not believe that they need to conduct an evaluation interview because they are in daily contact with their employees. These supervisors claim that their door is open at all times, but this approach is not enough. Many employees want a formal appraisal in which they receive a substantiated report on their performance. Also, employees may have some things on their mind that they do not want to discuss in the everyday contacts with the supervisor in the open office.

The supervisor must be well prepared for this review session. The appraiser must know what should be covered and achieved in this meeting and gather all the information relevant to the discussion. The various events that occurred during the evaluation period must be clear in the interviewer's mind. It may be advisable to prepare an agenda for this meeting. Thorough preparation enables the appraiser to be ready for any direction the discussion will take.

It is difficult to predict what will happen in this review session. It may be an uneventful meeting, and the appraisee's responses may be minimal—an occasional yes or no, or a nod of the head. Another meeting, however, may end up as a major bitter confrontation. Because of the importance and sensitivity of the performance review, the appraiser must not only be well prepared for this session, but also skilled in interviewing and counseling. The reviewer must ask the right question at the right time and be a constructive listener. In the review session, information must be shared. The appraisee must feel that his or her concerns are important. Success of this review session can be improved if the appraiser has empathy, listens constructively, asks the right questions at the proper time, and observes keenly. Last, the appraiser must allow enough time to conduct the interview.

The appraisal interview should be held shortly after the appraisal has been performed, and, as stated before, supervisors should refresh their memories regarding the reasons for the opinions expressed in the appraisal. Appraisees should be given enough notice so that they can prepare themselves for the interview as well. At the outset, the supervisor should state that the interview is to be a constructive and positive experience for both the appraisee and the appraiser and is being conducted for the benefit of the employee, the supervisor, and the institution. Some suggest that the supervisor ask the employee to appraise his or her own performance. This will give the supervisor a chance to refer to the progress the worker has made since the preceding counseling interview, compliment the supervisee on achievements, and then discuss areas that need improvement.

The formula of starting with praise, following it up with criticism, and ending the interview with another compliment is not necessarily the best method. Good and bad may cancel each other out, and the worker may forget about the criticism. A mature employee is able to take deserved criticism when it is appropriate.

By the same token, when praise is merited, it should be expressed. It is not always possible to mix praise and criticism effectively. Since the idea of being rated imposes some extra tensions and strains, feelings of friendliness and privacy in the interview are probably more important than at any other time. Since personal feelings and opinions most likely will be brought out in the discussion, the appraisee must be assured of privacy and confidentiality. The supervisor should not discuss specifics of the interview with the appraisee's coworkers even though some issues may have arisen in the session that will require further action. The employee should be assured that he or she will not be placed in the "tattletale" position. Also no distractions or interruptions should be allowed to occur during the session.

The supervisor should stress that everybody in the same job in the department is rated according to the same standards and that the employee has not been singled out for special scrutiny. He or she should be in a position to document the rating by citing specific instances of good and poor performance. The supervisor should be careful to relate the measured factors to the actual demands of the job. The rating must be geared to the present qualities of the employee's performance. This is particularly important if some employees are already doing good work and the supervisor is tempted to leave well enough alone. However, these are probably the very employees who are likely to make further progress, and to tell them simply to keep up the good work is not sufficient. These employees may not have major problems, but nevertheless they deserve thoughtful counseling. Such employees are likely to continue to develop, and the supervisor should be specific as far as future development plans are concerned. The appraiser must be familiar, therefore, with the opportunities available to the employee, requirements of the job, and the employee's qualifications. Whenever he or she is discussing a subordinate's future, however, the supervisor should not make promises for promotion that may not be possible to keep.

The interview should also give the employee an opportunity to ask questions so that the supervisor can answer them fully. Any misunderstanding cleared up at this time may avoid future difficulty. The appraiser should also clarify that further performance ratings and interviews are regular procedures with the enterprise. The supervisor should always remember that the purpose of the appraisal interview is to help employees to see their shortcomings and aid them in finding solutions. The real success of the interview lies in the employees' ability to see the need for their own improvement, stimulating in them a desire to change.

Since the appraisal interview is the most important part of the evaluation procedure, the supervisor should make certain that at its termination, the employees are clear on their performance and the ways in which they can improve. They also should have a desire to improve. It is hoped that employees will establish goals that are mutually satisfying to both themselves and the supervisor. An employee's commitment will provide some measurable goals against which future performance can be judged. At the end of the next period, both supervisor and subordinate will meet to evaluate how well the goals have been achieved and what the next objectives will be. This will give the subordinate a custom-made standard for evaluation. It provides him or her with a specified goal within a specified period. The employee will be that much more motivated, since the goal was a commitment on his or her part.

*Management by objectives* (MBO) has been discussed on several occasions in this text. The underlying concept of MBO is that identified, measurable, and workable objectives are agreed on by the supervisor and the employee, which leads to improved performance and a motivating environment. Management by objectives creates a participative climate because the subordinates help decide what their goals are. Although MBO is primarily a planning tool and a process that goes beyond performance appraisals, it can be logically and conveniently linked with performance evaluation and appraisal interviews. The review lends itself well to measuring the quality of an employee's on-the-job performance, achievements, and participation in setting new objectives. These new goals are to be achieved during the next period, and will be appraised and reviewed at the end of the period. Thus, the subordinate is judged by standards he or she helped determine.

Some experts strongly advocate that the annual performance appraisal review be separate from *salary review*. They suggest that discussing one's past performance, future potential, and further education and development as well as the coaching and counseling taking place should not be tainted by discussing pay and compensation. Whether a salary adjustment will be made does not depend only on the performance but also on the financial condition of the enterprise, wages paid elsewhere, the economic conditions, and many other factors. Most likely if both reviews are done together, the appraisee will interpret everything that is said in relation to future reward opportunities and possible promotions. A proposed solution is to have two separate review sessions. The first would be concerned with the review and employee development, and the second session, four to eight weeks later, would cover the compensation issue.

Appraisal forms customarily require the appraisee to *sign* the evaluation form on completion of the review. Usually a statement above the signature line says that the employee's signature merely confirms that the interview occurred and that the appraisee in no way approves or disapproves of the statements contained in the evaluation.

With this understanding, the subordinate will probably sign. If, however, the appraisee would like to state personal views, no harm is done in letting him or her do so. Many employees will not verbalize their disagreement with the rating, and signing the forms with such feelings can create resentment against the organization. The real purpose of the signature is to document for the supervisor's boss that the evaluation interview took place. As stated, many supervisors have mixed reactions about the appraisal interview. Since it provides essential feedback on the entire evaluation procedure, administration must make certain that it occurs, and the signature is the simplest way to confirm this.

| | |
|---|---|
| **AN EXAMPLE OF THE PERFORMANCE REVIEW PROCESS** | Robert Mager in his book *What Every Manager Should Know about Training*, offers the following checklists and guides to lead managers through this process. While doing performance evaluations may never be an easy process for managers, it is a necessary activity to ensure timely communication and constant improvement. Managers may find these checklists helpful in conducting disciplinary assessments as well since they encourage the manager to look beyond the individual's performance to other potential causes. |

| **Performance Analysis Checklist** |
|---|
| **1.** Whose performance is at issue? |
| **2.** What is the performance discrepancy?<br>  **a.** What is actually happening?<br>  **b.** What should be happening? |
| **3.** What is the approximate cost of the discrepancy?<br>  (What would happen if you ignored the problem?) |
| **4.** Is the discrepancy a skill deficiency?<br>  (Are they unable to do it?) |
| **5.** Yes . . . it *is* a skill deficiency:<br>  **a.** Can the job or task be simplified?<br>  **b.** Are the tasks performed often?<br>  **c.** Will other factors impede performance? |

6. No . . . it is *not* a skill deficiency:
   a. Are the performers being *punished* for doing it right?
   b. Are the performers being *rewarded* for doing it wrong?
   c. Are there no *consequences* at all to the performer for performing, either right or wrong?
   d. Are there *obstacles* to performing as expected?

7. List the causes of the discrepancy.

8. Describe solutions.

9. Estimate the cost of each solution.

10. Select the cost-effective solutions that can be implemented (those that are practical to implement).

11. Implement the solutions.

---

**Performance Problem Solution Checklist**

| Problem | Solutions |
|---|---|
| **They *can't* do it, and . . .** | |
| the skill is used often: | Provide feedback. |
| | Simplify the task. |
| the skill is used rarely: | Provide job aids to prompt desired performance. |
| | Simplify the job. |
| | Provide periodic practice. |
| Training will be required if the above remedies are inadequate. | |
| **They *can* do it, but . . .** | |
| doing it right leads to punishment: | Remove the sources of punishment. |
| doing it wrong is more satisfying: | Remove the rewards for incorrect performance. |
| nobody notices when they do it right: | Apply consequences to the *performer* for doing it right. |
| there are obstacles to performing as desired: | Remove the obstacles (or help people work around them). |

---

**Post-Training Follow-up**

Date of Training:_____ Date of Return to Work: _____
Skills/Knowledge learned:_____
_____
_____

Remember the following:

- **Be a Coach:** Be clear how the worker's performance should have improved from the training they just attended and encourage the worker to use their new skills and knowledge.

  EXAMPLES OF <u>WHERE AND HOW</u> THE SKILLS/KNOWLEDGE SHOULD SHOW UP:_____
  _____
  _____

- **Allow PRACTICE, PRACTICE, PRACTICE:** How will you schedule the worker's next month to fully use these skills?

- **Know what "IMPROVEMENT" looks like:** You know what mediocre is—now do you know what "best" looks like? Be specific with your worker on what highest quality looks like in the area they received training—*then look for it.*

  EXAMPLES OF EXEMPLARY PERFORMANCE IN THE AREA TRAINED ARE:
  _____
  _____
  _____

- **Reinforce Performance:** Do not forget to reinforce the worker when performance is at the level expected.

---

## ■ Proper Wages, Salaries, and Benefits

Although people want more from their jobs than just a wage or salary, the latter are basic necessities. Pay provides more than the means of satisfying physical needs; it provides a sense of accomplishment and recognition. Most people at work consider relative pay as very important, and real or imagined wage and salary inequities are frequent causes of dissatisfaction, friction, and low morale. It is top-level management's duty to pursue a sound policy of wage and salary administration throughout the entire organization; the goal is to have a sound nondiscriminatory compensation structure. By setting wages high enough, the healthcare center will be able to recruit satisfactory employees and motivate their present employees to work toward pay increases and promotions. Reducing inequities among employees' earnings will raise morale and reduce friction.

In most healthcare centers and other organizations, wage rates and schedules are set by top-level administration, and the supervisor's authority in this respect is quite limited. Nevertheless, it is a part of the supervisor's staffing function to make certain that the employees of the department are properly and equitably compensated. It is every manager's job to offer the amount of compensation that will retain competent employees in the department and, if necessary, attract good workers from the outside. Monetary rewards are an exceedingly important factor for all employees. However, many employees are much more concerned about how their salaries compare to the earnings of others than they are about their absolute earnings. No doubt many wage rates and schedules follow historical patterns, whereas others are often accidental or due to exceptions. For example, certain wage rates can be distorted when positions are difficult to fill, when individuals are retained due to certain knowledge or skill, or when the administration prefers different wage scale philosophies. In the long run such situations cannot be tolerated.

It is the supervisor's duty to see that the wages paid within the department are properly aligned *internally* and *externally*. *Internal alignment* means that the jobs within the department and institution are paid according to what they are worth. Internal consistency based on internal equity provides a system of compensation that is acceptable to the employees involved, resulting in satisfaction, and a desire to be promoted and to remain with the present employer. *External alignment* means that the wages offered for the work to be performed in the department compare favorably with the going rate in the community and area. External competitiveness refers to the pay relationships *among* organizations and the *competitive positions* reflected in these relationships. If wages do not compare favorably, the supervisor knows that some of the most experienced workers will leave and that it will be difficult to attract new ones from the outside. All of this applies also to an appropriate benefits program, often called fringe benefits.

## ■ Internal Alignment

To pay the various jobs within the department according to what they are worth, the supervisor should call on the help of the human resources department to conduct a *job evaluation*. Job evaluation is a method of determining the relationships between pay rates and the relative monetary value of jobs within a department. In such a procedure, a committee guided by the human resources staff evaluates the jobs according to various factors, devises an appropriate wage rate based on the worth of each job, and institutes an appropriate wage schedule. Of course, some questions will arise about what to do with exceptional cases, that is, those employees who are receiving either excessively high or exceedingly low salaries in relation to others. Once a plan has been designed, however, it is necessary to maintain it properly so that no new inequities arise.

The supervisor might request a job evaluation from the human resources department for his or her department if one has not been performed recently. Sometimes the help of an outside consultant is used. There are several methods of job evaluation. Although they are systematic, they are not totally precise because they involve questions of human judgment. In addition to the most widely used point system, other methods such as ranking, factor comparison, and job classification methods are typically used.

### External Alignment

If the wage and salary policy of the institution is to be externally competitive, pay rates must be approximately the same as those prevailing in the community. Thus, accurate wage and salary data must be collected through surveys. Job evaluations establish differentials between jobs based on different job content; *wage surveys* provide management with information on whether the organization's wage level is competitive externally and aligned. A wage survey involves collecting data on wages paid in the community for similar key jobs in similar or related enterprises. Without proper external alignment, the supervisor cannot recruit competent employees or prevent present employees from leaving for better-paying jobs.

To conduct such a survey is a rather costly and sophisticated procedure; performing one's own survey will probably produce the most meaningful results. Many other sources publish reliable surveys, including government agencies such as the Bureau of Labor Statistics, professional healthcare associations, and metropolitan hospital associations. The area usually considered in the survey is the geographical region within which workers seek employment and employers recruit workers without necessitating a change of residence.

Most enterprises also provide benefits for employees, such as pensions, insurance, educational benefits, healthcare, dental plans, maternity leave, daycare, vacations, pay for time not worked, and many others. They are often called fringe benefits, although at this time these benefits often account for 25 to 35 percent of the cash payroll. Most of these additional benefits are established by top-level administration as institutionwide measures. The supervisor has little to do with such benefits other than to make sure that the individual who has been evaluated understands how benefits operate and that each subordinate receives his or her fair share. It is advisable to include information along these lines in any wage survey.

To determine whether or not the rates offered by the department are competitive, the supervisor should request that the human resources department undertake such a wage and salary survey unless recent reliable information is available. Then, by comparing this information with the wage patterns, the supervisor can determine whether or not wages are properly aligned externally. A sound wage and salary pattern should always be of great concern to the CEO. Although the supervisor has very little direct authority in this area, pointing out such inadequacies and inconsistencies may bring the administrator to investigate.

In most instances, supervisors will not have enough authority to make wage and salary adjustments except within the framework of the departmental wage scale. However, they should definitely plead their case to top-level administration. To make an intelligent presentation, the supervisor must know the value of the various jobs within the department and also the going rate within the community. As every supervisor knows, proper compensation of employees is a significant aspect of the employee's continuing satisfaction and motivation. Without a sound wage and salary pattern, it is almost impossible for a supervisor to recruit competent employees or keep the subordinates motivated.

## PROMOTIONS

Promotions provide an internal source of potential applicants. A promotion is the reassignment of an individual to a higher ranked position. This higher-level job will entail more demands on the individual but results in higher pay, more authority and responsibility, more privileges, higher status, increased benefits, and greater potential for advancement. A promotion may also carry symbols of higher status, such as a more important job title, a larger office, a bigger desk, and a secretary. Although some people do not want to advance, promotions are sought by most people who have a high level of aspiration. It is part of our culture to start at the bottom of the ladder and rise in status and income as one grows older. Since most people in our society look on promotions in this way, it is essential that organizations develop and pursue sound promotion policies.

### ■ Promotion from Within

Organizations depend heavily on promoting their own employees into better and more promising positions. The policy of promoting from within the organization is one of the most widely practiced personnel policies today. This policy will help achieve the organizational objective of being a good employer and a good place to work. The latter is undoubtedly one of the many goals of all healthcare centers.

The policy of promotion from within versus recruitment from without is important to the enterprise and the individual employee. For the enterprise, it ensures a constant source of trained people for the better positions; for the employees, it provides a powerful incentive to perform better. After an employee has worked awhile for an enterprise, much more is known about that person than even the best potential candidate from outside the organization.

Internal promotion often is less expensive to the institution in time and money than luring applicants from the outside. Additional job satisfaction will result when employees know that with proper efforts they can work up to more interesting and more challenging work, higher pay, and more desirable working conditions. Most employees like to know that they can get ahead in the enterprise in which they are working and feel more secure in a setting that provides future job opportunities. All this provides strong motivation. On the other hand, little motivation exists for employees to do a better job if they know that the better and higher-paying jobs are always reserved for outsiders.

The internal promotion policy should be applied whenever possible and feasible. Most organizations are aware that under special circumstances outside people must be hired; sometimes strict adherence to internal promotion would do harm to the organization. For example, if there are no qualified candidates for the job, the internal promotion policy cannot be followed. If no one with the necessary skill is available, then someone from the outside has to be recruited for the position. Also, an organization may be forced to go outside because employees with inadequate potential for promotion have been hired in the past.

At times the injection of "new blood" into an organization may be necessary because it keeps the members of the enterprise from becoming too conformist. Bringing in new people is important primarily in high-level managerial jobs and for highly trained professionals but is less important in hourly paid jobs. Another reason the enterprise may have to recruit employees from the outside is that the organization cannot afford the expense of training and schooling current employees. A particular position may require a long period of expensive and sophisticated schooling, and the institution simply cannot afford this type of upgrading program. Only large organizations can afford such expenses. Another problem with promotion from within is that the organization must continue to live amicably with those who were bypassed. Such a problem, however, does not exist with an applicant from the outside who was rejected. In all this, considerations of equal employment opportunity and possibly affirmative action must be included.

On the other hand, the supervisor should remember that not every employee wants advancement; many people know their limitations. Some employees are quite content with what they are doing and where they are within the enterprise. They prefer to remain with employees whom they know and responsibilities with which they are familiar. These employees should not be pressured into better positions by the supervisor. The supervisor should also bear in mind that what he or she may consider a promotion may not seem like a promotion to the employee. A nurse may believe that a "promotion" to administrative work is a hardship and not an advancement. He or she may find the administrative activities less interesting than the professional duties and may be concerned about his or her professional future. The supervisor will have to provide promotional opportunities that do not entail compromising professional aspirations.

Sometimes a supervisor does not want to release an employee because he or she sees this employee as indispensable and does not want to release him or her to take a better job in another department. This could occur because the supervisor is extremely good in developing subordinates; for example, as soon as a head nurse has developed a number of outstanding nurses, they are generally promoted out of that unit. The head nurse may believe that the unit suffers because of the loss of these outstanding professionals. In such a situation, the administration should give credit to this head nurse for constantly and consistently developing promotable employees and show him or her that there will also be good employees entering the unit from other head nurses' units.

At times, the supervisor may be inclined to bypass someone for promotion because it would cause the supervisor some extra work in replacing the promoted employee and training a new employee. The supervisor may fear that the productivity of the department will suffer. This is shortsighted, since promotion from within is one of the prime motivators. Supervisors who are tempted to think this way should ask themselves where they would be today if their former superiors had had this attitude.

## ■ Basis of Promotion

Despite the objections just stated, there are usually more applicants for promotions than there are openings within the organization. Because of this, it is important for the organization and supervisors to formulate a sound basis on which employees are chosen for promotion. Since promotions are considered an incentive for employees to do a better job, it follows that the employee who has the best record of quality, productivity, and skill should be promoted. In many situations, however, it is difficult to objectively measure some employees' productivity, even though the supervisor has attempted to do so through merit ratings and performance appraisals. The most important criteria for choice are *merit* (current performance), *ability* (potential future performance), and *seniority* (experience).

### *Merit and Ability*

Since promotion is an incentive for good performance, the best-performing employees should be promoted. Our discussion of performance appraisals emphasized the difficulty in measuring performance. The differences in *merits* between different employees in a healthcare job are also often difficult to measure precisely. The person who was not promoted may feel that bias and favoritism were involved. Nevertheless, performance in one's present job is one of the criteria.

*Ability* and *potential* to assume the responsibilities of a higher-level position are additional criteria to consider. Consider the employee who has extensive public speaking experience outside of your organization in her volunteer role as chairperson of the Chamber of Commerce. This may be a skill that was captured during the development section of her performance appraisal. Now consider whether this person or another without public speaking skills would be better for a promotion into a public relations position. Or an individual who has a baccalaureate in science and a masters in gerontology. His education adds depth to his set of core competencies. If the organization decides to open or manage a continuing care community, this individual may have the competency to do so even though his current position does not utilize these competencies.

As you can see, the performance appraisal process is a major source of information. Performance appraisals are central to all organizational and management development. Generally, performance appraisals are used as a means of measuring performance in the past, but just as important is the appraisal of an employee's *potential*. Appraising a person's potential is based on the process and personal resources the employee uses to achieve results, that is, the ability to lead, intellect, and maturity. In appraising potential and future performance, the supervisor should evaluate the employee's oral and written communication, flexibility, and his or her decision-making, leadership, and planning abilities.

Since it has been recognized that traditional methods of selecting managers are fraught with many shortcomings and subjectivity, thousands of industries, and some healthcare organizations have adopted an *assessment center* approach for evaluating and selecting managers. An assessment center uses a process in which current employees or job applicants are evaluated as to how well they might perform in a managerial or higher-level position. Individual and group exercises are administered to a group of candidates who are seeking promotions to managerial jobs. The candidates are evaluated for their potential for success in management. The exercises and activities include job-related simulations such as interviews, in-basket exercises, tests, questionnaires, videotape exercises, group problems, and so forth. These exercises are designed to bring forth skills the organization considers critical to success. As the candidates go through these exercises, they are being observed by a group of specially trained observers (assessors, evaluators) who are members of the institution's management group. After the session, the candidates are evaluated by this panel of assessors to make selection recommendations or placement decisions, or to determine a candidate's future promotability. Generally, the composite performance evaluation is communicated to the candidate.

### Seniority

The exclusive use of merit and ability, which are to a great degree subjective criteria, often gives employees the feeling that promotions are not made fairly. Also, since many factors beyond an employee's control may affect productivity and performance, it would be unfair to base a promotion solely on these factors. Frequent charges of favoritism, bias, and possible discrimination have caused managers to search for more objective decision criteria that would not create morale problems. Since it is difficult to find objective criteria that completely eliminate favoritism and possible discrimination, it has been stated that the only objective criterion is length of service. Supervisors generally believe that their relations with their employees will be easier if they promote on the basis of seniority. Therefore, all organizations give some weight to seniority, whether they have a union or not. Unions stress that employees should be promoted on the basis of seniority. This approach is now regularly accepted even by those enterprises that do not deal with unions and is applied to those jobs not covered by union agreements.

Basing promotion on the length of service assumes that the employee's ability increases with service. Although this may be questionable, with continued service the ability to perform and the knowledge about the organization probably do increase. If management is committed to promotion based on length of service, it is likely that the initial selection procedure of a new employee will be made carefully and that the employee will get as much training as possible in the various positions. Most managers believe that an employee's loyalty is expressed by the length of service and that consequently this loyalty deserves the reward of promotion. On the other hand, some good employees may become discouraged and leave the organization, realizing that their chances for promotion are slim because of many long-service employees ahead of them.

### ■ Balancing the Criteria

Good supervisory practice will attempt to draw a happy medium between the criteria of merit and ability on the one hand and length of service on the other.

When the supervisor selects from among almost equally capable subordinates, the one with the longest service will no doubt be chosen. Then again, the supervisor may decide to promote an employee who is more capable or has more core competencies but has less seniority than another employee because the first stands "head and shoulders" above the one with longer service. If this is not the case, the one with more seniority will be promoted. These decisions become increasingly difficult, and it is easy to see why some supervisors have finally resolved the matter by making length of service the sole determinant of selection for promotion. The ideal solution is to combine both factors. Rarely will a supervisor choose a person with the greatest merit and ability from all eligible candidates without giving any weight to length of service.

Selection for promotion will also depend on the type of work involved, demands of the position to be filled, degree requirements prescribed by accrediting and professional associations, and many other factors. Most likely more and more emphasis will be placed on merit and ability when the position to be filled is a demanding and sophisticated job on a higher level, whereas more weight can be given to seniority for promotion into a lower-level position. Every organization must decide on the relative weight of these factors in each case when deciding who is to be promoted.

## TRANSFERS

Transfers are another internal source of recruitment. A transfer is a reassignment of an employee to another job of similar pay, status, and responsibility. It is not a promotion since it is a horizontal move, whereas a promotion is a vertical move in rank and responsibility. Transfers take place either because the organization makes it necessary or because the employee requests a transfer. Employees may want a transfer for various reasons, for example, to gain broader experience or to avoid some friction in a department. If an employee has problems that are causing friction, a transfer is not always the right solution unless these problems are resolved. Sometimes technological changes in one department free a number of employees for transfer into a unit where needs for employees are expanding.

Transferring an employee from one position to another within the healthcare institution often results in greater job satisfaction. For example, a nurses's aide may consider a job as an aide in the operating room to be more prestigious than being an aide on the nursing floor. The pay is the same and one cannot call it a promotion, but to the aide such a transfer means greater job satisfaction and constitutes an achievement. Transfers also provide employees with the opportunity to gain a broader knowledge of the institution's activities. It is necessary, therefore, that a healthcare institution have sound transfer policies and procedures so that those who desire a lateral transfer will be given the possibility of doing so, always considering equal employment opportunity provisions. The director of human resources together with the various line managers should design these policies and procedures and see to it that employees are prepared to make successful transfers.

It is probably best for the human resources department to act as a clearance center for interdepartmental transfers. If the responsibility is given to supervisors, the supervisee may be reluctant to request interdepartmental transfers.

Some supervisors may be understanding in these matters, whereas others may be resentful and not give their consent. Whatever procedure is instituted must have provisions that the employee inform the immediate supervisor of the desire to transfer. It is only fair that the present supervisor should be aware of the employee's intent. In the event that the immediate supervisor does not recommend the transfer, the employee should be able to appeal this decision to a higher line officer or possibly to the personnel director.

There also must be provisions as to whether transfers are to be made only within departments or between departments. The procedure must state whether the employee carries previous seniority credits with him or her and it must make provisions for the situation when two or more persons want to transfer to the same job. For example, should length of service be the sole determinant, or should capacity to handle the job be taken into consideration also? Good transfer policies and procedures must cover many additional aspects, such as equal employment opportunities. In any event, the opportunity must exist for employees to be transferred, since this will provide more job satisfaction and will motivate employees in much the same way as a promotion.

## SUMMARY

Performance appraisals are central to organizational and management development. Performance appraisals are formal evaluations of employees' job-related activities. Such a system not only guides management in gathering and analyzing information, but also provides guidance for merit increases, promotions, and coaching of employees. The purpose of the appraisal system is to provide a measure of the employee's job performance that leads to counseling and further development. An evaluation system consists of rating the employee and the appraisal interview, which usually occurs later. Although the appraisal interview between the supervisor and the employee may prove to be a difficult situation, the entire performance appraisal system is of no use if this aspect is ignored or not carried out appropriately.

An important source of candidates for job openings is the reservoir of employees who are currently with the institution. Whenever possible, promotion from within is one of the most rewarding personnel policies any enterprise can practice. It is of great benefit to the enterprise and to the morale of the employees. Although it is difficult to specify clearly the various criteria for promotion, it is normally acknowledged that a good balance between merit and ability should be used on one hand and length of service on the other. To be able to assess the ability, merit, and future potential of the employee, however, supervisors must remain aware of the employee's performance. Therefore, the supervisor must regularly appraise the performance of the employees in the department. A further internal source of recruitment is available from transfers.

In addition to all these duties, the staffing function includes making certain that the employees of the department are properly compensated and have a benefits program. Although much of this is out of the supervisor's domain, it is a supervisory duty to make certain that good internal wage alignment exists within the department, meaning that each job is paid in accordance with its worth and difficulties. To achieve this, a job evaluation is necessary. In addition to good internal alignment, the compensation pattern must also be competitive externally. This means that the wages paid must be high enough to attract people from outside the organization, if necessary, and to prevent present employees from leaving for higher wages. To do this, the supervisor must be familiar with the going rates being paid in similar occupations in the community. Such information can be obtained by wage and salary surveys conducted by the human resources department.

# PART VI
# INFLUENCING

# *Giving Directives and Managing Change*

*Chapter Objectives*

After you have studied this chapter, you should be able to:

1. Define the managerial function of influencing.
2. Describe the essential characteristics of good directives.
3. Compare and contrast the major techniques and theories of directing.
4. Relate the function of influencing to changing environments.

Influencing is the managerial function by which the supervisor evokes action from others to accomplish organizational objectives. It is the process that management uses to achieve goal-directed action from subordinates and colleagues in the organization. It is vital to implementing change. Influencing is a human resources function that is particularly concerned with behavioral responses.

The influencing function is also known as *leading, motivating, directing,* and *actuating.* Regardless of the terminology, however, it is the managerial function that the supervisor exercises to get the best and most out of the subordinates. At the same time, the supervisor strives to create a climate in which the subordinates find as much satisfaction of their needs as possible. In the past, managers depended largely on negative persuasion, disciplinary action, and a few incentive programs to influence their employees. The notion of organizational hierarchy dominated managerial thinking until the behavioral sciences brought about new understanding of human motivation and taught us better methods of influencing. Today every manager must understand some of the psychology involved in interpersonal relations.

It is the role of every supervisor to influence in order to get the work done through and with the help of employees. Influencing is the managerial function that *initiates* action. Without it, nothing, or at best very little, is likely to be accomplished. Influencing includes issuing directives, instructions, assignments, and orders, as well as guiding and overseeing employees. It also addresses the problems of how to motivate one's employees.

Moreover, the manager should consider the influencing function as a means not only for getting the work done and motivating the employees, but also for *developing* them. The most effective way to develop employees is diligent coaching and teaching by their immediate superior. Thus, influencing is more than just giving orders or supervising the employees to make certain that they follow directives. Influencing means building an effective workforce and inspiring its members to perform their best. Influencing is the function of getting the employees to work in a large enterprise as effectively as possible and with the same enthusiasm that they would display if they were working for themselves, either in their own enterprise or at a hobby. Only by appropriately influencing and supervising the employees will the manager be able to motivate them to work energetically on the job and at the same time to find personal satisfaction.

Influencing is the job of every manager, whether the CEO of a healthcare facility or the supervisor of one of its many departments. Every manager performs the influencing function, regardless of the position held. The amount of time and effort a manager spends in this function will vary, however, depending on the level, number of employees supervised, and other duties. The supervisor of a department will spend most of the time influencing and supervising, more so than the administrator of the institution.

Influencing is a continuous function of the supervisor that covers the day-to-day activities within the department. It is interconnected with the other managerial functions. Planning, organizing, and staffing can be considered preparatory managerial functions; the purpose of controlling is to find out whether or not the goals are being achieved. The connecting and actuating link between these functions, however, is the managerial function of influencing.

Influencing is largely affected by the type of employee the supervisor has selected while performing the staffing function. The plans that the supervisor has made and the organization has drawn up also have a bearing on the influencing function. The controlling function is likewise affected by influencing, inasmuch as control often involves identifying the causes of variances to plans, some of which may be human problems.

To get the job done, every supervisor spends much time and effort in giving directives to subordinates. Here we should recall the principle of *unity of command,* which means that in each department only one person has the authority to make decisions appropriate to his or her station. Each employee has a single immediate supervisor, who is in turn responsible to his or her immediate superior, and so on up and down the chain of command. This also means that a subordinate is responsible to only one supervisor.

The principle of unity of command further states that the supervisor is the only one who can give directives to the employees. All directives can come only from the immediate supervisor, and no one else should interfere in the guiding and overseeing of the employees. In other words, there is a direct line of authority from the supervisor to the subordinate, just as there is one from the CEO to the director of a service and from there to the supervisor of a department. The administrator's line, however, extends only to the director of a service and not to the supervisors and employees under these supervisors. Thus, all supervision of the employees in a department rests with the supervisor or the head of that department and must not be exercised by anyone else, except in emergencies. Otherwise, the principle of unity of command is violated; no person can serve two bosses.

In healthcare organizations the unity of command principle may be violated by the presence of two sets of instructions: one from an immediate administrative supervisor, and another from a patient's attending physician. Most times these instructions will not conflict, but if they do, the subordinate should refer the conflict to the supervisor. The supervisor or manager should confer with the physician if necessary to resolve the issue. If time does not permit for such deliberations, which is often the case in healthcare, the action that delivers appropriate clinical care to the patient should occur. Thus, the instructions that benefit the patient should be followed.

---

# CHARACTERISTICS OF GOOD DIRECTIVES

Because issuing directives is such a basic and integral part of the supervisor's daily routine, it has often been taken for granted that every supervisor knows how to give orders. We frequently assume that anybody can give orders. This is probably not true, but even if it were, there are some ways to issue directives more effectively than others. The experienced supervisor knows that faulty or bad order giving can easily upset even the best-laid plans, and, instead of coordination of efforts, a general state of chaos is created.

To the uninitiated outsider, it may seem that some supervisors can get excellent results even though they appear to break every rule in the book. Other supervisors may use all the best techniques of order giving and phrase their requests in the most courteous ways and still get only grudging compliance. The question of what is the most appropriate method of order giving depends on the employees concerned, work situation, supervisors and how they view their job, their attitude toward people, and many other factors. There are definite techniques for giving orders, however, and since the supervisor's own success depends largely on how the subordinates carry out the orders, the manager must possess the knowledge and skill for good directing. In other words, since directing is the fundamental tool employed by supervisors to start, stop, or modify activities, it is necessary for every supervisor to become familiar with the basic characteristics that distinguish good and accomplishable directives from those that are not. These characteristics are fulfilled when directives are reasonable, intelligible, worded appropriately, compatible with the objectives, and within reasonable time limits.

## ■ Reasonable Directives

The first essential characteristic of a good directive is that it must be *reasonable;* that is, you can reasonably expect compliance. Unreasonable orders will not only undermine morale, but will also make controlling impossible. The requirement of reasonableness immediately excludes orders pertaining to activities that physically cannot be done or are dangerous. In judging whether or not a directive can be reasonably accomplished, supervisors should not only appraise it from their own point of view, but should also try to place themselves in the position of the employee. The supervisor should not issue a directive if the capacity or experience of the employee is not sufficient to comply with the order. This becomes particularly important in the case of recent graduates who may have had an excellent education in many areas, but lack experience and even some of the basic knowledge required. Supervisors should not forget the value of their own on-the-job training.

It can easily happen that a supervisor issues unreasonable instructions. For instance, to please the superior, a supervisor promises the completion of a job at a particularly early time, and then issues such an order without considering whether the employee who is to carry out the order can actually do so. In this situation, the supervisor should make it clear that he or she will try to get the job done in time, but unreasonable pressure should not be put on the subordinate. The supervisor should place himself or herself in the position of the subordinate and ask if compliance reasonably can be expected under these limits. The decision will depend on many factors prevailing at the time. In some cases the directive may actually be intended to stretch the subordinate's capabilities a little beyond what had previously been requested. Then the question of reasonableness becomes a question of degree. Generally, however, a prime requirement of a good directive is that it can be accomplished by the employee to whom it is assigned without undue difficulty.

## ■ Intelligibility

Another requirement is that a good directive should be *intelligible* to the employee; that is, the employee should be able to understand it. The subordinate cannot be expected to carry out an order that he or she does not understand. For example, a directive in a language not intelligible to the subordinate cannot be considered an order. The same also applies if both speak English, and the supervisor uses words that the employee does not comprehend. This, then, becomes a matter of communication. (See chapter 5.) The supervisor must make certain that the employee understands, and it is his or her duty to communicate in words that the employee actually understands and not merely *should* understand. Instructions must be clear but not necessarily lengthy. What is clear and complete to the supervisor, however, is not always clear and complete to the employee. Also, sometimes the supervisor has not made up his or her mind as to exactly what he or she wants done. A supervisor simply cannot expect subordinates to carry out directives that have not been made clear and intelligible.

Ideally, the supervisor will ask the employee to repeat the directive in his or her own words. This way the supervisor can be assured the employee understands what is expected. If necessary, the supervisor should write down a list of brief steps or sketch the work flow for the employee when verbal instructions are lengthy or a certain series of steps must be taken in a prescribed order.

## ■ Appropriate Wording

Every good supervisor knows that the tone and words used in issuing directives significantly affect the subordinates' acceptance and performance of them. A considerate tone is likely to stimulate willing and enthusiastic acceptance, which is preferable to routine or grudging acceptance or outright rejection. In the patient care field, the word *order* in connection with the attending physician's directives is normally used without unpleasant connotations. However, most supervisors should refrain from using the term *order* as much as possible and instead use such terms as *directives, assignments, instructions, suggestions,* and *requests.* A directive followed by a sincere thank you is always appropriate.

## Requests

Phrasing orders as requests does not reduce their character as a directive, but there is a major difference in the reaction a request will inspire as compared to a command. With most subordinates, a request is all that is usually needed and used. It is a pleasant and easy way of asking an employee to get the job done. For example, "Mary, as time permits this morning, could you help Tina with her backlog of physician orders, so that she is caught up by 10:00 A.M.? Thanks for your assistance." This style of directing works well, particularly with those employees who have been working for the supervisor for some time and who are familiar with the personality of the supervisor, and vice versa. A request works best with this type of employee, and it usually does not rub anyone the wrong way.

## Suggestions

In other instances it might be advisable to place the directive in the form of a suggestion, which is an even milder form than a request. For example, the supervisor might say, "Mary, we are supposed to get all of this work done before noon and we seem to be a bit behind. Do you think we can make up for it?" Suggestions of this type will accomplish a great deal for the supervisor because they will be understood and accepted by responsible and ambitious employees. Such employees like the feeling of not being ordered around and of being on their own to get the job accomplished. This suggestive type of order, however, would not be advisable in dealing with new employees. They simply do not have the background of the department and have not been around long enough to have received sufficient training and familiarity with its activities. Suggestion is also not the proper way of giving orders to those employees who are less competent and less dependable. However, some subordinates must be told what to do simply because a request or suggestion might invite an argument as to why they should not do it or the employee will never get around to doing what was requested. For example, "Mary, I need the status on those two patient bills I gave you last Friday by 10:00 A.M. this morning. Before you go on break today, stop by my office with your report. Thanks." The command style leaves no room for questioning expectations.

Sometimes the *command* type of order is the only way to get things done. Everyone remembers commands from parents and schoolteachers as part of growing up. Most people, however, think that once they are adults, commands are no longer necessary. Thus, the best rule for a supervisor is to avoid commands whenever possible but to use them when necessary.

## ■ Compatibility with Objectives

A good directive must be compatible with the purposes and objectives of the organization. If the instructions are not in accord with these objectives, chances are the subordinate may not execute them adequately or may not execute them at all. Thus, when issuing directives that appear to conflict with the organizational objectives, the supervisor must explain to the employee why such action is necessary, or the supervisor should explain that the directive merely appears to be but actually is not contrary to the institution's objectives. Instructions must also be consistent; they must not be in opposition to orders or directives previously given unless there is a good explanation for the discrepancy.

## ■ Time Limit

An additional characteristic of a good directive is that it specify the time within which the instructions should be carried out and completed. The supervisor should allow a reasonable amount of time and, if this is not feasible, must realize that the quality of performance will only be as good as can be produced under the time limit. In many directives, the time factor is not stated, although it is probably implied that the assignment should be carried out within a reasonable time period.

These are some of the major characteristics that should be incorporated in a good directive. Because the performance of the employee depends to a great extent on the format and content of directives given, the supervisor should make certain that the directive is in accord with these most essential characteristics.

---

## MAJOR TECHNIQUES OF DIRECTING

In previous chapters, we mentioned various theories describing the supervisor's underlying managerial attitudes, such as Theories X and Y, autocratic and democratic leadership, participation in decision making, and broad or narrow delegation of authority. The following is a more detailed discussion of how these managerial attitudes manifest themselves in the daily working environment, in which the supervisor depends on the subordinates to get the job done.

Generally the supervisor may choose from two basic techniques of direction: *autocratic,* or *close, supervision* on the one hand and *consultative,* or *participative, general supervision* on the other. In our discussion we can clearly distinguish between these two extremes, but in practice the supervisor usually combines and blends the techniques. For example, the manager might use the autocratic technique for one situation and the democratic technique for another. For some employees, the supervisor might consider it more advisable to use one method and for other employees another technique. No one form of supervision is equally good in all situations. Whether it is better to apply a more autocratic or a more democratic type of supervision will depend on many factors: the type of work; current situation; attitude of the employee toward the supervisor; personality and ability of the employee; and personality, experience, and ability of the supervisor. A good supervisor is sensitive to all these factors and to the needs of each situation, so the style of supervision should be adjusted accordingly.

## ■ Autocratic (Close) Supervision

When the autocratic, or close, technique of directing is employed, the supervisor gives direct, clear, and precise orders to the subordinates with detailed instructions as to exactly how and in what sequence things are to be done. This, as we know, allows little room for the initiative of the subordinate. The supervisor who normally uses the autocratic technique will delegate as little authority as possible and believes that he or she probably can do the job better than any of the subordinates. The supervisor relies on command and detailed instructions, followed by close supervision. An autocratic supervisor believes that subordinates are "not paid to think"; they are expected to follow instructions. The boss alone is to do the planning and decision making; this is what he or she is trained and paid for. This type of supervisor does not necessarily distrust the subordinate but believes that without detailed instruction the subordinate could not properly carry out the directive. This person believes that only he or she can specify the best method and that there is only one way, the supervisor's way, to get the job done. In other words, Theory X management is practiced.

With most people, the consequences of autocratic supervision can be fatal. Employees lose interest and initiative; they stop thinking for themselves because no need or occasion arises for independent thought. They are obedient but silent and lack initiative, sparkle, and ingenuity. It becomes difficult for the subordinates to remain loyal to the organization and to the supervisor, and they secretly rejoice when the boss makes a mistake. This form of supervision tends to make the employees somewhat like automatons. Freedom is curtailed, and it is difficult for them to learn even by making mistakes. They justly conclude that they are not expected to do any thinking about their job, and, although they perfunctorily perform their duties, they find little involvement in the work. They are certainly not motivated.

Shortcomings of the autocratic technique of supervision are obvious. Generally, young men and women who have been brought up in a democratic society resent autocratic order giving. It is contrary to our traditional democratic way of life in America. No ambitious employee will remain in a position where the supervisor is not willing to delegate some degree of freedom and authority. Any subordinate who is eager to learn and progress will resent being constantly given detailed instructions that leave no room for his or her own thinking and initiative. The employee will be stifled and sooner or later will leave the enterprise if at all possible. This method of supervision does not produce good employees and will only chase away those who have potential.

On the other hand, one must not forget that under certain circumstances and with certain people a degree of close supervision may be necessary. This is the exception, however, not the rule. Suppose, for example, that the subordinate is the type of person who does not want to think for himself or herself and prefers to receive clear orders. Firm guidance gives reassurance, whereas loose and general supervision may be frustrating. Some employees lack ambition and imagination, and do not want to become at all involved in their daily job. Other employees have been brought up in an authoritarian manner by their families in the

United States or a foreign country, and their previous work experience leads them to believe that general supervision is no supervision at all. Moreover, a work setting sometimes is so chaotic that only autocratic techniques can bring order. Aside from these rather unusual situations, however, it can generally be assumed that autocratic, or close, supervision is the least desirable and effective method.

Also, the autocratic supervisor usually makes the basic Theory X assumption that the average employee does not want to do the job and that close supervision and threats of loss of the job are needed to get people to work. Such a supervisor believes that if he or she were not on the job and "breathing down their necks," all the subordinates would stop working. Under these conditions, they probably would. On the other hand, the supervisor who follows Theory Y and believes in general supervision assumes that the average employee is eager to do a good job, wants to do the right thing, and must have motivation to perform his or her best. Autocratic, or close, supervision is not conducive to motivating employees to perform their best; general supervision, however, is conducive to achieving maximum work potential.

## ■ Consultative (General) Supervision

The opposite of autocratic supervision is consultative supervision. Consultative supervision is also known as *participative, democratic,* or *permissive supervision.* It is similar to the concept of *general supervision* referred to earlier. Its basic assumption is that employees are eager to do a good job and are capable of doing so. The supervisor behaves toward them with this basic assumption in mind, and the employees in turn tend to react in a manner that justifies the expectation of their supervisors.

This democratic approach to the directing function manifests itself in the practice of general supervision when it comes to routine assignments within the department. When new jobs have to be performed and new assignments made, the democratic method of supervising will appear in the consultative, or participative, technique of directing. Both have the underlying assumption that employees will be more motivated if they are left to themselves as much as possible. We will first discuss situations that require consultation, then explore the meaning of general supervision for routine assignments.

### *Consultation*

The essential characteristic of consultation is that the supervisor consults with employees concerning the extent, nature, and alternative solution to a problem before the supervisor makes a decision and issues a directive. The supervisor who uses the consultative approach before issuing directives is earnestly seeking help and ideas from the employees and approaches the subject with an open mind. More important than the procedure is the attitude of the supervisor. A subordinate will easily sense superficiality and is quick to perceive whether or not the boss genuinely intends to consult him or her on the problem or only intends to give the impression of doing so.

Some supervisors are inclined to use such pseudo-consultation merely to give employees the feeling that they have been consulted. In many instances, supervisors ask for participation only after they have already decided on the directive. Here the supervisor is using the consultative technique as a trick, a device for manipulating people to do what he or she wants them to do. The subordinate will quickly realize that he or she is not being taken seriously and that this participation is not real. The results achieved will be much worse than if the superior had used the most autocratic method. To practice actual consultative management when issuing new directives and assignments, the supervisor must be ready to take it seriously and be willing to be swayed by the employee's opinions and suggestions. If the manager is not sincere, it would be better not to apply this technique in the first place.

If the subject matter concerns only the supervisor and one employee, the consultative, or participative, method can be carried out informally. Numerous occasions arise during the day to hold such private consultations; however, if this approach is used all the time, the subordinates may begin to doubt whether the supervisors have any opinions of their own and are able to make any decisions. Although some supervisors are incapable of making decisions, many go too far in using this philosophy of direction, and while implementing the technique of participation, they cannot retain the atmosphere of managing.

To reinstate the atmosphere of managing, one should recall that consultative direction does not lessen or weaken formal authority, since the right of decision making still remains with the supervisor. Moreover, the supervisor using this approach is just as concerned with getting the job done economically and expeditiously as the manager who uses another approach. Although the supervisor must not dominate the situation to the exclusion of any employee participation, this does not mean the supervisor cannot express an opinion. It must be expressed in a manner that indicates to the employee that even the supervisor's opinions are subject to critical appraisal. Similarly, participative consultation does not mean that the suggestions of the employee cannot also be criticized or even rejected. True consultation implies a sharing of information between the supervisor and employee and a thorough and impartial discussion of alternate solutions, regardless of who originated them. Only then can it be said that the manager really consulted the subordinate.

For such consultative practices to be successful, it is not only necessary that the supervisor be in favor of them, but the employee must also want them. If the employee believes that "the boss knows best" and that making decisions and giving directives is none of his or her concern, then it is not likely that the opportunity to participate will induce better motivation or morale. The supervisor must also keep in mind that the problems involved must be consistent with the subordinate's ability. Asking for his or her participation about topics that are outside the employee's scope of experience will make the employee feel inadequate and frustrated instead of being motivated.

In using consultation, the danger exists that at the end of an extended discussion the employee may not have a clear idea of the solution. It is therefore desirable and even necessary for the supervisor or subordinate to summarize the conclusions to avoid such a pitfall. This is even more essential if several employees participated in the consultation.

One of the obvious advantages of summarizing the results of the consultation is that the emerging directive does not appear to the employee as an order, but rather as a solution in which he or she participated. This ensures the subordinate's best cooperation and enthusiasm in carrying out the directive. It imparts a feeling of importance, since the ideas evidently were desired and valued. Active participation also provides an outlet for reasoning power and imagination and an opportunity for the employee to make a worthwhile contribution to the organization. Since there is considerable talent among employees, their ideas often prove to be valuable in improving the quality of directives.

An additional advantage of consultation is that it will bring the employee closer to the supervisor, which will make for better communication and understanding between them. Looking at these impressive advantages, it becomes apparent that consultation is by far the best method to use whenever the supervisor has to issue new assignments, directives, and instructions.

## General Supervision

This democratic, participative approach to directing subordinates leads to what we have already referred to as general, or loose, supervision when it comes to *routine assignments* and carrying out the daily chores involved in each employee's job. General supervision, as we know, means allowing the subordinate to work out the details of the job and make decisions on how best to do it. Through this process, workers will gain great satisfaction from being on their own and from having a chance to express themselves and make decisions. Instead of having a specified, detailed list of orders to comply with, the supervisor will just generally indicate what needs to be done and might make a few suggestions as to how to go about it. In so doing, the supervisor assumes that given the proper opportunity, the average employee wants to do a good job. The supervisor is primarily interested in the results. Once the subordinate is told what is to be accomplished and goals are established and limits defined, the employee is left on his or her own. This form of thinking and supervision can only lead to higher motivation and morale and ultimately better job performance. It gives employees the opportunity to satisfy their needs for self-expression and being their own boss.

### Explaining Directives

The supervisor who practices general supervision creates an atmosphere of understanding and mutual confidence in which the employee will feel free to call on the boss whenever the need arises without fear that this will indicate incompetence. Such a supervisor takes the necessary time to explain to the workers the reasons for general directives and why certain things have to be done. By explaining the purpose behind the directives, the employee will be able to understand the environment of the activities. This will make the employee better informed, and the better informed the subordinate is, the better he or she will be able to perform the job.

In many enterprises, a common complaint is that subordinates are kept in the dark most of the time and that supervisors hoard knowledge and information that they ought to pass on. In most instances, it is exceedingly difficult to issue directives so completely as to cover all particulars. If the person who receives the directive knows the purpose behind it, however, he or she is in a better position to carry it out than one who does not know. This will enable the worker to put the environment in total perspective and make sense out of it so that he or she can take firm and secure action. Without such knowledge, employees may feel anxious. Also, subordinates may run into unforeseen circumstances; if they know why the directive was given, they will probably be able to use their own good judgment and carry out the directive in a manner that will bring about proper results. They could not possibly do this if they were not well informed.

Sometimes a supervisor can overdo a good thing, however, and instead of clarifying the situation, provide so much information that the subordinate is utterly confused. Explanations should include only enough information to get the job done. If the directive involves a very minor activity and not much time is available, the explanation will probably be brief. Supervisors must use their own judgment in deciding how far they will go in explaining their directives. They will take into consideration such factors as the capacity of the subordinates to understand, the training they have had, the content of the directive, the underlying managerial attitude, and the time available. After evaluating these factors, the supervisor will be in a better position to decide what constitutes an adequate explanation.

**General Supervision Compared with "No Supervision"**

As mentioned, general supervision is not the same as no supervision at all. General supervision requires that the employee be given a definite assignment, but one that is definite only to the extent that the employee understands the results expected. It is not definite regarding the specific instructions that state precisely how the results are to be achieved. General supervision does not mean that subordinates can set their own standards. Rather, the supervisor will set the standards and will make them realistic, high enough to be a challenge, but not higher than possibly can be achieved.

Although general supervision excludes direct pressure, employees know that their efforts are being measured against these standards, and this knowledge alone should lead them to work harder. By setting the standards reasonably high, the supervisor does apply a degree of pressure, but it is quite different from that exerted by "breathing down someone's neck."

General supervision requires the supervisor to keep developing the potential of the employees. Everyone knows that active learning is more effective than passive learning. Employees learn more easily when they work out a solution for themselves than if they are given the solution. It is also known that employees learn best from their own mistakes. In general supervision, ongoing training of employees is an absolute necessity; the supervisor spends considerable time teaching employees how to solve problems and make decisions as problems arise at work. The better trained the employees become in basic problem-solving methods, the less need there will be for supervision. One way to judge the effectiveness of a supervisor is to see how the employees in the department function when the boss is away from the job.

General supervision, however, is a way of life that must be practiced over time, and the supervisor cannot expect instantaneous results if general supervision is introduced into a situation where the employees have been accustomed to close supervision. It will take time before the results can be seen. The "general" supervisor is just as much interested in results as any other supervisor, but he or she is also interested in the employee's individual development, which differentiates him or her from the "autocratic" supervisor.

Although the supervisor may be a firm believer in general supervision and will practice it whenever possible, under certain conditions firmness, fortitude, and decisiveness must be shown. Certain employees simply may not thrive under loose supervision. This, however, is the exception and not the rule. Although general supervision is not a cure-all for every problem, all research studies seem to indicate that it is more effective than close supervision in terms of productivity, morale, and achievements. General supervision permits the employee to acquire pride in the work and in the results achieved. It helps develop the employee's talent and capabilities, and permits the supervisor to spend less time with the employees and more time on overall management of the department. General supervision provides the motivation for the employees to work on their jobs with enthusiasm and energy, thus deriving full satisfaction from their work.

## EMPLOYEE PARTICIPATION TECHNIQUES

The quality circle, sometimes called the *quality control circle,* is one form of increasing employee participation in the daily work routine. Although the underlying ideas came from the work of McGregor, Maslow, Herzberg, Deming, Drucker, and others, the first practical applications were made in Japanese industry. This Japanese management technique claims much credit for high levels of productivity, quality, and worker satisfaction. Now as Total Quality Management (TQM), Continuous Quality Improvement (CQI), and Performance Improvement (PI) are becoming more prevalent in healthcare institutions, the quality improvement or quality management task force is being used to accomplish the goals of TQM and CQI.

A quality circle, or quality improvement team or task force, is a group of approximately eight to twelve employees (workers) and possibly a supervisor who may or may not be from the same work area, depending upon the topic or process the team has been asked to evaluate. These members strictly volunteer to meet regularly about once a week, during regular working hours, after hours, or both, to discuss work and quantity- and quality-related problems, and to stimulate innovation. They are either assigned a project to assess or are asked to try to identify problems, isolate the causes, and develop practical solutions or develop more effective methods to ensure that the work is accomplished error-free the first time; the supervisor may act as facilitator but often a worker or individual from outside the work team serves in this capacity or in the role of team leader.

Usually the team leader is first exposed to some basic training course in group dynamics, problem solving, and similar techniques. The members themselves are often given some training in problem-solving techniques, establishing priorities, brainstorming, and so forth. The underlying thought is to tap the minds of an organization's own workforce, realizing that the employees doing the job often know best why productivity may be hindered and why product quality is poor. Often they have excellent ideas and answers. These circle (or QI team) solutions are then presented to management or a QI (quality improvement) steering committee.

The quality circle idea fits into the existing organizational structures, following the existing channels of communication and authority. Since quality circles are an application of participative management, the concept can be introduced with success into any organization where administration's philosophy has been democratic, open, and participative. It is unlikely that quality circles would produce results in an environment that practices autocratic and highly centralized management. Many organizations have found the adoption of quality circles to be successful, whereas others have found them disappointing.

The QI Task Force or Team may have freedom to implement their recommendations without a presentation to management. In the TQM environment, much like that found in the Japanese culture, there is total trust between management and employees. Employees are encouraged to make changes and test their hypotheses of improving processes and output without fear of management repercussion. The employees are "empowered" to make decisions about their work environments. Management serves as a coach and facilitator of the brainstorming effort. This type of managerial attitude develops over a time period and creates a culture of mutual trust and freedom of communication in a facility. This cultural style is more closely identified with the Theory Z philosophy. Since TQM is fairly new in healthcare and the management culture it requires is different than most in the U.S., it may be several years before we see its results in our healthcare organizations.

Two approaches to problem solving are demonstrated in the chart developed by the Sisters of St. Mary (SSM) Healthcare System (see figures 19.1 & 19.2). The Process (Re-) Design Approach is used when a process or procedure for doing something, such as obtaining the information to register and the activities involved in registering a patient for treatment, becomes so cumbersome that it needs streamlining. The Problem Solving Approach is used when a problem or opportunity is presented to a team and the team is asked to improve upon the current situation.

Preparation of staff to participate in quality or performance improvement teams may consume some productive time, but must occur to make the process successful. All team members, whether they serve on the "steering" committee or the "team" assessing an opportunity to improve, must have a common vocabulary and utilize tools to transform data into meaningful information. Some of the tools often used are shown in figure 19.3.

CQI MODEL: PROCESS (RE) DESIGN APPROACH

**Team Information**

A PLACE TO:
- Show team name, members' pictures and names if desired.
- Post Team Project Planning Work Sheet.
- Display team meeting minutes.
- Solicit comments using self-stick notes.
- Recognize individuals who provided support to team.

**① Identify Opportunity**

OBJECTIVE:
Identify an opportunity for improvement and the reason for working on it.

KEY ACTIVITIES:
- Research the opportunity:
  —Review indicators.
  —Survey patients and other customers and suppliers.
  —interview individuals involved in the process.
- Consider patient and other customers and supplier needs to help select the opportunity.
- Schedule the CQI Model activities.

CHECKPOINTS:
1. The criteria for selection was customer oriented.
2. A schedule for completing the CQI Model steps was developed.

OUTPUTS:
- Mission Statement Form.
- Team Project Planning Work Sheet.

**② Conceptual Design**

OBJECTIVE:
Develop ideal process flows.

KEY ACTIVITIES:
- Design the ideal process flows.
- Perform customer needs analysis to define requirements at the hand-off and interfaces in the process.
- Write a clear outcome statement.
- Document mutually agreed upon requirements between customers and suppliers.

CHECKPOINTS:
3. The sequence of activities in the new process was documented.
4. The potential benefits of the new process were clearly identified.
5. Customers' valid requirements were identified.

OUTPUTS:
- Clear outcome statement of the process.
- Flowchart of the ideal process.
- Valid requirements of each customer/supplier relationship in the process.

**③ Analysis**

OBJECTIVE:
Design the control system for the process to prevent problems from occurring.

KEY ACTIVITIES:
- Consider potential problems.
- Consider potential causes.
- Develop methods for preventing potential problems.
- Design a measurement system.

CHECKPOINTS:
6. Potential causes of problems were identified and prioritized.
7. Appropriate actions were taken on major potential causes.
8. The measurement and control system is specific enough to pinpoint future problems.

OUTPUTS:
- Control system with measurable indicators.

**④ Implement New Process**

OBJECTIVE:
Put the new process in place.

KEY ACTIVITIES:
- Develop an action plan that:
  —identifies who, what, when, where, and how.
  —Reflects the barriers and aids needed for success.
- Obtain cooperation and approvals.
- Implement the process.
- Develop performance targets for the process.

CHECKPOINTS:
9. Action plan addressed who, what, when, where, and how.
10. Action plan reflected the barriers and aids necessary for successful implementation.
11. Cooperation of relevant managers in impacted organizations was obtained.
12. Performance goals/targets were identified.

OUTPUTS:
- Action Plan.
- Targets for measurable indicators.
- Implementation of new process.

**⑤ Measure Results**

OBJECTIVE:
Confirm that the process is working well and that the performance targets for the process have been met.

KEY ACTIVITIES:
- Compare results obtained to the target.
- Change the process, as necessary, if results are not satisfactory.

CHECKPOINTS:
13. Data was collected to measure performance relative to targets.
14. Results met or exceeded targets. (If not, specific follow-up was planned.)

OUTPUTS:
- Compare the results obtained to the target.
- Change the process, as necessary, if results are not satisfactory.

**⑥ Standardization**

OBJECTIVE:
Ensure that the process is still working and is incorporated into daily work.

KEY ACTIVITIES:
- Ensure that solutions become part of daily work:
  —Create/revise standards.
- Educate employees/medical staff on the process and/or standards and explain need.
- Establish periodic checks with assigned responsibilities to monitor the new process.
- Consider areas for replication.

CHECKPOINTS:
15. Method to assure process becomes part of daily work was developed.
16. All impacted personnel were trained (include explanation of need).
17. Periodic checks were put in place with assigned responsibility to monitor the proposed solutions.
18. Specific areas for replication were considered.

OUTPUTS:
- Education of people.
- Incorporation into standard operating procedures.
- Replication.

**⑦ Future Plans**

OBJECTIVE:
Plan what to do about any remaining problems and evaluate the team's effectiveness.

KEY ACTIVITIES:
- Analyze and evaluate any remaining problems.
- Plan further actions if necessary.
- Review lessons learned related to problem solving skills and group dynamics:
  —What was done well.
  —What could be improved.
  —What could be done differently.

CHECKPOINTS:
19. Plan for any remaining problems was developed.
20. Applied P-D-C-A to lessons learned.

OUTPUTS:
- Plan for the future of the team.
- Evaluation of the team and its work.

**Figure 19.1** Performance improvement CQI model: process (re) design approach.

CQI MODEL: PROBLEM SOLVING APPROACH

CQI MODEL: PROBLEM SOLVING APPROACH

| Team Information | ① Identify Opportunity | ② Current Situation | ③ Analysis |
|---|---|---|---|
| **A PLACE TO:** <br>• Show team name, members' pictures and names if desired. <br>• Posts Team Project Planning Work Sheet. <br>• Display team meeting minutes. <br>• Solicit comments using self-stick notes. <br>• Recognize individuals who provided support to team. | **OBJECTIVE:** <br>Identify an opportunity for improvement and the reason for working on it. <br>**KEY ACTIVITIES:** <br>• Research the opportunity: <br>—Review departmental or process indicators. <br>—Survey patients and other internal customers and suppliers. <br>—Interview individuals involved in the process. <br>• Consider patient and other customer supplier needs to help select the opportunity. <br>• Set indicator to track the opportunity. <br>• Determine how much improvement is needed. <br>• Show impact of the opportunity. <br>• Schedule the CQI Model activities. <br>• Describe the process used in the problem area. <br>**CHECKPOINTS:** <br>1. The criteria for selection was customer oriented. <br>2. The indicator correctly represented the theme. <br>3. The need for improvement was demonstrated using data. <br>4. A schedule for completing the CQI Model steps was developed. <br>**OUTPUTS:** <br>• Mission Statement Form. <br>• Team Project Planning Work Sheet. | **OBJECTIVE:** <br>Select a problem and set a target for improvement. <br>**KEY ACTIVITIES:** <br>• Collect data on all aspects of the process. <br>• Stratify the process from various viewpoints. <br>• Select a problem from the stratification of the process. <br>• Identify patient and other customer requirements. <br>• Write a clear problem statement. <br>• Utilize the data to establish the target. <br>**CHECKPOINTS:** <br>5. The situation was stratified to a component level specific enough to analyze. <br>6. Customer valid requirements were identified. <br>7. Problem statement addressed the gap between the current and targeted values. <br>8. The methodology in establishing goals/targets was identified. <br>**OUTPUTS:** <br>• Problem Statement. <br>• Indicator to measure desired improvement. <br>• Target for the indicator. | **OBJECTIVE:** <br>Identify and verify the root causes of the problem. <br>**KEY ACTIVITIES:** <br>• Perform cause-and-effect analysis on the problem. <br>• Continue analysis on the level of actionable root causes. <br>• Select the root causes with probable greatest impact. <br>• Verify the selected root causes with data. <br>**CHECKPOINTS:** <br>9. Cause-and-effect analysis was performed on the problem. <br>10. Root causes were taken to an actionable level. <br>11. Root causes with probable greastest impact were selected. <br>12. Data was used to verify the root causes. <br>**OUTPUTS:** <br>• Identification and verification of the root cause(s). |
| ④ Proposed Solutions | ⑤ Results | ⑥ Standardization | ⑦ Future Plans |
| **OBJECTIVE:** <br>Plan and implement proposed solutions that will correct the root causes of the problem. <br>**KEY ACTIVITIES:** <br>• Develop and evaluate potential solutions that: <br>—Attack verified root causes. <br>—Meet patient and other customer requirements. <br>—Prove to be cost beneficial. <br>• Develop an action plan that: <br>—Answers who, what, when, where, and how. <br>—Reflects the barriers and aids needed for success. <br>• Implement purposed solutions. <br>**CHECKPOINTS:** <br>13. Selected solutions attacked verified root causes. <br>14. Solutions were consistent with meeting customer valid requirements. <br>15. Solutions were cost beneficial. <br>16. Action plan answered who, what, when, where, and how. <br>17. Action plan reflected the barriers and aids necessary for successful implementation. <br>**OUTPUTS:** <br>• Proposed Solutions Matrix. <br>• Action Plan. <br>• Implementation of selected proposed solutions. | **OBJECTIVE:** <br>Confirm that the problem and its root causes have been decreased and the target for improvement has been met. <br>**KEY ACTIVITIES:** <br>• Confirm the effects of the proposed solutions, checking to see if the root causes have been reduced. <br>• Compare the problem before and after using the same indicator. <br>• Compare the results obtained to the target. <br>• Implement additional proposed solutions if results are not satisfactory. <br>**CHECKPOINTS:** <br>18. Root causes have been reduced. <br>19. Tracking indicator was the same one used in the identify opportunity stop. <br>20. Results met or exceeded target. (If not, cause was addressed.) <br>**OUTPUTS:** <br>• Comparison of the target improvement before and after the proposed solution(s) has been implemented. | **OBJECTIVE:** <br>Prevent the problem and its root causes from recurring. <br>**KEY ACTIVITIES:** <br>• Ensure that solutions become part of daily work. <br>—Create/revise the process. <br>—Create/revise standards. <br>• Educate employees/medical staff on revised process and/or standards and explain need. <br>• Establish periodic checks with assigned responsibilities to monitor the new process. <br>• Consider areas for replication. <br>**CHECKPOINTS:** <br>21. Method to assure solutions becomes part of daily work was developed (include applicable training). <br>22. Periodic checks were put in place with assigned responsibility to monitor the proposed solutions. <br>23. Specific areas for replication were considered. <br>**OUTPUTS:** <br>• Plan for replication. <br>• Action Plan to ensure all changes will become standard operating procedures. | **OBJECTIVE:** <br>Plan what to do about any remaining problems and evaluate the team's effectiveness. <br>**KEY ACTIVITIES:** <br>• Analyze any evaluate any remaining problems. <br>• Plan further actions if necessary. <br>• Review lessons learned related to problem solving skills and group dynamics: <br>—What was done well. <br>—What could be improved. <br>—What could be done differently. <br>**CHECKPOINTS:** <br>24. Any remaining problems of the theme will be addressed. <br>25. Applied P-D-C-A to lessons learned. <br>**OUTPUTS:** <br>• Plan for the future of the team. <br>• Evaluation of the team and its work. |

**Figure 19.2** Performance improvement CQI model: problem solving approach.

© SSM Health Care System CQI Manual. *St. Louis, MO. SSM Health Care, 1990. Reprinted with permission.*

| CQI Data Tools | Purpose/Description of Tool |
|---|---|
| *Brainstorming* | A discussion forum used to get a group of people to quickly generate, clarify, and evaluate a number of ideas that are listed regardless of their viability to support a solution to the problem. |
| *Cause-and-Effect (also known as the "fishbone" and Ishikawa Diagram)* 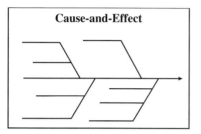 | A diagram that depicts causes of a problem and attempts to narrow the problem down to the most likely, or root, cause. Contributing issues to the problem are grouped together such as people, materials, machinery (equipment), and methods. |
| *Flow Charts or Process Diagram* 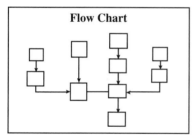 | Pictorial description of the flow or steps in a process to allow visualization of the tasks. |
| *Pareto Charts* 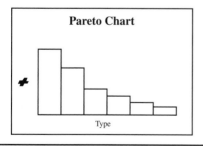 | These charts are used to display data in the order of its relative importance or weight. It identifies the "few major causes" of variation from the "trivial" to many. It comes from the 80–20 theory that 80% of the problem is directly related to 20% of the causes. For example, 80% of the delinquent medical records are for 20% of the physicians on the medical staff. |

**Figure 19.3** Commonly used performance improvement data tools.

*Continued.*

| **CQI Data Tools** | **Purpose/Description of Tool** |
|---|---|
| *Run Charts (Trend or Line graphs)* | This graph shows with a single line data or results occurring at different times for a time period. |

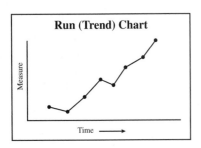

| *Histograms* | This graph, usually in "bar" format, displays the frequency with which something occurs. It shows a distribution that may or may not be "bell shaped." |
|---|---|

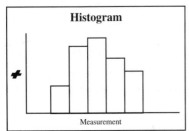

| *Scatter Diagram* | This diagram is used to demonstrate the relationship between two variables such as processing time and volume of specimens received. |
|---|---|

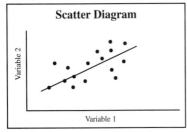

| *Control Chart* | This chart reflects the tolerances of something happening within limits. Normal limits are established and concern should rise when the number of occurrences outside of the limits increase. |
|---|---|

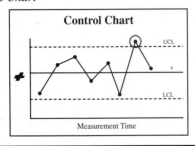

**Figure 19.3**   Continued.

In a CQI (continuous quality improvement) environment, teams generally follow a process including several steps:

| **Step** | **Who** | **QI Tool** |
|---|---|---|
| **1.** List and Prioritize Opportunities | Steering Committee | Data Collection, Pareto Analysis, Brainstorming, Flow Charts, Graphs and Charts |
| **2.** Identify Customer(s) and Expectations | Steering Committee and Team | Brainstorming, Flow Charts, and Data Collection |
| **3.** Define Project and Team | Steering Committee | Flow Charts and Graphs and Charts |
| **4.** Formulate Theories | Steering Committee and Team | Brainstorming, Cause-and-Effect Diagrams, and Flow Charts |
| **5.** Test Theories | Team | Flow Charts, Data Collection, Graphs and Charts, Pareto Analysis, Histograms |
| **6.** Identify Root Cause | Team | Flow Charts, Data Collection, Graphs and Charts, Pareto Analysis, Histograms |
| **7.** Identify Solutions and Control Systems | Team | Brainstorming, Flow Charts, Data Collection, Graphs and Charts, Cause-and-Effect Diagrams |
| **8.** Address Resistance to Change | Team | Brainstorming, Flow Charts, Cause-and-Effect Diagrams |
| **9.** Implement Solutions and Control Systems | Steering Committee and Team, and Others | Flow Charts, Graphs and Charts, Pareto Analysis, Histograms |
| **10.** Evaluate Performance | Steering Committee and Team | Data Collection, Graphs and Charts, Pareto Analysis, Histograms, Flow Charts |
| **11.** Standardize Process | Team, Steering Committee, Senior Management | Data Collection, Graphs and Charts, Pareto Analysis, and Histograms |
| **12.** Monitor Control Systems | Steering Committee, Senior Management | Data Collection, Graphs and Charts, Flow Charts, Pareto Analysis, Histograms |

The success of any process that places subordinates and supervisors together requires communication. To encourage communication without fear of reprisal the *nominal group technique (NGT)* is practiced. This technique tries to provide a way to give everyone in the group an equal voice in problem or process identification. And according to Witt,[1] the key questions that should guide the team or group must include:

- Who is the customer in the process?
- What is the desired outcome?
- What would the process look like under ideal conditions?
- What are key points where problems have been observed in the past?
- How can we design quality into the process, rather than inspecting for it after the fact?

For the healthcare supervisor, the most challenging part of any quality improvement process is the implementation of the improvement.

Healthcare organizations are on an evolutionary course to improve quality. In the 1970s the approach was one of retrospective review and pointing fingers to the source(s) of variation from expected. In the 1980s more participative approaches appeared with the use of quality control circles but still the method was one of recognizing a problem *after* it had occurred and then trying to fix it so it did not occur again. In the 1990s the continuous improvement strategy was one of looking at existing processes, regardless of whether they were faltering, and constantly trying to improve them. By doing so, all processes would constantly be undergoing streamlining, thus eliminating waste and associated costs, and resulting in an entity that could aggressively compete in a viciously competitive environment. Those who implemented a reengineering process within their institution recognize the need to continuously improve.

As you will recall from the chapter 13, reengineering requires you to focus on the customer's needs. By doing so, you are always looking to the customer (patient) for indicators of process modification. Once you begin reengineering you really cannot stop. You continuously improve and inevitably reach a point in time when your patient requirements will change, and guess what? You'll want to reengineer again, especially in healthcare, with its changing parameters and its constant reaching for better outcomes and measures.[2]

Learning the techniques, putting them to use, and continuously seeking input from employees have all taken time. Moreover, encouraging employees to be open and share criticisms constructively about processes established by their supervisors **and** supervisors not reacting negatively to the criticism have been major hurdles that only a few enterprises have successfully overcome. For

---

1.   James D. Witt, *"How to Implement Changes from Your QI Team,"* Occupational Health Management, *July 1996. v. 6, no. 7, July 1996, pp. 77–78.*
2.   *Deloitte and Touche LLP,* Health Care Review, *April 1996.*

healthcare organizations to flourish in the future, this type of equal exchange between employees and their supervisors must occur.

| **CHANGE AND INFLUENCING** | All organized activities are under continuous pressure for change. There are various reasons for change, but the most common are scientific and technological developments, people, competition, and communication. |

Supervisors' effectiveness in the influencing function is extremely important whenever they are faced with change. Since every enterprise operates in a larger context and a dynamic environment, change is inevitable and is a part of everyday life. In fact, the growth of most undertakings depends largely on the concept of change and the ability to accommodate it.

Although all organized activities are subject to change, the degree and complexity of change vary considerably from one activity to another. This is particularly so in the healthcare field, in which the speed and complexity of changes have continuously increased in the last few decades and will continue to do so in the future. There is little doubt that most of these changes have been beneficial. Hospital and ambulatory surgery centers are filled with patients benefiting from one new breakthrough or another. The healthcare center as a social system produces an ever-shifting equilibrium of forces because of the amazing changes in medical sciences and technologies, and in the social and economic environment. The supervisor's own department is a small social subsystem, interdependent on the larger system of the healthcare center. Any change imposed from outside is likely to shift the equilibrium of forces within each individual department, as well as within the organization as a whole.

The departmental supervisor is in the forefront of change, since he or she is the one in the daily work environment who has to make it a reality. The supervisor must "sell" the idea of change to the subordinates. Most often the supervisor has had little to do with the decision to make the change or with its timing; it originated higher up in the administration or somewhere else. However, the supervisor should understand and accept the change because now his or her duty is to introduce it, explain it to the subordinates, and report their reactions to the superiors. The supervisor will encounter reactions from the employees that range from ready acceptance to outright rejection and hostility.

Communicating the reasons for change may reduce to some degree rejection and hostility. Changes are often the result of outside events that force the enterprise to alter its practices. Sometimes changes must occur for the enterprise to stay alive.

When it comes to jobs and interpersonal relations many people tend to resist change. This is unfortunate because if an enterprise, especially in healthcare, is to survive, it must be able to react to the prevailing forces. Since resistance to change is a common phenomenon, the supervisor must recognize this and be familiar with ways to overcome it.

## ◼ Resistance to Change

The main reasons for resistance to change are: uncertainty, perception, loss, self-interests, and insecurity. One of the important factors of internal inflexibilities is psychological. Supervisors and employees may develop patterns of thought and behavior that are resistant to change. Supervisors are often frustrated in instituting a change by the unwillingness or inability of people to accept it. To overcome these inflexibilities, the supervisor must realize that it requires patient selling of the idea, education, careful dissemination of information, good leadership, and developing a tradition of change among the department's members. The supervisor must not fail to realize that even a trifling change may cause strong reactions within some of the employees.

This difficulty is further complicated because of *different perceptions*. For example, employees may believe that a new organizational arrangement will result in their loss of control or influence. This belief will cause resistance to change. The fact that the new structure will in no way reduce their influence does not diminish their resistance as long as they feel threatened or attacked.

To a large degree these sources of resistance to change center around a major consideration—*uncertainty* about the effects of change. An impending change is likely to cause anxiety and nervousness. The employees may worry about their being able to fulfill the new job demands. Also, the change may be fraught with weaknesses that have been overlooked or brushed aside.

Another reason for resisting change is that it disturbs the *equilibrium* of the current state of affairs. The assumption is that before the change, the employee exists within an environment where his or her *need satisfaction* has reached a high degree of stability; the change may threaten, prevent, or decrease the satisfaction of these needs. Therefore, it is natural for some employees to do whatever possible to thwart introducing a change. A further reason for resisting change is that any change is seen as a potential threat to the employee's *security and self-interests*. The subordinate must give up the known familiar routine for something new and unpredictable. For example, a new apparatus in the laboratory could make some of the technologists' previous skills superfluous. This could undermine their sense of occupational and professional identity. The change may require the technologists to upgrade their skills, and they may not be sure they can master the new responsibilities. At the onset, any new ideas and methods almost always present a threat to the security of the individuals involved in the change. Usually people fear change because they cannot assess or predict what it will bring in terms of their own position, activity, and future. It makes no difference whether the change is actually threatening or not. What matters is that the subordinate believes or assumes this.

Another reason for resistance to change is that it may threaten the employee's *status* within the organization and the existing social networks. The employee may fear that his or her status will be lowered and someone else's raised. Such feelings of loss have, for example, caused many new computer installations to be used less effectively than anticipated or to be slowed down in their effects on the overall organization. This resulted because employees in the controller's office, where computers were typically housed before the advent of PCs and networks, started to gain a different status in the organization once the computer became their domain. Its introduction caused what appeared to be threatening changes in the reporting relationships and status of numerous employees.

Often threats of an *economic* nature provide an additional reason for resistance to change. The subordinate may fear that the change will affect his or her job economically. The employee may not be willing to give up existing benefits because the costs of change will probably not be made up by the rewards. Many years ago hand-weavers in the Low Countries of Europe tried to destroy mechanical looms by throwing their wooden clogs (sabots) into the machinery (sabotage) because they feared that the machines would destroy their jobs and income. The same fears of loss still prevail today when it comes to the size of the paycheck.

In general, one may say that a change that causes great disturbance to one person may create little disequilibrium for another. The severity of the reaction that occurs in a particular situation will depend on the nature of the change and the person concerned. The important thing for the supervisor to recognize is that changes do disturb the equilibrium of the employee and that, when individuals become threatened, they develop behaviors that serve as barriers to the threat. Therefore, it is the supervisor's duty to facilitate the inevitable process of adjustment when changes are necessary. Let us see how this can be done.

## ■ Overcoming Resistance to Change

Fortunately there are several useful ways to overcome these difficulties. The supervisor should always remember that employees seldom resist change just to be stubborn. From the previous discussion we learned that there are valid reasons for resistance. Subordinates resist because the change affects their equilibrium socially, psychologically, and possibly economically. One of the factors that is particularly important in gaining acceptance of change is the relationship that exists between the supervisor who is trying to introduce the change and the employee who is subject to the change. If a relationship of mutual confidence and trust exists between the two, the employee is much more likely to go along with the change.

The supervisor should assume that a considerable amount of time is necessary to implement a change; a rigid timetable for change is unrealistic. The change must be planned far in advance, and its impact on each position and job should be anticipated. Even if the change is well thought out and carefully planned, some ramifications will probably be overlooked. The supervisor must leave room to discuss and accommodate them. With the proper attitude and the right techniques, however, the supervisor can facilitate the introduction of change. Involving subordinates in change discussions and decisions will help to overcome the various types of resistance.

### *Explanation and Communication*
The most important aspect in facilitating the introduction of change is the supervisor's duty to *explain* the change to the employees in advance. This should

begin long before the change is to be initiated. There should be ample time before the changeover to familiarize the employees with the idea, allow them to think through the implications and ramifications, and ask questions for more clarification. In other words, there must be sufficient time for feedback and additional *communication.*

In explaining the change, the supervisor should put himself or herself into the subordinate's position and discuss its pros and cons from the subordinate's point of view. This discussion should explain what will happen and why. It should clarify the way in which the change will affect the employee and what it means to that person. It should show that the change will not adversely affect the employee or that it will even improve the present situation. In this process of communication, the manager might want to interject what is often referred to as the *force-field analysis,* an approach to overcome resistance to change. In every change process there are forces acting for and against the change. The supervisor should comment on the pluses and minuses connected with the change from the employee's point of view, then try to tip the balance toward acceptance so that the forces for the change outweigh the forces against the change. All this information should be communicated to the entire department—those employees who are directly involved as well as those who are indirectly involved. Overstatements are ill-advised, however, and it is essential to be absolutely truthful. The supervisor cannot afford a credibility gap.

The supervisor must also try to communicate, explaining to the employees what they consciously and subconsciously want and need to know in order to resolve prevailing fears. Only then can employees assess and understand what the change proposal would mean in terms of their positions and activities. The supervisor must help the subordinate understand the need for the change. This will be easier if the supervisor has always been concerned with setting the proper stage and giving the proper background information for all the directives. In such a case, the employee is thoroughly acquainted with the underlying factors and is more likely to view the change as a necessary adjustment in a dynamic environment. The subordinate might ask a few additional questions about it, but then can quickly adapt to it and resume his or her previous behavior. The subordinate who has been informed of the reasons for change knows what to expect and why. Instead of blind resistance, there will be intelligent adaptation to the instructions; instead of insecurity, a feeling of security. It is not the change itself that leads to so much misunderstanding, but more the manner in which the supervisor introduces the change. In other words, resistance to change that comes from fear of the unknown can be minimized by supplying an appropriate explanation.

### Participation

Another effective way of reducing resistance to change is to permit participation in planning and implementing it. Playing a part in planning the change will reduce uncertainty and remove some of the fears and threats to social relationships and self-interests. Furthermore, those who are affected by the change may have something to contribute, since they are close to the situation and may see some weaknesses in the change proposal that management might have overlooked. Last, if the "plan" for change is *their* plan, acceptance by the employees is greater.

This participation may be in the form of *consultation,* whereby criticism and suggestions are sincerely solicited from the employees in relation to the contemplated change. In face-to-face conversations the supervisor discusses problems, asks questions, and tries to get the employees' ideas and reactions. One hopes management will then incorporate as much of this into the change as possible, and the employees will consider themselves partners in the change. A change imposed from above without participation is likely to generate resentment.

A more advanced stage of participation occurs when the supervisor lets the employees make the decision themselves. The supervisor defines the problem and sets the limits, but allows the subordinates to develop the alternatives and choose between them. *Group decision making* could also produce a better decision because pooled expertise is likely to identify and evaluate more alternatives than an individual could; those who are involved in this process are probably more deeply committed to the alternative selected. Therefore, group decision making is an effective means for overcoming resistance to change. Such an approach recognizes that if the employees who are threatened by a change have the opportunity to work through the new ideas and methods from the beginning and can be assured that their needs will be satisfied in the future, they will accept the new ideas and methods as something of their own making and will support the changes. Group decision making also makes it easier for each member to carry out the decision once it is agreed on, and the group will put strong pressure on those who have reservations or who do not want to go along.

Both types of participation should be encouraged because they help to facilitate the introduction of change. Of course, in trying to implement change in the department, the supervisor will make use of all means available—persuasion, discussion, participation, and group decision making. Participation is not always possible, however; in extreme situations, it may be necessary to make unpleasant changes unilaterally, impose them, and then help the subordinates understand and accept them.

## Survival during Change

Even though you as a supervisor "buy" into the reasons for change, and even if you are successful in influencing your staff to accept the change, adjusting to new circumstances can drain you. Pritchett and Pound recommend that good stress management techniques be practiced. "It makes sense now for you to work on managing your personal stress load. Keeping your sense of humor and controlling your attitude are steps in the right direction, but you also need to take care of yourself physically. Vigorous activity offers tension release and helps keep you healthy," they recommend.[3] They also suggest exercising such as running, swimming, aerobics, etc.

---

3.  *Price Pritchett and Ron Pound,* The Employee Handbook for Organizational Change *3rd ed. (Dallas): 38.*

**SUMMARY** The influencing function of the manager forms the connecting link between planning, organizing, and staffing on one side and controlling on the other. Issuing directives is perhaps the most important part of the influencing function because without them, nothing or at best very little would be achieved. Certain prerequisites insure that a directive will be properly carried out. A good directive must encompass the formula of who, what, where, when, how, and why. It should be accomplishable, intelligible, properly phrased, and compatible with the objectives of the enterprise. In addition, a reasonable amount of time should be permitted for its completion.

In issuing directives, the supervisor may employ two major techniques: the autocratic technique, which brings about close supervision, and the consultative technique, characterized by general supervision. For certain occasions, employees, and conditions the autocratic technique is probably more effective, but for most situations it is far better for a supervisor to apply consultative techniques to produce the highest motivation and morale among employees. This means that in the case of new assignments, the supervisor will consult with the employees as to how the job should best be done.

In directives primarily concerned with routine assignments and the daily performance of the job, the supervisor will employ a form of general supervision instead of close supervision. In so doing, the supervisor gives the employees the freedom to make their own decisions on how the job is to be done, after he or she has set the goals and standards to be achieved. This also gives employees the freedom to use their own ingenuity and judgment; experiences of this type offer continuous room for further training and improvement. In addition, general supervision motivates employees to the extent that they find satisfaction in their jobs. All indications are that general supervision produces better results than close supervision.

Since the healthcare field is dynamic, necessitating constant and often substantial changes, the supervisor is confronted with the problem of how to introduce change. To cope successfully with the average employees' normal resistance to change, the supervisor must realize that there are social, psychological, and possibly economic reasons for this resistance. By involving employees in change discussions and decisions, much of the resistance can be overcome. The supervisor is in the front line, and it is his or her responsibility to accommodate change and make it become reality.

# *Motivation*

## *Chapter Objectives*

After you have studied this chapter, you should be able to

1. Outline the major theories of motivation.
2. Describe the motivational processes.
3. Define perceptions, values and attitudes, and the factors that affect each of these.
4. Discuss the supervisor's duty in minimizing frustration and conflict.

Motivating employees is important to managers because it affects performance. Motivation is closely related to the crucial managerial function of influencing because it deals most intimately with the individual. Thus, we must understand something about what makes the human being tick, what motivates a person, and more basically what underlies a person's motivations.

Motivation is the process affecting the inner needs or drives that arouses, moves, energizes, directs, channels, and sustains human behavior. Generally, the motivational process begins the drive that impels individuals to work toward certain goals they believe will satisfy their inner needs. Once these goals are attained, we judge whether these efforts were worthwhile. If so, this works as reinforcement, and we continue to pursue these and/or other needs and drives. All this will be discussed in great detail later in this chapter. Understanding motivation will enable managers to help their employees achieve higher levels of job satisfaction and job performance.

---

## THEORIES OF MOTIVATION

Managers have been aware of how important motivation is for a long time. It has been a major concern for managers and psychologists, and many theories have been developed explaining how people are motivated. There are several different ways to interpret the concept of motivation; two of the major categories of contemporary motivational theories are the *content* theory and the *process* theory.

*Content theory* focuses on the question of what factor or set of factors moves, energizes, and starts the behavior of an individual. This theory discusses the concept of needs or motives that drive people and the incentives that cause people to behave in a particular manner. Three of the most publicized content theories of motivation are Maslow's hierarchy of needs, Herzberg's two-factor approach of satisfiers and dissatisfiers, and McClelland's needs for achievement, affiliation, and power. Each of these three content theories tries to explain individual behavior from a slightly different perspective.

On the other hand, *process theory* examines how and why people choose a particular behavior to accomplish a goal and how they evaluate their satisfaction after reaching the goal. Equity and expectancy are the two major process

**Figure 20.1** Model of the motivational process.

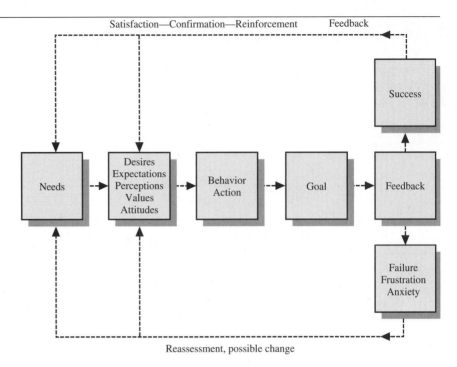

Modified from Theo Haimann, William G. Scott, and Patrick E. Connor, *Management,* 4th ed., Boston: Houghton Mifflin Co., 1982. Reprinted with permission.

perspectives on motivation. The first approach stresses the equity of effort in relation to the results; that is, there should be a balance in the amount of effort one must put forth for the resulting rewards—compensation, benefits, etc. The other approach emphasizes that one will put forth a certain level of effort if he or she expects to receive some reward, promotion, or recognition. If there is inequity or imbalance, staff will not be motivated.

## MODEL OF MOTIVATIONAL PROCESSES

Although the complete set of processes is very complex, a generalized model of basic motivational processes is presented in figure 20.1. This model shows five basic parts of the process: (1) needs; (2) desires, expectations, perceptions, values, and attitudes; (3) behavior action; (4) goal, and (5) feedback. At any point in time individuals are likely to have a mixture of needs, desires, and expectations. For instance, one subordinate may have a strong need to achieve and a desire to earn more money; this person expects that doing the job well will lead to the desired rewards. This expectation is likely to cause behavior that is directed toward specific goals. Achieving the goals serves as feedback on the impact of this behavior and reassures this individual that the behavior is correct; it satisfies the needs and expectations. On the other hand, it may tell the person that the present course of action is incorrect and should be altered.

This model of motivation is oversimplified because it does not take into account all influences on motivation; however, it shows the basic cyclical nature of the process. People are forever striving to satisfy a variety of needs and expectations, and the success of one effort triggers the pursuit of another need and desire. Once one need has been met, another need or desire emerges and stimulates further action.

## ■ Maslow's Hierarchy of Human Needs

One of the approaches to employee motivation is based on individual human needs. Every action is motivated by unsatisfied needs. These unsatisfied needs cause human beings to behave in a certain manner and to try to achieve certain goals in hopes of reducing the tensions that arise from unmet needs. A person eats because hunger creates the need for food. Someone else has a strong need to achieve and strives to advance in his or her field of work. In other words, there is a reason for everything that people do.

People are always striving to attain something that has meaning to them in terms of their own particular needs. It is often observed that human beings never seem satisfied; we are continuously fulfilling needs. After the successful fulfillment of one need, we will start on another round of pursuits. Indeed, we can say that life is a process in which needs constantly arise and demand satisfaction.

Probably the most widely known and accepted theory of needs and motivation is the model designed by Abraham H. Maslow consisting of *deficiency needs* and *growth needs.* Deficiency needs must be satisfied if the individual is to be healthy and secure. They are the physiological needs for food, water, clothing, shelter, etc.; needs for safety; and the feeling of belonging, love, and respect from others. Growth needs refer to development and achievement of one's potential. We should not think, however, that all needs are of the same order of importance. Many different kinds of needs exist, and some produce stronger motivation or demand more immediate satisfaction than others. Maslow suggests that these needs are arranged in a hierarchy. (See figure 20.2.)

Maslow's model contains five levels of needs that can be visualized as forming a pyramid. The most basic needs are *physiological needs.* Normally, in organizational settings, adequate wages and the work environment itself enable an individual to obtain the necessities and comforts of life that are vital to fulfilling these physiological needs.

When the physiological needs are reasonably satisfied, needs at the next higher level begin to dominate. These are usually called *safety needs,* such as safe physical and emotional environments. They are the needs we have for protection against danger and threat. Such needs are natural reactions to insecurity. We all desire more control over and protection from the uncertainties of life. In a work environment, these uncertainties would produce *security* needs caused by an unstable economic climate (recession), fear of arbitrary management action (i.e., decision to close a clinic), loss of job, favoritism, discrimination, unpredictable administration of policy, etc. Most enterprises today offer various

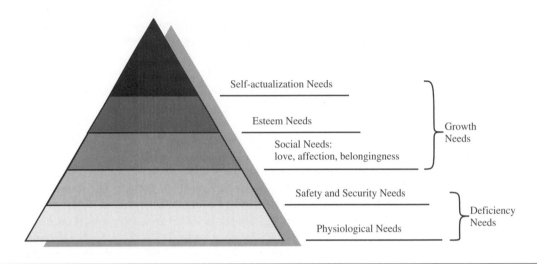

**Figure 20.2**   Hierarchy of needs.

programs that are designed to satisfy and fulfill these safety or security needs. For example, most enterprises have grievance systems, adequate medical and other insurance plans, provisions for retirement benefits, provisions for unemployment compensation, seniority benefits, etc. Especially during times of economic instability this need tends to dominate all employees' concerns. Therefore, the manager must attempt to respond to security needs when they arise.

Once the physiological and safety needs are satisfied, *social and belongingness needs* become important motivators. Social needs consist of belonging, association, acceptance by one's peers, and giving and receiving friendship and love. These needs are often identical with the needs people have for a feeling of group identity, being part of a group or team, and being accepted and respected by their peers. A supervisor must be aware of the existence of these needs, which can be fulfilled in organizational settings by informal groups. As we know, tightly knit, cohesive work groups will generally enable employees to gain greater on-the-job satisfaction and produce a better climate for motivation. This is why the supervisor should look at the positive aspects and strengths of informal groups. Often supervisors go to great trouble to control and interfere with the natural "grouping" tendency of human beings. This is ill-advised. When a person's social needs are thwarted and frustrated, this individual will behave in ways that are likely to hurt organizational objectives. The manager should always realize that social needs are fulfilled to a large extent by informal groups and informal organization, as discussed in chapter 15.

Once the first three needs, also known as *deficiency needs,* have been satisfied, people will generally attempt to satisfy growth needs. These are the needs for esteem and self-actualization. *Esteem needs* focus on one's desire to have a worthy self-image and receive recognition from others. Self-esteem includes the need for self-confidence, a positive self-image, self-respect, independence, achievement, competence, and knowledge. These needs are often fulfilled by mastery over part of the environment, for example, by knowing that you can accomplish a certain task.

However, a person also needs the esteem and recognition of others for his or her accomplishments. These needs relate to reputation, status, recognition, appreciation, and the deserved respect of colleagues. Many jobs in industrial settings offer little opportunity for satisfaction of such needs. However, many positions in the healthcare field are much more conducive to achieving these needs because of their challenging nature. The manager can help the situation by providing external symbols of esteem such as appropriate titles and offices. Of course, it is desirable that both aspects of the need for esteem are fulfilled. Frequently, however, the esteem of self comes before esteem from others.

The highest level of needs is the need for *self-actualization, self-fulfillment,* or *self-realization.* These are the needs for realizing one's own potential, for continued self-development, and for being creative in the broadest sense of the term. It has often been said that this is the need "to become what one is capable of becoming." Unlike the other four needs, which probably will be satisfied, self-actualization is seldom fully achieved. It is a process of becoming, and as one gradually approaches self-fulfillment, this process is intensified and sustained. Since this need probably can be met only from within, there is little the manager can do, except to provide an organizational climate conducive to self-actualization. Conditions of modern life give many people little opportunity to fulfill this need. Most employees are continuously struggling to satisfy the lower needs and must divert most of their energy to satisfy them. Therefore, the need for self-fulfillment frequently remains unfulfilled.

There seems to be a relationship between the hierarchy of needs and age. Physiological and safety needs are paramount in the life of an infant. As a child grows up, love needs become more important. When the adolescent reaches young adulthood, needs for esteem seem to take precedence. If the person is successful in life, then the move to self-actualization later in life is likely. Such a step does not necessarily follow because pressing circumstances may arrest the route of progress at the esteem level or at lower levels. Also, as we shall see later, this situation is often the basis of conflict between organizational and individual goals.

Maslow's hierarchy of needs has been and still is popular among managers and appeals to them. Since it is the supervisor's job to create a climate in which employees can satisfy the multitude of needs, this theory makes clear recommendations to management. Some of the specific dynamics of Maslow's theory may still be in question though, and have been challenged. Nevertheless, Maslow's hierarchy was the first clear theory urging managers to recognize the importance of higher-order needs. It caused a shift from the traditional lower-order motivators to higher motivators. Most healthy and normal employees probably have satisfied the lower-order deficiency needs (they are not hungry, feel reasonably secure, and have sufficient social relationships) but this fact does not negate the possibility of its existence. Consider a dietary worker who is the sole support of her extended family including her husband, three children, one grandchild, and her mother. Thefts of food items such as whole chickens or boxed items may require management to investigate employee lower-order needs.

Supervisors also must emphasize a working climate conducive to satisfying the higher-order growth needs. This means supervisors should stress some variety of duties, delegation of authority, autonomy, and responsibility so that employees can more fully realize their potential and their growth needs. Techniques to empower staff with levels of decision-making previously held only by supervisors allows them to satisfy some higher-order needs.

## ■ Two-Factor Motivation-Hygiene Theory

Another approach to the content theory of motivation as a need classification system was developed by Frederick Herzberg. Herzberg, a psychologist, has done much research on job satisfaction and has developed a number of conditions on which satisfaction is based. He distinguishes between those factors at the workplace that are unlikely to motivate employees (hygiene factors) and those that tend to motivate employees (motivators). In essence, he states that the hygiene rewards satisfy what are commonly known as lower-order needs, whereas the motivators satisfy higher-order needs. Herzberg identified the following groups as hygiene factors and as motivators:

| **Hygiene Factors** | **Motivation Factors** |
| --- | --- |
| The organization's policy and administration | Achievement |
| Technical supervision | Recognition |
| Interpersonal relations | The work itself |
| Working conditions | Responsibility |
| Salary | Advancement |

Herzberg measures satisfiers and dissatisfiers by how frequently they appear and how long they produce either a significant improvement or reduction in job satisfaction. (See figure 20.3.) The five hygiene factors are environmental. When they are at an unacceptable level, dissatisfaction will occur. When they are at an acceptable level, satisfaction results. The factors most frequently involved in events causing job dissatisfaction (dissatisfiers) are company policy and administration, supervision, interpersonal relations, and working conditions, and salary. When these factors are negative or lacking, they are considered to be *dissatisfiers.* Even when they are positive and appropriate, these factors do not tend to motivate people; it is almost as if they are expected. When positive, they are *satisfiers.*

This, however, does not mean that the hygiene factors are unimportant. They are essential because whether they exist or not is either satisfying or dissatisfying. Therefore, the manager must make certain that administration and policies are fair and suitable, that pay and benefits are appropriate, that technical supervision is acceptable, that working conditions are safe and healthy, and so forth. By

**Figure 20.3** Factors affecting job satisfaction.

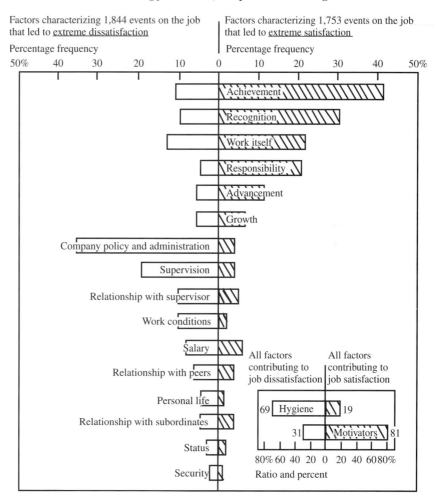

*Note: Figure 1 does not include duration data.*

providing these factors at the proper level, the manager does not give the employees the opportunity to feel motivated, but does keep them from being dissatisfied.

If managers really want motivated employees, however, they should use *motivators*. Herzberg's study indicates that the most frequently mentioned factors in improved job satisfaction are achievement, recognition, the work itself, responsibility, and advancement. These are the factors that, if present, truly motivate people. It is the opportunity for advancement, greater responsibility, the possibility of promotion, growth, achievement, and interesting work that make a job challenging, meaningful, and really motivating to subordinates. The manager, therefore, should give the employees an opportunity to experience these motivational factors in an environment conducive to growth. Such motivational factors are obviously associated with the higher-order needs of people—they are related to the work content, whereas the hygiene factors relate to the work environment.

Herzberg's findings have important implications for the supervisor. Although management strives for good organizational "hygiene" through sound wage administration, enlightened supervision, pleasant working conditions, appropriate fringe benefits, and so forth, these factors alone normally do not produce a motivational climate. If properly fulfilled, we merely minimize dissatisfaction; however, these factors are not motivators. What is actually required, therefore, is a two-way effort that is directed first at the hygiene factors and then at the development of motivation. In addition to the need to avoid unpleasantness that comes from largely dissatisfying conditions, the supervisor must produce positive motivation through a more sophisticated set of factors, which is closely related to the concept of self-actualization. Although it is difficult to apply these motivators in some situations, most positions in the healthcare setting provide ample opportunity to stress them.

## ■ Other Needs

Another approach to the content view of motivation concerns other important needs. David McClelland's research in organizational behavior led to what he has termed and is now commonly known as *need for achievement* (n *Ach*), *need for affiliation* (n *Aff*), and the *need for power* (n *Pow*).

The need for achievement is a need for personal challenge and accomplishment. It involves the desire to assume personal responsibility and pursue reasonably difficult goals, a preoccupation with the task, and specific and quick feedback as to accomplishment. This n *Ach* is obviously essential for a successful manager; one learns it from early childhood on and adults can learn it, too. McClelland defines it as behavior toward competition with a standard of excellence.

The need for affiliation is the need for human companionship, support, and reassurance. People with a strong n *Aff* look for approval and reassurance from others, are willing to conform to the norms and wishes of others, and are sincerely interested in the feelings of others. They are likely to do well in situations that include a lot of social interaction.

The third need is the need for power, or need for dominance. The n *Pow* is a need to influence others and to lead and control them. One of McClelland's studies concluded that all managers tend to have a stronger power motive than the general population and that successful managers tend to have stronger power motives than less successful managers.

### Levels of Aspiration

A person's level of aspiration is closely related to the order of needs. Level of aspiration causes an individual's goals to shift as various needs are satisfied. That is, once the needs on one level are satisfied, the individual tends to aspire to higher levels. For example, suppose an individual is highly motivated by the need to achieve, and attitudes and personality cause this person to look for such satisfaction by working as a nurse in a healthcare center.

Such a person will not be satisfied for very long by being a unit clerk. Once the position has been attained, this individual is likely to strive for the next higher position, such as charge or head nurse. After achieving the top position within the service, the objectives may shift to higher positions within the overall administration of the hospital; for instance, this person may seek to become an associate administrator or even the chief administrator. The objectives also may shift to something outside the hospital, such as governmental activities that present possibilities for the satisfaction of the achievement needs.

This endless search for alternatives to satisfy increasing aspirations is an important aspect of human motivation. If an organization can provide an individual with a wider range of need satisfactions, this person will have a greater commitment to the organization.

## PERCEPTIONS, VALUES, AND ATTITUDES

As we have said, all human behavior is motivated by unsatisfied needs. These needs spring from causes that are deep within the person and, together with other motives, attitudes, and behaviors, form the configuration usually called the *personality.* From this point of view, the motivation that contributes to personality can be defined as the potential to act to satisfy those needs that are not met. The phrase *potential to act* implies that some motives are stronger than others and thus more likely to produce action. The strength of motivation is determined by the strength of a particular need, the probability that the act required to satisfy that need will be successful, and the rewards forthcoming. An individual is more likely to act if his or her motive is stronger, the probability for success is high, and the reward is significant.

Other factors are also involved in producing human behavior or action. Motives do not stand alone. Closely related to them and significantly affecting their strength are *perceptions, values,* and *attitudes.*

We are constantly subjected to many stimuli from our environment—all of them compete for our attention. In our daily working environment there are noises, sights, sounds, smells, supervisors' instructions, memos, reports, physicians' directives, coworkers' remarks, people walking by, paging over the loudspeaker, phones ringing, posted signs, etc. All these and many more vie for our attention. The individual therefore has the problem of how to interpret and organize the more important stimuli, and how to respond to them.

The individual uses *perception* to screen, select, organize, and interpret stimuli to respond appropriately. This does not necessarily lead to an accurate portrayal of the environment, but to a unique picture, influenced by the perceiver's needs, desires, values, disposition, and frame of reference. Through the process of *perceptual selectivity,* certain stimuli catch one's attention and are selected, whereas one screens out those he or she does not want to bother with or that make the person uncomfortable.

The perceptual process plays an important role in all managerial activities, including decision making, appraising employees, communicating orally, and writing. It is important for the manager to understand the perceptual process and to realize that people perceive things differently.

*Perceptual organization* is how an individual categorizes, groups, and fills in information systematically. Once meaning has been attached to a certain stimulus, the individual can reach an appropriate response. Several *barriers* to accurate perception, however, can enter into these perceptual processes. Examples of barriers are the frame of reference, stereotyping, the halo effect, biases, perceptual defense, etc. (See chapters 5 and 17.) All the perceptual processes affect a person's attitudes and behavior at work.

Attitudes and values also play a role in all behavior. Attitudes are different from values. Values are closely held normative standards; the individual chooses them based on personal preference. "Values carry with them an 'oughtness' component. They are frequently defined as ideas about how everyone *should* feel or behave."[1] *Values* are broader, general, more encompassing concepts than attitudes; for example, most of us value freedom and equality. Our values of equality can be translated into our attitude toward minority groups.

*Attitudes* can be seen as "a *predisposition to respond in a favorable or unfavorable way* to objects, persons, concepts, or whatever."[2] They are the ways an individual tends to interpret, understand, or define a situation or relationship with others. Attitudes constitute one's feelings about something—likes and dislikes directed toward persons, things, situations, or a combination of all three. They are more than casual opinions, since they are heavily charged with emotional overtones. Attitudes may include feelings as well as intellectual elements. They also include evaluations and value judgments. Attitudes differ in type, strength, and the extent to which they are open or hidden.

Attitudes are revealed in two ways: by the individual's expressed statements or by behavior. An individual may express dislike for the manager he or she works for or may merely demonstrate this attitude by being absent excessively. Although we cannot see perceptions, values, and attitudes, their consequences can be observed in behavior.

## ■ Factors Determining Attitudes

Attitudes are learned from prior experiences. An infinite number of factors determine and influence an individual's attitudes. One major influence is a person's *biological,* or *physiological, makeup.* Such factors as sex, age, height, race, weight, and physique are important in determining the attitudes that contribute to overall personality structure. In addition, many psychologists believe that the very early years of life are crucial to attitudinal development. Freudian psychologists, in particular, believe that early childhood is the most critical period of all in shaping what a person actually becomes. This theory is often

1.  *Tereance R. Mitchell,* People in Organizations, *2d ed. (New York: McGraw-Hill Book Co) 1982, pp. 127–128. See also Richard M. Steers,* Introduction to Organizational Behavior, *3rd ed. (Glenview, IL: Scott Foresman & Co.) 1988, pp. 283–293.*

2.  *Ibid., pp. 127–128; see also Steers, pp. 283–293.*

referred to as *childhood determinism;* it maintains that such factors as feeding patterns, training patterns, and home conditions in early childhood are the primary determinants of personality structure.

Another area that influences a person's attitudes and personality is the *immediate environment.* Education, employment, income, and many other experiences that confront an individual as he or she goes through life will influence who this person is and eventually becomes. Furthermore, one should never forget that the *broader culture* of society also influences a person's attitudes. In the United States, people generally believe in competition, reward for accomplishment, equal opportunities, and other values that are part of the democratic capitalistic society. Individuals learn from their early years to strive for achievement, think for themselves, and work hard; they learn these roads lead to success. As the United States becomes more of "melting pot" for individuals from other less fortunate cultures, attitudes and beliefs may change. Some may be willing to compromise such values as freedom to do whatever they want and whenever they want to given the concerns about security that arose from the disastrous incidents in the mid-1990s—the ValuJet crash, the Unibomber, and the bombing in Oklahoma City, TWA on Flight 800, and at the Olympics. These events and other cultural influences affect a person's attitudes and thus behavior. Countless other factors also influence attitudes and personality; we have only touched on the more obvious ones.

## ■ Attitudes and Behavior

No matter what factors have caused their development, however, attitudes become deep-seated attributes of the individual's makeup. They are learned and acquired through all his or her life experiences. As stated, they do not have to be rational or logical. We hold firmly to our attitudes and resist forces that attempt to interfere with them. Attitudes can change, but they change very slowly. Attitudes do not exist only within individuals, but are also generated within groups. Often individuals accept the attitudes of the group to which they belong as their own.

As shown in figure 20.1, needs and motives do not stand alone as determinants of behavior. They are also influenced by the underlying attitudes and values of a person. Indeed, we can say that *values and attitudes will determine the route a person takes for the satisfaction of his or her needs.* Although basically the same needs are manifest in every person, individuals' attitudes will vary greatly and will affect their unique responses to their needs. In other words, attitudes help determine what motivates a person to take a certain action in order to fulfill a certain need. For example, many people may have a strong need for achievement. However, differing attitudes and values will motivate one individual to seek fulfillment of that need by working in a hospital, another by working in a government agency, yet another by working in industry, and a fourth person may seek fulfillment by teaching in a university or going into politics. Similarly, one individual will find fulfillment as a cook in a nursing home's kitchen while another will find it as a chemist in a hospital laboratory.

## MOTIVATION VERSUS FRUSTRATION

If the individual's chosen route results in goal accomplishment, the need will be satisfied and the attitudes reinforced. In other words, accomplishing the goal works as "feedback" to let the individual know that the needs are satisfied and the attitudes are reinforced. What happens, however, if the chosen course of action does not result in goal accomplishment? What happens when an individual wishes to pursue a certain course of action, but is prevented from doing so? This obstruction may be caused externally or internally.

Generally, actions that do not succeed in obtaining goals result in blocked satisfaction, frustration, and anxiety. As shown in figure 20.1, feedback notifies the individual that his or her needs are not being fulfilled. Hence, there is stress in the forms of frustration and anxiety instead of need satisfaction. There are five basic ways in which people usually resolve the problems of conflict and frustration: (1) problem-solving behavior, the best method; (2) resignation; (3) detour behavior; (4) retreat; or (5) aggression.

*Problem-solving behavior* is usually the most desirable way of meeting frustration. It is advantageous if a person can look at personal problems objectively and base his or her decisions on reasoned analysis of the situation. Unfortunately many people are not capable of doing this, and it is the supervisor's duty to help the employees learn problem-solving behavior. Suppose, for instance, that an LPN is eager to advance to a better position, but all better positions demand the RN degree as a prerequisite. The LPN is frustrated because he or she keeps running into this obstacle. In this case, an analysis of the situation and a thorough discussion with her supervisor could encourage the LPN to go to school and obtain the RN degree, which will enable her to move up within the hierarchy of nursing services. Such a route would constitute intelligent problem-solving behavior.

Another way to solve a conflict is by *resignation.* Suppose the same LPN were to think, "What else can I do? I have to stick it out." He or she seems resigned to her lot. This LPN will keep on working for the healthcare institution but may no longer consider herself a part of it. Once an employee has given up in the face of obstacles, it is difficult to rebuild morale to the point where institutional and departmental goals are really important. Some employees simply stay on the job listlessly until they are able to retire. Such employees who have resigned themselves to their lot are usually passive and resistant to change. They are difficult for the supervisor to deal with because new ideas do not excite or stimulate them. It is hoped that the supervisor can help such subordinates use problem-solving methods of reasoned analysis and objective evaluation. If, however, the supervisor does not succeed in this respect, he or she may try to restimulate the employee to strive either for past goals or toward some new and desirable goals. The supervisor knows that the result of resignation is usually inferior performance on the job, lowering of morale, and a climate that is not conducive to the best performance of the department.

A third way to solve a frustrating situation is to resort to *detour behavior.* Since the direct way of reaching the goal is barred, the employee will try to find another way to get there. Such detours, however, are often obscure and sometimes devious. For example, one kind of detour behavior is self-induced illness.

Children learn early in life that being sick gives them an acceptable excuse for getting out of doing an unpleasant task. Similarly, employees will often have painful and real physical disorders to evade conflict. Some people can stand conflict and frustration better than others, but sooner or later the strain begins to tell, and some sort of conflict resolution is necessary.

*Retreat,* or *leaving the field,* is a fourth way to meet the problems of conflict and frustration. Most people at one time or another have looked at their jobs and have wished that they could quit right then and there. They may believe that they are not getting the satisfaction they thought the position would bring, that no one realizes the difficulties involved in the job, that their supervisor does not appreciate all the things they are doing, and so on. Most people have such feelings sometime in their lives. In many instances an employee finds it necessary to leave the organization and find alternative employment, possibly in another town. Whether this reaction to frustration is good or bad, however, will depend on the major source of the conflict and frustration. If the major source is in the employee's personality and the conflict does not stem from the working situation, then leaving the field would not be the right answer. In other words, if the frustration is caused by the person's own peculiar psychological makeup, such a change probably will not bring about the desired result. If, however, the conflict is because of an unfavorable work situation, then leaving the field, quitting, or even leaving the city may represent a real solution to the problem. Often it is difficult for the individual to determine whether or not this is the case. Of course, it is not always necessary to quit the job or move to another city in order to "leave the field." Leaving the field may be displayed by daydreaming, spending a lot of time in the washroom, developing a high rate of absenteeism, resorting to alcoholism and drug abuse, or using some other form of symbolic escape. All these forms of retreat will cause the supervisor additional problems.

*Aggression* is the fifth way in which people may meet the problem of severe frustration. The individual feels frustrated and cannot find an acceptable, legitimate remedy. Sabotage, for example, is one common form of aggressive behavior. By aggression we mean not only overt hostile behavior aimed at harming other people such as that exhibited by some U.S. postal workers in the 1990s or hostile behavior to inanimate objects, but also merely the tendency to commit acts of aggression. This tendency may manifest itself in thoughts or words, or even in feelings that have not yet been put into words. In one situation, the staff of a dietary department used various forms of sabotage to express their frustration with management. Patients were served raw chicken and in some cases empty, but heated, plates. When I moved into the kitchen personally, my telephone line was cut daily for several days and less than friendly notes were left in or on my desk.

The supervisor should always remember that frustration and aggression are closely tied together and that all aggression stems from some form of frustration. As we have said, some individuals can stand more frustration than others and do not as easily respond with aggressive behavior. Moreover, many minor frustrations that could lead to aggressive behavior do not do so because people hold back and inhibit them. The job of the supervisor is to see that frustration is minimized and to provide constructive outlets for it. The supervisor should try to anticipate the sources of frustration and attempt to eliminate them. If this cannot be done, however, then the best the supervisor can do is see that the causes of frustration are not aggravated. Often patient listening will help to ease employee tensions, and it may enable the subordinate to seek the real source of the frustration. In fact, the kitchen staff and I spent many hours talking about their jobs, the importance of their positions, their role in patient care, and how much they were depended upon by their coworkers. When I moved back to my administrative office, many tears were shed—some by me.

A supervisor's talent can be measured by his or her ability to accurately determine when a subordinate needs patient listening *and* advice or patient listening *only*.

---

## CONFLICTS BETWEEN INDIVIDUAL AND ORGANIZATIONAL GOALS

Although many causes of frustration exist, a major cause arises when individual needs and goals conflict rather than coincide with those of the organization or, to be more specific, with those of the department. Much has been written about the conflict between the individual who seeks activity and independence and the climate in a bureaucratic, formalized organization that stifles a person's natural desire for freedom and self-determination. The consequences of such a climate manifest themselves in high turnover, waste, lower productivity, slowdown, lack of innovative and creative behavior, nonacceptance of leadership, and so on. The most serious consequence of a bureaucratic organization, however, is that it blocks the individual from attaining satisfaction of his or her needs.

Managers today are becoming more aware of these consequences and of the necessity for an organization to provide a climate that will enable its employees to find personal satisfaction. In fact, the need for an appropriate organizational climate is increasing because of the rising expectations of employees. This is especially true in the healthcare field, where organizations are confronted with an ever-advancing and more sophisticated area of activity. The highly skilled and educated employees are primarily professionals who expect to fulfill many of their needs right on the job. Since such employees tend to take high wages and appropriate fringe benefits for granted, it should be apparent that the key to long-term motivation for them rests in the satisfaction of the higher-level needs, that is, their esteem and self-fulfillment needs. It is management's duty to develop an organizational climate that will produce effective motivation and satisfaction of these needs, thereby helping to resolve the conflict between individual and organizational goals. Therefore, the supervisor's knowledge of the basic motivational processes is necessary because it will facilitate high levels of job satisfaction and minimize conflicts.

---

## SUMMARY

Influencing is the managerial function in which the supervisor creates a climate that enables subordinates to find as much satisfaction as possible while getting the job done. The influencing function is particularly concerned with behavioral responses and interpersonal relations. Only by appropriately influencing will the supervisor instill the motivation in the department's employees to go about their jobs with enthusiasm and also to find personal fulfillment of their needs. Therefore, it is necessary for supervisors to understand basic motivational processes.

Motivation is the force that arouses, energizes, directs, and sustains human behavior. All human behavior is caused by unsatisfied needs. These needs eventually stimulate the formation of goals that motivate people to take certain actions. Motivation, however, not only is caused by unmet needs, but also is largely influenced by an individual's perceptions, values, attitudes, and entire personality.

An individual's attitudes are formed beginning in early childhood. They affect and are affected by an infinite number of factors in the person's life. Attitudes will determine the individual route a person takes for the satisfaction of those needs. Although they vary in strength, most needs are basically the same in all people. Thus, Maslow speaks of a hierarchy of needs; in ascending order they are physiological needs, safety, social needs, esteem, and self-fulfillment. A person's level of aspiration is closely related to this hierarchy of needs.

People generally move from one level to the next in Maslow's hierarchy. McClelland focuses on describing other important human needs: achievement, affiliation, and power. Herzberg, in his two-factor approach, stresses the importance of motivators versus hygiene factors. He shows that the more important forces of employee motivation lie in factors related to work content and not work environment, or hygiene factors.

A person who is able to understand his or her needs and attitudes fairly well will be able to choose courses of action that result in achieving goals. Goal accomplishment serves as a feedback to the individual; the need is satisfied and the underlying attitudes are confirmed. If a goal is not attained, however, conflict often sets in. This is because action that does not succeed results in blocked satisfaction, frustration, and anxiety. Most people usually react to conflict and frustration in one of the following five ways: problem-solving behavior, resignation, detour behavior, retreat, or aggression.

It is the supervisor's duty to minimize frustrating situations, especially if they result from a conflict between individual and organizational goals. One way to minimize such conflicts is to realize that in the work environment various factors influence the realization of an employee's expectations. Some of these factors are merely satisfiers and dissatisfiers (Herzberg's hygiene factors), whereas others are motivators and are able to fulfill the higher-level needs and goals of people. These motivators include opportunity for advancement; greater responsibility; chance for promotion; growth, and achievement; and an interesting and challenging job. Supervisors, in their desire to create a good organizational climate, must make sure that in addition to satisfying hygiene factors, as many of these motivators as possible exist within the healthcare institution.

# *Leadership*

## Chapter Objectives

After you have studied this chapter, you should be able to:

1. Define the concept of leadership.
2. Discuss the major leadership theories.
3. Compare and contrast different leadership styles.

Because leaders can have a substantial impact on performance, leadership is one of the most popular and important topics in the field of management. It is a key process in any organization, and an organization's success or failure is largely attributed to it. Leadership is an essential component of the organizational climate; we have mentioned the term *leadership* repeatedly throughout this text, but merely in passing. Ultimately management leadership is responsible for establishing the type of climate that facilitates motivation and the successful performance of the institution.

The concept of leadership is still being widely researched and investigated. It is of great importance because every organization is concerned with attracting and developing people who will be effective leaders. Leadership plays an important role in organizational life. It fills in many areas not covered by organizational design or manuals. Leadership provides greater organizational flexibility, facilitates coordination and personal need satisfaction, and ultimately makes the difference between an effective and an ineffective organization.

We can define leadership as a process by which people are imaginatively directed, guided, and influenced in choosing and attaining goals. It is helpful to look at leadership in an organizational setting as a behavior, as something one person does to influence others. Leadership can also be defined as "the influential increment over and above mechanical compliance with routine directives of the organization."[1] Leadership is the process by which one person influences others to do something voluntarily rather than out of fear or due to coercion. This voluntary aspect is different from other processes, such as influence by authority or power.

In any organized activity a leader mediates between organizational and individual goals so that the degree of satisfaction to both is maximized. A manager also plays this mediating role but not necessarily in the same manner as a leader. Although the terms *manager* and *leader* are often used interchangeably, they are not synonymous. A person can be the manager but not the leader, and vice versa. A person who has formal positional authority may use formal legitimate authority and power to get things done; this individual certainly is a manager but may not be the leader. On the other hand, the individual who has no position of

---

1. *D. Katz and R. L. Kahn,* The Social Psychology of Organizations, *2d ed. (New York: John Wiley & Sons, Inc.) 1978, p. 528.*

formal authority, such as the informal leader, may use the leadership influence but is not the manager. Therefore, a manager can do a reasonably good job of managing without being a leader. From the view of organizational effectiveness, however, it is desirable for the manager to also be the leader. Thus, it is essential to learn what other qualities and prerequisites must prevail to be a leader as well as a manager.

| LEADERSHIP THEORIES | Many theories have been formulated as to what constitutes a good leader and what enables some people to be a leader and not others. We will look at a few of these theories briefly. |

## ■ The Early Genetic Theory

For hundreds of years observers recognized leadership as the ability to influence people in such a manner that they willingly strove toward an objective. It was believed that this ability was something apart from official position. This view held that certain people were born to be leaders, having inherited a set of unique traits, characteristics, or attributes that could not be acquired in any other way. This position, also known as the "great man" theory of leadership, concluded that leadership qualities were inherited simply because the leadership phenomenon emerged frequently within the same prominent families. In reality, however, strong class barriers made it impossible for anyone outside these families to acquire the skills and knowledge required to become a leader. In the beginning of the twentieth century, this belief in inherited leadership characteristics lost ground, although the belief in the significance of leadership attributes remained in the picture.

## ■ The Trait, or Attribute, Theory

As social and economic class barriers were broken down and leaders began to emerge from the so-called lower classes of society, the early genetic theory was modified. This modification primarily occurred because in the first half of this century behavioral scientists began to contribute to the literature on leadership. The first contribution was made by behavioral scientists who, rather than considering leadership only a function of inherited characteristics, held that it could also be acquired through experience, education, and training. Efforts were made to identify the traits great leaders throughout the ages had in common. These behavioral scientists tried to focus on all the traits, whether inherited or acquired, that were found in individuals regarded as leaders. Lists of qualities that recognized leaders had in common were compiled. These traits frequently included physical and nervous energy, above-average height, a sense of purpose and direction, willingness to accept the consequences, enthusiasm, friendliness and affection, integrity, technical mastery, decisiveness, verbal fluency, assertiveness, initiative, originality, intelligence, teaching skill, faith, ambition, and persistence.

The inadequacy of this approach soon became obvious. No satisfactory answer could be reached about which traits were most essential for leadership, or whether a person could be a leader if certain traits were lacking. Also, there was no suggestion about how to isolate and identify all the specific traits common to leaders. A further weakness of the trait approach was that it did not distinguish between those characteristics needed for acquiring leadership and those necessary for maintaining it.

Although the trait approach is partially discredited today, a considerable body of research shows that leaders have in common certain general characteristics. Some of these are intelligence, communication ability, sensitivity to group needs, and many of those previously mentioned. Such traits are interwoven in the personality of the leader.

These studies led researchers to question the validity of the trait approach as the predictor of leadership. Subsequent research determined that leadership style varies based on the managerial situation being confronted and/or the types of employees or skill levels they may have.

## ■ The Situational Approach

In their search for other variables, behavioral scientists discovered the importance of situational factors that make it easier for certain persons to acquire positions of leadership. This theory makes the assumption that leadership behavior varies in accordance with the situation. This approach, also known as the *contingency model* of leadership effectiveness, points out the interdependence between leadership style and the demands of the situation.

The proponents of the situational approach do not deny that the characteristics of individuals play an important part in leadership, but they point out that leadership is also the product of situational factors. Leadership in one group will differ from leadership in another group; in one situation a certain person might evolve as the leader, whereas under different environmental conditions someone else would emerge as the leader. For example, in a political meeting someone with good public speaking ability may rise to the top. In other words, the leadership characteristics and leadership behavior needed are a function of the specific situation.

In their desire to de-emphasize the traits approach, however, some behavioral scientists may have gone overboard in emphasizing the situation. In so doing, they may have ruled out the possibility that at least some characteristics *predispose* people to attain leadership positions or at least increase their chances of becoming leaders. Both characteristics and the situation are involved in the concept of leadership.

## ■ The Follower Approach

A still better understanding of leadership incorporates the input contributed by groups and followers. This approach maintains that the followers and the makeup of the group must also be studied because essentially it is the follower who perceives the leader and the situation and accepts or rejects leadership. Proponents of this approach further maintain that followers' persistent motives, points of view, and frames of reference will determine what they perceive and how they react to it. The follower approach emphasizes the importance of the group at a particular point, but it also acknowledges that certain characteristics will help one person emerge as the leader rather than another person. The satisfaction of the followers' needs, however, is an important aspect.

More specifically, the group and follower approach stresses the idea that the leadership function must be analyzed and understood in terms of a dynamic relationship, a social exchange process between the leader and the followers. They bring to the situation their personalities, needs, motivations, and expectations. The leader appears to the followers as the best means available for the satisfaction of their needs, whether those needs are emotive or task oriented. The group members will follow the leader because they see in that person the means for personal fulfillment. A leader is essential for influencing a group to act as a unit to move toward task accomplishment. The members look at this individual as their leader not only because he or she possesses certain characteristics, such as intelligence, skill, drive, and ambition, but also because of his or her functional relationship to the members of the group.

## ■ Leadership Roles

Most of us have had the occasion to observe individuals and the different roles they play in groups. One person may organize the group to achieve goals, whereas another plays the "devil's advocate," raising a stream of objections, and yet someone else is a "synthesizer" who puts together the ideas of all group members. These roles and many others are essential for group life. They fulfill the needs of the individual members of the group and are vital to the group's accomplishments. The group's leader is not necessarily expected to assume all these roles, but he or she is expected to fulfill some of them. Generally, leadership roles fall into two broad classifications, task-oriented roles and emotive leadership roles, in order to satisfy the followers' task and emotive needs.

*Task-oriented roles* are those used by the leader to organize and influence the group to achieve specified objectives. Usually in an organized activity these objectives are imposed on the group from above. In groups that arise spontaneously, however, tasks and objectives are generated from within the group itself. In both instances, the leader must facilitate the accomplishment of the group's goals. That is, the leader plays the role of getting the group to fulfill its tasks.

*Emotive leadership roles* are just as important as task roles. They are employee centered and provide satisfaction for the individual needs of the group's members. The emotional needs of people are of a social and psychological nature. A leader in the emotive role helps members of the group to gain satisfaction of these needs and at the same time prepares the way for task performance.

Frequently the ideal leader is one who plays both roles effectively. In some instances, however, leadership of a group can be shared without diminishing the group's performance or morale. In such a case one person plays the task role and another takes the emotive role. This would not be an unusual situation in a large healthcare institution. The formal organization of such an institution often forces a supervisor to be primarily concerned with getting the job done. He or she must concentrate largely on task leadership. Under these conditions, however, the groups will probably select another individual, the informal leader, who will function in the emotive role. The supervisor should not object to the informal leader's role. Rather, the supervisor should realize that it is a necessary part of the leadership process, one that fulfills important human needs and is an essential component of high employee morale. (See chapter 22.)

## ■ Conclusions

All three variables play a role in the leadership process: personal characteristics, the situation, and the followers. The leader is an individual perceived in harmony with the needs of the group and responsive to the group situation. However, because leaders must always be recognized as such by group consensus and because managers who are appointed do not necessarily reflect subordinate group choice, they are not generally regarded as leaders at the outset. They may become true leaders of the group, but they do not start out as such. It is desirable from an influencing standpoint that subordinates accept the manager as a leader and not merely as the head of the department.

## LEADERSHIP STYLE

Leadership style is of great importance because it influences acceptance of managers by subordinates. Generally, leadership styles can be classified into three broad categories: autocratic, democratic, and free rein.

### ■ Autocratic Leadership (Theory X)

Autocratic leadership usually reflects tight supervision, a high degree of centralization, and a narrow span of supervision. The autocratic style is repressive and normally withholds communication other than what is absolutely necessary for doing the job. Autocratic management makes decisions unilaterally and does not consult with the members of the department. Therefore, the autocratic style of leadership minimizes the degree of involvement by subordinates.

In more specific terms, autocratic leadership is described by Douglas McGregor as Theory X. According to McGregor, a Theory X manager leans toward an organizational climate of close control, centralized authority, authoritarian practices, and minimum participation of the subordinates in the decision-making process. One may consider this the "big stick" approach. As we already know, the reason that a Theory X manager accepts this combination is that he or she makes certain assumptions about human behavior.

McGregor's Theory X assumptions are as follows:

1. The average person dislikes work and will avoid it to the extent he or she can.
2. Most people have to be forced or threatened by punishment to make the effort necessary to accomplish organizational goals.
3. The average individual is basically passive and therefore prefers to be directed rather than take any risk or responsibility. Above all else, he or she prefers security.

## ■ Democratic Leadership (Theory Y)

The democratic style emphasizes a looser type of supervision and greater individual participation in the decision-making process. Authority is delegated as far down as possible, and a wide span of management is advocated. A free flow of communication is encouraged among all members of the department so that a climate of trust and confidence can be established.

In McGregor's terms, the democratic style is represented by Theory Y. The Theory Y manager operates with a completely different set of assumptions regarding human motivation. He or she maintains that an effective organizational climate uses more general supervision, greater decentralization of authority, democratic techniques, consultation with subordinates on departmental decisions, and little reliance on coercion and control. The assumptions on which this type of organizational climate is based include the following:

1. Work is as natural to people as play or rest, and therefore it is not avoided.
2. Self-motivation and inherent satisfaction in work will be forthcoming when the individual is committed to organizational goals; thus, coercion is not the only form of influence that can be used to motivate.
3. Commitment is a crucial factor in motivation, and it is a function of the rewards coming from it.
4. The average individual learns to accept and even seek responsibility given the proper environment.
5. The ability to be creative and innovative in the solution of organizational problems is widely, not narrowly, distributed in the population.
6. In modern businesses and organizations, the intellectual potentials of employees are only partially utilized.

McGregor underscores the notion that theories X and Y are beliefs held by management about the nature of human beings. As such, they constitute the foundation on which the organizational climate is built. The supervisor who follows Theory X has a basically limited view of people and their capabilities. He or she believes that individuals must be controlled, closely supervised, and motivated on the basis of money, discipline, and authority. Thus, the autocratic manager believes that the key to motivation is in the proper implementation of approaches designed to satisfy the lower-level needs of people.

The Theory Y supervisor, however, has a much different opinion of the capabilities and possibilities of people. He or she believes that if the proper approach and conditions can be presented, people will exercise self-direction and self-control toward the accomplishment of objectives. The Theory Y manager recognizes that the supervisor's activities must fit into the scheme of each employee's own set of needs. He or she also believes that the higher-level needs of people are more important in terms of personality and self-development. Thus, the supervisory skills are used to enable employees to achieve at least partial satisfaction of their needs for esteem and self-actualization on the job. This confronts the supervisor with the question as to which management philosophy and organizational climate will produce the best results. On the surface one is inclined to say that Theory Y would be more desirable than Theory X because it appears humanistic and less harsh. Also, it is more optimistic about human motives at work.

## ■ Theory Z Approach

A different managerial approach that has been widely discussed recently is the Theory Z approach, influenced by practices in Japanese industry. The success of Japanese industry in respect to productivity and quality has been attributed to a managerial philosophy about people and organizations that is different from ours. The Japanese organizational climate is based on lifetime employment, slow evaluation and promotion paths, nonspecialized careers, consensual decision making, collective responsibility, informal controls, and a holistic concern toward the firm. In brief, this approach fosters a trust relationship between workers and supervisors that results in high-quality output because fear of reprisal is absent and emphasis on teamwork dominates the workplace. This is contrary to many current practices in the Untied States, such as short-run employment expectations, rapid evaluation and promotions, specialized careers, individual decision making and responsibility, severe disciplinary actions for errors, and explicit controls. Theory Z is an approach that would incorporate some of the Japanese ideas into our present system as a possibility for increasing productivity and job satisfaction.

Quality circles and total quality management, discussed in chapter 19, are an outgrowth of the Japanese approach to management. Ironically, much of the Japanese management approach was taught to them by the Americans W. Edwards Deming and Joseph M. Juran after World War II. Today more healthcare CEOs are pursuing the Theory Z environment in their organizations, and those individuals exhibiting the related leadership traits are being sought.

## ■ Free-Rein Leadership

The free-rein style goes beyond democratic leadership and Theory Y. It is often called laissez-faire leadership because the climate of the organization is such

# *Morale*

## *Chapter Objectives*

After you have studied this chapter, you should be able to:

1. Discuss the supervisor's role in motivation and leadership and its bearing on the morale of subordinates.
2. Discuss the nature of morale.
3. Provide a basis for understanding the factors influencing morale.
4. Discuss the relationship between morale and productivity.
5. Review various morale assessment tools.

Understanding the supervisor's role in motivation and leadership has a great bearing on the morale of the subordinates. Some experts such as Herzberg do not speak of morale of the individual but refer to job satisfaction, emphasizing the satisfaction of needs. Others stress the social aspects of groups and friendships, and some are particularly concerned with attitudes toward coworkers, the organization, and supervision. Many writers link satisfaction with the needs and attitudes of an *individual,* whereas morale pertains to the spirit of a *group.* Although this distinction is precise, it is largely academic since the factors and methods used in measuring group morale are usually the same as those used in measuring an individual's satisfaction.

Although there are many definitions for morale, a particularly useful one is to describe it as a state of mind and emotion affecting the attitudes, feelings, and sentiments of individuals and groups toward their work, environment, administration, and colleagues. Morale is a composite of feelings, satisfaction, sentiments, and attitudes. It is the total satisfaction a person derives from the job, work group, boss, the institution, and the environment. "Morale pertains to the general feeling of well-being, satisfaction, and happiness of people."[1] When morale is high, the employees are likely to strive hard to accomplish the objectives of the enterprise; conversely, low morale is likely to prevent or deter them from doing this.

## THE NATURE OF MORALE

Supervisors often make the mistake of speaking of morale as something that is either present or absent among their employees. Morale is always present, however, and by itself has neither a favorable nor unfavorable meaning. Morale can range from excellent and positive through many intermediate degrees to poor and completely negative. If the attitude of the subordinates is poor, then the morale is also poor. If the subordinates are highly dedicated to strive hard for the best possible patient care, their morale is high. Employees with high morale find

---

1.   *Dale S. Beach,* Personnel: The Management of People at Work, *5th ed. (New York: Macmillan Publishing Co.) 1985, p. 307.*

satisfaction in their position in the enterprise, have confidence in their own and in their associates' abilities, and show enthusiasm and a strong desire to cooperate in achieving the healthcare center's objectives.

One cannot order employees to have high morale. It can only be created by introducing certain conditions into the work setting that are favorable to its development. High morale is not the cause of good supervision and human relations. Rather, it is the result of good motivation, respect and dignity of the individual, realization of individual differences, good leadership, effective communication, participation, counseling, and many other human resources practices. In other words, the state of morale will reflect how appropriately and effectively the administration practices good human relations and good supervision.

## THE LEVEL OF MORALE

Every manager, from the CEO down to the supervisor, should be concerned with the level of morale in the organization. A good supervisor knows it is a supervisory function to elicit and maintain the morale of the subordinates at as high a level as possible. The immediate supervisor, in the day-to-day contact with the employees, is the one who influences and determines the level of morale more than anyone else. Raising morale to a high level and keeping it there is a long-term project and cannot be achieved solely on the basis of short-term devices such as pep talks or contests. The supervisor will also find that although good morale is slow to develop and difficult to maintain, it can change quickly from good to bad. The level of morale varies considerably from day to day and is far more changeable than the weather.

Morale, moreover, is contagious. The higher the degree of individual satisfaction of group members, the higher is the morale of the entire group. This in turn tends to raise the overall level of morale even higher, since individuals get personal satisfaction from being in a high-morale group. Although favorable attitudes spread, unfavorable attitudes among employees spread even more quickly. It seems to be human nature to forget the good quickly and remember the bad.

Management is not alone in its desire for a satisfactory level of morale. Each employee of the institution is likewise concerned because bad morale is simply not as satisfying as good morale. A state of bad morale creates an unpleasant environment for the employees of the healthcare center, and they have as much at stake as the administration. Good morale, on the other hand, will make the employee's day at work a pleasurable and satisfying experience and not a misery. The employee will find satisfaction in working with the supervisors and associates. High morale is also important to the patient and the patient's family. They will quickly sense whether the employees of the institution are operating on a high or low level of morale, and they will respond accordingly. But what, we may ask, determines the level of morale?

**Figure 22.1**

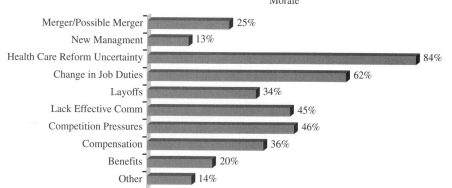

**MODERN HEALTHCARE**
Reasons for Decreased Employee
Morale

Merger/Possible Merger — 25%
New Managment — 13%
Health Care Reform Uncertainty — 84%
Change in Job Duties — 62%
Layoffs — 34%
Lack Effective Comm — 45%
Competition Pressures — 46%
Compensation — 36%
Benefits — 20%
Other — 14%

*Source: Deloitte and Touche LLP–Human Resource's*
*Strategies Group, Member of ABC Consulting,*
*Hospital Human Resource Survey–1995.*

## FACTORS INFLUENCING MORALE

Some of the factors cited in a Deloitte & Touche LLP survey are shown in figure 22.1.

Since morale is a composite of feelings, sentiments, attitudes, satisfaction, well-being, and happiness, almost anything can influence the morale of the employees. Some of these factors are within the control of the supervisor, whereas others are not. Although there are countless morale determinants, we can divide them into two broad groups: (1) those factors that arise primarily from situations external to the institution and (2) those factors that originate mainly within the realm of the supervisor's activities. Examples of both appeared in the Deloitte & Touche survey results.

### ■ External Factors

External factors affecting morale, those connected with events and influences outside the work environment and institution, are generally beyond the scope of the supervisor's control. Although they are external in origin, these factors nevertheless concern the supervisor, since everyone takes his or her problems to work and does not check them in the morning at the organization's door or leave them in the car. Examples of external factors are family problems, financial worries, associations with friends, car troubles, or a sickness in the family. Consider the impact on morale of those working at the local hospital when the only large employer in town, a mining company employing more than 35% of the town, closed. What happens away from the job may change the employee's feelings quickly; an argument before leaving home or an accident on the highway causing a long delay may set the emotional tone for the rest of the day. The morning news may be depressing, or it may produce high morale.

The supervisor can indirectly deal with these external factors primarily by doing a nondirective counseling interview, as discussed in chapter 17. The supervisor should try to sense such factors; often they are reflected in the work behavior of the subordinates. If something has happened to lower an employee's morale and if the supervisor is familiar with the cause, he or she should try to get the employee to forget the incident as quickly as possible by supplying an antidote. One of the best ways to help an employee get past a depressing incident is to encourage the employee to talk about it freely. Aside from a nondirective counseling interview, however, a supervisor can do little else to cope with outside factors affecting morale. The supervisor must remember that he or she or the institution itself is not the sole cause of shifts in the level of morale.

## ■ Internal Factors

Many important factors that affect the morale of employees are within the realm of the supervisor's activities. These include incentives, working conditions, and, above all, the quality of supervision. When considering incentives, the first thing that comes to mind is pay. Wages are exceedingly important, but aside from wages and fringe benefits, many other aspects are essential to the employee. Considerations such as job security, interesting work, good working conditions, appreciation of a job well done, chance for advancement, recognition, and prompt and fair treatment of grievances are all necessary components of a high-morale environment. (See chapter 20.) None of these will take the place of appropriate compensation in dollars and cents, but assuming that the pay properly reflects the job, these additional factors play a significant role. Although reasonable monetary incentives may be provided and the quality of supervision is high, morale can still sink quickly if, for example, working conditions are neglected. The important factor is that an honest attempt is made to improve working conditions whenever possible. Consider the cost of dry cleaning on an individual's income. A simple change to working conditions that permits employees to wear jeans every Friday as "casual day attire" may address both a comfort level and an employee's financial needs. In many cases, employees work under undesirable conditions and still maintain high morale, as long as the supervisor has made a serious effort to correct the conditions.

## ■ The Supervisor's Role

Aside from these on-the-job factors influencing morale, the most significant influence is exercised by supervisors in their immediate, day-to-day relationship with employees. The supervisor's overall manner of supervision, directing, leadership, interpersonal skills, and general attitude will, more than anything else, make for good or bad morale. Employees will put forth their best efforts when given an opportunity to satisfy their needs through work they enjoy and that at the same time achieves the department's objectives. Such job satisfaction will raise and keep morale at a high level. It can only be maintained if the supervisor lets the employees know how significantly they contribute to the overall goals of the healthcare organization and how their work fits into the overall effort.

Morale can also be maintained if the boss gives them a feeling of accomplishment in their work and allows them to be on their own as much as possible. The supervisor who practices democratic supervision, as discussed in previous chapters, and who "practices what he preaches" is likely to reduce the undesirable features of a job and create an environment in which the employees derive genuine satisfaction from the work they do every day. In addition, the supervisor should not forget the importance of social satisfaction on the job. The employees should have an opportunity to develop friendships and work as a team. In other words, one must not forget the positive contributions that informal groups and informal organization make.

The supervisor should bear in mind that the employees' morale is affected not only by what the supervisor does, but also by how it is done. If the supervisor's behavior indicates a feeling of superiority to the employees or the supervisor is suspicious of the employees' motives and actions, only a low level of morale can result. The supervisor should not forget how little it takes to make one's own spirits rise or fall. A word of appreciation from the boss or administrator can change the supervisor's outlook toward the whole work setting. He or she will become more cheerful, and in all likelihood so will the employees.

One may think of this as a "mirror-effect." If the hospital vice-president commends the department director on successfully completing a major project, for example, preparing for a JCAHO visit, the director will probably "mirror" the vice-president's actions with those departmental supervisors, staff, and secretaries who participated in accomplishing the project. The supervisors will then most likely "mirror" the director and share their appreciation with their line staff.

Supervisors also know that a frown or quizzical expression on their superior's face can have the opposite effect. The supervisor will begin to wonder what he or she did wrong, and morale will sink. Supervisors should remember that employees react the same way to them as they do to their bosses. Attitudes beget like attitudes. If the supervisor shows worry, the employees tend to follow suit. If he or she becomes angry, others become angry. When the supervisor appears confident in the operation of the department, employees will react accordingly and believe that things are going well. This does not mean that the supervisor should only see the good side of departmental operations and refuse to acknowledge difficulties and troubles. The supervisor should show the employees that as a leader he or she has the situation well in hand and that if anything goes wrong, he or she will give them an opportunity to correct the situation and prevent it from happening again.

In recent years, many organizations have developed what is called *employee assistance programs* (EAP) (See figure 22.2). These are staffed by professionals, such as social workers and medical and counseling personnel, who are trained in providing confidential, professional assistance to employees and their families. Some programs may also regularly use the services of an outside clinic. The purpose of the employee assistance program is to help employees who have

**Figure 22.2** Employee assistance plans

*Copyright 1996, USA TODAY. Reprinted with permission.*

# Employee assistance plans up

Percentage of employers offering counseling and referrals for personal problems:

58%
1989

81%
1995

Source: Foster Higgins survey of private and government, weighted to represent at U.S. employers

personal problems that may interfere with attendance and job performance—external influences; whether this counterproductive behavior is the result of work, home, or outside pressures is unimportant. Some of the more common problems are caused by alcoholism, drug dependency, financial worries, marriage or family difficulties, stress, and poor health. An employee can seek out this support on his or her own. However, most often the supervisor refers an employee to this program, or the referral might come from a medical person or from the union.

All visits and discussions must be handled in the strictest confidence. The objective of an employee assistance program is to help employees help themselves for humanitarian as well as economic reasons. In addition to the human rewards, such a program makes good economic sense for the institution because the cost of excessive absenteeism, reduced productivity, accidents, and other incidents can be substantial. Without violating the employees' confidentiality, the EAP counselor can also provide guidance and suggestions to the employees' managers.

Personal Performance Consultants, Inc. describe the benefit of EAP this way:

> *"When an employee with a proven record of performance begins to show signs of slippage, there is a good chance that the decline in attitude, attendance, or overall productivity is a result of a problem in the personal life of the employee.*
>
> *When you know how to confront the performance decline effectively, and how to offer the EAP, it can mean the difference between going through a long period of coping, or nipping the performance problem in the bud.*
>
> *That difference is an important one: to you . . . to the employee . . . and to your work group."*[2]

2. *Personal Performance Consultants, Inc.,* Employee Assistance Program Supervisor Resource & Training Manual, *1987 by Personal Performance Consultants, Inc.*

# THE EFFECTS OF MORALE

The question arises as to how high or low morale affects other variables, such as turnover, absenteeism, the rate of accidents, teamwork, and productivity. Much research has been done in this area, and we can draw some general conclusions from it. For example, high morale is moderately related to lower employee turnover. Probably the same holds true for a lowered rate of absenteeism. Furthermore, higher morale most likely also leads to other desirable consequences, such as fewer grievances, better mental and physical health, faster learning of new tasks, and possibly a lowered rate of accidents, although some apparent results have no relation whatsoever to high or low morale. Let us look at some other consequences.

## ■ Morale and Teamwork

The term *teamwork* is often associated with morale, but the two terms do not have the same meaning. Morale applies to the *attitudes* of the employees in the department, whereas teamwork is the smoothly coordinated and synchronized *activity* achieved by a small, closely knit group of employees. Although good morale is usually helpful in achieving teamwork, it is possible for teamwork to be high, yet morale low. Such a situation could exist in times when jobs are scarce and when the employees will put up with close and tight supervision for fear of losing their jobs. Also, teamwork may be absent even though morale is high; in such a case the employee, a solo performer, probably prefers individual effort and finds satisfaction in his or her own job performance.

## ■ Morale and Productivity

It is generally assumed that high morale is automatically accompanied by high productivity. Supervisors believe that as long as the morale of employees is high, their output will be correspondingly high. They are aware that the cooperation of employees is almost always necessary to get continuous superior performance. Moreover, some research evidence backs up the contention that there is a small but positive relationship between overall morale or job satisfaction and productivity. Every supervisor also believes, based on personal experience, that a highly motivated, self-disciplined group of employees will consistently do a more satisfactory job than a group where morale is low. Therefore, supervisors will do everything possible to keep morale high so that the department's performance remains high.

However, many studies show that this general statement does not hold true in all situations. There is proof that the morale-productivity relationships can appear in many forms: low morale and high productivity, high morale and low productivity, as well as high morale and high productivity, and low morale and low productivity. Much depends on other factors, such as the economic situation, the rewards, the job market, and the mechanical pace of the job. Thus, a supervisor cannot automatically depend on the positive relationship between morale and productivity; however, this is still a controversial issue.

## ASSESSING CURRENT MORALE

It is important for management to be familiar with the extent of job satisfaction or dissatisfaction of the employees. Much of the foregoing discussion has assumed that the level of morale is measurable, but one should realize that morale cannot be measured directly. Nevertheless, suitable indirect ways and means exist for determining the prevailing level of morale and its trends. Although some supervisors pride themselves on their ability to detect intuitively low or high morale, the wise supervisor would do better to approach this problem more systematically in either of two ways. One approach is through observation of activities, events, trends, and changes; the other method is to use what is usually referred to as attitude, opinion, or morale surveys.

### ■ Observation

Observation is a tool that involves watching people and their reactions. Although this tool is available to every supervisor, it is often not fully utilized. If the supervisor does observe the employees consciously and systematically, however, their level of morale and major changes in it can be appraised. The manager should watch the subordinates' behavior and listen to what they have to say; he or she should observe their actions and notice any changes in their willingness to cooperate. The supervisor will probably find it fairly easy to recognize through observation the extremes of high and low morale. Finer means of measurement, however, may be required to differentiate among the intermediate degrees. Personal observation can be used for obvious manifestations of morale, such as a facial expression or a shrug of the shoulder, but often these signs are difficult to interpret. It is also difficult to determine how far from normal the behavior must be in order to indicate a shift in morale. Thus, it takes an extremely sensitive supervisor to conclude correctly from such indicators that a change in morale has occurred or is currently taking place.

Moreover, the supervisor may not be able to make the detailed observations necessary for accurate morale appraisal. Although the closeness of the day-to-day working relationship usually offers much opportunity for supervisors to become aware of morale changes, they are often so burdened with work that they do not have time to look, or if they do look, they do not actually see. At times they may even be afraid to look for fear of what they might find. Although some supervisors may realize that changes are taking place, they are frequently inclined to ignore them. Only later, after a change in the level of morale is openly manifested, will they recall the first indications and admit to noticing them but not giving them much thought at the time.

To avoid such situations, the supervisor must take care not to conveniently brush aside any indicators. The most serious shortcoming of using observation as a yardstick to measure current morale is that when the events causing the low morale are recognized, the change has probably already occurred. The supervisor, therefore, should be extremely keen in his or her observation in order to do as much as possible to prevent such changes before they take place, or to quickly counteract them if they have already begun. The closer the supervisor's relationship with the employees, the more sensitive he or she will be to these changes, and the more quickly he or she will act.

## ■ Attitude Surveys

The other approach to assessing current morale is the use of attitude surveys, also called opinion or morale surveys. Many institutions use attitude surveys as a way of finding out how employees view their jobs, coworkers, benefits, wages, working conditions, quality of services, supervisors, the institution as a whole, specific policies, etc. Such a survey is a valuable diagnostic tool for management to assess employee problems. It is like taking the pulse of the organization. Surveys provide the most accurate indicators of the organization's human resources, as well as valuable upward communication because they allow employees to express their feelings about their jobs. As a result, administration will know the general level of satisfaction in the institution and which specific areas cause dissatisfaction. The attitude survey shows employees that management is truly concerned and at the same time gives them an opportunity to vent their opinions. This in itself will improve morale.

For surveys to be meaningful, however, administration must be committed to this undertaking. This means that management must be willing to invest effort, time, and money. Administration must be willing to follow through with action based on the results of the survey and be ready to communicate the major findings of the survey to the employees. Such a survey requires careful planning and professional development. Unless the institution's human resources department is large and has in-house professionals trained and experienced in attitude surveys, it is advisable to hire an outside consultant. This will ensure a well-designed instrument with appropriate validity, reliability, sampling, and statistical methods. The employees may have more confidence in an outside consultant's work than in their own personnel department doing the job. An outside consultant could also help in deciding whether a standardized survey, customized one, or a combination of the two would be more appropriate.

### *Taking the Survey*

Expressions of employees' opinions are requested in the form of answers to written questionnaires. These questionnaires must be prepared with great care and much thought. A good attitude survey measures the major variables of organizational life, such as leadership, supervision, administration, job satisfaction, job conditions and work environment, coworkers, pay, benefits and rewards, job security, advancement, and stress. The questionnaire should be written at a level appropriate for most of the employees. A cover letter from the CEO should accompany the questionnaire, encouraging the employees' participation and stressing the confidential and anonymous nature of the employees' involvement.

In a healthcare center, attitude surveys can cover the entire organization. At times it is appropriate to limit the survey to only one large department, such as nursing services, which usually accounts for half of all the employees. Full-scale attitude surveys should not be given in less than approximately three-year intervals; this allows enough time to indicate significant attitude changes.

Once an institutionwide survey is decided on, the administrator and all other managers must be prepared to endure criticisms because dissatisfactions will probably be expressed. More importantly, however, management must be prepared and willing to act on the complaints once they are revealed. Until the survey is taken, management can always plead ignorance, but after a survey, everyone knows that the administration has heard about the problems causing dissatisfaction. It is hoped that some of the complaints can be adjusted; at least a serious and honest effort must now be made. If the administration is not prepared or willing to act, it is far better not to take surveys. Once management asks the employees for their input and ideas and fails to take action, the employees will avoid expressing themselves in the future.

Questionnaires submitted to employees come in a variety of types. (See figures 22.3, 22.4, and 22.5 for example.) Three general forms are used most often. According to the format of the question asked, one can distinguish between *objective* surveys and *descriptive* surveys. An objective questionnaire asks the question and offers a choice of answers; there can be multiple choice or true and false questions. In objective surveys, the employees mark the one answer that comes closest to their feelings. In a descriptive survey, the question is asked, but the employees answer freely in their own words and ways. Since many employees may have difficulty expressing their opinions in writing, or may not want to take the time to write out answers, the best results are usually obtained on a form that enables the employees to check the box that seems to provide the most appropriate answer for them.

The survey forms can be filled out on the job or at home. Although there are many advantages to filling out questionnaires at home, a high percentage of them are never returned. It is better to have more meaningful answers, however, even if the number of replies is smaller. Some organizations are concerned that the rate of returned surveys might be low and prefer to distribute and collect the surveys the same day during working hours. The employees complete the survey forms on the premises and on company time. This procedure is likely to maximize the number of completed surveys.

Regardless of whether they are filled out on the job or at home, care must be taken that the questionnaires remain unsigned and that the replies cannot be personally identified. Respondents must be assured that the replies will be kept confidential. Employees are sometimes suspicious of the institution's motives, and they may respond in ways they believe the institution wants to hear. Therefore, it is essential that no individual identification information appears on the survey; otherwise, the employees believe that such numbers would identify them. However, it may be necessary to ask the employees to identify their work

Each question may be answered in several ways, any one of which will give us the information we need. Check only *one* answer that most closely expresses your true feelings. DO NOT sign the form. Seal your questionnaire in the accompanying envelope and drop it in the box in the Department of Human Resources on or before Sept. 15.

1. How would you rate the hospital as a place to work?

   ☐ Poor ☐ Not so good ☐ Better than most ☐ Good

2. Are you kept informed on the policies of the hospital and changes in them?

   ☐ Never ☐ Sometimes ☐ Usually ☐ Always

3. Do you feel that the policies of the hospital are fair to you?

   ☐ Never ☐ Sometimes ☐ Usually ☐ Always

4. Are you kept informed about what is going on at the hospital?

   ☐ Never ☐ Sometimes ☐ Usually ☐ Always

5. Where do you get most of your information about what is going on?

   ☐ Grapevine ☐ Local newspapers ☐ Bulletin boards ☐ Supervisor

6. Were you given a satisfactory introduction to and explanation of your new job before you started to work?

   ☐ No explanation ☐ Very little ☐ Fair amount ☐ Sufficient

7. Were you made to feel at home and at ease by your supervisor and fellow workers?

   ☐ Never ☐ Sometimes ☐ Usually ☐ Always

8. Do you like your job?

   ☐ Not at all ☐ Neither like it nor dislike it ☐ Fairly well ☐ Very much

9. How well do you feel your experience and abilities are used in your job?

   ☐ Poorly ☐ Not so well ☐ Fairly well ☐ Very well

10. What do you think of your department head and supervisor?
    Department head

    ☐ Poor ☐ Below average ☐ Above average ☐ Very good

    Why?
    Immediate Supervisor

    ☐ Poor ☐ Below average ☐ Above average ☐ Very good

    Why?

11. Are your duties and responsibilities clear to you?

    ☐ Never ☐ Sometimes ☐ Usually ☐ Always

12. Can you depend on your department head's and supervisor's promises?

    ☐ Never ☐ Sometimes ☐ Usually ☐ Always

13. Do your supervisor and department head give you full credit for suggestions you make about your job or department?

    ☐ Do not ☐ Seldom do ☐ Almost always do ☐ Always do

14. Do you get conflicting orders because of too many "supervisors"?

    ☐ Never ☐ Sometimes ☐ Usually ☐ Always

15. When your department head and supervisor criticize you or your work, is it done in a friendly and helpful way?
    Department Head

    ☐ Never ☐ Sometimes ☐ Usually ☐ Always

    Supervisor

    ☐ Never ☐ Sometimes ☐ Usually ☐ Always

(continued)

**Figure 22.3** Employee opinion survey.

16. Do your department head and supervisor give clear, exact, and easily understood instructions about your work?
    Department Head
    ☐ Never ☐ Sometimes ☐ Usually ☐ Always
    Supervisor
    ☐ Never ☐ Sometimes ☐ Usually ☐ Always

17. Do your department head and supervisor have a tendency to show favoritism?
    Department Head
    ☐ Does ☐ Usually does ☐ Seldom does ☐ Never does
    Supervisor
    ☐ Does ☐ Usually does ☐ Seldom does ☐ Never does

18. When changes are made in your work, are you usually given a reason for them?
    ☐ Never ☐ Sometimes ☐ Usually ☐ Always

19. Do your department head or supervisor take an understanding attitude toward your difficulties?
    Department Head
    ☐ Never ☐ Seldom does ☐ Usually does ☐ Does
    Supervisor
    ☐ Never ☐ Seldom does ☐ Usually does ☐ Does

20. If you are in trouble, whether it is your fault or not, what are your chances of a fair hearing and getting a "square deal"?
    ☐ No chance ☐ Very little chance ☐ Fair chance ☐ Good chance
    Why?

21. Do you feel that you can appeal to a higher authority if your immediate supervisor decides a point against you?
    ☐ I do not ☐ Reasonably so ☐ Almost always ☐ Always can
    If not, why?

22. Are your job and future secure if you work hard?
    ☐ No ☐ Fairly secure ☐ To a large extent ☐ Very secure

23. Are your associations with your fellow workers and superiors as pleasant as they should be?
    ☐ Not pleasant ☐ Fairly pleasant ☐ Almost always pleasant ☐ Mostly pleasant
    If not, why?

24. Do you feel that your fellow workers in your department are doing their fair share of the work?
    ☐ Very few ☐ About half of them ☐ Most of them ☐ All or almost all

25. Please list by number (1–10) items in the order of importance to you.
    ☐ Physical working conditions ☐ Doing something worthwhile ☐ Opportunity for advancement
    ☐ Like the job ☐ Job security ☐ Satisfactory relations with co-workers ☐ Wages
    ☐ Knowing what is going on ☐ Fair supervision ☐ Credit for work done

26. What do you like best about your job?

27. What do you like least about your job?

28. Length of service at XYZ Health Center (check one)
    ☐ One month or less ☐ 1 – 3 months ☐ 3 – 6 months ☐ 6 – 12 months
    ☐ 1 – 5 years ☐ 5 – 10 years ☐ 11 years or more

29. Age (check one)
    ☐ 16 –20 years ☐ 21 –25 years ☐ 26 –34 years ☐ 35 –45 years
    ☐ 46 –50 years ☐ 51 –70 years

(continued)

**Figure 22.3**—*Continued*

XYZ Health Center

30. Employed ☐ Part-time ☐ Full-time

Please add any additional information that you feel would make the hospital a better place in which to work.

_____

_____

_____

_____

_____

_____

_____

_____

_____

_____

_____

**Figure 22.3**—*Continued*

# EMPLOYEE OPINION SURVEY

DEPARTMENT NUMBER:_____

|  |  | AGREE | DISAGREE |
|---|---|---|---|
| 1. | I really feel a part of this organization. | ___ | ___ |
| 2. | Before changes are made here, management discusses them with employees. | ___ | ___ |
| 3. | If I have a complaint to make, I feel free to talk to someone "up the line." | ___ | ___ |
| 4. | My supervisor trusts me and lets me use my own ideas on the job. | ___ | ___ |
| 5. | I am paid fairly compared to other employees. | ___ | ___ |
| 6. | My supervisor is able to get good work from employees without threats or discipline. | ___ | ___ |
| 7. | This organization has a good benefit program. | ___ | ___ |
| 8. | Management sees to it that there is cooperation between departments. | ___ | ___ |
| 9. | Management encourages employees to make suggestions for improvements. | ___ | ___ |
| 10. | Management is really trying to make this organization successful. | ___ | ___ |
| 11. | My hours of work are OK. | ___ | ___ |
| 12. | Employees are treated fairly in promotions, job assignments, and discipline. | ___ | ___ |
| 13. | I have the right training to do my work. | ___ | ___ |
| 14. | My supervisor lets me know exactly what is expected of me. | ___ | ___ |
| 15. | My supervisor is fair regarding how much work he/she expects me to do. | ___ | ___ |
| 16. | My supervisor gives me credit and praise for work well done. | ___ | ___ |
| 17. | I feel free to talk to my supervisor about problems on the job. | ___ | ___ |
| 18. | Management is concerned about employee safety. | ___ | ___ |
| 19. | Management keeps employees informed about what is going on. | ___ | ___ |
| 20. | I trust my supervisor and I believe what he/she tells me. | ___ | ___ |
| 21. | The people I work with help each other out in order to get our work done. | ___ | ___ |
| 22. | My work team meets from time to time to discuss ways to improve our work and to make decisions regarding how things should be done. | ___ | ___ |
| 23. | I am really doing something worthwhile in my job. | ___ | ___ |
| 24. | I have lots of opportunities to use my abilities in this organization. | ___ | ___ |
| 25. | We have adequate staff in our department to handle our work responsibilities. | ___ | ___ |
| 26. | My supervisor tells me how I am doing on the job, good or bad. | ___ | ___ |

(continued)

**Figure 22.4**   Employee opinion survey.

*"HealthSouth Treasure Coast Rehabilitation Hospital, Vero Beach, FL"*

|  | AGREE | DISAGREE |
|---|---|---|

27. There is opportunity for advancement with this organization.      \_\_\_\_\_     \_\_\_\_\_

28. I enjoy coming to work in the morning.      \_\_\_\_\_     \_\_\_\_\_

What do you like most about working here?

_____

_____

What do you like least about working here?

_____

_____

What improvements would you recommend if you were the president?

_____

_____

What corporate benefits do you like best?

_____

_____

What corporate benefits do you like least?

_____

_____

Please use the following space to comment on any of the above questions or on anything else:

_____

_____

_____

_____

_____

_____

_____

_____

**Figure 22.4**—*Continued*

**EMPLOYEE OPINION SURVEY**
Anytown Health Center
Anytown, USA

Your employer is interested in your opinions and feelings about your work. This survey is one way to obtain your input about various aspects of your work. You should answer the questionnaire items honestly and frankly because it is totally **anonymous and confidential**. No one but you will know how you answered the question items. There are four parts to this survey. After you have completed one part, proceed to the next one until you have completed all four parts. After you have finished all four parts, place this completed form in the locked box at the front of this room and return your materials to the person administering the survey.

The results of this survey will be discussed with you at a later date by your supervisor and/or area manger.

**PART B**
The following statements concern specific aspects of the organization and your job here. Indicate your level of agreement with each statement by filling in the bubble to the right of the statement. Possible responses are:

| | |
|---|---|
| **1 = Strongly Agree** | **4 = Slightly Disagree** |
| **2 = Moderately Agree** | **5 = Moderately Disagree** |
| **3 = Slightly Agree** | **6 = Strongly Disagree** |

For example, if you "**moderately agree**" with a statement, you would fill in the bubble marked ② under the column marked Moderately Agree.

Again, your answers are **anonymous and confidential**, so please feel free to answer honestly.

| | | Strongly Agree | Moderately Agree | Slightly Agree | Slightly Disagree | Moderately Disagree | Strongly Disagree |
|---|---|---|---|---|---|---|---|
| 1 | I am proud to work for this organization. | ① | ② | ③ | ④ | ⑤ | ⑥ |
| 2 | I understand how the success of my department is measured. | ① | ② | ③ | ④ | ⑤ | ⑥ |
| 3 | My supervisor gives me clear working instructions. | ① | ② | ③ | ④ | ⑤ | ⑥ |
| 4 | Efficiency is highly valued in my department. | ① | ② | ③ | ④ | ⑤ | ⑥ |
| 5 | My department head sets clear goals for our department. | ① | ② | ③ | ④ | ⑤ | ⑥ |
| 6 | Communications among shifts in this organization are good. | ① | ② | ③ | ④ | ⑤ | ⑥ |
| 7 | I would have to make a bad mistake to be removed from my present position in this organization. | ① | ② | ③ | ④ | ⑤ | ⑥ |
| 8 | Employee promotions are handled fairly in this organization. | ① | ② | ③ | ④ | ⑤ | ⑥ |
| 9 | Compared to similar jobs in the community, I feel that I am paid fairly. | ① | ② | ③ | ④ | ⑤ | ⑥ |
| 10 | The organization's top management will use the information from this survey to make improvements. | ① | ② | ③ | ④ | ⑤ | ⑥ |
| 11 | My department head does a good job of running this department. | ① | ② | ③ | ④ | ⑤ | ⑥ |
| 12 | My job is challenging enough to suit me. | ① | ② | ③ | ④ | ⑤ | ⑥ |
| 13 | I am satisfied with this organization's sick leave policy. | ① | ② | ③ | ④ | ⑤ | ⑥ |
| 14 | I am happy with my current workload. | ① | ② | ③ | ④ | ⑤ | ⑥ |
| 15 | My supervisor discusses my productivity with me. | ① | ② | ③ | ④ | ⑤ | ⑥ |
| 16 | In my department, employees are well utilized. | ① | ② | ③ | ④ | ⑤ | ⑥ |
| 17 | My supervisor does a good job of running my area. | ① | ② | ③ | ④ | ⑤ | ⑥ |
| 18 | Absenteeism is no problem in my department. | ① | ② | ③ | ④ | ⑤ | ⑥ |

**Figure 22.5**  Employee opinion survey.

*Management Science Associates, Inc., copyright 1997.*

group (see figure 22.4) or to identify their department so management can focus its response to the source of the concern.

## Analyzing the Results

Once the forms have been filled out, the results must be analyzed. (See figures 22.6 and 22.7) Even if the survey is well designed, organized, and properly conducted, it can lead to a failure if it is improperly or superficially analyzed. The manner in which the data are analyzed is critical for the success of the survey. Only proper analysis will ensure that management will get a clear picture of the results so that the real problems will be addressed by action and appropriate solutions. A misdiagnosis of the survey results will lead to ineffective solutions.

A discussion of statistical approaches and concepts such as segmenting the survey, cluster analysis, and so forth is beyond the scope of this text. Briefly, the analysis must be thorough and instead of simple, straight-run statistics, it should produce more meaningful interpretations. For example, the interaction of organizational and demographic variables must be examined in relation to attitudes. Instead of simply stating that 65 percent of the subordinates have frequent communication with their boss and 35 percent do not, or that 75 percent of the respondents like their jobs and 25 percent do not, it would be better to state that of the 75 percent who like their jobs, 85 percent have frequent contact with their boss and 15 percent do not. At the same time, one can learn that among the 25 percent who do not care for their jobs, 55 percent claim that they have infrequent communication with their superiors. Also, for example, the results may determine whether females are more or less satisfied than males, young more than older employees, and so forth.

After a meaningful analysis and interpretation of the survey have been done, the results are presented to the top-level executive team. Then each executive will meet with his or her line managers to analyze and evaluate the survey results. Plans for action to correct the problems that surfaced should be formulated in these meetings. This process then moves downward throughout the hierarchy, first to all supervisors. Then the results of attitude surveys are used as discussion material with the rank-and-file employees in workshop meetings.

Besides this feedback of results to those who filled out the questionnaires, attitude surveys provide top-level administration, department heads, and supervisors with information to guide them in their overall efforts to improve morale. The surveys will reveal certain deficiencies, for specific actions should then be taken. For example, the questionnaire may show an overwhelming interest in and need for a child care center where young children would be cared for during the working hours of the parent. This obviously is an area of dissatisfaction, and administration should take immediate and specific action. Occasionally, however, the results of initial surveys are not so clear. They may raise many questions, and sometimes additional surveys are required to probe deeper. Survey techniques and analyses are becoming more and more sophisticated, and with their help management should be able to arrive at a solution to almost any morale problem that arises.

| Total Organization | 1992 | ORGANIZATIONAL PRACTICES BY DIMENSION | REPORT # 6111 |

Items included in WORKING CONDITIONS focus on the extent to which the physical environment and work procedures contribute to, rather than impede, job performance.

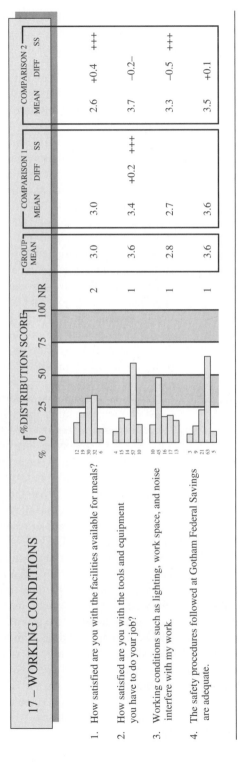

| 17 – WORKING CONDITIONS | %DISTRIBUTION SCORE 0 25 50 75 100 | NR | GROUP MEAN | COMPARISON 1 MEAN | DIFF | SS | COMPARISON 2 MEAN | DIFF | SS |
|---|---|---|---|---|---|---|---|---|---|
| 1. How satisfied are you with the facilities available for meals? | 12 19 30 32 6 | 2 | 3.0 | 3.0 | | | 2.6 | +0.4 | +++ |
| 2. How satisfied are you with the tools and equipment you have to do your job? | 4 15 14 57 10 | 1 | 3.6 | 3.4 | +0.2 | +++ | 3.7 | –0.2– | |
| 3. Working conditions such as lighting, work space, and noise interfere with my work. | 10 45 16 17 13 | 1 | 2.8 | 2.7 | | | 3.3 | –0.5 | +++ |
| 4. The safety procedures followed at Gotham Federal Savings are adequate. | 3 9 21 63 5 | 1 | 3.6 | 3.6 | | | 3.5 | +0.1 | |

**Figure 22.6** Employee opinion survey results.

© *Copyright Numerof and Associates, Inc. 1992. Reprinted with permission.*

**MANAGEMENT SCIENCE ASSOCIATES, INC.**
**Measure of Organizational Health Prepared for:**
**Anytown Community Hospital**
**Anytown, USA**

| Norm Group: National Norms | | | | Date of Survey: | 1 /97 |
|---|---|---|---|---|---|
| Organization Total | | | | Number of Respondents: | 1314 |

| Attitude Area/Question | Ind. Norm | Org. Norm | % Diff. | Very Pos. 1 | Mod Pos. 2 | Slgt Pos 3 | Slgt Neg 4 | Mod Neg 5 | Very Neg 6 | # Resp. |
|---|---|---|---|---|---|---|---|---|---|---|
| **A. JOB SATISFACTION** | 2.2 | 2.3 | -2 | | | | | | | |
| 1. Proud to Work for Hospital | 1.7 | 1.6 | 2 | 56% | 31% | 9% | 2% | 1% | 1% | 1314 |
| 2. Job is Challenging | 2.1 | 2.1 | 0 | 41% | 32% | 13% | 7% | 4% | 3% | 1310 |
| 3. Feeling of Satisfaction | 2.6 | 2.8 | -4 | 17% | 32% | 25% | 12% | 7% | 6% | 1313 |
| 4. Opportunity to Use My Abilities | 2.5 | 2.6 | -2 | 23% | 34% | 22% | 11% | 5% | 5% | 1295 |
| **B. JOB MOBILITY** | 3.2 | 3.4 | -4 | | | | | | | |
| 1. Opportunities to Transfer | 3.0 | 3.2 | -4 | 13% | 24% | 25% | 14% | 11% | 13% | 1268 |
| 2. Chances for Advancement | 3.4 | 3.7 | -6 | 7% | 16% | 25% | 23% | 14% | 15% | 1288 |
| **C. ADMIN/SR MANAGEMENT** | 3.0 | 3.0 | 0 | | | | | | | |
| 1. Resolves Employee Complaints | 3.3 | 3.4 | -2 | 8% | 20% | 29% | 19% | 11% | 12% | 1257 |
| 2. Overall Management of Hospital | 2.8 | 2.7 | 2 | 16% | 35% | 25% | 13% | 6% | 4% | 1284 |
| 3. Interest in Employees | 3.2 | 3.2 | 0 | 14% | 22% | 24% | 18% | 11% | 12% | 1287 |
| 4. Communicates Hospital Objectives | 2.7 | 2.7 | 0 | 18% | 29% | 30% | 14% | 5% | 4% | 1302 |
| 5. Use of Survey by Administration | 2.9 | 3.1 | -4 | 16% | 25% | 26% | 13% | 9% | 11% | 1299 |
| **D. DEPARTMENT HEAD** | 2.6 | 2.7 | -2 | | | | | 6% | | |
| 1. Understand How Dept/Unit Success Meas. | 2.5 | 2.7 | -4 | 20% | 34% | 23% | 13% | 8% | 5% | 1303 |
| 2. Sets Clear Goals for Department/Unit | 2.6 | 2.7 | -4 | 24% | 28% | 21% | 13% | 9% | 6% | 1301 |
| 3. Good Job of Running Department/ Unit | 2.6 | 2.6 | 0 | 28% | 28% | 19% | 9% | | 7% | 1305 |
| **E. SUPERVISION** | 2.7 | 2.9 | -4 | | | | | | | |
| 1. Gives Clear Instructions | 2.3 | 2.4 | -2 | 31% | 32% | 17% | 9% | 6% | 4% | 1306 |
| 2. Overall Management of Area | 2.5 | 2.6 | -2 | 32% | 25% | 16% | 8% | 9% | 9% | 1302 |
| 3. Handling Complaints | 2.9 | 3.2 | -6 | 20% | 22% | 18% | 14% | 9% | 16% | 1298 |
| 4. Administering Discipline | 3.0 | 3.2 | -4 | 18% | 23% | 20% | 15% | 11% | 14% | 1283 |
| 5. Feel Free to Tell What I Think | 2.6 | 2.7 | -2 | 33% | 24% | 16% | 8% | 8% | 12% | 1305 |
| 6. Does Not Play Favorites | 3.0 | 3.2 | -4 | 23% | 22% | 15% | 12% | 8% | 19% | 1299 |
| 7. Discusses Productivity with Me | 2.7 | 2.7 | 0 | 28% | 26% | 19% | 11% | 8% | 8% | 1305 |
| 8. Communications with Employees | 2.8 | 3.0 | -4 | 21% | 27% | 19% | 12% | 8% | 13% | 1303 |
| **F. COMMUNICATIONS** | 3.3 | 3.3 | 0 | | | | | | | |
| 1. Among Departments | 3.5 | 3.4 | 2 | 6% | 19% | 31% | 23% | 13% | 8% | 1289 |
| 2. Among Shifts | 3.2 | 3.1 | 2 | 9% | 29% | 28% | 15% | 9% | 8% | 1251 |
| **G. PERSONNEL/HR POLICIES** | 3.0 | 2.9 | 2 | | | | | | | |
| 1. Administered Consistently | 3.0 | 2.9 | 2 | 13% | 33% | 25% | 14% | 8% | 7% | 1273 |
| 2. Fairness of Promotion Policies | 3.2 | 3.2 | 0 | 9% | 27% | 27% | 16% | 11% | 10% | 1273 |
| 3. Satisfied with Personnel Policies | 2.7 | 2.6 | 2 | 16% | 40% | 25% | 11% | 5% | 4% | 1292 |
| **H. JOB SECURITY** | 2.6 | 3.1 | -10 | | | | | | | |
| 1. Takes a Lot to Lose Job | 2.6 | 3.0 | -8 | 22% | 23% | 21% | 14% | 10% | 10% | 1300 |
| 2. Feeling of Security | 2.7 | 3.2 | -10 | 16% | 25% | 21% | 15% | 10% | 13% | 1307 |
| 3. I Can Be Sure of a Job | 2.5 | 3.1 | -12 | 20% | 26% | 17% | 14% | 11% | 12% | 1309 |

**Figure 22.7** Employee opinion survey results.

*Management Science Associates, Inc., copyright 1997.*

**SUMMARY**   Morale is a state of mind and emotion affecting the attitudes, feelings, and sentiments of groups of employees and individuals toward their work environment, colleagues, supervision, and the enterprise as a whole. Morale is always present, and it can range from high to low. The level of morale varies considerably from day to day. Morale is contagious; that is, favorable attitudes spread quickly, and unfavorable attitudes spread even more quickly. High morale is not only the concern of the supervisor; the employees are just as interested in a satisfactory level of morale. Moreover, the effect of high or low morale is felt not only by insiders, but also by outsiders such as patients and visitors.

Morale can be influenced by many factors, which can be classified into two broad groups: those factors affecting the employee's activities that arise outside the enterprise and those factors originating within the job environment. The supervisor can do little to directly change the effects of outside factors on the subordinates' morale, but many internal factors, such as incentives, working conditions, and quality of work life, are within the supervisor's power to control. These factors can be used to significantly raise the level of subordinates' morale. If the supervisor succeeds in maintaining high morale, good teamwork and increased productivity probably will result. Recent research indicates that some interesting correlations exist between morale and productivity, turnover, absenteeism, and so forth.

An astute supervisor can sense changes in the level of morale by keenly observing the subordinates, but this is difficult. Often supervisors do not realize that a change has taken place until it is too late. Attitude surveys are primarily used as a way of finding out how employees view their jobs, coworkers, wages, benefits, supervisors, working conditions, etc. Surveys, once requested by management, often are instituted by outside consultants or by the institution's human resources department.

Surveys take the form of questionnaires submitted to the employees. Once a morale survey has been performed and properly analyzed, it is absolutely necessary that management do something about those areas of dissatisfaction that appear to contribute to a lowering of morale. It is also advisable to report the results to all those who participated and to discuss them in workshops throughout the organization in order to find solutions to the problems.

# *Positive Discipline*

*Chapter Objectives*

After you have studied this chapter, you should be able to:

1. Define the term discipline.
2. Discuss different techniques of administering discipline.
3. Describe different types of disciplinary actions.
4. Review the supervisor's role in disciplinary actions.
5. Outline the rights of employees in the disciplinary process.

The term *discipline* is used to express many different ideas and is understood in several different ways. To many, discipline carries the disagreeable connotation of punishing wrongdoers. When one hears the word *discipline,* one is often inclined to think immediately of authority enforcing obedience. There is a positive way of considering discipline, however, a way that is far more in keeping with good supervisory practices. Maintaining positive, sometimes also known as constructive, discipline and good influencing go hand in hand.

## ORGANIZATIONAL DISCIPLINE

For our purposes, discipline can be defined as a state of affairs or a condition of orderliness in which the members of the enterprise behave sensibly and conduct themselves according to the standards of acceptable behavior as expressed by the needs of the organization. Discipline is said to be good when the employees willingly follow the rules of the enterprise, live up to or exceed standards, and practice self-discipline. Discipline is said to be poor when subordinates either do this reluctantly or actually refuse to follow regulations, violate the standards of acceptable behavior, and require constant surveillance by their supervisors. Positive discipline thrives in an organizational climate in which management applies positive motivation, sound leadership, and efficient management.

### ■ Discipline and Morale

The level of morale can significantly influence the problems of discipline. Normally, fewer problems of a disciplinary nature can be expected when morale is high. By the same token, low morale brings about increased problems of discipline. A high degree of discipline can exist despite a low level of morale. Under these conditions, discipline is probably controlled by fear and sheer force. On the other hand, however, it is not usually possible to maintain a high level of morale unless there is also a high degree of positive discipline.

## ■ Self-Discipline

The best discipline is self-discipline—by this we mean the normal human tendency to do what needs to be done. In the healthcare setting, this means doing one's share and subordinating some of one's own needs and desires to the standards of acceptable behavior set for the enterprise as a whole. From early childhood on, people have been trained to respect rules, accept orders from those legitimately entitled to issue them, and realize that all organized activities set limits on the behavior of their members.

Experience shows that most employees want to do the right thing. Even before they start to work, most mature people accept the idea that following instructions and fair rules of conduct is a normal responsibility that goes with any job. Thus, most employees can be counted on to exercise a considerable degree of self-discipline. They believe in coming to work on time, following the supervisor's instructions, and signing the time sheet, and refraining from fights, drinking at work, stealing, etc. In other words, self-imposed discipline is based on the commitment of employees to conform with the rules, regulations, and orders that are necessary for the proper conduct of the institution.

Once the employees know what is expected of them and believe that the rules by which they are governed are reasonable, they usually will observe them without problems. The supervisor occasionally must check whether or not some of these rules and regulations are still reasonable. Times are changing, and certain rules that were once reasonable are no longer considered to be so. For example, the dress codes and codes of general appearance have most certainly undergone changes in the past decade. It would be unreasonable to request subordinates to comply with a dress and appearance code set up years ago.

When new rules are introduced, however, the supervisor must show their current reasonableness and need to the employees. For instance, short skirts may be fashionable, but they are not conducive to a nurse's appearance on the job. Instead of simply outlawing short skirts, however, a rule giving nurses their choice between wearing a certain length of hemline or uniforms with long pants might be considered a more reasonable dress code. Rules regarding hair length are relevant in some job settings, as in the surgical suite, but irrelevant in others. Therefore, since hair is a danger to asepsis, the supervisor and possibly the chief of surgery, infection committee, and director of nursing may need to work out rules that will make a hood or helmet-type covering mandatory for operating room personnel. Although no such device was previously regarded as necessary, past rules do not provide the necessary protection any longer. In other words, the supervisor must be alert to changing styles and mores, and must make certain that the rules and regulations truly respect them. Otherwise, rules are not enforceable, and many unnecessary disciplinary problems will arise.

If present, mores or the culture-driven expectations as well as the employees' strong sense of self-imposed discipline will exert group pressure on any possible wrongdoer, thus further reducing the need for the supervisor's disciplinary action. Work groups also set standards for conduct and performance; for example, fellow employees are expected by the group to carry their fair share of work, be at work on time, and so on. Group discipline reinforces self-discipline and will exert pressure on those who do not comply with group norms and standards.

Employees must also know that they will have the supervisor's unqualified support as long as they stay within the ordinary rules of conduct and their activities are consistent with what is expected of them. Proper discipline makes it necessary for the supervisor to give positive support to the right action and criticize and punish the wrong action. The subordinate must know that failure to live up to what is expected will result in "punishment."

The administration cannot expect employees to practice self-discipline unless it starts at the top. Similar restrictions must be imposed on all managerial personnel to remain within the acceptable patterns of behavior. For example, workers cannot be expected to impose self-discipline if supervisors do not show it. Proper conduct with respect to the needs of the organization requires the supervisor also to comply with the necessity to be on time, observe "no smoking" and "no drinking" rules, and dress and behave in a manner commensurate with the organizational and departmental activities.

Setting an example is a key responsibility of management. The "mirror effect" (see chapter 22) will pervade all levels of the organization if the example is displayed by all supervisors and managers. This role modeling by management can serve to tell all staff in a nonverbal way that "I only expect of you what I expect from myself."

## Maintaining Positive Discipline

Although the vast majority of employees will exercise considerable self-discipline, a few employees in every large organization occasionally fail to abide by established rules and standards even after having been informed of them. Some employees simply will not accept the responsibility of self-discipline. Also, a few unruly employees, probably because of their personality, background, and development, find it difficult to function within policies, rules, and regulations.

Since the job must go on, the supervisor cannot afford to let those few "get away with" violations. Quick and firm action is called for to correct the situation. Unless such action is taken, the morale of the other employees in the work group will be seriously weakened. At times like this, the supervisor has to rely on the power and force inherent in the managerial position, even though he or she may dislike doing so. In this situation, the supervisor must clearly realize that he or she is in charge of the department and is therefore responsible for discipline within it. If the supervisor does not correct the situation, some individuals who are merely on the borderline of being undisciplined may follow the bad example. When a defect in discipline becomes apparent, it is the supervisor's responsibility to take proper action and to resolve this employee-management conflict firmly and promptly.

## ■ The Purpose of Positive Discipline

When administering positive discipline, managers should remember that the purpose is to preserve the interests of the organization and to protect the rights of the employees. Discipline is not for the purpose of punishment or "getting even" with an employee. Rather, its purpose is to improve the employee's future behavior, to correct and rehabilitate, but not to injure. Discipline corrects the subordinate's breach of the rules and carries the notice of more serious consequences in the future. Discipline also serves as a warning for other people in the department. It reminds the disciplined individual's coworkers that rules exist and that violating them does not go unnoticed or without any action from the supervisor. Moreover, discipline reassures all those employees who respect the rules out of their desire to do the right thing. Discipline's primary purpose most certainly is not punishment or retribution.

Using the guides and checklists provided in chapter 18 may be beneficial when delivering discipline. The interests of the organization are best served when an employee understands what is expected of him or her and complies with those expectations. By doing so, the organization "salvages" a trained resource and avoids the expense of recruitment and loss of productivity resulting from a vacancy or from training a new employee.

The supervisor should administer discipline so that it motivates rather than demotivates. In other words, the boss must exercise positive discipline. This is not an easy task, since inherently the act of punishing a subordinate for violating a rule always presupposes that the subordinate was caught violating it. Yet many others who may have done the same thing go free, so to speak, because the supervisor did not catch them. This invariably injects a note of unfairness into the disciplinary process. Another reason that it is difficult to administer positive discipline is that any discipline is normally resented, and it places a strain on the supervisor-subordinate relationship. Sometimes all discipline does is make the subordinate double his or her efforts not to be caught again. Nevertheless, positive discipline will generally be successful and accepted if the supervisor follows a few simple rules when taking disciplinary action.

Jane Boucher's book *How to Love the Job You Hate* offers the following advice:[1]

## ■ Taking Responsibility

Normally, few occasions will arise that force a good supervisor to take disciplinary action. When it becomes necessary, however, it is the supervisor's job to do so. The supervisor is best qualified to handle the situation because he or she knows the employee, alleged violations, and circumstances. By being in charge of the department, the supervisor has the authority and responsibility to take ap-

---

*1.  Jane Boucher,* How to Love the Job You Hate *(Nashville: Thomas Nelson Publishers), pp. 163–166.*

---

**If You Must Criticize Someone**

Here are some suggestions for giving criticism in a way that motivates others to do a better job:

- **See yourself as a teacher or coach**—as being helpful. Keep in mind that you're trying to help someone improve.
- **Show you care.** Express your sincere concern about sharing ways the other person can boost his or her success.
- **Pick the right moment to offer criticism.** Make sure the person hasn't just been shaken by some incident.
- **Avoid telling people they "should do such and such" or "should have done such and such."** "Shoulds" make you appear rigid and pedantic.
- **Avoid giving the impression that you're more concerned with seeing your recommendations put into practice than in helping the other person improve.**
- **Show how the person will benefit from taking the actions you suggest.**
- **Give specific suggestions.** Being vague might only make the situation worse by creating anxiety and doubt.

*Tip:* Be sure you can take criticism yourself. If not, you may not be perceived as a credible source.

*From Jane Boucher,* How to Love the Job You Hate. *Thomas Nelson Publishers, Nashville, TN. Reprinted with permission of the publisher.*

---

propriate action. Although it may be expedient for the moment to let someone in the human resources department handle such unpleasant problems, the supervisor would be not only shirking and abdicating responsibility, but also undermining his or her own position if this were allowed.

The same result would occur if the supervisor were to ignore or conveniently overlook for any length of time a subordinate's failure to meet the prescribed standards of conduct. If such breaches are condoned, the supervisor is merely communicating to the rest of the employees that he or she does not intend to enforce the rules and regulations. Thus, the supervisor must not procrastinate in administering discipline. On the other hand, the supervisor must take caution against haste or unwarranted action. The first step is to obtain all pertinent facts. Before the supervisor does anything, it is necessary to investigate what has happened and why the employee violated the rule. In addition, the employee's past record should be checked, and all other pertinent information should be obtained before any action is taken.

## ■ Maintaining Control of Emotions

Whenever taking disciplinary action, the supervisor must not lose his or her temper. Regardless of the severity of the violation, the supervisor must not lose control of the situation, thus running the risk of losing the employees' respect.

This does not mean that the supervisor should face the situation halfheartedly or haphazardly. If he or she is in danger of losing control, however, action should be avoided until tempers have cooled down. Even if the violation is significant, the supervisor cannot afford to lose his or her temper. Moreover, the supervisor should follow the general rule of never laying a hand on an employee in any way. Except for emergencies, when an employee has been injured or becomes ill or when employees who are fighting need to be separated, such a gesture could easily make matters worse.

## ■ Discipline in Private

The supervisor must make certain that all disciplinary action takes place in private, never in public. A public reprimand builds up resentment in the employee, and it may permit unrelated factors to enter the situation. For instance, if in the opinion of the other workers a disciplinary action is too severe for the violation, the disciplined employee would appear as a martyr to the rest of them. A supervisor who is disciplining in public is bound to have his or her performance judged by every employee in the department. Employees expect to be treated with the same courtesy as they extend to their supervisor. Thus, just as a supervisor would expect private counselings, so should he or she extend the same courtesy to his or her subordinates.

Also, the employees will probably not know all the facts and may not agree with the facts on which the disciplinary action is based, and the supervisor may end up arguing with the other employees over what happened. Varying eyewitness reports probably will only confuse the situation. In addition, public discipline would humiliate the disciplined employee in the eyes of the coworkers and would cause considerable damage to the entire department. Therefore, privacy in taking disciplinary action must be the rule.

## PROGRESSIVE DISCIPLINARY ACTION

The question of which type of disciplinary action to use is answered differently in different enterprises. In recent years, however, most enterprises have accepted the idea of progressive discipline, which provides for an increase in the "penalty" with each "offense." First offenders get less severe penalties than repeat offenders; more serious infractions receive more severe penalties than lesser offenses. Unless a serious wrong has been committed, the employee would rarely be discharged for the first offense. Rather, a series of progressive steps of disciplinary action would be taken. The following steps, presented in ascending order of severity, are merely suggested; they are not the only means of disciplinary action, nor are they all necessary. Many enterprises, however, have found the progression of these disciplinary steps to be a viable approach: (1) informal talk, (2) spoken warning or reprimand, (3) written warning, (4) disciplinary layoff, (5) demotional downgrading, and (6) discharge.

## The Informal Talk

If the incident is minor and the employee has no previous record of disciplinary action, an informal friendly talk, also referred to as *counseling,* will clear up the situation in many cases. In such a talk, the supervisor will discuss with the employee his or her behavior in relation to the standards that prevail within the enterprise. He or she will try to get to the underlying reason for the undesirable behavior. If the institution has an employee assistance program, as discussed in chapter 22, the supervisor may refer the employee to it if indications show this program can help him or her. At the same time, the boss will try to reaffirm the employee's sense of responsibility and reestablish the previous cooperative relationship within the department. It may also be advisable to repeat once more why the action of the employee is undesirable and what it may possibly lead to. If the supervisor later finds that this friendly talk was not sufficient to bring about the desired results, then it will become necessary to take the next step, a spoken warning.

## Spoken Warning or Reprimand

In the reprimand interview, the supervisor should again point out how undesirable the subordinate's violation is and how it could ultimately lead to more severe disciplinary action. Such an interview will have emotional overtones, since the employee most likely is resentful for having been caught again and the supervisor may also be angry. The violation should be discussed in a straightforward statement of fact, however, and the supervisor should not begin with a recital of how the fine reputation of the employee has now been "tarnished." The supervisor also should not be apologetic but should state the case in specific terms and then give the subordinate a chance to tell his or her side of the story.

The supervisor should stress the preventive purpose of discipline by manners and words, but the employee must be advised that such conduct cannot be tolerated. In some enterprises a record is made on the employee's papers that this spoken warning has taken place. The purpose of the warning is to help the employee correct the behavior and prevent the need for further disciplinary action. The warning should leave the employee with the confidence that he or she can do better and will improve in the future. Some supervisors believe that such a verbal reprimand is not very effective. If it is carried out skillfully, however, many employees will be straightened out at this stage.

## Written Warning

A written warning is formal insofar as it becomes a part of the employee's record. Written warnings are particularly necessary in work settings where unions exist so that the document can serve as evidence in case of grievance procedures. The written warning must contain a statement of the violation and the potential consequences. A duplicate copy of it is given to the employee, and another duplicate of the warning is sent to the human resources department so that it can be inserted in the permanent record.

## ■ Disciplinary Layoff

A disciplinary layoff is the next disciplinary step when the employee has continued the offense and all previous steps were of no avail. Under such conditions the supervisor must determine what length of penalty would be appropriate. This will depend on how serious the offense is and how many times it has been repeated. Disciplinary layoffs typically extend over several days or weeks, and are seldom longer than a few weeks.

Some employees may not be impressed with spoken or written warnings, but they will find a disciplinary layoff without pay a rude awakening and probably will be convinced that the institution is really serious. A disciplinary layoff may bring back a sense of compliance with rules and regulations.

There are, however, several disadvantages to invoking a disciplinary layoff. Some enterprises do not apply this measure at all because it hurts their own productivity, especially in times of labor shortages when the employee cannot be replaced with someone who is just as skilled. Also, the employee might return from the layoff in a much more unpleasant frame of mind than when he or she left. Although most managers consider disciplinary layoff as a serious measure, some employees who frequently violate the rules may not regard it as such; they may even view a few days of disciplinary layoff as a welcome break from their daily routine. Although most institutions use it effectively, a number of institutions no longer use disciplinary layoffs. Instead, they move right on to discharge, or they practice the newer concept of discipline without punishment discussed later in this chapter.

## ■ Demotion

The usefulness of demoting an employee is seriously questioned, therefore, this disciplinary measure is seldom invoked. To demote for disciplinary reasons to a lower-level, less desirable, and lower paying job is likely to bring about dissatisfaction and discouragement. Over an extended period an employee downgrading is a form of constant punishment. The dissatisfaction, humiliation, and ill will that result may easily spread to other employees in the department. Sometimes this measure can be viewed as an invitation for the employee to quit, rather than be discharged. Many enterprises avoid downgrading as a disciplinary measure just as they avoid disciplinary layoffs or the withholding of a scheduled pay increase. If so, they will have to use termination of employment as the ultimate solution.

## ■ Discharge

Discharge, or corporate capital punishment, is the most drastic form of disciplinary action, and it should be reserved exclusively for the most serious offenses.

Supervisors should resort to it infrequently and only after some of the preliminary steps have been taken. Discharge is the ultimate penalty—is costly to the organization and causes real hardships to the person who has been discharged. When a serious wrong has been committed, however, discharge should be invoked at once. For instance, when an employee brandishes a loaded gun and threatens to shoot, immediate discharge would be in order. Even for lesser offenses, in some healthcare institutions the supervisor goes through the earlier steps of friendly and more formal spoken and written reprimands and then points out that the next measure would be discharge without any further discussion. In these institutions there is no intermediate penalty such as a several-day disciplinary layoff, which could hurt the superior-subordinate relationship. Discharge is the only step left in this progression. It is hoped that this severe penalty is invoked infrequently.

For the employee, discharge means hardship because it eliminates the seniority standing, possibly some pension rights, substantial vacation benefits, a high pay scale, and other benefits that the employee has accumulated in many years of service. Discharge also makes it difficult for the worker to obtain new employment. In regard to the enterprise, discharges involve serious losses and waste, including the expense of training a new employee and the disruption caused by changing the makeup of the work team. Discharge may also cause damage to the morale of the group. If the discharged employee is a member of a legally protected group, such as minorities or women, administration has to be concerned about nondiscrimination and quotas.

Therefore, because of these possibly serious consequences of discharge, many organizations have removed from the supervisor the right to fire. This has been reserved for higher levels in administration; in some institutions, the supervisor's recommendation to discharge must be reviewed and approved by higher administration and/or by the human resources director. With unions, management is concerned with possible prolonged arbitration procedures, knowing full well that arbitrators have become increasingly unwilling to permit discharge except for the most severe violations. Although situations may arise where there is no other answer but to fire the employee for "just cause," these cases will be the rare exception and not the rule.

## TIME ELEMENT

In all of the disciplinary steps previously discussed, the time element is significant. There is no reason to hold an indiscretion of past years against a person forever. Current practice is inclined to disregard offenses that have been committed more than a year previously if the person has reformed. For example, an employee with a poor record because of tardiness would start a new life if he or she maintained a good record for one year or maybe only for six months. This time element will vary, though, depending on the nature of the violation.

## DOCUMENTATION

It is essential for the supervisor to keep detailed records of all disciplinary actions, since they have the potential of becoming the subject of further discussions, disputes, and even litigation. The burden of proof is on the employer. The written record should cover the time of the event, details of the offense, the supervisor's decision, and action taken. It should also include the reasoning involved. If at some future time the supervisor or the institution is asked to substantiate the action taken, it is not sufficient to depend on memory alone.

At present, it is more important than ever to keep accurate detailed records because the aggrieved employee may file a lawsuit for wrongful discharge, based on discrimination, harassment, or similar reasons. If a union is involved, documentation is a must to justify a disciplinary measure if it is challenged by a formal grievance procedure. Regardless of any potential consequences, written documentation at the time of the event is essential for the institution and the supervisor's own records.

## THE SUPERVISOR'S DILEMMA

Throughout this book we have stressed the importance of the relationship of trust, confidence, and help between the supervisor and the employee. Disciplinary action is by nature painful. Therefore, despite all the restraint and wisdom with which the supervisor takes disciplinary action, it still puts a strain on the supervisor-subordinate relationships. It is difficult to impose discipline without generating resentment because disciplinary action is an unpleasant experience and puts a barrier between the supervisor and the employee. The question therefore arises as to how the supervisor can apply the necessary disciplinary action so that it will be given in the least resented and most acceptable form.

The supervisor must also be concerned about equity. It is imperative that discipline be equitably applied regardless of race, sex, age, position, etc. Sometimes we see exceptions being made because the employee is the son of a "high admitter" or a neighbor of the assistant director of plant operations or the daughter of a benefactor. These are not valid reasons for exceptions. Inequitable dispensing of discipline, or for that matter, praise or assignments because of associations unrelated to the work requirements, can destroy a manager's credibility and the staff's morale more quickly than any other reason.

### ■ The "Red-Hot-Stove" Approach

McGregor refers to what he calls "the red-hot-stove rule" and draws a comparison between touching a red-hot stove and experiencing discipline. When one touches a red-hot stove, the resulting discipline has four characteristics: it is *immediate,* with *warning, consistent,* and *impersonal.* First, the burn is immediate, and there is no question of the cause and effect. Second, there is a warning; everyone knows what happens if one touches a hot stove, especially if the stove is red hot. Third, the discipline is consistent; every time one touches a hot stove, one is burned. Fourth, the discipline is impersonal; whoever touches the hot stove is burned. A person is burned for touching the hot stove, not because of who he or she is.

This comparison illustrates that the act and the discipline seem almost as one. The discipline takes place because the person did something—because he or she committed a particular act. The discipline is directed against the act and not against the person. Following the four basic rules expressed in this "red-hot-stove" approach will help the supervisor take the sting out of many disciplinary actions. It enables the manager to achieve positive discipline and at the same time generate in the employee the least amount of resentment.

## Immediacy

The supervisor must not procrastinate; a prompt beginning of the disciplinary process is necessary as soon as possible after the supervisor notices the violation. The sooner the discipline is invoked, the more automatic it will seem and the closer will be the connection with the offensive act. As already stated, the supervisor should refrain from taking hasty action, and enough time should elapse for tempers to cool and for assembling all the necessary facts.

In some instances it is apparent that the employee is guilty of a violation, although the full circumstances may not be known. Here the need for disciplinary action is unquestionable, but some doubt exists as to the amount of penalty. In such cases the supervisor should tell the employee that he or she realizes what went on, but that some time will be needed to reach a conclusion. In other cases, however, the nature of the incident makes it necessary to get the offender off the premises quickly. Some immediate action is required even if there is not yet enough evidence to make a final decision in the case.

## Temporary Suspension

To solve this dilemma, many enterprises invoke what is called "temporary suspension." The employee is suspended, pending a final decision in the case. This device of suspension protects management as well as the employee. Suspension gives management a chance to make the necessary investigation and consult higher levels of administration or the human resources department, and it provides an opportunity for tempers to cool off. In cases of temporary suspension the employee is told that he or she is "suspended" and will be informed as soon as possible of the disciplinary action that will be taken.

The suspension in itself is not a punishment. If the investigation shows that there is no cause for disciplinary action, the employee has no grievance, since he or she is recalled and will not have suffered any loss of pay. If, on the other hand, the penalty is a disciplinary layoff, then the time during which the employee was suspended will constitute all or part of the layoff assessed. The obvious advantage of this device of temporary suspension is that the supervisor can act promptly without any prejudice to the employee. Nevertheless, temporary suspension should not be used indiscriminately; it should be invoked primarily when the offense is likely to call at least for a layoff.

## Advance Warning

To have good discipline and employees who accept disciplinary action as fair, it is absolutely essential that all employees be clearly informed in advance as to what is expected of them and what the rules are. There must be warning that a certain offense will lead to disciplinary action. Some enterprises rely on bulletin board announcements to make such warnings. These cannot be as effective, however, as a section in the handbook that all new employees receive when they start working for the institution. Along with the written statements in the handbook, it is advisable to include verbal clarification of the rules. During the induction process shortly after new employees are hired, they should be orally informed of what is expected of them and of the consequences of not living up to behavioral expectations.

In addition to the forewarning about general rules, it is essential to let the employees know in advance about the type of disciplinary action that will be taken. The various steps of disciplinary action should be clarified *before* employees could possibly become involved in an offense. There are considerable doubts, however, as to whether or not a standard penalty should be provided and stated for each offense. In other words, should there be, for example, a clear statement that falsifying attendance records will carry a one-week disciplinary layoff? Those in favor of such a list suggest that it would be an effective warning device and that it would provide greater disciplinary consistency. On the other hand, such a list would not permit management to take into consideration the various degrees of guilt and mitigating circumstances. In general, it is probably best not to provide a schedule of penalties for specific violations, but merely to state the progressive steps of disciplinary action that will be taken. It should be clearly understood that continued violations will bring about more severe penalties. Some enterprises do specify that certain serious offenses will bring the penalty of immediate discharge. For most violations, however, it is unwise to spell out a rigid set of disciplinary measures.

The practice of forewarning before taking disciplinary measures also applies to rules that have not been enforced recently. If the supervisor has not disciplined anyone who violated them for a long time, the employees do not expect these rules to be enforced in the future. Suddenly the supervisor may decide that to make a rule valid, he or she is going to make "an example of one of the employees" and take disciplinary action. Disciplinary action should not be used in this manner. Because a certain rule has not been enforced in the past does not mean that it cannot ever be enforced. What it does mean is that the supervisor must take certain steps before beginning to enforce such a rule. Instead of acting tough suddenly, the supervisor should give the employees some warning that this rule, previous enforcement of which has been lax, will be strictly enforced in the future. In such cases it is not enough to put the enforcement notice on the bulletin board. It is essential that, in addition to a clear written warning, supplemental verbal communication be given. The supervisor must explain to the subordinates, perhaps in a departmental meeting, that from the present time on he or she intends to enforce this rule.

### Consistency

A further requirement of good discipline is consistency of treatment. The supervisor must be consistent in the enforcement of discipline and in the type of disciplinary action taken. By being consistent, the supervisor sets the limit for acceptable behavior, and every individual wants to know what the limits are.

Inconsistency, on the other hand, is one of the fastest ways for a supervisor to lower the morale of the employees and lose their respect. If the supervisor is inconsistent, then the employees find themselves in an environment where they cannot feel secure. Inconsistency will only lead to anxiety, creating doubts in the employees' minds as to what they can and cannot do. At times the supervisor may be lenient and overlook an infringement. In reality, however, the supervisor is not doing the employees any favors, but only making it harder for all of them.

Mason Haire, a well-known psychologist, compares this situation to the relations between a motorist and a traffic police officer. He says that whenever we are exceeding the speed limit on the highway, we must feel some sort of anxiety, since we are breaking the rule. On the other hand, the rule is often not enforced. We think that perhaps this is a place where the police department does not take the rule seriously, and we can speed a little. There is always a lurking insecurity, however, because the motorist knows that at any time the police officer may decide to enforce the rule. Many motorists probably think that it would be easier to operate in an environment where the police would at least be consistent one way or the other. The same holds true for most employees who have to work in an environment where the supervisor is not consistent in disciplinary matters.

In addition, the supervisor faces another problem in trying to be consistent. On one hand, the supervisor has been cautioned to treat all employees alike and to avoid favoritism, whereas on the other hand, he or she has been told again and again to treat people as individuals in accordance with their special needs and circumstances. On the surface these two requirements appear to contradict each other. The supervisor must realize, however, that treating people fairly does not mean treating everyone exactly the same. What it does mean is that when an exception is made, it must be considered as a valid exception by the other members of the department. The rest of the employees will regard an exception as fair if they know why it was made and if they consider the reason to be justified. Moreover, the other employees must be confident that if any other employee were in the same situation, he or she would receive the same treatment. If these conditions are fulfilled, the supervisor has been able to exercise fair play, be consistent in discipline, and still treat people as individuals.

The extent to which a supervisor can be consistent and still consider the circumstances is illustrated as follows. Assume that three employees were engaged in horseplay at work. Conceivably the supervisor may simply have a friendly informal talk with one of the employees, who just started work a few days ago. The second employee may receive a formal or written warning, since he had been warned about horseplay before. The third employee might receive a three-day disciplinary layoff, since he had been involved in many previous cases of horseplay. All three situations must be handled with equal gravity. In deciding the penalty, however, the supervisor must take into consideration all circumstances.

### Being Impartial

Another way that a supervisor can reduce the amount of resentment and keep the damage to future relations with the subordinates at a minimum is to take disciplinary action as impartially as possible. In recalling the "red-hot-stove" rule, it is worth repeating that whoever touches the stove is burned, regardless of who he or she is. The penalty is connected with the act and not with the person. Looking at disciplinary action in this way reduces the danger to the personal relationship between the supervisor and the employee. It is the specific act that brings about the disciplinary measure, not the personality.

Keeping this in mind, the supervisor will be able to discuss the violation objectively, excluding the personal element as far as possible. The supervisor should take disciplinary action without being apologetic about the rule or about what he or she has to do to enforce it, and without showing signs of anger. Once the disciplinary action has been taken, the supervisor must let bygones be bygones. The supervisor must treat the employee as before and try to forget what happened. Understandably the person who has been disciplined will harbor some resentment, and the supervisor who meted out the discipline probably found doing it distasteful as well. Therefore, the supervisor and the employee may feel like avoiding each other for a few days. Such feelings are understandable, but it would be far more advisable for the boss to find some opportunity to show his or her previous friendly feelings toward the disciplined employee. This is easier said than done. Only the mature person can handle discipline without hostility or guilt.

## DISCIPLINE WITHOUT PUNISHMENT

Recently a number of organizations have tried to remove some of the shortcomings and resentment created by disciplinary action. In these entities it has been recognized that severe disciplinary action, such as unpaid suspensions, does not cause the desired change in behavior. It has frequently been observed that no employee comes back from an unpaid suspension feeling better about himself or herself, about the supervisor, or about the institution. Despite our discussion on how to reduce the supervisor's dilemma, many supervisors are not satisfied with a system of discipline in which they often suffer more pain than the employee who was disciplined. Frequently the supervisor is faced with hostility, apathy, martyrdom, reduced output, a decline in trust, and an uncomfortable personal relationship with a subordinate. Organizations such as healthcare institutions, with mostly white-collar professionals and highly educated technological employees, have often searched for a more palatable approach to discipline. An unpaid suspension for an operating room nurse, for example, has been deemed inappropriate by many supervisors.

For all these and other reasons, many organizations have resorted to a nonpunitive approach that is a more adult, more positive, and better way to encourage a disciplined workforce. This approach is known as *discipline without punishment*. The important feature of this concept is the *decision-making leave*. When counseling discussions have not produced the desired changes, management places the person on a one-day "decision-making leave." The institution pays the individual for the day to show the employer's desire to have him or her remain a member of the organization; this removes resentment and hostility usually produced by punitive action. The employee is then instructed to return the day following the leave with a decision either to change and stay, or to quit the job. Remaining with the institution is conditional on the individual's decision to solve the immediate problem and make a "total performance commitment" to good performance. When the employee returns to the job to announce the decision to stay, his or her supervisor expresses confidence in the individual's ability to live up to the requirements but also makes it clear that failure to do so will lead to dismissal.

The decision-making leave with pay shows the individual the seriousness of the situation and offers an opportunity for cool reflection. It puts the burden on the employee and clearly represents the institution's refusal to make the employee's career decision. This nonpunitive approach forces the individual to take responsibility for future performance and behavior. The employee also realizes that he or she is confronted with a tougher employer's response in case of failure to meet standards. The costs connected with paying the employee for the day are far less than those associated with disciplinary suspension without pay.

The use of decision-making leave has proved as powerful in the executive suite as on the nursing floor or in the clinical laboratories. The organizations that have adopted this nonpunitive approach show good results, since the responsibility for action is shifted from the supervisor to the employee. Also, the time frame changes from the past to the future. Nonpunitive discipline forces the problem employee to choose: "Become either a committed employee or a former employee."

## RIGHT OF APPEAL

In our society and legal environment an individual's wrongdoing is not judged by the accuser. The judge is not a party to the dispute between the accused and the wrongdoer. In industrial and healthcare settings, however, this is not the case. The line superior decides whether a violation has occurred, how severe it is, and what the penalty should be. If there is a union, the employee can appeal the case through a formal grievance procedure leading to binding arbitration. Nonunion organizations should also have a formal way of appealing a manager's decision because it is always possible that an individual in a position of authority might treat a subordinate unjustly. Thus, there must be a system to right such wrongs. Every enterprise must have a system of corrective justice that is concerned with maintaining a healthy organizational climate. A system for grievances must exist that will enable employees to obtain satisfaction for unjust treatment and to resolve such a conflict.

This right of appeal to higher authority should also exist in an enterprise that does not have a union. It must be possible for any employee to appeal the supervisor's decision in regard to disciplinary action. Following the chain of command, the immediate supervisor's boss would be the one to whom such an appeal would first be directed. From there, the complaining employee can usually carry the appeal procedure through various levels, ultimately to the chief executive officer of the organization as the final court of appeal. Unfortunately, in the contemporary organization, there is no system to separate the executive functions from a judicial review.

Probably all healthcare centers have provided for such an appeal procedure. However, great care must be taken that the right of appeal is a real right and not merely a formality. Some supervisors will gladly tell their subordinates that they can go to the next higher boss but will never forgive them if they do. Such statements and thinking merely indicate the supervisor's own insecurity in the managerial position. As a superior, he or she must permit the employee to take an appeal to the boss without any resentment. Sometimes the employee making the appeal may bring along a coworker or an ombudsman to plead his or her case. It is management's obligation to provide such an appeal procedure, and the supervisor must not feel slighted in the role as manager or leader of the department when it is used. Management's failure to provide an appeal procedure may even be a chief reason why employees take recourse to local, state, or federal agencies, or to unionization.

Undoubtedly, however, it requires a mature supervisor not to see some threat from appeals that go over his or her head. Such a situation should be handled tactfully by the supervisor's boss. In the course of an appeal, the disciplinary penalty imposed by the supervisor possibly may be reduced or completely removed. Under these circumstances the supervisor understandably may become discouraged and frustrated, since the boss has not backed him or her up. This usually happens in situations where doubt remains as to the actual events and where the boss cannot get two stories to coincide. In such cases the "guilty" employee normally goes free. Although this is unfortunate, it is preferable that in a few instances a guilty employee goes free instead of an innocent employee being punished. In our legal system the "accused" is presumed innocent until proven guilty, and the burden of proof is on management.

Another reason for the reversal of a decision by higher-level management is that the supervisor may have been inconsistent in the exercise of discipline or that not all the necessary facts were obtained before disciplinary action was imposed. To avoid such an unpleasant situation, the supervisor must adhere closely to all that has been said in this chapter about the exercise of positive discipline. If a supervisor is a good disciplinarian, the verdict will normally be upheld by the boss. Even if it should be reversed, this is still not too high a price to pay to guarantee justice for every employee. Without justice, a good organizational climate cannot exist.

## SUMMARY

Discipline is a state of affairs. If morale is high, discipline probably will be good, and less need will exist for the supervisor to take disciplinary action. A supervisor is entitled to assume that most of the employees want to do the right thing and that much of the discipline will be self-imposed by the employees. If the occasion should arise, however, the supervisor must know how to take disciplinary action. There is usually a progressive list of disciplinary measures, ranging from an informal talk or an oral warning to "capital punishment," namely, discharge. The supervisor should bear in mind that the purpose of such disciplinary measures is not retribution or humiliation of employees. Rather, the goal of disciplinary action is improvement in the future behavior of the subordinate in question and in the department's other members. The idea is to avoid similar violations in the future.

Nevertheless, taking disciplinary action is a painful experience for the employee as well as the supervisor. To do the best possible job, the supervisor must ensure that all disciplinary action fulfills the requirements of immediacy, forewarning, consistency, and impersonality. Moreover, the need for a good organizational climate makes it mandatory that a system of corrective justice exists, whereby any disciplinary action that an employee feels is unfair can be appealed.

# PART VII
# CONTROLLING

# *Fundamentals of Control*

## Chapter Objectives

After you have studied this chapter, you should be able to:

1. Define the managerial function of controlling.
2. Discuss different types of control systems.
3. Outline the basic requirements of a control system.

*Controls,* a term that often arouses negative connotations if it is not used properly, play an important role in the life of any organization. Everyone active in an organized activity depends on controls to make certain that the organization functions effectively. Controlling is an essential managerial function for all managers in the organization. It is the function of monitoring performance and taking corrective action when needed. Controlling is the process that checks performance against standards. Its purpose is to make certain that performance is consistent with plans; controlling ensures that the organizational and departmental goals and objectives are achieved.

The controlling function is closely related to the other four managerial functions, but it is most closely related to the planning function. When the manager performs the planning function, the direction, goals, objectives, and policies are set and become standards against which performance is checked and appraised. If deviations are found, the manager has to take corrective action, which may entail new plans and standards. This is how planning decisions affect controls and how control decisions affect plans, illustrating the circular nature of the management process.

## THE NATURE OF CONTROLLING

### Control and the Other Managerial Functions

Because the discussion of controlling comes last in this book, many readers may conclude that controlling is something that the manager does only *after* everything else has been done. This impression results from our thinking that controlling is a retrospective, or "after-the-fact," activity. That is because we often mistake inspection as control. When an activity creates a faulty service or product we expect the inspector to find the error before it negatively affects the success of the organization. However, it is much more appropriate to look at controlling as something that goes on *simultaneously* with the other functions. Although the relationship between planning and controlling is particularly close, controlling is interwoven with *all* managerial functions. The better the manager plans, organizes, staffs, and influences, the better the supervisor can perform the controlling function, and vice versa. As stated earlier, a circular relationship exists among all these functions, and their interrelatedness does not permanently place any one function first or last.

A supervisor cannot expect to have good control over the department unless sound managerial principles in pursuing the other duties are followed. Well-made plans, workable policies and procedures, a properly planned organization, appropriate delegation of authority, continuous training of employees, good instructions, and good supervision all play a significant role in the department's results. The better these requirements are fulfilled, the more effective will be the supervisor's function of controlling, and there will be less need for taking corrective action.

## ■ The Human Reactions to Control

Another important aspect of control is how people respond to it. As stated before, the word *control* often arouses negative connotations. In previous chapters we said much about work and human satisfaction; we spoke about tight versus loose supervision, delegation of authority, and on-the-job freedom in connection with motivation. Although controls are an absolute requirement in any organized activity, one must keep in mind that in behavioral terms control means placing constraints on behavior so that what people do in organizations is more or less predictable. Control systems are designed to regulate behavior, which implies loss of freedom. People react negatively to loss of freedom. The amount of control will determine how much freedom of action an individual has in performing the job. Complete absence of control, however, does not maximize an individual's perception of freedom. Some controls are needed to maximize the human perception of freedom. The reason for this is that controls not only restrict a person's behavior, but also the behavior of others toward him or her.

A certain amount of control, therefore, is essential for any organizational freedom. Neither the extremes of tight control nor complete lack of control, however, will bring about the desired organizational effectiveness. What is needed is a mixture between the two extremes that considers the amount of decentralization in the organization, management styles, motivational factors, the situation, the professional competence of the employees, etc. In other words, to arrive at the most desirable mixture of freedom and control, the manager must try to balance the goals of organizational effectiveness and individual satisfaction. These goals must be kept in mind whenever a manager is determining the degree of control.

## ■ The Supervisor and Control

The purpose of the controlling process is making certain that performance is consistent with plans, that plans and standards are being adhered to, and that proper progress is being made toward objectives. Also, if necessary, controlling means correcting any deviations. The essence of control for a supervisor is mainly the action that adjusts performance to predetermined standards if deviations from these standards occur. The supervisor is responsible for the results of the department. The manager must make certain that all functions within the department adhere to the established standards, and, if they do not, corrective action must be taken. At times, the supervisor may enlist experts within the organization for assistance in obtaining control information data and counsel. It would be inappropriate, however, for the supervisor to expect anyone else to perform the controlling function for him or her.

Planning, organizing, staffing, and influencing are the preparatory steps for getting the work done. Controlling is concerned with making certain that the work is properly executed. Without controlling, supervisors are not doing a complete job of managing. Control remains necessary whenever supervisors assign duties to subordinates, since the supervisors cannot shift the responsibility they have accepted from their own superiors. A supervisor can and must assign tasks and delegate authority, but, as stated throughout this text, responsibility cannot be delegated. Rather, the supervisor must exercise control to see that the responsibility is properly carried out.

The supervisor knows that the eventual success of the department depends on the degree of difference between what should be done and what is done. Having set up the standards of performance, the supervisor must stay informed of the actual performance through observation, reports, discussion, control charts, and other devices. The supervisor's job is to use these tools to evaluate the difference between what should be done and what is accomplished. Only then can the supervisor prescribe the necessary corrections that will bring about full compliance between the standards and the actual performance.

## ■ Anticipatory Aspect of Control

To a large degree controlling is a forward-looking function; it has *anticipatory* aspects. Management is concerned with controls that anticipate potential sources of deviation from standards. Past experience and the study of past events tell the supervisor what has taken place, and where, when, and why certain standards were not met. This enables management to make provisions so that future activities will not lead to these deviations. Unfortunately, the anticipatory aspect of controlling is not always sufficiently stressed, and often supervisors are primarily concerned with its *corrective* and *reactive* aspects. Deviations from standards are detected after they have occurred and are corrected at the point of performance, rather than anticipated.

Even if this is the case, however, the corrections will have an effect on the future. Normally, the supervisor can do little about the past. For example, if the work assigned to a subordinate for the day has not been accomplished, the controlling process cannot correct that. Some supervisors are inclined to scold the person responsible and assume that he or she was deliberately negligent. The good supervisor will look forward rather than backward. The supervisor must study the past, however, to learn what has taken place and why. This will enable him or her to take the proper steps to ensure corrective and ideally preventive action for the future.

Since control is a forward-looking function, the supervisor must discover deviations from the established standards as quickly as possible. Therefore, the supervisor's duty is to minimize the time lag between results and corrective action. For example, instead of waiting until the day is over, it is more advisable for a housekeeping supervisor to check at midday to see whether or not the work is progressing satisfactorily. Even then, the morning is already past and nothing can be done about it any longer. Although this is a painful thought to the supervisor, one cannot alter the fact that sometimes effective control must take place after the event has occurred. Such control is often unavoidable. Minimizing the time lag between results and doing something about them, however, will enable the supervisor to institute corrective action before the damage has gone too far.

## ■ Types of Control Systems

These considerations are the basis for three different types of control systems in relation to the time factor: controls that are in place before (anticipatory), during (concurrent), and after (feedback) the job is being done. Therefore we will distinguish between *anticipatory* (preventive or preemptive, preliminary or ahead of time), *concurrent* (in process, during the event, or steering), and *feedback* (reactive, post-action, after-the-process, or after-the-event) *controls.*

### Anticipatory Controls

Anticipatory controls are in place before the service activity or production starts. They anticipate potential problems and prevent their occurrence. Anticipatory control is a proactive, not a reactive, approach.

The supervisor should think through the entire process and task ahead of time and anticipate potential problems. In doing this, forward-looking control mechanisms will be built into the system, and mistakes are likely to be avoided. The purpose of preliminary controls is to anticipate and prevent mistakes by taking care of a potential malfunctioning in advance. For example, the supervisor will plan and arrange for a regular preventive maintenance program so that the equipment will not break down when needed. Another example of a preventive control is the sign on the curb of the street informing drivers that there is a two-hour parking limit.

Other examples of anticipatory controls are policies, procedures, standard practices, and rules. These are designed so that a predetermined course of action is prescribed to prevent mistakes or malfunctioning. For example, every hospital has established detailed plans and precise procedures in case of an emergency such as a fire. Disciplinary rules dealing with the problem of carrying a weapon on hospital premises constitute an anticipatory control mechanism because the rules serve as a deterrent. Other examples of preventive control mechanisms are warning signals on a piece of equipment or checklists before starting a test. Consider the extensive checklist an anesthesiologist goes through before administering anesthesia to a patient. Using this anticipatory approach to control will enable the supervisor to eliminate many of the daily crises.

## Concurrent Controls

Another group of control mechanisms are concurrent controls, which are capable of spotting problems as they occur. The purpose is to apply controls while the operations are in progress instead of waiting for the outcome. In these situations, the supervisor does not anticipate problems but monitors operations in process. For example, concurrent controls enable the supervisor to keep the quality and quantity of output standardized. There are numerous examples of concurrent control mechanisms all around the supervisor, such as simple numerical counters, automatic switches, warning signals, or even a sophisticated on-line computer system. Whenever the supervisor does not have such aids available, he or she will monitor the activities by observation and instruction, and also possibly by being helped by several other employees. Other examples of familiar concurrent control mechanisms are the fuel gauge in the car and the parking meter. As stated before, the purpose of concurrent controls covers a middle ground between anticipatory controls at the one end and feedback controls after the event, on the other end.

## Feedback Controls

A third group of control mechanisms, feedback controls, alert the supervisor after the event is completed. An example might be when the insurance company's Benefits Supervisor reviews an abandoned call report and finds callers abandoning the wait to speak to a customer service representative at the rate of 60% on Wednesday, but during the rest of the week the abandonment rate was under 10%. The feedback control system is the most widely used category. It takes place after the process is finished and the mistake or damage is done. Feedback control is the least desirable of the three alternatives. The purpose of this type of control is to improve *from* the point of damage and to prevent any future deviation and recurrence.

Feedback controls are most helpful in planning similar future activities. Examples of feedback controls are quality control, quantity of output, statistical information, opinion surveys or service surveys, and accounting reports. A common human resources feedback control is the exit interview performed with employees leaving the organization (see figure 24.1). The interview is performed to determine why the employee has chosen to look elsewhere for employment or to resign from his or her position. The feedback and information should go to the supervisor who is responsible for it and who will have to take action to improve future performances; the supervisor in turn will give as much information to the employees as possible.

Since control after the fact is the least desirable mechanism, the supervisor should make every effort to devise as many anticipatory and concurrent control mechanisms as possible. One method that has become popular of late is involving those staff members affected by the problem in discussion or brainstorming sessions to identify potential causes and solutions and then using a technique of

## EXIT INTERVIEW

The exit interview is a very effective evaluative tool used by Human Resources to ascertain controllable causes of turnover. Your comments, constructive criticism, any problems you may have incurred with the policies and procedures, salaries and benefits will assist us in future plans and programs for employees at T.C.R.H. Your remarks are confidential, for the Human Resources Department's use only and not a part of your personnel records. Thank you for your assistance and cooperation. Please return to Human Resources at the Outprocessing Procedure.

STAFF INFORMATION

Position ______________________________

Unit/Department ______________________

NEW POSITION

Company __________________

Position ____________________

Compensation _______________

COMMENTS AND SUGGESTIONS

What is the principal reason for your separation from employment?

How do you feel about T.C.R.H. as a place to work?

What constructive comments do you have to offer the Hospital regarding the overall work environment?

Were your training, skills, and experience utilized?

Did you feel you were a contributing member of the team?

Was your salary competitive for your particular position?

Were promotional opportunities available and were you informed of these opportunities?

Was your supervisor supportive in accomplishing your goals and objectives?

Would you recommend T.C.R.H. as an employer to prospective candidates? Yes _____ No _____
If not, please explain.

**Figure 24.1** An exit interview.

*"HealthSouth Treasure Coast Rehabilitation Hospital, Vero Beach, FL"*

voting that narrows the proposed solutions or actions that should be considered to a few or one. The supervisor should be able to convert many of the after-the-fact controls into on-line, during-the-process mechanisms or even to anticipatory controls with the help of up-to-date information systems and encouraging employee involvement in problem resolution. By empowering employees to take corrective action or, at a minimum, encouraging employees to contribute ideas and comments, some after-the-fact controls become unnecessary.

## ■ The Closeness of Control

Knowing how closely to control or follow up the work of a subordinate is a real test of any supervisor's talents. The closeness of follow-up from the subordinate's point of view is based on such factors as the experience, initiative, dependability, and resourcefulness of the employee who is given the assignment. Giving an employee an assignment and allowing him or her to do the job is part of the process of delegation. This does not mean, however, that the supervisor should leave the employee completely alone until it is time to inspect the final results. Delegation also does not mean that the supervisor should be "breathing down the subordinate's neck" and watching every detail. Rather, the supervisor must be familiar enough with the ability of the subordinate to determine accurately how much leeway to give and how closely to follow through with the control measures.

## BASIC REQUIREMENTS OF A CONTROL SYSTEM

For any control system to be workable and effective, it must fulfill certain basic requirements. Controls should: (1) be understandable; (2) register deviations quickly and be timely; (3) be appropriate, adequate, and economical; (4) be somewhat flexible; and (5) indicate where corrective action should be applied. These requirements are applicable to all services in all organized activities and to all levels within the management hierarchy. We will discuss them only in a general sense, since it would be impossible to spell out the specific characteristics of controls used in each department or service of a healthcare enterprise.

## ■ Understanding of Controls

The first requirement of a workable control system is that the control mechanisms must be understandable and fit the people involved, the tasks, and the environment. Both the manager and the subordinates must understand the data and what type of control is to be exercised. This is necessary on all managerial levels. The farther down the hierarchy the system is to be applied, the less complicated it should be. Thus, the top-level administrator may use a complicated system of controls based on mathematical formulas, statistical analysis, and complex computer printouts that are understandable to top-level administration. The control system for the lower supervisory level, however, should be less sophisticated. It must be designed to the level of the user. If the control system is too complicated, the supervisor will frequently have to devise his or her own control system that will fulfill the same need and will be understood by the employees as well.

## ■ Prompt Indication of Deviations

To have a workable control system, controls must indicate deviations quickly so that trends can be corrected without delay. As pointed out, controls are forward looking, and the supervisor cannot control the past. The sooner the supervisor is aware of such deviations, however, the sooner he or she can take corrective action. It is more desirable to have deviations reported quickly, even if substantiated only by partial information, approximate figures, and estimates. In other words, it is far better for the supervisor to have prompt approximate information than highly accurate information that is too late to be of much value. This does not mean that the supervisor should jump to conclusions or take corrective action hastily. The supervisor's familiarity with the job to be done, knowledge, and past experience will help him or her quickly sense when something is not progressing as planned and requires prompt supervisory action.

## ■ Appropriateness and Adequacy

Controls must always be appropriate and significant for the activity they are to monitor. Control tools that are suitable for the dietary department are different from those used in nursing. Even within nursing, the tools used by the director of nursing services are different from those the head nurse uses on the floor. An elaborate control system required in a large undertaking would not be needed in a small department; however, the need for control still exists, only the magnitude of the control system will be different. Whatever controls are applied, it is essential that they be appropriate for the job involved. They must be consistent with the organizational structure so that the person with authority to act will obtain the data.

## ■ Economics of Controls

Controls must be worth the expense involved; that is, they must be economical. At times, however, it may be difficult for management to ascertain how much a particular control system is worth and how much it really costs. One of the important criteria might be the consequences that would follow if the controls did not exist. Thus, the nurses' control of narcotics is stringent and exact, for example, whereas no one is too concerned with close control of bandages.

## ■ Flexibility

Since all undertakings work in a dynamic situation, unforeseen circumstances could play havoc even with the best-laid plans and standards. The control system must be built so that it will remain flexible. It must be designed to keep pace with the continuously changing pattern of a dynamic setting. The control system must permit change as soon as the change is required, or else it is bound to fail. If the employee seems to run into unexpected conditions early in the assignment, through no fault of his or her own, the supervisor must recognize this and adjust the plans and standards accordingly. The control system must leave room for individual judgment and changing circumstances.

## ■ Corrective Action

A final requirement of effective controls is that they must point the way to corrective action. It is not enough to show deviations as they have occurred. The system must also indicate *where* they have occurred and *who* is responsible for them. Supervisors must make it their business to know precisely where the standards were not met and who is responsible for not achieving the standard. If successive operations are involved, it may be necessary for the supervisor to check the performance after each step has been accomplished and before the work is passed on to the next employee or to another department.

---

**SUMMARY**  Controlling is the managerial function of monitoring performance; the manager checks performance against standards and takes corrective action if deviations exist. Control is most closely related to the planning function, but it is interwoven with all the other managerial functions as well. Control is essential in every organized activity, although in behavioral terms control means placing constraints on people. A good control system must be designed so that it will bring about organizational effectiveness without infringing on individual satisfaction.

In relation to the time factor, one can distinguish between anticipatory, concurrent, and feedback control mechanisms. There are several basic requirements for a control system to be effective. The supervisor must make sure that the subordinates fully understand the controls and that they are appropriate for the situation. Since control is anticipatory, a control system should be designed to report deviations as promptly as possible. Controls must also be worth the expense involved; they must be worth the effort put forth. A good control system also must provide for sufficient flexibility to cope with new situations and circumstances in a dynamic setting. Finally, a viable control system must clearly indicate where and why deviations have occurred so that the supervisor can take appropriate corrective action at the proper place.

# *The Control Process*

## Chapter Objectives

After you have studied this chapter, you should be able to:

1. Discuss the steps in the control process.
2. Review the purposes for measuring and comparing performance.
3. Describe corrective action techniques.
4. Review the basic managerial steps of setting standards, measuring performance, and taking corrective action.

**THE FEEDBACK MODEL OF CONTROLS**

The organizational control system can be viewed as a feedback model. Information on how the system is doing is obtained by the supervisor, or the sensor, who then monitors the system by comparing the actual results with the desired performance. Whenever the actual performance deviates from the standards set, the system triggers corrective action in the form of an input. (See figure 25.1.) This closed-loop feedback system works the same way a thermostat in the home functions. The thermostat is set at the desired degree of temperature. Whenever the room temperature falls below or rises above that temperature, the thermostat, continuously comparing room temperature to the desired temperature, corrects the variation by turning on or shutting off the furnace or air conditioner. This latter type of control is known as *cybernetic* because it monitors and manages a process with the help of a self-regulating mechanism.

**Figure 25.1** Closed-loop system of feedback.

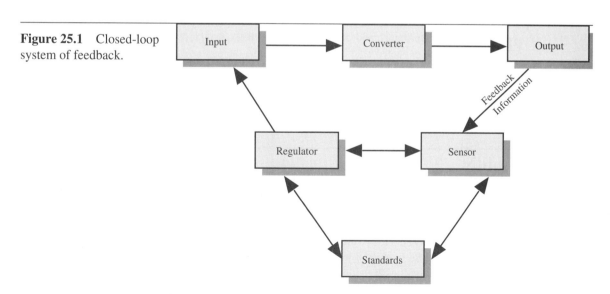

**Figure 25.2** Steps in the controlling process.

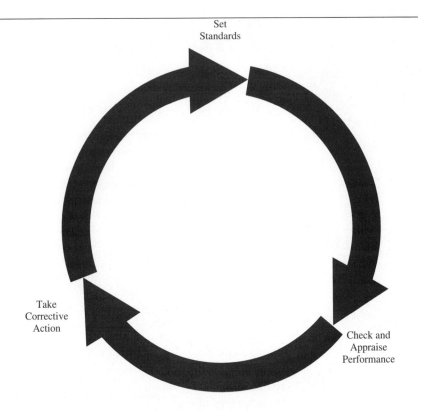

Set
Standards

Take
Corrective
Action

Check and
Appraise
Performance

## STEPS IN THE CONTROL PROCESS

In performing the controlling function, the supervisor must follow three basic steps. First, he or she sets the standards. Next, the supervisor must check and appraise performance and compare it against these standards to determine whether it meets the expected standards or not. If not, the supervisor must take corrective action, which is the third step in the controlling process. (See figure 25.2.) This sequence of steps is necessary for effective control. The supervisor could not possibly check and report on deviations without having set the standards in advance, and corrective action cannot be taken unless deviations from these standards are discovered.

## ESTABLISHING STANDARDS

The establishment of standards is the first step in the control process. Standards are criteria against which subsequent performance or results can be judged. Standards state what should be done. They are derived from organizational goals and objectives, and should be expressed in measurable terms. Control standards can be as broad or as narrow as the level to which they apply. In planning, the CEO sets the overall objectives and goals that the healthcare center is to achieve. These overall objectives are then broken down into narrower objectives for the individual divisions and departments.

The supervisor of a department establishes even more specific goals that relate to quality, quantity, costs, time standards, quotas, schedules, budgets, etc. These goals become the criteria, the standards, for exercising control. These examples are tangible; however, many standards are intangible. Although the latter are much more difficult to set and work with, a healthcare institution has to consider many intangible standards, especially concerning patient care. Let us look at both types of standards in more detail.

## ■ Tangible Standards

The most common tangible standards are physical standards that pertain to the actual operation of a department in which goods are produced (e.g., the dietary department) or services are rendered (e.g., nursing services, laboratories, and laundry). Physical standards define the amount of work to be produced within a given time span. Cost standards define direct and indirect labor costs, costs of the materials and supplies used, overhead, and many other items.

These standards are quantitative and qualitative. Not only do they define, for example, how much money can be spent per patient on food, supplies, and materials for three meals a day, but they also state what quality these meals are to have as far as nutritional values, taste, and aesthetic appeal are concerned. Likewise, there are standards on how much one pound of laundry should cost and how many pounds are to be processed in a certain time, taking into consideration the state of mechanization and automation of the laundry. Furthermore, the laundry will have qualitative standards as to sanitation and sterilization, cleanliness of the linens, color, and absence of stains. In another example, standards specify the number of nursing personnel on a floor in relation to the number of patients to be cared for. Such standards vary depending on the time of day, the nursing unit in question (e.g., an intensive care unit versus a regular floor unit), and many other factors. Standards also exist for the patient's comfort, physical needs, and safety and for the room's cleanliness and orderliness.

In setting standards, the supervisor is aided by experience and knowledge of the various jobs to be done within the department. A supervisor has a general idea of how much time it takes to perform a certain job, what resources are required, what constitutes a good quality of performance, and what is a poor job. Job knowledge and experience are the resources the supervisor uses to establish the standards against which to judge the performance and results of the department.

### Motion and Time Studies

There are also better, more scientific and systematic ways of establishing objective standards. In some activities the supervisor can call on industrial engineers who will use work-measurement techniques to help determine the amount of work an average employee should turn out within a given time period. There are many departments in a healthcare center, such as housekeeping, laundry, laboratories, dispatch office, dietary service, and possibly nursing services, where this approach is worth the effort and cost. Standards arrived at through work-measurement techniques help the supervisor distribute the work more evenly and judge fairly whether an employee is performing satisfactorily.

The supervisor, however, rarely conducts work-measurement analyses. They are usually assigned to an industrial engineer or perhaps to an outside consultant trained in doing motion and time studies. *Motion study* involves an analysis of the elements of the job and of how the job is currently performed with a view to changing, eliminating, or combining certain steps and devising a method that will be quicker and easier. Often flowcharts are drawn up that analyze the steps taken in performing the jobs; the workplace layout may be redesigned and hand motions revamped. After a thorough analysis of the motions and work-flow arrangements, the engineer will come up with what is considered the "best method" for doing the job in question.

Once the best method has been designed, *time studies* are then performed to find out the standard time required to do the job using this method. One or more qualified workers are timed with a stopwatch as they perform the prescribed work methods. Time studies are done scientifically and systematically by selecting an average employee for observation, measuring the times used for the various elements of the job, applying leveling and other corrective factors, and making allowances for fatigue, personal needs, contingencies. delays, etc. The combined result then leads to a standard time necessary to perform the job. Although this method is rather scientific, one must keep in mind that considerable judgment and many approximations will be used to arrive at the standard time. There is still the need for decisions involving judgment and discretion. Standard times, however, are a sound basis on which to determine objective standards. They also enable the supervisor to predict the number of employees required and the probable cost of the job to be done. In many activities outside the healthcare field, standards of this type serve as a basis for cost estimates and incentive plans.

If industrial engineers are not available, the supervisor can perform some of the studies simply by observing and timing the various operations and making the necessary adjustments previously stated. If the job to be performed in the department has never been done there before, the supervisor should try to base tentative standards on similar operations. If the new job has no similarity to any previous function, then the best the supervisor can do—unless the help of industrial engineers is available—is to observe the operation while it is being performed for the first few times. The supervisor will have to make approximate time and motion studies to arrive at a standard for the new function. Sometimes the manufacturer of a new piece of equipment can be helpful to the supervisor in providing standard data, for example, how long it will take an apparatus to perform a certain task.

## TIME LADDERS

Another approach to collecting data on productivity is the time ladder. This technique requires the employee to note what he or she does during 5-, 10-, or 15-minute increments of time throughout a day for several days. Employees who perform the same duties maintain separate ladders. The data tells the manager the average number of units one produces in a day and the types of interferences

**Observation Record for
Health Information Management Services**

| | Jane Super-visor | Lori Tran-scribe | Tara Tran-scribe | Susan Tran-scribe | Larry File Clerk | Kent File Clerk | Kim Coder | Mel Coder | John Coder | Totals |
|---|---|---|---|---|---|---|---|---|---|---|
| Supervisory activities | | | | | | | | | | |
| Technical (non-supervisory duties) | | | | | | | | | | |
| Transcribing | | | | | | | | | | |
| Handling transcribed work | | | | | | | | | | |
| Filing records | | | | | | | | | | |
| Sorting records | | | | | | | | | | |
| Pulling records | | | | | | | | | | |
| Coding | | | | | | | | | | |
| Abstracting | | | | | | | | | | |
| Idle, gone, non-productive activities | | | | | | | | | | |
| Totals | | | | | | | | | | |

Date of this sampling:
Observation Times:
1.        4.        7.        10.
2.        5.        8.        11.
3.        6.        9.        12.

**Figure 25.3**   Example of observation record form.

that an employee encounters, as well as nonproductive time (restroom visits, breaks, etc.). The method places the burden of data collection on the employee, but requires the supervisor to validate some of the data through other techniques such as direct observation.

## WORK SAMPLING THROUGH DIRECT OBSERVATION

In the direct observation approach, supervisors periodically observe employees and note whether they are working, what they are working on, or whether they are idle (including utilizing nonproductive time). The supervisor maintains a log that lists the employees along one axis and the key activities along the other. An example of the Observation Record Form is shown figure 25.3.

"Tick" marks are made during each observation, marking the activity the employee is performing at the time of the observation. Each observation is usually brief (10–15 minutes total) depending on the number of employees in the work area, the size of the work area, and whether the supervisor must walk around to adequately observe the staff. The observations occur several times a day (sampling).

Since the observation times are randomly selected, they could occur at virtually any time during the workday. After several days of the observation sampling, there will be adequate data to indicate what percent of the time employee X was engaged in each of his/her key activities, and so forth for each employee observed. This information provides the manager comparative information against which to compare production data. One might expect that if Kent files an average of 100 records a day and Larry files 250 a day and performs a comparable amount of sorting and pulling as Kent, that Larry may have a better method of doing his work. If so, the manager will want Larry to show Kent this method. Alternatively, the standard could be set at 250 and Kent would be encouraged to model Larry to achieve the standard.

Although they may not be absolutely scientific, standards are more likely to be effective if they are set with the participation of the supervisor and the subordinates instead of being handed down by a staff engineer, a manager, or an outside consultant. The purpose of any standard is to establish a specific goal for the employees to strive toward, and, as with all directives, employees are likely to be more motivated to achieve those standards in which they have had some part. Further, none of the above methods should be utilized without advising the staff in advance that the analysis is planned. Employee morale could be affected negatively if they feel they are being watched and do not know why.

## ■ Intangible Standards

In addition to tangible standards that can be expressed in physical terms, there are also standards of an intangible nature. In a hospital or related healthcare facility, some intangible standards are the institution's reputation in the community, the quality of medicine practiced, the excellence of patient care, and the degree of "tender loving care," including attention to the patients' psychological needs, and the level of morale of the employees. It is exceedingly difficult, if not impossible, to express the criteria for such intangible standards in precise and numerical terms. It is much simpler to measure performance against tangible standards, such as number of nursing personnel in relation to the number of patients.

Nevertheless, a supervisor should not overlook the intangible achievements even if it is difficult to set standards for them and measure their performance. Tools for appraising some of these intangible standards are being developed in the form of attitude surveys, questionnaires, and interviews. Although these tools are not exact, they should be helpful in determining to what extent certain intangible standards are being achieved. They also provide the manager with a sketch of the customers' expectations or perception of service quality. When patient questionnaires are returned indicating that the housekeeping service was poor, yet the housekeeping supervisor knows the room was cleaned daily, then it may be necessary to take other actions. Such actions might include having the housekeeper ask the patient before leaving the room what he or she found unacceptable.

## ■ How to Select Strategic Standards

The number of standards that can be used to ascertain the quality and quantity of performance within a department is very large and increases rapidly as the department expands. As the operations within the department become more sophisticated and complex and the functions of the department increase, it will become more difficult and time consuming for supervisors to check against all the conceivable standards. Therefore, they will need to concentrate on certain standards by selecting some of them as the *strategic* ones, those that best reflect the goals and whether they are being met.

For example, a billing manager making the rounds knows which strategic points to check first. She or he probably checks the bill lag or accounts receivable report and makes certain that the lag between discharge and bill drop has not lengthened, the accounts receivable are within expected limits, and the that the lag between discharge and coding has not significantly changed. She or he also observes where the billing personnel are and what they are doing. Each of these areas constitutes a strategic point of control for the billing manager. Unfortunately, there are no specific guidelines on how to select these strategic control points. The peculiarities of each departmental function and the makeup of the supervisor and employees will be different in each situation. Thus, only general guidelines can be suggested for selecting strategic standards.

One of the first considerations in choosing one standard as more strategic than another is *timeliness*. Since time is essential in control and controls are anticipatory, the earlier the deviation can be discovered, the better. This will help to correct problems early before errors begin to compound. Keeping this in mind, the supervisor can determine at what point in time and in the process activities should be checked. For example, in the maintenance department, the strategic control point may be after a crack has been repaired, but before it has been repainted.

Another consideration in choosing strategic control points is that they should permit *economic observations*. In chapter 24, we pointed out that a control system must be worth the expense involved; it must be economical. The same applies to the strategic control points. A further consideration is that the strategic standards should provide for *comprehensive and balanced control*. The supervisor must be aware that the selection of one strategic control point might have an adverse effect on another. Excessive control on the quantity of achievements often has an adverse effect on the quality. On the other hand, if expenses are selected as a strategic control point, the quality or quantity of the output may suffer. For example, the executive housekeeper must not sacrifice quality standards that have been designed to prevent infections in order to cut expenses. All these decisions will depend on the nature of the work within the department. What serves well as a strategic control point in one activity will not necessarily apply in another.

A supervisor may find it simpler to choose among many strategic control point options by prioritizing the options to monitor by identifying those that represent a majority of the work performed in the department (Pareto Principle described in chapter 19), those that, if not monitored, could place the department or organization at risk, and those that could affect the safety or security of the organization, its resources or assets, its staff, or patients. For example, the following is a list of strategic control options available for the Administrator of Small Town Hospital. Small Town is located in an agricultural community:

Number of patients hospitalized
Number of patients scheduled for surgery
Satisfaction of patients on 2 West
Satisfaction of patients on 2 South
Number of meals served by Dietary
Cash taken in today
Accounts receivable today
Cleanliness of the floor
Cleanliness of the parking lot
Number of nurses on duty
Number of magazines in the "to read" pile
Whether more than 5 volunteers are working in the gift shop
Inservices occurring throughout the hospital
Physicians in the hospital visiting their patients
Type of insurance each patient has today
Legislative action planned at the state capitol
Current corn price
Current cattle price
etc.

This Administrator has a number of variables he or she could monitor as strategic control points but many of the above neither do not our criteria. However, knowing the number of patients the hospital will serve in that day and whether there is adequate staff (nurses) to tend to the patients' needs may be two, while the accounts receivable and cash taken in may be two others. The first set of control points addresses services that represent the majority of services performed, while the second set speak to protecting the hospital's assets.

## ■ Standards and Individual Responsibility

For control to have an effective influence on performance, the supervisor must make certain that the goals and standards are known to all the employees within the department. The supervisor must clarify who is responsible for the achievement of standards so that he or she knows who to contact for deviations if the results are not achieved and who to praise if they are exceeded. After all, the supervisor is interested in having the standards and objectives reached. Only if each employee knows exactly what is expected concerning his or her own work can the subordinate try to achieve it. This is why the supervisor must link the standards with the individual responsibilities of each employee.

| **CHECKING ON PERFORMANCE** | ## Measuring and Comparing |

The second step in the process of control is to check on actual performance and compare measured performance against the standards. Observing and measuring performance is an ongoing activity for every manager. Work is observed, output is measured, and reports are compiled. Such checking activities are usually carried on by the supervisor after the subordinate has completed the function. Since the supervisor does not shift responsibility when assigning a duty to a subordinate and when delegating authority, he or she must make certain that enough controls are available to take corrective action in case the performance does not meet the standards.

There are several ways for a supervisor to *check on performance and measure:* (1) comparing performance with standards, (2) directly observing the work and personally checking on the employees, or (3) studying various summaries of reports and figures that are submitted to the supervisor.

### Comparing

As the manager observes and measures performance, the measured performance must be *compared* with the standards developed in the beginning of the control process. Such comparisons are an ongoing activity of the supervisor daily, weekly, and monthly. The observed performance may be higher, the same, or lower than the standards. In the first two situations, the supervisor obviously does not have any problems. If the performance does not meet standards, however, corrective action is required.

Since some deviation is expected in some activities, the question is how much deviation is acceptable before taking remedial action. This will depend on the activity; in some activities minor deviations may be acceptable. In other activities, such as nursing, deviations can be critical, and even a small one may not be tolerated. Furthermore, in some activities it is easy to measure performance, as in controlling sales and production; in other activities, as in many healthcare activities, measuring performance is not easy and comparisons are sometimes less clear-cut. (See the discussion on performance appraisal in chapter 18.) However, it is the supervisor's job to develop valid performance measures to control effectively and take corrective action when necessary.

### Direct Personal Observation

Observation is probably the most widely used technique for measurement. There is no better way for a supervisor to check performance than by direct observation and personal contact. Unfortunately personal observation is time consuming, but every manager should spend part of each day away from the desk observing the performance of the employees. For example, regular rounds are not only necessary for the head nurse; they are just as important for the director of housekeeping, the chief dietician, and the hospital administrator.

The nursing home administrator may make rounds in the resident areas less frequently, but even he or she should make some personal observations. For the supervisor, direct observations are the most effective way of maintaining close contact with employees as a part of their constant training and development. This opportunity for close personal observation is one of the great advantages of the supervisor's job; it is something that the top-level administrator cannot do to any great extent. The farther removed a manager is from the firing line, the less he or she will be able to observe personally and the more he or she will have to depend on reports.

Whenever supervisors observe their employees at work, they should assume a questioning attitude and not necessarily a fault-finding one. Supervisors should not ignore mistakes, but the manner in which they question is essential. They should ask themselves whether or not there is any way in which they could help the employees do the job better, more easily, safely, or efficiently. They should notice the way the employee is going about the job, whether it is up to par or substandard. Such observations can check specific areas, such as inadequate patient care, lack of orderliness, not meeting the physical needs of the patient, sloppy work, or poorly performed jobs. At times it may be difficult to convince an employee that his or her work is unsatisfactory. If reference can be made to concrete cases, however, it is not easy for the subordinate to deny that they exist. It is essential for the supervisor to make specific observations because without being specific, one cannot realistically appraise performance and take appropriate corrective action.

As stated, measuring performance through direct personal observation has some shortcomings; it is time consuming and means being away from the desk and office. Some other limitations also exist. The employee may perform well while the boss is around but drop back to a lower-level performance shortly after the boss is out of sight. Furthermore, it may be difficult to observe some of the activities at a critical time. Also, the supervisor should make an effort to see what is really happening and not only what he or she wants to see. Still, direct observation is practiced widely and is probably the best way of checking performance.

### Reports

Written reports, with or without oral presentation, and oral reports are good means of checking on performance if a department operates twenty-four hours a day, seven days a week, or if it is large or operates in different locations. When a department operates around the clock and one supervisor is responsible for it twenty-four hours each day of the week, this person depends on reports to cover those shifts during which he or she is absent. Even with reports, the supervisor should get to work a little earlier and stay a little later in the day so that there is some overlap with the night supervisor in the morning and with the afternoon supervisor later in the day. This gives the supervisors a chance to add some spoken explanations to their written reports. Reports should be clear, complete, concise, and correct. They must be brief but still include all the important aspects.

As the departmental supervisor checks these reports, he or she probably will find many activities that have been performed up to standard. The supervisor should concentrate on the *exceptions,* namely, those areas where the performance significantly deviates from the standard. Only the exceptions require the supervisor's attention. In fact, if the supervisor depends on reports from the various shifts, the subordinates may have been requested not to send data on those activities that have reached the preestablished standards, but to report only on those items that do not meet the standards or exceed them. In this way, the supervisor can concentrate all his or her efforts on the problem areas. This is known as practicing the *exception principle.* In such situations, however, a climate of trust must exist between the supervisor and subordinates so that they can freely report the deviations. Subordinates should know that the boss has full confidence in the rest of their activities even though there is no report on them.

If the supervisor does depend on reports for information, it is essential that they are reviewed immediately after they are received and that action is taken without delay when needed. It is demoralizing to send reports to a supervisor who does not even read them.

The nature of healthcare activities calls for reports that are accurate, complete, and correct, especially when patient care is involved. In all other areas as well, most employees will submit truthful reports, even if they are unfavorable to the employee. Much will depend on their relationships and the supervisor's reaction. The supervisor must check into the matter and correct any shortcomings. As long as the supervisor handles these reports constructively, stressing their honesty, the employees will continue to submit reliable reports instead of "stretching the truth." The supervisor must remember the importance of upward communication, and this is one opportunity to keep the channel open and flowing. (See chapter 5.)

## TAKING CORRECTIVE ACTION

The third stage in the control model is taking corrective action. If there are no deviations of performance from the established standards, then the supervisor's process of controlling is fulfilled by the first two steps—setting standards and checking performance. If a significant and worthwhile discrepancy or variation is found, however, the controlling function is not fulfilled until and unless the third step, appropriate corrective action, is taken. If the deviation is minor and acceptable and within a noncritical activity, it may be appropriate to do nothing except call it to the employee's attention and maintain the status quo. As always, data must be examined as quickly as possible after the observations are made so that timely corrective action can be taken to curb undesirable results and bring performance back into line.

The supervisor must first make a careful analysis of the facts and look for the reasons behind the deviations. This must be done before any specific corrective action can be prescribed. The supervisor must bear in mind that the performance standards were based on certain prerequisites, forecasts, and assumptions and that some of these may have been faulty or may not have materialized. A check on the discrepancy may also point out that the trouble was not caused by the employee in whose work it showed up, but in some preceding activity. For instance, a patient's infection might not be caused by the nursing activities or conditions on the nursing floor, but rather by conditions or actions in the recovery room or the surgical suite. In such a situation, the corrective action must be directed toward the real source. In this case the corrective action would emanate from the nursing director's office, assuming that the latter is the common line superior to all the departments concerned.

The supervisor might also discover that a deviation may be caused by an employee who is not qualified or who has not been given the proper directions and instructions. If the employee is not qualified, additional training and supervision might help, but in other cases finding a replacement might be in order. In a situation where directions have not been given properly and the employee was not well enough informed of what was expected of him or her, it is the supervisor's duty to explain again the standards required.

Only after a thorough analysis of the reasons for a deviation has been made will the supervisor be in a position to take appropriate corrective action concerning the employee in question. Again, it is not sufficient merely to find the deviation; controlling means to correct the situation. The supervisor must decide what remedial action is necessary to secure improved results in the future. Corrective action may require revising the standards, a simple discussion, a reprimand or other disciplinary action, transferring or even replacing certain employees, or devising better work methods. Corrective action, however, is not the final step. The supervisor must follow up and study the effect of each corrective action on future control. With further study and analysis the supervisor may find that additional or different measures may be required to produce the desired results, keep operations on line, or get them back on track.

## BENCHMARKING

A relatively new approach to improving an organization's operational performance is to identify another similar organization that seems to be performing better, visiting with the managers at that organization and discussing how they are able to achieve optimal performance. This process is known as *benchmarking*. Using the wisdom of the optimally performing organization, the managers can attempt to implement the same or similar practices at their own entity and hopefully experience some improvement in performance.

Benchmarking can begin at a macro level by comparing one's key statistics to those published by local, regional, or national organizations. (See figure 25.4.)

If your organization is a non-teaching institution and your case mix is substantially lower than those reported, the source of the survey may be contacted for further information, or you can convene a performance improvement team to evaluate the situation. Now look at figure 25.5.

This chart provides percentiles to better allow you to compare your facility's individual performance to those participating in the survey. Regardless of whether you compare your organization to those reporting in figure 25.4 or figure 25.5, it may result in the same final outcome—appointing an assessment team.

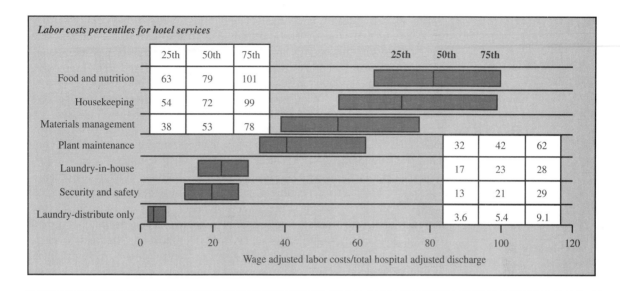

**Figure 25.4**   Example of benchmarking data.

*Reprinted, by permission, from* Using Operational Benchmark Data for Strategic Cost Management. *Copyright 1996 by the* HEALTHCARE FINANCIAL MANAGEMENT ASSOCIATION.

**Relationship between hospital characteristics and labor costs**

| Quadrant | Licensed beds | Average net operating revenue* per adjusted † discharge | Average net operating margin per adjusted discharge | Average all player case mix index | Average paid FTE per adjusted occupied bed | Average paid labor hours per adjusted discharge | Average percent net managed care revenue to net operating revenue |
|---|---|---|---|---|---|---|---|
| *Teaching hospitals* | | | | | | | |
| I | 487 | $7,041 | $543 | 1.30 | 4.72 | 162 | 56.19 |
| II | 481 | $11,381 | $218 | 1.52 | 6.05 | 231 | 38.94 |
| III | 611 | $9,388 | $500 | 1.33 | 6.17 | 250 | 50.27 |
| IV | 609 | $11,931 | $304 | 1.41 | 6.58 | 267 | 46.07 |
| Overall | 552 | $9,716 | $412 | 1.37 | 5.81 | 224 | 49.41 |
| *Non-teaching hospitals* | | | | | | | |
| I | 226 | $4,533 | $240 | 1.11 | 4.36 | 127 | 62.76 |
| II | 252 | $5,966 | $224 | 1.15 | 4.80 | 138 | 64.30 |
| III | 340 | $5,315 | $420 | 1.07 | 4.63 | 153 | 54.24 |
| IV | 294 | $6,875 | $94 | 1.10 | 5.01 | 166 | 50.85 |
| Overall | 273 | $5,600 | $236 | 1.11 | 4.68 | 145 | 58.11 |

*"Net operating revenue" excludes interest income. †"Adjusted" factor = total operating revenue/impatient revenue.*

**Figure 25.5**   Example of benchmarking data.

*Reprinted, by permission, from* Using Operational Benchmark Data for Strategic Cost Management. *Copyright 1996 by the* HEALTHCARE FINANCIAL MANAGEMENT ASSOCIATION.

This modeling effort, known as benchmarking, is really the seeking of "best practices" so that your organization remains competitive in the marketplace. However, as with any activity that may require reorganizing or possibly reengineering, the customer must always be considered first and your employees should always be involved in assessing the situation.

## SUMMARY

In performing the controlling function, the manager should follow three basic steps: (1) standards must be set, (2) performance must be measured and compared with standards, and (3) corrective action must be taken if necessary. In setting standards, the supervisor must be aware of both the tangible and intangible aspects. Many of the tangible standards can be established with the help of motion and time studies. It is much more difficult, however, to establish standards for intangible aspects of performance. Moreover, since the number of both types of standards is so large, the supervisor is the most qualified person in the department to determine which are the strategic control points. After establishing the strategic standards, the supervisor's function is to check and measure performance against them. In some instances the supervisor will have to depend on reports, but in most cases direct personal observation is the best means for appraising performance. If discrepancies from standards are revealed, the supervisor must take corrective action to bring matters back into line.

# Budgetary and Other Control Techniques

A budget is a written plan expressed in figures and numerical terms, primarily in dollars and cents, that extends for a specific time. It sets the standards to be met. The budget is the most widely used control device not only in healthcare centers, but for all phases of all other organized activities. Budgetary control is an extremely effective managerial tool, whether the manager is the chief financial officer (CFO) of an HMO or the supervisor of a department. For this reason it is essential that every manager learn how to plan budgets, live within their boundaries, and use them properly for control purposes. Of all available control devices, the budget, especially the expense budget, is probably the one the supervisor is most familiar with and has been coping with for the longest time.

As pointed out in chapter 7, budget making is a planning function, but its administration is part of the controlling function. Budgets are preestablished standards to which operations are compared and, if necessary, adjusted by the exercise of control. In other words, a budget is a means of control insofar as it reflects the progress of the actual performance against the plan. In so doing, the budget provides information that enables the supervisor to take action, if needed, to make results conform with the plan.

## THE NATURE OF BUDGETING AND BUDGETARY CONTROL

When all aspects of the institution's operations are covered by budgets and when all departmental budgets are consolidated into an overall budget, the enterprise practices *comprehensive* budgeting. When there is a budget only for specific activities, such as central/sterile supply or laboratories, it is called *partial* budgeting. Most enterprises practice comprehensive budgeting, including the overall budget for the organization and many subordinate budgets for the various divisions and departments.

Whereas the overall budget is of great concern to the CEO and the board of directors, the supervisor is mainly involved with the departmental budget, although overall budget considerations do have their effects on every departmental budget. The term *budgetary control* refers to the use of budgets to control the department's daily operations so that they will conform with the goals and standards set by the institution. Budgetary control goes beyond merely evaluating results in relation to established goals. Such control also involves taking corrective action where and when needed.

## ■ Numerical Terms

The budget states the anticipated results in specific numerical terms. Although the terms are ultimately monetary, at first not all budgets are expressed in dollars and cents. Many budgets are stated in nonfinancial numerical terms, such as labor hours, hours per adjusted patient day, quantities of supplies, operations per operating room (OR), bills per hour, or lab tests per diagnostic related group (DRG). Personnel budgets indicate the number of workers needed for each type of skill required, the number of hours allocated to perform certain activities, and so on. Although budgets may start out with numerical terms other than monetary values, ultimately every nonfinancial budget must be translated into dollars and cents. This is the common denominator for all activities of an organization, which is why one normally thinks of a budget as a plan expressed in monetary terms.

## ■ Improved Planning

Making a budget, whether it is financial or otherwise, leads to improved planning. For budgetary purposes, it is not sufficient just to make a general statement. One must quantify, date, and state specific plans in a budget. A considerable difference exists between making a general forecast on one hand and attaching numerical values to specific plans on the other. The figures in the budget are the actual plans that will become the standard of achievement. The plans are then no longer merely predictions. Rather, they are the basis for daily operations and are viewed as standards to be met.

---

## MAKING THE BUDGET

A complete budgetary program requires the involvement of all levels of management; it requires serious and honest considerations. Rigorous budgetary thinking is certain to improve the quality of organizational planning. Indeed, participation by all the managers and supervisors who will be affected by the various budgets is a prerequisite for their successful administration. Again, this is important because it is natural for people to resent arbitrary orders. Thus, it is imperative that all budget allowances and objectives are determined with the full cooperation of those who are responsible for executing them. In all the following remarks we assume that the institution practices what is typically known as traditional budgeting (later in this chapter zero base budgeting will be discussed).

# ■ Participation in Traditional Budgeting

As stated, the supervisor who must function under the departmental budget should play a significant role in preparing it. This increases the reliability, accuracy, and acceptance of the budget; the supervisor is closest to the activity, understanding all the elements going into the budget. He or she should be requested to submit a proposed budget and participate in what is commonly known as *grassroots budgeting*.

For example, as the fiscal year draws to a close, the supervisor of the operating rooms should sit down and gather together those figures that will make up next year's budget. In this endeavor the supervisor might need the help and assistance of his or her immediate line superior, in this case most likely the director of nursing services. The supervisor must gather all available information on past performance, expenses, salaries of nursing personnel, other wages, supplies, maintenance, etc. Then the supervisor should think of new developments, such as increases in wages, the increased costs of supplies, and additional personnel, before he or she can prepare an intelligent and realistic budget.

The full responsibility for preparing the budget does not lie with the supervisor alone. It is the administrator's and every upper-level manager's duty to work on budgets. They in turn, together with the controller's and accounting department's assistance and printouts, will give the departmental supervisor much information on past performance and future industry projections. The supervisor will use such information to substantiate future estimates and proposals in a free exchange of opinions with the line superior. After both reach a certain level of agreement, the line boss will then carry the overall departmental budget to higher administration.

For example, let us assume that the director of environmental services supervises three different areas of activity: housekeeping, dietary, and plant maintenance. The supervisors of each of these three activities work out their departmental budgets and discuss and substantiate them fully with the director of environmental services. Then the director combines all three inputs and comes up with a proposed budget for the entire environmental services division. This budget is submitted and discussed with top-level administration or whomever is the immediate line superior. Ultimately the final budget is adjusted and set by top-level administration. Its effectiveness is ensured, however, since true grassroots participation has taken place.

Such participation does not mean that the suggestions of the supervisors should or will always prevail. A careful and thorough analysis and study of the figures will be necessary. There should be a full discussion between the supervisor and the line superior, and the supervisor should have ample opportunity to be heard and to substantiate his or her case. The budget suggestions of subordinate supervisors will not be accepted if the superior believes the figures are unrealistic, incorrect, or inadequate. One of the shortcomings of broad participation is that the budget is loose.

Some subordinates are inclined to suggest budgets at levels that they hope to achieve without too much effort. This is obviously done for self-protection and because the supervisor wants to play it safe. The supervisor rationalizes that by setting the estimates of expenses high enough, he or she can be sure to stay within the allocated amount and will be praised if he or she stays well below the budget. This, however, defeats the purpose of grassroots budgeting. In a facility using TQM (Total Quality Management), to support the total trust environment and reduce the focus on the bottom line, management staff do not prepare budgets, thus over-budgeting is avoided and the quality of the product and/or service is emphasized. But in those facilities following traditional management methods, the line superior should remind the supervisor that the purpose of budget participation is to arrive at realistic budgets. The superior should explain that favorable and unfavorable variances will be carefully scrutinized and that the supervisor's managerial rating will depend, among other factors, on how realistic a budget proposal he or she submits. Many discussions will be needed before the budget is completed and brought to top-level administration for final approval.

## TYPES OF BUDGETS

Most budgets are for a period of one year. These are usually submitted at one time approximately three to four months prior to the year the budget takes effect. However, some organizations have established *rolling budget* approaches. Under this approach, the manager initially prepares the twelve months as he or she would in the traditional approach. When the first month of the new budget ends, the manager projects that month's budget for the following year. As the second month of the new budget ends, the manager projects the second month for the next year, and so on. This allows budget planning to occur every month rather than experiencing a massive flurry of work during a few weeks of the year.

While many organizations are steering away from what is known as *historical budgets*, they do exist. Under this approach, the amounts expended the prior year are increased by a certain inflation factor (or in some cases, decreased). The adjusted amounts become the manager's new budget. This approach does not consider one-time purchases and encourages managers to always spend their budgets.

### ■ Zero Base Budgeting

So far this discussion on budgeting has mostly referred to traditional, or conventional, budgeting. As demonstrated, under traditional budgeting management focuses its attention on planned changes from the previous year's level of expenditures.

Conventional budgeting involves projections for the following year based on current expenditures and the previous annual budget. This is often referred to as *incremental budgeting*. Although considerable effort goes into the development of these budgets, the most critical and analytical attention by top-level management is devoted to the year-over-year increment; the base is treated as though it were already authorized and requires no review.

This method assumes that the activities making up the historical base: (1) are essential, (2) must be continued, (3) are being performed effectively in a cost-efficient manner, (4) are more needed than new programs, and (5) will continue to be necessary and effective next year. Although some activities meet all these criteria, it is unrealistic to assume that for the new year all of them will. Furthermore, another potential problem exists—wasteful expenditures. If the department incurs less costs than budgeted, the department may try to spend the money even if there is no real need. Although this is reprehensible and not excusable, the fear of "losing" the money is great if the new budget is influenced by the current level of expenditures. Another potential shortcoming arises when a department that is currently operating efficiently is faced with an across-the-board edict to cut budget requests by a certain percentage. This penalizes the efficient supervisor, whereas it rewards the inefficiently run department.

Because of these limitations and the recent emphasis on cost containment, a need for better budgeting techniques has become more important. *Zero base budgeting* is a contemporary approach to budgeting. It was developed in early 1970 in industrial settings and then quickly introduced into state and federal government agencies. Today many major corporations are using zero base budgeting, and more and more healthcare institutions are introducing it. The increasing number of healthcare settings using zero base budgeting is due to changing healthcare priorities, constrained financial resources, changing technologies, available computer capabilities, and the emphasis on cost containment in particular.

Under zero base budgeting nothing is taken for granted; the budget for the new period ignores the previous budget. Every activity submitted for funding must be justified. This approach requires substantiation and justification of each budget item from the ground up. Zero base budgeting gives administration an excellent opportunity to reassess all activities, departments, and projects in terms of their benefits and costs to the organization. The great advantage is that each "package" has to be planned anew and costs are calculated from scratch; this avoids the tendency to look only at changes from the previous period. Ongoing programs are reviewed and have to be justified in their entirety.

Without going into details of zero base budgeting, in general terms the process involves seven steps. The first step is to define the *outputs* or *services* provided by the program/departmental area, such as correspondence or transcription services by the health information department. The second step is to determine the *costs* of these services or outputs, for example cost for transcribing home health notes for the home health service. Third, one identifies options for *reducing* the cost through *changes* in outputs or services, such as use of an outside contract transcription service. In the fourth step, the manager identifies options for producing the services and outputs more *efficiently.* In our example, the notes may be typed on self-adhesive sheets to allow the home health staff to stick the notes on the patient record in chronological order. The fifth step requires *determining the cost savings* associated with operations identified in steps three and four. The sixth step is assessing the risks, both qualitative and quantitative, associated with the identified options of steps three and four, for example, asking if the contract service will be timely. Last, the manager will select and implement those options with an acceptable cost/risk relationship.

All budgeting systems have some limitations, and zero base budgeting is no exception. The additional time necessary for budget preparation and the large amount of paperwork, especially in the initial implementation year may be viewed as offsetting the benefits. In subsequent years, however, the process will take much less time as managers become familiar with it. In the long run, the benefits of zero base budgeting seem to far outweigh the additional work and expenditures involved. Just as each item in the budget has been examined and justified by the benefits projected, the new procedure will be fully justified and worth its costs and efforts.

## DOING YOUR HOMEWORK TO PREPARE THE BUDGET

Many years ago the author was taught the three "P's" approach to preparing and promoting your budget: Preapproach, Proof, and Publication. The processes involved are:

### Preapproach

1. Identify demands for your services. Determine who your customers are and assess whether they are growing in number or declining. Are there other potential customers?
2. Evaluate your facility's economic climate. Discuss this with peer supervisors, other departments, the fiscal director, etc.
3. Locate internal competition for funds. Consider those departments that are providing similar services or planning to do so.
4. Establish a set of realistic budget expectations. If the patient activity is declining 10% do not submit a budget requesting 15% more resources.
5. Always start your budget preparation a year in advance. Do not wait until the notice arrives on your desk to begin data collection and budget preparation.

### Proof

1. Provide details and sources of estimates for your budget estimates.
2. Present past performance. How well have you achieved budget expectations in the past? How successful have you been in implementing new programs and reaching the goals planned?
3. Analyze and present applicable trend data that supports the activity levels projected. Remember to use written comments and graphs to enhance comprehension of your presentation.
4. Discuss the current status of prior programs implemented and/or goals assigned.

5. Prioritize new programs and/or services being proposed so you are ready, if asked to do so, to eliminate some programs and/or services proposed.

## Publication

1. Once the budget is approved, summarize the key new and ongoing programs authorized for your supervisor.
2. Update the status of each of these on a regular basis, no less often than quarterly. Try to discuss your report in person as well as providing a written report to your superior.
3. Identify any enhancements being considered to the approved or ongoing programs that may appear in the next budget in your quarterly updates.
4. Well in advance of the next budget notices being sent out, meet with your superior to discuss planned enhancements or new programs being considered and to begin the "preapproach" process.

Following these three simple steps will allow the supervisor to stay ahead of others competing for funds and ensure that one's boss is kept informed throughout the year.

## ■ Budget Director and Budget Committee

Although the authority and responsibility for the budget rest with the line officers and ultimately with the CEO and the board of directors, they will be helped in some cases by a staff unit headed by a budget director or the controller. This staff will provide the line managers with advice and technical assistance but should not attempt to prepare the budgets for them. The staff will be particularly helpful, however, in putting the various budget estimates together in final form so that top-level administration can submit it to the board.

Some institutions also have established a budget committee that serves in an advisory and supportive capacity in coordinating the various budgets. In this instance the budget committee clearly performs a staff function. This must be distinguished, however, from those budget committees to which the board has delegated the line function of setting, rather than just coordinating, the budget. In this situation the budget committee considers all departmental budget estimates and requests including expense and capital and makes the final decisions. This form of budget committee has ultimate line authority and responsibility for determining the budget instead of a single person such as the institution's top-level administrator or executive director. The budget is approved by the committee, and nothing can be done without its approval. If budget revisions and changes are requested, it is also up to the budget committee to allow or disallow them. Several arrangements are possible within these two extremes as to where the final authority for the overall budget rests. Usually it has to pass the CEO, the finance committee of the board, and eventually the board of directors.

## ■ Length of the Budget Period

Although the length of the budget period may vary, most healthcare enterprises choose one year. This period is then broken down into quarters, and many institutions will even divide it by months at the time of the original budget preparation. This is usually referred to as *periodic budgeting.*

Besides the annual budgets, healthcare institutions also typically have budgets extending over a longer term, such as three or five years. These budgets usually cover such items as capital expenditures, research programs, and expansions. Long-term budgets of this nature are not direct operating budgets and are of no direct concern to the supervisor other than for his or her role in projecting major capital needs (such as new chemistry analyzer, or an optical imaging system, etc.). Rather, they involve the chief administrator and the board of directors; they are planning, not controlling, tools. For most healthcare organizations it is difficult to plan much beyond five years because healthcare is so regulated and the regulations may vary greatly, depending on elected officials in Congress.

## ■ Flexibility of the Budgetary Process

The supervisor should keep in mind that budgets are merely a tool for management and not a substitute for good judgment. Also, care should be taken not to make budgets so detailed that they become cumbersome. Budgets should always allow the supervisor enough freedom to accomplish the best objectives of the department. There must be a reasonable degree of latitude and flexibility. In fact, one of the most serious shortcomings of budgeting is the danger of inflexibility. Although budgets are plans expressed in numerical terms, the supervisor must not be led to believe that these figures are absolutely final and unalterable. Realizing that a budget should not become a straitjacket, enlightened management builds into the budgetary program a degree of flexibility and adaptability. This is necessary so that the institution can cope with changing conditions, new developments, and even possible mistakes in the budget of human errors and miscalculations. Flexibility should not be interpreted to mean, however, that the budget can be changed with every whim, or that it should be taken lightly.

Nevertheless, if operating conditions have appreciably changed and there are valid indications that the budget cannot be followed in the future, a revision of the budgetary program is in order. Such circumstances may be caused by unexpected events, new legislation, unanticipated wage increases, or large fluctuations in demand. Consider, for example, the budget of the department of respiratory therapy, in which activities have been and are increasing constantly because of new applications, ideas, and technology. Revenues derived from this service are increasing rapidly at the same time. It would be absurd to expect the supervisor of this department to stay within the budgeted figures for salaries and supplies. If the department is expected to respond and supply the increased demand, this budget must be altered. In such a case the old budget has become obsolete; unless provisions are available to make the budget flexible, it will lose its usefulness altogether.

## ■ Budget Review and Budget Revision

Because of the potential to become obsolete, increasing attention has been given to ways of ensuring budget flexibility to avoid the danger of rigidity. Most enterprises achieve this by periodic budget reviews and revisions. At regular intervals of one, two, or three months the budget is reviewed. In meetings between the departmental supervisor and the line superior, actual performance will be checked and compared with the budgeted figures and the supervisor will be called on to explain the causes for any variations or inadequacies. A thorough analysis must then be made to discover the reasons for the deviation from the budgeted amount; this may lead to budget revisions or other corrective measures.

An unfavorable variation by itself does not necessarily require a budget change; it must be studied and explained. In the example just cited, however, the supervisor of the respiratory therapy department will not have any difficulties in proving the need for an upward budget revision. In some organizations such a revision can be made on the departmental level, whereas in other institutions it must be carried up to the CEO or even the budget committee. If the deviations are of sufficient magnitude, it is advisable to make the necessary revisions no matter how high up in the hierarchy they have to go or how much work they may involve. If the variation is minor, it may be more expedient to let it go instead of revising the entire budget, since it has been explained and justified.

No matter what decision is made, regular budget reviews and revisions seem to be the best way of ensuring the flexibility of the budgetary process. They prevent the budget from being viewed as a straitjacket and allow the supervisor to consider it a living document and a valuable tool for control purposes.

---

**BUDGETS AND HUMAN PROBLEMS**

Budgets necessarily represent restrictions, and for this reason subordinates generally resent budgets. Often subordinates have a defensive approach to budgets, an approach they acquire through painful experience. Many times the subordinates become acquainted with budgets only as a barrier to spending, or the budget is blamed for failure to get or give a raise in salary. Moreover, in the minds of many subordinates the word *budget* has often become associated with miserly behavior rather than with planning and direction.

The line manager's job is to correct this erroneous impression by pointing out that budgeting is a trained and disciplined approach to many problems and is necessary to maintain standards of performance. The budget must be presented to the supervisor as a planning tool and not as a pressure device. Most of the problems arise at the point of budgetary control. In other words, when deviations from the budget occur, subordinates are often censured for exceeding the budget. Such budget deviations necessitate explanations, discussions, and decisions. As stated before, the budget should not be looked on lightly. The subordinate should also know that in most enterprises enough flexibility is built into the budget system to permit good common-sense departures necessary for the best functioning of the institution.

Avoiding unnecessary pressures over the budget presupposes that a good working relationship exists between the supervisor and the immediate superior.

This in turn rests on clear-cut organizational lines and a thorough understanding that the line managers are responsible for control. Staff people are excluded from the process of controlling. They cannot take operating personnel to task for deviations in the budget; they can merely report the situation to the administrative officer. Effective use of budgetary procedures depends on the administration's attitudes toward the entire budgetary process, whether it will be an effective planning tool or a pressure device. Only with the planning-tool view will a supervisor believe that whatever can be done without a budget can be done much more effectively with a budget.

## COST CONTROLS   Cost Containment and Cost Awareness

Healthcare providers have been and still are under continuous unrelenting pressure to keep healthcare expenditures from spiraling. It is safe to predict that the drive to control costs will increase even more because of pressures from government agencies, legislators, insurers, and purchasers of healthcare, such as large corporations, health maintenance organizations (HMOs), preferred provider organizations (PPOs), and even enlightened individuals. In such an environment, control of costs is an ongoing problem for everyone from the president down to the lowest line supervisor; it is a problem that will never go away.

Cost control, better referred to as *cost awareness, cost consciousness,* or *cost containment,* should be viewed as a significant part of the supervisor's daily job. Supervisors must strive for cost consciousness with even emphasis. Sporadic efforts, crash programs, economy drives, etc., seldom have lasting results. Since cost awareness is an ongoing problem, the supervisor must set definite numerical objectives and make plans for achieving cost containment by a given date. Priorities must be clarified without infringing on the quality of healthcare; this is difficult to achieve, especially if there is more sophistication in patient care accompanied by general escalation of prices and wages.

To succeed in cost containment, it is essential to involve the employees of the department and make them realize that ultimately their actions will bring about results. All employees should consider cost consciousness as a part of their job. Most employees will normally try to do the right thing and will help save costs and reduce waste; most workers are not deliberately wasteful. Many employees can make valuable suggestions and contributions to cost-effectiveness. The supervisor should welcome employees' suggestions and not fault them for not having thought of these changes before. Cost awareness should be an ongoing challenge in everyone's daily job.

### ■ Allocation of Costs

Every supervisor must see that his or her department contributes effectively to the operation of the institution. In this context of overall controls we are not referring to the qualitative aspect, but to the financial operation of a department. The administration may tell a supervisor that his or her department is operating in the red and that it is losing money each year instead of contributing to a financial surplus. Consider, for example, an operating room supervisor who has been confronted with such a statement. The supervisor may be at a complete loss to understand this. Everyone is working as effectively as possible, the utilization of the operating rooms is high, there is no surplus of employees or waste of materials or supplies, and the supervisor is staying within the expense figures set out in the budget. The patient charges for using the operating room have been arrived at by the accounting department in conjunction with the administration. Still the overall figures at the end of the year indicate that the operating rooms are "costing" the hospital a great deal of money because this division ends up as a deficit activity.

The supervisor must realize that in a healthcare center, just as in all other organized activities, some departments are revenue producing, whereas others are not. Clearly the operating rooms and nursing services produce revenue. These patient care departments could not function, however, without the services provided by the other departments, such as housekeeping, dietary services, medical records, laundry, and administration. Admitting, collections, the executive offices, the human resources department, public relations, purchasing, and telecommunications are additional services without which no other department in the hospital could function. Although these are not revenue-producing departments, their costs must be carried if the hospital is to function on a fiscally sound basis. Hospitals must allocate such costs to those patient care departments that do produce revenue. The question arises as to *how* the costs of the many nonrevenue-producing departments are *allocated* to the revenue-producing departments. The supervisor has no control over this portion of a department's expenses, which can make the difference between ending up with a departmental surplus or with a deficit.

It is beyond the scope of this text to go into a detailed discussion of the various methods of cost analysis, contribution margin approach, and other bases for allocations. However, the supervisor should have a general understanding of the bases on which a department is being charged for these various expenditures. This is merely for the supervisor's own information, since in reality this person is powerless to influence the costs allocated to the department. The supervisor can readily understand the direct expenses (e.g., wages, salaries, supplies, materials), as well as some of the indirect expenses (e.g., Social Security and workers compensation taxes), charged to the department. The supervisor also probably understands that departments are charged with housekeeping based on the hours of service provided, maintenance figures on the basis of work orders, linen based on pounds of laundry, and so forth. When it comes to the allocation of many other charges, however, the supervisor should find out what the basis is. The healthcare institution will try to select a basis of distribution that is fair to all departments and feasible from an accounting point of view.

The overall financial performance of a department will be greatly affected by how these allocations for other expenditures are made, for example, administrative expenses, operation of the plant, depreciation, intern and resident service costs, in-service education, and interest expenses. Although all this is determined higher up in the administrative hierarchy, the supervisor is well advised to obtain some information and explanation on how it is done. Then the supervisor will understand how a department operates in the red, despite the effective work of the manager and its employees.

## ADDITIONAL CONTROLS

The supervisor's controlling function is closely related to and goes on simultaneously with all other managerial functions. Throughout this text many subjects were discussed as part of a particular function at the time, and now their meaning as an aid in the system of control can also be shown.

In chapter 7 standing plans such as *policies, procedures, methods,* and *rules* as basic tools for planning were discussed. At this point in the text, however, they can be viewed as anticipatory control devices. These tools are established with the hope and intention that they will be followed and that they work out as preventive controls. If they are violated, the supervisor, using feedback control, must take the necessary corrective action to get things back on track; in some cases disciplinary measures may be necessary.

We discussed *positive discipline* and *disciplinary measures* in chapter 23 as a component of the influencing function. In the controlling context, this topic can be viewed as a preventive and reactive control technique. If a rule has been violated, the supervisor must invoke disciplinary measures, which is synonymous with taking corrective action and sending a message to the employees about proper behavior on the job.

On various occasions *management by objectives* (MBO) was discussed. As mentioned, this is an agreement between the subordinate and the supervisor concerning a measurable performance objective to be achieved and reviewed within a given time period. This concept includes aspects of control. After mutually agreed-on objectives have been set, results are evaluated in the light of these standards, and, if necessary, shortcomings are corrected. This is another example of a control model mechanism.

*Performance appraisal systems,* the process of formally evaluating performance and providing feedback for performance adjustments, as discussed in chapter 18, can also be viewed as part of the organizational control system. Although performance evaluation measures were presented with the staffing function, they can now be regarded as a feedback control technique in the managerial control system.

These are just a few examples taken from previous discussions of the various managerial functions; they show how closely related controlling is to all the other functions. This confirms the statement that the better the supervisor plans, organizes, staffs, and influences, the better he or she will also perform the controlling function.

## SUMMARY

Budget making is planning, whereas living with the budget and budget administration fall into the manager's controlling function. Budgets are plans expressed in numerical terms that ultimately will be reduced to dollars and cents, since this is the common denominator used in the final analysis. Budgets are also preestablished standards to which the operations of the department are compared and, if necessary, adjusted by the exercise of control. Of all control devices, the budget, (primarily the expense budget) is the one most widely used and thus the one with which most supervisors should be familiar.

Since the supervisor is responsible for living up to the departmental budget, he or she must play a significant role in its preparation. Budget making is a line responsibility shared by the supervisor and the direct line superior. Ultimately all budgets are submitted to and approved by top-level administration, but it is essential that lower-level managers participate in making their own budgets and have sufficient opportunity to be heard and substantiate their cases.

Zero base budgeting is a relatively new approach to budgeting; under traditional budgeting, management's attention is primarily focused on planned changes from the previous year. Under zero base budgeting nothing is taken for granted and every activity and budget item must be substantiated and justified from scratch. For a budget to be a live document and not a straitjacket, the budgetary process must be flexible. There must be frequent periodic budget reviews within the normal one-year budgeting period and provisions for budget revision. Such provisions will lessen the human problems that budgetary controls often cause.

In addition to budgetary controls, the supervisor should be aware of other costs that will influence the overall performance of the department. Here the supervisor will be concerned with how the expenditures of the nonrevenue-producing departments in a healthcare institution are allocated to those departments that do produce revenues. The bases of these allocations can often make the difference between showing a departmental surplus and operating at a loss. Supervisors also play an important role in cost containment. Cost awareness and cost consciousness should be an ongoing consideration and part of the supervisor's daily activities.

Throughout this text we stressed the close relationship between the controlling function and the other managerial functions. Many of the managerial duties and activities discussed previously can now be viewed as additional controls, including policies, procedures, etc.; disciplinary measures; management by objectives; and performance appraisals. The most widely used control device, however, remains the budget and budgetary procedures.

# *PART VIII*
# *L*ABOR
# RELATIONS

# 27

# *The Labor Union and the Supervisor*

*Chapter Objectives*

After you have studied this chapter, you should be able to:

1. Review the history of collective bargaining and labor-related legislation.
2. Discuss the content of a typical labor contract.
3. Outline areas of concern for the supervisor.
4. Differentiate the role of the supervisor and the shop steward in organized labor environments.

Although labor unions have lost membership since the late 1970s, and the number of union members is stagnant, they are still an influential part of the workforce. At this time about 15 to 20 percent of the labor force in the United States are members of a labor union or some employee association. Therefore, it is essential for supervisors to be familiar with the role labor unions play in the workplace in order to be able to work with them properly.

Collective bargaining gained its major legal basis in 1935 with the enactment of the National Labor Relations Act, also known as the Wagner Act, which guaranteed workers the right to bargain collectively with their employers. In 1947 the Wagner Act was amended by the Labor-Management Relations Act, also known as the Taft-Hartley Act. In 1959 the Labor-Management Reporting and Disclosure Act, sometimes referred to as the Landrum-Griffin Act, was added. In 1974 these laws were extended to cover most healthcare institutions.

The union movement was primarily a blue-collar movement because there were more blue-collar workers in the United States' labor force than white-collar workers. Since the middle 1950s, however, the number of people in white-collar occupational categories and in service industries has been on the increase and has surpassed the blue-collar sector. With this change, labor unions have made in-roads in representing business services (e.g., computers), retail trade, finance, healthcare, government, and other sectors. A number of unions or employee associations have become the bargaining agents for teachers, college professors, nurses, airline pilots, nursing home employees, and various other white-collar workers. However, it is beyond the confines of this text to discuss the details of labor laws or give the full history of the union movement in the United States.

There is little doubt that the introduction of a union or an employee association into a hospital or related healthcare facility may be a trying experience for the supervisors, as well as for the chief executive officer (CEO). It may bring a time of tension during which constructive solutions to problems may be difficult. The issues, claims, and counterclaims are on everyone's mind and are present in the workplace, on the parking lot, and even in the local news media. The verbal battle may even accelerate into work slowdowns or stoppages. If the employees vote to join a union, managers are likely to believe that they have lost a battle and that their employees and union representatives have been victorious. It will take time for the ill feelings created during the organizing campaign to disappear.

Gradually, however, both the union and the administration must learn to accommodate and live with each other. Every manager must accept the fact that the labor union is a permanent force in our society. Every manager must realize that the union, just as any other organization, has in it the potential for either advancing or disrupting the common effort of the institution. It is in the self-interest of the administration to create a labor-management climate that directs this potential toward constructive ends. There is no simple or magic formula, however, for overnight cultivation of a favorable climate that will result in cooperation and mutual understanding between the union and management. It takes wisdom and sensitivity from every manager of the organization, from the administrator down to the supervisor, to demonstrate in the day-to-day relations that the union is respected as a responsible part of the institution.

In this effort to create and maintain a constructive pattern of cooperation between the healthcare institution and the union, the most significant factor usually is the supervisor of a department. Supervisors, more than anyone else, feel the strongest impact of the new situation because they make the largest number of decisions concerning unionized employees. The supervisor is the person in day-to-day employee relations who makes the labor agreement a living document, for better or for worse. To this extent, an article in *Textile World's* January 1995 issue discussed the movement away from unions and preference for cooperative labor/management committees. Of the 2,408 manufacturing employees polled, 63% opted for the committees, while only 22% chose unions. The survey also found that workers complained of a lack of participation in decisions and acknowledged the importance of management cooperating in achieving their goals.[1]

Supervisors are often confused as to how they should behave during an organizing campaign and after the election when the union arrives on the scene. The supervisor should realize that the subordinates usually decide for a union not because they were gullible or naive or because the union used deceit or strong-arm methods, but primarily because some of their major needs were not satisfied on the job. The supervisor should approach the union professionally and try to build a satisfactory relationship.

The supervisor should have received information and training in the fundamentals of collective bargaining and in the nature of labor agreements from the human resources department. This is essential for the development of good labor relations. The supervisor is involved in two distinct phases of labor relations: (1) the inception of unionization and the phase of negotiations; and (2) the

---

1.   James A. Morrissey, Textile World, *vol. 145, no. 1 (January 1995): 63(2).*

day-to-day administration of the union agreement, which includes handling complaints and grievances. Although the supervisor is primarily concerned with the second phase of relations with the union, he or she also plays a role in the first.

| UNIONIZATION AND LABOR NEGOTIATIONS | As soon as supervisors learn that union-organizing activities are starting, this information should be passed on to higher administration and/or the director of human resources. Often administration has already learned of such a campaign through other channels. This will enable the organization to plan its strategy, usually with the help of legal counsel. Supervisors should be aware of a number of legal restrictions that must be observed during the union-organizing efforts. The following remarks are only of a very general nature; supervisors will probably receive more detailed instruction from their administrators and lawyers. |
|---|---|

## UNIONIZATION AND LABOR NEGOTIATIONS

As soon as supervisors learn that union-organizing activities are starting, this information should be passed on to higher administration and/or the director of human resources. Often administration has already learned of such a campaign through other channels. This will enable the organization to plan its strategy, usually with the help of legal counsel. Supervisors should be aware of a number of legal restrictions that must be observed during the union-organizing efforts. The following remarks are only of a very general nature; supervisors will probably receive more detailed instruction from their administrators and lawyers.

Labor laws restrict what managers, including supervisors, are permitted to say and do during this critical period without the danger of their being involved in unfair labor practices. First, supervisors should continue to do the best possible job of supervision during this critical period. Administration should provide supervisors with information on the dos and don'ts during a union-organizing campaign (see figure 27.1). Generally, supervisors should not make any statements in reference to unionization that could be construed as a promise if the union fails or as a threat if the union is successful. Supervisors should not question their employees privately or publicly about organizing activities. When asked, supervisors can express their opinions about unionization in a neutral manner, if this is possible, without running into the danger of having the answer interpreted as a threat or promise.

These are only a few guidelines that the supervisor should keep in mind; there certainly are additional guidelines. Usually an election conducted by the National Labor Relations Board will determine the outcome of the organizing campaign. If the union loses the election, the employees will not have a union for the immediate future. If the union wins, management has to recognize the union as the bargaining agent and begin negotiations in good faith.

On the surface, it might not seem as if the supervisor is significantly involved in the negotiations of a labor agreement. As stated earlier, the period when a union first enters a department of a healthcare organization is usually trying and filled with tensions. Emotions run high, and considerable disturbance can result. Under such conditions, it is understandable that the delicate negotiations of a union contract are carried on primarily by members of top-level administration, probably assisted by legal counsel. There is usually an air of secrecy surrounding the negotiations, which often take place in a hotel or a lawyer's office.

Since a committee of employees may be participating in these negotiations, a direct line of communication exists between the other employees of the healthcare institution, but not necessarily to the supervisor. The supervisor often runs the danger of being less well informed about the course of negotiations than the employees. Therefore, the administrator must see to it that the supervisor is fully advised as to the progress and direction the negotiations are

**Figure 27.1** Do's and Don'ts for Managers and Supervisors During a Union-Organizing Campaign.

*Reprinted, by permission, from* Health Information: Management of a Strategic Resource. *Copyright 1996 by W. B. Saunders Co.*

**Do's and Don'ts for Managers and Supervisors During a Union Organizing Campaign**

**Do**

- Tell employees that the organization does not believe that they need union representation and that you would like them to vote no.

- Answer employees' questions about organizational polices and discuss the union campaign issues.

- Tell employees that if they join the union, they will be expected to pay union dues and fees.

- Assure employees that union or no union, management is going to continue to try to make the organization a good place to work.

- Explain to employees that the organization will recognize the union and bargain in good faith if the majority of the employees really want it, but that any improvements in wages and benefits are negotiable and not automatic, as the union might want them to believe.

- Administer appropriate disciplinary action or terminate any employee who threatens or coerces other employees, whether for or against the union.

- Request outside union officials to leave facility property if they try to solicit employees there. Escort them off the property or, if appropriate, call the police to have them removed.

**Don't**

SPIT
S—Spy on employees or conduct surveillance of any kind to determine the level of union sentiment.
P—Promise anything. You should not do anything to suggest that you are soliciting grievances.
I—Interrogate anyone. Asking questions about union sympathies or union activity is an unfair labor practice under the law.
T—Threaten, coerce, or intimidate any employee because of his or her union activity.

taking. In addition, the supervisor should be given an opportunity to express opinions on matters brought up during the negotiations. In other words, even though top-level management is representing the institution at the negotiating sessions, supervisors should be able to express their views through them, because ultimately it is the supervisor who bears the major responsibility for fulfilling the contract provisions.

The same necessity exists whenever renegotiations of the labor agreement take place. At that time, top-level administration should consult with the supervisors as to how specific provisions in the contract have worked out and what changes in the contract the supervisors would like to have made. Both the administrator and the supervisors must realize that although the supervisors do not actually sit at the negotiating table, they have much to do with the nature of the negotiations. Many of the demands that the union brings up during the negotiations have their origin in the day-to-day operations of the department. Many of the difficult questions to be solved in the bargaining process stem from the relationship that the supervisors have with their employees.

Therefore, a great amount of checking must occur back and forth between the administrator and the supervisor before and during the negotiation of a labor agreement. To supply valuable information, the supervisor must know what has been going on in the department and have facts to substantiate his or her statements. This points to the value of documentation, keeping good records of disciplinary incidents, productivity, leaves, promotions, etc. The supervisor should also be alert to problems that should be called to the administration's attention so that in the next set of negotiations these matters may be worked out more satisfactorily. It is in the interest of both the union and the institution to have as few unresolved problems as possible. If problems do arise, however, it is the supervisor's responsibility to see that administration is aware of them at the time of contract negotiations.

## CONTENT OF THE AGREEMENT

Once administration and the union have agreed on a labor contract, this agreement will be the basis on which both parties must operate. Since the supervisor is now obligated to manage the department within the overall framework of the labor agreement, he or she must have complete knowledge of its provisions and how they are to be interpreted. The supervisor is the one who can cause disagreements between the union and the healthcare institution by failing to live up to the terms of the agreement. Thus, the content of the union contract must be fully explained to and understood by the supervisor.

A good way to present such explanations is at a meeting arranged for top administration and all the supervisors, which is usually chaired by the human resources or labor relations director. The purpose of the meeting is to brief the supervisors on the content of the labor contract, giving them an opportunity to ask questions about any part they do not understand. Copies of the contract and clarification of the various clauses may be furnished to the supervisors so that they may study them in advance. Since no two contracts are alike, however, it is impossible to pinpoint specific provisions that the supervisor should explore. Normally all contracts deal with matters such as union recognition, management's rights, union security, wages, bonus rates, conditions and hours of work, overtime, vacations, holidays, leaves of absence, seniority, promotions, and similar details. Almost certainly there will also be provisions concerning complaint and grievance procedures and arbitration. In addition, there are likely to be many other provisions that are peculiar to each institution in question.

Besides the need to familiarize the supervisors with the exact provisions of the contract, it is just as important for the administrator to explain to them the philosophy of top-level administration in reference to general relations with the union. The supervisors should understand that the intention of the administration is to maintain good working relations with the union so that organizational objectives can be achieved in a mutually satisfactory fashion. The CEO should clarify that the best way to achieve good union-management relations in a hospital or any other institution is by effective contract administration. The experts in the personnel or the labor relations department will have a great deal to do with effective contract administration, but much will still depend on how the supervisor handles the contract on a day-to-day basis.

The supervisors must bear in mind that the negotiated contract was carefully and thoughtfully debated and finally agreed on by both parties. Thus, it is not in the interest of successful contract administration for the supervisors to try to "beat the contract," even though they may think they are doing the institution a favor. The administrator must make it clear that to achieve satisfactory cooperation, supervisors may not construct their own contractual clauses, nor can they reinterpret clauses in their own way. Once the agreement has been reached, supervisors should not attempt to change or circumvent it.

If the administrator fails to familiarize the supervisors with the provisions and spirit of the agreement, they should insist on briefing sessions and explanations before they apply the clauses of the contract in the daily working situation of the department. The advent of the labor contract does not change the supervisor's job as a manager. The supervisor must still perform the managerial functions of planning, organizing, staffing, influencing, and controlling. There is no change in the authority delegated to the department head by the administrator or in the responsibility the supervisor has accepted. The significant change is that the supervisor must now perform the managerial duties within the framework of the union agreement. He or she still has the right to require the subordinates to carry out orders and the obligation to get the job done within the department. Certain provisions within the union agreement, however, are likely to influence and even limit some activities, especially within the areas of job assignments, disciplinary action, and dismissal. In many instances these provisions of the contract undoubtedly will make it more challenging for the supervisor to be a good manager. The only way to meet the challenge is for the supervisor to improve his or her own managerial ability as well as his or her knowledge and techniques of good labor relations.

## APPLYING THE AGREEMENT

It is in the daily application of the labor agreement that the real importance of the supervisor's contribution appears. The manner in which the day-to-day problems are handled within the framework of the union contract will make the difference between positive labor-management relations and a situation filled with unnecessary tensions and bad feelings. At best, a union contract can only set forth the broad outline of labor-management relations. To make it a positive instrument of constructive relations, the contract must be filled in with appropriate and intelligent supervisory decisions. It is the supervisor who interprets management's intent by everyday actions. In the final analysis the supervisor, through decisions, actions, and attitudes, really gives the contract meaning and life.

In many instances the supervisor may expand on some of the provisions of the contract when interpreting and applying them to specific situations. In so doing, the supervisor sets precedents that arbitrators pay heed to when deciding grievances that come before them. Almost all labor agreements have a grievance procedure leading to arbitration. An *arbitrator* is a person called on by the union and management to make a final and binding decision in a grievance that the parties involved are unable to settle themselves.

It is impossible for the administrator and the union to draw up a contract that anticipates every possible situation in employee relations and specifies exact directives for dealing with them. Therefore, the individual judgment of the supervisor becomes very important in deciding each particular situation. This again illustrates the significance of the supervisor's influence on the interpretation of the labor agreement.

As a representative of administration, any error in the supervisor's decisions is the administration's error. The immediate supervisor has the greatest responsibility for seeing that the clauses of the agreement are carried out appropriately. This includes the supervisor's duty to ensure that the employees comply with the provisions, just as supervisors have to operate within them. Therefore, the administrator must realize how significant a role the supervisor plays in the contract administration. Likewise, it is just as essential for the supervisor to realize how far reaching his or her decisions and actions can become.

## PROBLEM AREAS

There are usually two broad areas where the supervisor is likely to run into difficulties in the administration of a labor agreement. The first covers the vast number of complaints that are concerned with single issues. These would include grievances involving a particular disciplinary action, assignment of work, distribution of overtime, as well as questions of promotion, transfer, downgrading, etc. In each situation the personal judgment of the supervisor is of great importance. As long as the contract provisions are met, the supervisor should feel free to deal with grievances as he or she sees fit. He or she must make certain, however, that the actions are consistent and logical even though they are made on the basis of personal judgment rather than on hard and fast rules.

The second area of difficulty in contract administration covers those grievances and problems in which the supervisor is called on to interpret a clause of the contract. The supervisor is placed in a situation in which an attempt must be made to carry out the generalized statement of the contract but finds that it is subject to varying interpretations. In such instances he or she would be wrong to handle the problem without consulting higher management first. Whenever an interpretation of the contract is at issue, any decision is likely to be long lasting. Such a decision may set a precedent that the institution, the union, or even an arbitrator would want to make use of in the future.

Therefore, if interpretation of a clause is in doubt, the question should be brought to the attention of higher management, the administrator, and possibly the human resources director. Although the supervisor may have been well indoctrinated in the meaning, philosophy, and clauses of the contract, his or her perspective is probably not broad enough to make a potentially precedent-setting interpretation. Since the supervisor did not attend the bargaining meetings, he or she cannot know the intent of the parties nor the background of this provision. For these and other reasons the supervisor should consult with superiors.

## ■ The Supervisor's Right to Make Decisions

In nonprecedent-setting situations and in the daily administration of the labor agreement, the supervisor must bear in mind that as a member of management, he or she has the right and even the duty to make a decision. He or she must realize that the union contract does not abrogate management's right to decide; it is still management's prerogative to do so. The union, however, has a right to protest the decision.

For example, the supervisor's job is to maintain discipline, and if disciplinary action is necessary, he or she should take action without discussing it with the union's representative. The supervisor should understand that usually there is no co-determination clause, and he or she should not set any precedent of determining together with the union what the supervisor's rights are in a particular disciplinary case. Of course, before any disciplinary measures are taken, a prudent supervisor will examine all the facts in the case, fulfill the preliminary steps, and think through the appropriateness of the action. This process is more fully discussed in chapter 28.

In a few cases the union contract will call for consultation or advance notice before the supervisor can proceed. Advance notice or consultation, however, does not mean agreement on the final decision. Repercussions or protests from the union can still occur, although prior communication on anticipated action can avoid some of them. In any event, the right to decide on day-to-day issues of contract administration still rests with the supervisor and not with the union.

## ■ The Supervisor and the Shop Steward

The supervisor will probably have the most union contact with the shop steward, who is the first-line official of the union and is sometimes referred to as *shop committee person, union delegate,* or *departmental chairperson.* The shop steward is not the same as a union business agent or business representative; these are normally full-time union officials who are employed and paid by the local or national union. At times the supervisor will also have to deal with them.

The shop steward normally remains an employee of the healthcare facility and is subject to the same regulations as every other employee. He or she is expected to put in a full day's work for the employer, regardless of having been selected by fellow workers to be their official spokesperson with both the institution and the union. This obviously is a difficult position, since the shop steward has to serve two masters. As an employee, he or she has to follow the supervisor's orders and directives; as a union official, though, he or she has responsibilities to coworkers.

Just as individuals vary in their approach to their jobs, so shop stewards vary in their approach to their positions. Some are unassuming; others are overbearing. Some are helpful and courteous, whereas others are difficult. Unless special provisions exist, the shop steward's rights are the same as those of any other union member. Moreover, the shop steward is subject to the same regulations regarding quality of work and conduct as the other employees of the department. However, certain privileges may be specified in the union contract such as how much "company" time the shop steward can devote to union business or other matters, whether or not solicitation of membership or collection of dues may be carried on during working hours, time off to attend union conventions, and similar questions.

As stated, the role of the shop steward will depend considerably on the makeup of the individual. Some will take advantage of their position to do as little work as possible, whereas others will perform a good day's work. The supervisor should always remember that the shop steward is an employee of the organization and should be treated as such. The supervisor should also remember, however, that the shop steward is the representative of the other employees; in this capacity, the shop steward learns quickly what the other employees are thinking and what is going on in the grapevine. Thus, the supervisor will come to understand and take advantage of the fact that the dual role can make the shop steward a good link between management and employees.

Although shop stewards perform a number of union functions, such as collecting dues, soliciting membership, and promoting political causes, the supervisor should realize that the shop steward's most important responsibility probably concerns employees' complaints and grievances. The shop steward's job is to bring such complaints and grievances before the supervisor. The supervisor's job is to settle them to the best of his or her ability, using the grievance procedures described in great detail in every union contract. Throughout these procedures, which we will discuss more fully in chapter 28, the supervisor represents management, and the shop steward represents the employees for the union.

In most cases, the shop steward is sincerely trying to redress the aggrieved employee by winning a favorable ruling. At times, however, the supervisor may be under the impression that he or she is out looking for grievances merely to stay busy. This may be partly true, since the shop steward does have a political assignment, and it is necessary to assure the employees that the union is working on their behalf. The shop steward must be able to convince the employees that they can rely on him or her, and therefore on the union, to protect them. On the other hand, an experienced shop steward knows that normally a sufficient number of real grievances must be settled. He or she sees no need to look for complaints that do not have a valid background and would rightfully be turned down by the supervisor.

Most unions will ensure that the shop steward is well trained to present the complaints and grievances so that they can be carried to a successful conclusion. The shop steward is usually well versed in understanding the content of the contract, management's obligations, and employees' rights. Before presenting a grievance, the shop steward should determine such matters as whether or not the contract has been violated, the employer acted unfairly, the employee's health or safety has been put in jeopardy, etc. In grievance matters, the union is usually on the offensive and the supervisor is on the defensive. The shop steward will challenge the management decision or action, and the supervisor must justify what he or she has done.

Because the shop steward's main interest is in the union, at times this may antagonize the supervisor. In some instances it will be difficult for the supervisor to keep a sense of humor and remain calm. Often the supervisor also will have difficulty discussing a grievance with a shop steward on an equal footing, since the shop steward is a subordinate within the normal working situation. When assuming the role of shop steward, however, the position as representative of the union members gives him or her equal standing. The supervisor should always bear in mind that the shop steward's job is political and as such carries certain weight. At the same time the supervisor should understand that a good shop steward will keep any supervisor on the alert and force him or her to be a better manager.

---

## SUMMARY

About 15 to 20 percent of the labor force in the United States are members of an employee association or a labor union. Since unions are attempting to represent more and more employees from services, it is essential that supervisors in healthcare undertakings are familiar with some basic aspects of labor union relations.

The supervisor's role in the union relations of a healthcare facility cannot be minimized. Although the supervisor is not normally a member of the management team that sits down with union negotiators to settle the terms of the labor contract, he or she does play an important indirect role in this meeting. Many of the difficulties and problems discussed at a negotiating meeting can be traced back to the daily activities of the supervisor. At best the union contract resulting from the negotiations can set forth only the broad outline of labor-management relationships. It is the day-to-day application and administration of the agreement that will make the difference between harmonious labor relations and a situation filled with unnecessary tensions and bad feelings.

The supervisor is the person who, through daily decisions and actions, gives the contract real meaning. He or she must therefore be thoroughly familiar with the contents of the contract and with the general philosophy of management toward the union. He or she must understand the difficult and important political role of the union shop steward, who serves in a dual capacity as one of the regular employees and as the representative of the union members. In grievance cases, the supervisor must learn to regard the shop steward as an equal, as one who is trained to present the complaints of union members as effectively as possible. The shop steward will challenge management's decision, and the supervisor must justify it. Although at times it may be difficult to keep a balanced perspective, the supervisor should always remember that an alert shop steward can serve to force him or her to be a better manager.

# *Handling Grievances*

## Chapter Objectives

After you have studied this chapter, you should be able to:

1. Define the term *grievance*.
2. Differentiate between the roles of the shop steward and the supervisor in responding to a grievance.
3. Review the process of handling a grievance.

A grievance can be defined as a complaint that usually results from a misunderstanding, misinterpretation, or violation of a provision of the labor agreement. This complaint has been formally presented to management by the union. Almost all union contracts contain provisions for a grievance procedure. The first step of the procedure begins at the departmental level, with the supervisor or the foreperson and the shop steward. If the grievance is not settled there, it can be appealed to the next higher level of management; at this point usually a chief steward or a business agent of the union will enter into the picture. At times the contract may provide for an appeal to an even higher level of management.

The grievance procedure usually sets a time limit for each of these steps to be finished. If the dispute cannot be settled by the first two or three steps to the mutual satisfaction of both parties, the agreement usually has an arbitration provision. This means that the issue may be submitted to an impartial outsider, an arbitrator. After hearing testimony and evidence, the arbitrator will render a final decision, which is binding on both parties.

The supervisor thus needs to be well qualified in handling complaints and settling grievances. Indeed, in a unionized setting one of the supervisor's most important duties is to make certain that most complaints and grievances are properly disposed of during the first step of the grievance procedure. Most organizations require that supervisors check and consult with a labor relations specialist in the personnel department when handling complaints. This is important because many complaints could have institutionwide or organizationwide implications. Grievances that refer to discrimination and equal employment opportunities could have legal implications for the entire organization.

Many additional reasons exist why the human resources department should be involved in the grievance procedure. The supervisor is not shirking responsibility or admitting ignorance by consulting and checking with these specialists. In some organizations management even has conferred on the labor relations staff (a division of the human resources department) the final authority to adjust grievances by giving them functional authority, as discussed in chapter 12.

The following discussion is based on an organizational setup in which the human resources and labor relations experts are in a strictly staff position, and the initial formal authority and responsibility to handle grievances rest with the line supervisor. In every unionized organization, line supervisors know that handling grievances is part of their job and that it takes judgment, tact, and often more patience than comes naturally.

Supervisors should not feel threatened by grievances. They frequently may think that too much of their time is taken up in discussing complaints and grievances instead of getting the job done in the department. They may also believe that they perform more as labor lawyers than as supervisors. Supervisors should also realize, however, that higher management regards the skill in handling grievances to be an important index of supervisory ability. The number of grievances that arise within a department is considered a good indication of the state of employee-management relations.

A fine distinction can be made between the terms *complaint* and *grievance.* From the supervisor's point of view, however, a grievance simply means a complaint that has been formally presented either to the supervisor as a management representative or to the shop steward or any other union official. As mentioned, a grievance usually is a complaint resulting from a misunderstanding, misinterpretation, or violation of the provisions of the labor agreement. The supervisor must learn to distinguish between those grievances that are admissible and those that are gripes and merely indicate that the employee is unhappy or dissatisfied. In every case, the supervisor should listen carefully to what the employee has to say in order to decide what action can be taken other than the grievance procedure to correct the situation. The grievance procedure, for the purposes of this chapter, means a process to resolve a misunderstanding, misinterpretation, or violation of the union contract.

## THE SHOP STEWARD'S ROLE

The shop steward (or union delegate) is usually the spokesperson for the employee in a grievance procedure. He or she is familiar with the labor agreement and has been well indoctrinated as to how to present the employee's side of the grievance. A good shop steward is eager to get the credit for settling a grievance. Therefore, the question arises as to what the supervisor should do if an employee approaches him or her without the shop steward or without having consulted the shop steward. In such a case it is appropriate for the supervisor to listen to the employee's story to see whether or not the case is of interest to or involves the union. If the indications are that the contract or the union are involved, then the supervisor should call in the shop steward to listen to the employee's presentation. Although it is unlikely that a union member would present a grievance without the shop steward, the supervisor will do well to notify the shop steward if this should happen.

Similarly, if the shop steward submits a grievance by himself or herself, the supervisor should also listen carefully and with understanding. It is always preferable, however, to listen to complaints when both the shop steward and the complaining employee are present. If the shop steward does not bring the employee along, it still is necessary to listen to what he or she has to say. Nothing can keep the supervisor from speaking directly to the employee later on, either with or without the shop steward. If the shop steward is not present, the supervisor should take great care not to give the impression that he or she is undermining the shop steward's authority or relationship with the union members. There should always be free and open communication between the supervisor and the shop steward, even though the shop steward's job is to represent employees and to fight hard to win their cases.

| **THE SUPERVISOR'S ROLE** | One of the supervisor's prime functions is to dispose of all grievances at the first step of the grievance procedure. This means that part of the supervisor's job, usually with help from staff people in the labor relations department, is to explore fully the details of the grievance, deal with the problems brought out, and then try to settle them. The supervisor will quickly learn that it pays to settle grievances early, before they grow from molehills into mountains. Occasionally some grievances will go beyond the first step and have to be referred to higher levels of management. Normally, however, if many grievances go beyond this step, it may indicate that the supervisor is not carrying out the supervisory duties properly. Unless circumstances are beyond his or her control, the supervisor should make every effort to handle grievances within reasonable time limits and bring them to a successful conclusion. To achieve prompt and satisfactory adjustments of grievances at this early stage, the supervisor should observe the following points in dealing with the grievance procedure. |
|---|---|

### ■ Availability

The supervisor must be readily available to the shop steward and to the aggrieved employee. Availability does not only mean being physically present. It also means being approachable and ready to listen with an open mind. The supervisor must not make it difficult for a complaining employee to see him or her and sound off. This does not mean that the supervisor must stop immediately what he or she is doing, but every effort must be made to set a time as quickly as possible for the first hearing. An undue delay could be interpreted by the employee and the union as stalling, indifference, or resentment on the part of management.

### ■ Listening Skills

Everything stated about communication (chapter 5) and interviewing (chapter 17) is applicable to the grievance procedure as well. When a complaint is brought to the supervisor, the shop steward and the employee should be given the opportunity to present their case fully. Sympathetic listening by the supervisor is likely to minimize hostilities and tensions during the settlement of the case. The supervisor must know how to listen well. He or she must give the shop steward and the employee a chance to say whatever they have on their minds. If they believe that the supervisor is truly listening to them and that fair treatment will be given, the complaint will not loom as large to them as it did. Halfway through the story the complaining employee may even realize that he or she does not have a true complaint at all. Sympathetic listening can often produce this result. Also, sometimes the more a person talks, the more likely he or she is to make contradictory and inconsistent remarks, thus weakening the argument. Only an effective listener will be able to catch these inconsistencies and use them to help resolve the case. Frequently supervisors are so preoccupied with defending themselves or trying to justify their point of view that they simply do not listen.

## ■ Emotional Control

The supervisor must take great caution not to get angry at the shop steward or the employee. The shop steward's job is to represent the employee even when he or she knows that the grievance is not valid. In such a situation the supervisor's job is to point out objectively that there are no merits in the grievance. The supervisor cannot expect the shop steward to do this since he or she must serve as the employee's spokesperson at all times. Sometimes a union deliberately creates grievances to keep things stirred up. Even this situation must not arouse the anger of the supervisor. If the supervisor does not know how to handle such occurrences successfully, he or she should discuss the matter with higher management and experts in the labor relations or human resources department. By no means, however, must the supervisor get upset, even if a grievance is phony.

If arguments, tempers, and emotional outbursts run high and make good communication difficult, the supervisor may want to terminate the meeting and reschedule it. He or she must use caution, however, not to participate in a shouting match. It is hoped that at the next meeting tempers will have cooled down and a calmer discussion will be possible.

## ■ Defining the Problem

Often the shop steward and the employee are not sufficiently clear in their presentations. It is then the supervisor's job to summarize clearly what has been presented and make certain that everyone understands the problem the complaint is trying to solve. Sometimes the complaint merely deals with the symptoms of the problem. The supervisor must know how deeply to delve in order to get at the root of the situation. It is necessary to define the employee's complaint and the extent of the problem precisely to determine whether a grievance is valid under the contract. Once the real problem is clarified and handled properly, it is unlikely that similar grievances will come up again.

## ■ Obtaining the Facts

All the facts should be obtained as quickly as possible to arrive at a solution of the problem and a successful adjustment of the grievance. The supervisor can probably get most of the facts by asking the complaining employee pertinent questions. In so doing, the supervisor should be objective and try not to confuse either the shop steward or the employee. He or she must ascertain who, what, where, when, and why. In other words, the supervisor must find out who or what caused the grievance, where and when it happened, and whether there was unfair treatment. He or she must also determine whether any connection exists between the current grievance and other grievances. Although it sometimes may be tempting to hide behind the excuse of searching for more facts, the supervisor must not do so. He or she must make a decision on the basis of those facts that are available and that can be obtained without undue delay.

Sometimes, however, it is impossible to gather all the information at once, and therefore the grievance cannot be settled immediately. In this case the supervisor must inform the aggrieved employee and the shop steward. If they see that the supervisor is working on the problem, they are likely to be reasonable and wait for an answer to be given at a specific future date.

## ■ Familiarity with the Contract and Consultation

After having determined the facts, the supervisor now must ascertain whether or not this is a legitimate grievance in the context of the contract. As mentioned earlier, a grievance is usually not a grievance in the legal sense unless provisions of the labor contract have been violated or administered inconsistently. Therefore, it is necessary to check the provisions in the contract when any reference to a violation is made. If the supervisor has any question about this, he or she should consult with someone in the personnel or labor relations department or higher management. Provisions in the labor agreement may not be clearly stated, and a question may exist about whether a certain provision in the contract is applicable at all. In such a situation, the complaining employee should be told that additional clarification in reference to the agreement is needed and that the answer will be delayed for a few days.

## ■ Time Limits

Usually the grievance procedure sets a time limit within which the grievance must be answered. The supervisor must see that all grievances are settled as promptly and justly as possible. Postponing an adjustment in the hope that the complaint may disappear is courting trouble and more grievances. Moreover, an unnecessary postponement is unfair because the employee and the shop steward are entitled to know the supervisor's position as quickly as the facts can be obtained.

Speed is definitely important in the settlement of grievances, but not if it will result in unsound decisions. If a delay cannot be avoided, the aggrieved parties must be informed by the supervisor instead of leaving them under the impression that they are getting the runaround. Waiting for a decision is bothersome to everybody concerned. In such a situation it may be a good idea to put the grievance in writing and sign it so the parties involved do not forget the details.

## ■ Adjustment of Grievances

Part of the supervisor's job is to see that all grievances are properly adjusted, preferably at the first step of the grievance procedure. As already pointed out, this is included in the managerial aspects of the supervisory function. It is far better to settle a minor issue at this stage before it escalates into a major issue. The only cases that should be referred to higher levels of management are those that are unusual, require additional interpretation of the union contract's meaning, contain problems that have not shown up before, or involve broad policy considerations.

## ■ Consistency of Action

In the adjustment of grievances, the supervisor must make certain that the rights of management are protected and that the policies and precedents of the institution are followed. If the supervisor must deviate from previous adjustments, he or she must explain the reasons to the employee and the shop steward. The supervisor must make certain that both of them fully understand that this exception does not set a precedent. In such cases the supervisor is always obliged to have this checked out and approved by higher-level administration and/or the human resources department before informing the parties involved.

## ■ Consequences of the Settlement

The supervisor should not reach a decision that is inconsistent with previous settlements. The supervisor must check previous settlements and make certain that the current intended decision is consistent with past decisions, the institution's policy, and the labor agreement. The supervisor should avoid making an exception because this decision is likely to become a precedent. In adjusting grievances, the supervisor must consider not only what effect the adjustment will have in this instance, but also its implications for the future. Whenever the supervisor settles a grievance, the possibility exists that this settlement will show up as part of the labor contract in following years. Also, if the case goes to arbitration, the arbitrator is likely to look for precedents, consider them almost as binding as the labor agreement, and use them as a valid basis for the final decision.

## ■ Providing a Clear Answer

The supervisor must answer the grievance in a straightforward, reasonable manner that is perfectly clear to the aggrieved parties. The answer must not be phrased in language that the aggrieved parties cannot understand, regardless of whether or not the adjustment is in favor of the employee. If the supervisor rules against the employee, the employee is that much more entitled to a clear, straightforward reply stating the reasons for the decision, not simply a no answer. Although the employee may disagree with such a reply, at least it will be understood.

Clarity is even more necessary if the supervisor has to reply to the grievance in writing. In that case, the answer must be restricted to the specific complaints involved, the words used must be appropriate, and any reference to a particular provision of the labor agreement or to the organization's rules must be clearly cited. Unless required, a written reply should not be rendered. If such a reply is required under the labor agreement, however, it is appropriate for the supervisor to discuss all the implications with higher management or with the human resources department so that a properly worded reply is given.

## ■ Non-Unionized Organizations

Many healthcare facilities have implemented grievance procedures regardless of whether the facility has a union or not. Grievances need to be heard by management in a timely fashion to avoid the possible introduction of a third party and to insure staff concerns are heard and given appropriate attention. To avoid the potential introduction of a third party, human resources departments in many facilities have developed detailed procedures that allow: (1) for first-level supervisors to investigate and attempt to remedy the concern, (2) for an appeal(s) process, and (3) for an ad hoc committee of peers and management to hear and recommend final action as it pertains to the grievance or concern. Each step has an associated time frame to ensure timely response to the complainant.

## ■ Record Keeping

It is essential for the supervisor to keep records and documents whenever a grievance decision is made. If the employee's request is satisfied, this decision may become a precedent. If the complaint cannot be settled in the first step, this grievance probably will go farther, possibly to arbitration or to a government agency, as in cases of discrimination. The case will certainly go to higher levels of management, and the supervisor should not defend the action by depending on memory. Diligent records of the facts, reasoning, and decisions should be available. With this documentation at hand, the supervisor will be able to substantiate the actions whenever asked.

Good records are an absolute necessity because the burden of proof is usually on the supervisor and management. Management has the right to decide, but the union has the right to submit a grievance. Whenever the employee or the union maintains that the supervisor has violated the agreement or has administered its provisions in an unfair or inconsistent manner, the supervisor must defend the action. Without good records and documentation, this will often be difficult, if not impossible.

Supervisors should familiarize themselves with all the previous points as aids in handling grievances. The supervisors' decisions and actions will have some impact on employee-union relations at the healthcare facility. For this impact to be favorable, supervisors not only must be familiar with the points just covered, but also must apply them during honest, face-to-face discussions with employees and the shop steward whenever grievances do arise.

---

**SUMMARY**  The labor agreement sets forth a broad, general outline of labor-management relationships. This outline must be filled in with intelligent supervisory decisions. Occasions to make such decisions arise mainly in the settlement of grievances. Indeed, the proper adjustment of grievances is one of the important components of the supervisory position. Whenever the supervisor settles grievances, the labor contract is referred to and interpreted. The settlements may have far-reaching implications because they set precedents. Much of what the union will discuss at the next contract negotiations originates with day-to-day supervisory decisions. If a grievance should go to arbitration, the impartial arbitrator will also attach great importance to precedents set by the supervisor.

Often it is not so much what the contract says that counts, but how it has been interpreted by management's front-line representative, the supervisor. This shows how important a role the supervisor actually plays in the adjustment of grievances and how necessary it is to gain considerable skill in the use of adjustment techniques. In most organizations, specialists in labor relations will be involved in arriving at the appropriate settlement.

To apply adjustment techniques appropriately, the supervisor should always be available and listen without losing his or her temper, even if the grievance is a "phony" one. The supervisor must learn to define the problem, obtain the facts, and then draw on a thorough knowledge of the contract's clauses. It is also important to avoid unnecessary delays and settle grievances at an early stage. Moreover, the supervisor must be fair in all decisions, protecting the rights of the institution and respecting the content and spirit of the agreement. The supervisor also must keep good records, give clear replies, and, above all, remain consistent.

Historically, unions have developed because management responded to the needs of their work force inappropriately. Today unions are established for similar reasons or at least because employees perceive a lack of attention to their needs on the part of management. Supervisors manage a variety of resources but their most productive, costly, and vocal resource is humans. Effective management will yield high quality, high productivity, and high morale. Recognizing that employees are inherently good and desire the facility to succeed will make the management of other resources (such as money, materials, and machinery) much easier.

# 29

# *Emerging Influences in Healthcare*

*Chapter Objectives*

After studying this chapter you should be able to:

1. Recognize the impact managed care has had on healthcare providers.
2. Distinguish between patient-focused care and teams.
3. Address the advantages of developing multiskilled practitioners.

---

**MANAGED CARE**     The 1960s and 1970s introduced an approach to healthcare that was touted as the answer to controlling healthcare costs—health maintenance organizations (HMOs). The pessimists predicted doom for this new approach, proclaiming its failure to recognize the patient's right to freedom of choice. Over the decades since its establishment, several generations of managed care have evolved. Now broader networks of providers such as preferred provider organizations coupled with smaller networks of HMO providers provide health insurance plan options for patients to move between levels of "freedom" by paying more for the care they seek. Some health plans permit three levels: the HMO, the preferred provider organization, and the full universe of providers available in an indemnity environment. The freedom to choose comes with a price tag but has responded to customer demand.

Why has this model succeeded? Prior to the mid-1970s, when healthcare was paid for regardless of cost both by insurers and the government, demand for services consumed supply. During this time, more hospitals were built, more high tech equipment was installed, and, as one hospital administrator stated, "you can get coronary artery bypass on any corner." How true this has become. But rising costs coupled with higher premiums summoned control, primarily by those paying the premium bills—the employers. Enter managed care.

Managed care considered the demands of consumers and compared them to the necessity. Initially limiting access to one or a few locations, requiring a primary care physician's (known as the "gatekeeper to care") intervention for any requested care, and instituting a co-payment for each service intervention helped to stem the demand and control the cost. For the government-supported consumers, the Medicare recipients, the costs were controlled for inpatient services by implementing the diagnosis-related group (DRG) reimbursement system in the early 1980s. Its impact has been tremendous.

Consumer demand however required more freedom. Employers willing to cost shift the premium increases to employees who were willing to pay a greater portion of the premium bill sought options to offer their employee groups. Preferred provider organizations (PPO) were established. These organizations included providers (physicians, home health services, hospitals, ambulatory care centers, etc.) willing to provide care to employee groups at a discounted rate, thus allowing the insurance premium to be established at a reasonable level.

Providers who were unable to eliminate unnecessary costs either failed under the DRG system and closed their doors or were unable to offer sufficiently discounted rates to the developers of preferred provider organizations and lost patient volume. Managed care pressures hospitals and other healthcare providers to deliver high-quality, low-cost services by becoming more efficient.

Managed care has forced every provider in the United State to re-evaluate its role, making each one overhaul its entire operation by:

- providing high-quality services at a lower cost to the payer;
- emphasizing outpatient care over costly inpatient services;
- reducing inpatient stays;
- merging and developing alliances with previous competitors to achieve economy of scale;
- downsizing; and
- establishing a variety of organizational structures such as physician hospital organizations (PHOs), integrated delivery systems (IDSs), etc.

The challenge for healthcare supervisors in the future will be in the design of cost-effective systems and nontraditional modes of healthcare delivery. Organizing skills will be imperative.

Even with its successes, managed care is not without faults. Some say that patients have been denied care to save money. Others believe that the really good providers have opted out of managed care programs so that they can deliver care to patients without interference, at a cost that is reasonable to do so. Yet several healthcare executives predict that a single-payer system will evolve to protect the economy from rising costs and also to provide some coverage for those 50 million uninsured Americans expected by the year 2000.[1]

In an attempt to streamline operations and reduce costs, healthcare organizations have considered team approaches to performing the daily work, thus eliminating the need for certain supervisory levels of personnel. Another approach that has been alluded to in this text is the "patient focus" system such as that implemented by Lakeland Regional Medical Center in Lakeland, Florida.

## TEAM DEVELOPMENT

At Lakeland Regional Medical Center, teams of staff are cross-trained to provide a wide variety of health services. The center has more than 75 teams. Patients formerly began their journey into the hospital by stopping at the registration area. This department, however, has now been eliminated. Now patients go directly to the patient care area in which they will stay. Lakeland has reduced the number of worker types that a patient encounters from 53 to 13 and anticipates a reduction of 15% of its workforce.

1. *Hospitals and Health Networks, "Special Report—Look at it this Way," July 20, 1996, p. 67.*

Before managers can carefully weigh the benefits of building teams within their organizations, they need to know exactly what they are getting themselves and their institutions into. Such buzzwords as *teamwork* and *team player* often are bandied about without being explained. So just what do they mean? In simple terms, a team is a group of individuals working together daily who possess individual expertise, share responsibilities, and work toward a common purpose.[2]

Teams can be divided into four categories:

- **Work teams,** sometimes self-managed, are charged with transforming organizations. These teams evaluate, improve, manage, or change ongoing work processes or dream up new ones.
- **Integrating teams** consolidate tasks organizationwide. For example, they might streamline purchasing processes across three locations.
- **Management teams** ensure that the organization's design helps rather than hinders it from accomplishing its mission.
- **Improvement teams** dissect the organization's design and suggest processes that will improve the way it functions.[3]

Organizations that have successfully implemented teams have been able to document their success by increased patient and staff satisfaction and by decreased costs.

## MULTISKILLED HEALTHCARE PROFESSIONALS

For teams to be successful in increasing staff satisfaction and reducing the number of workers a patient must come in contact with, a team must have a "one-stop shopping" composition. Therefore, all or many of the team members must be cross-trained and offer more than one skilled service to a patient. In many facilities, one person registers the patient, another takes her blood, another takes an X ray, another person measures blood pressure, and so on. Efficient care requires the elimination or reduction of *conveyor time,* that is the time wasted by multiple individuals capturing the same information (i.e., the patient's name) or lost time traveling between patients for one specified task when many tasks can be done by one person for the same patient at the same "stop" on the "conveyor belt." While this may sound like "factory" medicine, it is quite the contrast because it encourages establishing a rapport with the patient since the patient caregiver must spend more time with the same patient delivering multiple services.

The utilization of multiskilled health practitioners (MSHPs) is one method of enhancing employee productivity, cost effectiveness of health services delivery, and patient satisfaction. Some of the documented outcomes of establishing a multiskilled workforce are shown in table 29.1.

---

2. *Jill L. Sherer, "Tapping into Teams," Hospitals and Health Networks, July 5, 1995, pp. 32–34.*
3. *Ibid,, p. 36.*

**TABLE 29.1   The Impact of Multiskilled Health Practitioners and Associated Factors on Outcomes**

| Organizational Setting (author) | Program Characteristics | Outcomes |
|---|---|---|
| 1. St. Vincent's Hospital<br>Indianapolis, IN<br>(Anderson 1993)<br>(Brider 1992)<br>(Sagenick 1992)<br>(Weber 1991) | Cross-training teams of three<br>Work simplification<br>Work redesign<br>Decentralization | Reduced length of stay 15–20 percent<br>Reduced time to execute order from 90 to 19 minutes<br>Reduced number of steps for order from 46 to 12<br>Reduced infection rate<br>Reduced IV errors<br>Increased percent of time caregivers devote to direct patient care from 46 to 63 percent<br>65 percent of physicians very satisfied; 35 percent satisfied |
| 2. Bishop Clarkson Hospital<br>Omaha, NE<br>(Brider 1992)<br>(Sagenick 1992)<br>(Weber 1992) | Cross-training for respiratory treatments, phlebotomy, and EKGs | Admitting process time reduced from 7.5 hours to 23 minutes<br>Number of steps to start antibiotic regimen reduced<br>More direct patient care by nurses<br>Projected labor savings of 10 percent |
| 3. Lakeland Medical Center, FL<br>(Brider 1992)<br>(Watson et al. 1991)<br>(Sagenick 1992)<br>(Weber 1992) | Cross-training<br>Decentralization | High levels of physician satisfaction<br>Routine lab test time decreased from 157 to 48 minutes<br>Patient contacts with individual caregivers decreased from 54 to 14 on 4-day stay<br>Projected cost saving of 9.2 percent in pilot unit |
| 4. RWJ University Hospital, Central NJ<br>(Brett and Tonges 1990)<br>(Ritter and Tonges 1991) | Cross-training for clinical care nurse and primary nurse<br>Decentralization<br>Environmental redesign | Length of stay reduced 13 percent<br>Higher patient and nurse satisfaction<br>Higher quality of care<br>Favorable cost comparisons |
| 5. Public Health Satellite Clinic, SC<br>(Fearin and Alford 1990) | Cross-training nurses and clerks in care services | Decreased waiting time<br>Improved continuity of care<br>Increased employee loyalty to center<br>Higher levels of patient compliance<br>Kept appointments rose from 53 to 70 percent<br>Some staff turnover<br>Individual employee encounters drop from 56 to 18<br>Reduced cost per patient<br>Improved patient compliance |
| 6. Mercy Hospital, San Diego, CA<br>(Sagenick 1992) | Cross-training of pharmacy staff in various patient unit functions<br>Decentralized services | 10-15 percent projected labor savings |

**TABLE 29.1**—*Continued*

| Organizational Setting (author) | Program Characteristics | Outcomes |
|---|---|---|
| 7. Vanderbilt University Hospital, Nashville, TN (Sagenick 1992) (Anderson 1993) | Service associates cross-trained for transportation, dietary, supply management, and environmental services | 7.5 percent decline in cost per patient day<br>Favorable staff reaction to reduction in paperwork and increased collaboration |
| 8. Forbes Metropolitan Health Center, Pittsburgh, PA (Riley 1990) | Cross-training of nurses to perform in other areas of specialization | Reduction in OR nursing personnel by 10 percent<br>Reduction in ICU nursing personal by 18 percent<br>Reduction in use of agency personnel by 26 percent |
| 9. Aroostook Medical Center, Presque Isle, ME (McMahon 1992) | Cross-training of clinical personnel | Improved quality of care<br>Improved employee morale<br>Savings of $199,000 |
| 10. National Medical Enterprises, California (Ballard and Donnelly 1992) | Caregiver concept based on cross-training | Improved quality of service to physicians<br>Improved quality of service to patients<br>Higher level of job satisfaction for MSHP<br>Improved staff recruitment/retention<br>Better collaboration between physicians and professional staff<br>Decreased cost per patient discharge<br>Better integration of clinical services<br>Decreased length of stay |
| 11. St. Vincent Hospital, Green Bay, WI (Waggoner 1992) | Cross-training<br>Decentralization of authority | Improved quality of care<br>Improved employee retention |
| 12. National survey of 137 hospitals (Vaughan et al. 1991) | Cross-training | 93 percent indicated MSHP employees had a positive attitude<br>67 percent indicated MSHP employees found job more interesting<br>34 percent indicated cost-containment as a benefit<br>17 percent indicated staffing flexibility as a benefit<br>52 percent indicated no problems in utilizing MSHPs<br>53 percent indicated MSHP increased quality of care<br>40 percent expect to increase number of MSHPs while only 3 percent expect to decrease number or discontinue use |

## PATIENT-FOCUSED CARE

*Hospitals* magazine has defined patient-focused care (PFC) as "the redesign of patient care so that hospital resources and personnel are organized around patients rather than around various specialized departments." While none of the characteristics of the concept were universal, basic tenets include decentralization of services, cross-training of employees to create teams of multiskilled caregivers, intensified vertical and horizontal collaboration, and physical/geographical reorganization of delivery systems as services are brought closer to the bedside.[4]

Clearly the employment of MSHPs is a necessity in a patient-focused care environment. Fottler's discussion of PFC and MSHPs offers the following guidelines for implementation and management of a multiskilled health practitioner program. (See table 29.2.) Fottler contends that the MSHP should be adopted as part of an overall change process rather than as an isolated program unrelated to and not reinforced by other organization elements. More comprehensive approaches involving patient-focused care, development of teams/decentralization of support services, and cross-training of clinical personnel are likely to be more effective in the long run. They are also likely to involve a long-term commitment to changing the culture of the organization.[5] For the healthcare supervisor, the challenges will include introducing change to his or her staff, providing an environment for learning different skills while maintaining work flow, and supporting an evolving culture of teams.

## SUMMARY

Employer demands for lower healthcare costs coupled with insurers attempting to respond to its customers, the employers, have forced providers of care to ratchet down the cost of delivering care. These industry dynamics require supervisors to identify more efficient and cost effective ways to deliver patient care and services. One way is to reengineer processes as discussed in chapters 13 and 19. Another approach is to retrain staff to be able to provide a variety of services. This approach has lead to the creation of a multiskilled healthcare professional.

Further, supervisors have learned that "two heads are better than one" and by utilizing teams of employees to work through processes and develop solutions, the staff who are closest to the situation usually devise the best solution.

As the healthcare industry continues to change, the supervisor will be in a pivotal role to make things happen through the wise use of the resources at hand (staff and capital). To do so, he or she must be ready to emphasize a working climate conducive to growth by stressing some variety of duties, delegation of authority, and autonomy and responsibility so that employees can more fully realize their potential.

4.  Myron D. Fottler, Ph.D., *"The Role and Impact of Multiskilled Health Practitioners in the Health Services Industry, Hospitals and Health Networks, 41:1 Spring 1996, p. 63.*
5.  Ibid., *p. 72.*

**TABLE 29.2   Guidelines for Implementation and Management of a Multiskilled Health Practitioner Program**

*Planning*

1. Decide to implement MSHP program only if high level of commitment and support exists among the CEO and other members of the upper-management team.

2. Set up a multidisciplinary core committee to plan the MSHP program and decide what other elements (i.e., patient-focused care, organizational restructuring, cultural change, etc.) should be associated with program implementation.

3. Include physicians and other affected staff in program planning as well as the later implementation and evaluation.

4. Tailor the program to the skills needed in the particular employment setting.

5. Start the program in selected departments that are open to experimentation; add other departments incrementally as efficiency of the concept is demonstrated.

6. Begin the program with teams of 2 or 3 multiskilled caregivers in primary care departments that are operational 24 hours a day, with a large number of multidisciplined employees, and strong, stable leadership.

7. Avoid implementing the program concurrently with employee downsizing, cost-reduction programs, or other significant changes.

8. Develop job descriptions and career ladders for MSHPs.

9. As the program is implemented throughout the organization, eliminate or reduce the role of centralized departments by providing these services at the unit level.

*Communication/Motivation*

10. Clarify all roles, reporting relationships, and supervisory responsibilities through the core committee.

11. Establish one source of authority (often the head nurse) to rearrange the MSHP's priorities and activities on the unit.

12. Initiate a high volume of communications regarding "why," "how," and "who" among all affected parties.

13. Promote the program in terms of how it will benefit the affected physicians and other staff as well as the organization as a whole.

14. Institutionalize the program by modifying job descriptions and reporting relationships.

15. Continually "sell" the program at all levels.

*Recruitment/Selection*

16. Screen job applicants in terms of their interest, talents, and experience as team players.

17. Select candidates from multiskilled positions among volunteers based on their current performance, communication skills, interest in adding skills, adaptability, independence, self-motivation, and willingness to obtain additional training.

18. Select team leaders/supervisors who exhibit an ability to communicate with and delegate tasks to others.

19. Provide adequate staffing for the expected patient load.

*Continued*

**TABLE 29.2**—*Continued*

*Training/Development*

20. Provide on-the-job training or continuing education in the most appropriate places (external or internal) to prepare current clinical practitioners in needed skill areas.

21. Add a limited number of skills related to the original clinical skills of each individual so that competence can be maintained.

22. Provide intensive coaching in "team building" in order to reduce fears and resistance.

23. Recognize that cross-training is in "constant evolution."

*Compensation*

24. Determine compensation policies for MSHPs in advance of the program.

25. Provide additional compensation for employee development and utilization of additional skills that are higher level than the original position.

26. Provide recognition and other forms of nonmonetary compensation for MSHPs.

27. Provide incentives for supervisor to supervise, coach, and successfully utilize MSHPs.

*Performance Appraisal*

28. Appraise and give feedback to MSHPs frequently, based on their performance in their primary department with input from supervisors in other areas where they perform functions.

29. Continually monitor and check MSHP competence in infrequently performed functions.

*Evaluation*

30. Conduct an objective evaluation of the effects of the MSHP and other program elements (if applicable) in terms of quality of care, cost-effectiveness, and satisfaction levels of patients, physicians, MSHPs, and other staff.

31. Continually monitor quality standards in areas impacted by the MSHP.

32. Conduct an analysis to determine how often added skills are being used to determine whether to continue to provide training in all of these areas.

33. Modify skills developed, training methods, and management of MSHPs based on evaluation data.

34. Cultivate a willingness to experiment, to learn from implementation on each unit, and to modify the program based on experience.

# APPENDIX

## FORMAL

## ORGANIZATIONAL

## CHARTS AND MANUALS

# *Appendix*

Many conflicts in organizations are often caused by the employees not understanding their assignments and those of their coworkers. Proper use of organizational charts, manuals, and job descriptions defining and spelling out authority and informational relationships will help to reduce misunderstandings substantially and to clarify doubts. Organizational charts, manuals, and job descriptions are tools to clarify the organization's structure to everyone concerned. The healthcare institution's structure is formalized *graphically* in the chart and *in words* in the manual. These tools help explain to everyone involved in the organization how it works. To be helpful, they must be available all the time and be up-to-date, which means changes must be incorporated promptly.

Once the chief executive officer (CEO) has established the formal structure of the organization by setting up departments, teams, and levels, determining the span of supervision and deciding which positions are to be line and which are to be staff, the entire structure can be depicted graphically in organizational charts and in words by using manuals. These are important organizational tools because they provide a clear-cut picture of the overall institution that can be used by all levels of management. For the supervisor, organizational charts and manuals can be particularly helpful in understanding the formal organizing process and also the goals and intent of the administration. By studying them, the supervisors can see the positions and relations of their own department within the overall structure and learn about the functioning and relationships of all other departments as well. However, it should be mentioned that they do not show the informal organizational relationships discussed in chapter 15.

The responsibility for preparing an organizational chart rests with the CEO. A number of individuals, especially those in staff positions, will probably help in collecting information and preparing charts, but it is one of top-level administration's duties. Although the administrator is responsible for preparing charts and manuals for the institution as a whole, it will be necessary for the supervisor to devise some of these organizational tools on a departmental level if they are not available or not up-to-date. Thus, we must look more carefully at how such tools are prepared and at the information they supply.

## ORGANIZATIONAL CHARTS

Organizational charts are a means of illustrating the organizational structure at a given time; they provide a snapshot. The chart shows the skeleton of the structure, depicting the basic formal relationships and groupings of positions and functions. It maps the lines of decision-making authority. Most of the time the chart starts out with the individual position as the basic unit, which is shown as a rectangular box. Each box represents one function. The various boxes are then interconnected horizontally to show the groupings of activities that make up a department, division, or whatever other part of the organization is under consideration. They are connected vertically to show scalar relationships. Thus, one can readily determine who reports to whom merely by studying the position of the boxes in their scalar relationships. For example, we saw in the organizational charts in figure 10.1 some of the scalar relationships that can be found in a typical hospital.

## Advantages

One of the advantages of creating an organizational chart is the analysis and work that is necessary for its preparation, whether it is for the overall organization or a department. As the chart is prepared, the organization must be carefully analyzed. Such analysis might uncover structural faults and possibly duplications of effort, complexities, or other inconsistencies. One might also uncover cases of dual-reporting relationships (one person reporting to two superiors), overlapping positions, and so on. Moreover, charts might indicate whether the span of supervision is too wide or too narrow. An unbalanced organization can also be readily revealed.

Charts afford a simple way to acquaint new members of the organization with its makeup and how they fit into the entire structure. Most employees within the organization have a keen interest in knowing where they stand, in what relation their supervisor stands to the higher echelons, and so forth. Charts are also helpful in human resources administration. They can indicate possible routes of promotions for managers as well as for other employees.

Another advantage of charts is their assistance in developing better communications and relations. Charts can also be valuable for future planning purposes. A supervisor may want to have two charts for his or her department, one showing the existing arrangements and another depicting the ideal organization. The latter may be used so that all the gradual changes planned fall within the design of the ideal, representing the ultimate organizational goal of the department in the future. Charting shows what is changing and how the change affects the members of the organization.

## Limitations

There are also some limitations to charts, especially if they are not constantly kept up-to-date. It is imperative that organizational changes be recorded speedily because failure to do so makes charts outdated; managers often hesitate or neglect to redraft charts. Another shortcoming of charts is that the information they give is limited. A chart is a snapshot, not an X-ray film or a CT scan; it shows only what is on the surface, not the inner workings of the structure. It shows only formal authority relationships, not the many informal relationships that exist. (See chapter 15.) The chart also does not show the amount of authority and responsibility inherent in each position.

Another problem with charts is that individuals confuse authority relationships with status. Sometimes people read into charts interpretations that are not intended. For example, a person may interpret the degree of power and status by checking how distant a position is on the chart from the box of the CEO, or on which level it is shown. Despite these shortcomings, charts are still a very useful tool for every member of the organization.

## ■ Types of Charts

There are three main types of charts: vertical, horizontal, and circular. Of these, the vertical chart is the one used most often in organized activities.

Throughout this text and especially in figures 10.1 and 13.1, the charts shown and referred to are the vertical type. *Vertical charts* show the different levels of the organization in a step arrangement in the form of a pyramid. The CEO is placed at the top of the chart, and the successive levels of administration are depicted vertically in the pyramid shape.

One of the main advantages of the vertical chart is that it can be easily read and understood. It also shows clearly the downward flow of delegation of authority, chain of command, functional relationships, and how those activities relate to one another. As previously stated, there are a number of shortcomings with charts.

One of the disadvantages of charts is that the information conveyed is incomplete; the vertical chart can also convey a wrong impression about the relative status of certain positions. This is because some positions have to be drawn higher or lower on the chart, when in reality they are on the same organizational plane. For example, an incorrect impression can result if one division of an organization has more levels than another. An organizational unit of three levels may show a supervisor on the lowest level, whereas in a five-level unit that person would be on the third level.

In addition to the vertical chart, some healthcare institutions may occasionally prefer a *horizontal chart,* which reads from left to right. (See figure A.1.) The advantage of a horizontal chart is that it stresses functional relationships and minimizes hierarchical levels. The left-to-right chart of a matrix or project organization is a combination of these two arrangements. Horizontal relationships are superimposed on the vertical chart.

A *circular chart* can also be used. It depicts the various levels on concentric circles rotating around the top-level administrator, who is at the hub of the wheel. (See figure A.2.) Positions of equal importance are on the same concentric circle. This graphic portrayal eliminates positions at the bottom of the chart.

A few organizations might prefer an *inverted pyramid chart,* showing the chief administrator at the bottom and the associate administrators farther up. This type tries to express the idea of the "support" given to each manager by the "superior."

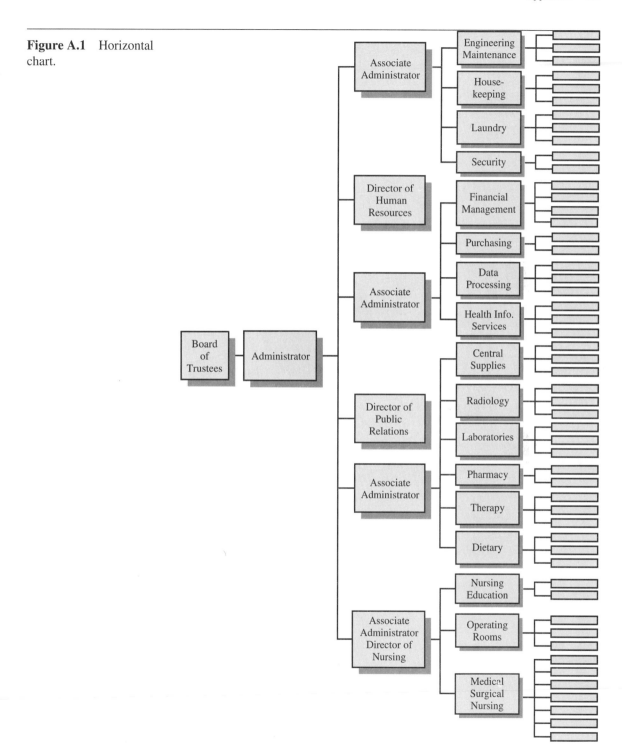

**Figure A.1** Horizontal chart.

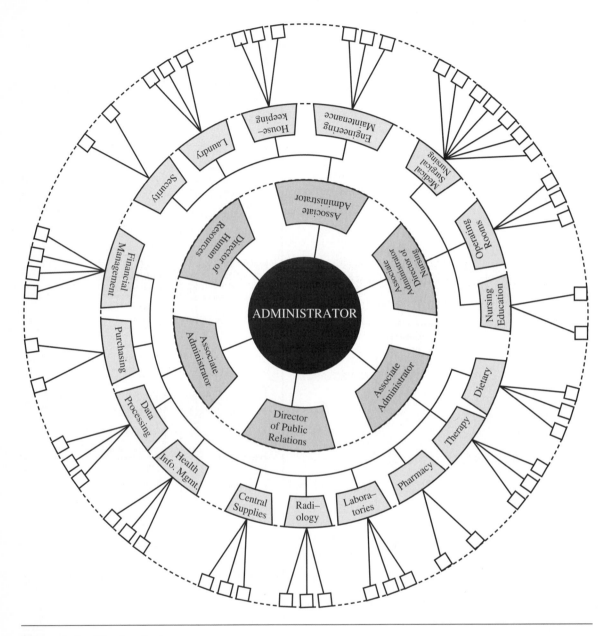

**Figure A.2** Circular chart.

# ORGANIZATIONAL MANUALS

The organizational manual is another helpful tool for achieving effective organization. It provides in comprehensive *written* form the decisions that have been made with regard to the institution's structure. It defines the institution's major policies and objectives, contains organizational charts of the institution and of specific departments; and provides job descriptions. Moreover, the organizational manual is a readily available reference defining the scope of authorities, responsibilities of managerial positions, and channels to be used in obtaining decisions or approval of proposals.

One of the chief advantages of a manual is the analysis and thinking necessary before it can be written. Another advantage is that the manual will also be of great assistance in the indoctrination and development of managerial personnel. The manual should clearly specify for each manager what the responsibilities of the job are and how they are related to other positions within the organization. In addition, it reiterates for the individual manager the objectives of the enterprise and of the department, and it provides a means of explaining the complex relationships within the organization. Supervisors should familiarize themselves with the contents of the institution's manual, especially those parts affecting their own department.

Organizational manuals are a valuable tool only if they are up-to-date. Since the manual is written, it is more difficult to change. Unless manuals are kept current and incorporate changes, they are more of a hindrance than a valuable aid. As stated before, another difficulty with a manual is the initial effort it takes to compile one.

## ■ Content

Although the content of the manual varies from one healthcare institution to another, almost all include statements of objectives, overall policies, job descriptions, organizational charts of the institution and specific departments, and possibly an explanation of titles.

## ■ Objectives and Policies

In the manual, as we have said, top-level management states the major objectives and goals of the institution. For a hospital the manual would state the institution's creed, philosophies, and broad policies in regard to patient care, the quality of medicine practiced, social responsibility, and many other areas of activities. The manual would mention, for example, the hospital's objectives concerning the education of medical and many other professionals, investigative studies, and possibly research in the fields of medical sciences and services. It may state for healthcare providers the objective: "to be alert and responsive to the changing needs of the community and the environment." The manual would also include a statement of overall hospital policies.

## POSITION DESCRIPTIONS

All manuals contain position descriptions, also known as job descriptions. There is some confusion, however, in the use of the term *job description* as compared to *job specification*. Generally, job descriptions objectively describe the elements of a position, that is, the principal duties and functions and also the scope and kind of authority. A job description is an accurate, up-to-date record of all pertinent information about a job as performed in a given department. Job specifications, on the other hand, specify the human qualities required—the personal qualifications necessary to perform the job adequately—such as education, training, experience, and disposition. In most enterprises, position descriptions are extended to include such human qualities.

Position descriptions in the manual will vary depending on the size of the departments and type of work involved. For instance, in the section for nursing services, all jobs starting with the director of nursing services down to the jobs of aides should be described. If a job is particularly complicated or involves numerous activities, its description will probably be rather lengthy (figure A.4); otherwise, most descriptions are fairly short. (See figures A.3 and A.5.)

Initially position descriptions should be written by the CEO and his or her staff as they proceed with the organizing process. If an institution does not have job descriptions, the departmental supervisors should see that they are drawn up. To help in this endeavor, the supervisors should be able to call on the human resources department, which has the necessary expertise to facilitate the job. Even when job descriptions are available, it is the supervisor's duty to become familiar with them to make sure they are realistic, accurate, and up-to-date. Job descriptions have a tendency to become obsolete, which can have serious consequences. Thus, it is necessary for the supervisor to check with employees who hold the various positions in the department and compare their jobs with those descriptions in the manual. If the manual is outdated or incorrect, the supervisor must have it revised. Times are changing, and in all likelihood the content of some jobs has changed without the administrator being aware of it. Furthermore, requirements for background, education, and training have undergone significant changes in many cases. All this should be recorded on the job description.

| BJC HEALTH SYSTEM POSITION DESCRIPTION | |
|---|---|
| **Position Title:** Supervisor, Reception, Evenings and Weekends | **Effective:** 07/01/94 |

**This Position Reports to (Title):** Manager (BJI-Systems)

**Dept:** Medical Record Services     **Entity:** Barnes/Jewish     **Job Grade:** 09

**Position Purpose:** Assumes responsibility for Central File and Reception areas of the department and for clinic support, payroll, ordering and scheduling functions to include coverage of alternate shifts (evenings, nights, weekends and holidays).

| Principal Accountabilities and Essential Duties of the Job: | % of Time |
|---|---|
| Monitors operations to ensure that "customers" are treated in a courteous and helpful manner, that services are provided in a timely fashion, and that high quality outcomes are achieved. | 30 |
| Acts as department coordinator of all patient record storage, retrieval, and filing functions. Coordinates medical record portion of any Medicare/Medicald/Blue Cross on-site audits. | 20 |
| Functions as Local Area Network (LAN) systems coordinator for record tracking system designing, installing and testing reports/output and troubleshooting errors as required by end users. Acts as Department resource for issues concerning hospitalwide clinical computer system (Technicon Data Systems—MIS). | 20 |
| Structures and modifies staffing as necessary to ensure coverage of delegated areas (weekdays) and of Department operations during alternate shifts (weekend/holiday days; 7-day evenings and 7-day nights). | 10 |
| Incorporates Total Quality Management principles into daily activities and implements quality control mechanisms to maintain integrity of services provided in all areas of responsibility. | 20 |
| Recognizes importance of strong positive customer/peer relations and works toward development of a service-oriented department. Reflects service orientation in procedures and employee evaluation tools. Monitors and responds to both positive and negative employee behaviors, as appropriate. | |
| Organizes and leads monthly in-service meetings for staff; distributes written guidelines, as indicated, between meetings. | |
| Completes special projects as assigned. | |
| Attach optional second page if necessary. | |
| The most significant duties have been included in this description. This does not preclude the assignment of occasional additional or developmental duties. The hospital reserves the right to modify this job description as needed to accurately reflect duties assigned. | |

**Figure A.3** Example: Supervisor, Reception, Evenings and Weekends. Weighted position description.

*Courtesy of BJC Health System's Medical Record Services, St Louis, MO.*

---

**Job Complexity:** * __ Level 1 __ Level 2 __ Level 3 __ Level 4 _X_ Level 5

---

**Impact of Decision-making Errors:** * __ Level 1 __ Level 2 __ Level 3 _X_ Level 4

---

**Position in the Organization:** * __ Staff __ Clerical __ Analyst __ Coordinator __ Lead __ Specialist
_X_ Supervisor __ Manager __ Director __ VP/Executive

---

**Age Category of Patients Served:** Check all age categories of patients served.
(Required by JCAHO for patient care givers.)
_X_ N/A __ < 1 Year __ 1–16 __ 16–49 __ 50 and over

---

**Exposure to blood/body fluid:** (Required by OSHA) __ Yes _X_ No

---

**Education and Experience:** Check the minimum requirements for education and experience. The education or experience preferred may be listed on the line provided.

**Education:**
__ Basic skill set
__ High school or equivalent (GED)
__ High school plus specialized training (minimum of 6 months to 2 years)
_X_ Associate degree
_X_ Bachelor's degree in _____
              (appropriate field)
__ Master's degree
__ Ph.D
__ M.D.

Preferred: _____

_X_ Certification/Licensure Required for Job: _____

**Experience:** (Check Appropriate Lines)

| Technical Field | Supervision |
|---|---|
| __ no experience | __ 0 to 2 yrs. |
| _X_ 3 months to 1 yr. | __ 3 to 4 yrs. |
| __ 1 yr. to 3 yrs. | __ 5 to 7 yrs. |
| __ 3 yrs. to 5 yrs. | __ 8 to 10 yrs. |
| __ > 5 yrs. | __ > 10 yrs. |

Preferred: _____

**Other Knowledge, Skills, Abilities Required:**
              Typing

---

**Physical Activity:** Check all that apply.

|  | NA | 0–25% | 26–75% | 76–100% | Avg. Lbs. |
|---|---|---|---|---|---|
| Lift/carry | __ | _X_ | __ | __ | ___ |
| Push/pull | __ | _X_ | __ | __ | ___ |
| Reach overhead | __ | _X_ | __ | __ | |
| Climb | __ | _X_ | __ | __ | |
| Squat/bend/kneel | __ | _X_ | __ | __ | |
| Sit | __ | __ | _X_ | __ | |
| Stand | __ | _X_ | __ | __ | |
| Walk/move about | __ | _X_ | __ | __ | |

---

**Working Conditions:** Check all the boxes that describe the environment.

_x_ Temperature _____ Heated and A/C office _____

_x_ Noise _____ Routine office noise _____

__ Chemicals or hazardous material/waste handled or present _____

Tools used _____

Equipment operated ___ Computer, printer, copy machine, fax machine _____

---

*For definitions see reverse side.

---

**Figure A.3**—*Continued*

# BJC HEALTH SYSTEM POSITION DESCRIPTION

**Position Title:** Registered Nurse

**Effective:** May, 1994

**This Position Reports to (Title):** Nurse Manager/Supervisor

**Dept:** Various Cost Centers     **Entity:** Barnes     **Job Grade:** 50, 51, 52

**Position Purpose:** Provides and directs patient care including assessment, diagnosis, planning, implementation and evaluation within the guidelines of the standards of nursing care and operational guidelines.

| Principal Accountabilities and Essential Duties of the Job: | % of Time |
|---|---|
| 1. Supports the continuous improvement of quality and service to ensure the organizational goal of excellence in outcomes and 100% consumer satisfaction. | (1) 20% |
| Identifies consumers and is professional and helpful in contacts. | |
| Identifies and manages problems to consumer satisfaction. | |
| Demonstrates understanding and applies primary nursing principles in daily practice. | |
| 2. Demonstrates appropriate assessment of the patient including age specific needs to promote optimal levels of wellness; documents patients assessment and teaching needs according to policy. | (2) 15% |
| Completes body systems assessment on assigned patients. | |
| Recognizes abnormal physical/psychological findings to determine appropriate nursing diagnosis(es). | |
| Assesses educational and discharge needs. | |
| 3. Plans patient care based on nursing assessment and diagnosis, medical interventions and patient/other's level of understanding; documents plans according to policy. | (3) 15% |
| Formulates a written plan of care. | |
| Collaborates with physicians and health team members. | |
| Documents patient's understanding of disease process and identifies needs with patient/others. | |
| 4. Provides patient care according to age-specific needs and nursing interventions to attain the patient's optimal level of wellness; documents care provided according to policy. | (4) 15% |
| Prioritizes and organizes care to complete tasks within a specific time period. Demonstrates competency in performance of basic nursing skills and specific skills relative to area of practice. | |
| Completes annual competency testing and skills demonstration. | |
| 5. Reviews and evaluates the patient and plan of care; documents evaluation according to policy. | (5) 15% |
| Evaluates and documents: | |
|   a.     Patient's progress toward achievement of expected outcomes. | |
|   b.     Effectiveness of nursing care/medical therapies. | |
|   c.     Effectiveness of teaching. | |
| 6. Maintains accountability for care of assigned patients. Acts with initiative, practices independently and provides direction to others. | (6) 10% |
| Is knowledgeable of and participates in the operational needs of the area. | |
| Is a role model and clinical resource for other staff. | |
| Meets the expectations of unit specific roles i.e. fall coordinator, infection control nurse. | |
| 7. Provides cost effective, appropriate patient care. | (7) 10% |
| Completes work activities without overtime. | |
| Charges for supplies and procedures performed. | |
| Evaluates products. Reduces supply waste. | |
| Utilizes financial indicators for measuring productivity. | |

*Attach optional second page if necessary.*

**Figure A.4**—Example: Registered Nurse position description.

*Courtesy of BJC Health System, St Louis, MO.*

Job Complexity: * ____Level 1 ____Level 2 ____Level 3 __x_Level 4 ____Level 5

Impact of Decision-making Errors: * ____Level 1 ____Level 2 __x__Level 3 ____Level 4

Position in the organization: * __x__ Staff ____Clerical ____Analyst ____Coordinator ____Lead ____Specialist
____Supervisor ____Manager ____Director ____VP/Executive

**Age Category of Patients Served:** Check all age categories of patients served.
(Required by JCAHO for patient care giver.)
__x__< 1 year __x__1-11 __x__12-18 __x__19-50 __x__51-64 __x__65 and over

**Exposure to blood/body fluid:** (Required by OSHA) __x__Yes ____No

**Education and Experience:** Check the **minimum** requirements for education & experience. The education or
Experience preferred may be listed on the line provided.

**Education:**
____Basic skill set
____High school or equivalent (GED)
____High school plus specialized training (minimum of 6 months to 2 years)
__x__Associate degree or Diploma School Program
____Bachelor's degree in_____
                    (appropriate field)
____Master's degree
____Ph.D
____M.D.

Preferred: ___BSN_____ Refer to page 3.

__x__Certification/Licensure Required for Job: Missouri RN License

**Experience:** (Check Appropriate Lines)
| Technical Field | Supervision |
|---|---|
| __x__no experience | ____0 to 2 yrs. |
| ____3 months to 1 yr. | ____3 to 4 yrs. |
| ____1 yr. to 3 yrs. | ____5 to 7 yrs. |
| ____3 yrs. to 5 yrs. | ____8 to 10 yrs. |
| ____> 5 yrs. | ____> 10 yrs. |

Preferred:_____

**Other Knowledge, Skills, Abilities
Required:**

**Physical Activity:** Check all that apply.

| | NA | 0-25% | 26-75% | 76-100% | Avg. Lbs. |
|---|---|---|---|---|---|
| Lift/Carry | ___ | _x_ | ___ | ___ | ___ 40 ___ |
| Push/Pull | ___ | ___ | _x_ | ___ | ___ 150 ___ |
| Reach overhead | ___ | _x_ | ___ | ___ | |
| Climb | ___ | _x_ | ___ | ___ | |
| Squat/Bend/Kneel | ___ | ___ | _x_ | ___ | |
| Sit | ___ | _x_ | ___ | ___ | |
| Stand | ___ | ___ | _x_ | ___ | |
| Walk/move about | ___ | ___ | _x_ | ___ | |

**Working conditions:** Check all the boxes that describe the environment.

__x__ temperature: Clean, air-conditioned environment

__x__ noise: Routine patient care area noise

__x__ chemicals or hazardous material/waste handled or present: Infectious patients, contaminated specimens, toxic
drugs and radiation

Tools Used: Usual Nursing-Medical tools

Equipment operated: CRT, Intercom and other hospital-provided equipment

**Figure A.4**—*Continued*

**REQUIREMENTS FOR CLINICAL SERVICES**

Graduate of accredited school of nursing and licensed to practice professional nursing in the state of Missouri. All services require individualized shells for their areas through competency testing in the core modules and shell reviews.

- Staff nurses employed in the Intensive Care Unit must successfully complete the Critical Care Course within six months of employment.

- Staff nurses employed in Neurosurgery must successfully complete the orientation course for neurosurgery within six months of employment.

- Staff nurses employed in Neuromedicine must complete the Neurology Competency testing within 12 months of employment.

- Staff nurses employed in the Cardiac Cath Lab/EP Lab must have previous Intensive Care, Emergency Room or Cath Lab experience and ACLS certification is preferred.

- Psychiatry prefers to hire staff nurses with experience in Geriatric, Adolescent, General or Adult Psychiatry. Staff nurses in Psychiatry must complete CPI certification within one year of employment.

- Staff nurses employed in Burn Trauma and PACU must complete ACLS certification within 6 months of employment and maintain annual certification.

- Staff Nurses in the Emergency Department must complete ACLS certification within 6 months of employment and maintain annual certification Eight hours of continuing education is also required annually.

- Staff Nurses employment in outpatient services should have a minimum of 2 years experience in an acute care setting. Prior experience in procedural areas, operating room and/or similar outpatient experience is preferred.

- Nurses employed in the West Pavilion Center and Digestive Disease Center required one year of Critical Care experience.

- Radiology prefers Staff Nurses to have a minimum of two years Critical Care experience and to attain ACLS certification within the first year of employment. ACLS certification must be maintained annually.

- Staff Nurses employed in the Pheresis area must have two years of general nursing experience in medicine, dialysis or intensive care. Additional experience in IV therapy is preferred.

- Staff Nurses working in the Oncology Clinical Service Line must complete Chemotherapy Certification within one year.

- Staff Nurses in Obstetrics and Neonatal areas must complete NOWS certification within one year of employment.

**EXPECTATION I Service and Quality**

Supports the continuous improvement of quality and service to ensure the organizational goals of excellence in clinical outcomes and 100% consumer satisfaction.
1.   Understands and participates in the continuous quality improvement process.
2.   Identifies patients, families, physicians and other departments as consumers and is friendly and helpful in contacts with these individuals.
3.   Communicates in a manner that demonstrates respect, courtesy and politeness.
4.   Maintains confidentiality.
5.   Recognizes consumer dissatisfaction, manages concerns quickly and to the satisfaction of the consumer or contacts the appropriate individual for follow up.
6.   Identifies problems early, offers suggestions for resolution and seeks input from other team members.
7.   Develops and maintains positive work relationships. Manages work related conflicts by communicating directly with team member or seeks assistance of manager when necessary.
8.   Participates in unit meeting to contribute to development of unit objectives. Willingly assumes new tasks/projects and assists others.
9.   Participates in assuring that unit quarterly indicator thresholds are met.
10.  Demonstrates understanding and application of primary nursing operational guidelines in daily practice.
11.  Achieves threshold or better on primary nursing audits.
12.  Develops and reviews goals for professional development with manager at evaluation conference.

**EXPECTATION II Assessment of Patients**

Assesses the patient including age specific needs, to promote optimal levels of wellness; documents patient's assessment and teaching needs according to policy.

1.   Completes a body systems assessment on assigned patients as well as an evaluation of discharge needs.
2.   Recognizes abnormal physical and/or psychological findings and factors that interfere with learning and/or discharge.
3.   Utilizes data gathered to determine an appropriate nursing diagnosis(es).
4.   The assessment data reflects the patient's status and interprets the information needed to identify each patient's requirements related to specific age needs.
5.   Evaluates patient's understanding of disease process, present condition or planned procedure.
6.   Documents assessment data in a thorough and concise manner according to policy.
7.   Evaluates clinical knowledge of staff. (Nurse Educator)
8.   Assesses staffing needs for safe patient assignments. (Charge Nurse)

**Figure A.4**—*Continued*

---

### BJC HEALTH SYSTEM POSITION DESCRIPTION

| | |
|---|---|
| **Position Title:** Director | **Effective:**  Sept., 1994 |

**This Position Reports to (Title):** Vice President

| | | |
|---|---|---|
| **Dept:** Heart Services | **Entity:** Barnes | **Job Grade:** 35 |

**Position Purpose:** Provide and directs patient care including assessment, diagnosis, planning, implementation and Evaluation within the guidelines of the standards of nursing care and operational guidelines.

---

| **Principal Accountabilities and Essential Duties of the Job:** | % of Time |
|---|---|
| 1. Directs and supports the continuous improvement of quality and service to ensure the Barnes goal of excellence in clinical outcomes and 100% consumer satisfaction. | (1) 20% |
| Directs the use of the quality improvement process to define and plan improvement for identified service problems. | |
| Organizes services to promote patient and consumer satisfaction with heart services. | |
| 2. Establishes high standards of performance for managers and staff. Facilitates innovation and manages change process effectively. | (2) 20% |
| Delegates authority and maintains manager accountability for outcomes. | |
| Demonstrates initiative and follow through. | |
| Promotes and contributes to education, research, and publication in healthcare. | |
| 3. Achieves the flow of ideas and information needed to reach goals and objectives. | (3) 20% |
| Uses oral and written communication methods effectively. | |
| Articulates expectations clearly. | |
| Maintains regular meeting with staff. | |
| 4. Demonstrates knowledge of strategic and operational planning theories. | (4) 20% |
| Monitors trends in healthcare and respective service. | |
| Utilizes accumulated information to establish effective program and fiscal plans. | |
| Develops effective business plans as appropriate. | |
| Develops financial plans appropriately. | |
| 5. Sets and achieves appropriate and challenging goals within the desired cost and time limit. | (5) 20% |
| Guides managers to accomplish appropriate goals and objectives. Meets deadlines consistently. | |

Attach optional second page if necessary.

The most significant duties have been included in this description. This does not preclude the assignment of occasional additional or developmental duties. The Hospital reserves the right to modify this job description as needed to accurately reflect duties assigned.

---

**Figure A.5**—Example: Director position description.

*Courtesy of BJC Health System, St Louis, MO.*

**Job Complexity:** *____Level 1 ____Level 2 ____Level 3 ____Level 4 ____Level 5

**Impact of Decision-making Errors:** *____Level 1 ____Level 2 ____Level 3 ____Level 4

**Position in the organization:** *____Staff ____Clerical ____Analyst ____Coordinator ____Lead ____Specialist
____Supervisor ____Manager _x_Director ____VP/Executive

**Age Category of Patients Served:** Check all age categories of patients served.
(Required by JCAHO for patient care givers.)
_x_ N/A ____< 1 year ____1–16 ____16–49 ____50 and over

**Exposure to blood/body fluid:** (Required by OSHA) _x_Yes ____No

**Education and Experience:** Check the **minimum** requirements for education & experience. The education or experience preferred may be listed on the line provided.

**Education:**
____Basic skill set
____High school or equivalent (GED)
____High school plus specialized training (minimum of 6 months to 2 years)
____Associate degree
____Bachelor's degree in_____
         (appropriate field)
_x_Master's degree in Nursing, Business or Health Care.
____Ph.D
____M.D.

**Preferred:**

____ Certification/Licensure Required for Job: <u>If RN, Missouri RN Licensure</u>

**Experience:** (Check Appropriate Lines)

| Technical Field | Supervision |
|---|---|
| ____no experience | _x_0 to 2 yrs. |
| ____3 months to 1 yr. | ____3 to 4 yrs. |
| ____1 yr. to 3 yrs. | ____5 to 7 yrs. |
| _x_3 yrs. to 5 yrs. | ____8 to 10 yrs. |
| ____> 5 yrs. | ____> 10 yrs. |

Preferred: _____

**Other Knowledge, Skills, Abilities**
**Required:** Leadership ability, effective communication skills and an understanding of planning and research skills.

**Physical Activity:** Check all that apply.

| | NA | 0–25% | 26–75% | 76–100% | Avg. Lbs. |
|---|---|---|---|---|---|
| Lift/Carry | ____ | _x_ | ____ | ____ | ____ 20 ____ |
| Push/Pull | ____ | _x_ | ____ | ____ | ____ 20 ____ |
| Reach overhead | ____ | _x_ | ____ | ____ | |
| Climb | ____ | _x_ | ____ | ____ | |
| Squat/Bend/Kneel | ____ | _x_ | ____ | ____ | |
| Sit | ____ | ____ | _x_ | ____ | |
| Stand | ____ | ____ | _x_ | ____ | |
| Walk/move about | ____ | ____ | _x_ | ____ | |

**Working conditions:** Check all the boxes that describe the environment.

_x_ temperature <u>Air-Conditioned environment</u>

_x_ noise <u>Normal office environment</u>

_x_ chemicals or hazardous material/waste handled or present <u>Infectious patients, toxic drugs and radiation</u>

Tools Used

Equipment operated <u>Personal computer, fax, telephone equipment</u>

**Figure A.5**—*Continued*

Many organizations have created criteria-based position descriptions.

| | |
|---|---|
| **CRITERIA-BASED JOB DESCRIPTION AND PERFORMANCE STANDARDS** | |

**Position Title**
Multiskilled Administrative Support Staff II
(MASS II)

**Hospital**
Lakeland Regional Medical Center

**Responsible To**
Within-the-Team Leader and/or
Department Leaders(s)

**Date**
November 16, 1995

**Department**

**Page**
1

**Typist**

**Approved by**

All the criteria-based duties and standards within this document will be performed according to established policies, procedures, and guidelines within the department and the Hospital.

■ Job Summary

The Multiskilled Administrative Support Staff (MASS II) is responsible to Within-the-Team Leader and/or Department Leader(s). Works as an empowered member of a self-directed work team committed to common purpose and goals, and holds self mutually accountable for team outcomes, under the general supervision of a Within-the-Team Leader. Shares 24-hour, 7 day/week responsibility for all aspects of department administrative support. Must be able to perform at the expert level in financial counseling and referral to entitlement agencies. Serves as a resource to other Multiskilled Administrative Support Staff (MASS). Performs miscellaneous duties as assigned.

■ Primary Job Duties

1. Makes decisions consistent with the principles and tenets of patient-focused care.
2. Demonstrates continuous learning and improvement of competence in own job role and actively participates in departmental performance improvement program so that outcomes are improved and costs are reduced.
3. Takes personal responsibility for self and accountability for actions in a self-directed work team environment, as well as sharing the work of the team.
4. Promotes patient, physician, and staff satisfaction.
5. Is able to perform the primary duties of a MASS.

6. Insures patients or their representatives are contacted regarding unfunded accounts or uninsured balances. Arrangements for appropriate deposits and/or payment schedules are made.

7. Insures information on alternate funding sources is provided and unfunded patients are referred to appropriate agencies as required.

8. Monitors in-house reports/folders and reviews complex case as required.

9. Performs reimbursement audit functions across the center to review accounts and practices that impact revenue.

10. Responsible for communicating changes in payor rules, regulations, and requirements and insures policies and procedures are amended as required.

11. Serves as a resource to MASS staff regarding all aspects of financial counseling as required.

---

## TEAM/UNIT QUALITY OF WORK-OUTCOME

**1.0** The following standards relate to the team's performance in the categories of quality, productivity and interpersonal relations. All performance demonstrates an understanding of the care of patients utilizing the principles of Patient-Focused care.

- Resources must be patient-focused and fully utilized.
- All operations must be responsive to patient and physician needs.
- Individuals at all levels must be accountable and satisfied.
- Patients must readily perceive value in their care.

**1.1  10%** Continuously improves the cost-effectiveness, efficiency, and quality of care to patients so that the OPIP unit or team relative value score is between 3.2 and 2.8. Distinguishes the OPIP trending data that is applicable to the MASS role and formulates improvement action plans.

**Source of Information:** Organizational Performance Improvement Plan
**Measurement Criteria:** Exceeds if relative value score is < 2.8

**1.2  10%** Consistently performs 100% of the Stage 2 behaviors in team development matrix, so that the team functions effectively to perform the total work of the team as evidenced by the use of Patient-Focused Tenets*.

| | |
|---|---|
| * Seek the Source | * Work it out |
| * Team with the docs | * Focus on care |
| * Serve the patient | * Lend a hand |
| * Keep it simple | * Keep it current |
| * Be the best | * Keep the continuity |

**Source of Information:** Supervisory Observation—10%
Documented Team Examples—50%
Input from patient/physician satisfaction surveys—30%
Peer Review—10%
**Measurement Criteria:**
Meets: Can demonstrate 100% of the behaviors at Stage 2 using 5 tenets consistently within/across team(s).

Exceeds: Consistently performs 100% of the behaviors at Stage 4 of Team Development.

1.3   10%   The team consistently demonstrates a willingness and flexibility to assume a workload level resulting in efficient/productive team utilization. All team members are flexible to provide coverage across all shifts and to adjust staffing related to the work of the unit as needed so that paid hours for the team are within budget.

**Source of Information:**
FTE management reports (monthly).
**Measurement Criteria:**
Meets: Team FTE/OT are 98–100% of budget.
Exceeds: Team < 98% of budget.

1.4   20%   Records are reviewed for complete and accurate documentation, including demographic, guarantor/insurance, and financial (i.e., charge posting) follow-up resulting in positive reimbursement outcomes.

**Source of Information:**
Team-based file review (2/member/yr) to be completed within the team—25%
MASS II review (2/member/yr)—50%
Number of reimbursement denials/errors. (Provided by finance)—25%
Total number of errors divided by the number of admissions.
**Measurement Criteria:**
Meets: Overall accuracy rate of 95–97%.
Exceeds: Overall accuracy rate is greater than 97%.

---

**INDIVIDUAL QUALITY OF WORK OUTCOMES**   2.0   Each individual must take personal responsibility for self through demonstrated competence, continuous learning, active participating in the departmental performance improvement program as well as sharing the work of the self-directed team. The process of continued team development is based on the success of this individual's development, which is measured in the performance standards below:

2.1   15%   Demonstrates technical competence of all primary job duties for MASS, as specified at the advanced beginner or competent level so that desired outcomes are met or continually improved.

**Source of Information:** Department—identified tools of assessment (written and oral tests, observed skills, demonstration, etc.). Team-based file review (2/member/yr) to be completed within the team—25%.
MASS II review (2/member/yr)—50%.
**Measurement Criteria:**
Meets: Advanced beginner/competent skills and file reviews indicate 95–97% accuracy.
Exceeds: Demonstrates expert performance with > 97% accuracy.

2.2   5%   Demonstrates positive interpersonal skills/relationships with both customers and peers as demonstrated by positive guest relations, good phone etiquette, offering assistance/direction to guest/peers, and initiating direct and honest communication.

**Source of Information:**
Supervisory observation—20%
Peer review—40%
Documented examples—40%
**Measurement Criteria:** See Subjective Criteria

2.3   5%   Optimize outcomes through appropriate follow-up, seeking appropriate resources as needed and initiating independent actions based on judgment. (i.e, Initiation of referrals to outside agencies for unfunded patient admission.)

**Source of Information:**
Documented examples—40%
Chart/folder review—40%
Supervisory observation—20%
**Measurement Criteria:** See Subjective Criteria

2.4   5%   Actively supports the LRMC Culture through consistent demonstration of the six fundamental components. Meets with Department Manager/Leader to: (1) ensure understanding of the Culture's fundamental components, (2) seek assistance in identifying opportunities for improvement, and (3) establish a personalized set of goals and objectives for continuous improvement.

**Source of Information:**
Direct observation by manager/leader, team feedback, patient/customer feedback.
**Measurement Criteria:**
Meets if consistently demonstrates five of the six fundamental components.

Exceeds if consistently demonstrates continuous improvement in at least three of the six components.

2.5    5%    Consistently meets job expectations and does not exceed budgeted authorized hours during performance appraisal period unless specifically approved by department manager.

**Source of Information:**
Department FTE and payroll reports.

**Measurement Criteria:**
Meets if hours paid are 98–100% of budgeted authorized hours. Exceeds if hours paid are less than 98% of budgeted authorized hours. Does Not Meet if hours paid are more than 100% of budgeted authorized hours.

2.6    15%    Acquires and reviews information regarding updates in Payor Rules, Regulations, and Requirements, and communicates these updates to the MASS staff as needed. Coordinates the education of appropriate staff as well as monitors the implementation of any changes. Serves as a financial counseling resource to MASS staff.

**Source of Information:**
Documented examples of attendance at education and training offerings.
Documented examples of communication of information to MASS staff.
Assessment feedback from Financial Liaison.
Assessment feedback from Within-the-Team Leader

**Measurement Criteria:**
Meets: Subjective criteria indicates a positive impact on collection errors.
Exceeds: Subjective criteria indicates a positive impact on collection errors with documentation that analysis resulted in the correction of $100,000 worth of errors.

*Courtesy of Lakeland Regional Medical Center, Inc., Lakeland, Florida.*

Categories of emphasis are defined in the position description, such as Quality of Work, Interpersonal Relations, Productivity and Personal Use of Time, Financial Contribution, and Support of Organization Culture. Examples of these have been seen in earlier chapters. Each category carries a weight, with all weights totalling 100. Within a category there may be several observable subcategories each with its own subweight totalling the category's weight. These positions descriptions can then be used to evaluate performance and directly tie the position description and the evaluation. Given the individual's performance, they may achieve up to 100 percent but often this does not occur. Therefore, it is necessary to establish ranges that tie to an action that will be taken when the performance evaluation is completed. Some organizations tie the percentage to pay increase amounts. (See figure A.6.)

**Figure A.6** HIM
Technician–Especially-
For-You Medical Center.

Primary Job Duties/Essential Functions

1. Analyzes medical records for items not meeting hospital, JCAHO, and state requirements. Identifies these deficiencies for each physician and enters in computerized system to allow monitoring until completion.
2. Pulls incomplete records for physicians upon request, and monitors records for after physicians have worked on them for completion of deficiencies.
3. Inserts lab data, test results, procedural notes, and dictated reports into records in their prescribed location and updates receipt of same in computerized system.
4. Identifies which physicians require notification or sanctioning; Verifies and assists with preparing these physician letters.
5. Expedites re-routing records with completed documentation to coders for billing.
6. Serves as primary department contact for/and continually assists and communicates with physicians in person and on telephone, so that records are complete within Medical Staff Bylaws, JCAHO, HCFA, and State mandated time frame.
7. Fully understands, trains, and assists physicians with the use of dictation systems and other computer based applications for HIM related functions.
8. Performs clinical pertinence studies for each clinical service, the Medical Record Department, and other health care activities in accordance of hospital performance improvement plan.
9. Summarizes results of Clinical Pertinence for Medical Record Committee and Quality Assurance.
10. Provides daily productivity log to Supervisor.
11. Performs miscellaneous duties as required.

Evaluation Components

| | | |
|---|---|---|
| **1.0** | **40%** | **Quality of Work** |
| 1.1 | 10% | Reviews records for timeliness and completeness of documentation so that quarterly reports are available to the Medical Record Committee. |
| 1.2 | 10% | Coordinates and communicates with physicians on all timeliness and completeness studies, record completion requirements, as well as special studies and projects. |
| 1.3 | 10% | Analyzes medical records accurately so that all deficiencies are recorded and entered into the computer system, and physician specific deficiency slips are attached to incomplete chart without exception, even complex, complicated records. Listens to dictation system and enters information in deficiency system as applicable. |
| 1.4 | 10% | Reviews record to make certain all component parts are present, updates deficiencies and assigns a visit to physicians in computer system, and sends to permanent file with no more than 2–3 exceptions per year. |

| | | |
|---|---|---|
| **2.0** | **45%** | **Individual Productivity/Time Usage** |
| 2.1 | 10% | Performs special projects and Clinical Pertinence studies. Reviews and assesses a minimum of 5% of each physician's annual admissions for completeness of documentation and timeliness of |

documentation. Compiles quarterly reports to show areas lacking documentation.

2.2   10% Communicates with physicians to assist with timely completion of medical records, and to assist with the coordination of timeliness and completion studies.

2.3   20% Analyzes inpatient and outpatient medical records and records deficiencies in computer system on current discharges at the rate of 20–30 records per hour. Facilitates special project records.

2.4   5% Facilitates the completion of medical records, with no more than 3 to 5 exceptions per year.

**3.0   15% Interpersonal Relations/Team Work**

3.1   10% Actively supports the hospital's customer service and organizational improvement mission through demonstration of its six fundamental components so that one's own behavior is continuously improved and care and services are provided to our customers in an empowered, interdependent, and team-oriented environment.

3.2   5% Performs miscellaneous duties as assigned to the satisfaction of the supervisor.

Range of Achievement for Each Category

**Exceeds:** In the evaluator's judgment and experience, this employee's performance is exceptional and is matched by very few employees. This employee provides a model and a resource person for other employees in the unit/area. The employee's demonstrated performance is at a level well beyond that normally expected of the majority of experienced employees in similar positions. Requires little or no oversight or supervision concerning this standard. Assign more than 75% and up to 100% of the percentage assigned to the category of performance.

**Meets:** In the evaluator's judgment and experience, this employee's performance meets the Hospital's high expectations for the job and is viewed as performing very well on this standard. Requires a normal amount of oversight and supervision regarding this standard. A definite asset to the Hospital. Assign 50%–74% of the percentage assigned to the category of performance.

**Does Not Meet:** In the evaluator's judgment and experience, this employee's performance is marginally acceptable and is in need of improvement. This employee is not meeting the expectations of the Hospital in this area. Requires more than the typical amount of oversight and close supervision on this standard. Assign 0–49% of the percentage assigned to the category of performance.

Adjustment Factor

| | *Total Percent Achieved All Categories* | *Wage Adjustment Percent* |
|---|---|---|
| Range: | 0–49% | 0–2% |
| | 50–74% | 3–4% |
| | 75–100% | 5–7% |

If they are kept current, position descriptions will prove invaluable to many people throughout the organization. They inform the incumbent (and whomever needs or wants to know) what he or she is supposed to do. The position description usually includes some statement of authority and informational relationships. It has many other additional benefits. For example, the human resources director will refer to the job description when requests are made by the supervisor to recruit applicants for an open position. Furthermore, someone in the human resources department will use them in the preliminary interview. The supervisor will also keep the job description in mind when applicants for positions in the department are interviewed.

Position descriptions help in drawing up candidate requirements. The new employee should have a chance to see the description of the job for which he or she has been hired. In some healthcare facilities, it is standard practice to hand new employees a copy of it for them to keep and study. In this respect, position descriptions serve as a basis of common understanding between employees and management. The job description is also used when the supervisor evaluates and appraises the employee's performance at regular intervals. For all of these reasons, both the supervisor and the administrator should be vitally concerned that the content of the position description is proper and current.

## TITLES

No standard agreement exists on the use and meaning of titles, especially in the upper echelons of healthcare centers. This is because of the recent trend toward the use of corporate titles for the top-level person. The role of the executive head has evolved from superintendent to hospital administrator to executive director to president. The job of the CEO in larger hospitals is no longer concerned only with the internal operations of the hospital, but also with the external relations in the larger field of community responsibilities. The title of president is gaining more and more acceptance, and the CEO of the healthcare center in the future will be known as the hospital president, just as is his or her counterpart in industry. This will assist those who are not familiar with healthcare operations to identify the president's organizational role properly. Before too long, the term *president* for the healthcare center's CEO will be the most appropriate designation. (Throughout this text the terms *president, chief executive officer,* and *administrator* have been used interchangeably.) This title will communicate to patients, relatives, visitors, physicians, and the general public that the president is the CEO in the organization.

Following corporate usage of titles, this would lead to an executive vice-president on the second level, several senior vice-presidents (e.g., for patient care and for fiscal affairs), then vice-presidents on the next level (e.g., vice-president of nursing, of professional services, of human resources, of environmental affairs, etc.).

Supervisors should not assume that every healthcare organization uses the same titles though. Nursing homes may use Administrator or Executive Director for their top employed position. Physician groups often use Executive Director or Practice Manager for their top employed position. Although the titles of the upper echelons vary from one healthcare institution to another, there must be internal consistency. Within a healthcare institution titles must be clear and consistent. The best way to do this is to use a basic title, such as director, and then add adjectives to indicate the rank and area of activity (executive, associate or assistant director, nursing, medical and surgical; or chief technologist, radiology, outpatient section).

The supervisor's job will be greatly facilitated by having all these organizational tools available. Charts, manuals, and position descriptions properly maintained and updated explain to everyone involved in the organization how it works and how the individual department and its members fit into the overall organization.

## CODE OF ETHICS

Many organizations have found it necessary to establish a written code of ethics. Supervisors will encounter enticements from equipment manufacturers and others to purchase their products. Sometimes the enticement is so subtle it goes unrecognized as something that could bias the supervisor's decision, such as tickets to a baseball game. Additionally, there have been occasions in which an overly zealous public relations manager slightly overstated the capabilities of the organization. While it may have been unintentional and without intent to defraud, inaccurately stating the organization's licensure, capability, and resources is fraudulent. These are just some examples of why institutions have found it necessary to define a Code of Ethics.

Components of the Code of Ethics will vary by organization, but some common categories are shown in the example that follows.

---

*Guide to Ethical Behavior*
*for the Staff of Small*
*Town Memorial Hospital*

This guide for acceptable conduct was developed to give all employees, physicians, suppliers, lenders, customers and prospective customers, and members of the general public an understanding of how Small Town Memorial Hospital's staff is expected to conduct the operations of this hospital and its affiliated clinics, home health agency, and services. For purposes of these guidelines, the use of Small Town Memorial Hospital means Small Town Memorial Hospital, Small Town Memorial Hospital Home Health Agency, Small Town Surgical Center, Small Town Clinics, and its rural health centers or physician office practices.

All members of the Small Town Memorial Hospital staff (employee, board, auxiliary, medical, and volunteer staffs) are expected to:

- carry out their activities responsibly;
- avoid any behavior that could reasonably appear to be improper or that could injure their own or Small Town Memorial Hospital's reputation for honesty and integrity in *all* its activities; and
- follow the policies listed below.

Failure by staff members to comply with these ethics guidelines; other codes provided upon employment, appointment or reappointment, or election; and acceptable standards of business conduct set forth by the hospital places it in a position of risk. When appropriate, the violator could be subject to disciplinary procedures, up to and including termination of the relationship the individual has with Small Town Memorial Hospital.

Alleged violation of or related dilemmas arising from these guidelines shall be referred to one or more of the following bodies for further action:

- Ethical issues related to patients or patient care shall be referred to the organization's multi-disciplinary Ethics Committee;
- Ethical issues related to physicians or medical staff services are referred to the appropriate medical staff committee; and
- Ethical issues related to employees, suppliers or any other not otherwise specified group or entity shall be reviewed by the Human Resources Director and Administrator.

*Employee Conflict of Interest*

Employees should refer to the Code of Conduct provided in the employee manual. One should have no personal, business, or financial interest that could compromise the objectivity, responsibility, and loyalty owed to Small Town Memorial Hospital. It is not possible to identify every activity that might cause a conflict of interest or an appearance of such conflict. Following are some examples of practices and circumstances in which conflicts might occur:

**Dealing with Suppliers and Customers**

Our goal must always be to obtain goods and services, and promote Small Town Memorial Hospital services on terms most favorable to the hospital when buying and selling. Neither you, nor any of your immediate family members should: (1) have or acquire by gift, inheritance, or other means, any interest in a supplier, customer, or its business (other than owning a small—five percent or less—percentage of the stock of a publicly held corporation); or (2) perform services for such a firm, unless properly disclosed. You should disclose any such holding or relationship to your immediate supervisor, department director, clinical service chief, or administrator, as such a relationship could appear to have the potential for biasing your judgment or activities.

**Dealing with Competitors**

You must disclose to your immediate supervisor, department director, clinical service chief, or administrator if you or any of your immediate family members: (1) receive by gift, inheritance, or otherwise, an interest in a competitor or its business; or (2) are performing services for a competitor of Small Town Memorial Hospital other than serving as a member of the medical staff of a competitor hospital.

**Outside Directors or Consulting**

If you are asked to serve as a director of or consultant to another corporation, you should first disclose this to your immediate supervisor, department director, or administrator, so that any possibility of the appearance of a conflict of interest or violation of antitrust or other laws can be evaluated.

**Compensation, etc., from Others**

You or any of your immediate family members should not accept compensation, loans, or entertainment having more than nominal value, commissions, property or anything else of personal financial advantage from any outside parties in connection with any transactions involving the hospital. This does not apply to personal loans from a recognized financial institution made in the ordinary course of business on usual and customary terms. At no time shall employees, volunteers, or auxiliary staff members accept cash or gifts of more than nominal value from patients or their families.

### Giving or Receiving Gifts

No gift (regardless of value) or other thing of value shall be given to or received from a customer representative with the intent to corrupt that person's or the employee's conduct.

### Political Payments

No funds or assets of Small Town Memorial Hospital shall be used for, or in aid of, any candidate or nominee for local, state, or federal political office in the United States or for, or in aid of, any political parties or committees in connection therewith unless allowed by law and authorized by the Administrator of Small Town Memorial Hospital. These prohibitions cover direct contributions and indirect assistance such as the furnishing of goods, services, or equipment to candidates, political parties, or committees.

### Other Opportunities for Personal Gain

Acquisition by you or your immediate family members of an interest or other financial advantage in real estate, patent rights, securities profit opportunity, or other right of property that results from or is directly connected with your employment should be disclosed to your immediate supervisor, department director, or administrator. It will not be approved if it might be adverse to the interests of Small Town Memorial Hospital or create an appearance of a conflict.

### Directors and Administrative Staff

Employment at Small Town Memorial Hospital in the capacity of key leadership and management carries with it the requirement of loyalty and fidelity to the institution, it being their responsibility to manage the affairs honestly and economically, exercising their best care, skill, and judgment for the benefit of Small Town Memorial Hospital. The matter of any duality of interest or possible conflict of interest can best be handled through full disclosure of any such interest.

The following policy of duality and conflict of interest is therefore implemented:

*Any duality of interest or possible conflict of interest on the part of any administrative or leadership individual should be disclosed to his or her superior and made a matter of record at the time of employment or when the interest actualizes. The need for any further action or prevention from being able to complete the responsibilities of the position will be determined at that time.*

*Board of Trustees Conflict of Interest*

### Board Policy

Board members of Small Town Memorial Hospital are expected and required to act legally and ethically in all relationships with the hospital, fellow board members, employees, patients, physicians, suppliers and contractors, competitors, financial institutions, government agencies, and the general public (See Board Bylaws Article VII, Board Code of Ethics, and Board Personal Financial Disclosure Statement).

*Medical and Other Professional Staff*

All members of the medical staff are guided by these Ethical Guidelines as are employees who are members of professions. Both groups are guided as well by their profession's code of ethics.

*Proprietary Information*

At the conclusion of your employment or affiliation with Small Town Memorial Hospital, you are required to return all Small Town Memorial Hospital documents and records. Even after leaving, you have a continuing obligation to safeguard such information.

*Accounting Systems: Books and Records*

Small Town Memorial Hospital policy requires that its books and records shall accurately reflect transactions and disposition of assets. Books and records will be kept in accordance with Generally Accepted Accounting Principles (GAAP) in the United States. No false, artificial, or misleading statements or entries shall be made in Small Town Memorial Hospital's books or records including, but not limited to, time reports, accounts, and financial statements. No unrecorded "slush" funds or secret assets of any kind shall be maintained for any purpose whatsoever. Staff are expected to follow the hospital financial and information management policies regarding retaining documentation in their area of responsibility.

*Quality and Integrity*

**Patient Rights**

It is the intent of Small Town Memorial Hospital to create an environment that provides for the continuum of care of patients within the constraints of its capabilities while at the same time its staff ensures that the basic rights of a patient are respected. In the case of a dependent minor, all rights and responsibilities will be made known to the parent(s) or guardian(s) of the minor. (See patient Bill of Rights).

**Marketing and Public Relations**

All marketing activities conducted and public relation statements issued by Small Town Memorial Hospital shall reflect only those services available through Small Town Memorial Hospital or its affiliated services, and its current licensure and/or accreditation status, when appropriate. Further statements shall be factual to the extent patient confidentiality and/or proprietary information is not violated. While Small Town Memorial Hospital is the only hospital in Small Town, this fact does not permit the hospital or its public relations department to exploit or exaggerate its capabilities.

**Patient Billings and Records**

All initial patient billings shall be itemized. Patients are entitled to receive an itemized bill upon request. Patients are also permitted to receive a copy of their record in accordance with the Medical Record Department policies and procedures. At all times, Small Town Memorial Hospital's staff shall abide by the patient Bill of Rights and the patient billing provisions outlined therein.

At least annually, the Patient Accounts Department will have an external agent audit a sample of the accounts to ensure proper billing practices have been followed and that adequate documentation exists to justify the billings.

At least annually, the Administration will evaluate it charges against the prevailing charges in the region to ensure its charges are consistent with others providing similar services.

**Admission, Transfer, and Discharge**

While patients are being treated at Small Town Memorial Hospital, staff will strive to ensure the same level of service and care is rendered dependent upon the acuity of the patient's condition. It is Small Town Memorial Hospital's policy to admit patients and give services without regard to race, color, national origin, age, sex, handicap, or ability to pay. Staff members found violating these basic rights of patients will be disciplined and may be terminated.

*Adapted from Lincoln County Memorial Hospital's Code of Ethics, Troy MO.*

### Confidentiality

As an employee of a healthcare organization you will inevitably be in contact with patient information. Some of this information will be very sensitive, while some items are readily available in the local telephone book. Your responsibility is to be able to decipher which is which and ensure that you and your staff do not inadvertently disclose personal, private, and otherwise confidential information inappropriately.

The right to privacy and keeping private information confidential have become a subject of congressional debate. Legislation has been proposed to protect patient information from unauthorized access regardless of the media on which patient records and information are stored (i.e., electronic records, optically stored, computer data bases and clinical repositories, or on paper). In addition, the legislature addresses information that has been transmitted to and is resident in third party computers such as those computers at insurance companies, in physician offices, or in contracted laboratories, for example.

The supervisor's role with regard to confidentiality includes:

- ensuring that his or her staff are properly inserviced and re-inserviced periodically about handling of confidential information;
- counseling staff who discuss patient information in inappropriate contexts, locations, or with individuals who have no need to know;
- maintaining security provisions with regard to patient record access, computer access, use of passwords, and establishing security levels to databases maintained within the department or organization's computer system; and
- obtaining an affirmation, annually, from his or her staff that they recognize their duties with regard to maintaining the confidentiality of patient and organization data.

An example of such a confidentiality statement is as follows:

---

*Confidentiality Pledge*

I have generally been informed and understand that I will come in contact with information concerning treatment of patients. This information is confidential and is not to be disclosed to any person or entity without appropriate patient authorization, subpoena, or court order. Further, I may have access to proprietary information about the organization's financial status, patient care volumes and statistics, and plans for future services or activities. I acknowledge that this information is confidential as well and will not disclose it to any person or entity unless authorized to do so by the Administrator.

I have been assigned a password to access certain computer files. The use of the data from these files will be for my work assignments only and no data shall be removed by copying it to another media without express authorization to do so and only for the purposes of performing my job. A log of any data files that have been duplicated will be kept current at all times and made available upon request.

---

I understand that confidential information or data is defined as any information in which the individual's, organization's, or any participating practitioner's name is identified or identifiable. As an employee, breach of confidentiality may be cause for immediate termination of my employment.

I have read this agreement and the confidentiality policies of this facility and will demonstrate my understanding and willingness to abide by these policies and procedures by affixing my signature and the date below. I will review this policy and document my compliance and understanding by reaffixing my signature and the date on an annual basis.

| Date | Signature | Supervisor's Initials |
|------|-----------|----------------------|
|      |           |                      |
|      |           |                      |
|      |           |                      |
|      |           |                      |
|      |           |                      |

*Adapted from Sample Confidentiality Pledge printed in* Medical Records and the Law— An Illinois Guide to Medico-Legal Principles and Release of Information, *by the Illinois Health Information Management Association, 1994.*

## SUMMARY

Supervisors have a challenging job in any organization but particularly in healthcare, where the product of the organization can be life or death. As a summary to this text, below is a list of the potential pitfalls that supervisors face daily as summarized by Richard G. Ensman, Jr. in the January 1996 issue of *Iron & Steel Maker* magazine. May you be successful in your career.

### Management Blunders:
### 10 Common Mistakes

1. **Failure to communicate.** Well-informed employees are the key to a healthy, upbeat workplace. When you notice problems, act. By talking about little things, rumors are prevented and gossip is silenced.
2. **Failure to delegate.** By delegating, employees have an opportunity to solve problems and grow professionally.
3. **Taking things personally.** Turning a work-related issue into a personal one can trigger animosity. Keeping professional objectivity and decorum is important.
4. **Failure to motivate.** Important motivators, besides the paycheck, are benefits, opportunities for professional growth, friendships on the job, and opportunities to broaden one's knowledge.

5. **Treating everyone the same.** No two employees possess the same skills, temperaments, or experiences. Some need a fixed routine; others demonstrate creativity. Treat each employee accordingly.

6. **Failure to demonstrate loyalty.** Loyalty is a two-way street. Demonstrate loyalty by paying attention to employees' personal needs.

7. **Failure to obtain information.** Incorrect or incomplete information leads to poor decisions. By keeping several information channels open, unpleasant surprises are minimized.

8. **Failure to plan ahead.** Mismatched priorities, poor schedules, and inefficient allocation of time result from poor planning. Set clear goals and objectives.

9. **Forgetting to say, "Thank you."** A word of praise for a job well done affirms an employee's value and boosts morale.

10. **Failure to set priorities.** Employees should understand what is expected of them.

# INDEX